T0330240

Challenging Social Inequality

Challenging Social Inequality

Selected chapters translated from the Portuguese by Miguel Carter

The Landless Rural Workers Movement and Agrarian Reform in Brazil

EDITED BY Miguel Carter

Duke University Press   *Durham and London*   2015

Library of Congress Cataloging-in-Publication Data
Challenging social inequality : the landless rural worker's movement and agrarian
reform in Brazil / Miguel Carter, ed. ; selected chapters translated from the
Portuguese by Miguel Carter.
p. cm.
Includes bibliographical references and index.
ISBN 978-0-8223-5172-6 (cloth : alk. paper)
ISBN 978-0-8223-5186-3 (pbk. : alk. paper)
1. Movimento dos Trabalhadores sem Terra (Brazil) 2. Land reform—Brazil.
3. Social movements—Brazil. I. Carter, Miguel, 1964–
HD1333.B6C47 2012
333.3'181—dc23   2012011604

Duke University Press gratefully acknowledges the support of the
UNESCO Chair in Territorial Development and Education for Countryside
and Fundação Editora da UNESP, São Paulo, Brazil, which provided
funds toward the production of this book.

United Nations
Educational, Scientific and
Cultural Organization

UNESCO Chair in Territorial Development
and Education for the Countryside

Book cover photograph: Occupation of the Giacometi estate in Paraná (1996).
© Sebastião Salgado / Amazonas Images.
Frontispiece: More than 12,000 people participate in a sixteen-day National March
for Agrarian Reform to Brasília, 2005. Photo courtesy of Francisco Rojas.

Property does not only have rights, but also has duties . . .
If I am elected, I will not separate the two issues:
the emancipation of slaves and the democratization of the land.
One complements the other.
It is not enough to end slavery alone.
It is necessary to end the consequences of slavery.

—JOAQUIM NABUCO, 1884,
Brazilian Abolitionist Leader

The São Paulo Landlord is no different from the Salisbury Landlord.
It is the same contempt for their fellow man:
the same adoration for their large landholding
and the same repulsion towards any altruistic and generous idea.
It is necessary at each moment to set limits with this Empire;
to compare the conservatives in Brazil with those in England:
the false liberals here and there (. . .)
The Abolition is marching triumphantly.
It is necessary, though, to give the Negro land.
We must demonstrate that Landlordism is a greater crime than Slavery.
We declared in Lua Conferences: "Slavery is a crime."
Now we will hold forth: "Large estates are an atrocity."

—ANDRÉ REBOUÇAS, 1887,
Brazilian Abolitionist Leader

If there is no struggle there is no progress.
Those who profess to favor freedom, and yet depreciate agitation,
are people who want crops without plowing up the ground.
They want rain without thunder and lightning.
They want the ocean without the awful roar of its many waters.
This struggle may be a moral one; or it may be a physical one;
or it may be both moral and physical; but it must be a struggle.
Power concedes nothing without demand.
It never did and it never will.

—FREDERICK DOUGLASS, 1849,
North American Abolitionist Leader

For Kristina,
Mi compañera de vida

For those who seek
social and environmental
justice in Brazil

CONTENTS

ACKNOWLEDGMENTS

All books are the result of a collective undertaking. Anthologies such as this volume, which engaged seventeen contributors from Europe, North America, and South America, amplify this collective process in a substantial way.

We owe our findings to hundreds, if not thousands, of people who have shared ideas and generated the information that helped shape the texts included in this volume. Our informants, research assistants, and many people who produced the data and studies employed in our assessments played an essential role in this enterprise. Moreover, during this time, we were all sustained—in different ways—by our families, friends, colleagues, and various host institutions. The book's final production, in turn, owes much to a team effort carried out by Duke University Press.

In all this, a special word of gratitude should be made to two academic centers that secured funding for this edition: the UNESCO Chair in Territorial Development and Education for the Countryside of the Universidade Estadual de São Paulo (UNESP) and the Brazil Study Program at the University of Oxford. Here, we are particularly obliged to Bernardo Mançano Fernandes and Timothy J. Powell.

Were it not for this broad and variegated support network, this anthology would have never been possible. It is with a warm heart, therefore, that we extend our appreciation to all the people involved in this vast undertaking. As the convener, editor and translator of this volume, it is my responsibility to acknowledge some of the individuals and institutions that helped make this project possible.

Tracing the genealogy of most books can be a rather difficult task, given the assorted web of ideas and experiences that can shape these literary works. Though centered on Brazil, this volume is in many ways a globalized text. Its contributors come from six different countries: Brazil, the United Kingdom, the United States, Mexico, Argentina, and Paraguay. In addition, editing this anthology involved tasks that crisscrossed many longitudes and latitudes around the globe. The book was conceived in Oxford, England, prepared in Washington, D.C., and Caacupé, Paraguay, and published in Durham, North Carolina.

The city of Oxford offered a lovely setting for two crucial moments in the volume's conception. The first took place in October 2003, when the Centre for Brazilian Studies at the University of Oxford sponsored an international conference on the Landless Rural Workers Movement (MST) and agrarian reform in Brazil that brought together several of the volume's contributors. I am thankful to those who sponsored this academic event and took part of its lively exchange, especially, Leslie Bethell, the Centre's director. Various people at the Centre provided assistance in setting up this meeting: Ailsa Thom, Sarah Rankin, Alessandra Nolasco, Margaret Hancox, and Julie Smith. I also want to express gratitude to the conference presenters and commentators: Anne-Laure Cadji, Bernardo Mançano Fernandes, Carlos Amaral Guedes, Elena Calvo-González, George Meszaros, Guilherme Delgado, Hamilton Pereira, Horacio Martins de Carvalho, Sue Branford, Wendy Wolford, David Lehmann, James Dunkerley, Joe Foweraker, Kathryn Hochstetler, Kurt Von Metteheim, and Laurence Whitehead.

A second *coup d'inspiration* took place at the White Hart, a quaint pub nestled in the village of Wytham, near Oxford. It was there, over a savory pint of local beer and an animated conversation that Leslie Bethell and I crafted the basic outline of this book. That evening I agreed to organize two editions of this volume, one in Portuguese and the other in English. Yet never did I imagine this would require as many years of arduous labor as it actually did. In hindsight, I realize I accepted this engagement with great innocence, impressed as I was with Leslie Bethell's contagious vitality and genuine enthusiasm for this initiative. Riding back on my bicycle to Oxford, on that dark and chilly autumn night, I vowed to lead the project to a worthy end.

My memorable *séjour* at Oxford was made possible thanks to the recommendations tendered by my mentors at Columbia University in New York: Alfred C. Stepan, Douglas A. Chalmers, Ralph Della Cava, and Albert Fishlow.

The Centre for Brazilian Studies offered an amiable and stimulating place for research and intellectual debate. During my year at Oxford I shared the good company, friendship and lingering conversations with Fiona Macauly, Marukh Doctor, Ronaldo Fiani, Marcos Rolim, Jurandir Malerba, Kathryn Hochstetler, Alexandre Parola, Lilia Moritz Schwarcz, Antonio Sérgio Guimarães, Nadya Araújo Guimarães, Matias Spektor, and Vanessa de Castro.

In Washington, D.C., I received the encouragement of various colleagues, students, and friends at American University: Louis Goodman, David Hirschmann, Deborah Bräutigam, Fantu Cheru, Daniel Esser, Robin Broad, Todd Eisenstadt, Philip Brenner, and Joe Eldridge. In turn, Joe Clapper, Ali Ghobadi, and the administrators of the International Development Program—Crystal Wright, Elizabeth Minor, and Amanda Rives—were graceful and efficient in their logistical assistance.

I am especially indebted to the generous and intelligent contributions made by my research assistants at American University: Enrique Gómez Carrillo, Lyndsay Hughes, Kristy Feldman, Kang Yue, and Erin Connor.

Significant revisions were made to the bulk of the contributions prepared for this volume. This was particularly the case with the eight chapters I translated from Portuguese. Throughout this seemingly endless task I received help from various colleagues, notably Patrick Quirk, Débora Lerrer, Eric Joseph, and Charlotte Cassey. Ralph Della Cava's steadfast support during this long and difficult process was exceptionally heartwarming.

A number of MST leaders and activists provided ample access to contacts and information on their movement, which greatly facilitated the preparation of this volume. Several of these individuals are acknowledged in different chapters that comprise this anthology. Others deserving a word of recognition are: João Pedro Stédile, João Paulo Rodrigues, Dulcinéia Pavan, Neuri Rossetto, Joaquim Piñero, Geraldo Fontes, Miguel Stédile, and Marina Tavares.

I am also extremely grateful to the photographers that helped illustrate this volume with stunning images, captured with deep human sensitivity. Among them are some of the best-known photographers of the Brazilian land struggle: Sebastião Salgado, João Ripper, Douglas Mansur, João Zinclair, Leonardo Melgarejo, Francisco Rojas, Verena Glass, and Max da Rocha.

Cristiane Passos located various pictures in the archives of the Pastoral Land Commission (CPT) and Prelacy of São Felix do Araguaia. Celeste Prieto helped with the final selection of photographs, while Anderson Antonio da Silva provided excellent assistance in preparing all the maps and several figures used to illustrate this volume. In addition, Ricardo Salles shared the André Rebouças quote used in the opening section of the book.

At Duke University Press, this book project was endorsed early on by Valerie Millholland. I am thankful to Jessica Ryan for her good patience and aid in preparing the manuscript for print. Three anonymous reviewers of the original manuscript offered insightful suggestions for revision.

My research work on Brazil's agrarian issues and rural social movements began in 1991. The innumerous visits and extensive travel throughout this country were financed by a number of institutions: The Tinker Foundation, the Inter-American Foundation, the Fulbright-Hays Dissertation Research Abroad Program, the Dorothy Danforth Compton Fellowship, the Nonprofit Sector Research Fund of The Aspen Institute, the University of Oxford's Centre for Brazilian Studies, and American University. A special recognition is extended here to all the organizations and individuals that subsidized my research and involvement in this project.

This anthology would not have been possible without the loyal support of my family, including the members of the Galland clan—Lilette Galland de Mira, Emilio Mira y López, Andrés Galland, Griselda Barrera Galland, and Leticia,

Eliana, and Fabiana Galland—who welcomed me with joy and kindness in Rio de Janeiro and Porto Alegre. My parents, John and Renée Carter, were a constant source of inspiration and encouragement, while my siblings, Nicolás and Yvette, were always there to lend a hand.

Raising a family and preparing books can be a tough act to balance. Over the years, Alma, Rafael, and David did their very best to keep things in perspective. By inviting my distraction, time and again, they lightened my load and nurtured a playful zest for life.

Kristina Svensson was the main anchor throughout the project. She accompanied the whole journey—from the conference in Oxford to the final edits—with *cariño,* patience, acumen, and generosity. The book is dedicated to her with all my love.

LIST OF FIGURES, MAPS, AND TABLES

ABRA   *Associação Brasileira de Reforma Agrária* (Brazilian Association for Agrarian Reform)

ACR   *Ação de Cristãos no Meio Rural* (Rural Christian Action)

AJUP   *Instituto de Apoio Jurídico Popular* (Institute of Popular Juridical Support)

ANCA   *Associação Nacional de Cooperação Agrícola* (National Association for Agricultural Cooperation)

ANMTR   *Articulação Nacional Mulheres Trabalhadoras Rurais* (National Network of Rural Women Workers)

APIB   *Articulação dos Povos Indígenas do Brasil* (Indigenous Peoples of Brazil)

ATES   *Programa de Assistência Técnica, Social e Ambiental à Reforma Agrária* (Program for Technical, Social, and Environmental Assistance for Agrarian Reform)

BNDES   *Banco Nacional de Desenvolvimento Econômico e Social* (Brazilian Development Bank)

CEAS   *Centro de Estudos e Ação Social* (Center for Studies and Social Action)

CEB   *Comunidades Eclesiais de Base* (Community Base Churches)

CEBI   *Centro de Estudos Bíblicos* (Center for Biblical Studies)

CEBRAP   *Centro Brasileiro de Análise e Planejamento* (Brazilian Center for Analysis and Planning)

CELAM   *Consejo Episcopal Latinoamericano* (Latin American Episcopal Council)

CEPAL   *Comisión Económica Para América Latina y el Caribe* (Economic Commission for Latin America and the Caribbean)

CEPLAC   *Comissão Executiva do Plano da Lavoura Cacaueira* (Executive Commission of the Cocoa Farming Plan)

CIMI   *Conselho Indgenista Missionário* (Indigenous Missionary Council)

CLACSO   Consejo Latinoamericano de Ciencias Sociales (Latin American Council of Social Sciences)

CLOC   *Coordinadora Latinoamericana de Organizaciones del Campo* (Latin American Coordinator of Rural Organizations)

CNA   *Confederação da Agricultura e Pecuária do Brasil* (Brazilian Confederation of Agriculture and Livestock). Prior to 2001, the CNA was known as the *Confederação Nacional da Agricultura* (National Confederation of Agriculture).

CNBB   *Conferência Nacional dos Bispos do Brasil* (National Conference of Bishops of Brazil)

COM   *Centro de Orientação Missionária* (Center for Missionary Orientation)

CONATERRA   *Cooperativa Nacional Terra e Vida* (Land and Life National Cooperative)

CONCRAB   *Confederação das Cooperativas de Reforma Agrária do Brasil* (Confederation of Agrarian Reform Cooperatives of Brazil)

CONIC   *Conselho Nacional de Igrejas Cristãs* (National Council of Christian Churches)

CONTAG   *Confederação Nacional dos Trabalhadores na Agricultura* (National Confederation of Agricultural Workers)

COPERAL   *Cooperativa Regional de Assentados* (Settler's Regional Cooperative)

CPA   *Cooperativas de Produção Agropecuária* (Farm Production Cooperatives)

CPT   *Comissão Pastoral da Terra* (Pastoral Land Commission)

CRAB   *Comissão Regional dos Atingidos por Barragens* (Regional Commission of People Affected by Dams)

CRB   *Confederação Rural Brasileira* (Brazilian Rural Confederation)

CTRIN-DTRIG   *Centro do Trigo Nacional – Departamento do Trigo* (National Wheat Commission of the Bank of Brazil and Department of Wheat)

CUT   *Central Única de Trabalhadores* (Unified Workers' Central)

ECLA   Economic Commission for Latin America

ELAA   *Escola Latino Americana de Agroecologia* (Latin American School of Agroecology)

EMBRAPA   *Empresa Brasileira de Pesquisa Agropecuária* (Brazilian Agricultural Research Corporation)

ENFF   *Escola Nacional Florestan Fernandes* (Florestan Fernandes National School)

ETR   *Estatuto de Trabalho Rural* (Rural Labor Statute)

FAO   Food and Agriculture Organization of the United Nations

FARSUL   *Federação da Agricultura do Estado do Rio Grande do Sul* (Agricultural Federation of the State of Rio Grande do Sul)

FEPASA   *Ferrovias Paulistas S.A.* (Paulista Railways, Inc.)

FERAESP   *Federação dos Empregados Rurais e Assalariados de São Paulo* (Federation of Rural Workers and Wage Earners of São Paulo)

FETAGRI *Federação dos Trabalhadores na Agricultura* (Federation of Workers in Agriculture)

FETAPE *Federação dos Trabalhadores na Agricultura de Pernambuco* (Federation of Agricultural Workers of Pernambuco)

FETRAF *Federação dos Trabalhadores da Agricultura Familiar* (Family Farm Workers Federation)

FETRAFSUL *Federação dos Trabalhadores na Agricultura Familiar da Região Sul* (Family Farm Workers Federation of the South Region)

FIESP *Federação das Indústrias do Estado de São Paulo* (Federation of Industries of São Paulo)

FTAA Free Trade Agreement of the Americas

FUNAI *Fundação Nacional do Índio* (National Indian Foundation)

FUNRURAL *Fundo de Assistência ao Trabalhador Rural* (Fund for the Assistance of the Rural Worker)

IAA *Instituto do Açúcar e do Álcool* (Sugar and Alcohol Institute)

IBAD *Instituto Brasileiro de Ação Democrática* (Brazilian Institute for Democratic Action)

IBAMA *Instituto Brasileiro do Meio Ambiente e dos Recursos Naturais Renováveis* (Brazilian Institute of Environment and Renewable Natural Resources)

IBC *Instituto Brasileiro do Café* (Brazilian Coffee Institute)

IBGE *Instituto Brasileiro de Geografia e Estatística* (Brazilian Institute of Geography and Statistics)

IECLB *Igreja Evangélica de Confissão Luterana no Brasil* (Evangelical Church of Lutheran Confession in Brazil)

INCRA *Instituto Nacional de Colonização e Reforma Agrária* (National Agrarian Reform and Colonization Institute)

INESC *Instituto de Estudos Socioeconômicos* (Institute for Socioeconomic Studies)

IPEA *Instituto de Pesquisa Econômica Aplicada* (Institute for Applied Economic Research)

IPES *Instituto de Pesquisas Econômicas e Sociais* (Institute for Economic and Social Research)

ITERRA *Instituto Técnico de Capacitação e Pesquisa em Reforma Agrária* (Technical Institute for Training and Research in Agrarian Reform)

JAC *Juventude Agrária Católica* (Catholic Agrarian Youth)

MAB *Movimento dos Atingidos por Barragens* (Movement of People Affected by Dams)

MAPA *Ministério da Agricultura, Pecuária e Abastecimento* (Ministry of Agriculture, Livestock and Supply)

MAST *Movimento dos Agricultores Sem-Terra* (Landless Farmers Movement)

MASTER   *Movimento de Agricultores Sem Terra* (Landless Farmers Movement)

MASTRO   *Movimento dos Trabalhadores Sem Terra do Oeste* (Movement of Landless Workers of the West)

MDA   *Ministério de Desenvolvimento Agrário* (Ministry of Agrarian Development)

MEB   *Movimento de Educação de Base* (Grassroots Education Movement)

MLST   *Movimento de Libertação dos Sem-Terra* (Liberation Movement for Landless Peasants)

MMC   *Movimento de Mulheres Camponesas* (Peasant Women's Movement)

MMTR   *Movimento das Mulheres Trabalhadoras Rurais* (Rural Women Workers' Movement)

MNLM   *Movimento Nacional de Luta pela Moradia* (National Movement to Struggle for Housing)

MPA   *Movimento dos Pequenos Agricultores* (Small Farmers' Movement)

MST   *Movimento dos Trabalhadores Rurais Sem Terra* (Landless Rural Workers Movement)

MTRUB   *Movimento dos Trabalhadores Rurais e Urbanos do Brasil* (Brazilian Rural and Urban Workers Movement)

MTSBST   *Movimento dos Trabalhadores Brasileiros Sem Terras* (Brazilian Landless Workers Movement)

MTST   *Movimento dos Trabalhadores Sem Teto* (Homeless Workers Movement)

MTV   *Movimento Terra Vida* (Life Land Movement)

MUST   *Movimento Unidos dos Sem-Terra* (United Landless Movement)

OCB   *Organização das Cooperativas do Brasil* (Organization of Brazilian Cooperatives)

OLC   *Organização de Luta no Campo* (Countryside Struggle Organization)

OTC   *Organização dos Trabalhadores no Campo* (Organization of Workers in the Countryside)

PAA   *Programa de Aquisição de Alimentos* (Food Acquisition Program)

PCB   *Partido Communista Brasileiro* (Brazilian Communist Party). Prior to 1962, the PCB was known as the *Partido Comunista do Brasil* (Communist Party of Brazil).

PCC   *Primeiro Comando da Capital* (First Capital Command)

PFL   *Partido da Frente Liberal* (Party of the Liberal Front)

PJR   *Pastoral da Juventude Rural* (Rural Youth Pastoral)

PMDB   *Partido do Movimento Democrático Brasileiro* (Brazilian Democratic Movement Party)

PNRA   *Plano Nacional de Reforma Agrária* (National Agrarian Reform Plan)

PROAGRO	*Programa de Apoio à Atividade Agropecuaria* (Program to Support Agricultural Activity)
PROCERA	*Programa de Crédito Especial para Reforma Agrária* (Special Credit Program for Agrarian Reform)
PRONAF	*Programa Nacional de Apoio à Agricultura Familiar* (National Program for the Strengthening of Family Agriculture)
PRONERA	*Programa Nacional de Educação na Reforma Agrária* (National Education Program in Agrarian Reform)
PSDB	*Partido da Social Democria Brasileira* (Party of Brazilian Social Democracy)
PSOL	*Partido Socialismo e Liberdade* (Party for Socialism and Liberty)
PT	*Partido dos Trabalhadores* (Workers Party)
RECA	*Projeto de Reflorestamento Econômico Consorciado Adensado* (Joint Consortium for Economic Reforestation Project)
RENAP	*Rede Nacional de Advogados e Advogadas Populares* (National Network of Popular Lawyers)
SCA	*Sistema Cooperativista dos Assentados* (Settlers' Cooperative System)
SENAR	*Serviço Nacional de Aprendizagem Rural* (National Service for Rural Learning)
SESCOOP	*Serviço Nacional de Aprendizagem do Cooperativismo* (National Service for Learning about Cooperatives)
SNA	*Sociedade Nacional da Agricultura* (National Agricultural Society)
SNCR	*Sistema Nacional de Cadastro Rural* (National Land Registry System)
SRB	*Sociedade Rural Brasileira* (Brazilian Rural Society)
STR	*Sindicato de Trabalhadores Rurais* (Rural Trade Union)
SUDAM	*Superintendência do Desenvolvimento da Amazônia* (Superintendence for the Development of the Amazon)
SUNAB	*Superintendência Nacional do Abastacemiento* (National Superintendece for Supplies)
SUS	*Sistema Único de Saúde* (Unified Health System)
TAC	*Curso Técnico na Administração de Cooperativas* (Technical Course in Coop Administration)
TCU	*Tribunal de Contas da União* (Court of Accounts of the Union)
TFP	*Tradição, Família e Propriedade* (Tradition, Family and Property)
UDR	*União Democrática Ruralista* (Rural Democratic Union)
ULTAB	*União dos Lavradores e Trabalhadores Agrícolas do Brasil* (Brazilian Peasant and Agricultural Workers Union of Brazil)
USP	*Universidade de São Paulo* (University of São Paulo)

Map 0.1. Brazil: States and places cited in the book

AN OVERVIEW

Miguel Carter

Brazil is one the most inequitable nations in the world. Its great disparities of wealth have deep historical roots. This volume addresses a critical legacy and enduring aspect of Brazil's social injustice: its sharply unequal agrarian structure. The following chapters probe the causes, consequences, and contemporary reactions to this situation. In particular, they shed light on the Landless Rural Workers Movement (MST), Latin America's largest and most prominent social movement, and its ongoing efforts to confront historic patterns of inequality in the Brazilian countryside.

This volume offers a wide-ranging picture of the MST and its engagement in the Brazilian struggle for land reform. The sixteen chapters included here were produced and revised between 2004 and 2008, following a conference sponsored by the University of Oxford's Centre for Brazilian Studies. All the contributors to this volume, an assembly of Brazilian, European, and North American–based scholars and development practitioners, have ample fieldwork experience on the subject. In concert, they offer a unique international and multidisciplinary perspective of this phenomenon. Its seventeen authors include five sociologists, two political scientists, two geographers, two anthropologists, an economist, as well as a lawyer, a journalist, and three development practitioners. Among the writers are eleven Brazilians, three Europeans, and three North American–based scholars. Together, they offer a sober and empirically grounded assessment of what is undoubtedly a complex and sensitive subject. The following comments present a brief overview of the anthology.

Chapter 1, "Social Inequality, Agrarian Reform, and Democracy in Brazil," by Miguel Carter sets the MST's mobilization for agrarian reform in a historical and comparative context. It underscores the sharp social disparities and contentious visions surrounding the MST's quest for land redistribution and appraises the movement's influence on Brazil's reform agenda. The prospects for enhancing development and democracy in Brazil, it asserts, are hampered by the nation's extreme and durable social inequities. Over the last three decades the country has experienced a conservative agrarian reform process—largely reactive and restrained in its response to peasant demands; sluggish, minimal, and ad hoc in its distributive measures; and conciliatory toward the nation's landlord class. Enduring oligarchic privileges, the underdevelopment of citizenship rights among the poor, and various other shortcomings of Brazil's democratic regime account for the nation's highly lopsided political representation in favor of the rural elite and explain the state's tepid land reform policies. The chapter concludes with a summary of the main positions in Brazil's contemporary debate over agrarian reform.

The ensuing fifteen chapters are divided into four parts. Part I, "The Agrarian Question and Rural Social Movements in Brazil," provides an essential background to the MST story. It examines Brazil's agrarian structure, state policies, and the formation of civil society organizations in the countryside. Part II, "MST History and Struggle for Land" and part III, "MST's Agricultural Settlements," build on a frequently made distinction between the struggle *for* land (*a luta pela terra*) and the struggle *on the* land (*a luta na terra*). The first refers to the mobilization undertaken by landless peasants to demand government land redistribution.[1] The struggle *on the* land takes place after the establishment of an official agricultural settlement. The main efforts during this phase are geared toward developing productive and meaningful rural communities. Each of these parts includes an introductory chapter followed by three case studies. All together, the six case studies cover four of Brazil's principal regions: the south, southeast, northeast, and Amazonian north.

Part IV provides a wide-ranging analysis of the MST, politics, and society in Brazil. It probes the movement's multifarious relations with recent governments and the rule of law. Moreover, it examines the MST's impact on other Brazilian social movements. The concluding chapter appraises current discussions over the MST and the future of agrarian reform in Brazil. In doing so, it presents some of the main findings of this volume. This is complemented by an epilogue and update on land reform trends in the late 2000s and early 2010s.

The Agrarian Question and Rural Social Movements in Brazil

Chapter 2, "The Agrarian Question and Agribusiness in Brazil," by Guilherme Costa Delgado offers a cautionary tale. His review of rural development policies since the 1950s shows how these policies have systematically favored the landlord class, notably during the military regime established in 1964. This government thwarted reforms in land tenure, while subsidizing the territorial expansion and technological modernization of the agrarian elite. This state-led capitalist transformation of agriculture fuelled the emergence of a powerful agribusiness class. Large-scale farmers and ranchers gained added economic relevance and power in the aftermath of the 1982 debt crisis. Under Brazil's "constrained adjustment" to the new global economy, agro-exports became a leading source of revenue to repay the nation's foreign creditors. Current prospects for implementing a substantial land reform, Delgado argues, are undermined by the neoliberal economic model adopted in the 1990s. This is compounded by the state's weak enforcement of agrarian reform laws and negligible efforts to put into effect tax provisions affecting large rural properties.

Chapter 3, "Rural Social Movements, Struggles for Rights, and Land Reform in Contemporary Brazilian History," by Leonilde Sérvolo de Medeiros also underscores the strength of Brazil's large rural proprietors, but, additionally, highlights the emergence of a variety of new peasant movements. These movements were started first in the 1950s and were reignited in the 1980s, during Brazil's political redemocratization. This second cycle of peasant mobilizations ushered in new social categories and public demands and fostered innovative forms of collective action. These peasant groups have sought to assert their public visibility, while demanding governments to fulfill various social rights. The MST's evolution, Medeiros insists, needs to be viewed in the context of previous and present-day struggles for citizenship rights in the countryside.

Chapter 4, "Churches, the Pastoral Land Commission, and the Mobilization for Agrarian Reform," by Ivo Poletto highlights the religious contribution to the organization and mobilization of the Brazilian peasantry. Stirred by the Second Vatican Council's *aggiornamento*, a theology of liberation, and human rights violations in the countryside, particularly in the Amazonian frontier, church agents established in 1975 a Pastoral Land Commission (CPT). The CPT was embraced early on by the National Conference of Brazilian Bishops (CNBB). Indeed, nowhere in the chronicle of world religion has a leading religious institution played as significant a role in support of land reform as has the Brazilian Catholic Church. Poletto shows how various church initiatives at the grassroots level helped nurture a vast network of rural social movements, the MST being its most prominent offspring.

MST History and Struggle for Land

Chapter 5, "The Formation and Territorialization of the MST in Brazil," by Bernardo Mançano Fernandes presents a broad view of the MST's history and territorial expansion to twenty-four of the country's twenty-seven states. This account presents a unique series of maps and discusses the MST's organizational resources and main mobilization strategies. Land struggles, Fernandes asserts, have been crucial to the development of the MST and the implementation of agrarian reform policies in Brazil. However, the surge in land distribution after the mid-1990s simply reduced the rate of land concentration in the hands of the agribusiness farmers. As a result, existing land reform policies have not altered the nation's agrarian structure in any substantial way.

Chapter 6, "Origins and Consolidation of the MST in Rio Grande do Sul," by Miguel Carter covers the history of the landless movement in one of Brazil's most developed regions. Land struggles in Rio Grande do Sul played a central role in the MST's formation, while generating many of its innovative practices. The movement's genesis, survival, and ongoing growth, Carter argues, are intimately entwined with its capacity for public activism—that is, an ability to engage in a type of social conflict that is organized, politicized, visible, autonomous, periodic, and basically nonviolent. The MST's orientation toward public activism is shaped by its enveloping conditions, notably its political opportunities and mobilizing resources. Carter builds on this framework and a comprehensive database on land mobilizations to examine the MST's historical trajectory in Rio Grande do Sul, from 1979 to 2006.

Chapter 7, "Under the Black Tarp: The Dynamics and Legitimacy of Land Occupations in Pernambuco," by Lygia Maria Sigaud offers an ethnographic account of land struggles in the northeast sugarcane region. Since the late 1990s, northeast Brazil has become the most active region in the fight for land. The MST's presence in Pernambuco ushered in a new mobilization technique characterized by Sigaud as the "encampment form." These precarious camps set up by unemployed rural workers are not an ad hoc gathering but a ritualized and symbolic instrument through which the rural poor have learned to establish entitlement claims. Sigaud demystifies prevailing views that depict these landless movements as intrinsically hostile to the state. The bellicose rhetoric between the state and peasant groups, she contends, masks a relationship that also includes elements of close cooperation and mutual dependency.

Gabriel Ondetti, Emmanuel Wambergue, and José Batista Gonçalves Afonso in chapter 8, "From *Posseiro* to *Sem Terra*: The Impact of MST Land Struggles in the State of Pará," appraise the MST's expansion into the Amazon region. Pará is noted for the fraudulent appropriation of much of its territory, high levels of rural violence, and a strong tradition of squatter (*posseiro*) land struggles supported by local rural trade unions and the CPT. The MST's early years in southeastern Pará proved to be difficult ones. The April 1996 police massacre of nineteen MST peasants near the town of Eldorado dos Carajás was a turning point in the movement's struggle. The massacre triggered national public outrage and prompted federal authorities to accelerate the pace of land distribution. Though relatively small in number, MST's actions in Pará caused a significant impact in the region. According to the authors, the MST helped revitalize Pará's land struggle and modernize existing "repertoires of contention." Moreover, it fostered the presence of the federal government in areas of the Amazon frontier where the state had been largely absent.

MST Agricultural Settlements

Land reform settlements differ greatly in their geographic setting, size, family composition, levels of economic development, political awareness, and cultural resources. Chapter 9, "The Struggle on the Land: Source of Growth, Innovation, and Constant Challenge to the MST," by Miguel Carter and Horacio Martins de Carvalho provides a synoptic view of the MST's efforts to enhance its agricultural settlements. These activities, they argue, are shaped by Brazil's conservative agrarian reform process, which has led to the dispersed and ad hoc distribution of land settlements. Prior to the election of President Luiz Inácio Lula da Silva, public policies were noted for their negligible assistance to these new communities. This situation led the MST to mobilize its settlers to insist that the government provide the houses, agricultural credits, schools, and other benefits established in the agrarian reform laws. In addition, the MST has organized thirteen specialized sectors to address the movement's various needs. These units—ranging from education, finances, communications, culture, and human rights to health, gender, production, cooperation, and the environment—operate at national, state, and local levels, adding great complexity and dynamism to the movement's decision-making process. These multiple and creative efforts, Carter and Carvalho conclude, have clearly bolstered the MST's organizational capacity.

Chapter 10, "Rural Settlements and the MST in São Paulo: From Social Conflict to the Diversity of Local Impacts," by Sonia Maria P. P. Bergamasco and Luiz Antonio Norder offers a comparative analysis of land reform settlements in Brazil's most industrialized and urbanized state. While emphasizing the assorted nature and impact of the agrarian reform process in São Paulo, the authors' findings concur with national surveys that suggest an overall improvement in the quality of life among the vast majority of settlers. The creation of land settlements, they argue, have favored the development of new social and political relations at the local level, while fostering alternative commercial arrangements, innovative technologies, and a gradual consolidation of public policies in support of peasant farmers. In contrast to São Paulo's highly industrialized agriculture, many of these communities have embraced a more sustainable and ecological model of rural development.

Chapter 11, "Community Building in an MST Settlement in Northeast Brazil," by Elena Calvo González presents an ethnographic account of the day-to-day dilemmas and frustrations that can take place in a new land reform settlement. Decisions over where to build new houses (together in an *agrovila* or in separate farm plots) and questions concerning the partial collectivization of land and labor stir power disputes within the settlement. Disappointments over the settlement's inadequate infrastructure contribute to shared feelings of failure and trigger extensive discussions and gossip over who is to blame. In this case study, regional MST leaders are reproached for exercising too much control and faulted for not doing enough. State officials are blamed by all parties, albeit in different ways. All this, Calvo-González observes, takes place amid feelings of nostalgia for the tight-knit community life experienced during the landless encampment.

Chapter 12, "MST Settlements in Pernambuco: Identity and the Politics of Resistance," by Wendy Wolford analyzes the impact of economic conditions, organizational strategies, and cultural views of the land on an MST community in Pernambuco's coastal region. The decline of the sugarcane industry in the mid-1990s facilitated the rapid growth of land reform settlements in this area. With the recovery of the sugar industry, after the 2002 surge in world sugar prices, the settlers chose to plant sugarcane instead of the alternative crops promoted by the MST and land reform officials. The MST lost sway over its members as a result of these disagreements. Unlike family farmers in other parts of Brazil, sugarcane workers have been traditionally connected to the land as wage earners, Wolford explains. For them, owning land is mainly about having a space to rest at ease, free from any controls. This individualist ethos hinders the MST's collective action efforts.

The MST, Politics, and Society in Brazil

Chapter 13, "Working with Governments: The MST's Experience with the Cardoso and Lula Administrations," by Sue Branford evaluates the MST's capacity to adapt to different political scenarios. The Cardoso government, she notes, brought mixed results to the MST: greater land distribution yet scant support for the new settlements. During Cardoso's second term a discernible effort was made to restrict MST protest and curb financial support for its activities. The 2002 election of President Lula, a longstanding MST ally, gave the movement a welcomed respite. Branford describes the unraveling of Lula's promise to implement a progressive agrarian reform program. The Lula government, she observes, feared upsetting agribusiness interests, alienating its conservative allies in Congress, and undermining its fiscal austerity program. Still, the Lula administration sharply increased funds for family agriculture and various projects aimed at improving the reform settlements. Faced with a difficult choice, the MST took the pragmatic decision to side with the Worker's Party's (PT) Left and attack the government's neoliberal policies, while sparing President Lula himself.

Chapter 14, "The MST and the Rule of Law in Brazil," by George Mészáros challenges orthodox ideas that assume a fundamental opposition between the MST's land mobilizations and the rule of law. Such views, he argues, oversimplify a complex situation and omit a fact relevant to many social movements around the world and throughout history, namely, their role as architects of an alternative legal order. The Brazilian justice system is manifestly unjust, cripplingly bureaucratic, extremely slow, and saturated with class bias, hence many of the MST's difficulties with the law. The 1988 Constitution espouses agrarian reform and qualifies property rights by their social function. Yet most judges insist on applying the Civil Code's absolutist approach to property rights. This closed legal methodology criminalizes MST activists. In a major victory for MST lawyers, though, a 1996 decision by Brazil's high court ruled that land occupations designed to hasten reform were "substantially distinct" from criminal acts against property. Far from simply disdaining legality, Mészáros concludes, the MST has actively contributed to shaping debates over the nature and function of law.

Chapter 15, "Beyond the MST: The Impact on Brazilian Social Movements," by Marcelo Carvalho Rosa argues that the MST has fueled the development of a new pattern of interaction between the Brazilian state and social movements. It assesses the MST's contribution to the formation of popular groups representing peasant women, people displaced by the construction of hydroelectric dams, small farmers, and homeless workers. Furthermore, Rosa examines the MST's impact on the National Confederation of Agricultural Workers (CONTAG) rural trade unions in the state of Pernambuco. Over the last quarter of a century, the MST's "movement form" and way of making collective demands on the state has become widely diffused throughout Brazil and legitimized by public officials.

The concluding chapter, "Challenging Social Inequality: Contention, Context, and Consequences," by Miguel Carter pulls together key themes and ideas in this volume and analyzes their main implications for social change in Brazil. It examines the principal arguments leveled against the MST's struggle for agrarian reform and delineates the broader contours of the debate at hand. Carter draws on the book's findings to suggest ways in which a sharper understanding of the landless movement can be reached. The chapter concludes with an assessment of the formidable obstacles to land reform in Brazil; the role of public activism in triggering and sustaining reforms aimed at reducing poverty and inequality; and the radical democratic implications of the MST's fight for social justice.

The Epilogue, "Broken Promise: The Land Reform Debacle under the PT Governments," by Miguel Carter provides a succinct assessment of Lula and Dilma Rousseff's conservative rural policies. These developments are set in context and reviewed in terms of their impact on the MST. The text closes by drawing out two paradoxes that emerge from this appraisal and weigh on the future of Brazil's democracy, its peasantry, and the ecological fragility of our planet.

Note

1. The term *peasant* is used in a broad sense throughout this volume. It refers basically to rural cultivators or "people of the land." These agricultural workers may or may not have control over the land they till. When they do, peasants usually engage in family labor practices on a modest parcel of land. For useful reviews of the definition of the peasantry, see Shanin (1987) and Kurtz (2000). The notion of a "landless peasant" deals with a variety of social categories of workers, mostly of rural origin, who aspire to cultivate a small plot of farmland. This concept is treated at length in various chapters in this volume, especially in chapters 3, 4, and 5.

1 Social Inequality, Agrarian Reform, and Democracy in Brazil

This chapter sets the Landless Rural Workers Movement (MST) and Brazil's mobilization for agrarian reform in context. It opens by juxtaposing two images of early twenty-first-century Brazil that illustrate in a vivid way the glaring social disparities and contentious visions enveloping the MST's quest for land redistribution. The text then offers a brief appraisal of the MST and its influence on Brazil's reform agenda. Thereafter, it probes some of the principal effects that deep and durable social inequality can have on development and democracy. This is followed by discussion of land reform experiences worldwide that situate the Brazilian case in comparative perspective. The ensuing two sections evaluate Brazil's prospects for agrarian reform and outline the main positions in the country's contemporary debate over land redistribution.

Early Twenty-first-Century Brazil: Two Distinct Images

May 2, 2005. And they marched. Carrying bright red flags in an orderly three-mile queue, 12,000 MST peasants embarked on an unprecedented sixteen-day procession across the hilly savannah leading up to Brasília. "Agrarian reform now!" chanted the men, women, and children assembled from far-flung corners of Brazil. The marchers had gathered the day before to celebrate a massive May Day labor rally. Their send-off from the sprawling modern city of Goiânia was blessed by the local archbishop and cheered on by other town leaders.

The logistical set up for the 125-mile mobilization was impressive.[1] Each night the marchers slept in large circus tents assembled on private ranches along the highway. The federal policemen accompanying the walk looked on rather anxiously each morning as the MST occupied the edge of a new estate to set up its camp. No violence was used, and all encampment areas were tidied up after the crowd's departure.

All participants were served three daily meals prepared by a cooking staff of 415 volunteers. Food donations from land reform settlements linked to the MST and contributions from church organizations, local and state governments, and other national and international sympathizers, assured the necessary resources for the mobilization.[2] Throughout the march, the MST's mobile radio station broadcast special programs available to participants through 10,000 small radio receivers on loan from the World Social Forum. More than sixty-five vehicles were employed to transport the circus tents, portable toilets, and personal belongings from one campsite to the next.[3]

Each stretch of the march began before sunrise. Protest songs, chants, and playful conversations with newfound comrades boosted morale along the daily eight-mile walk. Afternoons and evenings were reserved for consciousness-raising activities and amusement. Through the study of primers prepared by the movement's pedagogical team and lectures offered by various guests, the participants were invited to debate an assorted range of topics, including the MST's proposal for agrarian reform, Brazil's political juncture, present-day forms of imperialism, and the dangers of genetically modified seeds, among other environmental concerns.

After dinner, the camp offered "cultural nights," with performances by peasant musicians, dancers, and poets from all regions of the country. A massive screen was set up to exhibit movies and documentaries. One of the crowd's favorites was Walter Salles's *Motorcycle Diaries*, a gripping film about the South American travel adventures of young Ernesto "Che" Guevara. No alcohol was allowed on the camp premises.

As the march worked its way to the nation's capital, MST representatives were busy meeting with government ministers, congressional leaders, and judicial authorities. Aside from petitioning for land reform, they lobbied in support of several rural development projects and human rights protection. Over the course of two weeks, MST emissaries participated in fifty gatherings with twenty different federal ministries.

The government's fiscal austerity concerns, nonetheless, put a damper on the MST's negotiations. Prior to the march, the finance minister had slashed the budget for many social programs, including land reform. The restrictions on domestic spending undermined President Luis Inácio Lula da Silva's longstanding commitments to redistribute land. The same austere policies, coupled with soaring interest rates, enabled the financial industry to post record-high profits. In early 2005, government payments to service Brazil's public debt doubled the amount spent on all programs related to health, education, social welfare, agriculture, transportation, and public security.[4]

"We refuse to accept the fact," declared Fátima Ribeiro, a member of the MST's national board, after meeting with the minister of agrarian development, "that the 850 million dollar cutback for agrarian reform will be used to pay interest on the national debt, handing out yet greater profits to the bankers. Hope," she added, "is the last thing to die and that's why we are mobilizing."[5] The MST's arrival to the nation's capital was greeted by São Paulo's senior senator, Eduardo Suplicy, and four deputies of the Workers Party (PT). Upon their arrival in Brasília, the marchers held a ceremony to thank their federal police escort and gave each officer an MST T-shirt and cap. After spending the night next to the football stadium, they set up on their final protest through Brasília. The procession of 20,000 citizens was led by indigenous people and afro-descendants from the state of Bahia. First, they demonstrated in front of the US Embassy where they left a pile of "American trash" (mostly litter from McDonalds and Coca Cola products) and burned toy weapons to repudiate American consumerism and imperialism. At the Finance Ministry, the MST held another protest rally where calls were made for an "authentic Brazilian model of development." A large sign described the Finance Ministry as a *Fazenda do FMI* (an IMF estate).

Meanwhile, MST delegates were busy in Congress presenting petitions to the presidents of the Senate and the Chamber of Deputies, and attending an honorary ceremony for Dom Luciano Mendes, the former head of Brazil's National Bishops Conference and a lifelong advocate for agrarian reform. Outside the National Congress, Brasília's civil police provoked the only confrontation of the entire seventeen-day mobilization. The brawl began after a police car drove into a throng of marchers, crushing many of its participants. In response, some began to bang on the vehicle. The mounted police rushed in to beat back the protesters. Adding drama to the episode, a police helicopter hovered menacingly low over the crowd. Two senators scurried to the scene to appease the local police. Close to fifty people were reportedly wounded in the melee.

News depictions of the final day of the march focused largely on this brief incident. Prior to this, television coverage of the march had been largely negative. For days, the media fixated its attention on the donation of food and water by the governor of Goiás and the mayor of Goiânia. The evening news treated this story, and the provision of six ambulances to care for the marchers, as a major political corruption scandal. A public prosecutor's decision to investigate the contribution to the march was given prominent headlines, and encouraged a reporter for TV Globo's "Jornal Nacional," Brazil's leading news program, to describe this "unprecedented situation" as one where "the state was actually financing a movement against itself."[6] At other points during the march, press interest was generally sparse. The day the MST arrived to Brasília, only one of the country's five leading newspapers carried a front-page story of their mobilization.

At the Palacio da Alvorada, President Lula warmly welcomed a delegation of fifty MST members and supporters from the church, labor, student, and human rights organizations, as well as national celebrities. Lula delighted his visitors by putting on an MST cap. After intense negotiations, his government agreed to restore the budget cuts for land reform, hire 1,300 new personnel to refurbish the federal agency responsible for land distribution, and offer additional support for agrarian reform communities. Few other petitions made by the MST were actually met.

The marchers' last evening culminated with an ecumenical worship service, followed by a political rally and a music concert with well-known Brazilian artists.

The MST march to Brasília was an imposing event, comparable in scope to other great marches of the twentieth century: Mahatma Gandhi's twenty-three-day walk to the coastal town of Dandi, India, in 1930, where he defied British colonial rule by making salt; the twenty-seven-day Jarrow Crusade of unemployed workers from northeast England to London, in 1936, in the midst of the depression era; Martin Luther King Jr.'s five-day walk from Selma to Montgomery, Alabama, in 1965, at the height of the civil rights movement in the United States; and, the thirty-four-day indigenous march from the Bolivian Amazon to La Paz, in 1990, to demand land rights and protection of the rainforest. But, never in world history had there ever been a peaceful protest march as large, lasting, and sophisticated as this one.[7]

▬▬▬ June 4, 2005. Scarcely eighteen days after the culmination of the MST march a very different scene unfolded in São Paulo, Brazil's mega-city, industrial heartland, and financial capital.

A helicopter landed on the top of a four-story, neoclassical Italian palazzo with an impressive view of the city's skyline. Next to the heavily guarded, fifty-million-dollar building stood a shantytown; below flowed the melancholic, stench-filled Tietê River.

Stepping out on the helipad was one of Brazil's most important politicians. Inside, the crowd stirred with excitement. Geraldo Alckmin and his wife Lu had arrived. Soon, São Paulo's governor would be inaugurating the largest luxury goods department store in the world: a "temple of opulence," a "Disneyland for the rich," a "shopping bunker," according to local news accounts.

Inside the palazzo, Alckmin and Lu embraced their daughter Sophia. Alckmin was given the word: "Daslu represents the union of good taste and many work opportunities." He would certainly know. Sophia and his sister-in-law, like other young women of the upper class, were prominent Daslu employees. The ribbons untied, fifty musicians of the Daslu violin orchestra began to play. Impeccable, white-gloved waiters served champagne. Throughout the two-day festivity, Daslu treated its elite guests with 2,280 bottles of exquisite Veuve Clicquout champagne.

Strolling over Daslu's 20,000 square meters of marble floors, covering the size of three football fields put together, Alckmin, Lu, and Sophia stopped to appreciate the refined luxury items on display: a Dior crocodile leather hand bag for $16,660; a Prada mink coat for $19,600; Dolce & Gabbana jeans for $1,750;

Manolo Blahnik sandals for $1,250; and a Ralph Lauren T-shirt for $1,030. "This is all very colorful," observed Alckmin.

On the second floor, Sophia pointed out to her parents a helicopter hanging from the ceiling. "Look at this is beautiful motorcycle," said Lu, shortly after, as she gestured toward a Harley-Davidson valued at $81,300. Luxury cars, including a convertible Maserati tagged at $306,000, were on exhibit nearby. A few steps ahead, a handful of model yachts were on display, among them a Ferreti boat priced at $5.4 million. Daslu's real estate office even offered an island near the posh beaches of Angra dos Reis. The cost: $3.3 million.

Skiing equipment for those planning a trip to Chamonix, $8,000 bottles of wine, the latest home entertainment technology, and much more; Daslu has it all. A champagne bar, comfortable sofas, flowers, and espresso cafes are scattered throughout the store. Beautiful women, fluent in various languages—the store's Dasluzettes—pamper their customers with endearing Brazilian charm.

"This is our elite club," explained a dazzling socialite. "It's an apotheosis," chimed in her companion. "Chanel, Prada, Gucci, they are all here at Daslu." Champagne flute in hand, she recalled her largest shopping "extravaganza," a $100,000 Mercedes Benz purchased on a whim. "And at Daslu, it was during a sale. I started getting more and more excited and didn't stop until I had bought 20 clothing items, all of them top fashion names. Why, just today I reserved two Chanel shoes. I could spend the entire day lost in Daslu. This is the most marvelous place in the world to get lost."[8]

Daslu's grandiose opening was artfully designed to corner Brazil's booming luxury goods market. At $2.3 billion a year, it is the largest such market in Latin America, growing rapidly at 35% a year. São Paulo alone accounts for 75% of the business, reputedly one of the world's most profitable.[9] Indeed, the richest Brazilians appeared to be doing better than ever before. Merrill Lynch estimated that the country's millionaires had jumped from 92,000 to 98,000 between 2003 and 2004. And according to *Forbes* magazine, the number of Brazilian billionaires doubled to sixteen in 2005.

Alckmin was not the only renowned politician in attendance at Daslu's opening ceremony. Along with scores of high-flying businessmen, bankers, industrialists, soy bean kings, and sports and fashion personalities, were José Serra, the mayor of São Paulo, and Antônio Carlos Magalhães, the powerful senior senator and kingpin of Bahia, best known by his acronym, ACM. During the festivities, Alckmin and Serra kept fending off questions about their presidential candidacies. Daslu was blessed to have such influential patrons.

July 13, 2005. Five weeks after its glittering inauguration, Daslu's world was shaken by a rude awakening. That morning, over 100 federal police officers and tax agents raided the Daslu palazzo and detained its owner, Eliana Tranchesi, along with two business associates, on suspicion of tax fraud. The investigators alleged that Daslu had evaded more than $10 million in taxes over the past ten months by using fake companies to underreport the value of its imported goods. At customs, Louis Vuitton dresses worth over $2,000 at wholesale prices were being declared for $10 and fine Ermenegildo Zegna ties for only $5.

The police actions triggered alarm bells in Brasília and in São Paulo. Terribly upset with the news, ACM moved quickly to intervene on behalf of Eliana, a family friend who had hired the senator's granddaughter to work at Daslu. ACM voiced his outrage to the minister of justice, who spent much of the day handling angry phone calls from other VIPs. The senior senator then called Eliana, who was still in custody at the federal police office, and cried with her over the phone. Later, he made a scathing speech at the Senate podium criticizing the Lula government. His comments were echoed by his colleague Senator Jorge Bornhausen, president of the second largest party in Congress, the conservative Party of the Liberal Front (PFL), who described the Daslu raid as an "attack against the market." Eliana's arrest, he warned, could "generate an economic crisis by frightening foreign investments from Brazil."[10]

The country's leading business association, the Federation of Industries of São Paulo (FIESP) issued a forceful communiqué condemning the police arrest at Daslu. National news coverage of the affair gave prominent voice to its critics. The editorials of the country's most important newspapers supported Daslu and her owner. The media's depiction of the story prompted the ombudsman of Brazil's leading daily, *Folha de São Paulo*, to lament: "our newspaper could have published at least one little article defending or explaining the Federal Police's actions."[11]

▬▬▬ Two contrasting scenes, the MST's national march to Brasília and Daslu's inauguration in São Paulo, only a few days apart, provide pointed images of early twenty-first-century Brazil. Both events share a typically Brazilian air of grandiosity. One presents the largest long-distance protest march in world history. The other portrays the opening of the biggest luxury department store on earth. Their many differences, however, are compelling and emblematic.

Here stands a multiracial mobilization of the poorest strata of Brazilian society. There is an essentially all-white gala of its wealthiest pinnacle. One event is an act of protest, fueled by feelings of solidarity and the mystique nurtured by a sense of shared sacrifice. The other celebrates a business endeavor that caters to hedonistic temptations. Whereas the marchers live frugally, consuming mostly home-grown food staples, the Daslu crowd shares a feast sprinkled with imported sparkling wine, basking amid fashionable name brands and extraordinarily expensive products.

The contrasts continue. Progressive politicians back the MST mobilization, while the Daslu inauguration is well-attended by conservative ones. Their depictions in the mass media are disparate as well. The nation's leading news outlets treat public expenditures of $130,000 in food and water for the MST marchers as an act of political corruption, while tacitly condoning Daslu's scheme to evade $10 million in import levies. Whereas the MST needs to agitate for agrarian reform and other basic social rights, the Daslu crowd enjoys the necessary contacts, clout, and financial means to advance their interests in more discrete ways. The MST march challenges Brazil's status quo. The Daslu fête celebrates it with great opulence.

Brazil's sharp societal divide runs the gamut of this continental-size nation: the fifth-largest country in the world, both in territory and population, the ninth-leading economy, by the mid-2000s, and one of the globe's most unequal societies. According to a 2005 report, only war-ravaged Sierra Leone exceeded Brazil's income disparity. In Brazil, the wealthiest 10% of the population holds 46% of the nation's income, while the poorest 50% possesses only 13%.[12] The combined resources of its 5,000 richest families—that is, 0.001% of the population—adds up to 40% of the nation's gross domestic product (GDP).[13]

In the countryside, asset distribution is even more unequal. Scarcely 1% of the landholders control 45% of the nation's farmland, while close to 37% of the landowners possess only 1% of this same area. By all accounts, Brazil holds one of the world's highest concentrations of land.[14] Existing land tenure arrangements are rooted in Brazilian history. These were forged during its colonial period, with the vast land grants (*sesmarias*) to privileged Portuguese families and the institution of slavery. The sharp asymmetries were sustained, thereafter, under different political systems: empire, oligarchic republic, military rule, and political democracy.[15]

The MST and Daslu emblemize Brazil's disjointed society. Both worlds are interwoven, however. In their own way, each sheds light on the other. To confine the MST's place in Brazilian society as a movement merely engaged in the struggle for land or the search for alternative models of rural development is to miss out on the larger picture. The MST is not just a rural phenomenon. Looming behind its orderly marches and bright red flags is a specter that haunts Brazil's secular inequities. Though often exaggerated, the fears of change it elicits are not baseless. The MST rattles common-held perceptions, norms, and customs. It upsets "the natural order of things." It exposes, gives voice to, and channels tensions that underlie Brazilian society. Some view its agitation as a national anathema. Others sympathize with its disruptive thrust. Among the latter, many consider the movement a powerful Brazilian symbol and inspiration in the struggle to achieve equal rights and the full promise of citizenship.

The MST and the Struggle for Agrarian Reform in Brazil

During the twentieth century land distribution policies were undertaken in scores of nations. By the 1990s, however, the third world's trend toward urbanization and increasing agricultural yields through innovative technologies, coupled with the demise of communism and the rise of neoliberalism, had created a climate of opinion that sidelined land reform from the international development agenda. Amid all this, a curious countertrend began to take place in Brazil. Since the 1980s, an array of grassroots mobilizations has been pressing the Brazilian state for land reform, engendering in the process one of the longest sustaining social movements in history: the MST. By the mid-1990s the MST had become Latin America's largest social movement, and land reform had become firmly entrenched in Brazil's public agenda.

Brazil's first stirrings for land reform took place in the mid-1950s, in the country's poor northeast region. These mobilizations gained broader impetus during the early 1960s. The country's first national agrarian reform program was thwarted, nevertheless, by a conservative military coup d'etat in 1964, days after its promulgation. Thereafter, Brazil's nascent rural social movements and their leftist allies suffered extensive repression. The newly created National Confederation of Agricultural Workers (CONTAG) was placed under state corporatist control. Eight months after the coup, however, the new military president issued a moderately progressive land reform law. Although used mainly to further the government's colonization program in the Amazon, the legislation gave reform advocates—notably CONTAG, church, and opposition party leaders—a legal platform on which to defend squatters and call for land distribution.

CONTAG's rural network expanded rapidly with government support. By 1984, it included 2,626 unions with over nine million members. Although constrained by the authoritarian regime and its own bureaucratic ways, the rural trade union movement provided an important venue for the formation of class identity among the peasantry and the diffusion of citizenship rights. They also offered a space that allowed small farmers and rural workers to nurture social capital and leadership skills and to discuss agrarian matters. Despite the military's alliance with the landlord class, CONTAG and many of its unions found ingenuous ways to sustain an ongoing, often discrete, struggle for land in communities scattered across the countryside.[16]

A new landless movement erupted with force in the early 1980s, notably in Brazil's southern region. It emerged with the backing of a progressive religious network and the assistance of several rural trade unions, in a context shaped by intense agricultural modernization, growing demands for democracy by civil society groups, and the gradual demise of military rule. The MST was established officially in January 1984. A year later, Brazil witnessed the inauguration of a new civilian government that promised to carry out a land reform program.

Since its origins, the movement has developed a sophisticated grassroots organization, with a nationwide presence, an estimated 1.14 million members, over 2,000 agricultural settlements, a network of 1,800 primary and secondary schools, a national university, various news outlets, 161 rural cooperatives, including 4 credit unions, and 140 food processing plants.[17] By 2006, the MST had prodded the Brazilian government to distribute more than 3.7 million hectares, a territory nearly the size of Switzerland, or the state of West Virginia.[18] After the mid-1990s, the MST earned national fame as a leading critic of neoliberal policies and a forceful voice on behalf of Brazil's underprivileged majority.[19]

Through its ongoing activism and frequent workshops, the movement has inspired many other grassroots associations in Brazil and elsewhere in Latin America. An array of popular organizations, including CONTAG's rural trade unions, have assimilated MST tactics and taken courage from its actions.[20] Between 2000 and 2006, the Brazilian countryside had eighty-six peasant associations engaged in mobilizations for agrarian reform.[21] The MST is the most visible and elaborate of these movements. It remains predominant in the south. But the struggle in the northeast and Amazonian region has been led primarily by rural trade unions and various locally organized movements, including informal groups of squatters. In 2006, over a quarter of Brazil's 7,611 agrarian settlements were linked to the MST.[22] More than 90% of the land distributed between 1979 and 2006, however, resulted from activities undertaken by other peasant groups. This is particularly the case in the Amazonian region where roughly three-quarters of Brazil's land distribution has taken place.[23] The vast majority of these allocations have resulted from peasant land struggles.

In recent years, the MST has become an influential voice in international advocacy networks such as the World Social Forum and Vía Campesina, a coalition of family farmer associations in sixty-nine countries. By placing agrarian reform on Brazil's public agenda, the MST has helped stimulate growing global interest in land redistribution. A telling manifestation of this trend took place in early 2006, when the United Nation's Food and Agriculture Organization (FAO) convened its Second International Conference on Agrarian Reform and Rural Development. The last time the FAO had held a gathering on this topic was in 1979. The 2006 event was hosted by the Brazilian government in Porto Alegre, Rio Grande do Sul, not far from where the MST was born.[24]

Few issues have been as contentious in contemporary Brazilian politics as land reform. The MST's incisive role in the struggle for land redistribution has earned it glowing accolades on the political Left and spiteful comments among those with conservative views. In recent years, the Right has gone as far as to portray the MST's mass occupations of large, mostly idle farms as "acts of terrorism."[25] This sense of paranoia on the Right finds a natural counterpart in the romanticized depictions offered by the idealist Left. Both revel in the MST's revolutionary potential, albeit for opposite reasons. Each side exaggerates considerably. In doing so, they generally overplay the MST's influence on Brazilian affairs.

Though unusually long lived and complex for a social movement, the MST is essentially a poor peoples' association. It operates with limited resources and is susceptible to many of the collective action problems that can be found among grassroots organizations. The MST is not a "society of angels." Within the movement one can find many of the same human vices and blunders that have beset other social movements across the world.[26] Although large and broadly extended throughout Brazil, the MST comprises only a small fraction of its populace. Less than 1% of the nation's adult population and no more than 5% of its rural inhabitants are members of this social movement.[27]

Part of the MST's public recognition stems from an element of media aggrandizement. News coverage of the MST, though frequent, has been mostly negative, and at times blatantly hostile. The myths and misunderstandings about the MST constructed by the Brazilian press cannot be underrated.[28] The country's striking concentration of media power is partially responsible for this situation. It is estimated that nine family-owned conglomerates in Brazil control the media outlets that generate 85% of the country's news information.[29] Though staffed with many competent journalists, this press oligopoly and its attendant class biases hamper the diffusion of alternative views on the MST and other popular organizations.

Fear, fury, enchantment, and controversy over the MST should be of no surprise to students of land reform. After all, the redistribution of land, wealth, and power has sparked inevitable conflicts throughout world history. As Frederick Douglass presciently observed, such changes cannot take place without a measure of "thunder and lightning."[30]

Social Inequality, Development, and Democracy

Prevailing ethical views across the world, it is fair to say, abhor situations of steep social injustice. Gross disparities of wealth deeply offend most religious traditions and secular philosophies. Injunctions against hoarding food and other livelihood assets can be found in the Judeo-Christian tradition, Islam, Hinduism, Buddhism, Marxism, and various strains of liberalism.[31] These long-standing moral concerns have been reinforced in recent years by a growing awareness among scholars as to the harmful effects that durable inequities of wealth and other assets can have on economic growth, social development, and political democracy. The following comments synthesize several key ideas in this regard.[32]

1. *High inequality can slow economic growth.* Unfair access to credit means the economy misses out on profitable opportunities. Unequal educational opportunities lead to a loss of potential talent. Lopsided access to productive assets can leave entire segments of the population outside the market society,

because they are simply too poor to produce for the domestic market or consume the goods produced therein. The point is well illustrated in a study prepared by Nancy Birdsall and Richard Sabot comparing economic growth rates and social inequality in Brazil and South Korea, a country that experienced a radical land reform following World War II and invested substantially thereafter in developing its human capital. Using a simulation exercise, the study revealed that Brazil's economy would have grown an additional 17.2% between 1960 and 1985 if it had had South Korea's levels of social equality. Income disparity cost Brazil at least 0.66% of its yearly GDP growth. Deep social imbalances, then, reduce economic efficiency and progress.[33]

2. *High inequality hinders poverty reduction and can fuel further disparities.* Sharp and durable disparities of wealth make it much harder to reduce poverty through economic growth alone. According to a World Bank report, "Brazil could reduce poverty by half in ten years with 3% growth and an improvement of 5% in the Gini coefficient (the most common measure of income inequality)." Adding, "It would take the country 30 years to achieve the same objective with 3% growth and no improvements in income distribution."[34] Economic growth alone in highly unequal societies is more likely to fuel income disparity than bridge its gap. Brazil's "economic miracle" in the late 1960s and mid-1970s offers a poignant example of this. Between 1966 and 1976 Brazil's annual GDP growth averaged an impressive 9.2%, yet income inequality rose sharply. From 1960 to 1977 inequality increased from 0.50 to 0.62 on the Gini coefficient scale.[35]

3. *High inequality diminishes the overall quality of life, particularly in matters of personal security.* Every year one in three Brazilians is a victim of crime. The nation's homicide rate of 23.4 deaths per 100,000 people is nearly three times higher than the world average.[36] Steep disparities can make life miserable for all sectors of society. Whereas the Brazilian rich live in guarded mansions and condominiums, with private security around the clock, the urban poor are often victimized by the drug-related violence that has taken firm root in the nation's sprawling shantytowns (*favelas*). In 2007, only 6% of the Brazilian population felt their society was becoming safer.[37]

4. *High inequality tends to diminish social trust.* Stark class asymmetries nurture societal tensions and misgivings. According to the Latinobarómetro poll, Brazil has the lowest levels of social trust in the entire continent. Between 1996 and 2004, an average of less than 5% of Brazilians said they could trust other people most of the time.[38] High mistrust hampers the development of social capital. As Robert D. Putnam and other scholars suggest, a grave deficiency of social capital can hinder market activities, frustrate civil society efforts, and stifle the workings of political democracy.[39]

5. *High inequality engenders a dualistic pattern of development and produces a disjointed, apartheid-like society.* In 1974, economist Edmar Bacha coined the concept of "Belindia" to describe this phenomenon in Brazil: a small, rich, first-world Belgium coexisting with a large, poor, third-world India. Belindia thrives on the disparities between the formal and informal sectors of the economy, each nowadays occupying half of the nation's workforce. Brazil's social apartheid hampers the development of basic civil rights. Its great social distance fuels an ethos of disregard for human rights, notably in relation to the poorest social strata.[40]

6. *High inequities condition political power and cultural resources in society.* High inequities bias the political rules of the game and produce lopsided distributions of political strength and representation. They also skew access to education, mass communications, and other informational assets. These conditions fuel a cultural hegemony by facilitating dominant efforts to instill their ideas, values, and perceptions of what is to be considered "realistic," "feasible," and "desirable" in society. Politics and public policies are thus shaped to favor the interests of the privileged few; a view shared by two-thirds of the Brazilian population.[41] The extreme imbalance of political power and cultural resources creates a vicious cycle that encourages corruption, undermines competition and efficiency, and hinders the development of human capital among the poorest segments of the population, by restricting public investments in health and education.[42]

7. *High inequalities subvert the rule of law.* Societies with stark power imbalances are inhospitable to the development of a juridical system based on the fair, impartial, and independent application of legal norms. Acute disparities of wealth, as Oscar Vilhena Vieira underscores, "obliterate legal impartiality, causing the invisibility of the extremely poor, the demonization of those who challenge the system, and the immunity of the privileged." In such societies, compliance toward legal institutions is undermined by a lack of mutual responsibility among its members. The underprivileged see no reasons to "behave according to the rules of the game that systematically harm their interests," while the privileged feel "no social constraints on the maximization of their interests."[43] In Brazil, only 10% of the population believes they have equal access to the judiciary, the second lowest position in Latin America.[44]

8. *High inequalities undermine political democracy.* Unequal access to productive assets can engender distributional conflicts and foster instability.[45] In offering their people a lower quality of life, starkly unequal nations can fuel legitimacy problems. A 2002 survey found that 86% of Brazilians thought their society was unfair.[46] Such feelings of discontent, no doubt, influence public per-

ceptions of their political regime. Between 1996 and 2006, an average of only 41% of Brazilians indicated a support for democracy, and barely 24% of those surveyed claimed they were satisfied with their democracy.[47] In sum, democracies in highly unequal societies tend to be of dismal quality. These polities are often perceived as corrupt, are generally disliked by their people, and are potentially unstable.[48]

The foregoing discussion suggests that gross social inequities pose a distinct and serious challenge to development and democracy. Reducing such disparities can be a difficult task, yet the reforms needed to make this possible are no mystery. These include a wide range of redistributive policies related to taxation, credit, employment, education, health care, housing, social safety nets, and land tenure.

Land Reform

Land reform has been a classic instrument for redistributing wealth since antiquity. The Hebrews, Greeks, and Romans went through phases of land redistribution between the seventh and second centuries BC. In the modern era, the first major land reform began with the French Revolution's decrees repealing feudal tenures and freeing all persons from serfdom. By contrast, in England the eighteenth-century enclosure movement expelled the peasantry from their communal lands and into the growing industrial towns. Scandinavian peasants were entitled to hold their own property by the early nineteenth century. During the subsequent decades similar measures led to the termination of feudal arrangements in Germany, Russia, Spain, and Italy. In the United States, the Homestead Act of 1862, issued amid the Civil War, enshrined the ideal of the family farm and spurred the colonization of its western territories. In Canada, similar policies were pursued under the Dominion Land Act of 1872.

However, as a matter of public policy and political struggle, no other century has witnessed as much attention to the land question as did the twentieth century. Certainly, by any standard, the last century has been the epoch of land reform par excellence, during which land redistribution policies were undertaken in scores of nations.[49]

In a very broad sense, the twentieth-century surge in land reform efforts can be explained by a constellation of demographic, economic, societal, and political factors. Rapid global population growth made land a scarcer commodity. Despite the accelerated urbanization, most of the world's population throughout the twentieth century actually lived in rural communities and derived their livelihood from farming. Economic modernization during this period fostered pressure to transform traditional land patterns and raise agricultural productivity. Coupled with this, a gradual yet inexorable breakdown of rural isolation through technological changes in communication and transportation generated a distinct context for advancing changes in land tenure patterns. This epoch also marks the diffusion of new power configurations shaped by the state's growing presence in the countryside; the appearance in rural areas of an array of external actors advocating fresh ideas; and the development of novel forms of peasant organization and mobilization.

Twentieth-century land reforms, though ushered under a variety of political systems and ideologies, have largely been associated with and influenced in many ways by the political Left. Indeed, all governments of a Marxist persuasion enacted significant reforms, often through state collectivization schemes, as in the Soviet Union, China, most of Eastern Europe, North Korea, Vietnam, Cuba, and Ethiopia. After World War II, Japan, South Korea, and Taiwan implemented significant land redistributions. These reforms were firmly supported by the US government, yet were strongly affected by the Cold War era and the prevailing zeitgeist in support of state-led development policies. In the ensuing decades, other Asian countries, including India, Pakistan, Bangladesh, and Sri Lanka, followed suit by introducing ceiling laws that restricted their farm holding size.

Elsewhere, a variety of nationalist regimes, influenced by socialist ideas, expropriated large landholdings to the benefit of peasants in Mexico, Bolivia, Guatemala (however briefly), Egypt, Indonesia, Algeria, Syria, Iraq, Libya, Portugal, and Peru. Under the sway of strong left-wing political parties, democratic governments in Italy during the late 1940s and Chile after the mid-1960s executed land reallocations as well. Other Latin American countries, such as Venezuela, Colombia, and Ecuador, initiated timid efforts in this regard in the aftershock of the 1959 Cuban revolution and the radical transformation of its agrarian structure. In the 1980s, Nicaragua, after the Sandinista revolution, and El Salvador, amid a war with left-wing guerillas, also executed varying land transfer programs.[50]

A common form of advancing land reform in the second half of the twentieth century was through the introduction of land ceiling legislation. These laws set limits on the size of agricultural landholdings. Land ceiling laws have been applied in both capitalist and socialist economies. Table 1.1 presents a sample of countries that have enacted such policies.

The origin and type of land reforms can be accounted for by two basic thrusts—one societal-based (or "from below") and the other state-anchored (or "from above"). Very often the temptation has been to dichotomize these two thrusts and describe the genesis of some land reforms as stemming from above while treating others as arising from below. This approach, however, involves a very crude approximation to reality. In practice, no modern land reform could ever take place in the absence of a state. By definition, land reforms entail state involvement in restructuring property relations or regulating tenure arrangements in the countryside. In the absence of the state, such alterations could

Table 1.1. Land ceilings: A comparative sample

Country and legislation year	Ceiling level High	Ceiling level Low	Country and legislation year	Ceiling level High	Ceiling level Low
Japan (1946)	21	1	India (1972)	21.9	4.1
Italy (1950)	—	300	Sri Lanka (1972)	20	10
South Korea (1950)	—	3	Algeria (1973)	45	1
Taiwan (1953)	11.6	1.5	Pakistan (1977)	8	4
Indonesia (1962)	20	5	El Salvador (1980)	—	500
Cuba (1963)	—	5	Nicaragua (1981)	700	350
Syria (1963)	300	15	Bangladesh (1984)	—	8.1
Egypt (1969)	—	21	Philippines (1988)	—	5
Peru (1969)	150	15	Thailand (1989)	—	8
Iraq (1970)	500	10	Nepal (2001)	6.8	1.3

Sources: Table 1.1 was produced on the basis of the following sources for each country: *Japan*, Kawagoe (1999); *Italy*, King (1973); *South Korea*, Kuhnen (1971); *Taiwan*, Tseng (2004); *Indonesia*, Quizón and Debuque (1999); *Cuba*, Menjívar (1969); *Syria*, AllRefer. com (2006a); *Egypt*, Library of Congress (2003); *Peru*, Lastarria-Cornhiel (1989); *Iraq*, AllRefer.com (2006b); *India*, Zaheer (1980) and Indiaagronet–Agriculture Resource Center (2006); *Sri Lanka*, Singh (1989); *Algeria*, King (1977); *Pakistan*, Quizón and Debuque (1999); *El Salvador*, Wood (2003); *Nicaragua*, Kaimowitz (1989); *Bangladesh*, Quizón and Debuque (1999); *Philippines*, Lara and Morales (1990); *Thailand*, Quizón and Debuque (1999); and *Nepal*, Aryal and Awasthi (2006). A preliminary table and thoughtful discussion of the merits and difficulties of implementing land ceilings can be found in Yue (2004).

Note: All figures are in hectares (one hectare equals 2.47 acres). Variations between high and low ceilings are usually linked to the issue of land irrigation. As a rule, nonirrigated lands are accorded a higher ceiling than irrigated ones.

only take place through war, land grabs, and other expressions of naked force. The state may ultimately legitimize the results of these struggles. Nonetheless, in doing so it would prove the basic point: in the end, all land reforms must be sanctioned by the state.

Alternatively, no land reform could ever arise in a society that lacked expectations and demands for it. The intensity, scope, and way in which these claims are articulated and acted upon can vary immensely. Without them, however, land reform would become a nonissue, as certainly appears to be the case in the world's most developed countries. Hence, at bare minimum, societal voices are needed to trigger the initial impetus for any land distribution program. Clearly, then, the enactment of land reforms implies a combination of both state and societal thrusts.

Throughout the twentieth century, in most countries of the world, transformations in land tenure arrangements have been largely spearheaded by the state. This was notably the case in Japan and South Korea (under US occupation),

Table 1.2. Land reform in Latin America: A comparative index

Ranking	Country	Period	Land Reform Index[a]	Farmland distributed[b] (%)	Peasant beneficiaries[c] (%)	Reform years[d]	Democratic regime[e]
1	Bolivia	1953–1955	34.17	29.9	52.7	2.4	Mostly not
2	Cuba	1959–1963	34.08	81.2	75	4.6	No
3	Guatemala	1952–1954	18.00	17	19	2.0	Yes
4	Chile	1967–1973	9.86	40	20	6.1	Yes
5	El Salvador	1980–1984	7.45	19.6	12.7	4.3	No
6	Nicaragua	1979–1988	5.63	29.9	23.1	9.4	Mostly not
7	Peru	1964–1977	4.45	35.4	25.1	13.6	Mostly not
8	Venezuela	1960–1973	3.92	29.1	24.8	13.8	Yes
9	Panama	1968–1978	3.52	21.9	13.3	10.0	No
10	Mexico	1917–1940	3.21	22.5	54.1	23.8	No
11	Colombia	1962–1979	1.72	17.1	13.8	18.0	Yes
12	Honduras	1967–1984	1.14	11.2	8.8	17.5	Mostly not
13	Ecuador	1964–1983	1.11	9	10.4	17.5	Mostly not
14	Paraguay	1989–2002	0.78	2.3	8.3	13.7	Mostly yes
15	Dominican Republic	1962–1982	0.75	8.7	6.9	20.7	Mostly yes
16	Costa Rica	1962–1980	0.68	7.1	5.4	18.3	Yes
17	**Brazil**	**1985–2002**	**0.63**	**7.6**	**3.4**	**17.6**	**Yes**
	Brazil Ranking		*17th*	*15th*	*17th*	*13th*	

Notes:

a. The *Land Reform Index* gauges both the scope and intensity of the land redistribution process. It does so by adding the percentages of farmland distributed and peasant beneficiaries, and dividing this number by the reform years.[1]

b. *Farmland distributed* refers to the percentage of reformed land in relation to the total farmland available in the country. The total farmland area excludes reserved public domains and nonagricultural areas.

c. *Peasant beneficiaries* gauges the percentage of families benefited from the reform in relation to the nation's agricultural workforce.

d. *Reform years* refers to the time period it took to implement the main phase of land redistribution, developed by dividing all the reform months by twelve. This chart does not encompass all reform activities in each country.[2] Rather it focuses on their principal reform periods. Fewer reform years generally imply a more intense pace of land redistribution.[3]

e. The *democratic regime* classification is based largely on the existence or not of an electoral democracy, that is, a regime in which the main national leaders acquire or hold office through free and fair elections.[4]

1. The percentages for farmland distributed and peasant beneficiaries were drawn from various sources. These are listed by country according to the Land Reform Index ranking order. (1) *Bolivia:* Eckstein, Donald, Horton, and Carroll (1978: Appendix A); (2) *Cuba:* data from MacEwan (1981: 45–46) for land expropriated from May 1959 to mid-1963 and the total farmland, and from the Cuban Economic Research Project (1965: 235) for the land expropriated during the remainder of 1963, the estimate for the percentage of beneficiaries is from Kay (1998: 17); (3) *Guatemala:* Handy (1994: 93–95); (4) *Chile:* de Janvry (1981: 206–7); (5) *El Salvador:* data on reform area and beneficiaries are from Thiesenhusen (1995b: 154), total farmland is from Strasma (1989: 413), and the total agricultural workforce is from the 1980 census figures, published by International Labour Organization (2008); (6) *Nicaragua:* numbers on reform area

and beneficiaries are from Kaimowitz (1989: 385) for 1979–80 and Enríquez (1991: 91–92) for 1981–88, total farmland is from Reinhardt (1989: 460), while the total agricultural workforce is based on a 1980 official estimate published by International Labour Organization (2008), percentages for Nicaragua are close to those offered by Baumeister (1992: 21): 28% for the reform area and 22% for the beneficiaries; (7) *Peru:* figures for the reform area and beneficiaries are from McClintock (1981: 61), total farmland is from Eckstein, Donald, Horton, and Carroll (1978: Appendix A), and total farming families is from Thiesenhusen (1989b: 10–11); (8) *Venezuela:* statistics for the reform area, beneficiaries, and total farmland are from Eckstein, Donald, Horton, and Carroll (1978: Appendix A), total farming families is from Thiesenhusen (1989b: 10–11); (9) *Panama:* Thiesenhusen (1989b: 10–11); (10) *Mexico:* Eckstein, Donald, Horton, and Carroll (1978: Appendix A); (11) *Colombia:* the numbers for the reform area and beneficiaries are from Zamosc (1987: 266–69), the total farmland was obtained by adding Zamoc's data for land area distributed between 1970–77 to the farmland area registered in the 1970 agrarian census, the total agricultural workforce is from the 1973 population census, obtained from International Labour Organization (2008); (12) *Honduras:* data for the reform area and beneficiaries is from Brockett (1998: 194), total farmland is from Stringer (1989: 364), while the total agricultural workforce is from the 1977 population census, published by International Labour Organization (2008); (13) *Ecuador:* Thiesenhusen (1989b: 10–11); (14) *Paraguay:* Carter (forthcoming); (15) *Dominican Republic:* figures on the reform area and beneficiaries are from Stanfield (1985: 320–23), while total farmland and farming families is from Thiesenhusen (1989b: 10–11); (16) *Costa Rica:* Thiesenhusen (1989b: 10–11); (17) *Brazil:* numbers for reform area and beneficiaries are based on DATALUTA (2008), total farmland area and agricultural workforce are from the 1995 agrarian census, IBGE (1996). Other sources consulted for this chart include El-Ghonemy (2001), Grindle (1986), Ondetti (2008), and Sobhan (1993).

2. A handful of countries extended their land distribution program after their main reform period. In Mexico, reform activities dropped considerably in the 1940s but regained some momentum in the 1960s. By 1970, Mexico's reform area represented 34.1% of the total farmland, while its peasant beneficiaries amounted to 66.2% of the total agricultural families; author's calculations based on Eckstein, Donald, Horton, and Carroll (1978: Appendix A). Both El Salvador and Nicaragua had small redistribution programs in the 1990s that benefited former insurgents. In the Nicaraguan case, this took place amid a modest reversal of the Sandinista land reform.

3. For most countries, the reform period begins with the introduction of either a new or enhanced agrarian reform law, or the announcement of a specific program to carry out such reforms. The starting dates for the following countries are: Mexico (February 5, 1917), Guatemala (June 17, 1952), Bolivia (August 2, 1953), Venezuela (March 19, 1960), Colombia (December 13, 1961, though computed as starting in January 1962), Dominican Republic (April 27, 1964), Ecuador (July 11, 1964), Chile (July 28, 1967), El Salvador (March 6, 1980), Brazil (May 27, 1985). Costa Rica's reform period begins with the creation of the Instituto de Tierras y Colonización (ITCO), a government agency designed to implement its 1961 land reform law. Honduras's reform gained impetus in mid-1967 with the installation of a reformist leader at the helm of the Instituto Nacional Agrario (INA), much after the promulgation of a 1962 land reform law. Paraguay's reform era begins with the election of President Rodriguez on May 1, 1989, three months after the demise of the Stroessner regime. All reform periods close at the end of the calendar year, with the exception of Guatemala, which concludes on June 27, 1954, with the overthrow of the Arbenz government; Chile, which ends on September 11, 1973, with the military coup against the Allende government; and El Salvador, which closed its reform period in June 1984, at the end of the reform period's legal mandate. A reform month is counted only if it encompasses more than half of the days in a month.

4. The regime classifications presented in the chart draws on Smith (2005: 347–53) and Mainwaring, Brinks, and Peréz-Liñán (2007: 157–60).

Taiwan (after the Nationalist takeover of the island), and most of Eastern Europe (guarded by the Soviet army). Mexico experienced a strong societal surge for land distribution in the years that followed the 1910 revolution, yet the country's principal agrarian reform measures, introduced by President Lázaro Cardenas (1934–40) bore the patent marks of an active state. Contemporary cases where the primary drive for land reform is a societal one include Brazil, Paraguay, Honduras, Guatemala, the Philippines, Bangladesh, India, Indonesia, South Africa, and Zimbabwe.

Land reform can take place under autocratic and democratic political regimes. The most radical transformations have taken place in nondemocratic settings, usually after a social revolution or a foreign military occupation. In Latin America, four of the ten most extensive land reforms were implemented after social revolutions, in Mexico (1910), Bolivia (1952), Cuba (1959), and Nicaragua (1979). Only three of the top ten reforms were conducted by democratically elected leaders. These were in Guatemala (1952–54), Chile (1967–73), and Venezuela (1960–73). Guatemala's and Chile's reform, nevertheless, ended in right-wing military coups supported by the US government. Land distribution was reversed in both countries. The Venezuelan reform was less controversial since it was carried out mainly on public lands.[51] Compared to other Latin American experiences, Brazil's land reform process from 1985 to 2002 was one of the least significant in the hemisphere. It ranks last in the Land Reform Index presented in table 1.2. This index measures the scope and intensity of land reforms undertaken in seventeen Latin American countries during the twentieth century. In all these cases land distribution policies were preceded and accompanied by peasant land occupations and other pressure tactics.

Political democracies are unlikely to institute a revolutionary alteration of the land structure. Constitutional guarantees and mechanisms of due process temper the prospects of sweeping transformations. Still, the range of options available under this political regime can be broad. Table 1.3 conceptualizes two basic alternatives for redistribution under existing democracies: a conservative and a progressive approach to agrarian reform. The chart presents a distilled, ideal-type distinction, aimed at flushing out the underlying conceptual differences. Reality, of course, often blurs these categories. The analytical distinction, nonetheless, should help elucidate contemporary developments in Brazil.

Brazil's Prospects for Agrarian Reform

This section examines the contextual setting, politics, and prospects of agrarian reform in Brazil. It opens with a comparative framework aimed at situating the nation's development challenge in a global perspective. Brazil is not a poor country. As can be observed in table 1.4, its wealth and human development

Table 1.3. Agrarian reform in contemporary democracies: Two basic approaches

	Conservative	Progressive
Impetus	Reactive and restrained. Responds to social protest.	Proactive and engaging. Motivated by an agenda for social change.
Policy scope	Deals with specific demands, not systemic issues.	Structural orientation.
Main purpose	Appease rural conflicts. Limit social change.	Promote peasant agriculture. Transform agrarian structure and power relations.
Extent and rate of land distribution	Minimal and protracted. Benefits relatively few people. Land tenure pattern remains mostly intact. Reforms are implemented at a sluggish pace.	Substantial and rapid. Benefits a considerable proportion of peasants. Land tenure system experiences swift and discernable changes.
Patterns of land distributions	Ad hoc and dispersed. Favor state and landlord interests.	Strategic and concentrated. Propitious for peasant development.
Effect on popular sectors	Palliative. Destimulates new claims.	Invigorating. Favors the assertion of new entitlement claims.
Impact on large landholders	Neutral, or even positive. Landlords can profit through generous state compensations.	Negative. Terms of expropriation favor the public treasury over the agrarian elite.
Relation to the status quo	Fearful of upsetting landlords. Distribution does not alter prevailing power relations.	Prepared to confront landlords. Distribution seeks to change power configurations.
Relations between state and social movements	Tense and/or paternalistic. Criminalization of social protest. Human rights violations occur with impunity.	Constructive partnership. Respect for social movement autonomy. Protection of basic human rights.
State and land reform settlements	Meager support, if any. Aid responds mainly to social agitation.	Significant. State programs foster sustainability, including agro-ecology.

Table 1.4. Inequality, development, and land reform, Brazil and other leading developing countries: A comparative view.

Country	Inequality			Human Development Index
	Income/ consumption Gini	90th/10th percentile ratio	Land tenure Gini	
Brazil	0.59	16.25	0.85	0.800
South Africa	0.58	16.91	—	0.674
Colombia	0.54	15.00	0.80	0.791
Argentina	0.51	13.71	0.83	0.869
Mexico	0.49	11.87	—	0.829
Philippines	0.46	—	0.55	0.771
China	0.45	—	—	0.777
Iran	0.43	—	—	0.759
Nigeria	0.41	7.26	—	0.470
Thailand	0.40	5.56	0.47	0.781
Turkey	0.37	5.73	0.61	0.775
Egypt	0.34	—	0.65	0.708
Indonesia	0.34	—	0.46	0.728
India	0.33	—	—	0.602
South Korea	0.32	—	0.34	0.921
Russia	0.32	4.67	—	0.802
Poland	0.31	4.03	0.69	0.870
Pakistan	0.27	3.09	0.57	0.551
Brazil Ranking	**1st**	**2nd**	**1st**	**6th**

Sources: United Nations Development Programme (2007) for column 4; United Nations Development Programme (2005) for column 7; World Bank (2005) for columns 1, 2, 3, 5, 6; CIA (2008) for column 8; for column 9, see note below.

Notes: Argentina's income inequality refers only to urban areas, which comprise over 90% of its population. The column for land reform experiences in the twentieth century was prepared on the basis of an extensive literature review presented in the note to table 1.1 and note 50. The four-fold classification draws on two criteria: (1) the scope of the redistribution and (2) the maximum size of land ceiling laws. India, for example, had little land redistribution in the twentieth century, yet instituted fairly restrictive land ceiling laws which varied from state to state, oscillating between 4.1 and 21.9 hectares. By contrast, the Philippines's land ceiling law of five hectares was riddled with legal loopholes that exempted three-fourths of the nation's farmland. All currency figures are in US dollars.

	Wealth and poverty		Agriculture employment % in agriculture	Land reform experience during the 20th century
Gross national income at PPP	Population % below $2 per day at PPP	Child mortality under 5 per 1.000		
8,020	22.4	35	20	Low
10,960	34.1	66	9	None
6,820	22.6	21	23	Low
12,460	14.3	20	1	None
9,590	26.6	28	18	Moderate
4,890	47.5	36	35	Low
5,530	46.7	37	43	Extensive
7,550	7.3	39	25	Extensive
9,309	2.4	198	70	None
8,020	32.5	26	49	Moderate
7,680	24.7	39	36	None
4,120	43.9	39	32	Moderate
3,460	52.4	41	43	Low
3,100	80.6	87	60	Moderate
20,400	2.0	5	10	Extensive
9,620	7.5	21	11	Extensive
12,640	2.0	7	16	Extensive
2,160	73.6	98	42	Moderate
7th	**6th least**	**8th least**	**7th least**	**Low**

indicators rank moderately high in comparison to other large developing nations. Brazil, however, is the most unequal of all these countries. Only South Africa, a country that suffered a brutal system of racial apartheid during much of the twentieth century, rivals Brazil's income disparities.

Two suggestive findings can be gleaned from table 1.4. The first is that inequality and poverty are not inherently related. India, Pakistan, and Indonesia are illustrative of the fact that societies that are less unequal can also be quite poor. Extreme levels of income equality, in fact, can hinder economic growth by reducing work stimulus and other investment incentives. The Soviet Union's uniform wage structure exemplifies this point well.[52] Brazil, of course, presents the opposite extreme. Here, excessive inequality reduces economic output and sustains significant levels of social misery. A critical twenty-first-century challenge for Brazil, then, is to overcome its longstanding patterns of social exclusion by broadening access to wealth and other livelihood assets.

The second lesson suggests a connection between levels of societal equality and land tenure reforms. The most unequal developing nations listed in table 1.4 are those that have had little or no land reform during the twentieth century. Only two exceptions, Turkey and Indonesia, had a fairer land tenure system in place prior to the last century than that found in most formerly colonized areas of Latin America and Africa. Nearly all of the more egalitarian societies in this roster of nations had experienced a substantial process of land redistribution. Thus, as the world historical record shows, land reform can play an important role in reducing grave social disparities.

Brazil's social contrasts are palpable in many ways. In the countryside, a highly modernized and dynamic agricultural economy coexists with a pauperized society, in which more than half of the population lives below the national poverty line. The nation is a leading global producer and exporter of major agricultural commodities—notably sugar, coffee, oranges, soybeans, beef, and tobacco—yet nearly half of its population has experienced restrictions in accessing basic food necessities. According to a 2005 government survey, more than 25 million Brazilians, 14% of the population, had suffered from hunger in recent years.[53]

Adding to these contrasts, Brazil is also a land of strong regional differences. Indicators of its conspicuous north-south divide can be observed in table 1.5. Whereas the midwestern and southern half of Brazil enjoys a standard of living comparable to Mexico, Cuba, and Bulgaria, human development indicators in the northeast are similar to those of Indonesia and Syria, while the Amazonian north is akin to Iran and Paraguay. Yet on income distribution all five Brazilian regions fare among the nine most unequal nations of the world.[54]

Rural violence in Brazil is much higher in the north and northeast regions, where inequality and poverty are more prevalent. As noted in table 1.5, between 1988 and 2005, more than three-quarters of all rural killings, assassination attempts, and death threats over land conflicts took place in these two regions. The northern half of Brazil includes areas where state presence has either been historically absent or enmeshed in patrimonial fashion with large landholders. Landlords in these regions, and elsewhere in Brazil, have repeatedly used violence to deter the struggle for agrarian reform. According to the Pastoral Land Commission (CPT), Brazil's leading human rights organization in the countryside, between 1985 and 2006, 1,465 land reform activists and peasants, including dozens of children, were killed in different rural conflicts. Impunity with regard to these assassinations has been the norm. Only 8% of these cases were ever brought to trial, and fewer than twenty of the landlords who hired the gunmen to execute such crimes have been condemned by the courts.[55]

Since 1985, successive governments have undertaken land distribution measures, prompted largely by peasant mobilizations and public outrage over a few notorious killings in the countryside. By 2002, the Brazilian state had benefited close to 605,000 peasant families through the allocation of 27 million hectares in public and private land; a territory three times the size of Portugal.

Table 1.5. Poverty inequality and development in Brazil, by region

Regions	Poverty (%)	Illiteracy (%)	Human Development Index	Income distribution Gini	Land distribution Gini	Rural violence index
North	35	8	0.762	0.598	0.851	40
Northeast	50	18	0.718	0.617	0.811	37
Midwest	24	9	0.827	0.622	0.810	10
Southeast	17	7	0.834	0.586	0.757	8
South	20	5	0.831	0.572	0.712	6
Brazil	**28**	**11**	**0.801**	**0.609**	**0.843**	—

Sources: Gacitúa-Marió and Woolcock (2005b) for columns 1, 2, 4; Hoffman (1998) for column 5; CPT/NERA (2006) for column 6; see note for column 3.

Notes: The five regions of Brazil comprise the following states: north (Acre, Amapá, Amazonas, Pará, Rondônia, Roraima, and Tocantins); northeast (Alagoas, Bahia, Ceará, Maranhão, Paraiba, Pernambuco, Piauí, Rio Grande do Norte, and Sergipe); midwest (Brasília, Goiás, Mato Grosso, and Mato Grosso do Sul); southeast (Espírito Santo, Minas Gerais, Rio de Janeiro, and São Paulo); south (Paraná, Santa Catarina, and Rio Grande do Sul). Poverty figures are from the Fundação Getúlio Vargas based on a 1999 PNAD survey; illiteracy data draws on the 2001 census; Gini coefficient for income inequality is derived from data in the 2001 census, see Gacitúa-Marió and Woolcock (2005b: 27). The Gini coefficient for land inequality was produced on the basis of INCRA's 1998 Land Registry, see Hoffman (1998). The rural violence index presents the percentage of murders, death threats, and attempted assassinations, by regions, of peasants and land reform activists between 1988 and 2005. These data are based on CPT compilations by Bernardo Mançano Fernandes, director of the Núcleo de Estudos da Reforma Agrária (NERA) of UNESP Presidente Prudente. The Human Development Index (HDI) was prepared by the author on the basis of the following sources: life expectancy data for 2006, IBGE (2007a); adult literacy rates for 2006, IBGE (2007b); gross enrollment ratio based on 2000 data, Pontifícia Universidade Católica de Minas Gerais, Instituto de Desenvolvimento Humano and Programa das Nações Unidas para o Desenvolvimento (2004); GDP per capita at Purchasing Power Parity (PPP) dollars for 2005, IBGE (2005); and PPP conversion rate (IMF 2008). The formula used to produce the HDI was taken from UNDP (2007: 356).

Under President Lula's first government the total number of beneficiaries increased to 825,000 families, while land distribution reached a total of 41.3 million hectares; a territory as large as Sweden.[56] Despite the impressive numbers, the reform process has been an essentially conservative one, in the terms offered in table 1.3.

True, there have been some important differences. Under presidents Fernando Collor de Mello (1990–92) and Fernando Henrique Cardoso (1995–2002), the federal government was more hostile to landless movements than during the Lula administration. The Cardoso and Lula governments, on the other hand, distributed more land than their predecessors. The Lula government, however, has provided more resources for land reform settlements and peasant agriculture than all previous administrations. Still, despite these trends, the gist of agrarian reform policies in Brazil has been mostly reactive, restrained, and sluggish in its demeanor.

The reform's slow pace cannot be accounted for by any shortage of land or lack of potential beneficiaries. Quite to the contrary, scholarly studies suggest there are somewhere between 3.3 and 6.1 million families that could benefit from land reform. With children included, the number of potential beneficiaries could reach as many as 30.6 million Brazilians, a population the size of Canada.[57] Furthermore, according to the official land registry, Brazil has at least 231.3 million hectares (1.4 million square miles) of unproductive land, both privately and publicly owned. This estimate excludes all conservation areas and indigenous reserves. Altogether, Brazil's unproductive farmland comprises no less than 27% of the national territory; an area four times the size of France, or ten times the size of the state of Montana.[58]

Land reform measures enacted thus far have strived mainly to appease immediate claims, defuse local conflicts, and, above all, avoid major confrontations with large landholders. As such, they have refrained from taking forceful actions aimed at transforming the agrarian structure and its power asymmetries. The distributional impact of Brazil's land policies, though significant in some local areas, has had a minimal effect on the nation's land tenure arrangement. Even with the initiatives undertaken by Lula's first government, Brazil's land redistribution still ranks (in proportional terms) among the least significant reforms undertaken in Latin America. The total 1985–2006 reform efforts raised Brazil's position in the Land Reform Index (see table 1.2) to fifteenth place, only two notches above the last place. All told, this reform process has benefited 5% of the total agricultural workforce and distributed 11.6% of the total farmland.[59]

Brazil's conservative agrarian reform is the result of numerous factors addressed throughout the book.[60] One critical dimension deserves special attention here: the politics of Brazil's agrarian inequities. The current land structure originated during the colonial era and was maintained until the present period through various political practices. Brazil's early formation as an oligarchic society produced a powerful landlord class and a weak patrimonial state. Land concentration and slavery (a practice proscribed only in 1888, after 358 years of legal existence) produced a nation of sharp power asymmetries and autocratic rulers. This political system thrived on an export-oriented economy, structured around large plantations and extractive enclaves. Throughout Brazilian history, the agrarian elite reaped the benefits of state protection and privileged access to public resources. These patrimonial features established a highly exclusionary development model.

During the twentieth century, Brazil experienced an intense process of capitalist modernization, led by an invigorated state. Yet the secular inequities remained largely intact, especially in the countryside. The landlord class lost some of its national prominence with the rise of a thriving industrial, commercial, and financial bourgeoisie. Still, it retained significant political leverage, a result of its close ties to other business sectors and the media establishment, along with a large presence in the National Congress and an active engagement in state and local politics. The enduring strength of the landlord class has historically undermined efforts to democratize Brazilian politics and extend equal citizenship rights.[61]

Mainstream scholars such as Alfred P. Montero describe contemporary Brazilian democracy as an "oligarchical system of representation."[62] This system is the upshot of traditional elitist politics and institutional arrangements created during the twentieth century that undermined the political involvement of popular sectors. The stark disparities of power and access to public resources produced by this condition are illustrated in table 1.6.

Drawing on the data in table 1.6 one can establish the following findings. Between 1995 and 2006, the average political representation of landless peasants was one federal deputy for every 612,000 families. The landlords, on the other hand, had one federal deputy for every 236 families. Thus, the political representation of landlords in the Chamber of Deputies was 2,587 times greater than that of the landless peasantry. As a consequence of this lopsided distribution of power, between 1995 and 2005, each landlord had access to $1,587 in public expenditures to every dollar made available to landless peasants. Thus, extreme disparities in political strength have led to what John K. Galbraith wryly described as "socialism for the rich."[63]

Brazil's enduring oligarchic privileges were reinforced during the twentieth century through various practices that undermined the development of civil and political rights among the poor. In the last century, popular movements and progressive political parties endured the brunt of repression during Brazil's sixty-eight years of authoritarian rule.[64] Adding to this, the government hindered the formation of independent popular organizations by establishing a "state corporatist" structure for labor and peasant trade unions.[65] Instituted from the 1930s to the early 1980s, this framework legalized working-class associations in urban areas and, by the 1960s, in rural areas, while bringing them under state control. These developments, for the most part, constrained civil society expansion among the lower classes. Alongside these policies, Brazil's poor experienced the recurrent denial and violation of basic human rights, most dramatically through the intimidation, criminalization, and assassination of grassroots leaders. The "un-rule of law" among this segment of the population has deeply undermined trust and cooperation with law enforcement agencies.[66]

Various other mechanisms prevalent during the twentieth century led to the underdevelopment of poor people's political rights. The disenfranchisement of illiterates until 1985, along with extensive clientelistic practices and vote buying among the poor, contributed to the depoliticization of underprivileged

Table 1.6. Landless peasants, landlords, political representation, and public expenditures

	Landless peasants (and family farmers)	Landlords (and agribusiness)
Population Number of landless families and large landlords	6,120,000	22,000
Political representation Average number of federal deputies linked to each social sector, from 1995 to 2006	10	93
Public expenditures Total funds allocated by the federal government to each social sector, from 1995 to 2005 (in billions of US dollars)	10.2 bn	58.2 bn

Sources: Del Grossi, Gasques, Graziano da Silva, and Conceição (2001), and Ministério de Desenvolvimento Agrário (2003) for row 1; Vigna (2001, 2003) for row 2; Ministério de Planejamento, Orçamento e Gestão (2006) and Banco Nacional de Desenvolvimento (2006) for row 3.

Notes: Table 1.6 was developed on the basis of the following data and calculations. (1) *Population*: number of landless families assumes the higher estimate provided by Grossi, Gasques, Silva, and Conceição (2001). The number of large landlords is derived from INCRA's land registry data published by Ministério de Desenvolvimento Agrário (2003: Table 5.1.1.1). This figure includes all rural properties that are at least fifty times larger than the fiscal module established for Brazil's different regions. Fiscal modules are measurements set in the national agrarian law that vary in size according to regional characteristics. Near large urban metropolis a fiscal module usually equals five hectares of land. In distant parts of the Amazon, a fiscal module can include as much as 110 hectares. According to Brazil's agrarian law, any private estate above fifteen fiscal modules is considered to be a large property; see Teixeira (2005). (2) *Political representation*: number of federal deputies with organic ties to landless peasants is based on the average of three congressional periods. These included five representatives for the 1995–98 Congress; ten for the 1999–2002 period; and fifteen for the 2003–6 legislature. The number of federal deputies linked to the *bancada ruralista* (caucus representing large landholders and agribusiness interests), were the following: 117 for the 1995–98 congressional period; 89 during the 1999–2002 congress; and 73 during the 2003–6 legislative period. According to Edelcio Vigna, a rural policy expert at Brasília's Institute for Socio-Economic Studies (INESC), the figures for the landowners caucus should be treated as low estimates, since many other deputies are also direct descendants or relatives of large landholders, and thus inclined to cooperate with this group. In 2007, Vigna estimated that 120 federal deputies (23% of the lower house) and twelve senators were part of the bancada ruralista. I am grateful to Vigna's assistance in gathering this data. (3) *Public expenditures*: allocations to landless peasants are based on expenditures made by the Ministry of Rural Development. Allocations for large landholders include Ministry of Agriculture expenditures and agricultural credits provided by the Brazilian Development Bank (BNDES). The Ministry of Agriculture's expenditures and credit programs for small farmers, according to Vigna and other policy experts, is minute compared to the sums devoted in support of agribusiness farming and large cattle ranches. The Reais-US dollar exchange rate was calculated using data from the Federal Reserve Bank of St. Louis (2006).

sectors.[67] Moreover, Brazil's weakly institutionalized party system, costly election campaigns, and conservative media establishment, have bolstered elite interests while limiting the prospects for popular representation in politics. A highly fragmented party system, with weak party organizations and attachments, and intense personalist politics, has forged a political class deemed to be largely unaccountable to voters; albeit responsive to their wealthy campaign donors. "Weak parties," Scott Mainwaring writes, "have been a pillar of a system in which the state usually functions mostly for elites, in which these elites enjoy privileged access and favors," while "the poor suffer."[68]

The malapportionment of parliamentary seats in the National Congress has also buttressed the political strength of Brazil's large landholders. Election rules introduced by the military regime exacerbated federalist provisions limiting the democratic principle of "one person, one vote." This formula, in effect, enabled 13% of the national electorate to determine 51% of the Senate's composition and led to the overrepresentation of states with strong oligarchic traditions in both legislative chambers.[69] Due to their large presence in Congress, the landlords have been able to defeat various progressive initiatives on land reform, including pivotal measures in the 1988 Constitution. Further, their political clout has compelled all recent presidents to appease the landowners' caucus in order to sustain majority coalitions in Congress.

The obstacles to land reform and other redistributive policies in Brazil are compounded by the organizational fragmentation of its public administration and conspicuous bureaucratic politics. As Kurt Weyland underscores, these conditions have induced interest associations to "infiltrate" and "capture" many public agencies, and thus rendered state reform efforts vulnerable to elite opposition.[70] If anything, the "capacity of minority interests to block institutional change" has proven to be a resilient feature of contemporary Brazilian politics.[71]

The accumulated effects of Brazil's exclusionary development model and oligarchic system of political representation have greatly constrained the political participation and influence of popular sector groups. The last two decades of political freedoms and competitive elections have led to some discernible improvements, nonetheless. One of its stirring developments has been the rise of a new generation of popular movements, which, like the MST, have sought to organize and politicize their grassroots constituents. Since the mid-1990s, the MST has become Brazil's most expressive and incisive movement in the effort to contest the dominant system of elite privileges. Its contentious edge, brash tactics, and occasionally rough actions have stirred many reactions. Some intellectuals have accused the MST of being a "threat to democracy." Their views have had ample exposure in the mass media.[72]

A closer examination of the MST's actions, however, reveals a largely positive impact on Brazilian democracy. The MST has contributed much in advancing the prospects and quality of democracy by: (1) challenging the nation's stark social disparities, while generating constructive policy alternatives and valuable lessons in grassroots development; (2) strengthening Brazilian civil society through the organization and incorporation of marginalized sectors of the population; (3) facilitating the extension and exercise of basic citizenship rights—civil, political, and social—among the poor; (4) highlighting the importance of public activism—a form of social conflict grounded on pressure politics and bargaining with state authorities—as a catalyst for social development; and (5) engendering a sense of utopia and affirmation of ideals imbued in Brazil's long-term, complex, and open-ended democratization process.[73]

Brazil's prospects for substantial land reform remain uncertain. By international standards, Brazil is a world laggard on matters of wealth distribution. Even with a perceptible need and potential for reform, its current prospects face great political barriers. The long-term fate of agrarian reform will be shaped by multiple demographic, environmental, and economic trends, along with various political factors. In the coming years, much will depend on the balance of societal and political forces, the ideas articulated in the public sphere, and, ultimately, the political will of those at the helm of the state. Whatever the outcome, the social movement for agrarian reform has stirred and strengthened Brazilian civil society in ways that may well advance future struggles for democracy and social justice.

Agrarian Reform in the Twenty-first Century: The Brazilian Debate

The contextual analysis offered in the preceding section sheds light on the contemporary land reform debate in Brazil. This dispute is broadly divided into two camps. Standing on one side are longstanding opponents and newfound skeptics of land redistribution. On the opposite side are various proponents and sympathizers of agrarian reform. Their contrasting positions are tinged by varying perceptions of reality and shaped by different interests and value commitments. The following paragraphs outline the main arguments put forth by each camp.[74]

Opponents and skeptics argue that land reform has become an irrelevant policy for the nation's rural development given the technological modernization of agriculture, abundant food production, and profitable agribusiness farms. Further, they insist, the amount of unproductive land available for redistribution has diminished considerably, particularly in the southern and southeast regions of the country. Traditional land estates have been converted into agribusiness enterprises, which are currently responsible for two-thirds of the nation's agricultural output. In 2005, agriculture represented 42% of all Brazilian exports.[75] These exports are a leading source of foreign currency earnings needed to pay the country's external debt and reduce its reliance on international creditors. Thus, according to reform opponents, agribusiness' significant contribution to the national economy warrants the protection of all productive landholdings, regardless of their size. The government, therefore, should curtail all threats to existing property rights and refrain from land expropriations, even in cases where rural estates are known to employ slave labor.[76]

Adding to this, skeptics of agrarian reform underscore the fact that Brazil is nowadays primarily an urban nation. Only one-fifth of its population lives in the countryside and works in agriculture.[77] In their view, "the time for land reform has passed."[78] Modernization, they maintain, leads to an irreversible exodus from the countryside. This makes the peasantry a "moribund social class." Hence, instead of spending limited public resources on a "futile" economic cause, the government should focus on expanding its social welfare programs and generating urban jobs for the new migrants. Land reform, they maintain, is a very expensive way of doling out welfare assistance to the poor, particularly given the steep rise in land market values during the 2000s. At most, some argue, land distribution should be carried out only in Brazil's "backward" northeast region.[79]

To succeed in today's competitive market a family farmer needs specialized knowledge, modern technologies, and good management skills. Few land claimants, the critics contend, have the capacity to become successful farmers. In fact, most of them are undeserving "vagrants," "opportunists," and "cheaters."[80] Opponents assert that land reform settlements are an "economic failure" and usually describe these communities as "rural *favelas*." They believe the demand for land in Brazil is much lower than is often claimed and question official statistics on land concentration. These numbers, they suggest, are either inflated or irrelevant to the issues at stake.[81]

Finally, critics of land reform tend to be adamant in their opposition to the MST, which they portray as a "violent, authoritarian, and manipulative organization with a hidden revolutionary agenda." Land reform advocates, they claim, are driven by "ideological" views and informed by "outdated" ideas. Their "dangerous agitation," opponents sustain, jeopardizes Brazil's economic competitiveness, undermines the rule of law, and threatens its democratic institutions.[82]

The assorted supporters and sympathizers of agrarian reform, on the other hand, converge in their concern for Brazil's deep social injustice. Land reform, they contend, is an important policy for reducing poverty, fostering social inclusion, and bridging the country's vast inequality gap. Agrarian reform is a "historical debt" to Brazil's rural poor. Its implementation should be treated, many argue, as an act of reparation to the descendants of more than three centuries of slavery and longstanding restrictions to peasant land ownership. Despite the trend toward urbanization, Brazil still has a vast pool of potential land reform beneficiaries and extensive land availability, all of which makes land redistribution a contemporary and relevant policy. Large landholders, reform proponents insist, generally underutilize their properties and are routinely protected in this through acts of "state complicity." For example, they highlight the government's decision not to revise the more than three-decade-old productivity indexes used to determine if an estate can be expropriated for land reform. If the agribusiness producers are as "efficient" as they maintain, then, why not update these technical criteria? Agribusiness "success," critics point out, has been overhyped by a sympathetic media establishment, which masks the fact that this rural sector continues to benefit generously from public subsidies.

With adequate support programs, they assert, agrarian reform would stimulate rural productivity, especially for domestic consumption. The bulk of the food consumed by Brazilians, proponents highlight, is produced by family farmers, notably, manioc (92%), poultry (88%), bananas (85%), beans (78%), potatoes (77%), milk (71%), and coffee (70%). Moreover, family farmers are more productive per hectare than large-scale farmers and generate 87% of all rural employment in Brazil.[83] Land reform, they insist, is an effective and inexpensive way of generating employment. On average, each job created in a land reform settlement costs the government $3,640, whereas the cost of generating work in other economic sectors is substantially higher: 128% more expensive in industry, 190% in commerce, and 240% costlier in the service sector.[84]

By fostering needed employment in the countryside, they believe, land reform can deter the migration of poor people to the nation's vast and unmanageable urban slums. As such, it would help stem the drift toward social decomposition affecting many parts of the country, by mitigating rising crime rates and heightened expressions of urban violence. Strengthening rural communities through agrarian reform would help spur the revitalization of small towns, which have experienced a steady decline in many regions of Brazil. If land reform settlements were mere "rural *favelas*," they ask, then why is it that 91% of those surveyed in these communities say their quality of life has improved since acquiring land?[85] These and other findings, they suggest, reveal a great potential for strengthening poor people's social rights. As such, a substantial agrarian reform could help improve the overall quality of citizenship rights and democracy in Brazil.

Additionally, many supporters underscore the ecological advantages associated with peasant farming. Large-scale cattle ranching and industrialized agriculture, with its high chemical dependency, undermine environmental sustainability and create health hazards. Agribusiness farmers and other agrarian elites are responsible, they claim, for the destruction of much of the nation's natural heritage, including the Amazon rainforest. Peasant agriculture, by contrast, is usually "more ecological" and produces safer and more nutritious foods. From this point of view, agrarian reform would help foster a more "sustainable and endogenous pattern of development," grounded on principles of social justice and concern for the welfare of Brazil's vast contingent of marginalized people.[86]

Most proponents, however, do not see land reform as a magical panacea for

Brazil's social woes. They believe it can help solve some important problems, while catalyzing additional reform efforts. Agrarian reform, after all, is a highly charged and symbolic issue on the nation's public agenda. Over the last fifty years it has been a leading bellwether of Brazilian politics. Debates over concrete initiatives aimed at furthering land redistribution are one of the clearest indicators of the nation's contemporary political divisions between progressives and conservatives. Because of its symbolic weight, many advocates of agrarian reform feel that its progressive implementation could help trigger a broader "popular momentum" for social change.

The clash outlined above between opponents and supporters of land reform reveals markedly different ideas and values, as well as a contrasting tone in their overall argumentation. Critics of the reform agenda are generally more deterministic, defensive, and skeptical in their views of change. They underscore existing constraints in ways that rationalize the status quo. By contrast, land reform advocates tend to be more voluntaristic in their perceptions of change and are inclined to anchor their views on moral feelings and imperatives. These proponents challenge the status quo by decrying its injustice, while accentuating practical alternatives and potential benefits that could be obtained through reform. Whereas the opponents emphasize the historical novelties at stake, advocates for reform stress the intricate links between the past and present, and justify acts of historical reparation and accountability. Conservatives believe redistributive policies could establish dangerous precedents, while progressives see them as creating a positive impetus for further change.

Brazil's current debate over agrarian reform bears on matters that go well beyond the confines of topical discussions over land policies and rural development. The issues raise deeper questions about Brazilian society. At the dawn of the twenty-first century, land reform remains part of an intricate and contentious conversation over the future of Brazil—its promises, needs, fears, and dreams.

Notes

The author would like to thank Ralph Della Cava, Deborah Brautigam, and Kristina Svensson for their close reading of the text and valuable comments. A word of gratitude is also due to Erin Connor, Elizabeth Minor, and, especially, Kang Yue and Enrique Carrillo Gómez, for their important research assistance.

1. This depiction of the MST's 2005 national march draws on a close reading of all principal news accounts of the mobilization, including *O Estado de São Paulo*, *Folha de São Paulo*, *Jornal O Globo*, *Jornal do Brasil*, *Correio Braziliense*, *Agência Carta Maior*, and Sue Branford (2005). In addition, I consulted the transcripts of all the national television news coverage of the march; the MST's information service, posted at its website at http://www.mst.org.br/informativos/; and an MST video on the march, *Ergue a tua Voz: Marcha Nacional pela Reforma Agrária* (2005a). Conversations with people in-

volved in the mobilization were very helpful. I am particularly grateful for the generous assistance provided by Antônio Canuto and Geraldo Fontes.

2. The most visible supporters of the march were linked to the Catholic Church. Brazil's National Bishops Conference (CNBB) issued a communiqué conveying its "full solidarity" with the MST's march. Over ninety pastoral agents, bishops, nuns, friars, priests, and seminarians participated in the march, including the president of the CPT, Dom Tomás Balduíno, and theologian Leonardo Boff. Well-known musicians, theater troupes, and international solidarity groups also contributed to the mobilization. The ruling Workers Party (PT) issued a statement supporting the march. Furthermore, close to 1,000 municipal governments, where the MST has settlements, helped cover the transportation expenses for the peasants who joined the march in Goiânia.

3. The event was also supported by 325 MST health workers and other medical volunteers, along with sixty-five MST teachers who took care of the march's 115 children in a roving day care center.

4. The information refers to the first four months of 2005; see Banco Central (2005).

5. MST (2005b).

6. "Ministério Público quer investigar se houve uso de dinheiro público para a marcha do MST. "Jornal Nacional," TV Globo, May 9, 2005. Another telling comment was offered by Boris Casoy, the anchorman for the nightly news program of TV Record: "It is not fair that those who pay taxes—all of us—be used to sustain the MST's propaganda, a political movement, very often violent, that insists on not legalizing itself to escape the rigors of the law." "Poder público precisa respeitar um pouco mais o dinheiro do contribuinte." "Jornal da Record," TV Record, May 5, 2005.

7. In comparative terms, no other social movement has organized as many long-distance marches as the MST. Gandhi's Salt March started out with 78 men and endured for 240 miles; see Wikipedia (2006). The Jarrow Crusade consisted of 200 men and completed 280 miles; see Colette (2006). The Selma-Montgomery civil rights march began with 3,200 people and covered 54 miles; see Branch (1998). The indigenous march from Trinidad to La Paz started with 300 men, women, and children and crossed 350 miles, see Healy (2001: 361–94). By contrast, the MST's 1997 national march to Brasília mobilized 1,300 people for 64 days, from three different starting points: the city of São Paulo, Governador Valadares in Minas Gerais, and Rondonópolis, Mato Grosso, covering 640, 447, and 576 miles, respectively; see Chaves (2000) and Dos Santos, Paula, Ribeiro, and Meihy (1998). The MST's first long-distance march took place in 1986, when 250 landless peasants walked 27 days on a land reform pilgrimage to Porto Alegre; see Carter (chap. 6, this volume) on Rio Grande do Sul. In October 2007, landless peasants in India organized the world's largest long-distance march yet. For 27 days, 25,000 lower-caste and indigenous people walked 200 miles to New Dehli to demand land reform.

8. The description of Daslu's inauguration is based primarily on Bergamo's (2005b) news chronicle. Unless otherwise noted, all of the Daslu quotes are from this article. The depictions provided here are also informed by the author's visit to Daslu on July 25, 2005.

9. Benson (2005) and Downie (2005).

10. Bergamo (2005a).

11. Beraba (2005).

12. The data on social inequality are from a Brazilian government think tank, Instituto de Pesquisa Econômica Aplicada (IPEA) (2005: 50–61). Subsequently, IPEA published a study that noted a reduction in Brazil's Gini coefficient for income inequality. According to this report, between 2001 and 2005, the Gini measurement for income inequality

dropped from 0.593 to 0.566; see Barros, Carvalho, Franco, and Mendonça (2006: 108). The latter figure, however, still situates Brazil among the nine most unequal nations in the world, considering the 123 countries computed by the World Bank (2005).

13. Campos, Barbosa, Pochmann, Amorin, and Silva (2005: 29).

14. This data are from Brazil's 1995 agrarian census; see Instituto Brasileiro de Geografía e Estatística (IBGE) (1996).

15. For helpful historical reviews of Brazil's agrarian structure and politics, see Buainain (2008); Costa and Santos (1998); Faoro (1957); Forman (1975); Guimarães (1982, 1989); Martins (1981, 1991, 1996, 1997); Medeiros (1989); Schmink and Wood (1992); Silva (1996); and Stédile (2006, 2005a, 2005b, 2005c, 1999, 1997).

16. Rural trade union statistics are from Maybury-Lewis (1994: 219–20), who offers a valuable overview of CONTAG's history under the military regime. Further insights on the rural trade union movement can be found in Medeiros (chap. 3, this volume) and Rosa (chap. 15, this volume); also see Houtzager (2001), Medeiros (1989), Pereira (1997), Ricci (1999), and Welch (1999).

17. The number of MST members is admittedly uncertain. The MST has no formal roster. No surveys have ever been taken to quantify the movement's actual membership. By the end of 2006, the MST is estimated to have helped settle over 135,000 families. In mid-2007, the movement claimed to have an additional 150,000 families mobilized in encampments scattered throughout Brazil, see MST (2007b). Based on these numbers and an estimate of four adults (and adolescents) per family, one could project the MST membership to approximately 1.14 million people. Needless to say, levels of commitment among MST members are quite variable. The number of settlements and MST settlers presented here is based on the author's calculations derived from DATALUTA (2008) for total land reform settlements and families in 2004 and 2006, and MST (2007a) estimates for the number of land reform settlements affiliated to the movement. DATALUTA offers one of the most comprehensive databases on land reform issues in Brazil. Its findings are generated by the Núcleo de Estudos da Reforma Agrária (NERA) of the Universidade Estadual de São Paulo (UNESP) Presidente Prudente, a research center directed by Bernardo Mançano Fernandes. All figures on cooperatives and agro-industries are from the MST (2009). For sources and further data on the MST's accomplishments in education and communication, see Carter and Carvalho (chap. 9, this volume).

18. Area occupied by MST settlements is based on the author's estimates for 2006 derived from DATALUTA (2008) and MST (2007a). For further details on these estimates, see Carter and Carvalho (chap. 9, this volume).

19. Key sources on the MST's history and evolution include: Branford and Rocha (2002); Caldart (2002); Carter (2002); Fernandes (2000); Morissawa (2001); Ondetti (2008); Stédile and Fernandes (1999); Wolford (2010); and Wright and Wolford (2003). A useful review of the recent literature can be found in Welch (2006). The MST is treated as a social movement on the basis of Tarrow's (1998: 4) standard definition of this phenomenon as "collective challenges based on common purposes and social solidarities, in sustained interaction with elites, opponents and authorities." Social movements are also characterized as a form of contentious politics by McAdam, McCarthy, and Zald (1996); McAdam, Tarrow, and Tilly (2001); and Tilly (2004b).

20. More details on the MST's impact on other popular movements can be found in Rosa (chap. 15, this volume).

21. For further information on these peasant groups see tables 5.4 and 5.5 in Fernandes (chap. 5, this volume).

22. The number of settlements is based on the author's estimates derived from DATALUTA (2008) and MST (2007a). State-by-state data on MST settlements is provided by Carter and Carvalho (chap. 9, this volume).

23. These figures are based on the author's calculations derived from DATALUTA (2008). The estimate for the Amazonian region covers all the states that are part of what is officially known as "legal Amazonia," including large parts of the states of Mato Grosso and Maranhão.

24. FAO's 2006 land reform conference in Porto Alegre came on the heels of the 2004 World Forum on Agrarian Reform, held in Valencia, Spain, with representatives from seventy-two countries; see Carta Maior (2006). Both events, in turn, were shaped by the growing number of Asian, African, and Latin American countries that have been experiencing struggles for land reform; see Akram-Lodhi, Borras, and Kay (2007); Deere and Royce (2009); Borras, Edelman, and Kay (2008); Moyo and Yeros (2005); and Rosset, Patel, and Courville (2006).

25. A noted exponent of this view of the MST is Xico Graziano, a former advisor to Fernando Henrique Cardoso, who acted briefly, in 1996, as head of the federal government's land reform agency. A former federal deputy for the Party of Brazilian Social Democracy (PSDB), Graziano currently runs an NGO dedicated to the promotion of agribusiness and writes a regular column for three of Brazil's leading newspapers. On May 23, 2006, he published an opinion piece titled "Agrarian Terrorism" in which he treated the MST as the rural equivalent of a criminal gang known as the First Capital Command (PPC), responsible for a violent rampage that killed over three dozen police officers and prison guards in São Paulo that same month. Earlier, in November 2005, a commission of the National Congress controlled by the *bancada ruralista*, an influential caucus comprised of large landholding interests, issued a document describing the MST in similar terms.

26. For thoughtful examinations of some of the MST's recurring collective action problems, see Carter and Carvalho, Calvo-González, and Wolford (chaps. 9, 11, and 12, this volume), as well as Branford and Rocha (2002) and Caume (2006).

27. These percentages are based on IBGE's (2001: 96) 2000 census data for the population fifteen years and older, both nationally and in rural areas only.

28. Lerrer (2005), Hammond (2004), Comparato (2000), and Berger (1998) offer informative accounts of the Brazilian media's portrayal of the MST. A glaring example of the press' hostility toward the MST can be found in *Veja*, Brazil's best-selling weekly publication. Veja's caustic articles on the landless movement include the following titles: "As Madraçais do MST" (The MST's Madrassas), September 8, 2004; "A Esquerda Delirante" (The Delirious Left), front cover of the June 18, 2003, issue; "A Bagunça Promovida pelo MST" (Disorder Fostered by the MST), April 3, 2003; and "A Tática da Baderna" (The Riot Tactic), front cover of the May 10, 2000, issue.

29. Intervozes—Coletivo Brasil de Communicação Social (2005: 21).

30. Frederick Douglass's statement is from an 1849 letter to an abolitionist associate cited in Bobo, Kendall, and Max (1996).

31. The words of the prophet Isaiah speak eloquently for the Judeo-Christian heritage: "Shame on you! You who add house to house and join field to field, until not an acre remains, and you are left to dwell alone in the land. The Lord of Hosts has sworn in my hearing: Many houses shall go to ruin, fine large houses shall be uninhabited. Five acres of vineyard shall yield only a gallon, and ten bushels of seed return only one peck." Isaiah 5: 8–9 (New English Bible). In Islam we find similar admonishments:

"Woe to every slanderer, defamer. Who amasses wealth and takes pleasure in continuously calculating his wealth, thinking that his wealth would make him last for ever. Nay! He shall most certainly be thrown into Hell." Qur'an 104: 1–4. Both religious traditions condemn the excessive accumulation of riches but are not opposed to the creation of wealth per se. Rather, their religious contempt is toward the "love of wealth," which leads to an estrangement from God's imperative to seek justice and help those in need. I am grateful to Amin Mohseni for his sharing his thoughtful insights on Islam.

32. Inequality is a complex concept with multiple dimensions and meanings. The problems raised here refer fundamentally to situations of stark inequities of wealth and other basic livelihood assets that restrict the opportunities and capabilities for human development. For relevant conceptual discussions, see Sartori (1987); Sen (1992, 1997, 1999); and Tilly (1998, 2005). More generally, on inequality and development, see Cornia (2004); Selligson and Passé-Smith (2003); Tulchin (2002); Wilkinson and Pickett (2009); and the World Bank (2005). The literature on social inequality in Latin America has grown in recent years. Valuable information and assessments can be found in Berry (1998); Birdsall, Graham, and Sabot (1998); Chalmers, Vilas, Hite, Martin, Piester, and Segarra (1997); Ferranti, Perry, Ferreira, and Walton (2004); Ganuza, Barros, Taylor, and Vos (2001); Justino, Litchfield, and Whitehead (2003); Karl (2003); Lustig (1995); Morley (2000); and Tokman and O'Donnell (1998). More specifically on inequality in Brazil, see Campos, Barbosa, Pochmann, Amorin, and Silva (2005); Gacitúa-Marió and Woolcock (2005a); Henriques (2000); Hoffmann (2004); Schwartzman (2004); Weyland (1996); Wood and Carvalho (1988); and World Bank (2004).

33. Birdsall and Sabot (1994).

34. Ferranti, Perry, Ferreira, and Walton (2004: 4).

35. Average for GDP growth was obtained from IPEA (2006). Gini coefficient figures are from Fishlow (1972) and Barros, Henriques, and Mendonça (2000).

36. IPEA (2005: 108–21).

37. Corporación Latinobarómetro (2007: 102).

38. Corporación Latinobarómetro (2004: 32).

39. Putman (1993) and Edwards, Foley, and Diani (2001).

40. Bacha (1976). Cristovam Buarque has written extensively on Brazil's social apartheid; in particular see his discussion of the concept of *apartação*, or apartation (1994). On the disregard for human rights in societies with extreme disparities of wealth, see O'Donnell (1999).

41. Corporación Latinobarómetro (2004: 17).

42. This general point is well articulated by Karl (2003) and Rueschemeyer (2005). More broadly, on the politics of inequality, see Chalmers, Vilas, Hite, Martin, Piester, and Segarra (1997); O'Donnell (1998); and Tilly (1998, 2005).

43. Oscar Vilhena Vieira (2007: 2, 21).

44. Corporación Latinobarómetro (2007: 101).

45. On the relationship between social inequality and political violence, see Muller and Seligson (1987).

46. Data from the Corporación Latinobarómetro's 2002 survey, table 3.5, cited in Ferranti, Perry, Ferreira, and Walton (2004: 295). A 2007 survey found a nearly identical percentage, with only 13% of Brazilians perceiving their societies as "fair," see Corporación Latinobarómetro (2007: 39).

47. Corporación Latinobarómetro (2006: 72–74).

48. According to Przeworski, Alvarez, Cheibub, and Limongi (2001: 171), rising inequalities

can reduce the life expectancy of democracies to twenty-two years. In countries with diminishing inequalities, the recent trend in Brazil, the life expectancy of democracies can reach eighty-four years.

49. Some authors make a distinction between "land reform" and "agrarian reform." Land reform is defined as a state-enacted measure that redistributes "property in land for the benefit of landless workers, tenants and small farmers." Agrarian reform, on the other hand, is conceived as a broader policy initiative that embraces land tenure reforms along with efforts to improve social conditions for peasants through a variety of support programs such as credit, education, technological assistance, infrastructural development, and cooperatives. Land reform, in this view, can take place without a more comprehensive agrarian reform; see King (1973: 2–3). Each can vary significantly in quality and scope. The distinction is well taken. Throughout this book, however, land reform will be treated as largely synonymous to agrarian reform. This owes much to the fact that contemporary agrarian policies, in Brazil and elsewhere, generally assume that any effort to redistribute land must be accompanied by other support measures. Moreover, in Portuguese both terms are usually translated into the same term, *reforma agrária*.

50. These appreciations are based on an extensive review of the comparative land reform literature. The texts consulted on this matter include: Akram-Lodhi, Borras, and Kay (2007); Basset and Crummey (1993); Bermeo (1986); Bingswanger-Mkhize, Bourguignon, and van den Brink (2009); Brockett (1998); Colburn (1989); De Janvry (1981); De Janvry, Gordillo, Platteau, and Sadoulet (2001); Desai (1986); Dorner (1992); Eckstein, Donald, Horton, and Carroll (1978); Fox (1990); Ghimire (2001); Grindle (1986); Handelman (1981); Hooglund (1982); Huntington (1968); Inayatullah (1980); Kay (1998); King (1973, 1977); Lipton (2009); Menjivar (1969); Montgomery (1984); Moyo and Yeros (2005); Paige (1975); Pausewang (1983); Prosterman and Riedinger (1987); Riedinger (1995); Rosset, Patel, and Courville (2006); Sobhan (1993); Swinnen (1997); Thakur (1989); Thiesenhusen (1989, 1995); Williams (1992); Wolf (1973); and Zamosc, Martínez, and Chiriboga (1997).

51. Almost three-fourths of all land distributed in Venezuela between 1960 and 1973 involved a colonization program on state-owned land; see Eckstein, Donald, Horton, and Carroll (1978: Appendix A). A similar situation also took place in Colombia, where 90% of the reform area and 88% of its beneficiaries were settled in public domains; author's calculation taken from Zamosc (1987: 266–69).

52. On the adverse effects of extreme income equality, see Cornia (2004: 44–46).

53. Rural poverty data are from the World Bank (2005: 278); agricultural productivity rankings are from Flake (2006). For statistics regarding access to food, see IPEA (2005: 56).

54. Standard-of-living comparisons are based on UNDP's (2007) Human Development Index; comparisons on income inequality draw from the Gini coefficients for 123 countries published by the World Bank (2005: 280–281).

55. Comissão Pastoral da Terra, CPT (1988–2013).

56. Author's calculations made from DATALUTA (2008). Fifty-five of a total of 7,575 settlements established by INCRA between 1985 and 2006 were eliminated from the final tally presented here. These fifty-five settlements are essentially extractive reserves located in the Amazonian rainforest, namely in the states of Acre, Amazonas, Amapá, Pará, and Rondônia. All together, these enclaves make up an area of 18,339,543 hectares that has benefited 35,957 families; forty-seven of these extractive reserves were created during the first Lula government. DATALUTA's settlement figures for 1979–2002 are akin to those of Instituto Nacional de Colonização e Reforma Agrária (2003).

Its number of beneficiaries reflects the amount of land plots made available, not the actual number of settlers recorded in INCRA's database. They are biased, in other words, toward the highest possible number of land reform beneficiaries. Official data on land distribution in Brazil have been the source of controversy in recent years, in part due to the efforts made to "massage" these numbers for political gain. Former president Cardoso (2006: 539), for example, claims to have benefited 635,000 peasant families. Other official sources, however, suggest numbers that oscillate between 482,500 and 524,380 families. Closer examination of settlement data produced under the Cardoso administration found that many of the communities cited in its statistics were counted twice, while others existed only "on paper." Further, these statistics also included beneficiaries from two government programs that did not promote actual land redistribution. One of these programs facilitated the provision of land titles to farmers with de facto landholdings. The other offered a special credit line for farmers interested in purchasing land, often from other small rural proprietors. Reviews of relevant debates over land reform statistics can be found in Delgado and Fernandes (chaps. 2 and 5, this volume); also see Sauer and Souza (2007); Melo (2006: 220–23); and Scolese (2005: 81–84). The Lula administration presented data indicating it had settled 381,419 families between 2003 and 2006; see Ministério do Desenvolvimento Agrário (2006: 62). These figures, however, also computed beneficiaries of the government's land titling and credit programs. After an extensive review of INCRA's settlement data, DATALUTA concluded that the number of beneficiaries from Lula's 2003–6 land distribution policies reached 254,249 families. Of these, 33,643 families were settled in huge extractive reserves in the Amazonian rainforest, rather than regular farm plots, and thus excluded from the land reform tally presented here. For an appraisal contrasting the Cardoso and Lula government's land reform programs, see Deere and Medeiros (2007).

57. The estimate of potential beneficiary families is from the best academic study on this topic, prepared by Del Grossi, Gasques, Silva, and Conceição (2001). The 30.6 million figure presented here assumes a family composition of five, and multiplies this number by the study's high estimate of 6.120 million families.

58. These estimates are based on INCRA's land registry, published in a government-commissioned proposal for President Lula's National Agrarian Reform Plan; see Sampaio et al. (2005: 43 and Table 5.1.1.1). The 231.3 figure was obtained by adding 120.4 million hectares in large private estates (which the owners themselves declared to be unproductive) and 110.9 million hectares of unregistered public land. This study discounted 57 million hectares of unregistered public land that were overcounted in INCRA's land registry. The same report indicated that as much as 36% of Brazil's territory, that is, more than 311 million hectares, could be considered unproductive farmland. For a useful review of these findings, see Melo (2006: 203–214). Brazil's great land availability is corroborated by a US Department of Agriculture report that notes that the country only utilizes 5% to 7% of its land mass for agriculture. Pasture areas and other potentially productive land for agriculture amount to 38% of its territory, excluding nonarable areas (5%) and forested regions (52%); see Flake (2006).

59. Reform area and beneficiaries are derived from the author's calculus based on DATALUTA (2008). The data for total farmland and agricultural workforce used to produce these percentages are from the preliminary results of the 2006 agrarian census; see IBGE (2007).

60. On the main elements of Brazil's conservative agrarian reform see principally the chap-

ters in this volume by Delgado; Medeiros; Fernandes; Carter and Carvalho; Branford; and Carter's concluding chapter and epilogue.

61. On Brazil's contemporary landlord class, see Mendonça (2006) and Bruno (1997). Its historic influence on the formation of Brazilian society is treated at length in Cardoso (1977), Faoro (1957); Lamounier (1989), Martins (1996, 1997), and Prado Jr. (1994). The landlord class has long been regarded as an essentially negative force for democratization. A classic statement in this regard is Moore (1966). For more recent and nuanced appraisals of this issue, see Rueschemeyer, Stephens, and Stephens (1992), and, especially, Huber and Safford (1995).

62. Montero (2005: 71).

63. Galbraith (1977: 279).

64. The sixty-eight years of authoritarian rule is from Smith's (2005: 349) regime classification. It includes the 1900–1929 period, which Smith describes as a "republican oligarchic" era.

65. Schmitter (1971).

66. The "un-rule of law" is given extensive treatment in Méndez, O'Donnell, and Pinheiro (1999); Pinheiro (1997); and Pereira (2000). More broadly, on the problematic development of civil rights in Brazil, see Carvalho (2006). Recurrent infringements of human rights in the countryside are meticulously recorded in the CPT's annual reports on rural conflicts, published regularly since 1990. The class biases of the Brazilian judiciary and its implications for the MST are carefully analyzed in Meszaros (chap. 14, this volume).

67. On Brazil's voting restrictions for illiterates and electoral clientelism, see Lapp (2004: 119–53), Mainwaring (1999: 174–218), Martins (1996: 19–51), and Avelino Filho (1994). For a classic study of this political phenomena, see Leal (1993).

68. Mainwaring (1999: 335).

69. Stepan (2001: 345). On the problem of legislative malapportionment, also see Snyder and Samuels (2004).

70. Weyland (1996).

71. Montero (2005: 51).

72. Leading intellectual critics of the MST in recent years include Rosenfield (2006), Graziano (2004), Martins (2000a, 2003c), and Navarro (2002a, 2002b). Their views are further examined in Carter's concluding chapter in this volume.

73. These points are discussed in Carter (2009, 2010). Matters concerning the quality of democracy are given extensive treatment in O'Donnell, Cullell, and Iazzetta (2004). On the importance of social movements for the development and extension of citizenship rights, see Foweraker and Landman (1997) and Tilly (2002, 2004b). The long-term approach to democratization suggested here draws on Whitehead (2002).

74. For a useful review of the contemporary land reform debate, see Lerrer's (2003) interviews with fifteen leading government officials, civil society leaders, and scholars representing a broad spectrum of ideas.

75. Agricultural production data are from the Departamento Intersindical de Estatística e Estudos Socioeconônmicos (DIEESE) (2006: 180); export figure is from Flake (2006). Also see the interview with Lula's first minister of agriculture, Roberto Rodrigues, former head of an agrarian elite association, in Lerrer (2005).

76. Brazil's problem with modern slavery in rural areas is addressed in Medeiros (chap. 3, this volume); also see Breton (2002), CPT (1999b), and Sutton (1994). Efforts during the 2000s to pass legislation mandating the expropriation of estates that use slave labor have been blocked by the landlord caucus (*bancada ruralista*).

77. According to CEPAL (2004), 15% of Brazil's population resides in rural towns of less than 20,000 inhabitants.
78. Navarro's interviews are found in Scolese (2003) and Lerrer (2003: 258–59).
79. Navarro's interview is found in Lerrer (2003: 252); see also Graziano (2004: 38–39).
80. Graziano (2004: 156, 161).
81. See the interviews with two landlord representatives, Samapio Filho and Hein, as well as Navarro, in Lerrer (2003: 166, 201, 264).
82. A review of this "threat" argument can be found in Carter's concluding chapter to this volume.
83. Oliveira (2004: 32–62). This study is based on data from the 1995 agrarian census. Its definition of family farmers applies to all agricultural producers with less than two hundred hectares of land.
84. The cost of generating jobs through land reform is from an INCRA study conducted in 2004, which reported significant regional variations. This data and the comparative figures provided here are from Leite (2006a: 152–54). Each land reform plot is assumed to generate three jobs, a conclusion reached by one of the most comprehensive studies on land reform settlements in Brazil; see Heredia, Medeiros, Palmeira, Cintrão, and Leite (2004).
85. The survey data on land reform settlers are from Heredia, Medeiros, Palmeira, Cintrão, and Leite (2004: 347).
86. For an assessment grounded in these ideas, see Leite (2006b).

PART I

The Agrarian Question and
Rural Social Movements in Brazil

2 The Agrarian Question and Agribusiness in Brazil

Brazil's vast inequalities have roots in the consolidation of land in the hands of a few and the ability of the landed elites to influence the country's political system to protect their interests. This dynamic, however, did not go unchallenged, giving rise to the agrarian question of how to reform existing land tenure arrangements. This chapter focuses primarily on the post–World War II period, when a variety of theoretical and political arguments in favor of agrarian reform emerged. The opposing interests and visions for the future of Brazil's agricultural sector catalyzed some of the most intense political struggles of this time.

Those opposed to agrarian reform called on the state to promote the technical modernization of agriculture, a policy adopted by the military regime following the 1964 coup. This ushered in a process of "conservative modernization" in the countryside. Public debate over the agrarian question reemerged with the country's redemocratization, and particularly, the new civilian government's decision, in 1985, to promulgate Brazil's first National Agrarian Reform Plan. The progress made under this new political regime and the democratic Constitution established in 1988 was offset by the neoliberal policies adopted during the 1990s. This economic orientation undermined in many ways the state's role in enforcing the agrarian social rights enshrined in the Constitution, which prescribes that land ownership should fulfill a social function.

The efforts to counterpose agrarian reform with the technical modernization of agriculture, advanced by conservatives who supported the 1964 military coup, regained prominence in the late 1990s, albeit in a different political context. Under President Fernando Henrique Cardoso's second term (1999–2002) and in President Luis Inácio Lula da Silva's first government (2003–6), significant efforts were made to revitalize an agribusiness model for rural development. This strategy was designed to generate trade surpluses through agricultural commodity exports, and thus earn the foreign currency needed to pay Brazil's creditors.

The Cardoso administration decided to promote agro-exports in the wake of the 1999 devaluation of Brazil's currency and in a context of heightened external pressure to maintain a tight fiscal grip on the country's balance of payments. This agricultural policy gave utmost priority to agribusiness expansion, to the detriment of efforts to change the nation's agrarian structure. In fact, it reinforced business strategies geared toward maximizing profits derived from farmland assets and market speculation in these holdings. This mode of economic development has undercut the movement for agrarian reform and diminished the prospects of promoting alternative rural policies aimed at supporting peasant farming.

Political debates over the agrarian question have always been entangled with strong ideological positions. Amid these contentious views, nonetheless, one can find an interesting public discussion on this matter. This chapter strives to reconstruct this debate from the 1950s to the early 2000s, and shows how it has been shaped by different economic and political contexts. Yet despite these variations, the agrarian question has exhibited a clear line of continuity, marked by the preservation of a highly unequal structure of land ownership, both during the country's industrialization phase (1930–82) and its subsequent period of relative economic stagnation (1983–2005).

This chapter draws on two distinct historical and methodological approaches. The first section reconstructs the history of ideas and debates over the agrarian question from 1955 to 1982, a period of strong economic growth. It examines, in particular, the main arguments advanced to justify Brazil's conservative model of agricultural modernization. The second section analyzes the political economy of Brazil's agrarian structure from 1982 to 2005. During this phase the country experienced a "constrained adjustment" process to the new global economy, restored its democratic regime, and witnessed the rise of several new social movements for land reform, including the Landless Rural Workers Movement (MST).

The Agrarian Debate, 1955–1964

Brazilian economists and intellectuals began to debate over the nation's agrarian question in the mid-1950s, amid growing peasant mobilizations for land redistribution. This public conversation became more stylized by the early 1960s, with the publication of various important texts and rising political conflict over agrarian reform. The theoretical debate centered around four main perspectives, that of the Brazilian Communist Party (PCB), reformist sectors of the Catholic Church, economists linked to the United Nation's Economic Commission for Latin America (ECLA), and a group of conservative economists from the University of São Paulo (USP), led by Professor Antonio Delfim Neto. The first three supported agrarian reform, but the USP economists disagreed sharply with this position and even criticized the mildly reformist ideas espoused by economist Roberto Campos.

Three intellectuals linked to the PCB stood out for their Marxian contribution to the nation's agrarian debate: Caio Prado, Jr., Ignácio Rangel, and Alberto Passos Guimarães. Prado centered his critique on the social consequences of land and labor relations in the countryside, which imposed subhuman living conditions on most of its population. He championed higher rural wages, social welfare policies, and labor laws to protect farm workers, and thought that land reform should be treated as a second priority to these other reforms.[1] Guimarães, on the other hand, viewed large estates as "feudal remnants" within Brazilian agriculture. As such, land reform was needed to foster the capitalist transformation of the country and create conditions for a communist revolution.[2] Rangel, in turn, was primarily concerned with the countryside's overpopulation and risk of producing a crisis, "either because the rural sector fails to free up labor for other sectors, or on the contrary, provides it in excess."[3] In his perspective land reform was a peripheral issue since the problem of rural overpopulation would be resolved through urbanization and the expansion of foreign trade.

The development ideas advanced by the United Nation's Economic Commission for Latin America (ECLA) were forcibly articulated in Brazil by economist Celso Furtado. The nation's unequal agrarian structure and outmoded rural labor system produced structural tendencies toward inflation and recurrent crisis in the nation's food supply, given its inability to respond to growing urban and industrial demand. Land reform, he insisted, was necessary to stave off such predicaments.[4]

Catholic bishops and intellectuals also played an influential role in Brazil's agrarian debate and initiated a process that would lead to important changes within the church regarding its position on land reform. The church drew on its social doctrine to legitimize the principle of the "social function of rural property." This concept became part of the country's first land reform law—the Land Statute—enacted by the military government in November 1964. It replaced the notions of rural property established in the Land Law of 1850, which treated farmland as a mere commodity. During this time, church officials began to depict Brazil's agrarian structure as a source of grave injustice and social exclusion.[5] The church's new engagements in the countryside were also fueled by its intense rivalry with the Communists, who were seeking to influence the country's budding trade unions among peasants and farm workers (see also Poletto, chap. 4, this volume).

Delfim Neto and his colleagues at USP centered their attacks on Celso Furtado's arguments regarding the rigidity of agricultural supply. Drawing on ample statistical evidence they disproved ECLA's position and showed that Brazil's agricultural supply responded adequately to demand pressures. From this, they concluded that the nation's agrarian structure was not the main obstacle to rural production. This technocratic view, in fact, gave no consideration to the ethical and social issues that figured prominently in the church's social doctrine and the humanist vision of Caio Prado, Jr.'s.

Conservative economists at USP did not see the large disparities in land access and precarious labor conditions in the countryside as relevant economic problems. In their view, the existing agrarian structure was fine as long as it fulfilled the basic functions of agriculture in economic development. According to the basic tenets of American economic functionalism, these roles included: (1) providing labor power for industry without reducing food production, (2) creating a market for industrial products, (3) expanding exports, and (4) generating capital to help finance the national economy by transferring real income to the urban sector.[6]

Those debating the agrarian question before 1964 discussed problems that were, in Rangel's words, "primarily agrarian," in that they dealt with the mode of production in the countryside and its land structure, along with the socioeconomic and political consequences derived from this. Yet they also sparred over matters that Rangel described as "secondarily agrarian," such as the supply and demand of agricultural products, and their effects on prices, employment, and foreign trade. These issues impinged on the agrarian question, but were not central to its mode of production.

In sum, progressives framed the nation's agrarian crisis in relation to its unequal land structure, its oppressive labor relations, and their harmful effects on the nation's economy, society, and politics. Conservatives, by contrast, discounted many of these concerns and argued that Brazil did not have an agrarian crisis. In their view, this "crisis" could only exist if the agricultural sector caused negative effects on the country's inflation rate, trade balance, and industrial production.

The 1964 military coup cut this lively debate short. In the ensuing years, it gradually imposed Delfim Neto's arguments in favor of agricultural modernization without land reform.

Conservative Rural Modernization under the Military Regime, 1965–1982

Economic debates under the first military government, led by Marshal Humberto de Alencar Castello Branco (1964–67), were largely confined to intellectuals who had supported the 1964 coup d'etat. Delfim Neto's group offered an ultra-conservative critique of the economic analysis adopted by the military's first planning minister, Roberto Campos. Agriculture, according to the USP economists, was growing at adequate levels and not affecting inflation rates. Moreover, the nation's agrarian structure was not an obstacle to future economic growth. Hence, in their view, the land reform provisions established in the 1964 Land Statute were simply unnecessary. At best, land redistribution could be restricted to a few backward areas in the northeast, where the agrarian system was unresponsive to existing price mechanisms. For these conservative scholars, the government's focus should be to steer a process of "technical modernization" of agriculture. As per Delfim Neto, the sector's expansion needed policies oriented by a specific ranking of priorities, geared toward enhancing (1) the technical capacity of farmers, (2) agricultural mechanization, (3) fertilizer use, and (4) establishing an efficient agrarian structure.[7]

Delfim Neto was appointed to head the powerful Ministry of Finance in 1967, whereupon he began to put his ideas into practice. His support for a conservative rural modernization process was anchored on the expansion of a federal farm credit program, designed to bolster the nation's agricultural production. During this time, the agrarian debate became entirely dominated by the state's agenda and its efforts to accelerate agricultural growth.

Under the military regime, the state adopted various new agricultural policies designed to promote agro-exports and generate a foreign trade surplus, while maintaining commodity price and real wage stability. Furthermore, it made significant investments to upgrade the techniques and technology used for farm production. These policymakers sought to integrate agriculture with industry and link both to the international economy. Many of these measures required extensive state subsidies.

The technical modernization of Brazilian agriculture was carried out through the increased use of industrial inputs (fertilizers, pesticides, soil acidity management or liming, improved seeds, and petroleum-based fuels) and machinery (tractors, harvesters, irrigation equipment, and other farm gear). All this followed the basic tenets of the Green Revolution. In addition, various efforts were made to integrate commercial farmers into the industrial sector, including grain millers and manufacturers of cooking oil, sugar and ethanol, paper and cardboard, tobacco, textiles, and various beverages.[8] Over time, these agro-industrial firms would become an essential part of Brazil's agribusiness strategy, with close ties to various multinational corporations.

Brazilian agriculture experienced its golden age of capitalist development between 1965 and 1982, under the state's tutelage and strong financial support. This conservative rural modernization began with the repression of the land reform movement and its political defeat following the 1964 coup. The measures undertaken by the military government were also a reaction to the agricultural policies of the 1950s, which were driven by coffee exports and the quest to maintain the country's foreign exchange regime. The state thus sought to diversify and increase the nation's farm and agro-industrial exports, which had stagnated for nearly two decades at $1 to $1.5 billion per year. In addition, these rural policies were considered useful for tackling Brazil's urban and industrial growth.

Table 2.1. Agricultural credit, 1969–82:
Indexes for actual growth increase and implicit subsidy

Year	Real Growth Index	Annual inflation rate (%)	Highest nominal interest rates for rural credit (%)
1969	100.0	20.8	18.0
1970	119.0	19.8	17.0
1971	137.5	20.2	7.0
1972	170.5	17.0	15.0
1973	240.6	15.1	15.0
1974	297.6	28.7	15.0
1975	433.8	27.7	15.0
1976	444.9	41.3	15.0
1977	396.7	42.7	15.0
1978	403.4	38.7	15.0
1979	503.1	53.9	38.0
1980	481.1	100.2	45.0
1981	417.3	109.9	45.0
1982	404.1	95.4	60 to 80

Source: Delgado (1985: 81).

While the United States and Western Europe initiated their agricultural modernization in the late nineteenth and early twentieth centuries, Brazil did not start this process until the late 1960s, except for the state of São Paulo, which began in the 1950s. Brazil's turning point took place in late 1965, with the creation of the National Rural Credit System. This federal program channeled massive public subsidies to finance the country's Green Revolution (see table 2.1). Furthermore, it allowed the state to reorient the agricultural institutes set up by the Getúlio Vargas government, in the 1930s and 1950s, to promote and regulate prices for specific commodities such as sugar, coffee, wheat, and cocoa. These agricultural boards were closely aligned with the interests of regional-based landlords.[9]

In short, the Brazilian state sought to create a market for rural goods by providing incentives and protecting commercial farmers from the risks inherent to agricultural production that resulted from farm output and price fluctuations. Together with the National Rural Credit System, it founded and rekindled various public programs and agencies designed to funnel state resources to the benefit of the agrarian elite. These included the Price Guarantee Policy; various rural extension initiatives, including the Brazilian Agricultural Research Corporation (EMBRAPA), instituted in 1973; and the Program to Guarantee Agricultural Activity (PROAGRO), set up in 1974. Adding to its generous credit policy and support for agro-exports, the state offered lavish tax incentives to

Table 2.2. Technical indicators of agricultural modernization, 1960–80

Years	Consumption of NPK fertilizers (thousand tons of nutrients)	Fleet of four-wheel or conveyer farm tractors (units)
1960	198.4	61,345
1967	444.9	n/a
1970	999.0	145,309
1975	1,980.0	323,113
1980	4,066.0	545,205

Source: Delgado (1985: 36).

Note: NPK fertilizers refer to the combination of nitrogen, phosphorous, and potassium.

Table 2.3. Macroeconomic and land price variations, 1965–2003

Periods	1 Average GDP growth rate (%)	2 Average agriculture GDP growth rate	3 Ratio of trade surplus to GDP (%)	4 Ratio of net income sent abroad to GDP (%)	5 Real price increase for farmland (%)
1965–1980	8.10	4.60	0.38	1.34	35.3*
1983–1993	2.27	2.35	4.13	3.95	1.9
1994–1999	2.82	3.56	(–) 0.19	2.10	(–) 9.1
2000–2003	1.60	4.61	2.07	3.53**	5.7

Source: Fundação Getúlio Vargas (2004).

Notes: *Real price increase for farmland between 1970 and 1976; calculations derived from FGV data cited in Resende (1981). **Average for 2000–2002.

large landholders by providing exemptions on the national Income Tax and Rural Land Tax.

Brazilian agriculture underwent a process of intense modernization from the late 1960s to the early 1980s, as recorded through various indicators, including those offered in table 2.2. Rural production increased and diversified. Yet this transformation also deepened the many disparities found in the Brazilian countryside. The adoption of modern technology and techniques were concentrated largely in the country's south and southeastern regions, along with certain pockets of the midwest, which was still considered part of the nation's agricultural frontier. The rates of technical modernization were far lower in the Amazon and northeast regions.

This technical modernization process reinforced the landed oligarchy's close ties to the Brazilian state, notably through its agricultural institutes, various public subsidies, and support programs that helped maintain the nation's large landholdings (*latifúndio*) of mostly unproductive estates. The conservative nature of this modernization project can also be ascertained by the extraordinary increase in the value of these territorial assets, which, as shown in table 2.3, rose far beyond the nation's real economic growth.

The Agrarian Question in the Era of Agribusiness, 1983–2005:
External Adjustment, Political Opening, and Neoliberal Rule

Brazil's conservative rural modernization faced a sudden jolt in the early 1980s as a result of the nation's foreign debt crisis, the ensuing economic stagnation, and the demise of the military regime. This decade ushered in a transitional yet contradictory period for Brazil's agrarian question. The nation's political democratization facilitated the rise of a progressive network in the countryside propelled by new social movements, religious organizations, and trade unions. Their struggle for agrarian reform, however, was offset by government policies designed to promote agricultural exports in order to manage the country's debt crisis.

During the 1980s, the Brazilian countryside experienced a process of civil society resurrection (see Medeiros, chap. 3, this volume, and Poletto, chap. 4, this volume). These developments included the birth of the MST and a number of other peasant movements, the reorganization of the National Confederation of Agricultural Workers (CONTAG), and the consolidation of the church's Pastoral Land Commission (CPT). These groups, along with several non-governmental organizations (NGOs), eventually formed a broad coalition known as the National Forum for Agrarian Reform and Justice in the Countryside. All these land struggles and activities put agrarian reform back on the nation's public agenda. The promise to carry out a land redistribution program became part of the formal agreement that led to the election of President Tancredo Neves in 1984 and launched Brazil's New Republic. This pledge was ratified with President José Sarney's 1985 proclamation of the country's first National Agrarian Reform Plan. The 1988 Constitution, in turn, reaffirmed the Land Statute's principle legitimizing rural properties by their social function.

All these political changes, nonetheless, took place amid an emerging global economy that would significantly affect the policies and orientations of Brazil's ruling political elite. Mexico's 1982 decision to suspend payments on its foreign debt triggered a global financial crisis that had far-reaching effects on Brazil's economy. As a result, the Brazilian government adopted a series of measures that led to the nation's constrained adjustment to the new global economy, one characterized by heightened international and domestic restrictions on the country's economic development, an upshot of its large public debt and foreign dependency. The policies undertaken to cope with these restrictions were unable to solve the nation's debt problem. Instead, they plunged the Brazilian economy into a period of stagnation that lingered on for more than two decades.

Economic policymakers sought to manage the country's debt crisis by promoting agro-exports to generate the trade surpluses and foreign currency reserves needed to pay the nation's creditors.[10] This made the state dependent on the success of large commercial farmers and agro-industrial firms. Consequently, the measures taken to solve Brazil's foreign debt crisis ended up reinforcing the country's land concentration, while increasing market speculation over these rural holdings.

Farm-generated income dropped noticeably between 1994 and 1998, in the aftermath of Brazil's monetary stabilization program (known as the Plano Real), and in a context of high capital liquidity in the international financial markets. The global monetary crunch triggered by the Asian (1997) and Russian (1998) financial crises set off Brazil's 1999 currency devaluation and new debt crisis. This scenario prompted the government to reinstate its agro-export promotion policies in order to service the country's foreign debt.

Between 1983 and 2005 Brazilian authorities instituted a number of structural adjustment measures to deal with different demands imposed by the new global economic order. These international trends played a crucial role in shaping the political economy of Brazil's agrarian question by effectively stacking the deck against the prospect of implementing a substantive land reform program. The following section reviews three different historical phases in this development.

The First Global Adjustment Crisis and Brazilian Response, 1983–1993

The international financial crisis set off by Mexico's 1982 moratorium of its foreign debt thrust the Brazilian economy into a deep recession, bringing the nation's long cycle of economic growth—with an average 8.1% GDP yearly increase between 1965 and 1980—to an abrupt end. In response to this crisis, the military government's planning minister, Delfim Neto, adopted an economic strategy designed to maximize Brazil's trade surplus by expanding agricultural exports. This hastened the incorporation of new farmland in the agricultural frontier areas of the country's midwest region. Moreover, it revitalized several policies favoring export-oriented sectors of the economy, knowing these would generate the hard currency required to pay the country's foreign creditors. Table 2.3 shows that between 1983 and 1993 the national trade surplus and net income sent abroad hovered close to 4% of the GDP; a much higher rate than the 1965–80 period.

The effort to build up a large trade surplus in order to service the country's foreign debt led to an anomalous situation. It supported economic policies benefiting sectors that required few imported goods, and as such fueled agricultural growth. This strategy, nonetheless, led to a decline in farm income and rural property values (see table 2.3). Moreover, unlike other export-oriented economies, the large trade surpluses generated in Brazil did not stimulate domestic growth, since the export earnings were sent abroad to service the country's foreign debt, rather than reinvested at home. Consequently, the overall Brazilian economy remained stagnant during this period.

The Neoliberal Surge, 1994–1999

The government's monetary stabilization plan adopted in 1994 was undertaken in a context of abundant capital flows to emerging economies. The Plano Real, in fact, became a neoliberal instrument to attract foreign capital to Brazil. Under these circumstances, policymakers set aside the goal of maximizing trade surpluses, as the external constraints underpinning this strategy had largely dissipated. During these years of high liquidity, international financial markets increased their lending practice to emerging market economies.

This context induced the government to liberalize its foreign trade by overvaluing the nation's exchange rate, removing import tariffs, and dismantling its support programs for industrial development and agriculture. This pendulum shift, however, soon led to a negative trade balance. Brazil's escalating current account deficit, in turn, triggered a sharp rise in the nation's foreign debt (see table 2.4). Between 1994 and 1998, the current account deficit averaged close to 3.5% of the GDP per year, reaching close to 30% of the nation's GDP in 2003. In fact, during President Cardoso's eight years in office the net foreign debt rose to $173 billion.[11] As seen in table 2.3, the structural adjustment measures adopted during Cardoso's first term in office also caused a drop in farm earnings and land prices.[12]

The devaluation of farmland assets had an ambiguous effect on land reform. On the one hand, the lower cost of land facilitated government expropriation of unproductive estates and their redistribution among the rural poor. Diminished land values thus had the effect of demoting the economic power of landlords. On the other hand, the economic recession and dearth of state policies supporting family farmers hindered efforts to construct an alternative rural development model; an effort that would require, at minimum, substantial public sector support.

The drop in farm income and land values was driven by a sharp decline in agricultural prices. This situation was aggravated by the government's decision—starting in the early 1990s—to phase out various rural subsidies. All these developments had devastating effects on Brazil's family farms, many of which were abandoned, sold, or reduced to subsistence farming. Indeed, the 1996 agrarian census registered one million fewer farms than it had in 1985.

The economic foundation of the neoliberal trade and financial policies adopted between 1994 and 1998 were actually quite weak. These measures produced a large current account deficit and foreign debt. All of this came to a head at the end of Cardoso's first term in office, amid a global financial crisis set off by developments in Asia and Russia, which led to a massive capital flight out of Brazil. In early 1999, Brazil was forced to devalue its national currency. In the ensuing economic downturn, the Cardoso administration reigned in some of its neoliberal policies and adopted an agro-export promotion strategy to generate the currency reserves needed to service the country's foreign debt. This constrained adjustment to the global economy—based on export-oriented policies similar to those adopted between 1983 and 1993—would remain almost intact during President Lula's administration.

Relaunching the Agribusiness Strategy, 2000–2005

Brazil's 1999 economic crisis compelled the government to readjust its economic policies and accept three successive IMF loan-rescue operations (in 1999, 2001, and 2003) to cope with the country's current account shortfall. This deficit had increased sharply in 1998 and 1999 as a result of capital outflows led by short-term, speculative investors. To tackle the new debt crisis, the Cardoso administration reintroduced basic elements of the agro-export strategy devised by the military government in the wake of the 1982 debt crisis. This brought capitalist agriculture—rebranded as "agribusiness"—to the forefront of Brazil's international trade and domestic rural policy agenda.

Unlike his military predecessors, Cardoso's agro-export strategy began with weaker levels of public sector support for agriculture. In the preceding years, many of the state programs crafted to provide farm credit, guarantee prices, promote agricultural research, offer technical assistance, and develop port and road infrastructure to facilitate exports had been dismantled or weakened. These impediments and the lingering effects of Brazil's overvalued currency delayed the full resumption of rural development policies forged under the military regime, which favored the technical modernization of agriculture without land reform, until the early twenty-first century. In effect, the country's new trade policies would only generate the intended surplus by 2002 (see table 2.4).

The second Cardoso administration instituted various actions designed to revitalize the country's agribusiness sector, comprised by an amalgam of large landholders, big agro-industries, and global agro-food corporations operating in partnership with finance capital and the Brazilian state.[13] The Cardoso government (1) prioritized public investments in road and transport infrastructure to create development hubs, which incorporated new territories into the agro-export economy and formed trade corridors for agribusiness commodities;[14] (2) reorganized the state-sponsored Brazilian Agricultural Research Corporation (EMBRAPA), enabling its close collaboration with global agribusiness corporations such as Monsanto and Syngenta; (3) maintained a lax enforcement

Table 2.4. Macroeconomic indicators, 1983–2005

Years	GDP growth rate (%)	GDP growth rate for agriculture (%)	Current accounts deficit/balance (% of GDP)	Trade balance (% of GDP)
1983–1993	2.3	2.4	(–) 0.40	4.13
1991	1.0	1.4	(–) 0.35	2.61
1992	(–) 0.5	4.9	1.59	3.94
1993	4.7	(–) 0.1	(–) 0.13	3.09
1994	5.3	5.5	(–) 0.31	1.93
1995	4.4	4.1	(–) 2.55	(–) 0.50
1996	2.2	3.1	(–) 3.00	(–) 0.72
1997	3.4	(–) 0.8	(–) 3.76	(–) 0.83
1998	0.1	1.3	(–) 4.24	(–) 0.84
1999	0.3	8.3	(–) 4.72	(–) 2.39
2000	4.3	2.1	(–) 4.00	(–) 0.12
2001	1.3	5.7	(–) 4.55	(–) 0.51
2002	2.7	5.8	(–) 1.70	2.86
2003	1.1	5.0	0.81	4.51
2004	5.7	5.8	1.76	5.10
2005	3.2	2.3	1.58	5.09
1995–2000	2.4	3.1	(–) 3.71	(–) 0.90
2001–2005	2.8	4.9	(–) 0.40	3.41

Sources: IPEA data (www.ipeadata.gov.br) for column 1; IBGE for columns 2 and 3; Ministério de Desenvolvimento (www.desenvolvimento.gov.br) for column 4.

of the nation's agrarian laws and land market, facilitating the illegal usurpation of public lands and preservation of unproductive large rural estates; and (4) set up an exchange rate conducive to agribusiness exports and Brazil's constrained adjustment to the global economy.

The agribusiness sector found ample territory on which to expand, notably for feed-grain production. Corn and soybeans alone accounted for 80% of the nation's grain cultivation, which spread significantly in parts of the midwest, northeast, and Amazon regions. Driven by foreign demand, Brazilian agriculture grew by 4.9% between 2000 and 2005, well ahead of the national GDP, which increased by only 2.8%. The country achieved a foreign trade surplus by 2002, which continued to grow in the ensuing years, as noted in tables 2.3 and 2.4.

These trade surpluses, however, were not reinvested in Brazil, but were used primarily to service the country's foreign debt. Hence, despite the increase in agribusiness production, the national GDP remained stagnant. This pattern of development did not stimulate the national economy as a whole due to its acquiescence to global financial interests. Foreign trade surpluses are usually known to boost national income and domestic demand for goods and services. In Brazil, however, these gains were mostly sent overseas. Its main domestic beneficiaries were confined to the export-oriented agrarian elite.

Brazil's Constrained Adjustment to the Global Economy and the Agrarian Question

The Brazilian economy remained relatively stagnant between 1982 and 2005, with an average yearly GDP growth rate of 2.5%—unlike the average 7.5% annual growth rate from 1948 to 1980.[15] Amid the sluggish economy between 1982 and 2005, agribusiness earnings experienced significant oscillations. Its contractions and periods of exuberant growth were the upshot of Brazil's constrained adjustment to the global economy. Agribusiness profits surged after 1982 following the adoption of state policies geared toward repaying the country's foreign debt. These earnings shrunk with the implementation of the Plano Real and the influx of foreign capital, and re-expanded as a consequence of the country's currency devaluation in 1999 and new debt crisis.

Among the peasantry—namely, family farmers disengaged from the prevailing capitalist mode of agricultural production—the ebbs and flows of farm income amplified their socioeconomic distance from the agribusiness sector. These oscillations, in fact, fueled the expansion of Brazil's rural subsistence economy, a sector characterized by non-wage-earning economic activities and labor relations that provided a source of livelihood for a large portion of countryside dwellers.[16]

The agricultural downturn that followed the introduction of the Plano Real led to a contraction of the rural subsistence economy. Peasant farmers, however, continued in a slump during the agribusiness boom that started in 2000, even though their recession was less obvious. This underscores the fact that agribusiness growth in Brazil produced a constrained expansion of both the agrarian and national economy, given its propensity to undercut domestic demands for goods and services, limit job growth, and preserve vast areas of unproductive farmland. All three restrictions were strongly affected by Brazil's constrained adjustment to the global economy and hampered the nation's development prospects. Domestic demand for goods and services, including basic food necessities, was reined in to generate trade surpluses needed to service the foreign debt. This constrained adjustment also required restrictions on domestic imports in order to maintain a positive trade balance.

In turn, the capital-intensive nature and advanced technology used by agribusiness farmers curtailed opportunities for job creation in the countryside. The size of Brazil's rural labor force underscored the social problem at stake. According to the 2000 Census, close to 35% of the national population lived in

Table 2.5. Rural and small town inhabitants, 1970–2000 (%)

Population in rural and rural-like conditions	1970	1980	1991	2000
Total population in municipalities with less than 20,000 inhabitants	28.0	23.9	19.5	19.8
Rural population in municipalities with more than 20,000 inhabitants	31.7	24.7	19.7	15.1
Total	59.7	48.6	39.2	34.8

Source: Prepared by author based on Brazilian census bureau data, see IBGE (2005).

the countryside and in small rural towns with less than 20,000 inhabitants (see table 2.5). Because of agribusiness' low labor to capital ratio and limited capacity to absorb unskilled rural workers, this segment of Brazil's population has been compelled mostly to subsist through informal activities, amid persistently high levels of unemployment.[17]

Brazil's agribusiness model of rural development created strong incentives among the agrarian elite to preserve and accumulate vast tracts of uncultivated farmland, especially in the nation's agrarian frontier. Greater profit margins in agriculture raised farmland prices, encouraged landlords and agribusiness firms to maintain and acquire large stocks of unproductive land as reserve value, both for future use and land market speculation. The state, however, could have curtailed these practices by enforcing the nation's agrarian and rural property tax laws. The Brazilian Constitution, after all, mandates the government to expropriate all rural estates that do not fulfill a "social function." Yet the state's historic deference toward the agrarian elite and protection of its interests has thus far prevented all Brazilian governments, including the Lula administration, from undertaking substantive measures to redistribute wealth through land reform and rural tax policies. Whenever applied, Brazil's agrarian laws were often used to increase the landed elites' wealth by inflating the value of their estates well beyond market prices. This will be discussed in more depth below.

The state's lax enforcement of agrarian and rural property tax laws helped expand and empower Brazil's agribusiness sector. In doing so, it created conditions that fueled the decline of the country's family farms, while diminishing abilities to carry out a progressive land reform. Rural policies designed to benefit small farmers in Brazil, thus, need to be aware of the structural restrictions affecting the development of its peasantry, and contest the economic arrangements that undercut domestic demand for goods and services, limit job growth, and preserve vast areas of unproductive farmland.

Brazil's historic agrarian inequities were reinforced in the last half century through state policies designed to modernize agriculture and integrate the national economy into the new global order. In effect, the state's model of economic development undermined the possibility of carrying out the social rights guaranteed by the 1988 Constitution, including those favoring land redistribution. This wide gap between the country's legal edifice and actual practice has undermined efforts to reduce the nation's stark social disparities.

Sharp agrarian inequities have persisted under Brazil's democratic regime, despite the existence of a legal framework that actually supports land reform. All three branches of the state have played a complicit role—through acts of commission and omission—in sustaining these inequities. In doing so, they have helped erode the legitimacy of the nation's constitutional order, particularly with regard to land rights.[18] The state's reluctance and failure to regulate the land market and enforce constitutional laws meant to redress the country's agrarian problems has been compounded, no doubt, by Brazil's constrained adjustment to the global economy.

There is ample evidence to back these assertions. For one, Brazil's high land concentration has been amply documented, particularly through the Gini indicators (the most common measure used to gauge inequality) offered in table 2.6.[19] The state's weak enforcement of agrarian laws, nevertheless, requires a more fine-grained analysis. One way of doing this is to contrast Brazil's constitutional principles regarding land rights with the country's actual farmland use.

Building on the 1964 Land Statute, the 1988 Constitution established that rural properties have to fulfill a social function, defined by three criteria: "rational and adequate land use," "environmental preservation," and "suitable labor conditions." The 1993 agrarian law, however, only addressed the first clause

Table 2.6. Land distribution in Brazil, 1950–95 (as measured by the Gini coefficient)

Regions and Brazil	1950	1960	1970	1975	1980	1985	1995
North	0.944	0.944	0.831	0.863	0.841	0.812	0.820
Northeast	0.849	0.845	0.854	0.862	0.861	0.869	0.859
Southeast	0.763	0.772	0.760	0.761	0.690	0.771	0.767
South	0.741	0.725	0.735	0.733	0.734	0.747	0.742
Midwest	0.833	0.901	0.876	0.876	0.878	0.861	0.831
Brazil	**0.840**	**0.839**	**0.843**	**0.854**	**0.857**	**0.857**	**0.856**

Source: Gasques and Conceição (1998).

Table 2.7. Types of rural landholdings in Brazil, 2003 (in millions of hectares)

	National territory (total land mass)	100%	850.2
1.	Areas registered in the SNCR	51.4	436.6
1.1.	Unproductive areas (based on owner's declaration)	(14.2)	(120.4)
1.2.	Land reform settlements*	(4.7)	(40.0)
2.	National parks	12.0	102.1
3.	Indigenous reserves	15.1	128.5
4.	Other registered public lands	0.5	4.2
5.	Unregistered public land (*terras devolutas*)**	20.3	173.0
	Subtotal (1+2+3+4+5)	99.3	844.3

Source: Ministério de Desenvolvimento Agrário (2003a: Tables 5.1.11 and 5.2.2.1).

Notes: *INCRA data on all land reform areas administered by the federal government.
**Data obtained by subtracting all areas with landholding titles, including urban and
public infrastructure areas, from the total land mass.

and left the environmental and labor criteria undefined. "Rational and adequate land use" is determined by two indicators, one measuring the "degree of land use," the other the "degree of economic exploitation."[20] This legislation put the National Agrarian Reform and Colonization Institute (INCRA) in charge of overseeing the implementation of all land reform and rural property tax laws.

In Brazil, rural land can be held in five different ways: (1) private land, registered in the National Land Registry System (SNCR) and subject to the constitutional norms regarding its social function; (2) public lands, parks, and preservation areas, registered with the federal government; (3) indigenous reserves, also registered with the federal government and administered by the National Indigenous Foundation (FUNAI); (4) areas controlled by various state agencies, not recorded with the SNCR; or (5) nonregistered public land (*terras devolutas*), usually illegally usurped.[21]

The main elements of the nation's agrarian structure can be discerned through the data presented in table 2.7. This classification allows us to measure the degree to which landholdings in Brazil are under public ownership and fulfill the social function established in the National Constitution. In effect, rankings 1 through 5 in table 2.8 highlight the public and social orientation of landholdings, while the inverse ranking, from 5 to 1 in table 2.8, underscores the degree of privatization and commoditization of Brazilian farmland.

The weak enforcement of agrarian laws in Brazil is made evident in table 2.8. Its fifth category—which adds unproductive landholdings (according to the owner's sworn statement) and unregistered public land, usually seized by illegal land grabbers—comprised more than one-third of the national territory in 2003. Landholdings in the fourth category, declared "productive" by their own-

Table 2.8. Ranking of public-private rural landholdings, 2003 (%)

1. Indigenous reserves and national parks	27.1
2. Land reform settlements	(4.7)*
3. Other registered public lands	0.5
4. Private landholdings registered with SNCR, compatible with the constitution's social function (based on owner's declaration)	37.2
5. Unproductive private holdings and unregistered public land	34.5

Note: *Areas expropriated for land reform settlements belong to the federal government pending the settlers' completion of all payments due for their land parcel. During this time, the settlers retain legal custody of the land, and receive the final title only after making the last payment.

ers, are based on productivity indicators derived from the 1975 Agricultural Census. In the early 2000s it became clear that the farm output of many estates rested on greatly outdated values, given the significant technological advancement of Brazilian agriculture in the previous two decades. Still, all efforts to update these indicators under the Lula government were blocked as a result of the concerted national pressure of agribusiness associations, their political representatives, and allies in the media establishment.[22]

Unregistered public lands in Brazil have been appropriated mostly by large land grabbers, often with fake property tittles, in a process known as *grilagem*. These areas also include squatter peasants, occupying more than fifty hectares of land in the Amazon region. The country's unregistered public lands have rarely been the object of state control and taxation.

By adding categories 4 and 5 in table 2.8 one can infer that, in the early 2000s, nearly 72% of the national territory was under ineffectual state dominion. In truth, this estimate is probably low, for it does not consider the fact that many indigenous reserves and national parks—which comprised all together 27% of the national territory—were threatened or even occupied illegally by large cattle ranchers, planters, loggers, miners, and drug smugglers.[23]

Aside from the obvious discrepancy between Brazil's constitutional norms and actual land use, the state has shown a remarkable weakness in handling its Rural Land Tax. Enforcement of this levy has actually been negligible, as have been all efforts to set up a progressive toll on unproductive farmland. During the early 2000s, this tax amounted to just 0.1% of the federal government's revenue. In fact, the cost of levying this duty was roughly equal to the value of all the revenue collected through this tax.[24] All this suggests that a substantial portion of the country's rural legislation and tax policies have existed mainly, as the classic Brazilian aphorism would put it, *para o inglês ver* (for the English to see).

The state's reluctance to enforce the nation's agrarian laws prompted various peasant movements to engage in successive waves of land occupations, targeting mostly unproductive farms and estates set up illegally on public lands. These mobilizations were quite effective during President Cardoso's first term in office and prompted a notable increase in government land expropriation, particularly in the aftermath of two police massacres of landless peasants in Corumbiara (1995) and in Eldorado dos Carajás (1996). Between 1995 and 2002, the Cardoso administration practically doubled the land area allocated for agrarian reform, from 2% to 4% of the national territory.[25]

In the late 1990s, nonetheless, the Cardoso administration decided to take a strong stance against peasant land invasions (see Fernandes, chap. 5, this volume, and Branford, chap. 13, this volume). Among other measures, Cardoso issued a presidential decree (Medida Provisória 2027/98) prohibiting INCRA from surveying any estate occupied by landless peasants to determine the area's level of productivity. Land occupations have been the main leverage used by peasants to compel the state to expropriate unproductive farms. By inhibiting this protest tactic, the Cardoso government effectively paralyzed Brazil's land reform process in the early 2000s.

Obtaining land is a crucial step to any agrarian reform process. The Brazilian Constitution authorizes the state to expropriate rural properties that do not fulfill their social function. In addition, the state can repossess unregistered public lands, purchase farmland directly from the estate owners, or support a land-credit program. The latter two draw on market principles. In theory, these would be used in exceptional circumstances, given their higher cost to the national treasury and tendency to drive up rural property values.

Various omissions and actions taken by all three branches of the Brazilian state have undermined the effectiveness of the legal process required to carry out land expropriations. Different financial procedures and court decisions have greatly overvalued the compensation paid for many land expropriations; a fact well documented in table 2.9.[26] These distortions can be illustrated through the following case. A rural property bought in the land market at a hypothetical value of 100 in 1994 would have dropped to 60 in 1999, due to the agricultural recession and decrease in farmland prices. The state, however, would have expropriated the same property for 141 in 1999, more than double its market price. This sharp increase owes much to the adjustments for inflation and annual 6% interest rate paid on the government's agrarian debt bonds, the debt titles issued to compensate for the expropriated land.

The agrarian elite have found various ways to use these agrarian debt bonds to their own benefit, distorting in the process the principles underpinning the country's agrarian laws. The Brazilian Constitution established that these bonds are redeemable over a twenty-year period, with their real value preserved and updated according to the estate's market price. This system, however, has been distorted by the fact that bonds can actually be redeemed much earlier. Moreover, the added 6% interest rate and full protection against inflation greatly in-

Table 2.9. Public expenditures on agrarian debt bonds, 1996–2002 (in millions of Brazilian reais, 2001)

Year expenses time	Agrarian reform (1)	Agrarian debt bonds			Court-injunctions (3)	(2 + 3)* in %
		Amortization	Interest	Total (2)		
1996	1,424.3	66.8	116.4	183.2	445	44.1
1997	1,706.5	1,127.6	526.0	1,652.8	420	121.5
1998	1,512.2	371.3	221.8	593.2	110	46.5
1999	1,113.4	578.4	470.7	1,049.1	102	103.4
2000	534.7	545.7	205.0	750.7	41	148.5
2001	543.7	541.3	179.0	720.3	2	133.0
2002	—	224.0	69.0	293.0	—	—

Source: Gasques and Villa Verde (2003: 27).

Note: *The sum of items 2 + 3 corresponds to actual expenditures on agrarian debt bonds.

creased the bonds' value.[27] As a result of these procedures, agrarian debt bonds evolved from operating as a long-term public instrument, linked to market land prices, to a highly prized short-term asset, open to easy transaction in the financial market.

Such distortions have perverted the constitutional principles on which these agrarian debt bonds were created. These bonds, in effect, have become a short-term dividend that gives landlords a net cash premium for their unproductive land. Adding to this warp, the state has often been compelled to pay much higher values for its land expropriations due to court injunctions issued by judges inclined to give the large landholders a sympathetic hearing. All these developments have driven up the cost of land reform and saddled the Brazilian state with significant debt. Instead of promoting family farms through land redistribution, these legal instruments have been used to greatly augment the compensation given to Brazil's rural elite.

To conclude, there is ample evidence to suggest a widening gap—particularly since the early 1990s—between the state's concrete actions on agrarian matters and its legal principles concerning rural property rights in Brazil. This juridical and institutional vacuum has created fertile ground for the accumulation of both productive and idle land by the country's new agrarian elite—notably, its global agribusiness and financial conglomerates.

Agrarian Reform and Family Farming in the Early Twenty-first Century

Brazilian peasants and land reform proponents were at a crossroads during the onset of the twenty-first century. Few had doubts as to the magnitude of Brazil's agrarian problems. More than one-third of the nation's farmland remained idle and/or subject to illicit land-grabbing practices. Furthermore, the number of land claimants continued to be high. By 2003 close to a million families were living in landless camps and/or had registered with INCRA to receive a land parcel. Moreover, various demographic studies had revealed a much larger number of potential land reform beneficiaries.[28]

Adding to this, land reform advocates had developed a pretty sharp diagnosis of the country's agrarian dilemma. This highlighted the fact that land concentration and an agribusiness rural development model had intensified Brazil's problem with rural unemployment and poverty. Under this development model, the agrarian elite were allowed to accumulate vast stocks of idle farmland while marginalizing rural workers and peasant farmers from the agricultural market. All of these issues—along with the intense peasant mobilizations of 2003—put agrarian reform back at the top of the nation's public agenda. Despite this momentum, the Lula government adopted a diffident policy toward land reform. It sought to appease peasant protestors by offering some land redistribution and substantially increasing the public monies available for family famers and agrarian reform settlers. Still, it retained the policies that helped consolidate Brazil's agribusiness sector, while supporting an economic framework aligned with the nation's constrained adjustment to the global order.

In other words, the balance of forces in Brazilian society in the early years of the twenty-first century was tipped to favor the status quo. The renewed strength of the country's agrarian elite, in alliance with financial capital and influential sectors of the state, had created highly adverse conditions for Brazil's land reform movement. This was compounded by internal rifts within the peasant movement, mostly over whether to collaborate with, or contest the power of, agribusiness firms. Moreover, the Catholic Church's bishops' conference and social outreach agencies had lost some of the vigor with which they once had embraced land reform policies. Adding to this, the country's left-leaning political parties—heirs of the old Communist Party's agrarian traditions—had become part of the national government in 2003. These political leaders were disinclined to challenge Brazil's economic model and constrained adjustment to the global order. Instead, they sought to manage this process. Through their various actions and omissions, many of these political representatives ended up adopting positions akin to those championed by agribusiness interests. Such trends were reinforced by ideas fostered in academic and technocratic circles, influenced by the allure of technical progress associated with the agribusiness production model. These views were widely diffused through the nation's mass media.

For all their combativeness and increased organizational capacity, the MST and other peasant movements did not have the resources needed to mobilize larger segments of Brazil's marginalized population and prevent the rapid expansion of corporate agriculture. This dynamic, along with the Lula government's refusal to adopt more progressive actions on land redistribution, made it very difficult to reignite the country's land reform movement. These circumstances exacerbated the problems of social exclusion, violence, and criminality in the countryside. Its many victims included an array of informal, enslaved, and underaged farm workers; indigenous and maroon communities; impoverished, unemployed, and landless peasants; environmentalists; people displaced by the construction of hydroelectric dams; land reform settlers; and those afflicted by the nation's thriving drug trade.

Unlike the agribusiness firms, who could pursue their agenda through access to vast sums of money and close ties to power, marginalized people in the Brazilian countryside, were, on the whole, poorly organized and greatly underrepresented in both civil and political society. They lacked the resources needed to build coalitions and present their demands on the national stage and challenge the agribusiness model with a stronger voice.

Rural policies under the Lula government reflected this asymmetrical balance of social forces. Though saddled with internal discrepancies and constant tussles between the Ministry of Agriculture, the Ministry of Agrarian Development, and the Ministry of Social Development, the bulk of its funding went to support the agrarian elite and other well-to-do farmers. The priority given to this segment—including family farmers linked to the agribusiness production chain and a few exemplary land reform settlements—meant that close to 75% of all family farms ended up receiving a much smaller share of these public funds, if any at all.[29]

Brazil's constrained adjustment to the global economy strengthened the nation's agribusiness model of rural development. This approach to development has thrived on the country's lax enforcement of agrarian laws and taxes, low rates of domestic consumption, and the social exclusion of large segments of the rural population. Early twenty-first-century economic trends have thwarted attempts to overcome these restrictions and reinstate a cogent national development strategy—that is, a development process centered on the productive inclusion of its marginalized people and the preservation of the country's natural resources. This quest must incorporate efforts to deconstruct the ideological, political, and economic conditions sustaining Brazil's constrained adjustment to the global order. In addition, it must take bold steps to ensure the state's commitment to an audacious enterprise among the nation's poor: to build human capabilities and provide sustainable sources of livelihood.[30]

Conclusions

Brazil's contemporary debate over the nation's stark agrarian inequities, and the policies needed to reform this situation, began in the mid-1950s. The 1964 military coup, however, stifled this public conversation and imposed the conservative ideas advanced by a group of USP economists led by Delfim Neto, who served as an influential minister during the autocratic regime. Under the military, the state instituted various policies designed to promote the technical modernization of agriculture without land redistribution. Agrarian reform was brought back to the nation's public agenda with the country's redemocratization in the 1980s. In the early years of the twenty-first century the church and left-leaning political parties continued to support land reform, albeit with less fervor than in previous decades. Since the mid-1980s, the driving force in favor of agrarian reform has come from an array of peasant movements, notably the MST.

Conservatives have remained strong proponents of policies that support the technical modernization of agriculture without land reform. In the 1950s and early 1960s, this position was backed by the traditional clout of the country's rural elite. After the 1964 coup, the military government embraced this project and bankrolled it with generous public subsidies, to the delight of the nation's wealthy landowners. Lest there be no doubt, Brazil's agribusiness model of rural development is an enduring and powerful piece of the country's autocratic past. This model is backed by a triple alliance between large landholders, global agribusiness and financial conglomerates, and the Brazilian state. It is buttressed further by the landed elite's strong representation in Congress through a multiparty caucus known as the *bancada ruralista,* which hold close to one-third of all legislative seats.

Brazil's constrained adjustment to the global economic order in the wake of the 1982 debt crisis created favorable conditions for the expansion of agribusiness interests, given the need to stimulate agro-exports to generate the trade surplus required to service the country's foreign debt. This pattern of development aggravated the problems of social exclusion and environmental degradation. It created few jobs among unskilled rural laborers and marginalized over 75% of the nation's family farmers, most of whom remained mired in Brazil's large subsistence economy. By contrast, the agribusiness boom of the 1990s and 2000s bolstered the rural elite's historic influence and close ties with the political elite.

Even under the Lula government, the agribusiness approach to economic growth fueled the nation's dependency on primary commodity exports, deepening Brazil's subordinate role in the international division of labor. All this thwarted the prospects of pursuing a model of national development grounded on principles of economic inclusion and social equality.

Notes

The author is grateful to Miguel Carter for his constructive input in editing this chapter and for the assistance of Eric J. Eggleston in preparing the English translation. Translated from the Portuguese by Miguel Carter.

1. Prado (1966).
2. Guimarães (1989), published originally in 1963.
3. Rangel (1961: 25).
4. Furtado developed these arguments in the Triennial Plan, prepared while he was serving as planning minister for the João Goulart government (1961–64); see, in particular, Presidência da República (1962: 126, 140, 149).
5. The Catholic Church's contribution to this debate was less theoretical than that of other groups, since its ideas were articulated mainly through statements issued by its bishops and the Vatican's social encyclicals. For an analysis of the church's position during this period, see Pierruci, Souza, and Camargo (1986), and Carvalho (1985).
6. For an influential text outlining the main ideas of American economic functionalism, see Johnston and Mellor (1961); also Delfim Neto et al. (1969).
7. Delfim Neto et al. (1969: 113–14).
8. The efforts to integrate industry, agriculture, and trade policies are examined further in Delgado (1985).
9. These institutes included government bodies like the Sugar and Alcohol Institute (IAA), established in the early 1930s; the Brazilian Coffee Institute (IBC), created in 1952; the Executive Commission of the Cocoa Farming Plan (CEPLAC), set up in 1957; and the National Wheat Commission of the Bank of Brazil and Department of Wheat (CTRIN-DTRIG) of the National Superintendency of Supplies (SUNAB), instituted in 1967. This agricultural trade board held a national monopoly on all wheat marketing until 1990.
10. Agricultural sector imports were always lower compared to other economic segments, which made its trade surpluses far more impressive, especially in comparison to industry. Further insights on this matter can be found in Delgado (1985: 26–33).
11. Brazil's foreign debt figures are derived from the deficit/surplus of the Current Transactions' Account balance payment for 1994–99.
12. On land market prices during Cardoso's first presidency, see Delgado and Flores Filho (1998).
13. Large-scale financial investments in Brazilian agriculture began in the 1970s, with the state's decision to promote a Green Revolution through tax and credit subsidies. This development led to a sharp increase in land values; see Delgado (1985).
14. Cardoso's second administration adopted a multiyear plan called "Brazil in Action," designed to build highways, railways, and ports in an effort to incorporate new agricultural territories and facilitate agro-exports. Although the public investments were lower than expected, this program was one of the highest priorities of the Cardoso government.
15. Instituto de Pesquisa Econômica Aplicada (IPEA) (2009).
16. For a conceptual review and analysis of Brazil's "subsistence sector," see Delgado (2003).
17. Unemployment rates in rural areas and small, mostly agricultural towns increased from 2.1% in 1980 to 15.0% in 2000, a higher rate than that found in the nation's metropolitan areas. As noted in table 2.5, municipalities with less than 20,000 inhabitants made up close to 20% of the national population in both the 1991 and 2000 censuses.
18. The "social function" of rural property is established in one of the immutable clauses (cláusulas pétreas) of the Brazilian Constitution: article 5, sections 22 and 23; and formally defined in articles 184 and 186. These were subsequently regulated by Law 8629/93. Together, these legal principles provide the normative basis on which the executive is entrusted to regulate Brazil's land tenure system.

19. Statistical studies of land concentration in Brazil, using various databases—including the agricultural censuses and national household surveys of the Brazilian Institute for Geography and Statistics' (IBGE) and INCRA's land registry—reveal persistently high levels of extreme land inequality since the 1950s, with a Gini coefficient larger than 0.8, as can be seen in table 2.6; also see the useful econometric studies produced by Rodolfo Hoffman (2001, 2004). These numbers, however, have been an occasional source of controversy in Brazil, as when the Ministry of Agrarian Development (MDA) published data showing an unprecedented 5% reduction in the Gini coefficient between 1999 and 2000, from 0.848 to 0.802. In truth, though, these figures were the result of a faulty methodology, based on the removal—for the 2000 calculus—of all data for areas believed to be in the hands of large land grabbers, along with other alterations of INCRA's land registry. These methodological changes impaired all comparisons with previous years. In contrast, the IBGE data offer a far more consistent picture, with minimal variations over various agricultural censuses. At best, these figures suggest that the land reform settlements created between 1985 and 2000 reduced the Gini coefficient for land inequality by merely 0.1%; see IPEA (2001: 95).

20. "The degree of land use" required to meet the social function principle is based on an 80% or higher ratio between the "area under exploitation" and the "exploitable area," which excludes legal forest reserves, areas with construction, water, infertile soils, and the like. "The degree of economic exploitation" is defined by comparing the yearly and regional rates of agricultural and livestock production with the technical indexes established by the federal government for each region.

21. This classification was developed in collaboration with staff and technical advisors to the MDA, during the preparation of the National Agrarian Reform Plan, coordinated by Plínio de Arruda Sampaio; see Ministério de Desenvolvimento Agrário (MDA) (2003).

22. During the Lula government, various attempts were made to alter the technical indexes used for land expropriation. These, however, were blocked through relentless pressure from the main large landholding associations, notably the National Confederation of Agriculture (CNA), and their allies in the national press, who published raging editorials on the subject, arguing that such changes would produce "chaos in the countryside."

23. The 2004 invasion of indigenous territories by commercial farmers in Mato Grosso and Roraima—particularly in the "Raposa Terra do Sol" reserve—illustrates the long history of precarious protection for native people's lands in Brazil.

24. A 1996 law established a progressive hike on rural property taxes based on the actual amount of farmland use. This legislation, nonetheless, has not had any major effect on the real tax revenue, which hovered around $100 million per year, from 1996 to 2003. As a portion of federal revenue, the Rural Land Tax exhibited a constant decline, from 0.27% in 1996 to 0.18% in 1999, to 0.11% in 2001 and 2003 (see www.receita.fazenda.gov.br). Half of all the revenue collected by this national tax is transferred to the federal states and municipalities.

25. Under Cardoso's two terms in office the federal government distributed close to 21 million hectares of land, mostly in the Amazon region; see IPEA (2003: 106).

26. As can be gleaned from table 2.9, payments made on the Agrarian Debt Bonds for 1996 and 2001—including court-mandated compensations—were higher than the total monies spent on land reform in four out of six years.

27. This additional payment for bond expropriations was established in July 1991 by President Fernando Collor de Mello, in July 1991, who was clearly sympathetic to large landholders.

28. A summary of these studies can be found in Ministério de Desenvolvimento Agrário (MDA) (2003).

29. The 2000 demographic census revealed that merely 3.6% of all rural households had a monthly income higher than ten months' minimum wages, and only 11.6% earned more than five months' minimum wages. Drawing on the 1996 agricultural census, the Ministry of Agrarian Development calculated there were 4.14 million family farms in Brazil, of which 77% had an annual production value of twelve months' minimum wages, roughly at US$80 per month; figures based on Instituto Brasileiro de Geografía e Estatística (IBGE) (2007a).

30. In 2000, more than 54% of Brazil's labor was in the informal and subsistence sector of the economy; 28% of these workers were unemployed, and 34% toiled without the protection of the national labor card (*carteira de trabalho assinada*). Further analysis of the rural and urban subsistence sector can be found in Delgado (2003: 33).

3 Rural Social Movements, Struggles for Rights, and Land Reform in Contemporary Brazilian History

The rise of new social conflicts in the Brazilian countryside during the second half of the twentieth century triggered a growing public debate over agrarian reform and the role of agriculture in the nation's development. These disputes led to increasing discussion over the rights of rural workers. All this took place amid a complex and contentious effort to shape novel social arrangements, assert new political identities, and define the meaning of the term *rural worker.*

The new wave of peasant land struggles that emerged in the late 1970s appeared in a context shaped by previous disputes over land and rural labor rights. This historical context is crucial to the analysis of Brazil's current debate over agrarian reform. By the late 1970s, Brazil had already set up a legal framework and various state institutions and associations designed to represent the interests of rural workers. The country had also experienced different forms of popular struggle in the countryside and established different ways of making claims, framing debates, and identifying the adversaries at stake. In effect, this history had left a clear mark on the nation's legal edifice, public perceptions, and discourse over its rural conflicts. The study of these developments can shed light on the diverse identities, demands, and perceptions of rural workers that surfaced with the resurgence of peasant mobilizations in the 1980s.

This chapter provides a broad overview of this social history. It highlights crucial elements of the struggle for citizenship rights in the countryside prior to and after the 1964 military coup d'etat. The final section reviews the main developments in the 1980s, when a broad range of rural actors and demands appeared on the scene, adding great complexity to Brazil's agrarian debate.

Background

In Brazil, the struggles for land and to improve living conditions for those who toil on it for others have always been closely entwined. During the time of slavery, slaves often fled plantations and set up their own *quilombolas* (maroon communities), where they established dominion over the land. With the abolition of slavery and the assimilation of free labor on the large plantations, access to land for planting subsistence crops became a matter of frequent contention between landlords and peasants, and provoked various disputes within these estates.[1]

Prior to the mid-1900s, land conflicts were sporadic, based mainly on local grievances, and treated as a private affair. State intervention, if ever called on, employed police and military forces to invariably repress mass peasant uprisings, as in the case of Canudos (1897), in Bahia's *sertão* (semi-arid hinterland) region, and the Contestado revolt (1912–16), in the interior of Santa Catarina.

The 1920s ushered in a period of significant changes in Brazil, with the beginning of its industrialization process, and growing public discussion over labor rights and the nation's development model. In 1922, three events in particular underscored the country's novel and animated public conversation, while giving added impetus to various social, political, and cultural undertakings. The first event, the Modern Art Week celebrated in São Paulo, triggered prolific intellectual debates over Brazil's national identity. The second, the emergence of the *tenentismo* (lieutenants) movement led by young army officers, introduced demands for greater state centralization and democratic reforms, by calling for secret ballots and other initiatives. The third, the creation of the Brazilian Communist Party (PCB), ushered in the idea and call for major societal transformations, and placed the role of the working classes squarely at the heart of this discussion. While these events addressed different rural issues and their significance for the nation's historical formation, these were generally treated as matters of lesser importance. In the ensuing years, discussions over questions related to the Brazilian countryside lingered discretely on the nation's political agenda, while the country embarked on a process of substantial socioeconomic and political change.

The post-1930 period was marked by attempts to construct "a new concept of work and worker, a counterpart to that fashioned in the urban industrial sector: a depoliticized, disciplined and productive worker."[2] This involved an effort to create a state corporatist order that promoted collaboration among different social classes. This "legal strategy of establishing compulsory associations and creating corporatist trade unions sought to control the working class and align it to the interests of those in power."[3] It was under this corporatist formula that industrial workers gained access to basic labor rights in Brazil in the 1930s.

The government of Getúlio Vargas (1930–45) made sporadic efforts to extend labor rights to rural workers, and on several occasions expressed concern over the need to improve living conditions among the peasantry and ease their efforts to remain on the land. In 1937, the Chamber of Deputies debated a proposal to establish a Rural Code that would regulate rights and obligations in the countryside. The proposal defined the terms of what constituted a "rural employee" and tried to regulate the stores owned by the sugar plantation owners and labor relations involving rubber tappers in the Amazon.[4] The bill was never voted on, but discussions over the creation of different legal categories of rural workers remained on the nation's political agenda as part of existing debates over the right to form associations. Unlike the laws covering the industrial sector, where employers and workers had the right to join parallel union structures, the Ministry of Agriculture and landlords called for a hybrid form of association in the countryside. As a leading proponent of this view, Pericles Madureira Pinho, argued:

> while urban occupations constitute distinct units, in agriculture the uniformity of work does not allow such differentiation. The same people gather together every day during the hours of work, mixing "occupational activities" with familial and religious ones. . . . The natural harmony of agricultural tasks, wherein the owner identifies with the worker, and is in many cases his co-worker, cannot favor or encourage the formation of separate occupational groups . . . agricultural employers assume a tacit responsibility to assist their workers. In scenarios like ours, there are no antagonisms that can justify the creation of distinct occupational categories.[5]

In 1941, an interministerial commission was set up to study the inclusion of agricultural workers under the corporatist trade union structure.[6] During one of its meetings, representatives from the Ministry of Agriculture and the leading association of large landholders, the National Agricultural Society (SNA), upheld the same position in favor of a "mixed union," in order to prevent "disharmony among the agricultural classes." They also claimed it would be impossible to form unions among rural workers given their "intellectual and economic shortcomings" and the difficulty of defining the concept of *rural worker*. Their arguments, however, were defeated in 1944 when the commission approved a proposal submitted by the Ministry of Labor, Commerce and Industry, which supported the creation of separate unions for rural employers and workers. The Vargas government then issued a decree allowing rural workers to form their own trade unions. Under this law, those who worked for others were to be considered *employees*. The Ministry of Labor would be responsible for recognizing these unions.

The new law, however, was repealed shortly afterward, in 1945, with a new government decree that authorized the creation of mixed rural associations, comprised of large landowners and their rural workers. The law required that these new associations be set up on a territorial basis, one for each municipality, and include state-level federations and a national peak association. Following the state corporatist model, all these organizations would be subordinate to the Ministry of Agriculture, which was responsible for appointing all national board members.[7] The reversal of the legislation supported by the Ministry of

Labor offered clear evidence of the SNA's political clout in Brazil. It also ratified the state's separate treatment of rural and urban workers.[8] Supporters of the law insisted, nonetheless, that it would provide needed health care and education to the countryside man (*o homen do campo*), while "harmonizing" the interests of rural bosses and laborers.

On matters concerning land distribution, the Vargas government instituted the March to the West program, which encouraged peasants to colonize the country's frontier regions and backed efforts to increase the number of family farms, set up rural cooperatives, and ensure that peasants were able to remain on the land.[9] As President Vargas declared in one of his May Day speeches:

> The benefits conferred to [urban workers] should also be extended to rural workers, to those living in isolation in the *sertão*, far from the advantages of civilization. If we do not do this, we run the risk of seeing an exodus from the countryside and overpopulation of the cities—an imbalance of unforeseen consequences. . . . We cannot maintain such a dangerous anomaly, with peasants not having a farm plot in a country where fertile valleys . . . remain uncultivated or uninhabited.[10]

Vargas's actual colonization program was limited to a few settlement clusters in the states of Goiás, Paraná, Mato Grosso, and Pará. Some model farms were also created in the lowlands surrounding Rio de Janeiro (an area known as Baixada Fluminense), in order to alleviate food shortages in this city.[11]

Debates during the Vargas era showed a discernible tension between the recognition of subordinate relations in the countryside and efforts to enshrine a rural development model based on small-scale family farms. The legal arrangements instituted during this period underscored the significant political power of Brazil's landlord class, even with the sharp decline of agricultural exports during the Second World War. These debates were molded, in effect, by a handful of government ministries and a single civil society association representing the interests of the agrarian elite: the SNA. For the SNA and its state allies, rural workers were essentially "incompetent people," in need of constant tutelage.[12] Despite some concern for the country's unequal agrarian structure, Vargas's Estado Novo (New State) made no attempt to redistribute land beyond a few colonization settlements on Brazil's agricultural frontier. In all other parts of the country the landlords' power remained supreme.

The Emergence of Rural Workers and Peasants as Political Actors, 1950–1964

Brazil's redemocratization in the immediate postwar period brought many latent rural conflicts to the fore. Gradually, various contentious issues— particularly peasant land struggles—started to appear on the nation's public scene. Though hardly new, these peasant actions began to elicit arguments in support of tiller land rights and merged with other local fights into a broader demand for agrarian reform. These calls introduced a critique of the nation's high land concentration, while infusing the term *latifúndio* (large landholding) with negative connotations, which were linked to an exploitative and violent system grounded on the preservation of vast and idle rural properties.[13] At the same time, sugarcane workers began to mobilize for basic labor rights, first in São Paulo, and eventually in the northeast. These rural workers sought to obtain the same rights extended to urban workers: eight-hour work days, minimum wages, paid vacations, social security, and the right to form trade unions. Brazilian Communists, in particular, played a key role in supporting these rural labor movements.

The term *camponês* (peasant) acquired a newfound political identity during this process. Similarly, a new grammar was created to depict these different local conflicts in a language that would imply a much broader struggle for social transformations, as put forth by the Brazilian Communist Party (PCB) and other leftist groups. All these developments facilitated the formulation of a more cogent and visible set of demands, which helped overcome the largely diffuse and hidden nature of the grievances involved.

The PCB's organizing activities in the countryside led to the establishment of the Peasant and Agricultural Workers Union of Brazil (ULTAB) in 1954.[14] Its founding meeting in 1954 included delegations from São Paulo, the host state, and other states where the PCB had been involved in various rural conflicts, notably Rio de Janeiro, Pernambuco, Paraiba, Ceará, Maranhão, and Goiás.

The first association of what became known as the Ligas Camponesas (Peasant Leagues) was organized in 1955, on a sugarcane plantation in Pernambuco, where tenant farmers (*foreiros*) were struggling to forestall their eviction from the land. This peasant movement expanded considerably in the following years under the leadership of Francisco Julião, a lawyer who championed the tenant's cause, and with the support of progressive intellectuals and politicians in northeast Brazil. By the early 1960s the Peasant Leagues were the PCB's main competitors in mobilizing rural workers. Both organizations differed in their organizational template, their political ideas regarding the prospects of achieving a Brazilian revolution, and, consequently, their demands and priorities regarding the struggle for land.[15]

The claims and petitions advanced by ULTAB and the Peasant Leagues generated what Eder Sader describes as a "new discursive matrix."[16] This can be clearly discerned by analyzing the representations made at ULTAB's meetings, from the 1953 First Farmworkers Congress to the 1963 creation of the National Confederation of Agricultural Workers (CONTAG). This discursive matrix was disseminated through various grassroots activities and news publications directed at this rural audience, notably, the PCB's *Terra Livre*, published between 1949 and 1964, and the Peasant Leagues's *Liga*, distributed in 1962 and 1963.

The PCB, for instance, played a critical role in framing the grievances of agricultural laborers—the *moradores* on the sugarcane plantations and the *colonos* of the coffee farms—who lived on large estates and were assigned a small fraction of land to grow their own food, as claims made by rural employees striving to extend the nation's labor laws to the countryside. These demands ushered in a series of novel labor rights for plantation workers, including the *carteira de trabalho* (a labor and social security card), an eight-hour work day, two days of rest on weekends, paid vacations, and the cancellation of wage reductions for housing provided on the estate. While these workers often cultivated a small plot to produce their own food, the PCB normally insisted on assessing their situation through the prism of capital-labor relations, and therefore favored the use of strikes as the main mobilization tactic.[17] PCB activists were inclined to apply existing labor laws to frame the claims made by rural workers and did so in ways that suited the political discourse of the Brazilian Left. In actual practice, though, the Communists were more ambiguous than their rhetoric would suggest. For example, in Paraíba the PCB strongly supported plantation workers who were struggling to access a land parcel in the estate to cultivate their own food, and in doing so repeatedly called for agrarian reform during their protest mobilizations.[18]

Other categories of rural workers also began to advance their claims through legal references. The terms *arrendatários* (tenant farmers) and *parceiros* (sharecroppers) were adopted to describe various land arrangements based on cash or in kind payments. Tenants on the northeast sugarcane plantations were known as *foreiros*, while in other regions of Brazil they were treated as *rendeiros*. Sharecroppers, in turn, were described as *meeiros* and *agregados*. These rural workers mobilized initially to demand that their land leases be capped at 20% of their production. These petitions drew on the example of a handful of state constitutions that included similar laws, instituted in 1946 at the behest of Communist politicians.[19] Farm tenants also fought for longer land leases and against the widespread practice of being forced to plant grass for cattle pastures in the third year of their lease, thus becoming itinerant workers, unable to grow permanent crops and develop a sense of stability on the land.

In addition, peasant squatters (*posseiros*) framed their rights to possess a farm plot on the basis of the hard labor and other investments made to cultivate the land. Posseiros usually drew a distinction between their efforts and the idle and speculative land use of the *grileiros* and *latifundiários* (large land grabbers and landlords). During the 1950s one of the main squatter land conflicts took place in Formoso, Goiás, where a group of well-organized peasants were able to wrest control of a large territory and pressure the state government to recognize their possession of the area. Squatter struggles were also quite intense in Rio de Janeiro's Baixada Fluminense, some of which involved armed clashes with gunmen hired by these large landholders.

These categories of rural workers were amenable to shifts and alterations. Squatters, for instance, demanding land rights vis-à-vis a grileiro might have once been tenants or sharecroppers in the same area. The term *posseiro*, in fact, was more than just an objective social category. Over time, it also became a political identity deployed to assert a set of social rights.[20]

Land rights advanced by squatters, sharecroppers, and tenants were woven gradually into a broader call for agrarian reform and a poignant critique of the nefarious effects of land tenure inequality on Brazil's development. Peasant struggles helped put these issues on the public agenda and secure their right to form rural trade unions. These mobilizations to attain basic civil rights led rural workers to formulate demands for better labor and living conditions, calling for the provision of public health and education services, and the same social security benefits made available to urban workers.

In 1961, amid intense political disputes on the national scene, the ULTAB convened a National Peasant Congress in Belo Horizonte, with participants from various rural social movements.[21] The event's central theme—land reform—triggered heated debates. The Communists and Peasant League activists were deeply divided over the need to regulate sharecropping and tenant arrangements. ULTAB supported these regulations, while the Peasant League argued for a radical land reform program that would eliminate the need to legalize what they viewed as provisional and precarious forms of land access.

The quarrel between the Communists and Peasant Leagues took place in a context that regarded radicalism as a positive political value. Both groups, in fact, vied for this label. This contest was played out in the content of their agrarian reform program and concrete actions undertaken to promote their platforms. These actions fueled a series of novel land occupations that reaped fervent praise in the nation's left-wing news outlets, as in the 1961 occupation of the Imbé sugarcane plantation, an area presumed to have been usurped by grileiro landlords in Campos, Rio de Janeiro. Other mobilizations included the Peasant Leagues' land occupations following the evictions of tenant farmers, as well as the creation of landless camps in Rio Grande do Sul by the Landless Farmers Movement (MASTER) in 1962 and 1963.

The Catholic Church also stepped up its activities in the Brazilian countryside during the early 1960s, supporting land reform and the formation of rural trade unions, albeit in competition with the Communists and the Peasant Leagues. The church legitimized demands for social reform but strived to do so in a way that would avert "class conflict."[22] In particular, it embraced calls to provide social security, public schools, and health care to the nation's rural population.

Landlord Reactions

The same momentum that prompted the peasantry to forge a new political identity also spurred large landholders to raise their involvement in the nation's public debates. Indeed, their associations participated actively in discussions over the agrarian question and rejected the label of latifundiários. Their organizational capacity was enhanced by the 1945 decree that authorized the formation of "mixed" rural associations, which was composed of landlords and estate workers. This decree encouraged the rural elite to create a large number of municipal associations and statewide federations, which gave the landlord class further clout in civil society, adding to the strength of the SNA and the Brazilian Rural Society (SRB), a traditional association comprised mostly of coffee growers. These new groups began to exercise significant influence in local and state politics. Some of its federations were actually quite prominent in national politics, especially the federations from São Paulo, Rio Grande do Sul, and Minas Gerais. The Brazilian Rural Confederation (CRB), founded in 1954, stood at the apex of this associational structure. The CRB's political weight can be discerned by the fact that its representatives sat on the boards of all the main state agencies dealing with rural development, including the bureau for Rural Social Service.[23]

These rural associations championed the interests of export-oriented farmers and in doing so supported policies to promote agricultural mechanization, while opposing land redistribution and the extension of labor rights to rural workers. In the CRB's view, Brazil's main rural problems were the result of its low agricultural productivity, due to inefficient farming methods, poor soil conservation, and unstable conditions for rural production. This volatility was the consequence of insufficient access to credit, storage, and transport facilities, along with low profit margins and poor living standards in the countryside, which led to an exodus of both landowners and rural workers.[24] The CRB, therefore, frequently petitioned the Rural Social Service bureau to improve living conditions for the country's rural inhabitants. Along with other landlord groups, the CRB also called for state policies and credit programs designed to capitalize and support the productive capacity of rural entrepreneurs.

In their views, the emerging rural proletariat was the result of inadequate levels of capital and savings to buy and maintain a farm, due to the scarcity of credit and devalued national currency. Agriculture's low profit margins led to low wages. Rural poverty, therefore, was the result of insufficient levels of state support for agriculture. The agrarian elite made sure to convey these demands for greater public finance of agriculture as "rural producers," not as "latifundiários."

Landlord groups also opposed the institution of rural labor rights, contending such measures were inopportune due to the adverse economic situation in the countryside. Their arguments against the formation of rural trade unions underscored the belief that peasants were ignorant and spatially dispersed, and could be manipulated through these associations to make dangerous demands. What's more, they insisted in treating labor laws as an attack on the free enterprise system.

The prospect of changing the Constitution to authorize land reform elicited a wide array of counter-legal arguments among the agrarian elite. Some emphasized the need to safeguard rural property rights as an essential component of the free market system. Others noted the futility of such alterations given that Brazil's 1946 Constitution included a clause stating that rural land use must benefit the well-being of society. Among the rural elite, the prevalent view was that land reform was nothing but a pretext to promote the political uprising of the "agricultural proletariat" in alliance with urban Communist agitators.

Rural workers gained newfound public visibility and political recognition between 1950 and 1964. Still, landlord associations were no less effective during this time. The rural elite retained strong influence over the Ministry of Agriculture and played a decisive role in the civil society networks, activities, and conspiracies that led to the 1964 military coup. Their actual participation in the plot to overthrow the nation's democratic regime took place through their involvement in two think tanks that had a significant role in organizing the coup: the Brazilian Institute for Democratic Action (IBAD) and the Institute for Economic and Social Research (IPES).[25]

Recognition and Repression: The Rights of Rural Workers

The Brazilian state recognized important new rights for rural workers during the early 1960s. Despite strong objections by the agrarian elite, rural trade unions were legalized in 1962. Both trade unions and landlord associations were set up under the state corporatist model established during the Vargas era. In 1963, after more than a decade of sporadic debate, the National Congress approved the Rural Workers Statute, which extended to the countryside a series of labor rights obtained by urban workers in the 1930s.

Soon after the 1964 coup, the military government promulgated the Land Statute (Estatuto da Terra), the country's first land reform law, and passed a constitutional amendment that allowed the government to pay for land expropriations with special treasury bonds. Indeed, the law's main provisions have had a lasting legacy in shaping the contours of Brazil's land reform debate and experience.[26]

All these legal developments established a political acknowledgment of the country's different rural interests; their distinct forms of representation; and the need for state intervention to attenuate their social conflicts. Both large landholders and rural workers gradually consolidated their associations. The predilection, however, of the so-called small producers—in matters concerning their legal standing, political identity, and main social demands—remained up for dispute among these two contending forces. Popular demands for agrarian reform played a major role in the military's decision to overthrow Brazil's democratic regime in 1964. The military regime, nonetheless, ushered in various legal and institutional innovations. These were obviously influenced by the rural conflicts preceding the coup, which had transformed rural workers into political actors. Upholding these new rights, however, proved to be a difficult task under Brazil's authoritarian regime. All the nation's leading peasant leaders were arrested, killed, or forced to go underground in the wake of the 1964 coup. Some of the rural trade unions were intervened by the government. Others were taken over by leaders who were unfamiliar with previous rural struggles. Adding to all this, the autocratic regime effectively dismantled the social networks and organizational structures that helped catalyze Brazil's new peasant and rural labor groups.

At the same time, a vast portion of rural workers was obliged to migrate from the countryside in search of work as a result of the swift and intense technological modernization of agriculture and decreasing use of manual labor. Many of these rural migrants settled on the outskirts of small and mid-sized towns, where they engaged in temporary farm work, cutting sugarcane, or harvesting oranges, cotton, and coffee; were employed in construction; or held various odd jobs. Among this population, labor rights were rarely, if ever, observed.[27] The advent of the *bóia-fria* (daily agricultural worker) in the country's southeastern and southern regions, and the *clandestino* (informal sugarcane worker) in Pernambuco, underscored the forceful nature of the expropriation process underway in much of rural Brazil. In effect, during this period an incalculable number of squatters, sharecroppers, tenant farmers, and indigenous people were evicted from the lands on which they lived.

This transformation of the Brazilian countryside was made possible through the active role of the state. Though initially apprehensive of the military government's enactment of the 1964 Land Statute, rural entrepreneurs were buoyed soon thereafter when the state began to adopt the agricultural policies they had championed in the preceding years. The state offered tax incentives and ample credit subsidies to spur the technological modernization of traditional estates and direct large capital investments to the Amazonian frontier, to the detriment of its native inhabitants.[28] Moreover, despite CONTAG's complaints and sporadic acts of resistance, the state essentially ignored the Land Statute's provisions for land expropriations and the protection of sharecroppers and farm tenants.[29] The Ministry of Labor, in turn, rarely bothered to enforce the laws that applied to rural workers.

In sum, the legal rights granted under the military regime were effectively undermined by its repression of rural workers movements and its decision to bolster its alliance with the nation's agrarian elite. This context hampered the ability of peasants and farm workers to organize and defend their rights. As Vera Telles observes, the legal framework alone was incapable of establishing a pattern of "social interaction in which various parties acknowledge the other as having valid interests and relevant values linked to legitimate demands."[30]

However unsatisfactory, this situation did not lead to a complete disregard for rural workers, given the military government's need to cope with persistent conflicts in the countryside and reduce precarious living conditions among its inhabitants. The army, for instance, carried out various social programs in a paternalistic fashion among the peasantry, notably in the Amazon region, where land conflicts were most intense.[31] These and other initiatives expanded Wanderley Guilherme dos Santos' notion of a "controlled citizenry" to include social security rights, which were extended to the rural population in 1971 under the Rural Worker Assistance Program (FUNRURAL). In addition to providing retirement and disability pensions equal to one-half of the minimum wage, this program also covered basic health services and funeral expenses.[32]

Rural trade unions were put in charge of administering these services, by setting up clinics and hiring doctors and dentists, while processing retirement and disability claims, and providing funeral subsidies. The trade unions, thus, became widely perceived as a conduit for public assistance, rather than a venue by which to organize union members and advance their interests. As Regina Novaes points out, most union leaders were disinclined to support grassroots mobilizations and were regarded as a "cautious" generation within the rural trade union structure. Many of these leaders adopted clientelistic practices within the trade unions and used this asset to garner political support for local elites.[33]

This conservative demeanor was not always well received among rank-and-file members, many of whom held on to the progressive legacy of previous union organizers and appreciated CONTAG's efforts to nudge its trade associations in support of activities that raised awareness of workers' rights in the countryside. While unable to forestall the harmful consequences of Brazil's conservative rural modernization, CONTAG played an important role in disseminating basic notions of citizenship rights, while nurturing feelings of injustice among its members. These ideas and sentiments helped foster a culture of resistance that led to sporadic land conflicts in the 1970s and lawsuits to uphold labor rights, especially in Pernambuco. All these developments fueled a much wider resurgence of rural mobilizations in the 1980s. The rural trade unions, Moacir Palmeira explains, also helped diffuse and politicize the term *rural worker*, a designation imposed by the state to define trade union membership. This term ended up encompassing a wide range of groups of people who tilled the land, including squatters, small landholders, sharecroppers, tenants, and farm workers hired on a permanent or temporary basis.[34]

These developments were laced with many contradictions. Palmeira and Sérgio Leite note that greater state presence in the countryside, via its new legal arrangements and agricultural subsidies, undercut some of the traditional powers of local caudillos and fostered conditions that enabled the rise of new intermediaries. As such, clientelistic controls became,

> mediated by the power exerted over certain echelons of the state apparatus—which had become much more centralized—thus adding greater complexity to their *quest for domination*. Amid the mass exodus of rural workers from the large plantations, the landlords found they could no longer rely on patronage alone as a mechanism for connecting the peasantry with the state and society. This opened the possibility for the rise of new caudillos and *different patterns* of interaction, while undermining the traditional system of domination by creating space for the rise of alternative groups.[35]

During the 1970s, sectors of the Catholic Church began to promote awareness of basic rights in rural communities without rural trade unions, or with conservative union leaders, aligned with local elites, and thus unwilling to support grassroots organizing efforts. Pastoral agents inspired by liberation theology and involved in the creation of Community-Base Churches (CEBs) took an active role in disseminating notions of rights grounded in national laws and religious teachings. Progressive church leaders drew on various biblical passages to support land rights for squatters and landless peasants, and often framed their struggles in terms of the Israelite quest for the Promised Land. These different activities helped breed an opposition movement within the rural trade union structure that challenged the paternalistic demeanor and conservative leadership of many local union bosses. This movement offered an alternative model of organization that fueled the active participation and mobilization of rural workers. As Ivo Poletto (chap. 4, this volume) explains, the church's pivotal player in this regard was the Pastoral Land Commission (CPT), established in 1975. All these developments allowed the church to exert an influential position in Brazil's agrarian debates.

A New Cycle of Rural Struggles: The 1980s

A new phase of rural mobilizations emerged in the late 1970s and early 1980s, as a result of the profound changes taking place in Brazil's agricultural development, and the advent of new actors and ideas on the rural scene. These changes ushered in novel concerns, along with new social struggles and categories. Some groups of peasants began to challenge their displacement due to the construction of large hydroelectric dams. Others reacted to the expansion of cattle ranches that destroyed forested areas inhabited by indigenous and squatter communities. Yet others sought to overcome the detrimental impact of large-scale, industrial agriculture on peasant farmers. This new cycle of mobilization took place amid Brazil's political redemocratization and a resurgent civil society led by industrial workers in São Paulo, activists demanding amnesty for political exiles and prisoners, and various other popular movements. These different protests weakened the military regime and fueled a process of political liberalization. This opening prompted a campaign for direct elections (the 1984 Diretas Já movement), which led to a democratic transition with the installation of the "New Republic," in 1985.

This new cycle of mobilization involved elements of continuity and rupture with the past. Demands for agrarian reform regained prominence during this period, as did calls to protect labor rights and expand social security entitlements to all rural workers. Furthermore, these struggles triggered a critical reappraisal of traditional trade union practices and galvanized the formation of new social identities and associations that challenged the idea of a single "rural worker" category, confined mostly to union-related activities.

Agrarian struggles during this period unfolded amid various overlapping trends. Squatter land conflicts gained intensity in the north and northeast regions of the country. At the same time, new rural identities started to flourish with the mobilization of landless peasants and family farmers displaced by the construction of hydroelectric dams. In the Amazon, the rubber tappers and harvesters of *babaçu* coconuts began to assert their rights through various protest campaigns. All these groups introduced new forms of struggle, while articulating critical views and espousing alternative values vis-à-vis the dominant rural development model.

These new conditions spurred multiple innovations in the repertoire for collective action. Conscious efforts were made to gain public visibility, frame their claims in the language of legal rights, and negotiate their demands with state authorities. These acts generated petitions to enforce established rules, such as the Land Statute. In other situations, popular struggles helped to prompt the reinterpretations of existing laws or, more strikingly, generate political conditions that led to new legal arrangements and the creation of novel rights. A telling example of this can be gleaned from the rubber tapper (*seringueiro*) movement in the Amazonian state of Acre. With state subsidies and support, Acre's landed elite had been setting up large cattle ranches, and in doing so destroying vast areas of the Amazon rainforest. This devastation threatened the livelihood of forest gatherers who collected Brazil nuts and harvested sap from rubber trees. The seringueiros started by couching their claims in terms of provisions set in the Land Statute. But as the movement gained greater visibility and support—thanks to the dramatic mobilization of hundreds of rubber tappers and their families to block the tractors used to raze the forest—new legal instruments were created, leading to the formation of various extractive reserves in the Amazon region.

The construction of large hydroelectric dams sparked another conflict scenario in the late 1970s, with the displacement of thousands of peasant families, notably in Pernambuco and Paraná, where the Itaparica and Itaipu dams were built. Both struggles were supported by progressive religious actors. In Pernambuco, peasant resistance led to the formation of a strong coalition of rural trade unions. In Paraná, the CPT helped organize a precursor to the MST, the Movement of Landless Workers of the West (MASTRO), formed by squatters and farm tenants disregarded by Itaipu's resettlement policies. These mobilizations shared similar claims and tactics. The petitions would generally start with calls for better compensations and end with demands for farm plots close to the reservoir. The peasants publicized these claims through various acts of civil disobedience, including sit-ins at the offices of energy companies, road blockades, and removals of reservoir boundary markers. In the 1980s, different local disputes over the construction of hydroelectric dams were eventually organized into a national Movement of People Affected by Dams (MAB) (see Rosa, chap. 15, this volume).

Adding to these mobilizations, landless peasants in southern Brazil began to organize land occupations and protest camps in the late 1970s and early 1980s, leading to the creation of the MST (see Fernandes and Carter, chaps. 5 and 6, this volume). Peasant land occupations fostered new legal understandings that questioned the legitimacy of large rural properties, rather than their actual ownership, on the basis of their low or negligible productivity. Such arguments helped reassert the principle of the "social function" of the land, as established in the Brazilian Constitution of 1946 and in the 1964 Land Statute, and reaffirmed in the 1988 Constitution.[36]

As João Pedro Stédile, one of the MST's main leaders explained it:

If we do not occupy, we cannot prove that the law is on our side . . . the law is enforced only if there is a social demand . . . the law comes after this social action, never before. In the struggle for land reform this social action involves land occupations. It's the way (our) people make their claims and seek to have the laws enforced.[37]

The number of land occupations increased rapidly after the mid-1980s and became a standard feature of the MST's repertoire for collective action. This was fueled in many ways by its demonstrated success in pressuring the state to carry out land expropriations, and by the support it elicited from various civil society groups who were galvanized by the MST's bold actions.

Rural wage earners, in turn, reappeared on the national scene with a series of labor strikes in the late 1970s and mid-1980s that stirred part of the northeast. By this point most rural workers and families had already moved off the sugarcane plantations.[38] The Federation of Agricultural Workers of Pernambuco (FETAPE) led the first major strike in 1979, in the Zona da Mata region, which was noted for its historic sugar production. A second strike held the following year was backed by almost all of the state's sugarcane workers. This mobilization led to wage increases and the restitution of a wage table won by sugarcane workers in a 1963 strike. This table was established to reduce landlord abuse (*roubos do patrão*) that took place by miscounting the size and weight of the sugarcane harvest, and did so by establishing different wage rates for each specific task. Furthermore, the trade unions were able to restore the law that gave plantation workers living on the estate the right to grow subsistence crops on a two-hectare plot.

The 1980 strike was followed by more discrete yet ongoing struggles to ensure the actual implementation of these agreements. Rural workers clashed frequently—sometimes violently—with local landlords, while trade union leaders fought the plantation owners in court to their ensure their compliance to these agreements.

These strikes created a model for similar mobilizations in other Brazilian states with large sugarcane production, notably Paraíba, Rio Grande do Norte, Minas Gerais, and Rio de Janeiro. Rural trade unions played a crucial role in supporting these developments. In some areas, though, the strikes erupted prior to the union's involvement. For instance, in Guariba, São Paulo, the cane cutters strike of 1984 started with a wave of looting and violence, before the unions were able to take charge of the situation.

In southern Brazil, a new generation of small-scale farmers began to assert new political roles. In the 1980s they organized a series of protests and took on greater leadership roles in the rural trade union movement. These new dispositions were influenced by the church's liberation theology–inspired consciousness-raising activities in the countryside. It also reflected a growing awareness of the inability of peasant agriculture to compete with large commercial farmers and agribusiness firms, and improve their living conditions under the industrial model of farm production. These groups also nurtured a growing critique of CONTAG's bureaucratic ways. This context fueled the birth of an opposition movement within the rural trade union structure. This group employed more forceful tactics—such as blocking highways and access to ports, banks, and government buildings—to publicize their demands and pressure state authorities to negotiate with them. Peasant efforts to democratize rural cooperatives, dominated by large commercial farmers, proved to be an uphill battle, with few successes. In addition, small farmers sought to improve contract negotiations with agribusiness firms by setting up specific trade unions for tobacco, hogs, poultry, and other farm products.

As small farmers gained greater prominence within the rural trade unions, they re-framed longstanding claims into calls for a "new development model," distinct from the agribusiness-led model. While identifying themselves as rural workers, these peasant groups also underscored their specific needs and attributes. Church and NGO-sponsored workshops and international exchanges help spur many of these developments.

All these changes activated a growing academic debate over the economic and social importance of family farmers. These ideas were communicated to the rural trade union movement by their intellectual advisors, and were soon adopted as a centerpiece of the movement's public platform.[39] Thus, the category of "small farmers"—widely used by trade unionists in the 1980s—was quickly replaced by the notion of "family farmers." This came with new policy discussions supporting the creation of producer associations, agro-industries, and alternative commercial arrangements. In addition, these events stimulated debates over new agricultural technologies and their effect on the environment.

National peasant mobilizations such as the Cry of the Earth (Grito da Terra) gave these demands added public visibility. Started by CONTAG in 1991, with initial support from the CPT, MST, MAB, and other groups, these annual protest gatherings allowed CONTAG and its allies to begin a round of negotiations with state authorities, while generating civil society support for its petitions. These mobilizations led to various new government policies, among them, the National Program for the Strengthening of Family Agriculture (PRONAF), which was instituted in 1996.

The trade union movement suffered a serious internal crisis as these developments were taking place. Critics questioned its organizational model, approach to social conflict, and capacity to represent rural workers. This coincided with the rise of trade union leaders linked to family farmers, to the detriment of those closer to rural wage earners. As a result, CONTAG's unions undertook various reforms. Moreover, two new peasant organizations emerged in this context: the Movement of Small Farmers (MPA), in 1996, and the Federation of Workers in Family Farming in the South (FETRAFSUL), in 2001, reestablished in 2005 as FETRAF-Brazil. The new rural identities and interests asserted through these organizations invigorated a critique of Brazil's model of agricultural development and shared a budding appreciation for agro-ecological approaches to farming.

By the mid-1990s family farm policy debates were no longer confined to southern Brazil. The new national focus owed much to the growth of peasant associations in other parts of the country, many of which were set up through state incentives funded by regional development programs established under the 1988 Constitution.[40] Though sharing a common background and critique of Brazil's unequal agrarian structure and exclusionary development process, landless and small farmer associations did not always agree on political strategies and tactics by which to advance their cause.

Adding to this complex scenario, the 1988 Constitution opened new possibilities of influencing rural development policies at the local government level. Because of these trends toward state decentralization, peasant groups became involved in a variety of municipal development councils and actively engaged in electoral politics, by sponsoring candidates for local and state government positions. As a result, the rural trade unions and peasant movements began to broaden their agenda to include issues related to public education, health care, gender equality, youth participation, and leisure.

Rural wage earners began to lose prominence in the rural trade union movement after the mid-1980s, due to the sugar industry crisis in northeast Brazil and the growing mechanization of sugarcane plantations in other parts of the country. This crisis led to a substantial drop in the number of sugarcane cutters, which weakened the trade union's capacity to mobilize and demand that basic labor rights be enforced. As Lygia Maria Sigaud, Wendy Wolford, and Marcelo Rosa (chaps. 7, 12, and 15, this volume) explain, the MST's expansion to northeast Brazil sparked a revival of the struggle for land reform. In the sugarcane regions the bulk of these participants were unemployed plantation workers, organized by the MST, local trade unions, or a host of new landless groups. A similar development took place in the sugarcane region of São Paulo, and was led mostly by the Federation of Rural Employees and Wage Earners of the State of São Paulo (FERAESP).[41]

During the 1990s, efforts were made to expose Brazil's enduring problem with rural slave labor. Through its careful documentation work and human rights campaigns, the CPT was able to present a striking portrait of the state's weak enforcement of the basic rights of wage earners. *Slave labor* refers to situations in which workers are hired to toil in areas far from their place of origin and obliged to accrue debts—a cash advance to their family, travel expenses, food, medicines, and work tools charged at exorbitant prices—that cannot be paid off with their meager wages. At this point, the rural worker is compelled to engage in coerced labor practices and forbidden to leave the estate.[42] Their sense of helplessness is compounded by their physical isolation from other workers, friends, and family members. The CPT, in particular, has played a crucial role in denouncing these human rights violations and prompting federal authorities to rescue enslaved workers.

Landlord Associations in the 1980s

Brazil's agrarian elite benefited greatly from the military regime's rural modernization policies, as did various large industrial and financial conglomerates, who used generous public subsidies to purchase vast tracks of land in the Amazonian frontier. As such, the state helped forge an alliance between traditional landlords and large capitalist firms, thus bolstering the nation's vested interests in maintaining its starkly unequal land structure.

Landlord associations gained more political visibility as a result of growing peasant mobilizations—particularly its land occupations—and the nation's polarized agrarian debate. In the early 1980s, groups like the National Agricultural Confederation (CNA) focused mainly on calls for more agricultural subsidies. But the government's announcement of an ambitious agrarian reform program—unveiled by President José Sarney in 1985, at CONTAG's Fourth National Congress—provoked strong reactions from the landed elite.

Large landowners held a congress in Brasília scarcely a month after this proclamation to reject the government's plans to redistribute land. In doing so they employed a modernized version of their traditional discourse. Underscoring the close ties between agriculture and the agro-industrial complex, they argued that industrial agriculture should be carried out by those with access to capital to pay for these investments. Hence, in their view, the government's agrarian policies had to support an agribusiness model of rural development. Land reform policies, they insisted, would hinder this development approach, by dampening farm production and undermining the nation's free enterprise system.[43]

The same gathering in Brasília also prompted the creation of a new, more militant landlord association, the Rural Democratic Union (UDR). Though close to other agrarian elite groups—namely, the CNA, SRB, SNA—the UDR took on a particularly strident and confrontational opposition to land reform. As Regina Bruno points out, some sectors linked to the CNA and SRB felt that some land distribution would be inevitable and made a case for maintaining this program under elite control. Other landlord groups, however, espoused a radical opposition and called for a direct confrontation with the land reform movement. The violent rhetoric in all this was scarcely concealed.[44] In fact, one of their mottos—"For each estate invaded, a dead priest"—was widely publicized by the news press. The UDR's militant position was embraced primarily by cattle ranchers in São Paulo, Goiás, Mato Grosso, Pará, and Maranhão.

Between 1985 and 1989, the UDR became the most visible actor in the fight against agrarian reform. It organized rallies and cattle auctions to raise funds, and formed an influential lobby in Congress. During these years the UDR invested considerable efforts to elect its own representatives in Congress and state legislatures, and even fielded a presidential candidate in 1989. Many local UDR leaders rekindled traditional practices among Brazil's landed elite, sponsoring violent acts of reprisal against land reform activists. This, however, was done in a "modern way," by hiring gunmen in the guise of private security contractors.

The UDR's impetus galvanized Brazilian landlords and allies to thwart the implementation of the government's land reform plan. Furthermore, during the 1988 Constitutional Assembly, UDR representatives mustered enough votes to bar the expropriation of productive rural properties, and defeat other proposals for land redistribution. The consolidation of Brazil's agribusiness sector in

Table 3.1. A chronology of rural social history in Brazil, 1944–2005

Year	Event
1944	Decree 7038/44 establishes a separate model of union representation for rural workers and landlords.
1945	Decree 7449/45 defines the terms under which rural associations can be created. These must be "mixed organizations," based on territorial jurisdictions rather than professional or class criteria.
1945	First peasant associations are created.
1949	*Terra Livre* (Free Land) newspaper is published for the first time.
1953	The First Congress of rural workers takes place.
1954	The Second Congress of rural workers leads to the establishment of the Union of Farm and Agricultural Workers of Brazil (ULTAB). The Brazilian Rural Confederation (CRB) is created.
1955	The government institutes a bureau of Rural Social Service.
1955	The Peasant Leauge of Galiléia (Pernambuco) is formed.
1960	The Landless Farmers Movement (MASTER) emerges in Rio Grande do Sul.
1961	The National Peasant Congress of Belo Horizonte takes place.
1962	The Peasant Leagues begin publishing their newspaper *Liga* (League).
1963	The National Federation of Workers in Agriculture (CONTAG) is founded.
1963	The Brazilian Congress ratifies the National Statute for Rural Workers. Sugarcane workers organize a massive strike in Pernambuco.
1964	The military overthrow the democratic regime in coup d'etat (March 31). Congress approves the Land Stature (November).
1971	FUNRURAL is set up by the military government.
1975	The Pastoral Land Commission (CPT) is created in Goiânia.
1979	The fist land occupations are organized in southern Brazil.
1979	Sugarcane workers go on strike in Pernambuco, initiating a cycle of rural worker strikes that would be repeated in the following years in Pernambuco and in other states of the Northeast and Southeast regions.
1984	The Landless Rural Workers Movement (MST) is formed in Cascavel, Paraná. The Guariba strike unfolds in São Paulo.
1984	The *Diretas Já* Movement takes to the streets of Brazil.
1985	The military government relinquishes power to a new civilian president. The new government presents Brazil's First National Agrarian Reform Plan.
1991	CONTAG and other rural movement organize the first *Grito da Terra*.
1996	The Movement of Small Farmers (MPA) is founded in Rio Grande do Sul.
2001	The Federation of Family Farms Workers in the South (FETRAFSUL) is set up.
2005	FETRAFSUL is reestablished as national organization, FETRAF-Brasil.

the ensuing decade would build on the political strength of the nation's agrarian elite, along with a growth in capital investments, and close ties to agro-food corporations that control global markets for seeds, chemical inputs, trading, food processing, and retail.

Conclusions

The incorporation of rural workers into Brazil's political arena—during the latter half of the twentieth century—proved to be a groundbreaking development in the nation's history. Their struggles have since become an established feature of the country's political landscape. As such, rural workers have drawn on different mobilization cycles to propel their demands onto the public agenda and call on the state to fulfill various civil and social rights.

All these struggles led to the development of new patterns of collective action and novel social identities. The MST's birth and evolution needs to be viewed in the context of previous and contemporary peasant mobilizations; their impact on political institutions and popular sector organizations, and their main elite adversaries in the countryside. This, after all, is the conflictive context in which different social actors intersect and are mutually constituted.

A new rural Brazil has emerged from these clashes. Among rural workers this is symbolized by the refusal to accept precarious living conditions, and the struggle to configure the nation's public arena, in an effort to be seen and heard, and thus break their anonymity. In the end, as Hannah Arendt observed, "Being seen and being heard by others derive their significance from the fact that everybody sees and hears from a different position. This is the meaning of public life, compared to which even the richest and most satisfying family life can offer only the prolongation or multiplication of one's own position with its attendant aspects and perspectives."[45]

Notes

Translated from the Portuguese by Miguel Carter.

1. On historic patterns of landlord-peasant conflict in Brazil, see Alier and Hall (n.d.), Martins (1979), and Palmeira (1977).
2. Lenharo (1986a: 15).
3. Lenharo (1986a: 22).
4. Lenharo (1986a: 85–86). The reference to the rubber tappers was due to the large migration of rural workers from the northeast to the Amazon region.
5. Pinho (1939: 58–59).
6. The 1941 interministerial commission was nominated by President Getúlio Vargas and chaired by the director of the National Agricultural Society (SNA). This commission included representatives from the ministries of Justice, Labor, Industry and Commerce, and Agriculture and delegates from the cattle ranch, agriculture, and agro-industrial

sectors. Asked by the envoy from the Ministry of Labor why there was no delegation of rural workers, the SNA chairman responded that the commission was based on regional representation rather than social class. The minutes of these meetings can be found in SNA (1943).

7. Stein (1991).

8. This kind of state selectivity, according to Offe (1984), is not random but is determined by power constellations and possibilities, whereby certain groups, interests, and issues are included or excluded from the scope of what is politically thinkable.

9. Vargas's colonization program covered the transportation costs of disaffected urban dwellers who wished to return to the countryside; see Lenharo (1986b).

10. Cited in Neiva (1942: 237).

11. Lenharo (1986b).

12. On the history of different forms of political exclusion and tutorage of the Brazilian peasantry, see Martins (1981).

13. Novaes (1997).

14. According to the newspaper *Terra Livre*, ULTAB's creation was preceded by twenty-five regional preparatory congresses; see Medeiros (1995).

15. Camargo (1973) and Medeiros (1983, 1995).

16. Sader (1988).

17. In research conducted in the archives of *Terra Livre*, at the National Library of Brazil, I registered 119 rural labor strikes between 1949 and 1964, mostly in São Paulo's coffee plantations, followed by the northeast's sugarcane region. These strikes were of different size and scope. The most significant one, no doubt, was the 1963 strike in Pernambuco's Zona da Mata region, which paralyzed sugarcane production in almost all sugarcane estates and mobilized thousands of workers; see Medeiros (1995).

18. On the struggles led by rural workers in Paraiba, see Novaes (1997).

19. Loureiro (1982).

20. Grynszpan (1987), Novaes (1997), and Cunha (2007).

21. In the early 1960s, the largest number of rural worker associations in the country belonged to ULTAB. The 1961 National Peasant Congress included representatives from MASTER, a landless peasant movement supported by the governor of Rio Grande do Sul, Leonel Brizola. An analysis of this meeting can be found in Medeiros (1995).

22. Novaes (1997) and Carvalho (1985); also see Poletto (chap. 4, this volume).

23. The Rural Social Service was created in 1955 as an autonomous government agency under the Ministry of Agriculture to improve access to public education, health care, and housing; promote rural associations and cooperatives; and provide agricultural extension services

24. The Brazilian Rural Confederation's main arguments are well summarized in its official magazine, *Gleba* (Confederação Rural Brasileira (CRB) 1955: 26).

25. For a detailed review of the roles played by IBAD and IPES in organizing the 1964 military coup, see Dreifuss (1981).

26. On the ambiguities in the Land Statute, see Martins (1984), Medeiros (1989, 2002b), and Bruno (1997).

27. According to CONTAG, in the early 1980s close to 80% of Brazil's rural workers subsisted in the informal labor market, mostly as day laborers. Most were agricultural workers employed on a daily basis.

28. Delgado (1985).

29. The Land Statute allowed for the expropriation of latifúndios based on their size (over

600 rural modules) or underutilization (fewer than 600 rural modules with low productivity rations for the property's location). This law required that all land payments be made through government-issued Agrarian Debt Bonds. The Land Statute also set minimum time frames and basic contract obligations for farm tenants and sharecroppers.

30. Telles (1994: 91).
31. Martins (1984).
32. Santos (1979).
33. Novaes (1997).
34. Palmeira (1985: 50).
35. Palmeira and Leite (1998: 128), emphasis in the original.
36. The idea of the "social function of the land" was first introduced in the 1946 Constitution but was left undefined. The 1988 Constitution stipulated that "the social function is fulfilled when rural property simultaneously meets, according to criteria and standards prescribed by law, the following requirements: I—rational and appropriate use; II—appropriate use of available natural resources and environmental preservation; III—compliance with the provisions governing labor relations; IV—exploitation that promotes the welfare of owners and workers" (article 186). For further details on this constitutional clause, see Mészáros (chap. 14, this volume).
37. Stédile and Fernandes (1999: 115).
38. Sigaud (1986).
39. For relevant discussions on "family farmers," see FAO/INCRA (2000), Schneider (2003), Abramovay (1992), Veiga (2001), and Wanderley (2000).
40. The special regional development funds set up under the 1988 Constitution were assigned to the the north, northeast, and midwest regions of Brazil.
41. The Federation of Rural Employees and Wage Earners of the State of São Paulo (FERAESP) was created by a group of dissident trade unionists from the state's sugarcane region, after a breaking with CONTAG's affiliate in São Paulo.
42. On the problem of slave labor, see Figueira (2000, 2004); Barelli and Vilela (2000); and Esterci (1994).
43. Medeiros (1989) and Bruno (1997).
44. On the UDR, see Bruno (1997); also Payne (2000).
45. Arendt (1987: 67).

4 Churches, the Pastoral Land Commission, and the Mobilization for Agrarian Reform

Citing Popol Vuh, Eduardo Galeano says that when the gods created human beings, before the discovery of corn, their true essence, they made them out of wood. These people appeared to be human, yet had no feelings and did not respect the land. The gods believed they had been eliminated, but no: they continue to exist and are the ones who rule the world. The people made of corn, however, are also alive, and, like a flower that breaks through the asphalt, continue to sprout.

—Silvia Ribeiro

An attempt to "break through the asphalt" was evident in Brasília, in November 2004, as more than 10,000 people—representing indigenous groups, landless peasants, family farmers, and *quilombolas* or maroon communities, formed by the descendants of runaway African slaves —gathered to take part in Brazil's first Land and Water Conference. President Luiz Inácio Lula da Silva and his minister of Agrarian Development, Miguel Rossetto, declined their invitation to attend the event. The only cabinet member who agreed to speak at the conference, the minister of Mines and Energy, Dilma Rousseff, experienced moments of great difficulty in reaching her audience, many of whom were visibly displeased with her message.

The Land and Water Conference was sponsored by a broad coalition of forty-five civil society groups involved in the National Forum for Agrarian Reform and Justice in the Countryside; and actively supported by three religious organizations: the Pastoral Land Commission (CPT), the Pastoral Social (the social outreach agency) of the National Conference of Bishops of Brazil (CNBB), and *Cáritas Brasileira*, a social justice outfit linked to the CNBB. Their participation signaled the church's ongoing commitment to the rural poor and their struggle to access two vital sources of life: land and water.

Brazilian politics has experienced significant changes since the 1970s. Yet for all its years of democratic opening, the nation has failed to address the root causes of the country's severe inequities in the countryside. At the dawn of the twenty-first century, Brazil was mired at once in a drive toward neoliberal modernization, while holding a rural population of nearly four million landless peasant families, and a few thousand landowners—entrenched in power through various oligarchic arrangements—controlling the bulk of the nation's farmland.

A Land and Water Conference of the kind held in Brasília would make sense in any country of the world, given the threat posed to humanity by those who seek to exploit these two life-essential goods as simple market commodities. This conference illustrates in many ways the general concerns and stance taken up by Brazilian popular movements engaged in a longstanding struggle to alter the state's conservative rural policies. Moreover, they also reveal the dilemma faced by progressive grassroots actors dealing with a government they elected to undertake broad social transformations, at a time when the impetus for such changes appear to have diminished, or even been abandoned by the nation's political leaders.

Indeed, by the end of Lula's second year in office, his administration had showed clear signs of acquiescence to the forces pressuring the new government to uphold a conservative economic policy. In doing so, it undercut the longstanding promises made by Lula's Workers Party (PT) to create new social opportunities for the majority of Brazilians. The official justification regarding the need to prioritize agribusiness and other primary export sectors to generate a trade surplus and regain confidence among Brazil's international creditors could be accepted during the first year. By 2004, however, this argument failed to convince the nation's more progressive sectors. All this led various popular groups to search for ways in which they could intensify pressure on the Lula government to change its economic and rural development policies. The Land and Water Conference convened in Brasília stemmed from this political impasse and strategic awareness, and conveyed a growing sense of discontent shared by the nation's leading popular movements.

The active religious presence at the conference underscored a historical trend dating back to more than a half century of Brazilian public life—namely, the enduring commitment among prominent sectors of the Catholic and Protestant churches in support of agrarian reform. This chapter provides a historical review of this religious involvement in the mobilization for land redistribution and the promotion of citizenship rights in the Brazilian countryside. In doing so, it reveals the Catholic Church's internal tensions regarding these developments. It also examines the context that led to the creation of the CPT in 1975—an ecumenical agency that became the main religious organization engrossed in the struggle for human rights and social justice in rural Brazil. The chapter concludes with an appraisal of the CPT's main challenges and achievements over the course of its thirty-five-year history. In doing so, it shows how the Brazilian churches helped nurture a vast network of rural social movements, the Landless Rural Workers Movement (MST) being its most prominent offspring.

Churches and Peasant Land Struggles

To understand the churches' involvement in Brazil's land struggle, it is necessary to bear in mind key traits of these religious institutions. Many assume that a church's position on a given matter can be discerned from the formal documents and public statements made by its leading authorities. In the case of the Catholic Church, everything approved, published, or conveyed by its bishops is treated as an official policy. This perspective, however, disregards the relevance of ideas and actions advanced by various movements and pastoral groups within a church. Though undoubtedly important, the church's official point of view is inadequate for the analysis at hand.

Close relations between ecclesiastical and state institutions have often induced religious leaders to uphold positions that undercut the interests and basic rights of the majority of the population. This took place when the Brazilian military overthrew the nation's democratic government in March 1964 and imposed an authoritarian regime. Almost all of the country's main Christian leaders supported the coup d'etat, and in doing so forfeited their freedom of action and their ability to criticize the persecution and violence suffered by many progressive religious activists. In the ensuing years, some churches asserted a degree of autonomy vis-à-vis the military regime, as a result of increased state repression and pressure from various bishops and lay groups within the church.

A church, in other words, cannot be treated as a monolithic bloc. The words uttered by its leaders cannot be viewed as the only stance, interpretation of reality, or course of action endorsed by a religious institution. The plurality of ideas within the Brazilian Catholic Church can be discerned, for example, by an event that took place in 1973, with the creation of an "informal caucus" of progressive bishops, which remained active still in the 2000s. Rather than make public analyses and decisions at odds with the CNBB's official stance, this group sought to enrich internal church discussions by offering what it considered more evangelical ways of carrying out its core mission.[1] In fact, this was the venue used by progressive prelates to get the CNBB to endorse the CPT's creation and help change the church's position on the land reform.

Experience teaches us that churches maintain their unity through diversity. Even under churches organized in an autocratic and centralized manner, people of Christian faith have always had—and still have—the freedom to think for themselves, notably through acts of prayer and meditation. These instruments can allow people to seek their own ways of remaining faithful to Christ's mission. Though disapproved by the religious hierarchy, the persistence of these ideas and sentiments can open up opportunities for subsequent changes in the church's official position. Churches, in other words, are complex institutions. Only by taking these intricacies into account will one be able to discern their full impact on Brazil's social history.

Renewal That Comes from the Periphery

Brazil's main churches supported the military coup in 1964 in the belief that this would keep the country from being taken over by communist ideology. Many Christians disagreed with this position. Indeed, some were actively engaged in social and political activities that were viewed by the authoritarian regime as acts of "naïve collaboration with the forces eager to implant communism in Brazil." Imprisoned and tortured by the regime, these Christian activists were abandoned by most of the church hierarchy.

This was particularly so with the Catholic Action movement. This Catholic network of lay movements worked with various social sectors, organizing university and high school students, urban workers, middle-class youth, and young countryside dwellers through the Catholic Agrarian Youth (JAC).[2] With the support of various bishops, JAC and other Catholic Action activists invested significant efforts to promote the church's social doctrine among the country's rural population. In doing so, they helped organize peasant groups that became involved in the early struggle for land reform. Their involvement in these mobilizations were deemed "subversive" and led to the violent persecution of many of these Catholic activists.

At that time, the engagement of young and adult Christians activists— backed by clergy who served as their "spiritual advisors"—in support of the creation of a rural workers movement, was treated as a novelty. Peasants and plantation workers, after all, were not allowed to form trade unions in Brazil until early 1963.[3] In the years prior to this, all efforts to organize the peasantry were considered acts of insubordination, subject to police repression. In effect, at the time, social relations in the Brazilian countryside were largely characterized by domination, dependence, and clientelism. Landlords ruled over their workers and inhabitants of their vast estates, including the sharecroppers who were generally obliged to surrender half or more of their harvest to the landlord. With the support of its allies in government, the agrarian elite succeeded in creating a hegemonic consensus based on the false premise that peasants were a "humble and peaceful" lot, who lived "a happy and orderly life" under their "benevolent tutelage." This myth was reinforced by efforts to promote the idea that peasants were too "culturally backward" to set up and run their own organizations (see also Medeiros, chap. 3, this volume).[4]

The 1964 military coup was strongly propelled by the conservative backlash against the peasant struggle for agrarian reform. This explains the extreme harshness with which peasant movements and their leaders were treated in the aftermath of the coup. Fledgling peasant unions were repressed throughout the country under the suspicion of being led by communists. Other rural movements were essentially wiped off the map, among them, the Peasant Leagues, which were particularly active in the northeast, and the peasant communes or "republics" of Trombas and Formoso, in northern Goiás.[5]

State repression unleashed against peasant leaders and popular educators in the countryside killed and imprisoned scores of progressive Christian activists, and effectively dismantled their network. Rather than protect their flock, the church hierarchy held fast to many of the misgivings and accusations made by the military regime, and used these charges to justify the closure of various Catholic Action groups. Even so, many pastoral agents and church activists, especially in the northeast and southeastern regions of the country, kept their commitments to social change alive, sometimes with the backing of local bishops and parishes. At other times, they operated covertly, concealing their activities from both state and religious authorities.

The progressive church network fostered through the Catholic Action movement and popular education projects inspired by Paulo Freire's literacy training program were among the CPT's main precursors. In the early 1960s, Freire's idea of promoting an active citizenry through a participatory pedagogical process influenced the creation of various "study circles" among illiterate peasants and the church-sponsored Grassroots Education Movement (MEB). Created by the CNBB in 1961, MEB's Freire-like literacy program for rural inhabitants in the Amazon and northeast regions survived the 1964 coup and continued operating in a discreet manner under the authoritarian regime.

The Community-Base Churches (CEBs) are also crucial to this history. These grassroots Bible study groups were spearheaded in the wake of the Catholic Church's Second Vatican Council (1962–65), and encouraged mostly by bishops who opposed human rights violations under the military dictatorship. These bishops, in turn, were often supported by pastoral agents who had taken part in Catholic Action and other popular education activities. The CEBs usually congregated small groups of people to read and discuss the Bible in light of their community problems and to seek collective solutions to these and other societal dilemmas. These religious groups encouraged its members to join popular movements, trade unions, and progressive political parties, to forge a bottom up struggle for democracy and social justice. The church's sustained investment in organizing and raising critical consciousness among popular sectors played a major role in reinstating Brazil's agrarian question onto the national public agenda. During the 1970s, this process was abetted by the fact that scores of radical activists—many of secular origin—were compelled to seek alternative forms of engagement within the church's progressive network, due to the intense political repression in many parts of the country.

Thus, the CPT's formation in 1974 and 1975 must be understood in the context of the calls for change coming from below and from the margins of the established church. These initiatives were spurred by concrete appeals to Christian solidarity and the broader religious renewal that followed the proceedings of the Second Vatican Council and the 1968 meeting of the Latin American Episcopal Council (CELAM), in Medellin, Colombia. These two critical events provided the theological and pastoral guidelines on which these novel practices were set up. Though discernible in the church's official discourse, as always, the real innovative work was propelled by religious people, communities, and local churches motivated by a strong commitment to change.

Changes in the Catholic Hierarchy

The Catholic Church in Brazil experienced an important transformation since the 1960s. These developments influenced the views of its hierarchy and, in doing so, helped advance the nation's popular struggle for land reform in significant ways. During the 1950s and early 1960s the CNBB supported agrarian reform as part of a broader strategy that sought to modernize the country. This position was in sync with prevailing development ideas at the time: ones that favored active state involvement in economic planning and the introduction of basic social reforms needed to fuel Brazil's capitalist modernization and allow the country to catch up to the wealthy industrial economies. The CNBB's support for these reforms was motivated by the desire to create better living conditions for the majority of Brazilians and forestall a socialist revolution.[6] A small group of bishops, however, took an adamant stance against the church's position and published a book, titled *Agrarian Reform: A Matter of Conscience*, that condemned land redistribution as an attack on the natural rights to property, which they considered to be of divine origin.[7] These bishops coalesced around an ultra-conservative church association known as Tradition, Family and Property (TFP), while the Catholic Action movement, especially the nascent JAC, along with other pastoral agents involved in organizing peasant unions, defended the CNBB's position on land reform.

The military's promulgation, in November 1964, of the country's first land reform law—the Land Statute (*Estatuto da Terra*) eased the CNBB's decision to endorse the regime's new leaders. While containing some reformist provisions, this law was used mainly to uphold the military's conservative agrarian policies. In the ensuing years, the CNBB's support for land redistribution was reduced to making ineffective petitions that called on the state to enforce the Land Statute. The church hierarchy, though, became more critical of the regime after military hardliners took over the government and introduced the Institutional Act 5 (AI-5), in December 1968. The new wave of repression activated by this measure led to the violent treatment of a handful of bishops and several pastoral agents.[8]

It was in this context that an informal group of bishops convened in São Paulo, in 1973, and agreed to publish a series of documents criticizing the authoritarian regime and its development policies. The meeting's main instigator was Dom Tomás Balduíno, the Bishop of Goiás, who traveled to various parts of the country with a team of advisors to invite other prelates to take part in this gathering. These pastoral letters were signed by various groups of bishops, heads of Catholic congregations, and missionaries. All of these signatories were prominent individuals unlikely to be physically harmed by the repression they were condemning. The documents were published under precarious conditions. Some were even printed in clandestine fashion. These included the 1973 letters: "I Heard the Cries of My People," signed by bishops and heads of Catholic congregations in the Brazilian northeast; "Marginalization of a People: The Cry of the Churches," prepared by bishops from the midwest region; and "Y-Juca-Pirama: The Indian, the One Who Must Die!" written by bishops and missionaries working with indigenous peoples.[9] These documents drew on biblical and theological reflections to present a sharp critique of the human rights violations and the development model advanced by the military regime. Moreover, by underscoring the importance of popular participation and labor rights, these letters signaled the newfound commitment of sectors of the Catholic Church in support of grassroots efforts to create a democratic society by equalizing access to property, culture, and power.

The CPT was created in June 1975, at a time of growing opposition to the military dictatorship, and amid signs of a budding collaboration between various bishops and pastoral agents dedicated to serving the country's poor. The CPT's formation proved to be a turning point in the Catholic Church's approach toward the country's rural population and in its support for their land struggles. The CPT encouraged the CNBB to undertake important changes that led it to (1) validate the work of several dioceses that had long suffered persecution for defending peasant rights; (2) support the CPT's activities as an independent church agency; and (3) embrace the call to serve as a "voice of the voiceless," by denouncing the violence inflicted on the rural poor and the state's complicit ties with agrarian elites, including large national and multinational corporations that had purchased vast tracks of land in the Amazon region.

Relations between the CNBB and CPT, however, were not always harmonious. In October 1976, scarcely a year after it was founded, the CPT was summoned to a meeting of the Permanent Council of the CNBB to explain its activities and organization. The same invitation was extended to the Indigenous Missionary Council (CIMI), which had been defending the rights of indigenous peoples since 1972. The move against the CPT and CIMI was led by bishops and priests linked to TFP, who viewed these groups as acting in utter contempt of the church's doctrine upholding the natural rights to property. Their stance was supported by large landholders and high-ranking military officers. Overall, though, the dialogue with CNBB leaders ended with a positive recognition of the pastoral activities undertaken by the CPT and CIMI.[10]

The CNBB continued to offer steady support for the CPT in the ensuing years. It did so in a mature way, offering constructive criticism if deemed necessary, while respecting its organizational autonomy. The CPT, in turn, earned and maintained the CNBB's trust and respect thanks to the sobriety and rigor with which it presented its accusations and detailed reports on human rights violations in the countryside; the authentic commitment and courage of its activists; and the many accomplishments inspired by its adherence to the Gospel of Jesus, grounded on sound theological and social reflection. All these factors explain the CNBB's reliance on the CPT to represent the church on various rural policy forums. An early illustration of this took place in 1977, when the CNBB asked the bishops in charge of the CPT to participate in the first Parliamentary Commission of Inquiry on the Agrarian Question organized by the lower house of Congress.[11] Their testimonies impressed the legislators by offering an incisive account of the land disputes taking place in various parts of Brazil. At this hearing the CPT bishops denounced the violence sponsored by rural landlords, criticized the government's economic policies and disinterest in land reform, and suggested alternative ways of pursuing a more inclusive development model.

Fueled by dramatic conflicts in the countryside and the CPT's rising influence in public debates over the agrarian question, the CNBB chose to make the nation's land problem a central theme for its 1980 General Assembly. The preparation of the CNBB's pastoral letter, "The Church and Land Problems," was preceded by extensive discussion among the bishops over the church's own vision and practice on this matter. The document's doctrinal content proved to be groundbreaking. In it, the bishops asserted that rural property rights were not absolute, but qualified by social obligations. The text differentiated between those who use the land "for work" and those who appropriate it "for business" and thus regard the land as a commodity amenable to speculation and abuse. The first approach was legitimate because it placed the land at the service of life. The second was illegitimate since it enabled the owner to benefit from the land without meeting its social obligations.[12]

The CNBB document took a strong stance in support of agrarian reform, and committed the church to the grassroots struggle needed to achieve this transformation. The bishops agreed to redistribute nonessential church properties to landless peasants,[13] and demanded effective steps to redistribute the nation's farmland. They also endorsed the CPT's pastoral work among the rural poor, and pledged to strengthen popular organizations in the countryside. Here they argued that the formation of peasant, farm workers, and rubber tapper associations were vital to securing their citizenship rights.[14]

Since 1980, the CNBB has consistently supported land reform, through its public pronouncements, documents, and various pastoral activities, such as the Fraternity Campaigns held during the time of Lent. During the 1987–88 Constitutional Assembly the CNBB joined a broad coalition in support of a progressive agrarian reform. In doing so, it helped shore up support for this measure by spearheading a nation-wide petition that collected 1.2 million signatures. Though defeated by the rural oligarchy's entrenched powers in the assembly, and fierce landlord opposition led by the Rural Democratic Union (UDR), this national campaign sowed the seeds for the formation of Brazil's main civic alliance for land reform, the National Forum for Agrarian Reform and Justice in the Countryside. Established in 1995, this coalition enjoyed the solid backing of the CPT, CIMI, and other religious organizations.

The CNBB retained a reformist stance throughout the 1990s and 2000s, insisting that politics be governed by ethical principles, that quality of life issues take precedence over economic growth, and that the rights of all people prevail over the interests of a privileged minority. Internal church differences, particularly on whether or not to cooperate with the MST and other landless movements, have tempered its actual contribution to the mobilization for agrarian reform. Still, the CNBB and its social agencies (the *Pastorais Sociais*) have underscored the church's firm and continued support for land redistribution through a number of activities, such as the Brazilian Social Week (*A Semana Social Brasileira*), the Cry of the Disenfranchised (*Grito dos Excluídos*) protest gatherings, and the Mobilization to Overcome Misery and Hunger (*Mutirão pela Superação da Miséria e da Fome*).[15]

The church's progressive involvement in the countryside triggered numerous acts of persecution and violence against pastoral agents. Still, the main credit for this religious engagement should be given to the peasants who elicited local church participation in their acts of resistance and pleas for justice. These, after all, were the concrete initiatives that enabled the church, and especially the CPT, to serve as a catalyst for change. This collaboration enhanced self-confidence among rural workers and fostered a sense of critical awareness, creativity and capacity for self-organization. All this provided Brazilian peasants with unprecedented access to tools and resources needed to confront historic patterns of social exclusion and rural violence.

The CPT's Quest to Transform the Brazilian Countryside:
Genesis, Mobilization, and Impact of an Evangelical Service for Rural Workers

The CPT's founding steps were taken under the government of General Emilio Medici Garrastazu (1969–74), responsible most repressive period under Brazil's authoritarian regime. In the name of "national security," the military government promoted the violent persecution of all those considered "enemies of the homeland." Churches involved in fostering grassroots associations were inevitable targets of the regime. Religious workers engaged in the church's *pastoral popular*, serving the rural and urban poor through Gospel Groups (*Grupos de Evangelho*), CEBs, and popular education activities, were often viewed as "subversives" by the forces of repression who monitored these groups closely and arrested several of their leaders. In 1972, the military regime went as far as to imprison all of the pastoral agents—priests, nuns, and lay workers—of the Amazonian Prelacy of São Felix do Araguaia, including its newly appointed bishop, Dom Pedro Casaldáliga.

These acts of persecution revealed the existence of numerous grassroots activities among popular sectors, sponsored by progressive parishes and religious congregations in different parts of the country; some of which were scorned, and evenly sharply contested, by the local bishop. Over time, several of these pastoral groups began to recognize their isolation, and suspect this could be part of a regime strategy to weaken and discourage their efforts. This coincided with a growing recognition that church activists needed to forge stronger networks to share experiences and ideas, and cooperate on common engagements in order to enhance their impact.

The impetus for collaboration among church progressives gained added momentum with the success of the three pastoral letters published in 1973 by the bishops and heads of religious congregations in the Brazilian northeast, midwest, and Amazon region. The informal group of progressive bishops that fueled this initiative convened another meeting at the end of 1973 to evaluate and plan its activities. This led to the organization of a meeting of popular educators and progressive pastoral agents from across Brazil, involved in community organizing among the urban and rural poor. Their gathering took place in February 1974, at the Jesuit Centre for Studies and Social Action (CEAS), in Salvador, Bahia, amid various precautions taken due to the security risks involved. At the event, participants mapped out a wide range of grassroots actions taking place throughout Brazil and proposed the creation of thematic networks to address specific problems, along the lines of CIMI, the church agency set up to support the country's native inhabitants.

After this gathering, an active participant of the informal group of progressive bishops, Dom Pedro Casaldáliga, persuaded the CNBB to sponsor a pastoral meeting on the Amazonian region. The intense harassment of pastoral agents in Dom Pedro's Prelacy of São Felix do Araguaia, led him to seek out closer collaboration with other church groups. His prelacy had gained notoriety in 1971 for issuing the first strongly worded critique of the government's development policies in the Amazon, in a document, titled, "A Church in the Amazon in Conflict with *Latifúndios* and Social Exclusion." Dom Pedro's epistle—his first pastoral letter as bishop—became a landmark text in the church's defense of squatter's rights against powerful agribusiness firms, which, thanks to generous state subsidies, had moved into the Amazon region to install huge cattle ranches.

The CPT was formally established in June 1975, at the Pastoral Meeting of the Amazon region, held in Goiânia, Goiás. From the outset, this agency was conceived of as part of an effort to increase the church's ability to serve the Amazonian people, rather than attend to its own institutional needs. In theological terms, the point of reference on which to discern God's calling were the lives of the people threatened by profoundly unjust policies, implemented by an autocratic state to shore up the interests of the nation's agrarian elite. Most perceptively perhaps, this meeting crystallized the notion that the people afflicted by these injustices had to organize at the grassroots and mobilize themselves to overcome their oppression. Since its very beginning, then, the CPT was envisioned as an instrument of church service to the rural poor, charged with raising their awareness of basic citizenship rights and fostering associations led by the rural workers themselves.

To accomplish this mission, the CPT developed a network of pastoral agents engaged with peasant groups, and provided advice and motivation for their work. As such, it sought to persuade local churches to embrace the defense of peasant rights as part of their religious duty. The CPT pursued these undertakings by creating spaces—namely, meetings, workshops, and assemblies—where pastoral agents could to share experiences and learn from each other, and improve their knowledge of social reality. These spaces also facilitated opportunities for the CPT to evaluate and revise its activities, and reflect on the theological meaning of its efforts to promote peasant rights.

Various CPT branches were established in the Amazon region soon after the 1975 meeting in Goiânia. These hubs were extended to the rest of Brazil in the ensuing years. By 1979 the CPT had set up local offices and networks in all federal states. In 1995, the CPT had 1,062 agents working throughout the country.[16] Though generally disparaged by agrarian elites, the CPT has played an influential role—at local, state, and national levels—in shoring up church support for land reform.

Another hallmark of the CPT is that it was fashioned early on as an ecumenical agency, inspired by the Catholic Church's innovations as a result of the Second Vatican Council. The strongest ecumenical relationships were forged with the Evangelical Church of Lutheran Confession in Brazil (IECLB), notably in the states of Paraná, Espírito Santo, Rondônia, Roraima, and Mato Grosso. Other churches have also worked closely with the CPT, including some of Pentecostal origin, especially in the state of Rio de Janeiro. This ecumenical dimension has played an important role in affirming the CPT pluralist values, self-image, and sense of religious mission. Despite occasional qualms on the part of the CNBB, the CPT has continued to embrace an ecumenical ethos in its day-to-day work.[17]

The CPT's Impact in Brazil

Writing in the late 1980s, sociologist José de Souza Martins noted that Brazil's land struggles were at risk of "consecrating a liberationist political space." Such consecration, however, was not the result of the church's well-known defense of agrarian reform, but rather the consequence of "capitalist expansion during the last twenty years." This development "changed the relationship between land and power: capital became associated with land ownership, and developed into a conservative and anti-reformist force." The church, in contrast, felt compelled "to mobilize as a result of the conflicts generated during process" of structural change. The "consecration of this political space," added Martins, was

> closely associated to the fact that political action among poor and margin-
> alized people was confined to dealings with the immediate and local power
> structure. Yet this is precisely where the fundamental locus of political power
> is set. It is here that oligarchic forces sustain their clientelist ties of patronage
> and domination. This is also the place where the practical and immediate
> clash over the property rights that sustain oligarchic domination, and now
> associate land and capital, are first revealed.[18]

This was the context that directed many Christian activists to pursue their religious commitment to the rural poor in ways that imbued the struggle for land with a "sacred aura." The CPT was formed to overcome the dispersed and fragmented character of these local struggles. All this raised a crucial dilemma regarding the church's continued support for the peasantry given the alternative possibility: a gradual return to a conservative pact with landed oligarchy allied with the forces of capital.[19]

In 2005 the CPT celebrated thirty years of existence, a significant accomplishment in a country as large and complex as Brazil. In all these years the CPT remained particularly active in the Amazon region, with its vast tropical rainforest and urgent deforestation problems; its great rivers and struggles against the privatization of water in the city of Manaus; its riverine communities dependent on the livelihoods of its artisanal fishermen, keen on promoting both aquatic and land reforms; the rubber tappers, fighting to establish extractive reserves in forest areas, instead of a family farm; and small farmers, struggling to benefit economically from the land without destroying the environment. Amid this assorted scenario one also finds large cattle ranches, burgeoning soy bean fields, and huge mining operations, all engrossed in the drive to obtain short-term profits through export dividends, with no regard for the accelerated destruction of the Amazon's fragile ecology.

The CPT's presence in the Brazilian northeast has also been historically strong. This region contains the country's main semi-arid territory, along with pockets of more humid and extremely fertile land. This part of Brazil has been traditionally dominated by a rural oligarchy. Though many are nowadays considered to be "modern agribusiness entrepreneurs," these agrarian elite families are still as fiercely protective of their landholdings and power base as ever, and willing to do most anything to maintain the status quo. The CPT has also remained active in Brazil's immense midwest region, where the existence of the Cerrado eco-system is under serious threat due to the predatory nature of its economic development. Since the 1980s this has been fueled by the expansion of large commercial farms that rely on monoculture and intense pesticide use to produce agricultural commodities for export.

Finally, the CPT has had a long involvement in the south and southeastern sections of the country, the territory where Brazil experienced its first wave of agricultural modernization, inspired by the technical breakthroughs that paved the way for the "Green Revolution." This process, however, has become increasingly dominated by a handful of global agro-food conglomerates. The southern part of the country is also the place where the CPT helped organize the Landless Rural Workers Movement (MST).

The CPT has embraced many challenges during its more than three-decade involvement in the Brazilian countryside. These have often overlapped and rarely appeared in chronological order, thus illuminating a multifaceted quality to the CPT's work. The following section highlights this quality by reviewing seven dimensions of the CPT's mission to serve the rural poor. This includes its efforts to support: peasant squatters (*posseiros*), people displaced by hydroelectric dams, landless peasants (*sem terra*), small farmers, temporary rural workers (*boias-frias*), and enslaved farm laborers, as well as its actions to preserve the environment and protect human rights.[20]

Posseiros: In Defense of the Land Tillers

The CPT's origins were closely entwined with the plight of the posseiros in the Amazon region, and their resistance to the violence with which large landholders and capitalist firms sought to appropriate the land where these peasants lived and toiled. As described earlier, the CPT was founded at a pastoral meeting to discuss these rural conflicts in the Amazonian frontier and actually set up its first field offices in this part of the country.

Posseiros are peasants who occupy and cultivate plots of land but hold no property titles or legal agreements to farm this area. Squatters usually lack land titles because they are unable to pay for and/or navigate through the bureaucratic process required to secure this document. Traditional customs and mores regarding land use in the Brazilian interior also affect this situation. Historically, it has been common for peasants living in the agricultural frontier— where land was neither cultivated, fenced in, or showed any discernible signs of ownership—to clear a small parcel of the rainforest, grow crops for the family's consumption and sale at local markets, and if needed, after a while, move on to establish another farm. This peasant tradition always viewed the rights to land as defined by labor. Those who cleared and prepared the land for planting, tended the field, and collected the harvest were considered its legitimate owners. Underpinning this popular conception of the land was a deep sense of moral economy. In this view, the earth was created by God for the benefit of all of humanity, and thus, no one could stake an absolute claim over it, because "God did not put the earth up for sale."

As such, posseiro land conflicts revealed sharp disparities in the way land, work, and legal rights were conceived by different actors in dispute; all of which aggravated the lopsided nature of the struggle at stake. The business entrepreneurs who arrived to the Amazon region saw land as an asset to be bought (or even swindled) in the land market. In their perspective, labor was a separate market, in which individuals are amenable for hire at the lowest wage possible, to ensure high business profits. Moreover, for these entrepreneurs, landownership was essentially determined by the possession of a title deed, acquired through direct purchase, or by falsifying land titles, a widespread practice in many parts of Brazil known as *grilagem*.[21] In sum, capitalistic expansion into the Amazon territory was premised on the view that land was a useful means of production and speculation, and, inevitably, a source of status and power, particularly at the local level.

The arrival of new alleged landowners bearing proper or fraudulent title deeds wreaked havoc on the lives of the posseiros. These new landlords would soon order the squatters to leave the property. If needed, threats would be made and gunmen hired to attach the peasants, by destroying their fields and homes, and using torture and other forms of violence. Hundreds of posseiros were killed during this process. The landlords would often count on the local police and even the army to protect their interests. All of these human rights violations were carried out with great impunity, since the legal system was deeply biased in favor of any large landowner who could produce a property title. The posseiros, in other words, were obliged to confront the full force of Brazil's authoritarian state, which took pride in promoting the occupation of the Amazon region by agribusiness farmers and various capitalist firms, as one of the cornerstones of its national development policy.

The CPT's first major actions in this area were to offer humanitarian protection, legal defense, and support in organizing the posseiros. This was literally the CPT's baptism by fire. Its pastoral agents faced constant threats and acts of persecution. Some were even killed for their work in solidarity with the posseiro communities. The assassinations of Father Josimo Tavares, who defended peasant rights in the Bico do Papagaio region of north of Goiás (now part of the state of Tocantins), and Eugênio Lyra, a lawyer and activist in Santa Maria da Vitória, Bahia, are two emblematic examples.[22] In the 1970s and 1980s, posseiro conflicts began to appear in practically every region of Brazil. Aside from the

Amazon, squatter struggles peppered many parts of the Brazilian northeast, southeast (especially in Minas Gerais), and midwest. All this reinforced awareness of the fact that such land disputes were a problem of national scope, resulting from the country's starkly disparate land tenure system, and the illicit appropriation of a substantial portion of the Brazilian territory.[23]

Working closely with the posseiros, the CPT was instrumental in organizing the first peasant associations in the Amazon region: the rural trade unions, as Gabriel Ondetti, Emmanuel Wambergue, and José Batista Gonçalves Afonso underscore in their case study of Pará (chap. 8, this volume). The CPT also played a vital role in publicizing the posseiros' struggles, and documenting human rights violations and other injustices committed by Brazil's autocratic state and the new capitalist landlords that were taking over their farmland.

People Displaced by Dams: Organizing Resistance to Large Hydroelectric Projects

The CPT's first organizing efforts in the state of Paraná began in 1978, under the leadership of a Lutheran pastor, involved in supporting more than 8,000 families evicted from their farms with the construction of the Itaipu dam, close to the city of Foz do Iguazú. Those displaced by the dam—small farmers with land titles, posseiros, and tenants—insisted that the companies responsible for building the huge hydroelectric plant, shared with neighboring Paraguay, provide fair compensation for their rural properties and farm investments. The conflicts were aggravated by disputes over the ways in which compensation payments were made and other peasant demands, including access to new farmland, electricity, and additional public benefits. The construction companies knew that the sheer force of the water filling up the dam's reservoir would oblige even the most stubborn farmers to abandon the area. As such, they purposefully dragged out their negotiations with displaced families in order to obtain deals that would maximize their business profits.

A similar dynamic took place during the construction of the Sobradinho dam in Bahia and the Itaparica dam in Pernambuco, erected on the São Francisco River; the Tucuruí plant on the Tocantins River in Pará; and the Balbina dam in the state of Amazonas. This predatory pattern of development regarding nature, local peasants, and riverbank communities has continued under the PT governments elected since 2002; upheld, as always, in the name of "progress." In all these disputes over the construction of massive hydroelectric projects, local communities have achieved few victories. As a rule, the state has protected the interests of large construction companies by restraining—even through repressive measures—those actively opposed to the creation of these dams. To influence public opinion, the state and construction companies have often portrayed their critics as "backward" and "atavistic," even though a number of competent studies have suggested viable energy alternatives, less harmful to the environment and the rights of rural communities.

In spite of their sparse success, the CPT has continued to support resistance to massive, top-down development projects, as in the case of the enormous Carajás mining complex set up in the Amazon region during the 1980s, which disrupted scores of peasant and indigenous communities.[24] In all these activities, the most important accomplishment was the rise of the Movement of People Affected by Dams (MAB). Founded initially in 1980, as a local commission in Rio Grande do Sul, MAB later expanded to most Brazilian states. By the 2000s, the movement had become an influential participant in global networks opposed to the construction of large hydroelectric plants. Aside from championing the rights of people displaced by river dams, MAB has made important contributions to the development of an alternative energy matrix, based on sensible ecological ideas and policy proposals.

The Landless: Conquering the Land That Belongs to All

The CPT's active involvement in the struggle for agrarian reform dates to its founding meeting, where it took up the mission to help rural workers establish their own organizations to fight for land redistribution and other basic rights. One of the CPT's early tasks was to disseminate information among the peasantry on the nation's agrarian laws, especially the Land Statute. Unlike the posseiros, landless struggles involved people who did not have access to land. Among these, one would often find the sons and daughters of small farmers; tenants and sharecroppers who cultivated other people's land in exchange for a fraction of the harvest; rural laborers expelled from their homes in large plantations or cattle ranches; posseiros evicted from their land parcels; temporary rural laborers (*boias-frias*); and even unemployed urban workers, who for the most part were of rural origin. In sum, the term *landless* came to represent an amalgam of diverse social categories that seek to improve their life and family prospects by accessing a farm plot on which to toil. This quest has fueled their demand for the democratization of land ownership.

During the early 1980s, the CPT played a key role in supporting peasant land mobilizations in the south of Brazil. In order to strengthen these local landless groups, the CPT created a network to coordinate various land struggles dispersed throughout the region. In time, this network became the basis for the formation of the MST. The first landless groups in the state of Paraná originated with the efforts to organize peasants displaced by the construction of the Itaipu dam, and particularly by the families unable to obtain a new farm. In Rio Grande do Sul, the landless movement started with the land occupations carried out by small farmers expelled from an indigenous reserve. The CPT assisted these and many other land mobilizations across Brazil, which usually involved setting up landless camps at the edge of country roads and on the outskirts of urban centers.[25]

With the CPT's backing, the network of landless groups in southern Brazil decided to scale up their struggle into a national movement. The MST was founded amid this impetus, in early 1984, and ratified its intentions to establish a nationwide presence the following year, when it held its First National Congress, in Curitiba, Paraná.

The CPT's own development was greatly enriched by the MST's growth into an influential force in the quest to bring about the social transformation of Brazil and the world beyond. Since its early days, the CPT longed to see a popular movement of this caliber arise in Brazil. This owes much to the fact that the CPT never conceived of itself as an outfit that could substitute for the associations created and run by the rural workers themselves. Indeed, its principal mission has always been to strengthen popular organizations by helping existing ones become more authentic and by supporting the formation of new associations when called for by the rural working class.

After 1985, the MST began to forge greater autonomy from the CPT, as it moved to develop its own organizational strategies and priorities. A number of CPT agents had difficulties accompanying the MST's growth with a spirit of wisdom, solidarity, and constructive criticism. Various moments of tension surfaced during these years, as the CPT grappled to redefine its support for the movement, and MST cadres exhibited signs of political immaturity and insularity. Over time, though, the MST and CPT were able to establish a close partnership based on mutual respect and frequent collaboration on various practical endeavors.

Family Farmers: Guaranteeing the Right to Remain on the Land

The CPT has traditionally worked closely with small farmers, especially in the south and northeast regions of the country, but also in areas of more recent colonization, such as the states of Rondônia, Mato Grosso do Sul, Mato Grosso, and Acre. This aspect of the CPT's work, however, grew in significance some years after its founding, in response to the challenge of tackling the precarious conditions that compelled many peasant farmers, including land reform settlers, to sell off their land parcels.

Family farmers have always produced the bulk of the food consumed by Brazilians and also contributed significantly to the nation's agricultural exports. This fact, however, had never been duly recognized by the state, and much less encouraged through its agricultural policies. Small farmers often lacked the confidence and resources needed to develop alternative forms of production and commercialization, appropriate for their circumstances. Moreover, their organizations were generally quite precarious. Rural trade unions usually fell well short of providing the level of support needed by its members, while rural cooperatives were all too few, and, wherever present, usually poorly run. In spite of a growing awareness of the importance of family farms in Brazilian society, these producers were hamstrung in the quest to gain effective public recognition.

CPT actions in this regard have centered on improving the livelihood of the country's most impoverished and precarious family farmers. It has done so by nurturing collective efforts among these farmers and generating alternative strategies for agricultural production and trade, to ensure adequate conditions and incentives for these peasants to remain on the land. This has clearly been an uphill struggle. For all the progress made, the number of small-scale farmers who abandon their land parcels continues to outnumber those who are able to establish new family farms.

President Lula's 2002 election initiated a period of greater political recognition and state support for peasant farmers. Two policies stand out in this regard. First, the program initiated in 2003 to purchase farm products directly from land reform settlers and other small farmers to provide food at various public institutions, such as school lunch programs, prisons, hospitals, and the like. Second, is the nearly eight-fold increase in federal funding to support family farmers, from US$ 0.7 billion to US$ 5.52 billion, between 2002 and 2006. While this amount pales in comparison to the public subsidies given to large-scale agribusiness farmers, these developments show the potential for greater government support of peasant farming.

The newfound interest in family farms was reinforced in mid-2004 with a large meeting held in Brasília to launch the organization of a new national association of family cultivators, the Federation of Family Farm Workers (FETRAF), affiliated with Brazil's main labor confederation, the Unified Workers' Central (CUT). FETRAF-Brasil/CUT was officially established in late 2005. By the end of the decade it had active chapters in eighteen federal states. Peasant associations gained added strength in the 2000s with the consolidation of the Peasant Women's Movement (MMC), originally founded in 1995, and the expansion of the Small Farmers Movement (MPA), created in 1996, both of which later joined the international Via Campesina network.

All these trends are indicative of the peasantry's greater capacity for political organization. They are also illustrative of the new issues that have come to the fore of these movements, related to gender equality, agro-ecology, and the struggle to preserve native seeds, in opposition to the rapid expansion in the use of genetically modified seeds (GMOs). By joining these efforts, the CPT has expanded its outlook and sharpened its awareness of the earth's essential value to human life.

Temporary Farm Labor and Slave Workers: Seeking to Restore Human Dignity

The CPT's defense of temporary farm workers (*boias-frias*) and laborers in the Amazonian cattle ranches, who have often endured slave-like conditions, dates back to its founding years in the mid-1970s.[26] True, at the time the main focus of its Amazon work revolved around the posseiro land conflicts. But the rising number of boias-frias in the ensuing decades, and their palpable needs, renewed the CPT's engagement to protect their basic human rights.

It was in the Amazonian state of Pará, notably in its southeastern rim, that the CPT began its campaign against the use of enslaved rural workers. After the mid-1990s, this drive expanded well beyond the state of Pará. Contemporary slave practices in the Amazon were spurred by the capitalist appropriation of this territory, notably through the installation of large agribusiness cattle ranches. The pursuit of profit as an absolute value led several of these firms—a few owned by prominent banks and multinationals—to treat their impoverished workers as having no human or labor rights worthy of respect, hence the abusive treatment to which they were subjected.

The CPT has been outspoken in denouncing these human rights violations and has compelled the courts and federal government to take action on these matters. Through such efforts and the careful documentation of these abuses, it has helped expose and raise awareness of this problem within Brazilian civil society. As a result, the federal government has become more effective in combating this type of crime. Still, the impunity for those engaged in such practices remains high. For one, hardly any of the rural properties involved in the use of slave workers have been expropriated by the state. Efforts to pass a law in Congress that would make this expropriation mandatory were repeatedly blocked during the 2000s by the *bancada ruralista*, the powerful legislative caucus that champions the privileges of large landholders as though they were absolute rights.[27]

Preserving Nature to Guarantee Life

The CPT's core mission in the early twenty-first century has revolved around the trilogy of land, water, and rights. Though concerned with the ethics of land cultivation since its origins, it was not until the 1990s that the CPT began to incorporate a more explicit concern—in both its biblical and theological reflections—for the environmental destruction taking place in Brazil. These concerns have underscored the existential integrity that binds land, water, and agriculture in practices that seek to sustain life for all people and for future generations.

Within the CPT, the efforts to preserve the environment have varied over time and place. Three types of peasants, in particular, have shaped its ecological insights and practices: the posseiros, the riverbank fishermen and women (*ribeirinhos*), and the rubber tappers (*seringueiros*). The crucial linkage between land, labor, and food production in the posseiro communities helped refine the CPT's ideas on rural property rights. Amazonian ribeirinhos nudged the CPT to embrace their defense of water rights and calls for aquatic reform. In struggling with the ribeirinhos to protect the rivers and sanctuary lakes—where the fish spawn their eggs—the CPT has come to recognize the profound ecological wisdom found among the inhabitants of these riverine communities. Rubber tappers, in turn, pioneered the concept of preserving the Amazon rainforest as a necessary condition for sustainable economic activity, and did so by fighting to create extractive reserves. Many lives were lost in this crusade, most memorably that of Chico Mendes, a seringueiro trade union leader, assassinated by cattle ranchers in 1988.

All these popular mobilizations and novel ideas fueled the CPT's efforts to promote sustainable development practices. An early example of this can be found in the Joint Consortium for Economic Reforestation (RECA), a colonization project established with church support in 1989, to recover a deforested area in the Amazon region. The peasants involved in this project planted new trees and employed agricultural techniques that preserved the new rainforest, thus improving the quality of life of the families living in this rural settlement.[28]

Organic agriculture and the need to protect water resources and seeds as a "heritage of the people for the good of humanity," in La Via Campesina's appropriate term, were incorporated into the CPT's popular education work through an ongoing learning process. The CPT has formed many partnerships in its quest to promote an ecological rural development model. It has joined groups fighting the massive expansion of agro-industrial mono crops; the clearing of vast swaths of rainforest to set up cattle ranches; the misuse of water through wasteful irrigation systems; and the introduction of GMO crops, which have made farmers dependent on a handful of global corporations that control this technology.

An illustration of the CPT's heightened ecological interest can be discerned in the way its annual Land Pilgrimages (*Romarias da Terra*)—which were started in 1978, in Rio Grande do Sul and extended thereafter across the country— became known after 1999 as the "Land and Water Pilgrimages." In recent years, these religious mobilizations have cultivated a spiritual attachment and ethics of care toward Mother Earth, through prayers, songs, words, and other symbolic gestures conveyed at these large gatherings. The pursuit of ecological justice has without a doubt enriched the CPT's pastoral mission and reinforced its vital commitments to agrarian reform, the right to democratic participation in politics and society, the ideals of solidarity and cooperation, and the fundamental value of life.[29]

Advancing Human Rights, Inspiring Hope at the Grass Roots

The struggle for human rights has permeated the CPT's history and continues to be its defining hallmark. This mission was made explicit in the agency's founding charter and can be discerned in all of its activities. Many of the issues and rights involved have changed over the years. Yet the CPT's core effort to defend the rural poor and uphold their individual and collective rights has remained the same.

For the CPT, the notion of rights cannot be confined solely to the rights made available under the nation's legal framework, as upheld in some conservative and positivist interpretations. The rule of law in Brazil has always been deeply permeated by class biases and strongly influenced by rural oligarchic interests (see also Mészáros, chap. 14, this volume). Brazil's stark disparities in wealth are at the heart of the nation's unequal enforcement of laws. To compensate for this, since its beginning, the CPT has provided legal services to defend the posseiros and other rural workers and invested considerable effort to educate peasants with regard to their legal rights. In 1996, CPT attorneys played an active role in setting up a novel National Network of Popular Lawyers, dedicated to the promotion of human rights.

Adding to these activities, the CPT has gained wide recognition in various national and international settings for its meticulous documentation of rural conflicts and human rights violations in Brazil. Starting in 1985, the CPT has published detailed annual reports on these issues, which has led this church agency to become the nation's most authoritative voice on matters of rural violence, judicial impunity, and slave labor.

▬▬ Building on its holistic view of human rights, the CPT has tried to make sure that land and water—two indispensable sources of life—be defined and upheld as a common good for all people. Hence, its insistence that the access to these natural resources be granted on the basis of labor, the creation of equal social opportunities, the democratization of power, and the production of food with technologies that can guarantee a decent quality of life for all people today and for future generations.

In the religious sphere, the CPT has helped the National Council of Christian Churches (CONIC), comprised of the Catholic and mainline Protestant churches, and the Catholic Church in particular, to eschew conservative attempts to bestow religious legitimacy on the nation's unequal agrarian structure and its rural oligarchy. Despite some internal setbacks, these churches have remained, by and large, unswervingly committed to their support for land reform, the MST, and other rural popular movements struggling for social justice.[30]

The CPT has remained steadfast to its prophetic calling for more than three decades. Today, it continues to inspire hope at the grassroots by working closely with Brazil's popular movements and bolstering their democratic demands for land redistribution and for state support for peasant farming and agro-ecology. As in the early days, the CPT's motivation in all this draws deeply from its spiritual inspiration and religious values, nourished in the promise of hope and liberation for the downtrodden people of the earth.

The forces opposed to land reform are still dominant in Brazil. Yet thanks to the MST and other popular groups, the struggle to democratize land rights are much stronger today than they were when the CPT got started. Indeed, since

1975, the CPT has helped guarantee that an expressive segment of Brazil's Catholic and Protestant churches continue—in Silvia Ribeiro's fitting metaphor—to "break through the asphalt" and pursue the structural transformations needed to ensure that the earth becomes a source of justice for all.

Notes

The author wishes to acknowledge Miguel Carter's careful review and observations in preparing this text. Translated from the Portuguese by Miguel Carter.

1. Poletto (2002b: 115).
2. The Catholic Action branch for adults in the countryside, the Rural Christian Action (ACR) movement, was particularly active in the northeast region; see Silva (1985).
3. The Rural Workers Statute was signed into law on March 2, 1963. By contrast, urban trade unions obtained legal recognition two decades earlier, under the 1943 Labor Law; see Pessoa (1999: 66).
4. Peasants, nonetheless, had carried out major insurrections, such as the Canudos Revolt in Bahia (1893–97) and the Contestado War in Santa Catarina (1912–16), both of which were defeated by military forces; see Martins (1981).
5. On the 1964 coup and anticommunist influence in the Catholic Church, see Dreifuss (1981). On the repression of peasant movements following the coup, see Martins (1981).
6. For a review of the church's position on land reform in the 1950s and early 1960s, see Carvalho (1985) and Martins (1989: 24–35).
7. Sigaud, Mayer, Oliveira, and de Freitas (1960).
8. For an informative account of this historical period, see Serbin (2000).
9. The first two documents were published in the magazine *SEDOC*; see Bispos e Superiores Religiosos do Nordeste (1973) and Bispos do Centro-Oeste (1973).
10. The conclusions reached at the CNBB's meeting with CPT and CIMI representatives were published in the CPT's (1976) news bulletin.
11. See CPT (1977).
12. Conferência Nacional de Bispos do Brasil (CNBB) (1980: 83–93).
13. On the church's rural properties and the redistribution of some of this land, see Lenz (1980), and Guanziroli and Fernandes (1987).
14. Conferência Nacional de Bispos do Brasil (CNBB) (1980: 94–104).
15. The *Semana Social Brasileira* (Social Brazilian Week) is an ecumenical initiative promoted by the CNBB's Pastoral Social to foster dialogue among a wide range of civil society actors. The Fourth Semana Social Brasileira took place between 2004 and 2006. During this time it helped coordinate and mobilize various groups through a Grassroots Initiative for a New Brazil. The *Grito do Excluidos* (Cry of the Disenfranchised) is an annual mobilization sponsored by various religious groups and popular movements, including the CPT and the MST. It originated during the CNBB's Second Semana Social Brasileira in 1994 and spread to other Latin American countries in 1999. The Grito dos Excluidos builds on the historic Cry of the Ipiranga, which led to Brazil's independence in 1822. The *Mutirão pela Superação da Miséria e da Fome* (Effort to Overcome Misery and Hunger) was instituted by the CNBB in 2002 to engage the CEBs and other civil society groups in endeavors to reduce Brazil's social disparities and create effective opportunities to end poverty. On the CNBB's multiple activities in support of agrarian reform, see Poletto (2003).

16. CPT (1997: 273). On the origins of the CPT, see the collection of testimonies assembled in Poletto and Canuto (2002). This book seeks to make up for the lack of documentation on the CPT's early formation, a consequence of the repression in the political climate in the 1970s.

17. The book, *Teologia da Terra* (Barros and Caravias 1988), offers an important review of the theological and spiritual insights that have inspired the CPT's work. Its main ideas are influenced by liberation theology and the "prayerful Bible readings" sponsored by the Center for Biblical Studies (CEBI).

18. Martins (1989: 62).

19. Martins (1989: 66).

20. These seven dimensions of the CPT's work draw on Canuto (2002).

21. The term *grilagem* comes from the Portuguese word for crickets, *grilo*, which are used to forge land titles. This was done traditionally by placing the crickets in a box with the fake deeds and letting them secrete a chemical substance that makes the papers look old in a matter of days. One of the early and best studies of Brazil's ongoing problem with large land grabbers (*grileiros*) was written by Victor Asselin (1982), a Canadian priest who served as the CPT's first vice president.

22. On the life of Father Josimo Tavares, see Aldighieri (1993) and Breton (1997).

23. Tavares dos Santos (1993).

24. State support for huge development initiatives was not limited to Brazil's energy sector. The military government's pursuit of rapid economic growth set in motion various large-scale projects in agribusiness, commercial fishing, mining, and industry—all of which were supported by tax breaks and other public subsidies, to the detriment of alternative programs that could have helped remedy many of Brazil's social ills.

25. Stédile and Görgen (1993). On the origins of the MST, also see Fernandes and Carter (chaps. 5 and 6, this volume).

26. Esterci (1987).

27. Breton (2002).

28. RECA was set up on a colonization project for 500 peasant families, on the border of the state of Acre and Rondônia. The CPT, along with various national and international NGOs and Brazil's Ministry of the Environment, have shored up RECA's efforts to generate a new agro-forest development model; see Projeto de Reflorestamento Econômico Consorciado e Adensado (RECA) (2003).

29. For a review of the CPT's ecological concerns in the 1990s, see Barros and Peregrino (1996).

30. A mid-2000s sample of the church's ongoing commitment to land reform can be gleaned from its decision to (1) help organize the 2004 Land and Water Conference; (2) highlight the importance of agrarian reform, family farming, and agro-ecology during CONIC's 2005 Fraternity Campaign, carried out during the weeks of Lent; and (3) participate with dozens of religious activists in the MST's National March for Agrarian Reform in May 2005.

PART II

MST History and Struggle for Land

5 The Formation and Territorialization of the MST in Brazil

I still remember the young activist of the Landless Rural Workers Movement (MST) who came to speak with me in 1989. He asked about the possibility of carrying out a land occupation in the Pontal do Paranapanema, a region located in the westernmost part of the state of São Paulo. I had just moved to the area to start teaching at the State University of São Paulo (UNESP) Presidente Prudente campus. The young activist and I decided to meet with supporters of the popular struggle: the progressive Catholic priests and the labor union leaders affiliated with the Unified Workers' Central (CUT).

After three months of discussions, the priests and labor organizers concluded that the conditions were not ripe to begin the MST land struggle in the Pontal do Paranapanema. The possibilities for organizing landless families and occupying large rural estates in the region would be severely restricted, they believed, given the government's hopeless agrarian reform policy and the powerful political leverage of local landlords led by the Rural Democratic Union (UDR), an association well-known for its use of violence against landless peasants. The decision disappointed the MST leader, who soon thereafter returned to his rural settlement in the neighboring state of Paraná.

A few months later, however, to my great surprise, the MST carried out their first land occupation in the Pontal region. Close to 800 families from various parts of São Paulo and Paraná entered the Nova Pontal cattle ranch on July 13, 1990. While visiting the landless camp set up within the estate, I came across the same MST activist who had shortly before left the Pontal area disheartened with the assessment made by the movement's allies. I asked him point-blank why they had decided to undertake the occupation under such bleak circumstances. "Look," he responded, with self-confidence and poise, "if the conditions aren't set, we must create them. Without land occupations the government will never carry out agrarian reform. Land occupations are our way of fighting the power of the landlords."

The Nova Pontal occupation prompted a series of land mobilizations through-out the area, which gained widespread media coverage. Between the early 1990s and mid-2000s the Pontal do Paranapanema had more land occupations than any other part of Brazil. By 2006, 6,500 peasant families had received a farm plot in 112 settlements established as a result of these mobilizations. With courage and conviction, the young MST activist helped change the region's history.[1]

■■■■ The struggle for land in Brazil has persisted with or without the existence of an agrarian reform plan. Land mobilizations are a popular struggle, while agrarian reform is a public policy carried out by the state. The struggle for agrarian reform includes two main political manifestations: land occupations, which are a daily occurrence and the main form of access to land in Brazil, and various mobilizations undertaken by different peasant organizations to pressure the state to implement policies designed to offer agricultural credit, education and housing, and other public benefits. This struggle has put land reform on the nation's public agenda. Until now, though, the Brazilian state has not carried out a redistribution program aimed at altering the country's starkly unequal land tenure. State involvement is essential to this process, yet the state in Brazil has not pursued such reforms in a decisive or proactive way. Rather, the state has consistently followed on the coattails of peasant mobilizations.

This chapter examines this argument through an analysis of the MST's historical development under various governments, from the military regime to the Lula administration. Brazil's agrarian conflicts stem from its highly concentrated landholding structure and the pattern of agricultural modernization engendered therein. This conflict has led to a paradoxical situation: peasant exclusion from the process of formulating rural public policies has fueled, in turn, repeated demands for peasant inclusion and access to basic citizenship rights.

The Brazilian state's approach to agrarian conflicts has focused on addressing specific demands, rather than pursue structural reforms. As a result, its oscillations have been affected largely by the peasantry's capacity to mobilize under varying political and economic junctures. This adverse situation for land redistribution is the upshot of the enduring political strength of Brazil's agrarian elite, who have historically undermined the development of peasant agriculture. Their traditional influence over the state's rural policies led to a process of agricultural modernization that preserved the nation's highly unequal landholding structure. Indeed, the military dictatorship set up in 1964 in many ways cemented the power of Brazil's landlord class (see Delgado, chap. 2, this volume).

Shortly after coming to power, the military government issued Brazil's first agrarian reform law: the 1964 Land Statute. The government's intent, nonetheless, was not to carry out land reform, but to use the legal instrument as a way of controlling agrarian conflicts. Its agricultural policies, in turn, were based on the Green Revolution, which sought to increase rural production through technical modernization. This model was geared toward improving the competitiveness of large commercial farmers within the capitalist system, while disregarding peasant farmers.[2] The military regime undertook various efforts to mitigate land disputes by fostering colonization projects in the Amazon. Yet their attempts to foster peasant migration did little to minimize rural conflicts in other parts of the country. From its onset, the authoritarian regime used threats and acts of violence to deter popular mobilizations demanding access to land and better working conditions in the countryside.

The MST was born in the context of a waning military regime and mounting societal pressure for political democratization. This chapter analyzes the movement's formation and territorialization across Brazil through land struggles and the creation of agricultural settlements. The landless camps and rural settlements provide a territorial space in which peasants can solidify their social identities and practices, and diffuse the land struggle by establishing or invigorating other peasant movements. This view of the land struggle underscores the fact that social organization and territory are inseparable components of peasant struggles. Territorialization is crucial to the analysis offered in this text given its centrality to the MST's historical development.

Four stages in the development of the MST's organization and territorialization can be identified as: its early formation, consolidation, institutionalization, and globalization. All of these phases were shaped by decisions taken within the MST, amid varying political circumstances and economic conditions, both in Brazil and at the global level.

The MST's early formation (1979–84) preceded the movement's official founding, but is essential to understanding its evolution. The movement's consolidation (1985–89) included a process of national expansion and organizational development. Its subsequent institutionalization (1990 and onward) enabled the MST to become the main interlocutor vis-à-vis the federal government on matters related to land reform and gain wide international recognition. This historical review is followed by a closer analysis of the MST's land struggles and organizational structure. The movement's fourth phase was shaped by its 1996 decision to join La Via Campesina, a global network of peasant associations. La Via Campesina's expansion in the late 1990s, and staunch position against the World Bank's market-based policy for land distribution, helped globalize the MST's struggle for agrarian reform.[3] The chapter concludes with an evaluation of the Lula government's land reform policy and the prospect of reducing land concentration in a period of heightened agribusiness power.

The MST's early stirrings in the late 1970s emerged in the wake of fifteen years of political repression under Brazil's military regime. This took place in a context of growing popular mobilization—in both urban and rural areas—to reclaim basic rights and democratize the country. In the countryside, the church's Pastoral Land Commission (CPT) strongly supported these activities. Land reform was reinstated on the nation's public agenda during this period, after its suppression by the 1964 military coup. This was largely the result of struggles led by squatter peasants and rural trade unions in the Amazon region, and land occupations carried out in other parts of the country, notably in the south and northeast regions.

In the main urban centers, strikes undertaken by metalworkers, teachers, bank employees, and others led to the emergence of what became known as the "authentic union movement," which created the CUT and gave rise to the Workers' Party (PT). Popular struggles for democratization during the 1980s, spearheaded by various movements and trade unions, transformed the PT into one of the most important political parties in Brazil.

The PT helped connect an array of popular groups that had surfaced autonomously, yet interacted frequently, each with their own organizational structure. All of these associations shared a common origin and purpose: the struggle to defend the rights and interests of working-class people. During the 1980s, the PT supported efforts made by various rural social movements and the CPT to put land reform on the nation's agenda and legitimized peasant land struggles.

The MST's genesis did not start with the movement's founding at the First National Meeting of the Landless People, in 1984, but rather with the first land occupations organized in southern Brazil in the late 1970s. During this time, landless peasants, squatters, and tenant farmers in the states of Rio Grande do Sul, Santa Catarina, Paraná, São Paulo, and Mato Grosso do Sul began to resist their evictions by carrying out land occupations and other forms of organized opposition.

In northern Rio Grande do Sul, squatters who had been forcibly removed from an indigenous reserve occupied the Macali and Brilhante estates in September 1979. Amid the expansion of cattle ranching in western São Paulo, squatters from the Primavera estate resisted their eviction from an area that had been illegally usurped by a local landlord and secured their land rights through a presidential decree signed in 1980. In the neighboring state of Mato Grosso do Sul, tenant farmers from the municipality of Naviraí resisted their eviction by local cattle ranchers. Other peasants from the same area occupied the Baunilha estate in May 1981. In southwestern Paraná, the construction of the Itaipu dam displaced thousands of peasant families from their land and sparked the formation of a landless movement in this region. In western Santa Catarina, landless peasants occupied the Burro Branco estate in May 1980 and drew on the active support of the Catholic diocese of Chapecó to prevent their removal by local authorities. Among all the early mobilizations, the landless camp set up in 1981 at Natalino's road crossing in Ronda Alta, Rio Grande do Sul, generated the largest national impact. The military's decision to take over the camp and thwart the rise of a landless movement stirred the involvement of a wide range of social and political forces opposed to the authoritarian regime. All this brought the budding land reform movement into the limelight (see Carter, chap. 6, this volume).[4]

The CPT played a crucial role in the MST's early formation by supporting these popular mobilizations and helping develop a network of landless peasants. It sponsored meetings that brought together various groups engaged in land struggles across southern Brazil, thus enabling them to overcome their isolation and become more effective. The first major gathering of CPT agents and landless peasants took place in July 1982, in Medianeira, Paraná. The second was held in September 1982, in Goiânia, with peasant representatives from all regions of Brazil. A committee was set up at this event to coordinate activities for the creation of a national landless movement. The CPT sponsored two additional meetings in 1983, leading up to the MST's official formation in January 1984, at an assembly convened in Cascavel, Paraná. A year later, the MST held its first National Congress with representatives from twenty-three of Brazil's twenty-seven federal states.

Early on, the MST made the tactical decision to organize on a national scale. It did so in the context of various meetings facilitated by the CPT to assess the country's political transition and review the experience of previous peasant mobilizations in Brazil and elsewhere. Several consultations were held with former leaders of rural movements that had been wiped out by the military regime, such as the Peasant Leagues (*Ligas Camponesas*), the Peasant and Agricultural Workers Union of Brazil (ULTAB), and the Landless Farmers' Movement (MASTER).[5] This historical assessment helped the new MST leaders and advisors to recognize the importance of building a national organization in order to strengthen the movement's capacity to confront its opponents. Adding to this, the MST drew on the lessons gained from its first land occupations and landless camps—namely, the different task teams and coordination bodies created to sustain these mobilizations—to forge a unique decision-making framework.

All of these developments helped shape the movement's organizational model. Key principles adopted by the MST included the need to set up coordination and leadership councils based on collective decision-making processes; ensure compliance with the decisions made by these bodies; maintain the movement's political autonomy; promote education and political awareness; preserve the unity of both economic and political struggles;[6] and cultivate organic ties between movement members and leaders. The MST's expansion throughout Brazil drew on these principles and the experience gained from its first mobilizations.

MST Consolidation, 1985–1989

The struggle for land advanced as the struggle for agrarian reform receded. In 1985, Brazil's first year of redemocratization, President Sarney presented an agrarian reform plan that promised to settle 1.4 million families. By the end of his term in 1989, however, only 84,852 families had been settled, merely 6% of the anticipated total. These land allocations were mainly the result of occupations carried out by peasant groups rather than the upshot of any serious government policy. In truth, the MST was skeptical of Sarney's agrarian plan from the onset of his administration.

During the 1988 Constitutional Assembly the landlord and agribusiness caucus (*bancada ruralista*) devised a clever strategy to thwart the presidential decrees needed to expropriate large estates: they inserted a clause in the Constitution that required an additional law to specify the procedures under which the state could expropriate unproductive farmland. The new agrarian reform law, however, did not go into effect until 1993, thus halting all land expropriations for five years. Thereafter, the rural elite worked to prevent the government's appropriations of many estates and fought to overturn through the courts expropriations already signed by the president. Moreover, they found ways to exploit land reform proceedings to their own financial advantage by getting the government to pay above-market prices for the expropriation of large unproductive estates.[7]

During this period the MST branched out to all of the states in the southeast and northeast regions of the country and made inroads in the midwestern state of Goiás and the Amazonian state of Rondônia (see map 5.1). The MST's formation in the Brazilian southeast began in the state of São Paulo, in 1984. It subsequently organized its first land occupations in Espírito Santo in 1985 and in Minas Gerais's Vale de Jequitinhonha in 1987. The first efforts to set up the MST in Rio de Janeiro, in 1985, were called off in 1987 due to internal organizational problems. The movement only began to reorganize in Rio de Janeiro in 1993.

In the northeast, the MST's organizing efforts in southern Bahia started shortly after the movement's first statewide meeting in 1986. Its first land occupation in this state took place in 1987, in the historic municipality of Prado, on a largely unproductive eucalyptus plantation run by the state-owned mineral conglomerate, the Companhia Vale do Rio Doce. That same year, the MST carried out its first land occupations in the states of Alagoas and Sergipe. The MST started operating in Sergipe in 1985, through the involvement of people who had taken part in land occupations sponsored by the CPT and rural trade

Map 5.1. MST territorialization in Brazil, 1979–1999

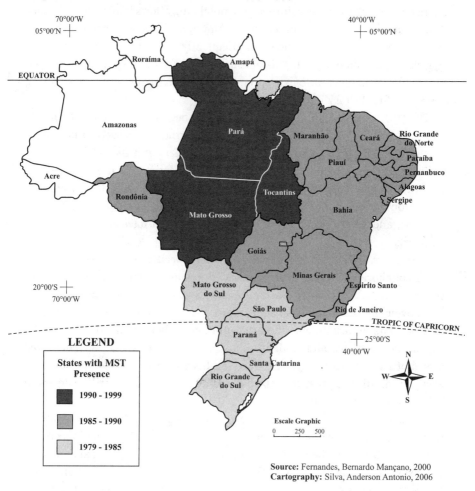

LEGEND

States with MST Presence

- 1990 - 1999
- 1985 - 1990
- 1979 - 1985

Escale Graphic
0   250   500

Source: Fernandes, Bernardo Mançano, 2000
Cartography: Silva, Anderson Antonio, 2006

unions supported by the diocese of Própria. The MST's first land occupation in Pernambuco, in 1985, proved to be a success, yet this group eventually left the movement. It was not until the arrival of landless activists from neighboring states in 1989 that the MST was able to reestablish itself in Pernambuco. The movement's first land occupations in the states of Paraíba, Rio Grande do Norte, Ceará, and Piauí took place in 1989. Initial activities to organize the MST in Maranhão were carried out with the help of the Rural Workers Education and Cultural Center (CENTRU), a non-governmental organization (NGO) linked to rural trade unions from the region of Imperatriz. These two groups, nonetheless, split in 1988 due to tactical differences. The MST undertook its first land takeover in the region soon thereafter and occupied three other cattle ranches the following year.

The bishop of Goiás, Dom Tomás Balduíno, and local CPT activists helped shore up the MST's first recruitment and mobilizing efforts in the state of Goiás. The occupation of the Mosquito ranch in May 1985, however, ended with a police eviction. The landless camp was subsequently transferred to the Civic Plaza of Goiânia, the state capital. This unusual act prompted the governor and federal land reform officials to expropriate the ranch in August 1986, thus scoring the MST's first victory in the state of Goiás.

The MST's incursion into the Amazon region began in Rondônia. The movement's 1985 land occupation in this state, nevertheless, proved to be unsuccessful. Its real birth, therefore, took place in 1989, with the takeover of the Seringal ranch in the municipality of Espigão do Oeste. This unproductive estate, though, was only expropriated after additional land occupations, sit-ins at the regional offices of the National Agrarian Reform and Colonization Institute (INCRA), and several armed clashes with gunmen (pistoleiros) hired by local landlords.

Various groups helped support the MST's territorialization across Brazil. The CPT's collaboration, in particular, provided a pivotal force through its extensive ecumenical network of pastoral agents and Catholic bishops. Moreover, the movement's national expansion received support from various rural trade unions, some Protestant churches, CUT-affiliated labor unions, the PT, human rights organizations, and student groups. Adding to this, the MST deployed scores of its own activists, often from southern Brazil, to help organize land occupations, diffuse other mobilization tactics, and establish the movement in different parts of the country.

The MST became a national movement and consolidated its main organizational traits and sense of identity between 1985 and 1989. Of particular concern during this time was the quest to establish the movement's political autonomy and avert organizational dependency by expanding the scope of its alliances. Delegates discussed this matter at length during the MST's Second National Meeting, in December 1985. Wherever it went, the movement sought to create local partnerships to assist its land struggle. At times, though, some of these allies would try to direct the MST's actions, prompting the movement to insist on its autonomy. These situations sometimes triggered a sense of malaise between the MST and its partners.[8] To strengthen its political autonomy, the landless movement decided to provide periodic workshops to train the cadres responsible for furthering land struggles in each state.

Efforts to prepare these young activists were coupled with a range of activities that helped develop the movement's culture and political identity. In 1987, at its Third National Meeting, the MST adopted one of its principal symbols—its red-colored flag—and agreed to sponsor an internal competition for the composition of its anthem. This song was selected in 1989, at the MST's Fifth National

Meeting. A significant process of identity construction took place during the movement's consolidation phase, engendering a culture of resistance that became a vital part of the movement's mobilizations and daily activities.

In sum, the MST's consolidation was the result of its recurrent efforts to train its activists and thus strengthen its internal organization and ensure the movement's territorialization throughout Brazil. It did so by establishing an autonomous national network and forging a culture of peasant resistance. By the end of this period, the movement had garnered enough stamina and resilience to face the different acts of state repression that would take place in the ensuing decade.

MST Institutionalization, 1990 and Onward

This phase ushered in various challenges in the MST's relations with the Brazilian state. Fernando Collor de Mello's presidency, following his election in December 1989, in the first direct vote for president after the military regime, proved to be short-lived. He resigned in December 1992 amid impeachment proceedings in Congress over charges of corruption. Collor was replaced by his vice president, Itamar Franco, who governed until 1994.

Under the Collor administration, the state used violence to repress the MST, invading its offices and arresting its leaders in different parts of the country. This compelled the MST to recoil and curb its land occupations. To offset these restrictions, the movement focused on strengthening its newly created land reform settlements by setting up cooperatives and supporting the development of these territories. Despite many difficulties, these activities helped boost the MST's internal organization. In 1993, MST leaders met with President Itamar Franco to lobby for land distribution, along with access to farm credits and other resources needed to shore up its rural settlements. This was the first time the movement had ever been received by a sitting Brazilian president, and as such was considered an historic event for the MST.

Itamar Franco's successor, Fernando Henrique Cardoso, was elected president in 1994 and reelected in 1998. Under Cardoso's first term, Brazil experienced the largest increase in land reform settlements in all its history (see figure 5.1).[9] Throughout this time, though, his government dismissed the fact that Brazil still had many *latifúndios* (large unproductive estates) and maintained that it had a relatively small number of landless peasants.[10] The administration believed it could quickly solve the nation's agrarian problem by settling all the families living in the existing landless camps. This view, however, was soundly refuted by the rapid and visible surge of new encampments and land occupations during Cardoso's first term. Between 1994 and 1998 the number of families living in landless camps grew from 20,000 to 76,000. It was during this

Figure 5.1. Families in land occupations and agricultural settlements in Brazil, 1988–2006

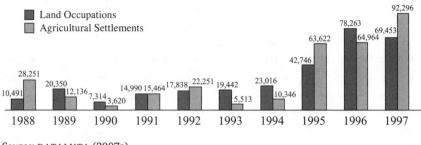

- ■ Land Occupations
- ▨ Agricultural Settlements

Source: DATALUTA (2007a).

surge that the police massacres of landless peasants occurred in Corumbiara, Rondônia, in 1995 and in Eldorado dos Carajás, Pará, in 1996.

Cardoso's second administration ushered in a new and more repressive strategy toward the MST. It criminalized various tactics used to mobilize for agrarian reform and established a market-based policy for land distribution. In 2001, the government issued two decrees. One ruling prohibited all rural settlers from acting in solidarity with the landless families by taking part in their land occupations. The other measure barred INCRA from initiating its proceedings to expropriate an occupied estate for two years if occupied once, and four years if occupied more than once. To draw people away from the landless camps, it created a program to register land claimants through the national postal service and the Internet. Close to 840,000 families signed up in less than two years, though none received a farm plot through this initiative.

With World Bank support, the Cardoso government set up the *Banco da Terra* (Land Bank), a credit program designed to form rural settlements through land purchases carried out by landless farmers. During Cardoso's second term, this program gained headway amid a reduction in land expropriations. This administration also canceled a special credit line and technical assistance program for land reform settlers, to the detriment of hundreds of thousands of families. Furthermore, it cut funding for educational programs designed to assist the settlers, created at the MST's behest. All this led to a significant decline in the number of land mobilizations between 1999 and 2002, the second drop of its kind since the restoration of Brazilian democracy.

While claiming to have carried out Brazil's largest land reform program, Cardoso's agrarian policies generated two distinct results: (1) a steep rise in the number of families living in landless camps and rural settlements, with the number of encamped families reaching 180,000 by 2004; and (2) precarious conditions in the settlements created under his administration. As detailed by Miguel Carter and Horacio Martins de Carvalho (chap. 9, this volume), the bulk of these communities received very little government support in terms of infrastructure

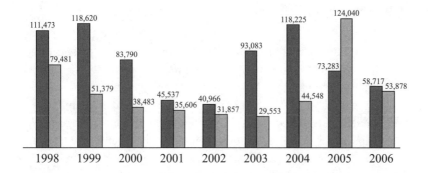

development, schools, and farming credit. This situation led to the decapitalization and impoverishment of hundreds of thousands of peasant families.

All of this suggests that the Cardoso government did not have a real agrarian reform plan. In fact, during his two terms in office, the majority of the settlements were established as a result of land occupations.[11] The second Cardoso administration, however, sought to criminalize these land mobilizations and even the peasant movements themselves.[12] This led to a decline in the number of land occupations and consequently the number of settlements created during this period. To meet the goals set by the government, the Ministry of Agrarian Reform began to falsify land reform statistics by "cloning" settlements created earlier by the federal or state governments and recording them as settlements constituted under Cardoso's second administration. These actions brought such havoc to INCRA's statistics that by 2003 this federal agency could not determine the actual number of land reform settlements established in Brazil.

During its institutionalization phase, the MST started organizing mobilizations in the Federal District of Brasília in 1992, and carried out its first land occupation in the state of Mato Grosso in 1995, with the support of movement activists from various states, CPT agents, the Bishop of Rondonópolis, human rights organizations, and university professors and students. The MST also began to assert its presence in the Amazonian state of Pará in 1990. Later, in 1999, it initiated its first mobilizations in the state of Tocantins. By the end of the 1990s, the MST had a footing in twenty-three Brazilian states.

During this period, the MST became known as the country's leading peasant movement in the struggle for agrarian reform and gained considerable international recognition, notably after the mid-1990s. Amid these developments, it expanded its organizational structure in significant ways, creating a network of cooperatives, schools, training and research centers, and task teams dealing with a variety of issues, from gender and culture to agro-ecology and human rights.[13] In effect, the MST became Brazil's main popular voice and state interlocutor on matters dealing with agrarian reform.

Peasant land struggles involve a territorial phenomenon, given that the take-over of large landed estates and their conversion into rural settlements alters the landholding structure. Land distribution significantly increases the number of people in a particular territory. This new reality changes the patterns of spatial and labor organization, which alter the forms of social and political interaction. Land is essential to the peasantry. Its access ensures their main source of livelihood, helps preserve their identity, and sustains their family enterprise.[14]

Over the last half-century Brazil's land struggles have been led mainly by squatters (*posseiros*) and landless peasants (*sem terra*). Squatters usually occupy land in areas along the agricultural frontier. These peasants mobilize to resist the territorialization of capital, spearheaded by large landholders, loggers, and agribusiness firms, who usually grab land through various illegal tactics known as *grilagem*. Landless peasants, on the other hand, mostly occupy areas in parts of the country where capital has already been territorialized. These groups organize takeovers of large rural properties, such as estates linked to agribusiness production, in addition to areas obtained through grilagem or fraudulent schemes.[15] These two kinds of peasant struggles differ in one crucial respect: whereas the landgrabber (*grileiro*) landlord or agribusiness firm arrive where the squatter lives, landless peasants go into areas already controlled by these elite forces.

As a form of popular struggle, land occupations are not a new phenomenon in Brazil, but are rather part of the longstanding history of its peasant population. These occupations have been their main form of access to land and thus a vital component of the peasantry's social reproduction from the time of the Portuguese colony.[16] Since the 1980s, land occupations have taken place in practically all of Brazil's federal states.

In addition to the MST and squatters on the agricultural frontier, several other peasant organizations have engaged in land occupations throughout Brazil, as revealed in tables 5.4 and 5.5 (also see Rosa, chap. 15, this volume). Table 5.4 registers eighty-six peasant groups that have mobilized for land between 2000 and 2006. A geographic representation of the presence and intensity of all these land occupations can be found in maps 5.2 and 5.3. Moreover, map 5.4, and 5.5 offer geographical data on land reform settlements in Brazil.

A comparison of the maps 5.3 and 5.5 depicting the geography of land occupations and rural settlements reveals a clear difference between the agrarian policies ushered in by recent governments and demands made by peasant movements. Whereas the Brazilian state has prioritized land distribution in the Amazon region and parts of the northeast, the largest number of peasant land occupations has actually taken place in the south, southeast, and northeast regions. This disparity underscores the fact that Brazil's agricultural modernization has

Map 5.2. Land occupations in Brazil, 1988–2005:
Number of families in occupations per state

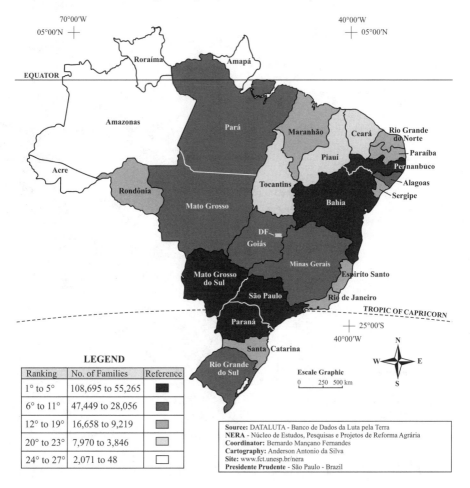

LEGEND

Ranking	No. of Families	Reference
1° to 5°	108,695 to 55,265	■
6° to 11°	47,449 to 28,056	■
12° to 19°	16,658 to 9,219	▨
20° to 23°	7,970 to 3,846	▢
24° to 27°	2,071 to 48	□

Source: DATALUTA - Banco de Dados da Luta pela Terra
NERA - Núcleo de Estudos, Pesquisas e Projetos de Reforma Agrária
Coordinator: Bernardo Mançano Fernandes
Cartography: Anderson Antonio da Silva
Site: www.fct.unesp.br/nera
Presidente Prudente - São Paulo - Brazil

Rank	State	No. Families	Rank	State	No. Families
1°	PE	108,695	15°	RN	14,204
2°	SP	81,193	16°	PB	13,155
3°	MS	64,712	17°	RJ	9,605
4°	PR	58,754	18°	RO	9,521
5°	BA	55,265	19°	ES	9,219
6°	PA	47,449	20°	PI	7,970
7°	RS	45,061	21°	CE	6,615
8°	GO	36,606	22°	TO	4,331
9°	MG	35,586	23°	DF	3,846
10°	AL	32,759	24°	AC	2,071
11°	MT	28,056	25°	AM	2,024
12°	SC	16,658	26°	AP	120
13°	MA	14,484	27°	RR	48
14°	SE	14,369			

Map 5.3. Land occupations in Brazil, 1988–2005: Number of families in occupations per municipality

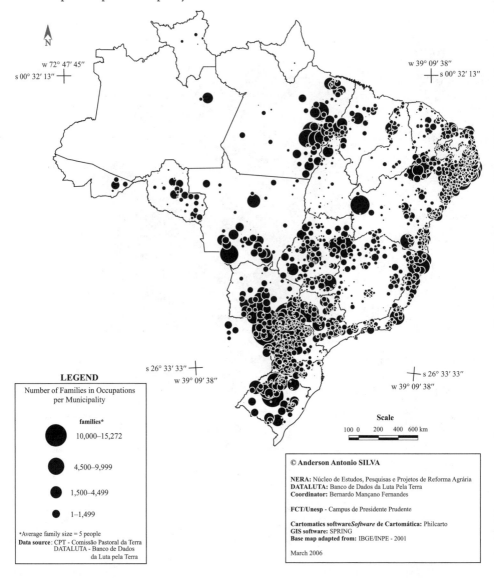

LEGEND
Number of Families in Occupations per Municipality

families*
- 10,000–15,272
- 4,500–9,999
- 1,500–4,499
- 1–1,499

*Average family size = 5 people
Data source: CPT - Comissão Pastoral da Terra
DATALUTA - Banco de Dados
da Luta pela Terra

Scale
100 0   200   400   600 km

© **Anderson Antonio SILVA**

NERA: Núcleo de Estudos, Pesquisas e Projetos de Reforma Agrária
DATALUTA: Banco de Dados da Luta Pela Terra
Coordinator: Bernardo Mançano Fernandes

FCT/Unesp - Campus de Presidente Prudente

Cartomatics software*Software* de Cartomática:** Philcarto
GIS software: SPRING
Base map adapted from: IBGE/INPE - 2001

March 2006

not solved the nation's historic agrarian problem. In this country, agribusiness firms take over land farmed by peasants in regions where agriculture is more developed, while the government encourages peasants to settle in regions where agriculture is less advanced, namely in the Amazon. Yet even in those regions, peasants and agribusiness firms have engaged in intense disputes over existing farmland.

Map 5.4. Land reform settlements in Brazil, 1985–2005: Number of beneficiary families per state

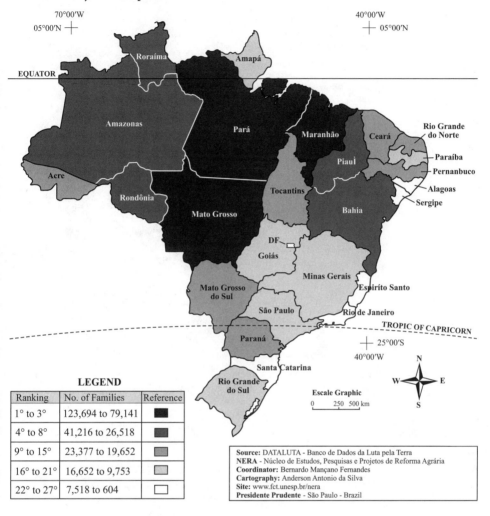

LEGEND

Ranking	No. of Families	Reference
1° to 3°	123,694 to 79,141	■
4° to 8°	41,216 to 26,518	■
9° to 15°	23,377 to 19,652	▨
16° to 21°	16,652 to 9,753	▨
22° to 27°	7,518 to 604	□

Source: DATALUTA - Banco de Dados da Luta pela Terra
NERA - Núcleo de Estudos, Pesquisas e Projetos de Reforma Agrária
Coordinator: Bernardo Mançano Fernandes
Cartography: Anderson Antonio da Silva
Site: www.fct.unesp.br/nera
Presidente Prudente - São Paulo - Brazil

Rank	State	No. Families	Rank	State	No. Families
1°	PA	123,694	15°	RN	19,652
2°	MA	101,826	16°	GO	16,652
3°	MT	79,141	17°	MG	15,243
4°	RO	41,216	18°	SP	13,790
5°	BA	39,803	19°	PB	13,485
6°	AM	28,446	20°	RS	12,122
7°	RR	27,648	21°	AP	9,753
8°	PI	26,518	22°	AL	7,518
9°	PE	23,377	23°	SE	7,434
10°	CE	23,048	24°	RJ	6,285
11°	PR	21,929	25°	SC	5,368
12°	MS	21,710	26°	ES	3,688
13°	AC	21,699	27°	DF	604
14°	TO	20,635			

Map 5.5. Land reform settlements in Brazil, 1985–2005: Number of beneficiary families per municipality

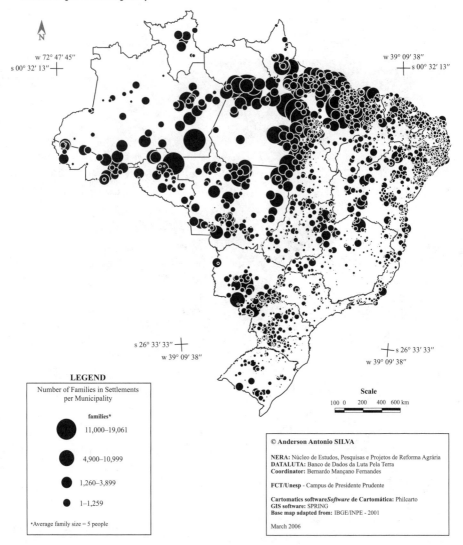

N

w 72° 47' 45''
s 00° 32' 13''

w 39° 09' 38''
s 00° 32' 13''

s 26° 33' 33''
w 39° 09' 38''

s 26° 33' 33''
w 39° 09' 38''

LEGEND

Number of Families in Settlements per Municipality

families*

11,000–19,061

4,900–10,999

1,260–3,899

1–1,259

*Average family size = 5 people

Scale

100 0   200   400 600 km

© **Anderson Antonio SILVA**

NERA: Núcleo de Estudos, Pesquisas e Projetos de Reforma Agrária
DATALUTA: Banco de Dados da Luta Pela Terra
Coordinator: Bernardo Mançano Fernandes

FCT/Unesp - Campus de Presidente Prudente

Cartomatics software*Software* **de Cartomática:** Philcarto
GIS software: SPRING
Base map adapted from: IBGE/INPE - 2001

March 2006

▬▬ MST territorialization through land occupations constitutes a process of peasant confrontation, resistance, and class formation.[17] During its early years, MST struggles were spearheaded mostly by landless peasants, along with squatters and tenant farmers resisting land evictions. In the following period, a large number of farm workers began to join the movement to access their own farm plot and thus escape precarious labor and living conditions. Starting in the 1990s, the MST began to recruit members from urban shantytowns.[18] All these struggles promoted the resocialization of workers who had never had land. Various sources of motivation helped propel this process, among them: the quest to meet basic subsistence needs; the pursuit of material advantage; feelings of indignation and pride; political consciousness; a sense of peasant identity and moral economy of the land; and a drive to overcome existing obstacles forged through the movement's collective dynamics.

Aside from being a territorial struggle, the fight for land is also a family struggle, since it generally engages all family members in various activities. Even in situations where only some family members take part in an actual land occupation, the rest of the family is usually actively involved in supporting those who are absorbed by the mobilization. In each land occupation, the participating landless families set up coordination councils and task teams responsible for securing food supplies, ensuring access to health and education for the youth and children, handling public relations and negotiations, and motivating movement participants. In essence, MST struggles are indistinguishable from its social organization.

Land occupations can be pursued through two main strategies. In some cases, the MST mobilizes to obtain a specific large-landed estate. After settling as many landless families as possible, those unable to obtain a farm plot go on to occupy and struggle for another area. Under this logic, families mobilize to try to capture a particular ranch or plantation. In other situations, several land occupations can be carried out simultaneously with the goal of settling all of the families involved. These multiple, mass-scale occupations can lead to the creation of various new settlements. This second approach has strengthened efforts to territorialize the MST, by transforming its land occupations into a continuous struggle for land. Families who receive a farm plot are replaced by new landless peasants who join the families already engaged in the struggle. These mass occupations cluster families together from various municipalities and even neighboring states, thus superseding formal territorial boundaries.

Land occupations can be implemented in many different ways. Some times, the peasants will occupy a small part of a rural estate, set up a landless camp, and negotiate over their claim to the entire area with state authorities. In other cases, they occupy a large ranch or plantation, divide it into family plots, and start to cultivate the land individually. In yet other situations, peasants have opted to grow their own food collectively within the occupied estate.[19] Though usually well-planned, land occupations are always riddled with uncertainty and risk, given the diverse and dynamic contexts in which they take place. Over the years, the MST has developed a rich tactical repertoire for handling these mobilizations. Still, each new land occupation has its own peculiarities and can present fresh challenges.[20]

Since its early days, the MST has combined various forms of struggle. In addition to land occupations, the movement conducts long-distance marches and hunger strikes, occupies public buildings, sets up road blockades, and carries out demonstrations, usually in front of government offices or state-owned banks. These protests help energize the struggle and improve the movement's negotiating power vis-à-vis the state. In the MST's view, land mobilizations are a heterogeneous popular struggle, forged through praxis.

MST praxis begins by organizing at the grassroots level. This is set in motion through the creation of family clusters, which are then linked to other family groups who agree to take part in the same landless camp. The struggles that led to the movement's formation created a generation of young activists who helped extend its grassroots work to other parts of the country. Organizing the poor, creating landless camps, and occupying large rural estates generate spaces for political socialization. In these face-to-face encounters amid the land struggle, peasants have the opportunity to exchange life experiences, sharpen a sense of awareness of their status as dispossessed and exploited rural workers, and develop an identity as landless peasants. These moments allow them to review their own life history and condition, reflect on the balance of social and political forces affecting their struggle, and establish various networks and alliances. The political consciousness raised through this process has shaped and galvanized various generations of MST activists who have played a crucial role in sustaining the movement since the early 1980s. These multiple spaces for political socialization, then, have inspired the landless to take action and gain awareness of their citizenship rights, and fortified their collective efforts to overcome poverty.

Adding to all this, the struggle for land in Brazil needs to be understood in the context of recurrent problems of rural violence, human rights violations, and impunity. The use of violence against peasants in this country has a long-standing history. The CPT, as Ivo Poletto explains, was the first organization to systematically record this violence and the widespread impunity related to crimes committed against rural workers (see chap. 4, this volume). Table 5.1 reveals that between 1988 and 2005, 903 people were assassinated over rural conflicts in Brazil. Fewer than ten of the landlords responsible for hiring the killers have been put on trial. Still, despite continuing death threats and assassination attempts, land struggles have persisted throughout Brazil. While violent acts against rural workers involved in land and labor disputes have occurred in all

Map 5.6. Assassinations of rural workers in Brazil, 1988–2005: Number of murders registered per state

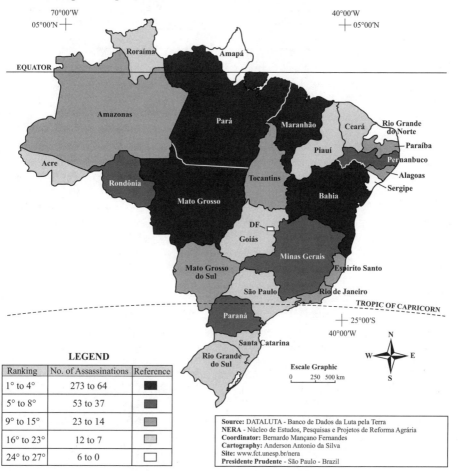

LEGEND

Ranking	No. of Assassinations	Reference
1° to 4°	273 to 64	
5° to 8°	53 to 37	
9° to 15°	23 to 14	
16° to 23°	12 to 7	
24° to 27°	6 to 0	

Source: DATALUTA - Banco de Dados da Luta pela Terra
NERA - Núcleo de Estudos, Pesquisas e Projetos de Reforma Agrária
Coordinator: Bernardo Mançano Fernandes
Cartography: Anderson Antonio da Silva
Site: www.fct.unesp.br/nera
Presidente Prudente - São Paulo - Brazil

Rank	State	No. Deaths	Rank	State	No. Deaths
1°	PA	273	15°	ES	14
2°	MA	72	16°	GO	12
3°	MT	68	17°	AC	11
4°	BA	64	18°	PI	11
5°	PE	53	19°	SP	10
6°	PR	43	20°	SC	9
7°	RO	37	21°	RR	8
8°	MG	37	22°	RS	8
9°	AM	23	23°	CE	7
10°	TO	23	24°	AP	6
11°	RJ	19	25°	RN	3
12°	PB	18	26°	SE	3
13°	AL	16	27°	DF	0
14°	MS	16	–	N.I*	39

*Assassinations in unidentified places

Table 5.1. Rural violence in Brazil:

Number of assassinations, attempted murders, and death threats, 1988–2005

Region and state	Assassinations No.	Assassinations %	Murder attempts No.	Murder attempts %	Death threats No.	Death threats %
North	**361**	**42.2**	**22.3**	**25.7**	**1,197**	**41.0**
Acre	11	1.2	19	2.2	63	2.2
Amazonas	23	2.5	12	1.4	140	4.8
Amapá	6	0.7	0	0	12	0.4
Pará	273	30.2	147	17.0	756	25.9
Rondônia	37	4.1	21	2.4	49	1.7
Roraima	8	0.9	8	0.9	36	1.2
Tocantins	23	2.5	16	1.8	141	4.8
Northeast	**247**	**27.4**	**345**	**39.8**	**1,085**	**37.2**
Alagoas	16	1.8	17	2.0	30	1.0
Bahia	64	7.1	70	8.1	179	6.1
Ceará	7	0.8	31	3.6	39	1.3
Maranhão	72	8.0	74	8.5	421	14.4
Paraiba	18	2.0	58	6.7	82	2.8
Pernambuco	53	5.9	60	6.9	115	3.9
Piauí	11	1.2	32	3.7	187	6.4
Rio Grande do Norte	3	0.3	1	0.1	3	0.1
Sergipe	3	0.3	2	0.2	29	1.0
Midwest	**96**	**10.6**	**96**	**11.1**	**241**	**8.3**
Distrito Federal	0	0	1	0.1	1	0.0
Goiás	12	1.3	13	1.5	26	0.9
Mato Grosso	68	7.5	56	6.5	190	6.5
Mato Grosso de Sul	16	1.8	26	3.0	24	0.8
Southeast	**80**	**8.9**	**110**	**12.7**	**175**	**6.0**
Espírito Santo	14	1.6	2	0.2	36	1.2
Minas Gerais	37	4.1	61	7.0	81	2.8
Rio de Janeiro	19	2.1	21	2.4	34	1.2
São Paulo	10	1.1	26	3.0	25	0.9
South	**60**	**6.6**	**60**	**6.9**	**152**	**5.2**
Paraná	43	4.8	51	5.9	119	4.1
Santa Catarina	8	0.9	5	0.6	17	0.6
Rio Grande do Sul	9	1.0	4	0.5	16	0.5
*Other**	*39*	*4.3*	*33*	*3.8*	*67*	*2.3*
Brazil	**903**	**100.0**	**867**	**100.0**	**2,918**	**100.0**

Source: CPT, National Secretariat, Documentation Sector (2006).

Note: *"Other" refers to people victimized in an unidentified place.

Table 5.2. MST organizational structure

Representational arenas	Sectors and task teams
National Congress	National Secretariat
National Meeting	State Secretariats
National Coordination Council	Regional Secretariats
National Board	Mass Front Sector
State Meeting	Political Education Sector
State Coordination Council	Education Sector
State Board	Production, Cooperation and Environment Sector
Regional Coordination Council	Communications Sector
Settlement Coordination Council	Finances Sector
Landless Camp Coordination Council	Projects Sector
Local Nuclei	Human Rights Sector
	International Relations Collective
	Health Sector
	Gender Sector
	Culture Sector
	Youth Collective

Formal associations
National Association for Agricultural Cooperation (ANCA)
Confederation of Agrarian Reform Cooperatives of Brazil, Ltd. (CONCRAB)
Technical Institute for Training and Research in Agrarian Reform (ITERRA)
Florestan Fernandes National School (ENFF)

parts of the country, they have been particularly intense in the Amazon region, including the states of Mato Grosso and Maranhão, and a handful of northeastern states (see map 5.6).

MST Organizational Structure and Identity

The MST's institutionalization helped sharpen its organizational structure, which includes three interactive domains, its: (1) representational arena, (2) sectors and task teams, and (3) formal organizations (see table 5.2). The first two spheres came about as a result of extensive reflection over the models of organization adopted by previous peasant movements.[21] Together, they embody the movement's multidimensionality and underscore the variegated spheres for collective decision making that have been vital to the MST's development and struggle. The third domain encompasses various associations that are formally registered, and thus able to operate bank accounts, establish legal contracts, and channel funds for different development projects.

The MST's representational arenas include various instances and levels of participation, from the local nuclei to different coordination councils, boards, meetings, and the National Congress. One level elects or appoints representatives to the next tier. The entry point to this process is the local nuclei made up of families in the landless camps and agricultural settlements. Each of these communities elects their coordination council, which then selects its regional coordination council, which appoints its representatives to the state coordination council, which in turn selects its delegates to the national coordination council. These state and national coordination councils elect their own boards to manage various affairs. Day-to-day decisions within the MST are made in its local nuclei, coordination councils, and boards.

The movement sets its basic policies and priorities at its National Meetings and National Congress. National Meetings are held every two years. Local, regional, and state meetings are held annually. The National Congress is generally held every five years. These MST gatherings provide a venue for sharing ideas and experiences, planning its activities, and making decisions on various matters, while offering a space for symbolic commemorations, festive celebrations, and the promotion of peasant culture.

Members engaged in MST activities can participate in its various decision-making arenas and deliberate on the initiatives to be carried out by the movement's sectors and secretariats. These sectors and secretariats provide an administrative and executive conduit for the implementation of development projects in the landless camps and settlements. The sectors operate at different levels. The Education Sector, for example, is organized at the level of local encampments and settlements, as well as at the regional, state, and national levels. At each tier, the participants in this sector collaborate with their counterpart on the coordination councils, secretariats, and boards, in order to pursue policies that benefit MST members.

The movement's sectors and formal associations intersect its organizational structure. For instance, the Culture Sector involves people from other sectors, along with its own members, notably the musicians and organizers of the symbolic rituals and commemorative gatherings—known in MST circles as místicas (moments of mystique)—that help inspire all movement meetings. In a similar fashion, the International Relations Collective is supported by members from other sectors and representational arenas, especially from the National Coordination Council. Those involved in the formal associations collaborate regularly with various sectors to help set up development projects dealing with agriculture, livestock, education, health, and infrastructure for the settlements.

The National Association for Agricultural Cooperation (ANCA), the Confederation of Agrarian Reform Cooperatives of Brazil (CONCRAB), the Technical Institute for Training and Research in Agrarian Reform (ITERRA), and the Florestan Fernandes National School (ENFF), were established to assist the MST's development policies. These associations allow the movement to pursue agricultural research and policies supportive of peasant farming, grounded on an agro-ecological model for rural development. By combining scientific research, political education, and technical training, the movement has helped boost analytic capacity and practical skills among movement activists. All these activities have furthered the MST's recognition as one of the best organized popular movements in Latin America.

The MST's organizational structure is multifaceted, plural, and hybrid. It is both formal and informal in character, and offers an amalgam of old and new patterns of grassroots association. Its breadth has enabled the movement to address a wide range of issues, dealing with the social, economic, cultural, environmental, and political dimensions of its struggle. The MST's defining trait is not embedded in its structure, but rather in its movement, that is, its versatility and flexibility. Its multidimensional and adaptable character has allowed it to be simultaneously present in different political arenas and facilitated its efforts to create new spaces for action. This multifaceted structure, with various levels of collective decision making, has also helped protect the MST, by making it more difficult for hostile forces to co-opt, control, or repress the movement.

This multidimensionality has strengthened the movement's ability to organize, but has also created enormous challenges. One of the MST's guiding principles has been the struggle against the domination of large landholders and powerful business corporations. In doing so, the movement has had to cope with the challenge of trying to experiment with new ways of overcoming the disaggregate nature of family farm labor, while striving not to reproduce capitalist relations among its settlers. This oppositional principle has been a cornerstone of the movement's political identity. It explains why the MST is admired and hated in different political and intellectual circles.[22] It also provides a framework for interpreting the movement's ebbs and flows.

Over the years, the MST has forged a strong sense of identity. The movement has cultivated this through the use and display of various symbols, including its red flag, red cap, slogans, and anthem. These symbols provide an indication of people's organic attachment to the movement and are visibly present at its meetings, schools, cooperatives, land mobilizations, and settlements.[23] They are a hallmark of the MST's territorial identity.

The slogans developed by the movement have played an important role in framing its struggle and shaping its political culture. These popular phrases have resulted from deliberations at the movement's state and national meetings. New phrases have emerged in response to different political scenarios and MST strategies. The main slogans used by the movement since its early years can be found in table 5.3. These slogans convey the concerns of a peasant struggle carried out amid varying political junctures—notably, the disenchantment with Sarney's 1985 agrarian reform plan; the need to occupy and conquer land,

Table 5.3. MST slogans: A chronology

Year	Origin	Slogan
1979	Catholic Church Campaign for Agrarian Reform	Land for those who toil on it
1984	First National Meeting	Land is not handed out, but conquered
1985	First National Congress	Without agrarian reform, there is no democracy Occupation is the only solution
1990	Second National Congress	Occupy, resist, produce
1995	Third National Congress	Agrarian reform: A struggle for all
2000	Fourth National Congress	For a Brazil without *latifúndio*
2007	Fifth National Congress	Agrarian reform: For social justice and popular sovereignty

and resist eviction orders; and bring the country's large landholding system to an end. They also acknowledge of the breadth of the MST's fight for agrarian reform and underscore its vital impact for Brazil's democratic development.

MST symbols—its slogans, flag, songs, crosses, farming tools, food produced in its communities, books, and reference to historic leaders of other popular struggles—are part and parcel of its language of political resistance; a source of counter-hegemonic discourse to Brazil's status quo. The families linked to the movement draw on these symbols to bolster their peasant identity and culture, and do so by taking part of MST mobilizations, festive gatherings, and meetings. Recognizing the importance of this symbolic language and the emotional power it holds, the MST formed a collective within the Culture Sector to promote the movement's values and sense of mística. The development of the MST's strong identity has been intimately related to its territorialization process and the consolidation of its organizational structure.[24]

MST Globalization: La Via Campesina, 1996 and Onward

The MST's development was strengthened after the mid-1990s with its involvement in the creation of a global peasant movement. During the 1990s, agribusiness firms began to expand rapidly in various parts of the world, threatening peasant territories and sources of livelihood. In the early part of that decade the MST started to forge closer relations with peasant movements in Latin America, and subsequently other continents. In 1996 it joined La Via Campesina, a network of peasant associations created in 1993, which by 2008 had grown to include 168 organizations from sixty-nine countries in Asia, Africa, the Americas, and Europe.[25] La Via Campesina's main space for political deliberation and decision making is its International Conference. Its governing structure also includes an international coordinating committee, various political committees, and an international secretariat. The political committees are organized around five thematic clusters: food sovereignty and international commerce; agrarian reform and rural development; gender and human rights; sustainable peasant agriculture; and biodiversity and genetic resources. Each of these committees is responsible for planning global campaigns and peasant mobilizations in various parts of the world, while participating in debates and protest activities at different international forums and meetings.

The formation of La Via Campesina has strengthened peasant movements worldwide by fostering a transnational network of peasant activists and encouraging their mobilization through global struggles. The MST hosted the Fourth International Conference of La Via Campesina in São Paulo, in June 2004. Within Brazil, members of La Via Campesina include the MST, the Small Farmers' Movement (MPA), the Movement of People Affected by Dams (MAB), the Peasant Women's Movement (MMC), the CPT, and the Catholic Church's Rural Youth Pastoral (PJR).[26]

La Via Campesina champions the idea of "food sovereignty" as a right of all peoples and their countries. Food sovereignty prioritizes local food production and consumption. It gives countries the right to protect local farmers from cheap imports and control production. La Via Campesina advocates for agricultural trade policies rooted in principles of solidarity and international governmental agreements aimed at curbing the power of corporate agribusiness. As such, La Via Campesina has strongly opposed the World Trade Organization's (WTO) neoliberal policies regarding international agricultural commerce.

In 1996, La Via Campesina launched a global campaign for agrarian reform that mobilized various peasant movements and NGOs, particularly in Latin America, and gained the attention of several governments and international organizations. This campaign strengthened global resistance to the World Bank's market-based programs for land distribution. La Via Campesina upholds a rural development model based on family farms and agro-ecological practices that seek to guarantee biodiversity and protect genetic resources.

In addition, La Via Campesina has taken an active role in the protests carried out during the WTO meetings in Geneva (1998), Seattle (1999), Cancun (2003), and Hong Kong (2005) to insist that the WTO remove agricultural products from its trade negotiations. La Via Campesina has introduced various innovative tactics, such as holding simultaneous peasant mobilizations in various cities across the world. This transnational advocacy network has emboldened peasant resistance to rural policies that favor corporate agriculture. In the process, La Via Campesina has gained recognition as a leading spokesperson for peasant interests in various national and international policy arenas.

Agribusiness, the Lula Government, and Prospects
for Agrarian Reform in Brazil

Brazil and the world have undergone substantial changes since the MST's formation in the early 1980s. The neoliberal policies adopted in Brazil during the 1990s have had a significant effect on the country. These led to the privatization of a large number of state enterprises, the deregulation of various sectors of the economy, and the elimination of many labor rights, all of which have bolstered the nation's structural unemployment. These changes weakened Brazil's trade union and peasant movements and had a strong effect on the PT's political positions.[27] The PT's decision to build a broad coalition of left- and right-wing political forces to elect Luís Inácio Lula da Silva as president in 2002 was undoubtedly shaped by this context.

New trends in rural development have also reconfigured Brazil's agrarian debate. In the early 1990s, the main obstacle to land reform and peasant agriculture began to shift from the old latifúndio system to the new agribusiness complex. To undermine the popular struggle for land, agribusiness supporters instituted a market-based land reform program. This initiative sought to depoliticize and demobilize the struggle for agrarian reform by establishing market mechanisms for land adjudications, an arena in which the power and interests of agribusiness firms and landlords would clearly prevail.

Land occupations undercut agribusiness' logic of capital accumulation and domination. To counter these threats, Brazil's agrarian elite and its allies have invested considerable efforts to criminalize peasant land struggles through a variety of legal measures. The rural elite's interest in commoditizing land reform is explained by the fact that it allows privileged actors the ability to control and restrict the ways in which peasants can obtain a farm plot. From the standpoint of agribusiness, land should only be accessible to those who abide by market rules and are able to purchase it from willing sellers. This logic would ensure land availability to large commercial farmers interested in maximizing profits.

Agribusiness supporters have sought to demonize land occupations through their substantial influence on Brazil's main news outlets. Moreover, it has engaged the nation's legal system to curb landless mobilizations. Agribusiness interests have also sought to shore up their public image and convince small farmers to collaborate with them by sponsoring land credit and/or land lease programs.

The ascent of neoliberal policies and corporate agriculture in Brazil during the 1990s ushered in theoretical arguments favoring the integration of peasant farmers with agribusiness firms. This school of thought, known as the "agrarian capitalism paradigm," championed public policies geared toward assimilating a segment of the peasantry into prevailing market arrangements, and claimed these measures would resolve the country's agrarian problem.[28] These views were countered by the "agrarian question paradigm," which highlighted the unequal and contradictory features of rural capitalist development. In societies as starkly asymmetrical as Brazil's, it argued, this development model actually hindered efforts to resolve its main agrarian problems.[29]

The agrarian capitalism paradigm had a perceptible impact on the academic and public debate over Brazil's rural problems. Aside from creating several new euphemisms—such as substituting "family agriculture" for "peasant agriculture" and "agribusiness" for "capitalist agriculture"—it contributed to a linear understanding of agricultural development. Moreover, it facilitated the formation of new rural groups, known as "family agriculture" associations, such as the Southern Federation of Family Agricultural Workers (FETRAFSUL), linked to Brazil's main labor confederation, CUT.

Political forces on both the Left and Right found reassurance in the idea that the nation's agrarian question could be resolved through public policies supporting market mechanisms for land adjudication, and peasant integration with agribusiness firms. At the same time, Brazil's print and broadcast news media gave ample coverage to intellectuals who advocated such ideas. Soon, these arguments became predominant among journalists, scholars, and politicians, including several PT leaders. Brazil's agrarian problem, in their view, could not be resolved in a capitalist society, and since there were no alternatives to this, the problem had become essentially obsolete.

These developments explain the significant changes that took place in the PT's land reform program between 1989 and 2002. In its 2002 election proposal the PT failed to mention the number of families that would benefit from agrarian reform policies and suppressed its historic critique of the country's latifúndio system and high land concentration.[30] The PT had clearly toned down its earlier discourse, offering a conciliatory, developmentalist approach to resolving the nation's problems. Adding to this, the Lula government decided to maintain the market-based land reform program established under Cardoso and incorporate various policies designed to assimilate family agriculture into the agribusiness development strategy. All of these elements were highly indicative of the PT's major turnabout on these issues.

Following Lula's election, the nation's main media outlets—TV Globo, the newspapers *O Estado de São Paulo, Folha de São Paulo, Jornal O Globo,* and *Jornal do Brasil,* along with *Veja* and other weekly magazines—played a discernible role in keeping the government's rural policies aligned with the agrarian capitalism paradigm. These news outlets, for the most part, obscured the grim realities of the Brazilian countryside: its stark and rising inequities, extensive poverty, and growing numbers of peasants and native peoples who had lost their land in recent years. Moreover, they mostly ignored the huge number of landless families camped at the side of the nation's highways or in large rural estates. Their reports on the precarious conditions of land reform settlements set up under the Cardoso administration rarely, if ever, included any attempts to understand the political factors that led to this situation. Adding to this, its portrayal of the nation's rural conflicts was largely decontextualized, with little to no reference as to their root causes. Instead, mainstream news media repeatedly found ways to blame peasant movements, particularly the MST, for the predicaments it decided to expose. These depictions and omissions in the nation's main news sources have played an influential role in shaping public opinion, including the ideas of many politicians and intellectuals. In doing so, they successfully framed the main problem in terms of the rural conflict itself, while overlooking the actual causes driving this dispute.

President Lula's election enabled peasant movements to propose candidates for second-tier positions within his administration. The MST and the CPT influenced the appointments of various INCRA officials, while CONTAG and FETRAF-SUL carried greater weight in the selection of top personnel at the Ministry of Agrarian Development (MDA). The Lula government reinstated the educational and technical assistance programs for land reform settlers cancelled during Cardoso's second presidency. It also instituted new farm credit and infrastructure development programs designed to uplift rural settlements largely abandoned by the Cardoso government. In mid-2003, under pressure from the MST and other Via Campesina movements, the MDA entrusted Plínio de Arruda Sampaio to coordinate preparations for Brazil's Second National Agrarian Reform Plan. The proposal developed by Sampaio and a team of specialists called for the settlement of one million families over a five-year period.[31] The Lula government, however, decided not to adopt this plan. It feared the initiative would trigger a confrontation with the agrarian elite and its powerful congressional caucus, and elicit hard-hitting attacks from the nation's main news outlets and other agribusiness supporters. In fact, a majority of the PT politicians appointed to the MDA sympathized with the agrarian capitalism paradigm. As such, they shared the PT's growing disposition to keep to the agrarian question under social control rather than address its root causes.

In November 2003, the minister of Agrarian Development, Miguel Rossetto, obtained President Lula's approval for an alternative, far more modest, agrarian reform plan. Rossetto's proposal sought to settle 400,000 landless families by 2006, instead of the 600,000 suggested by the Sampaio team. It also promised to settle an additional 150,000 families in 2007, much less than the 400,000 families offered in Sampaio's plan. Rossetto's proposal also pledged to provide a farm plot to another 130,000 families through a land credit program rejected by Sampaio's team, which viewed "market-based land reform" as having a spurious impact on the nation's agrarian structure. Sampaio's proposal used INCRA's land registry to estimate the volume of land available for redistribution at 310 million hectares. The alternative, official plan, however, was based on substantially lower figures. The two proposals, however, agreed on the importance of treating agrarian reform as a process of territorial development, geared toward improving the quality of life in all new land reform settlements.[32]

As these developments were taking place, the agrarian elite made certain that its nominees would head all the main posts of the far more powerful Ministry of Agriculture, and ensure the continuity of its pro-agribusiness policies initiated under the military regime. Large landholders reacted vigorously to the sharp increase in land mobilizations under Lula's first term, holding countermarches to oppose land expropriations, while garnering sympathetic coverage from the nation's main press outlets. The Supreme Court's decision to annul President Lula's first land expropriation—an unproductive estate of over 13,000 hectares in São Gabriel, Rio Grande do Sul—had a strong symbolic impact. The landed elite also stepped up its use of violence, prompting a large increase in the number of assassinations of peasant activists.[33]

Lula's land reform program focused largely on the number of beneficiary families, rather than the areas selected for these settlements. As noted previously in figure 5.1, the largest number of families settled between 1988 and 2006 took place in 2005. In fact, the average number of families settled per year under Lula's first government—63,000 families—was higher than Cardoso's yearly average of 57,000 families. Between 2003 and 2006 the Lula government settled 252,019 families.[34] On closer inspection, though, these figures reveal important limitations to Lula's reform program, since the bulk of land distribution took place in national parks and extractive reserves in the Amazon region.

In order to meet Lula's land reform goals, INCRA began to settle a substantial portion of the landless families on public lands, including existing land reform settlements. This practice undercut the redistributive character of Lula's agrarian program. Substandard land and agricultural policies for peasant farmers— upheld by all Brazilian governments, including the Lula administration—have compelled many settler families to leave their farm plot, and in doing so make the way for new ones. Rather than resolve the core problems at stake, this process merely perpetuates them.

Agribusiness' rapid territorialization since the 1990s has deterritorialized peasant agriculture. From 1992 to 2003, the area controlled by corporate agriculture grew by fifty-two million hectares, while the area under family farms increased by thirty-seven million hectares, thanks to the twenty-five million hectares expropriated for agrarian reform.[35] This situation has aggravated peasant impoverishment and structural unemployment, deepening rural inequities and leaving landless cultivators with little choice but to occupy land in order to preserve their peasant lifestyle.

Brazil's land reform policies have not altered the nation's agrarian structure in any substantial way. Rather, they have simply reduced the rate of land concentration in the hands of agribusiness farmers. Without the hundreds of land occupations carried out to pressure the state to redistribute land, the properties linked to agribusiness farming would have increased by seventy-seven million hectares between 1992 and 2003, while family farms would have grown by only twelve million hectares. Land concentration, in other words, would have been much higher. The average annual expansion of agribusiness farms would have jumped from 4.7 to 6.5 million hectares, while the growth rate for peasant farms would have dropped from 3.4 to 1.1 million hectares. In the absence of land reform, the territorialization of corporate agriculture would have been five times larger than that of family farms. With land reform, this territorial expansion only doubled the rate of family farm growth.[36] In sum, Brazil's agrarian reform has merely reduced the pace of, instead of reversing, the country's pattern of land accumulation and disparity. Such trends were at the core of Brazil's agrarian question in the first decade of the twenty-first century.

Table 5.4. Peasant organizations involved in land struggles (number of groups by state, 2000–6)

Region and state	No. of groups	Region and state	No. of groups
North	15	**Northeast**	21
Acre (AC)	2	Alagoas (AL)	5
Amapá (AP)	1	Bahia (BA)	6
Amazonas (AM)	1	Ceará (CE)	3
Pará (PA)	7	Maranhão (MA)	2
Rondônia (RO)	5	Paraiba (PB)	1
Roraima (RR)	2	Pernambuco (PE)	13
Tocantins (TO)	4	Piauí (PI)	4
		Rio Grande do Norte (RN)	4
Midwest	17	Sergipe (SE)	1
Distrito Federal (DF)	3		
Goiás (GO)	7	**Southeast**	40
Mato Groso (MT)	7	Espírito Santo (ES)	3
Mato Grosso do Sul (MS)	7	Minas Gerais (MG)	16
		Rio de Janerio (RJ)	4
South	19	São Paulo (SP)	25
Paraná (PR)	14		
Rio Grande do Sul (RS)	6		
Santa Catarina (SC)	2	**Brazil**	86

Source: DATALUTA (2007a).

Notes: Total for regions and Brazil exclude all double-counting of the same group. Of these 86 peasant associations, sixty-two were active in just one state. Only fourteen organizations were engaged in land mobilizations in more than two states. This table does not include informal groups of peasant squatters, found mostly in the Brazilian north.

▇▇▇ This chapter has shed light on a lesser known quality of Brazil's peasantry: its vital role in the struggle for its own survival, and the impact this force has had on improving the quality of life of hundreds of thousands of peasant families. The Brazilian state did not spearhead these reforms. Instead it followed consistently on the coattails of peasant mobilizations. This insight allows us to draw two major conclusions. One underscores the crucial importance of peasant movements to this reform process, as it recognizes their limitations given the power imbalance with their main nemesis: the agribusiness complex. The other lesson highlights the discernable clout exerted by these agro-capitalist forces over the Brazilian state and the nation's model of development.

This account of the MST's territorialization from the late 1970s to the mid-2000s reveals that—despite unprecedented levels of popular mobilization and wide recognition as the best-organized peasant movement in the nation's history—this popular organization has not been able to change Brazil's agrarian structure. All this substantiates the complex and indeterminate nature of Brazil's agrarian question. The territorialization process driven by both peasant movements and agribusiness forces are creating new conflicts that will refashion the agrarian question in the years to come. The new internationalized context, shaped by global agribusiness corporations and transnational peasant networks and their allies, will become a critical reference for understanding the new conflicts to arise in the cities and countryside of Brazil.

Table 5.5. Main peasant organizations engaged in land struggles, 2000–6

Name	Acronym	No. states	Federal states
		Territorial presence	
Landless Rural Workers Movement (*Movimento dos Trabalbadores Rurais Sem Terra*)	MST	24	AL, BA, CE, DF, ES, GO, MA, MG, MS, MT, PA, PB, PE, PI, PR, RJ, RN, RO, RR, RS, SC, SE, SP, TO
National Confederation of Agricultural Workers (*Confederação Nacional dos Trabalhadores da Agricultura*)	CONTAG	17	AC, BA, CE, DF, ES, GO, MA, MG, MS, MT, PA, PE, PI, PR, RJ, RN, TO
Organization of Workers in the Countryside (*Organização dos Trabalhadores no Campo*)	OTC	9	CE, GO, MG, PA, PR, RO, RS, SP, TO
Land, Work and Freedom Movement (*Movimento Terra Trabalho e Liberdade*)	MTL	7	AL, BA, GO, MG, PB, PE, RJ
Liberation of the Landless Movement (*Movimento de Libertação dos Sem-Terra*)	MLST	6	AL, GO, MG, PE, RN, SP

Notes

The author would like to thank Miguel Carter for his detailed review and valuable comments in the preparation of this text. Translated from the Portuguese by Miguel Carter.

1. Statistics are from DATALUTA (2008).
2. For a detailed analysis of the military regime's development plans, see Fernandes (1996a).
3. This chapter builds on extensive fieldwork carried out between 1996 and 1998, and participation in various activities linked to the MST and Via Campesina. It also draws on a considerable review of the relevant literature; see Fernandes (2000).
4. On the MST's origins, see Fernandes (2000) and Carter (2002).
5. For a brief history of rural social movements in the 1950s and 1960s, see Medeiros (chap. 3, this volume). Further historical detail on the Peasant Leagues; ULTAB, tied to the Brazilian Communist Party (PCB); and MASTER, a landless movement in Rio Grande do Sul influenced by the Brazilian Labor Party (PTB), can be found in Fernandes (2000); Medeiros (1989); and Stédile and Fernandes (1999).
6. The MST's early decision to maintain close linkages between its economic and political struggles became a hallmark of its identity. Because of this, it has been common to find land reform settlers actively engaged in organizing landless camps and supporting land occupations. This principle, no doubt, facilitated the MST's territorialization.
7. Insights on the various mechanisms used to thwart the enactment of Brazil's agrarian laws can be found in Delgado (chap. 2, this volume) and Meszaros (chap. 14, this volume).
8. This was a difficult moment in the MST's formation. Its main allies came from the ranks of rural and urban trade unions, churches, progressive political parties, and NGOs. In some states, the MST's insistence on its organizational autonomy and right to make its own decisions strained relations with its allies. The bulk of these disagreements dissipated over time. In effect, the movement's consolidation facilitated the renewed collaboration with various partners in the struggle for agrarian reform.
9. DATALUTA statistics on land occupations are drawn from five sources: the CPT and the National Agrarian Ombudsman's Office, both of which record data at the national level. It also includes state-level data produced by the following research groups: the Center for Agrarian Reform Studies, Research and Projects, for São Paulo; the Agrarian Geography Laboratory, for Minas Gerais; and the Geography Laboratory for Struggles in the Countryside, for Paraná. DATALUTA statistics on land reform are produced with data from INCRA, the São Paulo Land Institute, and the Mato Grosso Land Institute.
10. Cardoso (1991: 10).
11. In Brazil, land occupations have been the main form of peasant access to a farm plot, a point well underscored in Fernandes (2000: 301) and Leite et al. (2004: 43).
12. The criminalization of the landless struggle was spearheaded mostly by conservative judicial activists, aligned with agrarian elite interests, and well inclined to use their legal powers to order the imprisonment of landless leaders and other punitive measures. A clear example of this conservative judicial activism took place in São Paulo's Pontal do Paranapanema region; see Fernandes (1997) and Fernandes, Meneguette, Fagundes, and Leal (2003).
13. Three important institutions created during this process were CONCRAB; the Technical Institute for Training and Research in Agrarian Reform (ITERRA); and the Florestan Fernandes National School. The MST's institutionalization phase is difficult to characterize given its continued development during the 2000s.

14. On the concept of territorialization, see Fernandes (2000, 2005) and Fernandes and Martin (2004).

15. *Grilagem* takes place through the illegal appropriation of public land (*terras devolutas*) and falsification of land titles. These areas are usually subdivided and sold off as land parcels despite the land title's shady origin.

16. This point draws on the author's fieldwork in thirteen Brazilian states in 1998; see Fernandes (2000: 301).

17. As can be seen in figures 5.2 and 5.3, the greater part of Brazil's land occupations between 1988 and 2005 took place in states where capitalist agriculture was most advanced—in areas affected by high rural unemployment due to the mechanization of agriculture.

18. Lima and Fernandes (2001).

19. The decision made by landless peasants to occupy an estate and cultivate its land can be considered a radical act. Though usually carried out without the consent of either government authorities or the landowner, this action can also result from negotiations conducted among the three parties, as they await the formal completion of the land expropriation process.

20. Fernandes (2000: 291–92).

21. Stédile and Fernandes (1999).

22. An illustration of this hatred toward the MST can be found in the writings of Zander Navarro (2002a, 2002b), who served as an advisor to the Cardoso government. Navarro's efforts to demolish the MST, though, through a patchy, nonempirical, and politicized analysis of the movement has had negligible impact in Brazilian academic circles.

23. The movement's organic quality is a political construct and resource. This reflects the degree to which the landless families are linked to the MST. As a rule, the higher the number of participants in its activities and mobilizations, the greater the strength of this attribute.

24. A very useful website on the MST's culture of resistance, prepared by the School of Modern Languages at the University of Nottingham, can be found at http://www.landless-voices.org.

25. On La Via Campesina's formation, see Desmarais (2007, 2009); see also Fernandes and Martin (2004).

26. Further information on the social movements that make up La Via Campesina can be found in Rosa (chap. 15, this volume).

27. For the PT's historical evolution on these positions, see Partido dos Trabalhadores (1998). During the Lula government it was no small irony to observe the PT—the party who had roundly criticized the Cardoso administration for subordinating the nation's interests to the neoliberal global economy—adopt many of Cardoso's policies as their own.

28. For an illustrative text of the agrarian capitalism paradigm, see Abramovay (1992).

29. On the paradigm of the agrarian question, see Fernandes (2001).

30. Partido dos Trabalhadores (2002).

31. The land reform plan proposed by Plínio Arruda Sampaio's team, of which the author was a member, established the goal of 1 million beneficiary families based on the 839,715 families who had registered for a land parcel through the national postal service—through a program sponsored by the Cardoso government—and the 171,288 families living in landless camps across Brazil, in October 2003. Sampaio was a well-known and respected PT leader, who had served as federal deputy, public prose-

cutor, university professor, and consultant to the United Nation's Food and Agriculture Organization, and had led the PT's Agrarian Secretariat. At the end of 2005, Sampaio left the PT to join the new Socialism and Liberty Party (PSOL), created by PT dissidents. Sampaio's plan viewed agrarian reform as a process that should prioritize: (1) territorial development, rather than a policy to appease rural conflicts through the creation of ad hoc and widely scattered rural settlements; (2) land expropriations geared toward reducing agrarian inequality, rather than a market-based land reform; and (3) efforts to strengthen rural settlements through the provision of ample financial support at all stages of their development. In sum, this plan matched the main elements of Carter's definition of a "progressive agrarian reform," offered in the introduction to this volume.

32. The proposal prepared by the Ministry of Agrarian Development and accepted by President Lula was entitled, "Second National Agrarian Reform Plan: Peace, Production and Quality of Life in the Countryside." Further details on the debates surrounding this plan can be found in Branford (chap. 13, this volume).

33. According to the CPT (2004), the number of assassinations over rural conflicts soared by 70% in 2003.

34. Carter and Carvalho (in chap. 9, this volume) offer a different calculus for the number of families settled under Lula's first administration. Their lower figure discounts the families placed in forty-seven extractive reserves created in the Amazon region, between 2003 and 2006.

35. Fernandes (2005).

36. Fernandes (2005).

1. Occupation of the Cuiabá estate, in Sergipe, 1996.
© Sebastião Salgado / Amazonas Images.

2. Occupation of the Giacometi estate, in Paraná, with 12,000 people, 1996.
© Sebastião Salgado / Amazonas Images.

3 and 4. Close to eight hundred landless families march to São Gabriel, Rio Grande do Sul, 2003. Photos courtesy of Leonardo Melgarejo.

5. National March to Brasília. One hundred thousand people took part in the final rally, 1997. Photo courtesy of Douglas Mansur.

6. Over seven hundred landless families occupy the Boqueirão estate, Rio Grande do Sul, 1995. Photo courtesy of CPT Archives.

7. Land pilgrimage with 20,000 people, Natalino's Crossing, Rio Grande do Sul, 1982. Photo courtesy of Zero Hora.

8 *(opposite, top)*. Landless families camped at Natalino's Crossing, Rio Grande do Sul, 1982. Photo courtesy of Zero Hora.

9 *(opposite, bottom)*. Landless camp in Rio Bonito, Paraná, 1996. Photo courtesy of João Ripper.

10 *(above)*. Landless camp with 1,900 families in Viamão, Rio Grande do Sul, 1998. Photo courtesy of Leonardo Melgarejo.

11 and **12.** More than 12,000 people participate in a sixteen-day National March for Agrarian Reform to Brasília, 2005. Photos courtesy of Francisco Rojas.

13 and **14.** Over 1,500 delegates take part in the MST's First National Congress, in Curitiba, Paraná, 1985. Photos courtesy of CPT Archives.

15. Commemorating the movement's cultural diversity at the MST's Fifth National Congress, in Brasília, with 18,000 participants. Photo courtesy of Leonardo Melgarejo.

6 Origins and Consolidation of the MST in Rio Grande do Sul

Evicted from their lands, their homes destroyed, the peasants flocked to the parish house for relief. A Catholic priest let them in. He knew of their suffering. In May 1978, they had been forcibly removed from their farms by a warring band of Kaigang Indians, struggling to recover their indigenous reserve in Brazil's southernmost state, Rio Grande do Sul. Close to 1,100 squatter families lost their homes and crops overnight. Half of these were sent to the Amazon on a government colonization program. Another group was settled near the Uruguayan border. Over 400 landless families remained in the vicinity of Father Arnildo Fritzen's parish, in the village of Ronda Alta.

When the landless families knocked on the priest's door, they had been living in borrowed stables and precarious shacks for almost a year. At the parish house, Father Arnildo and his forty impoverished guests shared simple meals and a modest roof. Over the next few days, they read the Bible, sang, prayed, and reflected on their lives. A passage from the book of Exodus struck them deeply:

> I have seen the misery of my people in Egypt. I have heard their outcry
> against their slave-masters. I have taken heed of their sufferings, and have
> come down to rescue them from the power of Egypt, and to bring them up out
> of that country into a fine broad land; to a land flowing with milk and honey.[1]

Suddenly, amid their meditations, a moment of epiphany dawned upon the group. They realized their suffering was akin to that of the Israelites under the pharaoh's oppression. Like the Hebrew people, they too had to escape from slavery, break their chains of misery, and march to the Promised Land. United, they would have the strength of Moses. An air of excitement took over the austere parish kitchen. Instilled with a new sense of hope, the peasants vowed to help organize their landless kin and struggle for freedom.

A week later, Father Arnildo received a new group of visitors. Four young professionals from Porto Alegre, the state capital, arrived in a Volkswagen bus.

They had heard of Father Arnildo's involvement with a new progressive church network that supported family farmers and were there to engage his support. Prior to this, they had spent several weekends visiting the families who had been forced to leave the Indian reserve. The young men were part of an informal group devoted to the study of agrarian issues. Among the progressive activists was João Pedro Stédile, an energetic economist of peasant origin who would later become the landless movement's most visible leader.

These meetings in May 1979 produced a dynamic team. By July, the priest, peasants, and young professionals had generated a local network that helped organize three different assemblies among the landless families. Drawing on political contacts, they were able to arrange a meeting with the state governor Amaral de Souza, on August 1. During their amiable exchange, one of the peasant representatives asked the governor point-blank: "What if we invade the Sarandi estate?" The area had been expropriated by a progressive state governor in 1961. After the 1964 military coup, part of the estate was subdivided into two government-owned farms—Macali and Brilhante—and rented to wealthy planters through a crony deal. The governor's playful response to the startling question took everyone by surprise: "Why, I'd go with you!" By the end of the meeting, he assured them a land settlement in thirty days.[2]

Five weeks later, with no solution in sight, the landless families made good on their warning. They boarded old trucks and followed Father Arnildo's Volkswagen Beetle to the Promised Land. At 2:30 in the morning they occupied the Macali farm. Unbeknownst to all, on that starlit eve of September 7, 1979, Brazil's National Independence Day, these humble country folk, young activists, and a sympathetic priest had set in motion the organization of Latin America's leading social movement—the Landless Rural Workers Movement (MST).

■■■ Rio Grande do Sul has been a vital state in the national development of the MST. A mere statistical glance, though, would belie this fact. Since the mid-1990s, the largest numbers of people in MST landless camps were in the Brazilian northeast. Moreover, after a quarter of a century of land struggles, less than 2% of Brazil's land reform beneficiaries were located in this southernmost state.[3] A review of the historical record, nonetheless, shows that the MST in Rio Grande do Sul has had a major qualitative impact on the national movement, notably as an incubator of novel strategies and a wellspring of movement activists.

This part of Brazil is where the landless organized their first planned occupation (1979), protest camp (1981), massive land occupation (1985), and long-distance march (1986), among other mobilization tactics. Rio Grande do Sul is also where the MST's newspaper, the *Jornal dos Trabalhadores Rurais Sem Terra* (1981), got started, along with the movement's first encampment school (1982), collective farm (1984), statewide cooperative confederation (1990), teacher training program (1990), labor cooperative to raise funds for the landless struggle (1996), itinerant school to accompany the children during marches and other camp relocations (1997), and organic seed production cooperative (1997). It was in this southern state that the MST first experimented with the idea of a "permanent encampment" (2003), aimed at training shantytown dwellers to become farmers, and organized the movement's first statewide news agency (2005).

A discernible portion of the MST's cadre is of *gaúcho* (natives of Rio Grande do Sul) origin. The movement installed its first national headquarters in Porto Alegre, before moving to São Paulo in 1986, where it continued to staff much of its office with gaúchos. Since the mid-1980s, hundreds of gaúchos have helped extend the MST across Brazil.[4] The movement's leading pedagogues are also gaúchos, as are its main specialists in agricultural cooperatives. The land struggle in Rio Grande do Sul, therefore, is crucial to understanding the MST's capacity for innovation.

This chapter examines the conditions and dynamics that fashioned the landless movement in this southern Brazilian state. It contends that the movement's genesis, survival, and expansion stem from its ability to mobilize through public activism—a form of social conflict grounded on pressure politics and bargaining with state authorities. The chapter's initial review of the concept of public activism is followed by an analytic narrative of the movement's development in this state. This account explains how varying conditions in Rio Grande do Sul shaped the MST's mode of public activism over three distinct historical phases. The conclusion shows how the movement's strategic conduct and resilient ethos affect its ongoing disposition toward public activism.

Public Activism

A common depiction of the MST, propagated by leading Brazilian news outlets and influential scholars, holds that its contentious demeanor stems from its "zealous adherence to a revolutionary ideology." The landless movement, in this view, has "canonized" its orientation toward "collective action" as a result of its "fundamentalist" approach to politics.[5] Over three decades of struggle the MST has undoubtedly forged a combative ethos and self-image. Yet the suggestion that its protest activities are propelled mainly by its strong beliefs greatly oversimplifies the issues at stake. Such accounts typically analyze MST ideas and tactics in a vacuum. In doing so, they underrate the movement's capacity for strategic innovation and overlook the ways in which the circumstances enveloping its struggle influence its actions and dispositions.

This chapter builds on a robust literature in social movement theory to argue that the landless movement's contentious ideas and tactics need to be examined in light of the existing political opportunities, mobilizing resources, and strategic perceptions at any given historical juncture. The chapter's central thesis is premised on this groundwork.[6]

The MST's development in Rio Grande do Sul has been intimately entwined with its capacity to engage in a distinct form of social conflict, defined here as *public activism*. This approach to social struggle is substantially different from that of an armed insurgency, a scattered riot, or what James C. Scott defines as "everyday forms of resistance," to describe informal, discreet, and disguised forms of popular aggression.[7] Unlike these other patterns of social confrontation, the MST's public activism involves an organized, politicized, visible, autonomous, periodic, and nonviolent form of social conflict.[8]

Actions carried out through public activism are geared toward drawing public attention; influencing state policies, through pressure politics, lobbying, and negotiations; and shaping societal ideas, values, and actions. Typically, mobilizations of this kind employ an array of modern repertoires of contention, such as demonstrations, marches, petitions, group meetings, hunger strikes, protest camps, and election campaigns, along with acts of civil disobedience such as sit-ins, road blockades, building takeovers, and organized land occupations.[9] Unlike other approaches to social conflict, public activism's nonviolent thrust makes it essentially compatible with civil society and provides a legitimate democratic vehicle for propelling social change.

Public activism requires certain facilitating conditions, namely, enhanced political opportunities for collective action and substantial access to mobilizing resources. *Political opportunities* refer to the power configurations within a given polity that can enable or disable grassroots participation. These are usually shaped by variables such as regime tolerance, state capacity, elite instability, government disposition, political allies, and public attention, particularly through press coverage. *Mobilizing resources* describes the formal and informal web of human, material, and ideational assets that propel and sustain the collective vehicles used for mobilization. These resources can be generated through external and internal inputs.[10]

Together, enhanced political opportunities and mobilizing resources create a set of incentives that persuade contentious groups to make demands on the state and bargain with public authorities. Moreover, they encourage the development of partnerships with civil and political society groups in order to strengthen these demands and improve negotiations. Under these conditions, social conflict is basically channeled into nonviolent forms of interaction with the state and other societal forces. The prospects for public activism increase when actual and perceived political opportunities and mobilizing resources are relatively high (see figure 6.1).[11]

This chapter traces the development of the MST's public activism over three different phases of the land struggle in Rio Grande do Sul: the origins of the movement (1979–84), followed by a decade of heightened confrontation and

Figure 6.1. Forms of social conflict

		Mobilizing resources	
		Low	High
Political opportunities	High	Scattered riots	Public activism
	Low	Everyday forms of resistance	Armed insurgency

Figure 6.2. Modes of public activism

		Mobilizing resources	
		Low	High
Political opportunities	High	Rowdy confrontation	Sustained critical engagement
	Low	Entreating appeals	Aggressive struggle

struggle for survival (1985–94), and the consolidation of a sustained pattern of mobilization (1995–2006). All three historical periods exhibited a contentious dynamic grounded on the core twin elements of public activism: pressure politics and bargaining with state authorities. Yet each phase also revealed a distinct mode of public activism, as seen in the various dispositions, tempos, and tactics that prevailed in each period. The matrix presented in figure 6.2 shows how these were largely shaped by their surrounding circumstances. This diagram refines the analytic framework developed in figure 6.2 to demonstrate how diverse combinations of political opportunities and mobilizing resources can engender four different types of public activism, characterized by a predominant orientation that inclines groups to establish their contentious claims through entreating appeals, aggressive struggle, rowdy confrontation, or a sustained critical engagement.

Generally speaking, each of the movement's three historical phases was characterized by a different mode of public activism. During the first period (1979–84), landless demands were normally conveyed through "entreating appeals," aimed at garnering broad public sympathy and eliciting charitable responses from church and government leaders. In the second phase (1985–94), the MST began to assert its claims through defiant transgressions of the established order and other manifestations of "aggressive struggle." New, more incisive tactics were forged to overcome obstacles to land distribution, a process that abetted and sharpened the movement's class identity. During the third period (1995–2006), the landless movement exhibited elements of a more stable, mature, yet no less assertive form of interaction with state agencies and relevant civil society forces, defined by a pattern of "sustained critical engagement." This dynamic enabled the MST to adopt a broader agenda for social change and strengthen its organizational capacity.[12] A graphic synthesis of this historical evolution is displayed later in the chapter, in figure 6.5. The following analytic narrative will demonstrate that the MST's public activism—in all three scenarios—was not propelled by "dogmas," but deployed primarily to overcome specific obstacles and pursue concrete demands in the most effective way possible.

The Origins of the MST, 1979–1984

The September 7, 1979, occupation of the Macali estate unleashed a series of land mobilizations in the Ronda Alta region. Soon thereafter, over 240 landless families, organized in two competing groups, occupied the adjacent Brilhante estate. Eighty of these families received a homestead in this area after living for eight months in improvised tents and making repeated trips to Porto Alegre to plead their case before state authorities. In early October 1980, around 100 of the remaining landless families occupied a neighboring ranch, the Annoni estate. This action, though, prompted a swift and violent eviction by the police, who arrested various peasants and two government advisors to the Macali and Brilhante settlers. News of these events prompted a public scandal in Porto Alegre. A month later, with the support of church groups, state legislators opposed to the military regime, labor leaders and human rights activists, several of these families set up a week-long protest camp in front of the Governor's Palace. The governor's decision to quell their appeals through the purchase of a nearby ranch stirred, unwittingly, a climate of anticipation in the Ronda Alta environs.

By the end of 1980, 270 families had obtained a farm plot as a result of the Macali occupation and ensuing land struggles. These events, in the words of local peasants, "cleared the horizon" and "opened the frontier" for the massive mobilization that would reinstate agrarian reform on the nation's public agenda: the landless camp set up at the entrance of the Macali settlement, at a red-earth country road juncture known at Natalino's Crossing.[13]

The MST's formation in Rio Grande do Sul was enabled by the state's suitable conditions for public activism. This was one of the most developed regions in the country at the time, as gauged through a host of indicators, such as state capacity, education, income, industry, transport and communication facilities, and social capital. Intense European migration to the northern half of the state, after the mid-1800s, endowed the area with a strong family farm legacy that fostered an active and resourceful civil society. More specifically, the landless movement's emergence in the Ronda Alta region was spurred by previous land mobilizations in the early 1960s, supported by populist governor

Leonel Brizola, which set an important historical precedent. It was also an up-shot of the accelerated agricultural modernization process that began in the mid-1960s and left many small farmers outside of the land market.[14] Further-more, the military regime's gradual *abertura* (opening) in the late 1970s had im-proved political opportunities for mobilization. The Catholic Church, in turn, offered substantial mobilizing resources, notably through its new generation of progressive bishops, priests, and nuns, inspired by a new theology of liberation and other innovations ushered-in after the Second Vatican Council (1962–65).[15]

The church's Pastoral Land Commission (CPT), in particular, played a key role in the formation of the MST in Rio Grande do Sul. The *gaúcho* branch of the CPT was established in June 1977 by pastoral agents involved in a broader progressive church network that promoted grassroots empowerment through the creation of Bible study groups, known as the Community-Base Churches (CEBs).[16] Although a minority within the church, liberation theology activists wielded significant influence among their religious cohorts, thanks to their solid organizing skills and strong commitment to social justice.

Between 1979 and 1984, conditions in the gaúcho countryside were suitable only for a more modest and restrained form of public activism. Brazil, after all, was still under military rule, while the landless peasants were barely organized and greatly dependent on external mobilizing resources provided by the Cath-olic Church and other civil society groups. Thus, during its early and weakest years, the landless movement regularly couched its demands as "entreating ap-peals" that underscored a deferential attitude toward state authorities and its religious benefactors. As a rule, these petitions framed the *sem terra* (landless peasants) as a group of poor and suffering country folk, in order to elicit broad public sympathy and a charitable response to their quest for land.

This disposition was palpable in the land struggle that started in April 1981 with the formation of a landless camp at Natalino's road crossing. Its mile-and-a-half stretch of precarious straw and plastic-covered huts set up near the village of Ronda Alta sent shock waves across the region. News outlets rushed to cover the unusual story. Even those who had worked surreptitiously with Father Arnildo to get the mobilization started were taken back with the size of the ensuing land rush.[17] By July more than 600 landless families had pitched their tents at the camp. Most were extremely poor. Almost one-third of the family heads were illiterate. Only a handful had completed their elemen-tary education.[18]

The makeshift gathering at Natalino's Crossing evolved rapidly into a well-structured grassroots organization. In less than four months, the peasants at the camp had set up a multilayered, collective decision-making process; car-ried out several activities to raise consciousness among the participants; and invested efforts to forge a common identity as "sem terra" and nurture a sense of *mística* (mystique) within the movement.

The church's progressive network played a pivotal role in fostering these developments and securing resources to sustain the mobilization.[19] The camp drew on the CEBs participatory model of organization to develop a collective decision-making process and various task teams. Movement organizers recognized early on that this collective model would help protect the camp from government efforts to co-opt or coerce its leaders. A stewardship council, elected by all adult participants, was responsible for delegating practical chores to specific task teams that dealt with sanitation facilities, health care, food distribution, the collection of firewood, negotiations with state authorities, and religious worship. All these collective undertakings enabled people to augment their sense of responsibility and disposition to participate in the struggle.

Pastoral agents, notably Father Arnildo and a handful of nuns who worked at the camp, spearheaded the efforts to raise political awareness among the sem terra. For this, they employed several primers prepared by CPT colleagues. Several of these texts matched the peasants' struggle with biblical passages, such as the Exodus story. Others promoted the study of Brazilian social reality and land reform laws. The convergence made between the laws of God and the nation sharpened convictions among the peasants as to the righteousness of their cause. Every late afternoon the landless gathered at the foot of the camp's massive wooden cross to sing, pray, and hold their assembly meetings. These collective rituals offered a subtle yet powerful source of inspiration. As one of the participants described it, "It was in the assemblies, in the prayer meetings that we'd extract strength. Some days we'd be really sad, but after the prayer meetings we'd return to our huts really animated."[20]

Faced with mounting news coverage of Natalino's landless movement, Brazil's conservative military rulers made an early decision to forestall any land redistribution in Rio Grande do Sul. Undercover agents soon infiltrated the camp. At the same time, several government officials made palpable efforts to discredit, demoralize, dissuade, and intimidate the peasants. Despite the government's hostility, the sem terra recognized they had no viable recourse outside the state's legal framework. In a modern setting like Rio Grande do Sul, land redistribution could only be achieved through state intervention. Alternative forms of land struggle, such as squatting and other everyday forms of resistance, prevalent in the Amazon frontier, were simply unavailable in Brazil's southern region.

The Natalino movement's penchant toward public activism was forged in this political context and reinforced by the significant mobilizing resources provided by a solidarity network that included Catholic and Protestant churches, urban and rural trade unions, human rights groups, university students, and opposition party leaders. Their combined strength created a balance of forces that inclined state officials to treat the new landless movement with greater toleration.[21]

All this suggests that public activism was embraced from the very onset as a practical tool, rather than an ideological construct. The prevailing strategic assumption held that only a combination of pressure politics and bargaining could alter the government's policies and contest the dominant landlord interests that lay behind them. Based on this understanding, the Natalino peasants generated twenty-three noteworthy protest gatherings and made no less than eighteen well-publicized trips to Porto Alegre to lobby officials at the Governor's Palace, the State Assembly, and the federal government's land reform bureau, INCRA.

The massive July 25, 1981, rally at Natalino's Crossing, in particular, triggered alarm bells in Brasília. The Porto Alegre press heralded the gathering of over 15,000 people as "the largest demonstration of agricultural workers" in Rio Grande do Sul's history.[22] The event included a religious procession led by the camp's massive wooden cross and a lively roster of speakers, folk musicians, and troubadours. At the closing homily, Dom Tomás Balduíno, bishop of Goiás, delivered a thundering sermon in which he epitomized the Natalino struggle as the rural equivalent of the dramatic labor strikes that roused the metropolitan region of São Paulo, between 1978 and 1980.

Five days after this event, Brasília placed Natalino's Crossing under National Security Rule and dispatched a military force to disband the landless camp. The mission was entrusted to the army's top counterinsurgency specialist, Colonel Sebastião Rodrigues Moura (popularly known as Colonel Curió). Curió had earned fame in the Amazon for defeating a communist guerrilla movement in the early 1970s and imposing order at the world's largest gold rush, the Serra Pelada. Under Curió's command, Natalino's Crossing took on the air of a prison barrack. The military operation restricted access to the area, disrupted the camp's internal organization, and sought to bribe its leaders. Military officers also threatened to remove the sem terra through violent force. Even so, Curió failed to convince most peasants to abandon the camp. The landless movement survived this treacherous moment thanks to its influential allies, internal cohesion, religious mystique, and the deep conviction of its right to fight for land in Rio Grande do Sul.

Curió's departure from Ronda Alta at the end of August made headlines on all of Brazil's main press outlets.[23] The military's high-profile action enabled the Natalino struggle to become a cause célèbre for the country's resurgent civil society and a high point of convergence for those opposed to its authoritarian regime. More importantly, it helped catapult agrarian reform back onto the nation's public agenda.

The camp's final success involved a long drawn-out process. In February 1982, over 20,000 people gathered at Natalino's Crossing for a land pilgrimage organized by the CPT. Six Catholic bishops and 300 priests took part in a procession with the camp's large cross.[24] The following month, in an unprecedented decision, the gaúcho Catholic hierarchy agreed to purchase a nearby farm to establish a safe haven for the sem terra. The transfer to the Nova Ronda Alta camp was a major boost for the landless movement. All remaining 170 families were settled in September 1983, after months of slow-grinding pressure on a newly elected governor, who had promised during his campaign to secure a farm plot for each sem terra family.

Natalino's struggle was a decisive turning point in the genesis of the MST. It handed the budding landless movement its first major political victory, and enshrined its disposition toward public activism. It also served as an incubator for many of its mobilization tactics.

Starting in mid-1982, the Natalino leaders and advisors became actively involved in a CPT-sponsored network of landless people in southern Brazil that would give rise to the MST. Two parishes in Rio Grande do Sul were crucial to this development: Father Arnildo's community in Ronda Alta and the parish of Três Passos, led by two Franciscans, Father Plinio Maldaner and Friar Sergio Görgen. Located in the northeastern corner of the state, the Três Passos church had played a dynamic role in supporting the region's progressive rural trade union movement. In December 1983, these two groups organized the first statewide assembly of the landless movement, at a Catholic seminary near Três Passos, a month before the MST's official formation in Cascavel, Paraná. By this time, activists linked to both CPT parishes were already engaged in a discrete yet intense effort to recruit and organize the groundwork for a new landless surge.

Heightened Confrontation and the Struggle for Survival, 1985–1994

On the night of October 29, 1985, more than 200 trucks, buses, and cars converged from thirty-two different municipal districts in northern Rio Grande do Sul to occupy a mostly idle, 9,200-hectare cattle ranch known as the Annoni estate. More than 6,000 people participated in what was then the largest and most thoroughly planned land occupation in Brazilian history. By morning, they had erected a sprawling village of black tarp tents and organized a security team to prevent police eviction. Drawing on the Natalino experience, the peasants set up an elaborate internal organization: a network of family groups, various task teams, a coordination council, and leadership committee. Everyday life at the encampment was a busy hive of activities and meetings. Next to a patch of dense forest, the landless gathered daily by a big cross for prayers, religious and protest songs, announcements, and hearty words of encouragement from an array of supporters. A vast solidarity network was established to further the landless cause. Shortly after the occupation, the local Catholic bishop and eighty priests showed up to bless the Annoni camp—located just a mile-and-a-half away from Natalino's road crossing.

Approximately 1,250 families obtained a land parcel as a result of the concerted pressure and long-sustained mobilization that followed this occupation. The piecemeal and scattered settlement of all the Annoni families, however, was completed only in 1993.

Conditions for mobilization between 1985 and 1994 proved to be adverse, in spite of the restoration of civilian rule and President José Sarney's plans, announced in May 1985, to carry out a substantial agrarian reform program. In fact, the initial glimmer of hope soon turned into a climate of disappointment. The increasing number of human rights violations in the countryside and the sluggish pace of land distribution, due to the intense opposition of landlord groups, triggered the resignation of progressive government officials responsible for implementing the land reform plan. Sarney's decision to close down INCRA, in October 1987, ended any expectations of goodwill on the part of federal government. Adding to this, the following year, land reform advocates lost key votes in the Constitutional Assembly. As a result, they were obliged to cope with a five-year moratorium on all land expropriations, on account of the legal vacuum established under the new Constitution.[25]

Luis Inácio Lula da Silva's defeat to Fernando Collor de Mello in the 1989 presidential race compounded the movement's feelings of distress. The MST had enthusiastically supported Lula's Workers Party (PT), given its promise to carry out an extensive agrarian reform and implement other progressive policies. Collor's neoliberal administration relegated such policies to the back burner. Its repeated efforts to criminalize MST activities amplified the movement's perceptions of dire threat. Stédile vividly described this period as the movement's "baptism by fire." Adding, "We could have ended there. Had Collor remained for his five-year term and repressed us a bit more, he could have destroyed us."[26]

All these constraints, however, did not stop the MST from shoring up its mobilization resources. During this time, its membership and organizational capacity increased significantly, and expanded into new regions of Rio Grande do Sul and Brazil. From 1985 to 1994, the gaúcho MST carried out 206 mobilizations, including seventy-one land occupations. These struggles forged a new generation of landless activists and led to many tactical innovations. The MST also established various rural cooperatives and set up programs to train its cadre and educate its members. After the mid-1980s, all this took place amid a heightened quest for autonomy, the development of a sharper sense of class identity, and the electoral gravitation toward the PT.[27] These elements, coupled with the unfavorable political climate for land reform, led to a decline in the MST's external support. The movement's greater isolation, though, was more than compensated by its substantial buildup of in-house mobilizing assets.

The MST's more confrontational demeanor during this period was shaped by this context. Indeed, more than any set of beliefs, it was the confluence of three factors—adverse political opportunities, relative isolation, and growing capacity for self-mobilization—that induced the movement to adopt a mode of public activism characterized mostly by an "aggressive struggle" for growth and survival.

The Annoni struggle offers an instructive view of crucial moments and trends that defined this phase. In July 1985, the MST convened a three-day protest camp that gathered close to 10,000 people in Palmeira das Missões, to demand that the government execute its land reform plan. This mobilization was the result of nearly two years of grassroots organizing in northern Rio Grande do Sul. The many petitions and negotiations held with government officials during this time ended producing a string of empty promises. This situation brought about the MST's decision to occupy the Annoni estate—an idle cattle ranch bogged in a legal quagmire since 1974, after INCRA expropriated the area to resettle farmers displaced by the construction of a hydroelectric dam. MST organizers assumed, correctly, that these circumstances would minimize public objection to their first major transgression of private property rights.

The Annoni struggle involved a broad range of essentially nonviolent collective action measures, varying from countless lobbying efforts with state officials, including three trips to meet with national authorities in Brasília, and an array of high-profile, protest tactics. The statistics of the struggle undertaken by the Annoni occupants are quite revealing. In the eight years it took to settle all the families, landless people from the Annoni estate were engaged in thirty-six land occupations; at least thirty major protest rallies; nine hunger strikes; two lengthy marches; three road blockades; and nine building takeovers, six of these at the Rio Grande do Sul INCRA office in Porto Alegre and three at the State Assembly. Ten human lives were lost in these struggles, including seven children who died from precarious health conditions at the camp and a young mother who was killed during a demonstration in Sarandi, in March 1987.[28]

During these years, the gaúcho MST introduced several new protest tactics, which were then emulated in other parts of Brazil. The movement's February 1986 occupation of the INCRA building in Porto Alegre was the first sit-in of its kind in Brazil. The 280-mile march to Porto Alegre, however, carried out between May and June 1986, was with no doubt the movement's most publicized innovation. Close to 250 sem terra, accompanied by Father Arnildo and other CPT agents, participated in this twenty-seven-day mobilization, known as the *Romaria Conquistadora da Terra Prometida* (Conquering Pilgrimage to the Promised Land). Upon their arrival in Porto Alegre, the marchers received a hero's welcome by the city mayor and over 30,000 well-wishers. The sem terra held a large demonstration in the city's main public square, the *Praça da Matriz*. Shortly thereafter, they occupied the hallways of the adjacent State Assembly, following an agreement made with prominent legislators. Close to 200 landless activists camped out in the state capitol for three months. During their stay in

Map 6.1. Rio Grande do Sul

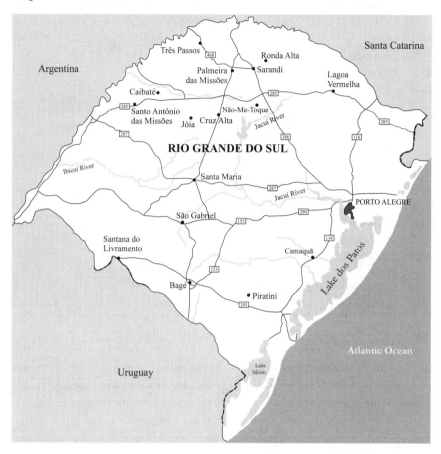

Porto Alegre, the sem terra invested considerable efforts in shoring up public sympathy for agrarian reform by visiting schools, churches, trade unions, and other civic groups. The peasants also held daily processions through the city center, bearing the camp's wooden cross.[29]

Brewing frustration over the federal government's meager pace of land distribution, exacerbated tensions within the gaúcho MST. The decision taken in late September 1986, to end the occupation of the State Assembly and dismantle the eight-month camp next to the INCRA building, triggered sharp disagreements. These and other disputes over tactical choices led to a rift within the movement, notably between influential advisors like Father Arnildo and a group of young, more radical cadres.[30] This fracture also exposed a newfound quest among MST organizers to assert their autonomy vis-à-vis the church and embrace an ad hoc ensemble of socialist ideas. Still, the new sem terra leaders remained close to several CPT agents, especially Friar Sergio Görgen. This was the context in which the movement began to craft its new symbols and

Table 6.1. Landless contingents in Rio Grande do Sul, 1979–98

| Date established | | Initial camp | | Families |
Year	Month	Locale	Municipality	involved
1979	September	Macali	Ronda Alta	110
1979	September	Brilhante	Ronda Alta	170
1981	April	Natalino's Crossing	Ronda Alta	600
1984	August	Agricultural Station	Santo Augusto	72
1985	October	Annoni Estate	Sarandi	1,500
1987	November	Itati Estate	São Nicolau	1,000
1989	November	Salso Estate	Palmeira das Missões	1,500
1991	August	FEBEM	Cruz Alta	1,850
1992	July	Caaró Sanctuary	Caibaté	980
1993	November	Barrestos	Lagoa Vermelha	450
1995	February	Ponte Queimada	Cruz Alta	1,000
1995	December	Exit to Panambi	Palmeira das Missões	1,800
1995	December	Banhado do Colégio	Camaquã	830
1997	January	BR 295	S. Antônio das Missões	2,700
1998	February	Rondinha Settlement	Joia	1,700
1998	February	BR 293	Piratini	800

Source: Carter (2007).
Note: All landless camps were sponsored by the MST or precursor groups.

self-image, by replacing its religious emblems and metaphors of resistance for a more defiant, class-based identity. By 1987, it had substituted the movement's white flag displaying the Natalino cross for a bright-red flag showing a machete-wielding peasant couple and a map of Brazil as its emblem.[31] In the face of all these changes, the MST retained an important liberation theology–inspired practice: the desire to cultivate a sense of *mística,* by drawing on the movement's symbolic repertoire—its flag, songs, chants, theater, poetry, and stirring speeches.

The MST's turn to a more aggressive strategy after mid-1987 was taken in response to a series of setbacks that included a growing climate of stagnation and in-fighting at the Annoni camp. To counter these predicaments, the movement decided to scale-up its activities in Rio Grande do Sul, and began to resist court orders evicting the sem terra from its land takeovers.[32] Between 1987 and 1993, it intensified its recruitment work and expanded its land occupations. Six new landless contingents, comprising a total of 7,280 families, were organized during this time, tripling the number of sem terra involved in the movement (see table 6.1). In the course of these seven years, the MST conducted sixty-eight land occupations, nearly one-third of all the land occupations it carried out between 1979 and 2006.[33]

The movement's decision to resist court eviction orders was put to a dramatic test in March 1989, following the occupation of the Santa Elmira estate in Cruz

Alta, a region well known for its influential landlord class. Since its formation in late 1987, this sem terra contingent had taken part in three other land occupations, and had endured a string of false promises made by different public officials. In February 1989, a fumigation plane hired by local farmers sprayed toxic pesticides over the landless camp, killing four children and sending fifteen more to the nearest emergency ward. The incident sparked feelings of anger and exasperation at the camp, but received scant coverage in the gaúcho press. At the Santa Elmira ranch, the peasants tore up the local judge's eviction papers, hoping their resistance would buy time for negotiations with authorities in Porto Alegre. Egged on by local landowners, the state military police resolved to execute the judge's orders right away. Accompanied by armed militants of the Rural Democratic Union (UDR), a belligerent landlord association, the police force unleashed a brutal repression of the landless group. Over 400 sem terra, two CPT agents, including Friar Sergio, and five policemen were injured during the eviction. Nineteen peasants, including three children, were taken to the hospital with bullet wounds. Several sem terra were tortured by the police after their arrest. The Santa Elmira episode provoked intense public outrage and prompted an emergency meeting of the Catholic bishops' conference of Rio Grande do Sul, which emphatically condemned the repression.[34]

Land mobilizations peaked briefly in 1989, in the course of Lula's presidential campaign. In September, the MST mounted an encampment with close to 1,850 families, the largest ever, at the time, in Rio Grande do Sul. Subsequent camps were somewhat smaller and suffered retention problems due to the grim conditions for landless mobilization under President Fernando Collor de Mello. The 1991 camp organized in Palmeira das Missões began with 1,500 families, but dropped to 650 families in a year's time. The landless contingent formed in Santo Antônio das Missões in July 1992 started with 980 families yet decreased to 600 families by the end of the year. The encampment established at Lagoa Vermelha in late 1993 was organized with only 450 families. Despite their smaller size, these groups were quite combative in character. In two-and-a-half years, the Palmeiras camp engaged in five land occupations, six road blockades, two building takeovers, and a 310-mile march to Porto Alegre that received scant media coverage.

The most violent phase in the gaúcho land struggle took place between 1989 and 1992. In June 1990, following the Santa Elmira incident, police shot and critically wounded a sem terra during a peaceful march near Cruz Alta. Two months later landless activists clashed with the police in Porto Alegre during an eviction from the Praça da Matriz. An off-duty policeman was killed during the melee, and seventy-two other people were wounded, among them fifty peasants and twenty-two police officers.[35] In addition, two landless peasants were killed during clashes over land occupations, one at a ranch near Bagé, in August 1991; the other at an estate in São Miguel das Missões, in November 1992.

Mario Lill, a prominent MST leader in Rio Grande do Sul, appraised this period in the following terms:

> With the UDR attacking the National Agrarian Reform Plan and Sarney's retreat on the promise he had made to implement the Plan, the landlords got bolder. Collor arrived to power and vowed "to finish off this little landless movement." His government was the harshest we experienced. Itamar Franco was milder. The Collor era was much more complicated. In those years the movement was close to doing crazy things. It's a lot easier to make mistakes when you are defending yourself or trying to counterattack under great pressure. I wouldn't say that we were more "radical" then. I wouldn't consider a peaceful march less radical than an act of physical confrontation. Sometimes a peaceful mobilization can be far more radical in its results than a direct clash. Back then we were more aggressive and combative. We had a stronger fixation about this. Today, we recognize clearly that it wasn't a good period for us. We didn't see many improvements then. Even when we fought back physically, we didn't make great progress. Our most combative actions were taken at a time when we were simply struggling to survive.[36]

Consolidation and Sustained Struggle, 1995–2006

The MST acquired a new momentum in Rio Grande do Sul when it set up a landless camp at the outskirts of Cruz Alta, in February 1995, with close to 1,000 families. This was the first sem terra group formed through various public announcements made on local radio stations and by distributing thousands of fliers across the state. This was also the first camp given a public welcome by Cruz Alta's mayor at a ceremony held at the city's main square. By this time MST leaders had developed closer ties with INCRA officials, as well. However, despite the movement's constant lobbying efforts, all new land expropriations remained stalled.

In early September, the landless families agreed it was time to put more pressure on state authorities, hence their decision to occupy the neighboring Boqueirão estate. News reporters rushed from across Brazil to cover the tense standoff between MST activists and the police, who were poised to carry out an eviction order. At the Boqueirão ranch, the sem terra constructed an elaborate set of trenches to deter the police from executing this mandate. Experienced MST activists and CPT agents also arrived on the scene to advise the landless cohort and negotiate on their behalf with police commanders, the local judge, and INCRA officials. Press accounts highlighted the fact that this was the first land occupation to use cell phones and issue daily reports on the Internet.

Fourteen days later, an exhausted contingent of over 700 landless families agreed to leave the estate peacefully, after receiving new assurances that

INCRA would make land available to all. MST leaders heralded the event as the "revival of the land struggle in Rio Grande do Sul."[37] Stirred by the impetus generated by this mobilization, the MST moved swiftly to organize two new landless camps. In just three months, they recruited 2,600 families from all parts of Rio Grande do Sul, including some of its urban shantytowns.

All in all, the period between 1995 and 2006 offered improved conditions for the land struggle in this state, notwithstanding the large obstacles in place for land redistribution. Because of great MST pressure and state response, the pace of land reform increased considerably between 1996 and 2002. During this time, the federal and state governments created two-thirds of all land reform settlements established in Rio Grande do Sul from 1979 to 2006. These developments were certainly influenced by the national scandal that followed the April 1996 massacre of nineteen MST peasants in the Amazonian hamlet of Eldorado dos Carajás. In fact, this incident prompted President Fernando Henrique Cardoso to institute a new Ministry of Agrarian Reform and accelerate land distribution throughout Brazil.[38] Adding to this, the benign depiction of the landless struggle in the highly popular television soap opera, O Rei do Gado (The King of Cattle), aired two months after the massacre by TV Globo, Brazil's mass media mogul, helped generate widespread support for land reform. Opinion polls taken in April 1997 showed that 94% of the population felt the struggle for agrarian reform was just, whereas 85% indicated support for nonviolent land occupations as a way to accelerate government reform efforts.[39]

As Bernardo Mançano Fernandes (chap. 5, this volume) and Sue Branford (chap. 13, this volume) explain, Cardoso's second administration (1999–2002) was far more hostile toward the MST and less supportive of land reform. This was influenced by the government's renewed efforts to promote agribusiness exports to pay off Brazil's foreign creditors in the wake of the country's sharp currency devaluation in early 1999 (see Delgado, chap. 2, this volume). Land market values soared under these policies, reducing the government's capacity to purchase additional farmland. Moreover, in the late 1990s, cattle ranchers linked to the Agricultural Federation of the State of Rio Grande do Sul (FARSUL) began a series of mobilizations to block INCRA's efforts to examine and determine the productivity levels of large landholdings, a required step for land expropriations. The gaúcho rural elite also marshaled its allies in Congress, the judiciary, and in the federal administration. On the heels of a May 2002 meeting between President Cardoso and FARSUL, Cardoso actually ordered INCRA to halt all expropriation proceedings affecting large rural properties in Rio Grande do Sul.[40]

The conservative onslaught under Cardoso's second term was largely offset in Rio Grande do Sul thanks to the 1998 election of Governor Olivio Dutra, the former PT mayor of Porto Alegre and a close MST friend.[41] The movement campaigned enthusiastically for Olivio and was perceived by many to have made a crucial contribution to his election. At Olivio's request, the MST desig-

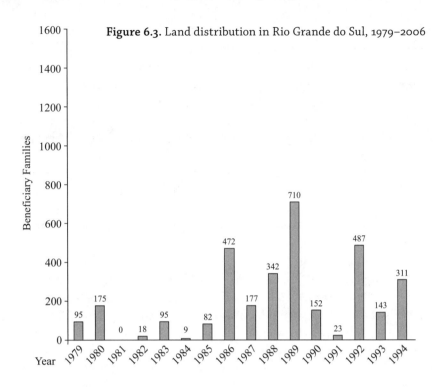

Figure 6.3. Land distribution in Rio Grande do Sul, 1979–2006

nated Friar Sergio Görgen to direct the state government's new agrarian reform agency. During his tenure, Friar Sergio negotiated a series of novel agreements with the Ministry of Agrarian Reform that enabled the Olivio government to allocate staff and funds for INCRA land purchases. Between 2000 and 2002, the state government financed 88% of all settlements created in Rio Grande do Sul. All told, the Olivio administration allotted land to 3,100 gaúcho families; 29% of all its recipients since 1979.[42]

These benefits allowed the gaúcho MST to augment its mobilizing resources in a significant way. Throughout this phase, its membership base tripled, as did its number of well-motivated and disciplined cadres. This growth led to the development of a complex organizational network.[43] The movement gained widespread national and international recognition after the massacre at Eldorado dos Carajás and highly publicized mobilizations such as the 1997 national march to Brasília. These developments greatly enhanced the MST's access to external mobilizing assets. This broadened the scope of its domestic and global allies, and helped generate new funding for its cooperatives, agro-industries, schools, media outlets, and health projects, furnished mostly by the Brazilian state and foreign non-governmental organizations (NGOs). The gaúcho MST bolstered its political capabilities and self-confidence in this period, and developed a sophisticated view of the new challenges at stake.

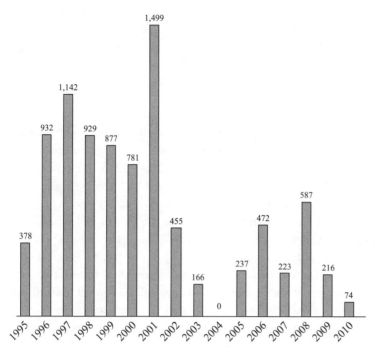

Source: INCRA-RS (2003b, 2005, 2008) and DATALUTA (2013).

This context of enhanced political opportunities and mobilizing resources created incentives for the MST to orient its public activism toward a pattern of "sustained critical engagement" with the political process. Its reliance on pressure politics remained unabated. But its ability to cooperate with the state and fashion broad coalitions with other popular groups led the movement to adopt a more temperate demeanor, while maintaining many of its core radical principles. Buoyed by these conditions, the MST began to embrace a more comprehensive, holistic agenda for social change, open to long-term solutions. Several new concerns were added to its class-based analysis of Brazilian reality, notably gender equality, human rights, agro-ecology, food sovereignty, youth empowerment, and the democratization of the nation's mass media. By weaving these themes together the movement has been able to articulate a robust critique of Brazil's exclusionary and predatory model of development, and the global forces underpinning this.

Far from "receding after 1994," as some scholars suggest,[44] MST mobilizations in Rio Grande do Sul expanded significantly in the ensuing years, as did the number of land reform settlements created in this state. Between 1995 and 2004, MST land mobilizations increased by 55% over the previous decade, while the number of beneficiary families nearly tripled (see table 6.2 and figure 6.3).

The considerable gains made during this period were the upshot of a persistent combination of pressure politics and bargaining with state authorities. In effect, all landless contingents formed at this time endured a life of struggle, duress, and peril. As an illustration, the sem terra involved in the 1995 Cruz Alta camp took part in three land occupations, two lengthy marches, ten demonstrations, two highway blockades, a hunger strike, and numerous negotiations with local, state, and federal government officials, in order to receive a farm plot.

Their occupation of the Santo Antão estate, in January 1996, was attacked by an armed UDR militia that discharged several rounds of automatic gunfire at the camp and injured a peasant woman. The following day, the sem terra thwarted a new attack by hurling a homemade gasoline bomb, laced with firecrackers, through a large sling tied between two trees. The explosive device produced a big thunder as it crashed on an empty hill near the estate's mansion. The UDR group promptly denounced the "infiltration of Shinning Path agents" at the MST camp. Local radio stations made bold captions out of these false accusations. Officials from INCRA, in turn, reacted swiftly to prevent a forceful police eviction. Soon thereafter, it announced the formation of ten new settlements. After eleven days of resistance the sem terra greeted the good news in jubilant celebration, before dismantling their occupation camp. In total, it took twenty-two months to settle all remaining 650 families from the Cruz Alta group.[45]

MST camps enjoyed greater police protection under the Olivio administration (1999–2002). During this period, the movement organized smaller encampments, and spread them out across the state. Under the previous governor, Antônio Britto (1995–98), who was hostile to the MST, the movement felt the need to organize bigger camps and involve large numbers of families in each land occupation, in order to forestall an easy police eviction. By contrast, the more liberal policing tactics employed by Olivio's government allowed the movement to increase its mobilizations in a substantial way (see table 6.3 and figure 6.4). The bulk of these protest actions were directed at the Cardoso administration. As a rule, the MST's reliance on pressure politics—even under sympathetic governments—stems from a basic view of the nature and the balance of forces in Brazil. In its eyes, public activism serves as a counterpoint to the power exercised by land reform's influential opponents, namely, landlord associations like FARSUL, right-wing politicians, and the media establishment, emblemized in Rio Grande do Sul by the RBS communications empire and its flagship, conservative newspaper, *Zero Hora*.[46]

After the mid-1990s, MST land struggles in Rio Grande do Sul became more visibly entwined with a variety of other claims, such as demands for agricultural credits, housing subsidies, and access to schools and electricity, along with other public investments needed to shore up its settlements. Its mobilizations also began to include calls to bolster INCRA's operating budget and staff. In addition, it engaged in various protests against human rights violations in the

Table 6.2. MST mobilizations and beneficiary families in Rio Grande do Sul, 1979–2004

Years	Total mobilizations	Land occupations	% Land occupations	Beneficiary families	% Beneficiary families
1979–1984	34	7	21	392	4
1985–1994	206	71	34	2,899	28
1995–2004	320	75	23	7,159	69
Total	560	153	27	10,450	100

Source: Carter (2007), INCRA-RS (2003a, 2005, 2008).

countryside, the legalization of genetically modified seeds (GMOs), neoliberal policies of state privatization, and proposals to implement a Free Trade Agreement of the Americas (FTAA). Critics viewed these developments as a sign of the movement's "undue politicization" and "deviation" from a more "wholesome past," in which its main preoccupation centered on gaining access to land.[47] Still, others have viewed this as a positive contribution that has helped enrich and expand the agenda for public discussion in Brazil, and thus maintain a substantial spectrum of dissent alive.[48]

After the mid-1990s the MST started targeting large global corporations to protest their growing influence in the *gaúcho* countryside and their easy access to public coffers. These actions reflected, in many ways, the movement's growing awareness of the new and complex set of obstacles to agrarian reform. Using disruptive stunts it began to expose corporate activities that, in its view, exacerbated the country's disparity of wealth and damaged the environment. The first emblematic example of this trend took place in July 1997, when the movement occupied an area that Governor Britto had assigned for the construction of General Motors' new car plant. This action helped rally public opposition to Britto's generous subsidies to GM and other big companies. The second event occurred in January 2001, during the first World Social Forum meeting in Porto Alegre, when the MST and its Via Campesina allies, led by José Bové, France's noted farm activist, destroyed part of a GMO soybean field near the town of Náo-Me-Togue, at an experimental station owned by Monsanto, the world's largest biotech corporation.[49] Adding to this, on March 8, 2006, International Women's Day, a group of 2,000 female activists from the MST and other Via Campesina groups sabotaged a seedling production unit owned by Aracruz Celulose, a giant pulp conglomerate, to protest against the creation of massive eucalyptus plantations in southern Rio Grande do Sul. The women denounced the firm's use of federal government funds to produce vast "green deserts" of monoculture, that undermined prospects for land distribution in Rio Grande do Sul. All three incidents provoked considerable public controversy, and triggered police investigations and court indictments. The Aracruz episode, in par-

Table 6.3. Land mobilizations and agricultural settlements in Rio Grande do Sul, 1979–2006: Basic statistics by presidential period

Period	President (& party affiliation)	Governor[a] (& party affiliation)	MST mobilizations Total	%[b]	Yearly average	MST land occupations Total	%[c]	Yearly average
1979–84	Figueiredo (PDS)	Souza (PDS) & Soares (PDS)	34	5	5.7	7	4	1.2
1985–89	Samey (PFL)	Soares (PDS) & Simon (PMDB)	83	13	16.6	30	18	6.0
1990–94	Collor & Franco (PNR)	Guazzelli (PMDB) & Colares (PDT)	123	19	24.6	41	24	8.2
1995–98	Cardoso 1 (PSDB)	Britto (PMDB)	86	13	21.5	17	10	4.3
1999–02	Cardoso 2 (PSDB)	Dutra (PT)	144	22	36.0	43	25	10.8
2003–06	Lula 1 (PT)	Rigotto (PMDB)	182	28	45.5	32	19	8.0
Total			**652**	**100**	**36.2**	**170**	**100**	**9.4**

Source: Carter (2007); INCRA-RS (2003a, 2005, 2008).

Notes:

a. Terms for Rio Grande do Sul's governors were as follows: Soares served from 1983 through 1986. Simon was succeeded by his vice governor Guazzelli in 1990. Collares became governor in 1991. Subsequent gubernatorial terms coincided with those set for the president.

b. Percentage based on total MST mobilizations.

c. Percentage based on total MST land occupations.

d. State government–sponsored settlements between 2000 and 2006 include 30 communities created jointly with INCRA, but driven mainly by the state government.

ticular, was roundly condemned by the nation's main press outlets and the Lula administration.[50]

Lula's 2002 election aroused high expectations among land reform activists in Rio Grande do Sul. Yet his first term in office proved to be a big disappointment. Between 2003 and 2006, the number of land recipients in this state dropped by 76%, compared to the previous term. No other Brazilian state had such a precipitous decline.[51] What's more, the gap between land mobilizations and beneficiary families was the starkest ever in the movement's history, in this southernmost state (see figure 6.4). Various constraints hampered land distribution in Rio Grande do Sul during this time. A steep rise in land values, fueled by high agro-commodity prices in the global market, and INCRA's own diminished workforce, hampered the bureau's capacity to obtain land. Under the Cardoso administration, INCRA's Porto Alegre office lost 85% of its staff, dropping from 378 to sixty employees. In 2003, the bureau had only three agronomists

Main settlement sponsor			Beneficiary families			Area distributed (in hectares)		
	Federal govt.	State govt.[d]	Total	Yearly average	% MST	Total	Yearly average	% MST
State	0	12	392	65	100	6,998	1,166	100
State	13	32	1,783	357	100	39,372	7,874	100
State	12	23	1,116	223	100	21,802	4,360	100
Federal	72	2	3,396	849	100	87,906	21,977	100
State	25	85	3,915	979	92	91,756	22,939	93
Federal	10	8	957	239	91	18,404	4,601	94
State	**132**	**162**	**11,559**	**642**	**97**	**266,239**	**14,791**	**97**

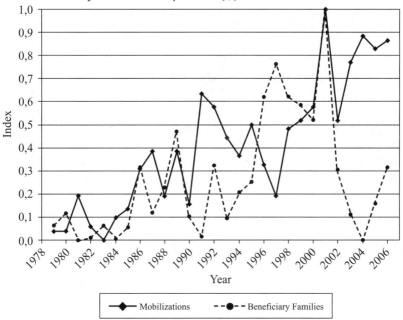

Figure 6.4. MST land mobilizations and beneficiary families in Rio Grande do Sul, a comparative intensity index, 1979–2006

Source: Carter (2007); INCRA-RS (2003a, 2005, 2008).

Notes: This index measures intensity levels by applying the formula of relative dispersion to year-by-year data on MST land mobilizations and beneficiary families.

to handle all land expropriations in Rio Grande do Sul.[52] This adverse situation was further complicated by FARSUL's combative efforts to block INCRA's land acquisitions.

The Supreme Court's August 2003 decision to annul Lula's first expropriation decree, which confiscated the Southall estate in São Gabriel, handed a blow to the new PT administration. The court's controversial ruling spared an unproductive, 13,000-hectare cattle ranch on spurious technical grounds, boosting the morale of gaúcho landlords who mobilized intensely to stop the expropriation.

Under President Lula, the federal government increased funding for family farmers and projects designed to improve conditions in existing land reform settlements, while maintaining much larger subsidies for export-oriented agribusiness farmers.[53] Unlike the second Cardoso presidency, the PT government dismissed right-wing calls to criminalize the MST. The Lula administration, nonetheless, was hampered by its choice of political allies in Congress. Above all, it feared taking measures that would incur the wrath of the rural elite and its media supporters, and thus upset the PT's conservative partners in Congress. An illustrative example of this was the refusal to revise the outdated index used to determine the productivity of large-landed estates, based on measurements derived from the agricultural census of 1975, despite repeated requests from peasant groups. All this led to a growing disenchantment with Lula among MST activists. As one leader put it during a personal conversation, "Lula has now become a friend of our enemies."

President Lula's election in 2002 set off a surge in land mobilizations, which reached their highest peak ever in Rio Grande do Sul (see table 6.3). At the same time, the MST was forced to alter some of its pressure tactics. The PT's defeat in the 2002 gubernatorial race made land occupations a riskier enterprise, hence their drop in numbers. Other protest measures, though, notably, demonstrations, road blockades, and building occupations, increased substantially. Many of these were conducted in synchronized fashion across the state. In mid-2003, the MST carried out a highly publicized sixty-seven-day march to press for the expropriation of the Southall estate and set up a camp in the vicinity.[54] Starting in 2004, the movement initiated a campaign to expropriate the Guerra estate, a 7,000-hectare ranch, situated close to the Annoni settlement. Aside from lobbying INCRA and garnering the support of twenty-three mayors from the region, the MST occupied the estate eight times between 2004 and early 2007. The 2006 gubernatorial election of Yeda Crusius, on a conservative alliance between the Party of Brazilian Social Democracy (PSDB) and the conservative Party of the Liberal Front (PFL), created an obstacle to these mobilizations. In close collaboration with the Crusius administration, the state judiciary instituted a number of unprecedented measures to criminalize and curtail MST activities. In December 2007, the state's High Council of Prosecutors went as far as to issue a secret report calling on the judiciary to "outlaw the MST" in Rio

Grande do Sul.[55] Prodded by these political threats and paltry response to their land requests, a number of sem terra—especially the younger activists—began to embrace their struggle with a more aggressive disposition.

Conclusion

This chapter has underscored the importance of reviewing contentious ideas, tactics, and actions in context. Decontextualized analyzes of contentious groups like the MST greatly impoverish our understanding of this phenomena. Moreover, they facilitate attempts to caricaturize these movements and treat them as a "fundamentalist," "irrational," and even "dangerous menace." It is easy to sit back and reflect on the MST as though it were an isolated group, devoid of a social milieu. Here, one is spared the task of probing the conditions under which it mobilizes, or of appraising its perceptions of threat and opportunity. What's more, these intellectual blinders disregard any analysis of how the movement might relate to Brazil's development model or to the country's enduring inequities in wealth and power. Insightful studies of popular organizations like the MST are not simple to produce, given the significant time and effort required to generate solid empirical data. Field research is essential for this. If conducted in a recurrent and meaningful way, these on-site visits can yield invaluable insights on how these patterns of contentious politics actually operate.[56]

This chapter has shown that the landless peasants in Rio Grande do Sul adopted public activism in a context that offered considerable political opportunities and resources for mobilization. It also demonstrated how different combinations of these two variables created conditions that explain the MST's varying modes of public activism between 1979–2006. This analytic framework helps distinguish three prevailing dispositions that shaped the movement's historical evolution in Rio Grande do Sul. During its weakest phase (1979–84), the sem terra movement made *entreating appeals*, couched in religious icons and language, to raise broad public sympathy and elicit a charitable response by church and state authorities. This was followed by a period (1985–94) of heightened frustration given the obstacles to agrarian reform, and a quest for autonomy and new self-identity, that led to an *aggressive struggle* for the movement's survival and expansion. The MST's third phase (1995–2006) involved a process of substantial growth, consolidation, and maturation, which inclined the movement to adopt a pattern of *sustained critical engagement*, as it pursued a broader and more holistic agenda for social transformation. A graphic synthesis of this argument can be found in figure 6.5.

The MST would have accomplished nothing in Rio Grande do Sul had it not made use of its democratic right to engage in public activism. Its disposition toward this form of social conflict was not driven by "dogmatic" principles or "outdated ideologies," as some would have it. Public activism served, first and

Figure 6.5. MST development in Rio Grande do Sul, 1979–2006

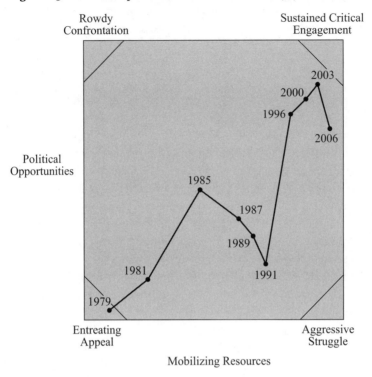

foremost, a practical tool. Pressure politics enabled a poor people's movement like the MST to stir public opinion and gain direct access to policymakers in a way that other, usually lopsided mechanisms of Brazilian democracy—electoral contestation, legislative representation, judicial review, media influence, and lobbying —would have rendered too costly, ineffectual or innocuous.[57] Given its alternative options, public activism was the MST's most rational and cost-effective strategy for obtaining government concessions.

Pressure politics, however, was more than just an instrument for exacting government concessions. Collective acts of struggle also strengthen the movement internally. By energizing its participants, they sharpen class consciousness, raise awareness of basic rights, build social networks of trust, nurture organizing skills, and cultivate new popular leaders. They also foster feelings of pride and ownership over the results achieved. As such, the movement's public activism has played a central role in the long run development of political capabilities among Brazil's rural poor.[58]

Finally, public activism helped galvanize the movement's passions, convictions, and sense of mystique that gives the landless movement its resilient ethos. Though engaged in efforts to acquire material benefits, MST mobilizations were often colored by what Max Weber defined as an ideal interest (or value-rational) orientation toward social action. Ideal interest behavior uses strategic means to pursue absolute ends. Within the MST one can find traces of this orientation in the tendency to view its struggle as a "fusion of striving and attaining" rather than optimizing results;[59] the strong feelings propelling and resulting from its mobilizations; and the powerful ways in which its collective experiences can alter the individual calculus of its members. The MST's ideal interests are often nurtured through its rich symbolic repertoire—of songs, chants, flags, theater, poetry, and stirring speeches—displayed in ritual gatherings that stimulate feelings of shared sacrifice, camaraderie, and idealism. These and other moments of fraternization and struggle can stir courage, persistence, and vitality among movement activists.[60]

Herein rests a major source of MST strength and endurance: the capacity to sustain and balance its steadfast ideals with a quest for practical solutions to everyday problems. This peculiar interplay has allowed the movement to mobilize with great impetus and maneuver at once with skillful adroit. Given the steep challenges ahead, this will be sorely needed in the years to come. Ultimately, though, the terms of the movement's course of action will be determined largely by its context. As Nelson Mandela rightly observed,

> A freedom fighter learns the hard way that it is the oppressor who defines the nature of the struggle, and the oppressed is often left no recourse but to use methods that mirror those of the oppressor. At a certain point, one can only fight fire with fire.[61]

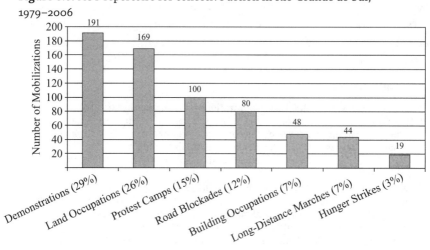

Figure 6.6. MST repertoire for collective action in Rio Grande do Sul, 1979–2006

Table 6.4. Landless repertoires of contention in Rio Grande do Sul, per year, 1979–2006

Year	Land occupations	Demonstrations	Protest camps	Road blockades	Building occupations	Long-distant marches	Hunger strikes	Total	% MST
1979	3	1	0	0	0	0	0	4	100
1980	1	3	0	0	0	0	0	4	100
1981	1	10	1	0	0	0	0	12	100
1982	0	3	1	1	0	0	0	5	100
1983	0	2	0	0	0	0	0	2	100
1984	2	3	1	1	0	0	0	7	100
1985	2	7	1	0	0	0	1	1	82
1986	3	9	1	0	2	3	3	21	86
1987	14	4	1	0	3	0	1	23	96
1988	3	7	2	1	0	0	1	14	86
1989	14	6	1	0	1	0	2	24	92
1990	3	1	2	0	2	2	0	10	100
1991	11	12	2	4	2	3	1	35	100
1992	17	2	5	5	2	1	0	32	100
1993	6	5	4	2	2	2	4	25	100
1994	4	4	4	4	1	3	1	21	100
1995	2	9	10	1	1	4	2	29	97
1996	4	9	0	1	2	3	0	19	100
1997	7	2	4	2	0	1	0	16	75
1998	11	5	6	0	1	8	0	31	87
1999	14	3	4	8	1	0	0	30	97
2000	11	4	8	4	5	0	1	33	97
2001	14	5	17	13	3	7	0	59	92
2002	16	6	4	5	4	2	0	37	78
2003	7	16	6	7	4	3	0	43	98
2004	11	28	8	8	6	2	2	65	74
2005	12	18	11	5	6	0	0	52	87
2006	8	14	5	20	6	0	0	53	89
Total	**204**	**199**	**109**	**92**	**54**	**44**	**19**	**721**	**91**
*% MST**	*85*	*96*	*92*	*87*	*89*	*100*	*100*		*91*

Source: Carter (2007).

Notes: This table records all popular mobilizations for land distribution in Rio Grande do Sul. It displays actions carried out by the MST and non-MST groups, including local landless organizations, peasants displaced by the construction of hydroelectric dams and the creation of indigenous reserves, as well as indigenous mobilizations for land.

*% MST is the percentage of total land mobilizations carried out by the MST, alone or with its allies.

The statistics presented here are from an extensive database on "Land Mobilizations in Rio Grande do Sul, 1978–2006," see Carter (2007). Information for this database was compiled from numerous sources, principally archival material found at the CPT offices in Goiânia and Porto Alegre. Other documents consulted include INCRA-RS (2003b); MST-RS (2003); various issues of the MST's Jornal Sem Terra and the CPT-RS Voz da Terra. Between 1991 and 2006 I con-

(Table 6.4 notes, continued)
ducted interviews with over 270 land reform activists, social scientists, church authorities, INCRA officials, and government representatives in Rio Grande do Sul.

This database only records public activities aimed at furthering land distribution. Mobilizations geared solely toward obtaining other benefits—such as agricultural credits and infrastructural support land reform settlements—are not computed. Contentious activities, however, demanding both land and other claims are computed as land mobilizations.

The mobilization categories used here were developed on the basis of the following criteria: (1) Land occupations refers to organized incursions of landless people on either private or publicly owned rural properties; (2) Protest camps denotes landless encampments that last for more than a week; (3) Long-distance marches consider mobilizations of people who walk a distance of twenty miles or more; (4) Building occupations entail sit-ins in urban constructions, namely government offices; (5) Demonstrations encompass a wide range of public protest gatherings, including short-distance marches and brief protest camps. This category does not include MST workshops or internal meetings; and (6) Hunger strikes includes groups of people fasting for twenty-four hours or more.

Notes

The author would like to thank Luiz Antônio Pasinato, José Rui Taglipietra, and Paulinho Lopes for their contribution in gathering relevant CPT and INCRA data, and the support of his research assistants, Enrique Carrillo Gómez and Kang Yue. A word of appreciation is also due to Kristina Svensson and Lyndsay Hughes for their valuable edits. This chapter is dedicated to the memory of Charles Tilly, with deep gratitude for his inspiring mentorship at Columbia University.

1. Exodus 3: 7–8.
2. This account of the movement's early formation builds on extensive interviews with Father Arnildo Fritzen, interview by the author, tape recording, Ronda Alta, RS, September 8, 1994, and Ronda Alta, RS, September 3, 2001; two of the young professionals, João Pedro Stédile, interview by the author, tape recording, São Paulo, SP, July 30, 2003, and Ivaldo Gehlen, interview by the author, tape recording, Porto Alegre, RS, August 1, 2005; and several peasant leaders of the Ronda Alta region. On the Macali occupation, see Gehlen (1983).
3. See table 9.9 in Carter and Carvalho (chap. 9, this volume).
4. In 2003, I found that nearly half of the staff at the national office were gaúchos. Approximately sixty gaúchos were involved in efforts to shore up the movement in various other parts of Brazil. Mario Lill, interview by the author, tape recording, Pontão, RS, June 6, 2003. For a historical review of this trend, see Lerrer (2008).
5. Navarro (2002a, 2002b), Martins (2000a), Graziano (2004), and Rosenfield (2006).
6. Tilly (1978, 2004b, 2006); Tarrow (1998); and McAdam, McCarthy, and Zald (1996).
7. According to James C. Scott, everyday forms of resistance include actions such as poaching, foot-dragging, evasion, discreet forms of land squatting, anonymous threats, sabotage, and arson (1985, 1990).
8. Nonviolence, here, refers to the absence of collective actions that strive to inflict physical harm on other people, or threaten to do so, and/or consist of willful acts to destroy substantial property assets. Under certain circumstances, this definition can include acts that lead to minor collateral or accidental damages to property.
9. On this theme, see Tarrow (1998) and Tilly (1979, 1983).
10. Key external resources include informal supportive settings and established solidarity networks. Internal assets address issues such as the movement's capability, autonomy,

and extension. A more detailed assessment of these variables can be found in Carter (2004b); also see Tarrow (1998) and McAdam, McCarthy, and Zald (1996).

11. This study shares Gabriel Ondetti's (2008) argument for a political process explanation of the MST's rise and fluctuation yet differs with his decision to treat various social movement theories in a competitive (either/or) fashion. Instead of dwelling on their differences, I believe one can gain greater analytic mileage by combining their main attributes in creative ways. Tables 6.1 and 6.2 are the result of my effort to bring together two of the leading social movement theories: political process, also known as *political opportunity structure* (Tilly 1978, 2006; McAdam 1982; and Tarrow 1998) and *resource mobilization* (Olson 1965; McCarthy and Zald 1977; and Oberschall 1973). The chapter is also laced with insights gleaned from framing process theories (Gamson 1992; Snow and Bedford 1992; and Zald 1996) and social movement studies that underscore the significance of emotional dispositions (Aminzade and McAdam 2001; Goodwin, Jasper, and Poletta 2001;). Efforts to combine these various approaches are not new to the field; see Jean Cohen (1985); Morris and McClurg Mueller (1992); McAdam, McCarthy, and Zald (1996), Tarrow (1998); and Goodwin and Jasper (2004). None of these studies, however, has produced a matrix akin to the one developed here.

12. "Rowdy confrontation" refers to patterns of conflict that tend to be rather disorganized and unruly. Because of its strong internal discipline, the MST in Rio Grande do Sul has not engaged in this form of contentious politics.

13. Angelin Antonio Campignotto (Antoninho), interview by the author, tape recording, Ronda Alta, July 27, 1994, and Etelvino Cupinger, interview by the author, tape recording, Ronda Alta, RS, August 16, 1994. This account of the MST's origins draws on Carter (2002).

14. On the capitalist modernization of the gaúcho countryside, see Brum (1988); Dacanal and Gonzaga (1979); Kleinmann (1986); and Martins (1991).

15. Key sources on the MST's early history include Carter (2002, 2003), Fernandes (2000), Gehlen (1983, 1991), Marcon (1997), and Stédile and Fernandes (1999). On the Catholic Church's involvement in support of the landless, see Poletto (chap. 4, this volume). More generally on the progressive aspect of Brazil's Catholic Church, see Beozzo (1994), Della Cava (1989), and Mainwaring (1986).

16. Rio Grande do Sul's CPT was organized during a meeting at the Center for Missionary Orientation (COM) of the Caxías do Sul diocese. The COM was started in 1970 to prepare missionaries heading to northern Brazil. It soon became one of the principal hubs for the gaúcho liberation theology network. By 1985, close to 40,000 pastoral agents and lay activists from all over Brazil had taken part in COM's progressive workshops (Goeth 1994). On the history of Rio Grande do Sul's CPT, see Góes (1997).

17. Father Arnildo and other activists who were engaged in the occupation of the Macali and Brilhante farms played a secretive yet crucial role in igniting the Natalino camp. Their goal was to foster a new, spontaneous-like mobilization that would pressure the government to expropriate one of the many idle cattle ranches in the vicinity. For security reasons, this aspect of the camp's origins was kept strictly confidential at the time. My insights on these covert efforts are based on interviews with three of its organizers: Father Arnildo Fritzen, Ivaldo Gehlen, and a peasant leader of the Brilhante occupation, Celso Pilatti, interview by author, tape recording Ronda Alta, RS, July 30, 2005.

18. Carter (2002: 134).

19. A handful of nuns were actively engaged in coordinating everyday activities at the camp, while Father Arnildo was widely recognized as the movement's spiritual leader.

Six progressive bishops visited the encampment during the first five months to bless and encourage the landless movement. Among these church visitors were two of the CPT's founding bishops, Dom Pedro Casaldáliga and Dom Tomás Balduíno. Church endorsement of the Natalino encampment, however, was far from unanimous. Two leading conservative detractors in Rio Grande do Sul were the local bishop of Passo Fundo, Dom Claudio Colling, and the Cardinal of Porto Alegre, Dom Vicente Scherer. For all their misgivings, both prelates still allowed their dioceses to organize food and clothing drives for the Natalino peasants.

20. Carlos Irineu Silva, interview by the author, Ronda Alta, RS, October 1, 1994.

21. Here, in a microcosm, we find Robert A. Dahl's classic axiom in full operation: "The likelihood that a government will tolerate an opposition increases as the expected costs of suppression increase" (1971: 15–16).

22. "Sem-terras decidem acampar no Palácio," *Folha da Tarde* (Porto Alegre), July 27, 1981.

23. At the time of Curió's departure, close to two-thirds of the Natalino families remained at the landless camp, while 137 agreed to join a colonization program in the Amazonian region. These figures are based on the federal government's own count; see Marcon (1997: 231).

24. "Mais de 20 mil pessoas participaram ontem da 5a. Romaría da Terra," *Zero Hora* (Porto Alegre), February 24, 1982. The Land Pilgrimage is an annual religious gathering organized by the CPT, which originated in Rio Grande do Sul, in 1978. A useful study on this subject is Dallagnol (2001).

25. On the politics of land reform during this period, see José Silva (1987, 1989) and Veiga (1990).

26. Stédile and Fernandes (1999: 105).

27. In 1986 the MST elected its first PT candidate, Adão Pretto, to the State Assembly of Rio Grande do Sul. Pretto was subsequently elected to the National Congress in 1990, where he served for five terms until his untimely death in early 2009.

28. The statistics for the Annoni camp are from Carter (2007). Its main sources are cited in Table 6.4, in the appendix. This account of the Annoni struggle is based on interviews with ninety-five participants.

29. Church support remained strong during the early years of the Annoni struggle and assured the movement vital mobilizing resources. In February 1986, over 50,000 people, among them a dozen Catholic bishops and 200 priests, gathered at the Annoni camp for the CPT's annual Land Pilgrimage. The march to Porto Alegre, later that year, was underwritten mainly through church donations.

30. The differences between the young MST cadres and advisors were essentially tactical and personal rather than political. Despite the rift, Father Arnildo continued to support the landless struggle and remained close to one of the Annoni groups.

31. For a thoughtful review of the MST's symbolic realignment during this period, see Hoffman (2002). On the confluence of various religious sentiments within the MST, see Görgen (1997).

32. The plan to resist evictions was enshrined subsequently in the maxim fashioned for the MST's Second National Congress in 1990: "*Ocupar, resistir e produzir*" (Occupy, resist and produce).

33. Carter (2007), as noted in tables 6.4 and 6.5.

34. On the Santa Elmira incident, see Görgen (1989) and Americas Watch (1991).

35. For detailed accounts of the Praça da Matriz episode, see Lerrer (2005) and Görgen (1991).

36. Mario Lill, interview by the author, tape recording, Pontão, RS, July 6, 2003.

37. This account of the Cruz Alta camp is based on interviews with eighty-five participants in this struggle and a close review of all relevant news articles.

38. Further details on the Eldorado dos Carajás massacre can be found in Ondetti, Wambergue, and Afonso (chap. 8, this volume); also see Nepomuceno (2007).

39. The Ibope polling figures were published in *O Estado de São Paulo* on April 16, 1997; see Comparato (2000: 190–91).

40. Cardoso's decision to support FARSUL's demands prompted the resignation of INCRA's superintendent in Rio Grande do Sul. For a detailed review of Cardoso's land reform policies, see Da Ros (2006: 197–271).

41. As a progressive leader of the Bank Tellers Union, Olivio Dutra was an early and active supporter of the Natalino struggle. Later, as mayor of Porto Alegre, during the Praça da Matriz incident in August 1990, he sheltered in the municipal palace scores of sem terra fleeing police violence.

42. INCRA-RS (2003b, 2005, 2008). The total number of beneficiary families for Olivio's land program includes 172 families settled in 2003 and 2004 as a result of funds committed by the PT administration prior to its departure. The percentage noted here is based on the total land beneficiaries from 1979 to 2004. Information regarding the additional 172 families was provided by an INCRA official in Rio Grande do Sul, Roberto Ramos; author's telephone interview, Porto Alegre, RS, January 21, 2008. For a comprehensive review of Olivio's land reform policies, see Da Ros (2006: 273–431).

43. For further insights on this organizational build up, see Carter and Carvalho (chap. 9, this volume).

44. Navarro (2002a: 207).

45. This account of the Santo Antão occupation is based on interviews with sixty-five sem terra involved in this mobilization and INCRA's superintendent at the time, Jânio Guedes Silveira, interview by the author, tape recording, Porto Alegre, RS, November 24, 2000.

46. Carlos Wagner, a veteran reporter on land reform issues for *Zero Hora*, southern Brazil's leading newspaper, claims that this daily took a decisively anti-MST position in the early 1990s and has remained a staunch conservative critic of the movement ever since. Carlos Wagner, interview by the author, tape recording, Porto Alegre, RS, July 1, 2003. In May 2002, the gaúcho MST decided to stop giving any interviews to *Zero Hora* and other RBS outlets as an act of protest against its repeated distortions and misuse of statements provided by movement leaders, along with its highly skewed coverage of its activities. In 2005, the gaúcho MST helped create an alternative news agency, *Agência Chasque*. Informative accounts of the media's portrayal of the MST in Rio Grande do Sul can be found in Lerrer (2005) and Berger (1998).

47. For relevant comments of this sort, see Graziano (2004: 73, 103, 278), Martins (2000a: 17–39, 112–15; 2007), Navarro (2002a: 201–12; 2007; 2009), and Rosenfield (2006: 227, 239, 252–53, 267).

48. Carter (2011).

49. La Via Campesina is an international peasant network, joined by the MST in 1996; see Fernandes (chap. 5, this volume) and Rosa (chap. 15, this volume). It is worth noting that four of the five Brazilian organizations involved in the national chapter of the Via Campesina originated in Rio Grande do Sul. These are the MST, the Movement of People Affected by Dams (MAB), the Peasant Women's Movement (MNC), and the Movement of Small Farmers (MPA). For background information on these movements, see Navarro (1996b).

50. Further details on the Aracruz incident can be found in Rosa (chap. 15, this volume). For an illustration of the scathing critiques made in the national press, see "Cangaço Revolucionário," *Folha de São Paulo*, March 10, 2006. For an alternative account, see the video documentary by Via Campesina, Brasil, *Rompendo o Silêncio* [Breaking the Silence] (2006); which can be found on YouTube.

51. This figure is drawn from data offered in table 6.3. The comparative ranking was developed by the author from DATALUTA (2008).

52. Information provided by a high ranking INCRA official in Rio Grande do Sul, José Rui Tagliapietra, interview by the author, tape recording, Porto Alegre, RS, July 3, 2003. A major structural constraint during this period stemmed from the rising levels of urbanization in this southernmost state, which reduced the number of potential land claimants and led the MST to intensify its recruitment efforts in the *favelas* (shantytowns) of the state's main urban centers. According to the Brazilian census bureau, the urban population in Rio Grande do Sul increased from 77% in 1991 to 84% of the state population in 2005. Excluding people who live in smaller rural towns, the population dwelling in the countryside was approximately 1.7 million.

53. Further information on the subsidies provided to agribusiness farmers can be found in Delgado (chap. 2) and Carter and Carvalho (chap. 9), in this volume. As an MST gaúcho leader explained it, "if before we were driving at 10 kilometers per hour, now with the Lula government we are driving at 30. But the others from the landlord class who were driving at 80 are now flying at 180 kilometers per hour." Isaias Vedovatto, author's interview, Pontão, RS, July 5, 2008.

54. On the march to São Gabriel and the struggle for the Southall estate, see Görgen (2004).

55. The report approved unanimously by the High Council of Prosecutors of Rio Grande do Sul was made public in June 2008 and was followed by a temporary lull in state hostilities. For a perceptive analysis of the legal mechanisms used to suppress MST mobilizations, see Scalabrin (2008).

56. Extensive interaction with MST participants is necessary to grasp how these movements perceive their situation. Indeed, this is crucial for the study of social movements, for as McAdam, Tarrow, and Tilly well observe, "No opportunity, however objectively open, will invite mobilization unless it is a) visible to potential challengers and b) *perceived* as an opportunity. The same holds for threats" (2001: 43) (my emphasis).

57. Further insights on how Brazil's extremely unequal democracy affects the politics of land reform can be found in the introduction (chap. 1) to this volume. The MST's rational demeanor in dealing with its strategic options and limitations is analyzed in greater detail in Carter (2011).

58. The notion of "political capabilities" draws on Whitehead and Molina (2003: 32), which, in turn, is inspired by the writings of Amartya Sen (1999).

59. The expression "striving and attaining" is borrowed from Albert O. Hirschman (1982: 85).

60. Max Weber's ideal interest concept is treated extensively in Carter (2002, 2003). For his brief characterization of value-rational behavior, see Weber (1978: 24–26). On the role of emotions within the MST, see Quirk (2008). Other social movement analyses that underscore the importance of passionate commitments can be found in Goodwin, Jasper, and Poletta (2001) and Aminzade and McAdam (2001).

61. Mandela (1995: 166).

7 Under the Black Tarp
The Dynamics and Legitimacy of Land Occupations
in Pernambuco

The act of establishing claims to a rural estate by occupying a small part of the area and setting up a camp of landless rural workers is a new phenomenon in Brazilian history.[1] True, there were some land occupations prior to the 1964 military coup, notably in Rio Grande do Sul and Rio de Janeiro.[2] These mobilizations, however, exhibited different traits from the ones that emerged in the 1980s, and were certainly not as widespread. In the early 1960s, many supporters of agrarian reform were apprehensive about these tactics and viewed them as an inappropriate way to press for change. Many of these skeptics favored alternative approaches, such as mobilizing for constitutional and other legal reforms.[3] The authoritarian regime installed in 1964 thwarted the possibility of organizing land occupations. In fact, almost all the areas obtained through these mobilizations were eventually returned to their original owners. During these years, many activists and defenders of the budding rural worker's movement became the targets of intense police and military repression.

Land occupations reappeared in Rio Grande do Sul in late 1979 and led to the formation of a new landless camp. These first peasant mobilizations were organized with the support of the church's Pastoral Land Commission (CPT), and subsequently led to the creation of the Landless Rural Workers Movement (MST) in 1984 (see Fernandes and Carter, chaps. 5 and 6, this volume). The movement's territorial expansion to other parts of Brazil facilitated the diffusion of land occupations as a rural protest tactic. The agrarian law passed by the National Congress in 1993, stipulating the terms under which unproductive farmland could be expropriated for violating the 1988 Constitution's requirement that rural properties "fulfill a social function," engendered an auspicious setting for the rise of a new wave of land occupations in the mid-1990s. These mobilizations were organized by the MST, the rural trade unions, and dozens of other, mostly local, landless movements, set up in this period in most Brazilian states (see Fernandes, chap. 5, tables 5.4 and 5.5). These developments stirred the National Institute for Colonization and Agrarian Reform (INCRA), the federal agency responsible for land expropriations, into action. In the ensuing years, hundreds of rural estates were redistributed to peasants and farm workers who had taken part in these landless camps, and who consequently became *parceleiros* (settlers), with a state-assigned farm plot. Land occupations, landless camps, and rural expropriations resulting from these mobilizations produced a distinct turnabout in the orientation of many rural associations and the Brazilian state.

This chapter examines this shift by probing the case of Pernambuco, the northeastern Brazilian state with the largest number of land occupations since the mid-1990s. This study centers on the Zona da Mata region, an area on Pernambuco's coastal rim that experienced a considerable number of land occupations, which led to the formation of numerous land reform settlements on a territory noted for its large sugarcane plantations.[4] It analyzes these mobilizations, and the development of a newfound sense of legitimacy regarding the use of land occupation tactics, in light of the region's recent history and social conditions. This study is based on empirical research carried out in sixteen land occupations that took place in the municipalities of Rio Formoso and Tamandaré, between 1997 and 2004.[5] Five of these landless camps were organized by MST, three by the MST in collaboration with rural trade unions, and eight by the rural trade unions alone.

The Encampment Method

The first occupation reported in Rio Formoso was organized by MST activists and local rural trade union leaders,[6] in April 1992, when close to 1,200 people (men, women, and children) entered and set up a camp at the Camaçari plantation to demand the area be expropriated and redistributed to the landless families. The occupiers believed the Camaçari estate was a property of the Federal Railway Company. But the owners of the nearby Cucaú plantation persuaded the local judge that the area belonged to them. As a result, hundreds of police officers were sent to the plantation to evict the occupiers of the landless camp. Many of its participants returned home. About 800 people, however, rebuilt the camp in Vermelho, in an area of small rural properties in Rio Formoso. From there they embarked on a succession of land occupations that targeted various sugarcane plantations deemed to be unproductive, and thus amenable to INCRA's expropriation. All these mobilizations were sponsored jointly by the MST and Rio Formoso's rural trade union. The unions only started organizing their own occupations in 1996.

By studying the formation of multiple landless camps one can detect common trends and dynamics. As a rule, the plantations were occupied at night or at dawn, after which the participants would establish their camps in an elevated and visible location, preferably near a forest patch and waterway. There, they built shacks with wood taken from the forest, covered them with leaves, and placed a black tarp on top. These precarious constructions were usually laid out in an orderly grid, with streets separating different rows of huts. The camp's assembly point included a high pole displaying the flag of the organization that had sponsored the camp.[7] In the early years only the MST raised its flag, since the rural trade unions had none of their own. The union's flag appeared only after the statewide Federation of Agricultural Workers of Pernambuco (FETAPE) began to promote land occupations to advance agrarian reform in this state.[8]

The number of people engaged in each land occupation varied considerably. More than 100 rural workers took part of the takeover of the São João plantation in 1996, while only nine people were involved in the occupation of the Brejo estate in 1997. After the initial land occupation, a landless camp can expand with the arrival of more people. The Brejo camp, for instance, grew to include more than sixty participants. Camps, however, can also shrink in size, as did the São João camp, that ended up with nineteen people, or the Liana camp, which after the initial occupation by eighty rural workers dropped to thirty-five participants. Such reductions can result from people deciding to leave the camp voluntarily for various personal reasons. In some situations, participants may be compelled to abandon the camp after engaging in unacceptable behavior, generally as the consequence of alcohol abuse or the resort to physical violence.

Adult males were usually predominant during the act of occupation. Women and children generally arrived afterward. To signal their engagement with a landless camp, the occupants were expected to erect a shack on the premises. It was uncommon for adults to stay at the camp the whole time, as most of them needed to earn an income to maintain their families. Many labored in the sugarcane fields. Others held odd jobs in construction, worked as security guards or street vendors, caught crabs in the mangrove swamps, and so on. A member or two of each family, though, would typically stay at the camp to care for the shack. Some participants would spend long periods away from the camp, and ask a relative or acquaintance to mind the family hut, or even let it stand empty. Still, these individuals had to return periodically to the camp to reaffirm their ties with the landless community.

Each camp created specific task teams to manage its division of labor. One team would handle security issues and guard the encampment at night. Others would administer food supplies or take care of health and sanitation matters, education, and other concerns. The *movements*, as the rural workers themselves would refer to the groups that sponsored land occupations, tried to obtain food for the landless families from government agencies, notably INCRA, local governments, and politicians, as well as churches. In addition, if needed, they would help organize roadside collections and food drives among local shop owners.

Most camp dwellers came from Pernambuco's sugarcane region. Some, however, were from the neighboring Agreste region, a semi-arid area further inland composed mainly of family farms. A majority had made a living toiling in the sugarcane fields. Others had worked as bricklayers, domestic servants, truck and tractor drivers, watchmen, and street vendors. The camps included families with small children and teenagers and single adults. Some were active workers and others retired pensioners. Many had joined the landless camp after receiving a personal invitation from an MST or rural trade union activist. Recruitment efforts were usually carried out at the *pontas de rua*, the street corners in the outskirts of small rural towns, where the manual laborers lived— the lowest social strata in the Zona da Mata. Recruitment activities would also take place in the sugarcane plantations, among rural workers who had formal labor contracts.

Each camp could last for different time periods. Some were dismantled after a few months' time, following the expropriation of the sugarcane estate. Others endured for many years, as did the Mamucaba camp, which was set up in 1998. This camp was evicted twice in 2006 and 2007, before relocating to the outskirts of the town of Barreiros, where it has remained active for fifteen years.[9] By contrast, some camps were erected for only a few hours or days. Almost all the landless groups endured court-ordered evictions from the occupied estates, based on legal petitions made by the landowners. After each removal, the landless would usually reassemble their camp in the same place or on a nearby roadside. Some landless communities suffered violent expulsions at the hands of private militias hired by landlords, as in the case of the Mascatinho, Jundiá de Cima, and Mato Grosso plantations. Indeed, violent threats and attacks against these camps were recurrent phenomena in this area.

The first occupation of a sugarcane estate established a demand for the property's redistribution. Its occupants would then become claimants to a parcel of this land. As a result, the landless community would become associated with this plantation and bear its name, even in situations where they had to relocate the camp outside the disputed territory. For example, the Cipó camp was destroyed shortly after its first occupation and re-established in the neighboring town of Vermelho, where it remained known as the "Cipó camp." In a similar way, the Mato Grosso camp was vacated after an armed attack, but was set up again as the same camp in an area of the Minguito estate that had already been expropriated. The Jundiá camp was dismantled after an attack by more than 100 gunmen hired by the landowner, yet reorganized soon after on an adjacent roadside.

Landless encampments and occupations generated their own special vocabulary. The verb *ocupar* (to occupy) was preferred over *invadir* (to invade), which was used by the media and landowners, and employed in common parlance. Workers described the actual occupation by using the verb *entrar* (go in). Whenever they arrived at a place with the idea of "going into" the plantation, they would ask the movement coordinator if there was a *vaga* (vacancy), as if they were looking for a job. The rural workers would occupy an estate in order to, in their expression, *pegar terra* (grab land). Their experience at the camp, in turn, was often described as living *debaixo da lona preta* (under the black tarp), a phrase meant to evoke a sense of material deprivation and exposure to the vagrancies of nature: rain, excessive heat during the day, and cold temperatures at night.

Landless camps, in other words, were not just a simple gathering of people to demand the expropriation of a large rural estate. These communities were formed through acts of land occupation that involved ritualized techniques. Moreover, they maintained a sense of spatial organization, and established etiquettes for joining the camp, rules for living together, a distinct vocabulary, along with the use of several symbolic markers to convey the existence of a landless camp, notably their flags and black-tarp-covered huts. This combination of elements amounts to a distinct method for establishing claims described here as the *encampment method*.[10] This model was created in southern Brazil, during the land mobilizations that led to the MST's rise in the early 1980s, and transferred subsequently to the northeast by landless activists from the south.

Between 1987 and 2003, INCRA expropriated 194 rural properties in Pernambuco, including sixteen sugarcane plantations in the municipalities of Rio Formoso and Tamandaré, which became a separate district in 1996. As required by land reform laws, the first to secure a farm plot on the former plantation were its workers and residents. INCRA would then incorporate families that had taken part of the landless camp. Fourteen of these estates were occupied by landless workers, a fact that shows a close link between the encampment method and land expropriations carried out by the federal government.

Belief in the Black Tarp

The rise and widespread use of the encampment method in Pernambuco's Zona da Mata was not an anticipated event. This region's recent history offers no empirical basis on which to expect that this territory ruled by powerful sugar barons would find itself occupied by scores of landless camps; that the MST would be able mobilize rural workers in an area where rural trade unions had enjoyed undisputed hegemony; that the rural trade unions themselves would start to occupy these private estates; and that their workers would accept the idea of occupying other people's property. To understand how these developments became possible, we need to set the occupations and encampments in a broader social and historical context.

Starting in the late 1980s, the Brazilian state began to liberalize controls over various sectors of the economy, including the sugar industry. In doing so, it put an end to a decades-old subsidy program for sugar and sugarcane prices. It also privatized exports monopolized previously by the Institute of Sugar and Alcohol and increased interest rates. These public measures, coupled with a severe drought, triggered a crisis in the sugar industry. Many plantations and sugar mill operators, unable to cope with this situation, filed for bankruptcy. Others tried to avert insolvency by downsizing their firms. Thousands of rural workers lost their jobs during this time.[11]

In the late 1990s, of the four sugar mills in the two districts studied here, only Trapiche, whose headquarters are located in Sirinhaém (a municipality next to Rio Formoso), was in a solid position. Cucaú, based in Rio Formoso, had just come out of bankruptcy. Santo André, located in the Tamandaré district, did not process the 1996–97 sugarcane harvest and had been paying its workers irregularly since 1995. Central Barreiros, located in Barreiros, south of Tamandaré, had had thirteen of its plantations (nine of these in Pernambuco and four in the state of Alagoas) repossessed by the Bank of Brazil to pay off its debts and qualify for new loans. This plantation mill alone had seen its sugarcane production drop from nearly 650,000 to 350,000 tons between 1988–89 and 1996–97.[12] Other sugarcane estates in the area experienced a similar plunge. At the Amaragi plantation mill, one of the largest in Rio Formoso, production capacity declined from 30,000 tons of sugarcane in the 1970s to only 6,000 tons in the mid-1990s. During this time, Amaragi and other plantations simply stopped paying their workers.

According to the local rural trade union, close to 3,000 agricultural workers in Rio Formoso alone were left without a job as a result of this economic slump. Amid this crisis, the groups organizing land occupations in this area began to target in a strategic way the properties held by bankrupt sugarcane barons. Because of their underutilized fields, these estates qualified as unproductive by INCRA's technical criteria. Given their newfound vulnerability, many landlords were unable to preserve their plantations. MST and trade union organizers, in turn, seized the opportunity made available by this crisis and began to invite unemployed sugarcane workers to join the landless struggle and occupy the estates that had been left fallow.

The MST's incursion into the Zona da Mata took place during this contest, amid its own efforts to extend the movement throughout Brazil.[13] On the southern coast of Pernambuco, MST activists formed an alliance with local rural trade unions and began occupying various sugarcane plantations. The activists brought a series of MST techniques forged during its land occupations and experience in setting up and managing its landless camps. The trade unions, for their part, provided cadres, contacts with rural workers, and access to basic resources, such as their union offices and vehicles.[14] The 1992 occupation of the Camaçari plantation, an event widely viewed as the land struggle's inaugural stamp in the region, was an offspring of this collaboration work. "It all started in Camaçari," as the leaders and workers who participated in this and other occupations would often say.[15] After this mobilization, the MST began to recruit several young people to develop a network of local activists in order to support its land occupations. José Augusto, nicknamed Cabeludo (Hairy), was one of these young activists. Born in 1970 and raised in Rio Formoso, he was the grandson of a renowned rural trade union leader. As he explained:

> I got to know the Landless Movement in 1992, I had left the plantation [Cucaú] and didn't have a job. . . . I took part in the last meeting [to organize the occupation of Camaçari]. . . . Then I became involved in activities at the camp. . . . MST leaders invited me to take part of one their little workshops. After that, well, I started becoming what you'd call a *militante* [militant] — I became a leader in the movement. I went home with my head held up high. I said, "That's it, now I'm going all the way, *ate of fim da linha* [to the end of the line]."[16]

The alliance between Rio Formoso trade unionists and the MST was a noteworthy affair. Although land reform had always been on the agenda of Pernambuco's rural trade union federation (FETAPE), nobody in the federation had ever proposed occupying land in order to obtain it. As Marcelo Rosa shows, this alliance was fuelled by different career aspirations within the rural trade union movement (chap. 15, this volume). Younger trade union leaders sought to promote land occupations with the MST to boost their standing within the union ranks, while senior leaders regarded it as an opportunity to build careers in local politics.[17] In 1996, trade union members began to set up their own landless camps in the region's sugarcane estates.

Union members involved in organizing these camps gradually pressured FETAPE's leadership to adopt these activities as part of the federation's platform. By then, FETAPE had lost the monopoly over rural workers representation, steadily acquired after 1962, when the state's first rural trade unions were formed. Many perceived this loss as a threat to the federation's clout and prestige in Pernambuco.[18] Driven by this new impetus, in 1997 FETAPE was already occupying as many properties as the MST.[19] The strength of Pernambuco's trade union movement helped increase the rate of land occupations in this state in a dramatic way. Between 1990 and 1994, Pernambuco ranked as the sixth highest Brazilian state in number of land occupations, with a total of 28 of these mobilizations out of a national total of 421. Moreover, it ranked fourth in the number of families involved in occupations, with about 5,000 families out of a total of nearly 75,000. Between 1995 and 1999, however, in the wake of FETAPE's increased participation in these actions, Pernambuco became the leading Brazilian state in the number of land occupations—with 308 out of 1,855 of these mobilizations—and in the number of families involved—which included 35,000 families out of a total of 256,000.[20]

Until the early 1990s, rural workers in Pernambuco's Zona da Mata would have treated the act of occupying part of a plantation without the owner's consent as an inconceivable idea. What's more, the thought of demanding the state to expropriate the area for redistribution would have elicited a sense of bewilderment. In their traditional understanding, workers could only move into a plantation if hired to provide services, and could only grow subsistence crops in a small plot within the estate if authorized by the plantation owner or manager. Prior to the 1990s one could have found utopian visions among the rural workers of a "free plantation," a place where they could cultivate a parcel of land, raise as many animals as they wished, and work for the landlord only when money was short.[21] Still, this vision presupposed the existence of a plantation owner and did not involve the notion of workers' land ownership. Thus, given these preconceptions, one cannot explain the occupation of sugarcane plantations as resulting from long-held desires to own a family farm plot.

The widespread unemployment caused by the crisis in the sugar industry provides an alternative and attractive account of the rise of land occupations in the Zona da Mata. This, in fact, is how trade unionists and MST activists often explained the influx of workers to their encampments. After losing their jobs, the argument went, the sugarcane cutters accepted the invitations made by these grassroots organizers and decided to join the land struggle. This explanation, however, stumbles with the problem of seasonal unemployment that surged regularly between March and August, during the winter lockdown between sugarcane harvests.[22] It is true, though, that the sugar industry's crisis in the 1990s affected the surge of land occupations at the end of each harvest season. Yet being unemployed was not a sufficient condition to prompt workers to join a landless camp. During this period, thousands of jobless sugarcane laborers preferred to subsist by taking on odd jobs rather than move to a landless camp and live in a black tarp shack. These workers refused to go to these encampments by saying they were "not interested in owning a piece of land." Cabeludo, the young MST activist, referred to the vicissitudes of recruiting people in poor communities by observing, "Some take it well, others take it badly. They say that the landless are good-for-nothing rabble-rousers, and that they don't want to die to get a little piece of land."

In Sauézinho, at the Santo André plantation, some workers were skeptical of the idea of converting the estate into a land reform settlement. At the Brejo camp, a worker who at the MST's request had tried to recruit more people for the mobilization, was told that they "didn't want to occupy someone else's land." In Serra d'Agua, the camp coordinator, Dinho, said that there were workers who were "afraid of the [land reform] movement because in other areas the landowners' militias shoot, right? They kill!" Moreover, some sugarcane workers had taken part in the occupation of estates that had hired their services, and had to find ways to reconcile their participation at the landless camp with their formal duties at the same plantation. This was the case with the employees of the Pedra de Amolar estate of the Cucaú mill, which formed the core group that occupied Rio Formoso's Mato Grosso plantation in 1999.

The rural workers who joined the landless camps between 1997 and 2000 claimed to have done so in order to "grab a piece of land." Their social background and life trajectories prior to joining the land struggle were quite heterogeneous. Some had lost their jobs; others had been made homeless after a major flood in Rio Formoso, in 1997. Yet others wanted to rebound with a new life after separating from their spouses, or experiencing serious illness or death in the family. Some were attracted to the camp by the presence of acquaintances and relatives, or by its proximity to their place of residence. Others accepted the invitation to join a land occupation because of their personal ties to and bonds of trust with MST activists or rural trade union leaders. The following cases help depict the diversity at stake.

Amaro Santino was at the Brejo camp in September 1997. He had joined the camp at the end of May, a month and a half after the occupation. He was forty-eight years old and had eighteen children, fifteen of whom lived with him. Born in Sirinhaém, he had lived for twenty-nine years in the Trapiche plantation. After a disagreement with his boss, he resigned his position and left the estate, and traveled to Tamandaré with his family to be close to his brother. He then heard about the Brejo camp on an MST-sponsored radio program: "I said to myself, 'the Brejo plantation is having trouble with INCRA. They are calling a lot of people to go there.' And there was this problem I had at the Trapiche mill. So I said to myself, 'I'm going there to INCRA's place' [the Brejo camp]."

Edmilson was one of the first to enter Brejo. On the actual day of the occupation he was going to the market when he ran into Dedé, an MST activist whom he knew by sight. Dedé invited him to the camp, saying it was a good movement and asked him to get more people. Although he had never participated in a land occupation, he had heard of these mobilizations at the regular trade union meetings he attended at the Ilhetas plantation, owned by the Central Barreiros mill, which like many other firms had stopped making wage payments.

Nazareno, a member of the Brejo camp, lived in Tamandaré and made a living selling fruit, crab, and fish cooked by his wife.

> I was there, walking around, always going by the camp. Then I saw this whole movement thing and Zezinho came to speak to me. Zezinho is an [MST] activist. He's a coordinator. So I started thinking and thinking [about what he had said]. Then one day I came here. So I told them and the boys told me to stay. . . . After that I made this little shack, here.[23]

Dalvino, a native of the Agreste region, was in the Mamucaba encampment in 1999:

> It was when I came back here, again, looking for work. I tried here, there, everywhere, couldn't find anything in the businesses firms, the sugar mills. I was about to head back to the *sertão*. But then this guy, a friend of mine, said, "let's go join the landless!" So I came here [to the Mamucaba camp].[24]

Traíra participated at the 1992 camps in São Manuel. But after they were disbanded he went to Cipó, where he eventually became a settler:

> I was in Tamandaré and this young fellow said, "Traíra, do you want to grab a piece of land? Aren't you crazy about getting your own land?" I said, "Why not, where is it?" He said, "Look, there is a man taking names of people to go into a plantation. I don't know where it is, but it is to get land." I said, "Well, I'll go right now." Then I left and got there as the man, called Paulista, was about to leave. I didn't get to speak with him 'cause he was on his way out. But as he left he told me, "You, come next Wednesday when we'll have another meeting." So I went there on Wednesday. I didn't know what it was to be "landless." Then he said, "We're going there to occupy the plantation. Afterward the land will be divided up among the people who occupied it." And I said, "Sure, I'll go."[25]

Gerôncio had joined the 1997 landless camp in Minguito, where he eventually became a settler:

> I was in the city, heading to the trade union office, when I heard people say, "Gerôncio, they're going to open up a camp there. Are you going to invade the property too?" I said, "Look, this business of invading someone else's land, I have never done it. But I'll go there anyways." It was somebody I knew from the trade union. I was a member too. I worked in the fields, I was part of the union, and paid my union dues. Then he said, "You've got nothing to do now, Gerôncio, don't you? So, what are you going to do? You have no land, no place where to live. Because there is this land that is going to belong to the government, to INCRA, only INCRA. Why don't you go and put up a shack there? It's going to be a good prize. It's a debt that the sugar mill owes the bank." I said, "You know what? I'll go there."[26]

In spite of their diverse backgrounds and personal histories, all of these people shared a common belief: that their standing in life would improve after spending a brief period of time living under the black tarp. This ritual of passage would enable them to access a farm plot to grow crops and raise animals, and access government credit to build a house and improve their farm production. Yet above all, this new situation would enable them to become independent laborers, free from any controls by their employer. As Amaro Santino, from the Brejo camp, explained it, "I want to get a plot of land to work with my children so we wouldn't have to depend on these [rural] bosses." Daniel Pedro, who was also at the Brejo camp, put it this way:

> Because I'm forty-four years old; forty-four years of suffering at the hands of the company, you understand? And I haven't got anything. I've worked this whole time for others and I haven't been able to buy anything for myself. And here I've been working and working. Now I'm going to try something different, because working for others got me nothing. Also I have nothing against trying one's luck. Because I've already lost as much as anyone can lose . . .
> I think the way to improve my future is right here, at the camp. And if I lose here, I won't be losing anything anyways. . . . So, I'll take a gamble on life and try my luck.

The belief that a better future could come from the experience of living under the black tarp is a decisive factor in accounting for the willingness of rural workers to occupy a plantation. This conviction, in all likelihood, was built up progressively, starting with the Camaçari occupation. Participants in that mobilization say that few people actually attended the first meetings to organize the occupation. They were wary of what they were told and fearful of what might happen to them. Over time, though, the size of the group began to increase, due in no small part to the presence of trade unionists from Rio Formoso. These union leaders played a key role by providing a clear roadmap for the struggle that lay ahead and helping people overcome their hesitations. INCRA's first land expropriations in the vicinity, in 1993, strengthened people's faith in the prospects of a positive outcome. It also diminished their fear of occupying a landlord's estate.

The novelty in all these developments is the belief that by "living under the black tarp" poor people could aspire to a better future. Prior to this, the main possibilities for a "better life" included migrating to the south or to Pernambuco's capital, Recife; changing jobs or employers; or getting a position in the formal sector of the economy.[27] In the 1990s, though, the notion of living under the black tarp became part of this repertoire of options. It was a new alternative, but no different in this regard to other alternatives. This line of interpretation can better explain facts that would remain obscure if the decision to join a landless camp was viewed solely as the result of "conversion to the land struggle," as some romantic analyses of these movements would suggest. This point can be pursued further by examining people's decisions to leave a landless camp. When an individual resolves to participate in an occupation, he or she is indicating a belief in—or a disposition to bet on—the likelihood of success of this mobilization. A wide range of obstacles, from land evictions and violent attacks by landowner militias to the wear and tear of a lengthy expropriation process ("this land will never come," as camp participants are known to say in these situations), can discourage many people. All these adversities can shake their conviction of having made a good bet. In such circumstances, a rural worker would not hesitate to leave the camp if he or she found a more attractive way to improve his or her life standing. Leaving the camp, however, does not mean the worker has lost all belief in its prospect. Over the years, I encountered several workers who had returned to the same camp after leaving it or who had joined another landless group some time later.

Many rural workers in the Zona da Mata region remained skeptical about joining a landless camp. Indeed, the idea that this venue could improve one's chances of moving ahead in life was far from universal among this populace. Such beliefs, however, can change over time. Between 1997 and 2004, I met workers who were appalled by the idea of "grabbing a piece of land," only to find themselves at a landless camp a few months or years later. Moreover, the belief does not produce automatic effects. Often people believe, but prefer to wait for a better opportunity. Edmilson, for example, thought of joining the Mascatinho occupation, but decided to stay back. He then joined the Brejo camp, which was located in an area he knew well and liked. From a sociological point of view, the key issue here is that, among poor people in Pernambuco's Zona da Mata region, this belief has become part of the realm of possibilities for improving one's footing in life.

In this part of Brazil, the rise of the encampment method was not caused by a single economic, political, or cultural force. Rather, it was the product of a change in the region's social figuration, to use Norbert Elias's term for the interdependent and dynamic processes that shape and reshape the balance of power among individuals over the long run.[28] This shift was made possible by a combination of various social conditions: the sugar industry crisis, MST actions, innovative rural trade union practices, and the development of a new belief. To identify these conditions, it was necessary to question the existence of the camps and ask "how did they become possible?" And to answer this question in light of the social history and modes of representation that have shaped the world of the sugarcane plantations in the Brazilian northeast.

A Foundational and Legitimizing Act

The land occupations organized in the Zona da Mata region were not preceded by any local land conflicts that could have served as an example for these mobilizations. In fact, prior to this surge there were no perceptible signs of rupture in the area's social fabric. Workers in the Amaragi, Sauezinho, Saué Grande, and Coqueiro plantations had problems with wage payments. The Cipó estate was in flux due to the landowner's death. The Brejo, Serra d'Água, Minguito, Mascatinho, and Jundiá de Cima plantations had been handed over to the Bank of Brazil to cover the debts owed by the Central Barreiros sugar mill. All these situations could have been handled in a conventional way, by taking the wage dispute to the Labor Courts or by waiting for a new plantation owner to take over the estate. The expropriation of these large landholdings was not an inevitable outcome.[29]

By organizing land occupations and camps, the MST and its allies in the rural trade union movement created a turnabout of events that shifted the terms in which the crisis of the sugar industry would be addressed. In other words, they created a land conflict where none had existed before and prompted INCRA's decision to expropriate these troubled estates. The purpose here is not to speculate why the MST chose to occupy these plantations, since it is a well-known fact that the movement's goal at that time was to promote the occupation of unproductive plantations and turn them into land reform settlements. All the sugarcane estates occupied during this period, with the exception of Serra d'Agua and Minguito, fit INCRA's technical criteria for land expropriation.[30] The noteworthy issue here is that the encampment method established a novel approach, which transformed a set of problems that could have been solved in customary ways, into a land conflict.

INCRA, in turn, conferred legitimacy on the encampment method. It recognized the MST and other movements as proper claimants, accepted their demands, and acknowledged the participants of occupations as legitimate petitioners by granting them small farm plots. Through its bureaucratic procedures and records, INCRA gave official recognition to these movements and the workers engaged in their camps. INCRA's documents referred to land occupations as "conflict areas," and its tabulations of these conflicts included columns with information on the location of the conflict, the size of the property, the number of families living at each camp, and the name of the organization that had sponsored the occupation. The forms used by INCRA to register future land beneficiaries used the term *acampado* to describe a camp participant (a category not formally recognized in Brazilian legislation), along with other legally inscribed categories, such as "rural worker" and "squatter."

More than 90% of Pernambuco's land expropriations were carried out in estates defined by INCRA as "conflict areas." The encampment method was crucial to this. Its land occupations and camps created the land conflict that made these expropriations possible.[31] The story of the Tentúgal plantation, owned by the Central Barreiros mill and located in the neighboring municipality of São José da Coroa Grande, offers an illustrative case. After the mill declared bankruptcy, the workers who lived in the plantation began to discuss the possibility of setting up a landless camp on the estate. Knowing it would be difficult to achieve a land reform settlement on their own, they invited local trade unionists to help them organize the camp. The shacks were dismantled, however, shortly afterward, a fact that was blamed on the union's meager assistance. When the plantation workers heard there were MST activists in the area, they asked for their help in setting up a new camp and pressured INCRA to expropriate the estate. The camp was reorganized in 1999. Yet because of their resident status on the plantation, these workers did not have to occupy the land per se. Still, they went through the ritual of putting up several black tarp huts and raised a red MST flag on a high pole to symbolize the existence of a land conflict. The landowners subsequently obtained a court order to have the camp dismantled, but none of the participants were evicted from the area since they were part of the estate's labor force. Hence, the eviction order was confined solely to the destruction of the shacks and confiscation of the MST flag. The camp was rebuilt several times before the Tentúgal's formal expropriation in 2002. While different from other land struggles in the region,[32] this case has the virtue of demonstrating how the encampment method became essential to the effort to redistribute land. It was simply not enough to petition INCRA to expropriate an area. These demands had to be presented in an appropriate, persuasive and emphatic manner.

Landless occupations and camps constitute a symbolic language. They enable its participants to assert their claims through action and establish a foundational act on which they can legitimize their demands. The act of occupying land and building an encampment gives the movement in charge an opportunity to convey clear messages to INCRA, the landlord, and other landless groups. It tells INCRA it wants the area to be expropriated for redistribution. It indicates they have a claim on the landlord's property. And it signals to other landless groups this occupation has an "owner." This language is understood by everyone involved. INCRA acknowledges the request and starts an expropriation process. The landowner realizes he might lose his estate and acts to defend his interests by demanding to restore full dominion of his property. In turn, other landless groups agree to respect the flag raised by the movement that has occupied the estate and not intrude on this area.

Landless movements, in sum, legitimize their demands through land occupations. A rural worker, in turn, establishes his or her need for land by building a shack at the camp. This act asserts a claim that involves various stakeholders. It calls on INCRA to select its land reform beneficiaries from among those residing at the camp. It asks the movement responsible for the camp to include his or her name on the list of petitioners that will be presented to INCRA. It also signals to others at the camp that this person is also trying to obtain land. In other words, the act of setting up a black tarp shack and living under it legitimizes the rural worker's quest for a family farm plot. These actions offer material proof of a person's desire to benefit from the government's land reform program.

Adding to this, the act of "living under the black tarp" is represented as a form of suffering that makes all those who submit to this experience worthy of the final reward: a parcel of land. A hierarchy of legitimacy could be found among rural workers encamped for several years, as observed in the Mamucaba occupation. These informal rankings were based on criteria such as length of time since the arrival at the camp and the amount of time actually spent therein, the level of engagement in its activities, and courage shown in times of evictions or confrontation with the private militias hired by the landlords to attack the camps.[33] These rankings had no effect on INCRA's selections. Rather, they served as an informal metric by which to classify individuals as more or less deserving of a farm plot.

In conclusion, land redistribution in Pernambuco's coastal region was the up-shot of a process triggered by land occupations and landless camps. These mobilizations created a series of situations that were identified by INCRA as "land conflicts." Thanks to INCRA's legitimation, the encampment method became the "appropriate way" to demand land reform. The state's consent to this mobilization tactic has had an inevitable impact on all those interested in stirring up a landless movement or obtaining a parcel of land. For, in effect, it has obliged them all to adopt the encampment method as a single formula for success.

Reciprocal Dependency and Competitive Relations

The bellicose rhetoric often heard between state officials—particularly from the Ministry for Agrarian Development and INCRA—and movement leaders suggests a highly confrontational relationship. Since the mid-1990s, the media has published frequent declarations by government authorities stating that land reform must be accomplished in a lawful manner and that all violations of the rule of law—notably the "invasion of private properties"—will not be tolerated.[34] The movements, in turn, regularly accuse the government of not following up on their promise to redistribute land and threaten to carry out new waves of land occupations and other protest measures. Such hostilities were no doubt more intense under the Cardoso presidency than under the Lula administration. Although revealing elements of tension, this rhetoric masks the close cooperation and mutual dependence that actually exists between the Brazilian state and rural social movements.

Despite favorable provisions in the 1988 Constitution and the 1993 Agrarian Law, state authorities in Brazil have refused to implement an extensive land redistribution policy, based on the expropriation of unproductive large land-holdings. Because of this, rural social movements have had to step up their efforts—through land occupations and camps—on the properties that should be reformed. Given this situation, these movements have effectively set up basic guidelines for the state's agrarian polices: the estates expropriated are the ones occupied by these groups. The close relationship between land occupations and expropriations can be discerned by comparing INCRA's list of land reform settlements, established under the Itamar Franco, Cardoso, and Lula governments, with the movements' own list of land occupations and camps. State officials validate land expropriations by asserting the need to pacify a "conflict area." This language emerged, in all likelihood, at a time when the state began to address the violent land conflicts taking place in the Amazon region, between *posseiros* (squatters) and *grileiros* (land grabbers), particularly during the 1970s and 1980s. In Pernambuco, however, the land conflict was effectively created by social movements, through their land occupations and protest camps. Here, then, the notion of "conflict areas" euphemizes the arbitrary issues at stake.

Rural social movements have continued to play a key role in designating the state's land beneficiaries, by ensuring that new settlers are selected from among those who participate in their land mobilizations. Contrary to the common view, Pernambuco did not have a large mass of destitute people yearning for land. The movements produced this demand by promoting the encampment method, which gave the rural workers an opportunity to attain something they would have never dreamed of before: their own farm plot.[35] By going to the encampment and demanding a parcel of land they began to identify themselves as a *sem terra* (landless). After all, this was the proper way of representing themselves at the camp. It was also the term used by other people, in the city and countryside, to depict people living under the black tarp. Poor people from the shantytowns and the outskirts of rural villages, surviving on odd jobs or employed by the sugarcane plantations, are normally not viewed as "landless," because they are not engaged in the land mobilizations that define this identity. Rural social movements, therefore, have played an essential role in stirring the social demand and conditions needed for someone to be considered "landless" and receive a land parcel from the state.

These movements, on the other hand, depend significantly on the state to carry out their land occupations. State programs designed to assist landless workers provided a powerful incentive for people to join these mobilizations. Rural workers often reported that the invitation to join a landless camp came with assurances that INCRA would be expropriating unproductive estates in the vicinity and redistributing it among camp participants. Movement recruiters also assured the workers that INCRA would provide basic foodstuff during their time at the camp;[36] as well as facilitate credits to build a new house and start their agricultural production once the new settlement got started. These promises were confirmed with each land expropriation and disbursal of government subsidies to new settlers, all of which enhanced recruitment efforts in the area. The dynamics of land occupations were thus very much entwined with and dependent on the state. Without the state's involvement, the movements would have had no reasonable expectations to offer to their audience, and thus experience great difficulties in attracting people to their camps. All of this would have greatly weakened the dynamics of landless movements in Pernambuco's Zona da Mata, which had gained strength and multiplied since the early 1990s to include, by 2004, nine different organizations engaged in land mobilizations.[37]

INCRA and each of these movements, then, were linked through ties of mutual dependence and tacit cooperation. These relations, however, were usually tense and complex given the fact that they are part of a social figuration, as Norbert Elias would observe, that involved individuals associated with various branches of the state, such as the judiciary, and other influential actors like the landlords. Hence, most land appropriations in the Zona da Mata were carried out as a result of the movements' intensified pressure on INCRA. For instance, the Sauezinho, Saué Grande, Coqueiro, Cocal, and Cocalzinho plantations that belonged to the Santo André sugar mill in Tamandaré were expropriated in late 1999, after more than 100 workers from these areas camped out for forty-five days on the sidewalk in front of the INCRA office building in Recife. INCRA's expropriation proceeding in Santo André had to contend with the mill owner's powerful political friends, with clout in Brasília. Media coverage of such events focused largely on the visible signs of tension and conflict. By contrast, this chapter reveals the discrete elements of mutual dependence and cooperation that undergird the encampment method.

In closing, the encampment method was also widely adopted as result of the dependency forged between the movements and the participants who gained a farm plot, as well as the competition among these different movements. Those who received land and other government benefits felt indebted to the group that sponsored their mobilization. These debts were depicted as a sign of *compromiso* (commitment), and implied obligations of loyalty and cooperation. It was thanks to these ties that the movements could draw on the assistance of seasoned activists—who had already obtained a farm plot through previous mobilizations—to organize and boost the number of participants in new land occupations, long distance marches, and other protest activities. Aside from this contribution, the movement activists would also teach the newcomers how to prepare a land occupation, while drawing on their own life story to instill the new recruits with a sense of hope as to the merits of their struggle. Indeed, different groups of settlers were involved in supporting all the land occupations that had taken place in the Zona da Mata.[38]

Land mobilizations and expropriations were widely recognized as the feats and victories that conferred the movements with symbolic capital (prestige) and relative power, given their ability to influence the balance of forces. Lest there be no doubt, the surge of land occupations in this part of Brazil owed much to the competition provoked between the many different movements engaged in the struggle for land reform.[39]

Conclusion

Land occupations in Brazil have been portrayed as an impressive feat, both at home and abroad. Many observers have treated these developments as the manifestation of a "struggle for land," a "new sign of rebellion of the oppressed," and a "natural reaction to a global order under neoliberal domination." This chapter has strived to explain how land occupations became possible in Pernambuco, by eschewing analyses that attribute this phenomenon to the "awakened consciousness of the landless masses" or the upshot of some "inexorable force of history." In doing so, the study made certain methodological choices. It started with an ethnographic review and comparison of landless camps that helped identify a common mobilization pattern. After this, it analyzed the conditions that facilitated the use of the encampment method. This led to a historical analysis of the social relations and motivations of camp participants. In assessing their need to take part of a *performance* that involved setting up black-tarp-covered shacks and hoisting the movement's banner on a tall flag pole, the study found that these symbolic acts were crucial to legitimizing land claims. The final section addressed the dynamics of land occupations in ways that underscored elements of mutual dependence and competition between the state, various movements, and the individuals engrossed in these mobilizations.

Land occupations in Pernambuco did not emerge out of a "struggle for land" per se. The demand for land was not a preexistent one. Rather, it was produced by movements and sustained by the state's response to their actions. As long as there were individuals willing to join these movements who believe in the opportunities made available by living "under the black tarp," they engaged in a set of activities that created a "struggle for land." This struggle had several effects. Among these one can underscore the fact the struggle generated conditions that enabled the Brazilian state to carry out a land redistribution program. The struggle also gave rise to, and strengthened, a wide range of rural social movements. Above all, though, it allowed hundreds of thousands of people to garner the attention of public authorities and improve their livelihoods by gaining access to land, credit, education, and other state services. Were it not for this struggle, many would have continued to be ignored by the state, as large segments of the Brazilian population have been throughout the nation's history. At best, they would have reaped the meager benefits of a temporary or emergency assistance program. The arguments made in this chapter are based on developments in the state of Pernambuco. A successful case study, though, can illuminate other situations, provide clues, and offer an analytical framework model for further research.

Notes

Translated from the Portuguese by Miguel Carter.

1. For an earlier and expanded version of this chapter, see Sigaud (2005).
2. On the land occupations that took place in the states of Rio Grande do Sul and Rio de Janeiro during the early 1960s, see Eckert (1984) and Grynszpan (1987), respectively.

3. Demands for agrarian reform prior to the 1964 military coup are examined in Camargo (1981).
4. Pernambuco's Zona da Mata is one of the oldest settlement areas in Brazil. The Portuguese set up sugarcane plantations there in the sixteenth century and began producing sugar. Since the mid-nineteenth century, sugarcane has been grown on large plantations owned by sugar mill proprietors and influential landlords. The sugarcane harvest season requires a considerable labor force. Until the mid-1950s most workers lived on the plantations. In the ensuing years, though, the majority of these people were compelled to find housing in the small rural towns that lie next to these estates. The Zona da Mata region covers 11% of Pernambuco's total area. Its population in the mid-1990s reached more than 2.7 million people, 37% of the state's total. The region's large landowners have traditionally played a pivotal role among Pernambuco's economic and political elite. On the social history of these plantations, see Andrade (1980, 2001), Eisenberg (1977), Mello (1975), Palmeira (1976), Sigaud (1979), Garcia (1983), and Heredia (1979).
5. A map of Pernambuco with the location of the towns cited in this text can be found in Wolford (chap. 12, this volume).
6. Rural trade unions are organized by municipal districts. In Pernambuco's Zona da Mata the vast majority of union members have been plantation workers. More generally, on Brazil's rural trade union movement, see Maybury-Lewis (1994).
7. See Smircic (2000: 29–55) for a detailed description of a 1999 land occupation in the Zona da Mata region.
8. FETAPE's decision to promote land occupations is analyzed in Rosa (2004a); also see Rosa (chap. 15, this volume).
9. The Barreiros camp was still in place in late 2012. This update on the Mamucaba group was appended by Miguel Carter, the volume editor, based on information provided by an MST leader in Pernambuco, Jaime Amorim, telephone interview, November 30, 2012.
10. Sigaud (2000).
11. For a review of the sugar industry's crisis, see Andrade (2001).
12. According to data published by the Sindicato das Indústrias do Açucar de Pernambuco (1999).
13. On the MST's national expansion, see Fernandes (2000), and Stédile and Fernandes (1999).
14. Rosa (2004a: 77).
15. The MST's arrival in Pernambuco in 1989 was beset by problems. Its first land occupation that same year ended in failure. The movement's origins in the Zona da Mata region are attributed mainly to its successful occupation of the Camaçari estate in 1992.
16. Testimony collected in September 1999 by Lygia Sigaud and Sergio A. Chamorro Smircic.
17. Rosa (2004a: 73–154).
18. The Zona da Mata's first rural trade unions were set up in 1962, the year a national law was passed authorizing the formation of these unions. For historical background on this period, see Camargo (1973, 1981), Bezerra (1979), and Wilkie (1964).
19. *Diário de Pernambuco*, Recife, June 11, 1997.
20. Fernandes (2000: 270–72). Data collected by Fernandes's UNESP research center should be treated with caution, since land occupations can be short-lived and its number of participants extremely variable.
21. On the utopia of the free sugarcane plantation, see Sigaud (1979: 205–22).

22. Sigaud (1979: 167–204).
23. All statements from the Brejo plantation were recorded by the author in September 1997.
24. All statements from the Mamucaba plantation were recorded by David Fajolles in September 1999.
25. Statement recorded by Marie Gaille and Alexandra Barbosa da Silva in September 1999.
26. Statement recorded by Benoit de L'Estoile in September 1999.
27. An analysis of how sugarcane workers made sense of the idea of migrating to the south can be found in Garcia (1990).
28. Elias (1982: 154–61).
29. The labor rights acquired by rural workers in 1963 allowed them to address their grievances against the plantation bosses in the labor courts. After the military coup, this practice became the rural trade union's most effective way of resolving disputes with their employers; see Sigaud (1999). One should also note that changes in plantation ownership were not infrequent in Pernambuco's Zona da Mata.
30. The Serra d'Agua and Minguito estates were considered productive under INCRA's criteria, but were included for land redistribution due to the fact that the plantations' bankrupt owner, the Central Barreiros sugar mill company, had handed them over to the state-owned Bank of Brazil.
31. Once the petition for a land expropriation has been made, the regional INCRA office sends a team of technicians to appraise the estate's level of productivity. If the land is found to be unproductive, the legal process goes on to Brasília, where the national INCRA office requests the president of the Republic to sign an expropriation decree, noting that the property does not fulfill the "social function" required by the 1988 Constitution. After this, the owner is compensated for the expropriated land in Agrarian Bonds (*Títulos da Dívida Agrária*) and receives cash payments for all improvements made on the estate.
32. The majority of the landless camps set up in Pernambuco's Zona da Mata were formed through the occupation of sugarcane plantations. A few camps, though, were started by workers who actually lived on these estates, as in the cases of the Amaragi, Sauezinho, Saué Grande, and Coqueiro plantations.
33. Fajolles (2000) identified this hierarchy of legitimacy among Mamucaba camp participants; also see Sigaud et al. (2006).
34. A sample of this public rhetoric can be gleaned from the press reports published during the MST's 1997 national march to Brasília; see Chaves (2000: 265–341).
35. This observation derives from extensive fieldwork in land reform settlements in Rio Formoso and Tamandaré, between 2002 and 2004.
36. The possibility of gaining access to food donations at the camp motivated many rural workers to join these mobilizations, even though these government provisions were often allocated in an irregular way.
37. Rosa (2004a: 172–73).
38. This type of loyalty was also observed in the encampments studied by Macedo (2003) in Rio de Janeiro, by Loera (2006) in São Paulo, and by Brenneisen (2003) in Paraná.
39. Smircic (2000), Sigaud (2000), Sigaud, Fajolles, Gautile, Gómez, and Smircic (2006), and Rosa (2004a).

Gabriel Ondetti, Emmanuel Wambergue,
and José Batista Gonçalves Afonso

8 From *Posseiro* to *Sem Terra*
The Impact of MST Land Struggles in the State of Pará

As it expanded across Brazil's vast territory, the Landless Rural Workers Movement (MST) encountered many local groups already engaged in struggles for land. One of the challenges facing MST militants was how to turn these groups into allies while also consolidating their own organization and its distinctive methods. This was not necessarily a simple task. Local activists often saw the MST, with its roots in southern Brazil, as an outside competitor for political influence and the loyalties of rural workers. The MST also brought its own methodology, based on a tight organization, strong discipline, and massive protest events. This approach often differed from indigenous traditions of struggle and was sometimes seen as ill-suited to local social and political conditions.

Nowhere was the preexisting movement for land more intense than in frontier areas of the Amazon, where poor squatters, or *posseiros*, had for years been waging life-and-death battles for land access with wealthy landowners and land grabbers. This struggle was particularly strong in the state of Pará, where the rapid opening of formerly inaccessible areas in the 1960s and 1970s had generated a chaotic settlement process marked by violence. The posseiros had their own methodology and a support network anchored by rural workers' unions and the Catholic Church. Because of the strength of the posseiro tradition, as well as the MST's early difficulties in the state, until well into the 1990s the MST's national leadership had doubts about whether their organization would ever become a major force in Pará.

Even by the mid-2000s, fully two decades after the MST's initial attempts to establish its presence in the state of Pará, its achievements remained rather modest if measured by the most obvious quantitative indicators. Since it began actively organizing land occupations in the state in the late 1980s, the MST has accounted for fewer than 15% of all such actions undertaken in Pará.[1] The land reform settlements linked to the MST constitute an even smaller proportion of the overall total. These achievements are greatly overshadowed by those of the rural workers' unions associated with Pará's Federation of Workers in Agriculture (FETAGRI), one of Brazil's most combative state rural union federations.

In this chapter we tell the story of the MST's development in Pará and we assess its overall impact on the struggle for land in this immense state, where more than one-fifth of all the land reform beneficiaries in Brazil are settled. We argue that the relatively modest progress made by the MST in terms of organizing land occupations and conquering new settlements is not an accurate indicator of this organization's true influence in Pará, since some of its major contributions are not reflected in these totals. When one takes into consideration the MST's less obvious impacts, it becomes clear that it has actually had a powerful, even transformative, role in the struggle for land. In particular, we emphasize the importance of two contributions.

One involves a change in what Charles Tilly has called the "repertoire of contention": that set of organizational forms and protest tactics culturally available to activists in a given place, at a given time.[2] The MST has helped to diffuse a new repertoire, involving more organized and visible tactics aimed at putting pressure on authorities by appealing to public opinion and the news media. The repertoire associated with the posseiro struggle, based on looser organization, smaller groups, and the wearing down of landowner resistance by sheer persistence and brute force, is still very much in use. However, land reform activists, including many rural union leaders, have gradually absorbed some of the MST's key methods, transforming the struggle for land into something more closely resembling a modern social movement.

The second and more important way in which the MST has influenced the struggle for land in Pará is by pressuring the federal government to intervene more aggressively in the state's landholding structure. Mainly by forcing a major confrontation with the local power structure, the MST has obligated federal authorities to accelerate land distribution in southern Pará or face mounting political costs. This confrontation was crystallized in the brutal police massacre of landless protestors at Eldorado dos Carajás in April 1996, which attracted national and international attention and deeply embarrassed the government of Fernando Henrique Cardoso. With the increasing resources available for agrarian reform, the number of landless families settled in the state has multiplied rapidly. In addition, the improved prospects for obtaining land have contributed to a revival of grassroots protest for land, affecting all the groups involved in the struggle.

This chapter is organized into three main sections. The first lays the groundwork for our analysis of the MST in Pará by discussing the origins and character of the posseiro struggle. We highlight, in particular, the role of the Brazilian military regime's Amazon "development" policies and the influence of the progressive church movement in shaping this struggle. In the second section, we provide an account of the MST's trajectory in the state. Among the themes we emphasize are the shifting relations between this organization and the posseiro struggle and the powerful, reciprocal causal influence between the MST's struggle in Pará and the political context for land reform at the national level. Finally, we assess the MST's overall impact on the struggle for land in this state, fleshing out the arguments outlined above.

The Posseiro Struggle

When the military took power in Brazil in 1964, most of the Amazon region was a remote backwater. Policies implemented by the dictatorship during the late 1960s and 1970s would accelerate the pace of change dramatically, however, transforming both the environmental and human features of the region. In no state was change more rapid and jarring than Pará, on the eastern edge of Amazonia. One of the most notable and tragic consequences of this transformation was the intensification of social conflict over land. The massive inflow of both rich and poor people seeking land in the state gave rise to numerous conflicts, many of them violent. With the help of Catholic activists, the poor became increasingly assertive in pursuing access to land in the 1980s. Significant victories were won, but at the cost of many lives.

The rubber boom of the late nineteenth and early twentieth centuries had linked Amazonia more closely to the national and international economies and drew many immigrants to the region. With the end of the boom, however, the region lost population and entered a period of relative stagnation. In 1964, when the military took control of the Brazilian state, there were few roads to break up the seemingly endless stretches of forest and savannah and much of the region's population, including most of Brazil's remaining indigenous groups, continued to live off a mixture of subsistence agriculture and petty extractive activities. One of the priorities of military authorities was to accelerate colonization and economic development in Brazil's share of the Amazon River basin. They sought not only to exploit its land, mineral, and energy resources, but to further solidify the country's territorial claims in the region. The rise of a Communist-led guerrilla movement in southeastern Pará in the early 1970s increased the military's security concerns in the Amazon. Although it was easily extinguished, the movement contributed to the regime's drive to strengthen the presence of the state in what would soon become an economically strategic corner of the region.[3]

A variety of initiatives were devised to meet these goals. From the point of view of struggles for land, three were most important. One was the granting of generous tax incentives to individuals and firms willing to invest in cattle ranching in the Amazon. Ranching had already begun to grow in the region before 1964, but the military's subsidies and road construction initiatives accelerated the trend. By 1980 more than a billion dollars had been doled out by the Secretariat for the Development of the Amazon (SUDAM).[4] The ranches were often enormous, averaging more than 20,000 hectares, and some landowners ended up grabbing more land than they were legally entitled to. The scale of SUDAM-funded projects was not matched by their productivity. A 1985 study found that, on average, they were achieving only 16% of their expected production.[5] To make matters worse, the ranches created little employment and accelerated deforestation.

Another policy initiative was aimed at benefiting poorer farmers. Since the early 1960s, when protest for land reform accelerated in the impoverished northeast, military authorities had been concerned about the implications of the country's high land concentration for "national security."[6] In response to this concern, in 1970 General Emilio Médici, president of Brazil, announced a program aimed at settling landless families from other, more densely populated regions in the Amazon. "Lands without people," went the regime's poetic slogan, would provide a haven for "people without land." Most would be settled along the Trans-Amazon Highway, a proposed roadway that would cut across the Amazon from east to west, extending some 5,000 kilometers.

The regime's colonization project began slowly and never reached its goals.[7] Pressure from the private sector helped push authorities to downgrade public colonization after 1973. However, the promises of land distribution ended up triggering a major influx of poor rural people into the Amazon in search of land. Unable to gain land in official projects, many families squatted on what they took to be public land, helping plant the seeds of future conflict. Combined, the growth of ranching and the failure of colonization served to concentrate control over farmland. In 1992 Pará had the second most unequal landholding structure of all the states, behind only Amazonas.[8]

The third initiative was part and parcel of the two already mentioned: the intensification of road construction. Traditionally, the major means of transportation in the Amazon had been its many rivers. Plans for developing the region, however, could not proceed without a larger, better system of roadways. The Trans-Amazon was the most ambitious project, but several other new highways were constructed during the 1970s and early 1980s, especially along the eastern and southern borders of the region. The roads provided access to areas that could be farmed, logged, or mined. With "land fever" running high, areas close to the new roadways were often claimed even before the road-building crews began their work.

During the early years of the regime, Pará was the state most affected by these changes. The construction of the Belém-Brasília Highway, completed in 1960, had already linked Pará to the southern half of the country. Running along the state's eastern border, the road facilitated the entrance of people interested in taking advantage of its resources. Many ended up in southeastern Pará, which, unlike the area surrounding the state capital, Belém, to the north, was still sparsely populated. The Trans-Amazon Highway cut across the middle of the state, further increasing access to southeastern Pará from the northeast. A number of federal colonization projects were located in this region. In addition, almost one-third of all SUDAM subsidies for agriculture and agro-industry were channeled to projects located in Pará.[9]

Other changes that occurred during the military era would also play an important role in drawing people to southeastern Pará and especially the area around Marabá, located halfway between Belém and the state's southern boundary. In the late 1970s, the regime initiated a huge mining project in the Carajás region, southwest of Marabá. Centered on what would become one of the world's largest iron mines, the project promised to create many jobs. About the same time, some 200 kilometers to the north, construction work was started on a massive hydroelectric project, the Tucuruí dam, which also promised employment. Finally, in 1980, prospectors made a huge gold strike at Serra Pelada, between Carajás and Marabá. By mid-decade close to 100,000 miners, or *garimpeiros*, were working to extract Serra Pelada's riches. The apparent opportunities offered by these initiatives were a magnet, drawing people into the region at an impressive rate. An expanding road network facilitated access and population centers sprang up in formerly uninhabited areas. Marabá, the most populous town in southeastern Pará, grew by 144% during the 1970s.[10]

Conflict over land in the Amazon also intensified during the course of the decade. Rapidly increasing access to the region spurred competition for control over public land and a weak state was unable to arbitrate effectively between competing claims. In the early years, most of the conflicts involved attempts by poor squatters to avoid expulsion from lands claimed by wealthier landowners or land grabbers (*grileiros*). Large landowners usually came from the more developed regions of Brazil, and a few of the largest were multinational companies. They often contracted armed men to "cleanse" their lands of posseiros. Facing the threat of violence or arrest, squatters usually moved on. Occasionally, however, a group would resist. Since their opponents were armed and posseiros could not expect assistance from authorities, who usually favored large investors, resistance typically involved armed force. These conflicts took many lives, alarming military authorities, who feared they might ignite a broader struggle.[11]

The Catholic Church gradually became more deeply involved in these battles. Influenced by the rising progressive tide within the Latin American church, Amazon clergy organized Community Base Churches (CEBs), recruited lay activists, and urged the poor to organize to defend their interests and pursue social justice.[12] The brutal social conflicts provoked by the military's Amazon

Map 8.1. Pará

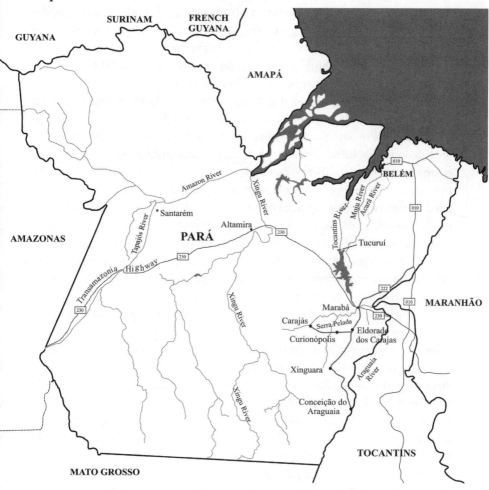

development policies helped to radicalize many members of the clergy. As Ivo Poletto explains in chapter 4, this volume, Amazon bishops were instrumental in the creation, in 1975, of the Pastoral Commission on Land (CPT), an organization devoted to defending the rights of poor people to farmland. Church officials were increasingly critical of the regime's policies in the Amazon and, at the grassroots level, clergy and religious lay people associated with the CPT provided various types of assistance to posseiros, including food, pressure on authorities, and legal assistance.

Over time, the character of land conflicts shifted.[13] Purely defensive struggles gave way to more offensive strategies, as groups of posseiros occupied lands known to be claimed by owners or grileiros. Through sheer determination and armed force they sought to outlast competing claimants. If the conflict was particularly intense, the state might step in and expropriate all or part of the property, rewarding the posseiros' efforts with a legal title. In addition, the activist network undergirding the struggle for land gained greater density. In some areas organized efforts were made to take over rural trade unions, which in most cases served mainly as conduits for the delivery of social services and to transform them into instruments of class struggle.

The shift in tactics responded to the declining availability of unclaimed land in accessible areas. In addition, it was a reaction to political changes. The gradual democratic opening at the national level, in the late 1970s and early 1980s, provided more political space for mobilization and protest. Also, the regime's efforts to attenuate conflict through selective distribution of land in response to the threat of violent conflict only seemed to provoke more land occupations.[14] Landowners responded by assassinating posseiro leaders and their allies, including members of the clergy. Conflict peaked in the mid-1980s, when José Sarney, the first civilian president in two decades, announced a major land reform plan. The program was eventually gutted under pressure from landowners, but the announcement encouraged poor workers to stake claims to land and landowners to resist them, often with deadly force.

In Pará the posseiro struggle was concentrated mainly in the southeast, where development initiatives and the inflow of migrants had been most intense. The best organized and most successful local movement was in the municipality of Conceição do Araguaia. There, poor workers conquered many large properties and, after a protracted struggle, captured the local rural workers' union in 1985. In the Marabá area to the north, conflict was also intense, but progress was slower. Posseiros faced a more established oligarchy, whose wealth had traditionally derived from the extraction of Brazil nuts.[15] Throughout southern Pará, land-related violence was extremely common throughout the late 1970s and 1980s. Largely as a result of conflict in this region, Pará alone accounted for almost one-fourth of the 1,687 deaths related to rural social conflict in Brazil between 1970 and 1989.[16] Few of the perpetrators were ever tried, much less convicted, reflecting the extreme weakness of the rule of law.

In 1987 union activists in Pará succeeded in taking over the state rural union federation, FETAGRI, and affiliating it to the Unified Workers' Central (CUT), Brazil's most leftist union confederation. By then, however, mobilization for land was beginning to taper off in most areas. The federal government's growing resistance to land redistribution served to discourage new occupations. Under President Fernando Collor, a right-wing populist who took office in 1990, expropriations of private farmland would grind to a virtual halt. In addition, in some municipalities years of violent attacks by landowners and their henchmen had taken their toll on the movement, sending many of its leaders to an early grave.

The MST in Pará

The MST first established a presence in Pará during the climax of the posseiro struggle in the mid-1980s. However, it would not become a truly autonomous and functioning organization until the 1990s. The MST's slow progress reflected a number of factors. One of the most significant was the strength of the pos-seiro tradition itself. Rural union activists were ambivalent about supporting the MST's growth in their state and the organization's methods were foreign to activists and rural workers alike. In addition, when the MST finally began organizing occupations of its own in Pará, the political context for land reform at the national level had taken a turn for the worse and concessions were hard to come by. Nevertheless, by the mid-1990s, MST had established a solid foothold in the state and had won some significant victories in the Marabá area, setting the stage for a showdown with the local power structure.

With the support of the CPT, union activists from Pará attended the MST's first national congress in Curitiba, Paraná, in 1985. At least in theory, a group of them took responsibility for establishing the MST in their home state.[17] The MST was given office space at the state CUT headquarters and the head of the CUT's rural secretariat represented Pará on the MST's National Coordination, its second highest leadership body. However, at least part of the state's rural union leadership was unenthusiastic about the MST, since they were build-ing their own movement through the official union structure, which the MST skirted.[18] Though the MST was nominally established in Pará, the activists as-sociated with it dithered, failing to organize land occupations using the MST's name or methods. According to a union activist who later joined the MST, their inaction mainly reflected the strength of the posseiro tradition:

> The union movement is the union movement and the MST is the MST. The union movement has its own way of acting, which is not the same as the MST. Big, organized occupations were not the practice of the union movement. It was not a question of disagreeing with the MST's methods as much as having one's own customs and ways of doing things.[19]

It was not until the late 1980s that, under pressure from the national leader-ship, activists began organizing land occupations under the MST banner. The first two occurred in the southeastern municipality of Xinguara.[20] Even then, local activists did not fully incorporate the MST's methods and failed to heed the national leadership's instructions to target a huge estate controlled by a prominent family, viewing the idea as unrealistic.[21] In any case, the families were quickly expelled from the properties occupied. In response, the MST lead-ership decided to lay down the law. Representatives of the National Board trav-eled to Pará in 1989 and told local activists that they would either have to start behaving like the MST or leave the organization.[22] It was also decided that the

MST would move its state secretariat south, from Belém to Conceição do Araguaia, then a major center for land struggles.

In 1990, with the help of several MST militants from nearby states, the MST conducted two land occupations in Conceição. Unlike the actions undertaken earlier in Xinguara, these were more faithful to the methods used by the MST in the rest of the Brazil.[23] Although the occupiers did not suffer expulsion, the MST experienced difficulties in both cases. In the first, the leadership's attempts to organize collective production in line with the MST's national policies met with resistance.[24] The CPT and rural unions had done relatively little to influence settlement organization or production methods and the MST's idea of setting up production cooperatives was foreign. The MST's initiatives divided the camp and caused tension with the CPT. The second occupation, meanwhile, provoked the entrance of a large number of squatters onto the property, when it became apparent that expropriation would occur. To avoid violent conflict between the groups, the MST ended up pulling out of the camp.

Through these efforts in Conceição the MST recruited a new group of young activists. However, its failures were damaging to its reputation. To make a fresh start, the leadership decided in early 1991 to move the secretariat north to Marabá. In terms of landowner power, Marabá was arguably a more difficult target than Conceição. Its ruling elite, led by the fearsome Mutran family, had been in place for decades and still controlled vast landholdings. However, other characteristics of the area were more promising. As a rapidly growing economic and population center, Marabá offered the chance to make a greater political impact. Federal policy initiatives in recent decades, including the massive Carajás mining project, had weakened the oligarchy's grip on power and immigration to the region had caused a huge buildup of landless workers.[25] The decline of the Serra Pelada goldmine, beginning in the late 1980s, had contributed to growing poverty and unemployment in the region. Finally, the union movement was not as strongly consolidated as in Conceição, meaning there was somewhat more political space for an organization striving to lead and shape the struggle for land.[26]

In Marabá, the MST resolved to target only properties located close to urban centers, with good market access, a choice that set it on a collision course with the area's elite. Its efforts in Marabá got off to a poor start. Under President Collor the federal police had begun to harass and arrest MST leaders in a number of states. The MST's plans to occupy a large property once owned by the Mutran family were foiled in June 1991, when federal police agents arrested seven militants. Since this group represented most of the MST's leadership, it effectively crippled the organization. The militants were only released several months later, following a concerted campaign by domestic and international human rights groups.[27]

The MST rebounded from this setback with impressive vigor. In 1992, activists recruited more than 500 families to occupy the Rio Branco estate, a massive property in the Carajás area controlled by the Lunardellis, a wealthy coffee-growing clan based in São Paulo and Paraná. The activists were expelled by the police and set up camp in front of the local federal land reform agency (INCRA) office in Marabá, where they stayed for several months before occupying the same property once again. In December 1993, INCRA expropriated half of the Rio Branco. Although the land could accommodate fewer than half of the MST families who had participated in the camp, the expropriation represented an important victory for the organization, its first in the state of Pará.

Over the next two years, the MST organized a number of additional camps and occupations. Two initiatives were particularly bold and helped to consolidate the MST as a significant new actor in the Marabá area. In June 1994, some 2,000 MST families occupied an area owned by the mighty Companhia Vale do Rio Doçe, a state-owned firm that operated the Carajás iron mine. They were quickly expelled by police. After camping in front of the Marabá INCRA office for several months, they occupied the remaining area of the Rio Branco in May 1995. This time, events at the national level worked in the MST's favor. In August, thirteen people had died in Corumbiara, Rondônia, when police tried to clear a land occupation. The incident made headlines all over Brazil and put pressure on newly elected president Fernando Henrique Cardoso to accelerate the pace of land reform, especially in areas with a high risk of violence. INCRA officials had declared the Rio Branco productive, and thus not vulnerable to expropriation, but the agency purchased the property in order to defuse the conflict.

By the mid-1990s, the MST had enlisted a significant group of young militants. Some of the union activists had dropped out. These, however, were replaced mostly by a mixture of rural workers recruited from camps and settlements and a few more urban people, some of them linked to Catholic organizations. Conspicuous mainly by their absence were the transplanted southern militants who had played an important role in the MST's expansion into other states. This was apparently a reflection of the low priority the national MST leadership placed on Pará. Because of the strength of the posseiro tradition, the National Directorate had judged that the MST's potential for growth in the state was limited.[28] That the MST had begun to make a name for itself was therefore a pleasant surprise to the organization's top brass.

The MST's advances had been achieved by organizing essentially the same social sector that had traditionally been involved in the posseiro struggle. These were mainly poor, often illiterate, workers with personal or family roots in the rural northeast, particularly neighboring Maranhão. They generally had some background in agriculture yet, unable to obtain land, many had worked in gold mines or saw mills or as wage laborers on ranches or in urban areas. Critics of the MST often said its recruits were more urban and had less of a "vocation for agriculture" than the posseiros, but there is not much evidence for these assertions. MST families came from urban areas because the rapid occupation of the land by vast cattle ranches had made the Amazon, unlike earlier agricultural frontiers in Brazilian history, a largely urban frontier.

What clearly set the MST apart from the posseiro tradition was its organizational methods and tactics, derived mostly from the MST's earlier experiences in southern Brazil. MST occupations tended to be larger than posseiro actions and more disciplined and collectivized. Whereas posseiros entered a property and immediately spread out, dividing the land into individual plots, the MST formed a single, compact encampment. This method facilitated collective organization. The families were usually broken down into smaller groups and each of these was represented on a commission, which helped coordinate the camp's activities and maintained a comparatively rigid code of discipline. The MST's struggle was also more politically centralized. Although they typically received advice and assistance from unions or the CPT, posseiro groups were often formed without consulting these allies and were essentially autonomous. In contrast, state MST leaders actively recruited families for its occupations and subsequently made most of the key tactical decisions, such as where and when to occupy.

Posseiro occupations tended to be, at least in the initial period after entering a property, all-male affairs. The MST, meanwhile, expected male "family heads" to bring women and children with them. In this way, they hoped to reduce the risk of repression and project a more wholesome image of the movement to the media and public. The MST's strategy of appealing to public opinion and building broader alliances was also reflected in its use of tactics other than land occupations. When expelled from occupied properties, the MST set up camps at the side of a public road or in front of the Marabá INCRA office. Marches, demonstrations, and occupations of INCRA offices were also common tactics used by the MST to exert pressure on authorities. Although these types of tactics were not unknown in the posseiro struggle, they were not very common. As an MST leader in Pará, Charles Trocate, put it, "The *posseiro* entered into conflict basically with the landowner. With the MST, there is conflict with the landowner but also with the INCRA and the state. The MST confronts the state with the problem."[29]

Finally, the properties targeted for occupation by the MST were different. Whereas posseiro actions usually went after relatively marginal land, the MST boldly focused on highly valued ranches, which were located near urban areas and often possessed good infrastructure. In some cases, the MST knew the areas they targeted were productive by the INCRA's low standards, but they sought to wear down both the landowner and authorities in order to force a government purchase of the property. As a result, top landowners came to see the MST as a greater threat to their interests.[30]

The Eldorado dos Carajás Massacre

If there is one event that clearly divides the contemporary history of the struggle for land in Pará into "before" and "after" periods it is the brutal massacre of nineteen MST protestors by state police forces on April 17, 1996, in Eldorado dos Carajás. This incident, stemming directly from the MST's efforts to force the expropriation of a massive and highly coveted group of estates in southeastern Pará, catapulted the state's land conflicts onto the national and even international stage and galvanized support for the MST and its struggle in the wider society. Although a tragedy for those directly affected by it, the massacre ended up transforming the struggle for land in southern Pará in ways that were beneficial to the region's landless population.

With their purchase of the Rio Branco estate in late 1995, INCRA officials had sought to defuse agrarian conflict in the Carajás region. To their dismay, the MST immediately organized a new mobilization aimed at conquering another giant landholding. This time the target was the Macaxeira complex, a 42,000-hectare tract spanning the municipalities of Curionópolis and Eldorado dos Carajás, near the Serra Pelada goldmine. Once owned in its entirety by the Pinheiro family of Marabá, part of the city's traditional oligarchy, the Macaxeira had been subdivided into a number of separate estates, at least one of which was still owned by members of the Pinheiro family. In November 1995 the MST set up a roadside encampment in the urban periphery of Curionópolis. MST activists boldly announced the establishment of the camp in poor neighborhoods using a loudspeaker, and some 1,400 families, including many former garimpeiros, gathered in the camp. The MST told the INCRA that their target was the Macaxeira. When the INCRA declared the complex productive in March, the families occupied one of the properties in the complex. With the MST so openly flaunting local authorities and elites, tensions mounted.

In early April 1996 a group of more than 1,000 people set out from the MST's Macaxeira occupation on a march to the INCRA office in Marabá. They demanded a meeting with Governor Almir Gabriel, a member of Cardoso's Party of Brazilian Social Democracy (PSDB). Although the march was part of a national MST protest campaign, the group's key demand was an eminently local one: to force the INCRA to expropriate the complex. Along the way the MST decided to block Highway 150, the main artery linking Marabá to the Carajás region to the southwest, to demand that the state government provide buses and food. Governor Gabriel, who had been feeling pressure from landowners to act more vigorously against the MST, initially agreed to these demands, but later refused. He then ordered local military police commanders to clear the roadway "no matter what."

Two groups of police arrived at the double curve where the MST had set up its blockade, one from each direction. They opened fire on the protestors, killing or injuring dozens. Several of the wounded were then finished off as they lay agonizing on the pavement, in some cases bludgeoned to death with their own farm implements. One young MST activist was hunted down in a roadside shanty and executed. In addition to the nineteen people killed at the scene, two died later and more than sixty were injured.

After the killing had stopped, one of the commanders, Colonel Mario Coláres Pantoja, reportedly told his troops, "Mission accomplished, and no one saw anything."[31] This statement was one of a number of pieces of evidence suggesting that the killings had been planned in advance.[32] In all probability, one of the causes of the massacre was the bad blood that had been developing between the MST and the local military police. Traditionally, the police had used violence and intimidation against poor rural workers virtually at will, but the MST's massive mobilizations, sometimes involving thousands of people and occurring in public spaces, made such tactics less viable. The police grew increasingly resentful at this affront to their authority.

There is also some evidence suggesting that local landowners may have played a part in the atrocity. For example, an informant reportedly told investigators that the police had been paid by landowners to commit the massacre in order to intimidate the MST.[33] Although the latter accusation has never been proven, it does not seem far-fetched, given the history of violence and police complicity with elite interests in Pará, as well as the tensions caused by the MST's advances in the region.

All of the military police officers involved in the incident were acquitted in a controversial trial in 1999. Pará's Supreme Court, however, annulled the verdict. The two commanders, Col. Pantoja and Major José Maria Pereira de Oliveira, were finally convicted of murder in 2002 and given long prison sentences. However, they were released pending appeal and the other 145 officers present at the massacre were acquitted. Even the 2002 trial was riddled with irregularities and many progressive groups called for the verdict to be annulled.[34] In late 2004, an appeals court confirmed both the conviction of the two commanders and the acquittal of the rest of the officers involved.

Although the justice system's response to the killings was characteristically sluggish, the reaction of the media and civil society was swift. Pantoja's assertion that "no one saw anything" was incorrect. A local television news crew following the MST march managed to record extensive footage of the incident. This footage, along with the efforts of the MST and other groups to spread word of the killings, helped make the massacre a major news story all over Brazil and beyond. In the days that followed, criticism of Cardoso's land reform policy intensified in the media and among progressive groups in civil society. The notion that he was doing little to address the land situation was politically damaging to Cardoso, both because of the widespread support for agrarian reform among Brazilians and because the president's prestige hung in part on his reputation as an enlightened reformer. Cardoso was also concerned about the massacre's impact on his government's image abroad.[35] Less than a week after the Eldorado massacre, he announced the creation of new ministry devoted exclusively to land reform, removing the INCRA from the grips of the conservative Ministry of Agriculture.

As the site of the Eldorado massacre and a chronic source of land-related violence, southeastern Pará was singled out for special measures. A few days after the killings, Cardoso dispatched army troops to maintain order in the region, in what some observers saw as an implicit federal intervention of the state. More importantly, the government announced that the INCRA office in Marabá would be transformed into a new regional headquarters to cover the southeastern part of the state. This change made Pará the only state with two INCRA regional units, substantially expanding the resources available for land reform. The INCRA's work was also facilitated by the establishment in Marabá of new federal courts and an office of the attorney general. Now, the judicial aspects of land expropriation could be processed locally, rather than in distant Belém. A new INCRA survey of the Macaxeira miraculously found part of it to be unproductive. The families who had occupied the complex were settled on it, forming a settlement project named "April 17" in honor of those killed in the massacre.

With the enhanced federal presence in Marabá, land reform accelerated. INCRA data suggest that more land (about 2.6 million hectares) was acquired for reform in Pará during the 1996 to 1998 period than in the entire decade that preceded it. The bulk of this activity was concentrated in the southern part of the state. Land occupations also surged powerfully in Pará in 1996, with the majority of these actions occurring after the massacre at Eldorado. Although occupations multiplied rapidly all over the country in the mid-1990s, the increase in Pará was particularly sharp.[36] The pace of mobilization and protest for land would continue to be intense through the end of the 1990s. Although the MST was an important actor, the bulk of the occupations continued to be by groups not linked to this organization.

Beyond forcing Cardoso to accelerate land reform in Pará, the incident at Eldorado dos Carajás had a number of other political benefits for the MST. It helped solidify support for the MST among progressive groups in Pará, especially in Belém, where civil society is more developed. In addition, the MST's relations with the rural unions, which had not generally been very close, improved. In previous years the MST and the unions had rarely communicated with each other and even more infrequently collaborated in their efforts to pressure authorities. MST activists sometimes looked down on the unions as backward and ineffective, while union leaders resented the arrogant attitude they perceived among MST activists, as well as the publicity this organization often attracted. The tragedy at Eldorado helped to bring the unions and the MST closer together and joint protest actions became more common. In 1997 the MST and FETAGRI together assembled a camp of some 8,000 people in front of the Marabá INCRA to push the agency to make good on its policy promises. In the following years, joint MST-FETAGRI mobilizations became a regular phenomenon. Within FETAGRI, the shift was facilitated through a regional leadership change in 1996, which placed a number of younger activists in power and fostered greater coordination among local rural workers' unions. In addition, because Eldorado had provoked sympathy for the MST's struggle abroad, it helped the state MST organization gain access to financial support from foreign nongovernmental organizations.

Eldorado dos Carajás was the largest single instance of deadly, land-related violence in recent Brazilian history. From a regional perspective, however, it was not very unusual, forming part of a series of massacres that have occurred in southeastern Pará since the 1970s. According to CPT data, between 1971 and 2004, 772 people were killed in rural (mainly land-related) conflicts in Pará.[37] Almost three-quarters of these murders occurred in the southeastern corner of the state, making this the most violent rural area in all of Brazil. The vast majority of the victims were poor rural workers. The weak presence of the state and the strong ties between landowning elites and the holders of political power has helped make judicial impunity the rule in these cases. In southeastern Pará only seven cases of murder related to rural social conflict have resulted in a conviction since the early 1970s. Although rural violence in Pará peaked in the mid-1980s, murders of rural workers and activists have continued to be commonplace.

The Move to Belém

At the end of the 1990s the MST began a new phase in its development in Pará, moving its state secretariat to Belém and initiating a series of land occupations in the metropolitan region. MST state secretariats are usually based in the capital city to facilitate contact with the INCRA, state officials, the media, and civil society. In Pará, however, the sheer size of the state had led the MST to locate its secretariat where the struggle for land itself was concentrated. Nevertheless, by the mid-1990s MST leaders had resolved that a stronger presence in Belém would be desirable, in order to avoid political isolation in the more conservative south. The massacre at Eldorado delayed the initiative, but in 1998 the MST began both to set up its secretariat in the capital and to organize the struggle for land in the surrounding region.

At least in terms of mobilization, the initiative has been a clear success. Through 2004, the MST had organized twenty-one land occupations in Belém and the surrounding region. These initiatives, involving some 5,800 families, have transformed northeastern Pará into the major locus of MST protest activity in the state. The targets have included three properties located in a rural district of the capital itself and another belonging to one of Pará's most powerful (and disreputable) politicians, Jader Barbalho. With regard to settlements, progress has been slower. Through mid-2005, the MST had secured three settlements in the region (including two in Belém), which are home to about 280 families.

Its campaign in the capital region has helped to counterbalance the difficulties the MST had experienced in southeastern Pará in the early 2000s. Between 1999 and 2004 the MST formed only four new groups of landless workers in this region and obtained no new settlements. The assassination of two key MST leaders in 1998 contributed to the MST's problems. A more important factor, however, has been the widely perceived failure of the ambitious agro-industrial and collective production projects undertaken by the MST in its local settlements, which undermined the organization's image at a time when the Cardoso government was undertaking a political offensive against it at the national level.[38] Doubts about the MST's strategy helped local conservative politicians, working with the INCRA, to provoke divisions in some settlements.[39] As a result, the MST was forced to devote more effort to preserving its influence over its existing settlements than to pressuring for new ones.

The MST and other progressive forces in Pará hoped that the election of Workers' Party (PT) candidate Luiz Inácio Lula da Silva as president in late 2002 would bring an acceleration of land reform efforts in the state. Occupations and encampments multiplied rapidly in 2003 and 2004 in anticipation of faster land redistribution. The MST's mobilization of new families intensified substantially, especially in the Belém region. However, the PT government dithered on keeping its historic promises. New expropriations became few and far between and worker mobilization was met with rising violence from landowners and their henchmen.[40]

Impact of the MST

As the preceding account suggests, the MST has been at least nominally present in Pará for close to two decades. The direct, quantitative contributions made by the MST during these years are not particularly impressive, at least in comparison to its achievements in states like Paraná, Pernambuco, Rio Grande do Sul, and São Paulo, where the MST has been clearly the dominant force in the struggle. It would be wrong, however, to conclude from this that the MST has not been an important actor in Pará. In fact, as we argue below, the MST has played a vital, transformative role. In addition to its obvious contributions in terms of occupations and settlements, the MST has impacted the struggle in two more indirect, but crucial ways: by shaping the "repertoire of contention" used by activists and by forcing the federal government to devote greater resources to land reform in the state.[41]

Land Occupations and Settlements

Between 1988 (the first year data are available) and 2004, the CPT recorded 272 land occupations involving 42,698 families in Pará. The MST accounted for almost 15% of these actions and about 38% of the families. These figures undoubtedly exaggerate the MST's role significantly, since non-MST occupations are often small and occur in remote areas, making them less likely to be registered by the CPT.[42] Local rural trade union or FETAGRI activists probably played some role in most of the other occupations. However, in Pará, as in other frontier states, land occupations are often organized at the grassroots level without the intervention of any pre-existing entity.

The MST also exerts political influence over only a small proportion of the more than 500 land reform settlements in Pará. MST land occupations have played a role in the creation of eighteen settlements with some 4,800 families. As of mid-2005, these figures represented 3.4% and 3.9% of the respective state totals. Thirteen of these settlements, home to about 3,000 families, continue to have relatively close ties to the MST today. In contrast, according to a FETAGRI official, about half of the land reform settlements in southeastern Pará have strong ties to rural unions.[43] Table 8.1 summarizes the data on MST land occupations and settlements in the state of Pará.

There are three main reasons for the MST's modest direct achievements in Pará. First, the posseiro tradition has continued to provide a culturally familiar and viable alternative for people wanting land. Over the years, posseiro tactics have become part of the popular stock of knowledge, which can be easily drawn upon. In addition, these tactics have continued to be relatively effective because of the persistent frontier character of much of the state. Successful occupations do not require the political force needed, for example, in the south or southeast, where land is more intensively cultivated and of higher economic value and where, in contrast to Pará, ownership over farmland is usually not disputed. Second, joining the MST is no small commitment. Recruits must accept its extensive rules and its radical ideology. Once land has been gained, the MST also intervenes more assertively in the organization of the settlement and expects monetary contributions. Although critical to the MST's success, these policies help to limit its mass appeal, especially where alternatives are available.

A third and final factor is the particular niche the MST has chosen to occupy in Pará. As we suggested earlier, the MST has targeted highly valued properties. In doing so, it has sought to give its settlements a better chance of becoming thriving rural communities. In terms of expanding the MST's physical presence in Pará, however, this strategy has some disadvantages. Relatively few properties meet these criteria and some are productive rural estates, invulnerable to expropriation. In addition, their owners are wealthy and influential. MST camps have thus had to endure long, hard battles, sometimes involving several police evictions and camps in front of the INCRA. In contrast, workers who oc-

Table 8.1. MST land occupations and settlements in Pará, 1988–2005

	MST	Non-MST	MST as % of total
Land occupations	40	232	14.7
Occupying families	16,343	26,355	38.3
Settlements established	18	519	3.4
Families settled	4,816	119,357	3.9

Sources: CPT, INCRA, and MST.

cupy marginal areas are less likely to face evictions (at least in the short term) and can begin working the land immediately.

Repertoire of Contention

One of the major indirect impacts the MST has had on the struggle for land in the state of Pará has to do with methods of organization and protest used by activists—what scholars have called the "repertoire of contention." Through its example, the MST has provoked a significant, if still only partial, transformation in this area. This change, we argue, roughly parallels the transformation in the general repertoire of contention noted by scholars such as Charles Tilly and Sidney Tarrow in Western Europe and in North America some two centuries earlier. Not coincidentally, this transformation also shares with the earlier one some facilitating structural factors, related to state expansion, development, and other changes that have occurred in Pará in recent decades.

Coined by Tilly, the concept of "repertoire of contention" refers to that universe of protest tactics and organizational forms that is readily available to political activists in a particular place and time.[44] The repertoire is a cultural concept, since it consists of a shared stock of knowledge about how to make demands on government officials and other power holders. At the same time, repertoires reflect underlying structural factors, such as working conditions, demographics, technology, and the character of the state, that delimit the range of actions that can be used effectively. Important episodes of mobilization can have a critical impact in terms of diffusing new tactical innovations. Enduring transformations of the repertoire, however, ultimately reflect changes in the structural context as well.

Tilly and Tarrow note such a transformation in Europe and North America in the late eighteenth and early nineteenth centuries. Moving away from a "traditional" repertoire based on local, grievance-specific, and relatively violent actions, protestors gradually adopted a "modular" one, involving more flexible and publicly oriented tactics that usually resulted in less violence, such as the strike, march, and demonstration.[45] The new repertoire made it easier for a movement to diffuse geographically and form broader alliances, helping give rise to truly national social movements. Tilly attributes the transformation to the expansion of state power and the spread of capitalism. As a result of these changes, local grievances were increasingly rooted in forces operating at the regional or national level. At the same time, according to Tarrow, related changes, especially the growth of the news media and civil associations, made it easier to form broad networks to coordinate protest activities beyond the local level.

The posseiro struggle bears a strong likeness to the traditional repertoire. Consisting mainly of attempts by local groups to gain control of particular pieces of land, sometimes using armed force, it largely fits Tarrow's characterization of this repertoire as "violent and direct, brief, specific and linked to the claims of participants."[46] Like the traditional repertoire, the posseiro struggle also tends not to occur in very public places or to involve massive protest events. The methodology imported to Pará by the MST, meanwhile, resembles the "modular" repertoire. The MST employs a highly public protest strategy that seeks to build alliances by appealing to sympathetic groups, directly or through the media. It uses tactics, such as the protest march and the mass demonstration, that are core elements of the newer repertoire. Even the MST's use of the traditional tactic of occupying land cannot be reduced to a specific claim to a particular piece of land. MST occupations often involve far too many families to be settled on the ranch targeted, so more than expressing a claim to that property, they convey a broader demand for agrarian reform. The use of roadside camps also represents a way of exerting pressure on authorities by making the social problems associated with land concentration evident to a wider audience.

The MST's style of struggle has not been adopted wholesale by other groups in Pará, but certain aspects of it have clearly caught on. Non-MST groups are now more likely to set up a single camp, as the MST does, rather than quickly dividing an occupied area into individual plots. Rural workers' unions have also tended to target areas closer to highways and urban centers, rather than in the backcountry. Roadside camps, which until fairly recently were almost exclusively associated with the MST, have increasingly caught on among non-MST groups. In recent years, finally, unions have stepped up their organizing efforts and carried out many public demonstrations and occupations of INCRA offices to pressure for land, credit, and other public goods. Although such actions were sometimes used in the past, today they are much more common. In some cases, as mentioned earlier, these actions have been mounted in concert with the MST. Francisco Ferreira Carvalho, a longtime union activist in Marabá, underscored the shift in union perspective and tactics since the MST's first major occupation in the region in 1992:

> Before '92, we did not think that urban society's response to the struggle
> would be positive. We thought mass struggle would be crushed by repression;

that it could not work. The MST demonstrated that it could. In '92 the *posseiro* struggle was strong, but it was isolated. Each union did its own struggle. Now we do more public mobilizations. We get on television and we make denunciations. We do marches and organize public acts. We learned that from the MST.[47]

Although this tactical shift was directly provoked by the MST's example, it has been facilitated by underlying structural changes in Pará society, ones not very different from those described by Tilly and Tarrow. The growing penetration of formerly isolated areas of southeastern Pará by roads, capital investment, and communications technology in recent decades has transformed this part of the state. While provoking social dislocations and violence, this process has also created a more urban society and one more closely linked to major population centers at the state, national, and even international level. The end of the military dictatorship also encouraged the development of the media and civil associations in Pará, as in other parts of Brazil, and raised the visibility and political costs of violent repression. These changes have made it increasingly possible for rural workers to wage their struggles by reaching out to public opinion and civil society and thus putting pressure on authorities to meet their demands.

Federal Land Reform Policy

A second major facet of the MST's impact on the struggle for land in Pará is even more far-reaching and consequential. By forcing a major confrontation with Pará's landholding elite and their defenders within the state apparatus, the MST essentially forced federal authorities to accelerate the pace of land reform in Pará, especially in the southeastern part of the state. This change has meant a major increase in the number of families receiving land. In addition, the increase in federal resources for land reform has helped to fuel a revival of grassroots mobilization for land in southeastern Pará. Both changes have benefited not only the MST but many other groups as well, including the FETAGRI and its affiliated unions.

The massacre at Eldorado dos Carajás was of fundamental importance in accelerating the pace of land reform activity in Pará. Because it focused public attention and concern on the land issue, this incident forced the Cardoso government to invest more heavily in land reform at the national level. Since it was the site of the killings, southeastern Pará received special attention. Particularly important was the establishment of a regional INCRA headquarters in Marabá, which greatly increased the resources available for land reform in this region.

The impact of this change on settlement production is striking. A national settlement count conducted in 2002 found 400 settlement projects in Pará established between 1985 and 2001, with 89,299 families living in them. Almost three-quarters (293) of these projects were located in the southern part of the state. Only forty-seven of them, or fewer than one in six, existed before 1995.[48] In many cases posseiros had de facto control of these areas several years before they were transformed into official settlements. Legalization of these holdings, however, has provided families with important benefits in terms of tenure security and access to government programs for settlers.

The acceleration of agrarian reform efforts in Pará since 1996 has not solved the problems of unequal land access in the state. Nevertheless, it has achieved substantial progress, especially in the southeast. The settlements identified by the Sparovek study in Pará have an area equivalent to one-fourth of all the farmland, as measured by the 1995–1996 Agricultural Census (Instituto Brasileiro de Geografía e Estatística). By comparison, Mato Grosso, with the second largest area in settlements, had only 8.3% of its farmland occupied by settlement projects. About one-third of the farmland in southern Pará is held by settlements. In some municipalities the figure is above 40%, even taking into account only settlements established through 1999.[49]

The MST must take a large share of the credit for bringing this change about, since the killings at Eldorado were a response to the unprecedented challenge the MST had been mounting to the interests of local elites and their political allies. In addition, the MST's disciplined national structure and unparalleled public relations capacity were important in maximizing the political impact of the incident. The fragmented and less politically audacious approach characteristic of the posseiro struggle would probably not have triggered such a massive instance of repression in such a public place, where it could easily be caught on film. It is also hard to imagine the plodding and politically heterogeneous National Confederation of Agricultural Workers (CONTAG) doing as effective a job of publicizing the massacre and developing it as a symbol of injustice in the Brazilian countryside.

Because it deserves much of the credit for forcing federal authorities to intensify land reform efforts in Pará, the MST should also receive a large share of the credit for another change that occurred in the mid-1990s: the revival of grassroots mobilization for land reform. More than 80% of all the land occupations in Pará during the 1988 to 2004 period occurred after 1995. This represents an impressive revival of the struggle, which, as we mentioned earlier, had begun to fade in intensity in the late 1980s. More than one factor has contributed to the growth of land occupations since the mid-1990s. The decline of gold mining and the completion of the Tucuruí dam project, for example, played a role by giving rise to a larger pool of poor, unemployed, landless workers in southern Pará.

However, the most important factor in the movement's revival during the last decade was the increase in federal capacity for undertaking land reform in

Pará, particularly the establishment of a new INCRA regional headquarters in Marabá. Because it greatly improved the prospects for obtaining legally sanctioned access to land in southern Pará this change encouraged workers and activists to attempt new occupations.[50] Both the MST and the rural unions freely admit this. Although the MST has been the key force behind this change, it is only one of its beneficiaries. Non-MST occupations have greatly outnumbered those of the MST. In fact, the rural unions have undergone a kind of renaissance as a result of the renewed occupation activity and the growth of land reform settlements linked to them. Although its leaders are not always willing to recognize it, the newfound dynamism of the rural union movement after 1996 owes much to the political impact of the MST in Pará and at the national level.

The MST's influence in Pará, combined with its national visibility and media savvy, have even managed to change the name given to those who struggle for land in the state. Today, the word "posseiro" has begun to fall into disuse, even to describe the relatively small, loosely organized land occupations traditionally associated with the rural unions. Increasingly, poor people who struggle for land in Pará are referred to as *sem terra*, even if they are not affiliated with the MST—hence, the title of this chapter.

Conclusion

The MST did not invent the struggle for land in the state of Pará. Nor has it become the dominant actor within the movement, at least in the most obvious quantitative terms. FETAGRI and the rural trade unions associated with it continue to be a vital force in the state and the main organized group behind mobilization for land. Yet, as we have argued in this chapter, the MST has played a fundamental role in the struggle for land in Pará. It has deeply influenced the character of mobilization and it has made a critical contribution to the acceleration of federal settlement efforts. It has helped spur a revival of the grassroots movement for land reform and it can take much of the credit for the major increase in land reform settlements since the mid-1990s, which has affected the lives of tens of thousands of families.

Conquering new settlements will continue to be a key goal of the MST and other pro–land reform groups. Much usable land remains to be distributed. Nevertheless, an increasingly critical element of the struggle for agrarian reform in Pará (as well as elsewhere in Brazil) will involve demonstrating to opinion leaders and the broader public that this policy actually works to reduce poverty and enhance local development. Only by showing that settlements are a viable and cost efficient strategy for addressing these issues will proponents of land reform obtain the lasting political support they need to institutionalize this policy and achieve momentum for its future expansion.

This is just as great a challenge as getting the state to redistribute land in the first place. Authorities must be pushed to provide settlers with the infrastructure, extension services, and credit that they need to achieve a modest, but dignified, standard of living. Many of these goods and services must be provided by municipal governments, which are often quite conservative and corrupt and have little interest in devoting resources to settlements. At the same time, the media and public opinion must be convinced to judge the success of land reform settlements by a realistic standard. Given recent development trends, the most likely alternative for many poor, undereducated, landless people in Pará is not a well-paying factory job or a prosperous small business, but a desperate, itinerate existence that in many cases leads women to sell their bodies and men to submit to work conditions differing little from slavery.

The MST cannot achieve this goal alone. It must be pursued by a broad front of groups representing the interests of small farmers, agricultural workers, and other poor people. In the state of Pará, the FETAGRI, the CPT, and other progressive groups will be essential participants. However, the MST, with its national structure, organizational discipline, broad strategic vision, and undeniable charisma, is particularly well positioned to lead this struggle.

Notes

1. The data on land occupations cited in this chapter come from the Pastoral Land Commission (CPT), which has published an annual report on rural social conflict and human rights violations since 1986. We believe its data for Pará augments somewhat the MST's share of land occupations, but consider the CPT's data set, nonetheless, to be the most comprehensive one available.
2. Tilly (1986).
3. Wambergue (1999).
4. Schmink and Wood (1992: 60).
5. Costa (1998: 62).
6. Cehelsky (1979).
7. Branford and Glock (1985); Ozório de Almeida (1992).
8. Hoffmann (1998: table 4).
9. Costa (1998: 50).
10. Schmink and Wood (1992: 157).
11. The military's earlier experience fighting the Araguaia guerrilla movement in southeastern Pará helped foment concern about the potential for rebellion in the region; see Wambergue (1999).
12. Martins (1981); Adriance (1995); Wambergue (1999).
13. Wambergue (1999).
14. Schmink and Wood (1992: 80–83).
15. Emmi (1985).
16. Oliveira (1999: 31).
17. Advonsil Cândido Siqueira, interview by Gabriel Ondetti, Belém, PA, November 9, 1999. Siqueira is the former president of the CUT-Pará and former member of the MST National Coordination.

18. Leroy (1991: 167).
19. Joaquim Daniel Alves Barbosa, interview by Gabriel Ondetti, Conceição do Araguaia, PA, November 18, 1999.
20. There is disagreement about when the Xinguara occupations occurred. CPT data suggest that both occupations were undertaken in 1989, while current and former MST leaders insist that at least one of them occurred in 1988. Both sources agree that roughly thirty-five families were involved in the first occupation.
21. Advonsil Cândido Siqueira, interview by Gabriel Ondetti, Belém, PA, November 9, 1999.
22. Charles Trocate, interview by Gabriel Ondetti, Marabá, PA, July 15, 2005. Trocate was a member of the MST National Board at the time of the interview.
23. Charles Trocate, interview, July 15, 2005.
24. Joaquim Daniel Alves Barbosa, interview by Gabriel Ondetti, Conceição do Araguaia, PA, November 18, 1999.
25. Emmi (1985); Petit (2003).
26. Progressive forces were able to take over the STR in Conceição do Araguaia in 1985, while in Marabá it took until 1993.
27. Wambergue (1999).
28. Jorge Neri, interview by Gabriel Ondetti, Marabá, PA, November 6, 1999. Neri was a member of the MST National Board at the time of the interview.
29. Charles Trocate, interview by Gabriel Ondetti, Marabá, PA, July 15, 2005.
30. Dr. Carivaldo Ribeiro, interview by Gabriel Ondetti, Marabá, PA, November 17, 1999. Riberiro is a former president of the Marabá landowners' union.
31. "Motorista diz ter visto 2 sem-terra presos" *Folha de São Paulo*, June 23, 1996.
32. Another was the fact that the officers involved in the incidents were apparently not wearing their required name plates, presumably to avoid identification.
33. "Massacre foi encomendado por R$100 mil, diz testemunha," *Folha de São Paulo*," April 26, 1996.
34. CPT (2003: 148).
35. See the column by Janio de Freitas, "A Omissão Confessada," *Folha de São Paulo*, April 21, 1996.
36. The total number of land occupations in Brazil increased by 173% between 1995 and 1996. In Pará, they increased by 371%, with most of the occupations in 1996 occurring after the Eldorado dos Carajás massacre.
37. CPT archives.
38. In May 2000 Cardoso announced a series of legal measures to halt land occupations and criminalize MST activities. Further discussion on these issues can be found in Branford (chap. 13, this volume).
39. In 2000, conservative forces founded an entity called the Federation of Association Centrals of the State of Pará (FECAP), intended to represent settlers vis-à-vis government agencies and thus compete with the FETAGRI and MST for their loyalties. FECAP has gained influence in a substantial number of settlements in the region.
40. CPT (2004).
41. Another important MST contribution to the struggle for agrarian reform in Pará relates to the emphasis it has placed in improving the quality of life in existing land reform settlements, notably by pressuring authorities for a variety of support policies, including credit, infrastructure, and technical assistance. Pará's rural unions have been strongly influenced by the MST's example in this area.

42. Undercounting of occupations was more pronounced before the mid-1990s, when, in response to the rapid growth in such actions nationwide, the CPT became more rigorous in its data collection.

43. Francisco de Assis Soledade da Costa, interview by Gabriel Ondetti, Marabá, PA, July 16, 2005. Costa was the Southeast Regional Coordinator for FETAGRI at the time of the interview.

44. Tilly (1983, 1986).

45. Tarrow (1998: 29–42).

46. Tarrow (1998: 36).

47. Francisco Ferreira Carvalho, interview by Gabriel Ondetti, Marabá, PA, October 11, 1999. Carvalho is the former president of Marabá's rural trade union.

48. Sparovek (2003: 42). These figures, of course, do not include the colonization projects created on public land during the military years. By now, however, these represent only a small percentage of the total number of settlement projects in the state of Pará.

49. Heredia, Medeiros, Palmeira, Cintrão, and Leite (2006: 283–84).

50. The massacre also helped increase the pace of land occupations in Pará by making the state government more reticent toward undertaking police evictions of occupations, for fear of provoking new massacres. Local police battalions, in particular, have been prohibited from engaging in such actions.

PART III

MST's Agricultural Settlements

9 The Struggle on the Land

Source of Growth, Innovation, and Constant Challenge
for the MST

Jonas Iora's story is not much different from that of other Landless Rural Workers Movement (MST) activists. A son of peasants, at age thirteen he
left school and became a farm laborer. The work was heavy, more than twelve
hours a day. He visited his first landless camp at the request of neighbors who
asked for a ride to the camp on a truck he had borrowed from the local government. Jonas stayed at the camp for a few days.

Then I started enjoying the environment, the camaraderie, soccer games and
discussions. I became interested and started thinking: "If I go back I'll be
doing the same work as always." Then, in the early days of the camp I was
asked to serve as one of its coordinators. I didn't want to get too involved. But
I ended up helping the health care team. From there on I just kept going.

When I returned home to pick up my mattress and other stuff, my folks
didn't want to let me go. My mother cried a lot. But I had decided to join
the camp. After this, I started getting to know the history of the movement,
taking classes and understanding the organization's principles, its goals, what
the movement stood for. I became passionate about its cause. I got involved in
various movement activities. Afterward I went to its national training school
in Caçador [in the state of Santa Catarina]. I met a woman comrade there. We
live together nowadays on a land reform settlement.

I have a small farm plot that I really like. Oh my God! I feel a deep passion
when I till the earth. Yet we know our struggle is much bigger. We learned
this by taking part in the movement's struggles. The movement is now my
family. Of course I also love my biological family. Today my parents and
siblings have a very different view of the movement. They admire the fact
that my companions and I went to the landless camp, took part in its struggle,
obtained land, and are now living well, with dignity.[1]

The access to land brings considerable changes to the lives of peasants who mobilized in its quest. Landless families celebrate the state's creation of a land reform settlement, and the distribution of land tenure titles to its beneficiaries, as an invaluable "conquest." This victory, though, opens up new and significant challenges. In the words of its protagonists, it marks the passage from "the struggle *for* land" to "the struggle *on* the land." This chapter provides an analysis of the latter process and its impact on the MST. To understand this development, one needs to establish first the broader conditions that envelop the movement's actions. A central task here will be to assess the conservative nature of Brazil's agrarian reform.

The MST's growth after the mid-1980s owes much to the ambivalent features of the Brazilian context. Four elements, in particular, have shaped the nation's struggle over agrarian reform: first, a democratic regime offering important political freedoms and competitive elections, amid an "oligarchic system of representation"[2] and sporadic protection of human rights, especially among the nation's poor; second, an exclusionary model of rural development, fashioned under the lingering clout of large landholders and the rise of powerful agribusiness conglomerates; third, a society characterized by extreme levels of inequity and the marginal subsistence of large segments of the population; and fourth, a peasantry mobilized through public activism, in ways that seek to bring social pressure and advance negotiations with government authorities.[3]

The MST's progress and constraints must be examined in light of the obstacles and opportunities forged under these conditions. The state's conservative inertia and inadequate public assistance prompted the MST to boost its capacity to obtain government benefits and offer alternative services to its members. Rather than diminish or weaken its struggle, these constraints induced the movement to fortify its internal structure, broaden its agenda, and cement a willingness to fight for the social transformation of Brazil. State concession to MST demands, however delayed and partial, facilitated the movement's recruitment efforts among the nation's large number of destitute people.

The state's meager support for agrarian reform settlements prompted the movement to generate various strategies to secure the benefits accorded to settlers under existing land reform laws. In doing so, the MST was able to unite its struggles *for* and *on* the land. The latter was pursued in two complementary ways. First, the movement remained engaged in a continuous process of pressure politics, lobbying, and negotiations with state authorities. Second, it began to establish a number of educational centers, cooperatives, and other programs designed to support its members and train its cadre. The movement's growing sophistication was thus fueled by the need to mobilize its members and organize various activities to substitute for inadequate public services. As a result of all these endeavors, the MST developed seven major sources of power—namely its: mobilization capacity, multifaceted yet flexible organization, strategic creativity, quest for financial independence, resourceful allies, investment in popular education, and mystique and discipline.

This chapter flushes out this argument in five parts. First, it analyzes the conservative character of Brazil's agrarian reform, in relation both to the struggles *for* and *on* the land. Then it evaluates the result of this process on the precarious implementation of rural settlements. After that, it examines the impact of this dynamic on the MST's organizational development. This is illustrated with a review of the evolution of three of the movement's thirteen task teams, those dealing with education; production, cooperation, and the environment; and communication. The MST's growth and sophistication is then analyzed in light of its main sources of power. The chapter ends with an assessment of the constant challenges faced in the movement's struggle on the land.

Conservative Agrarian Reform

Brazil's existing legal framework and state institutions designed to handle rural affairs, including the judiciary, were set up under a balance of political forces that favored traditional dominant interests in the countryside. This balance of forces was a legacy of the authoritarian regime that preceded the formulation of the country's agrarian laws. Brazil's conservative agrarian policies also reflect important autocratic legacies that paved the way for the military government installed in 1964, notably its long history of oligarchic politics led by a powerful landed elite.

Building on the typology in the introduction chapter to this volume, we define a "conservative agrarian reform" as one driven by a reactive and restrained impetus to land redistribution, rather than a proactive effort to further social change. A conservative reform strives mainly to appease rural conflicts, rather than promote family farming through measures that seek to transform the agrarian structure and its power relations. This approach treats land reform as an isolated social problem and policy concern, of marginal value to the nation's development. Its agricultural settlements are consequently set up in a dispersed and ad hoc way, and bear negligible effects on the nation's land-tenure pattern. Governments influenced by this disposition are unwilling or fearful of taking actions that would confront or upset the dominant forces in the countryside, its large landowners and agribusiness corporations.[4]

Brazil's conservative agrarian reform can be clearly discerned in the nation's large tracts of unproductive farmland that are rarely, if ever, subject to redistribution, despite existing laws that oblige the state to expropriate such areas for land reform. The same forces that constrain such reforms also penalize, in assorted ways, those who mobilize for land distribution.[5] According to Brazilian government sources, at the outset of the twenty-first century, there were at least 231 million hectares—a territory six times the size of Germany—

available for land reform, and up to 6.1 million families who could benefit from it.[6]

The MST and their allies in the National Forum for Agrarian Reform and Justice in the Countryside have long favored a "progressive agrarian reform," anchored on an alternative rural development model and espouse a "progressive agrarian reform." Their goal is to change the nation's land tenure system and alter the balance of forces in the countryside through a substantial and vigorous land distribution program. This would seek to eliminate the nation's large estates through the imposition of legal limits on the size of rural properties; democratize access to land, credit, and public services for poor countryside dwellers; and break up the oligopoly of major multinational corporations that support an agricultural model based on large-scale industrial farming, social exclusion, and environmental degradation. A progressive agrarian reform, they believe, can only be carried out by a strong state, aligned with popular interests. This would enable the government to offer extensive support for land reform beneficiaries and other small farmers, through a wide array of ancillary programs related to farm production, commercialization, rural cooperatives, education, health, public infrastructure, and technical assistance aimed at promoting agro-ecology.[7]

With the restoration of democratic rule in 1985, Brazil witnessed the election of five civilian presidents from various political parties and persuasions. Still, in one way or another, all of them—from José Sarney to Luis Inácio Lula da Silva—maintained a conservative agrarian policy. While supportive of land reform in their public statements, in practice all of these governments: first, allocated land under social pressure; second, created land reform settlements through a sluggish and complicated administrative process; third, kept a distant demeanor regarding frequent human rights violations in the countryside and widespread judicial impunity on this matter; fourth, favored a residual distribution of land, in remote places and in a dispersed and ad hoc manner; and, finally, offered meager support to land reform settlements, or did so largely in response to pressure exerted by peasant movements. The following paragraphs examine these basic traits of Brazil's conservative agrarian reform in greater detail.

1. *Land Allocations Conducted under Social Pressure.* Among agrarian experts there is broad consensus that land distribution would have never taken place in Brazil without peasant struggles.[8] A study conducted in various regions of the country found that 96% of the ninety-two agricultural settlements surveyed emerged from peasant land conflicts. In 72% of cases studied, peasant groups had taken part in land occupations. By contrast, only 11% of the settlements were created through state-led initiatives.[9] Land struggles have been a regular feature in the Brazilian countryside, notably since the mid-1980s. Between 1987

and 2006, the Pastoral Land Commission (CPT) registered 7,078 land occupations across the country, involving more than one million families throughout this period.[10] This count does not include the scores, possibly hundreds, of discrete land occupations carried out by squatters in the Amazon region. Social pressure is also conveyed through the formation of landless protest camps and the organization of marches, hunger strikes, occupations of public buildings, and other demonstrations. The magnitude of these activities has been impressive. Between 2003 and 2006, Brazilian peasants organized 3,129 protest camps and demonstrations, mobilizing nearly 2.4 million people to advance land reform and pro-family farm policies.[11]

2. *Sluggish and Complicated Administrative Process.* Even under relentless pressure for reform, the bureaucratic proceedings needed to establish a new agricultural settlement can take several years. This process will vary in speed depending on the government's political will and the rise of any legal hurdles. In the 1990s and early 2000s it took an average of about four years of continuous mobilization before a peasant family was able to gain access to a farm parcel.[12] During this time, the federal land reform agency, INCRA, must undertake various administrative steps, beginning with a formal survey of the property in dispute to verify its qualification as a *latifundio*, or large unproductive estate. This process ends with a presidential decree that declares the area of public interest for land reform and orders its expropriation. The judiciary can put a hold on these lengthy proceedings at any juncture through court injunctions filed by the landowners. All these hurdles and delays are indicative of a trait found in conservative agrarian reforms: its legal and bureaucratic architecture are designed first and foremost to protect the interests of large landholders rather than facilitate the redistribution of these rural estates.

3. *Human Rights Violations and Impunity.* Conflicts over land in Brazil have produced repeated acts of violence against peasants and activists engaged in the mobilization for agrarian reform. The data presented in table 9.1 denotes a systemic problem. Despite some variations, all governments that succeeded the military regime witnessed a high number of murders, attempted assassinations, death threats, torture, beatings, and arrests of people involved in the struggle for agrarian reform.

The number of killings in rural conflicts dropped noticeably after the Sarney administration, but remained significant thereafter (see table 9.2). A large number of those murdered were peasant leaders, trade unionists, and religious clergy engaged in the fight for agrarian reform. The selective character of these assassinations reveals a determined effort to intimidate and dissuade people from mobilizing for land distribution. The use of violence exerted by elements of the landed elite reflects a longstanding practice, rooted in authoritarian so-

Table 9.1. Human rights violations in rural Brazil, annual average per presidential period, 1988–2006

President	Period	Murders	Assassination attempts	Death threats	Torture	Physical attacks	Arrests
Sarney	1988–89	84	84	144	36	1,016	334
Collor	1990–92	90	74	202	69	2,215	252
Franco	1993–94	50	50	183	63	2,148	303
Cardoso 1	1995–98	43	49	106	31	1,020	465
Cardoso 2	1999–2002	30	56	139	31	233	347
Lula 1	2003–2006	47	73	256	34	449	495
Total	1988–2006	49	63	172	42	1,041	382

Source: Compiled by the authors based on annual reports by the CPT. For more details, see table 9.13.

Table 9.2. Murders over rural conflicts, Brazil, 1985–2006, by presidential period

President	Period	Total	%	Annual average
Sarney	1985–89	561	43	112
Collor	1990–92	179	14	60
Franco	1993–94	99	8	50
Cardoso 1	1995–98	172	13	43
Cardoso 2	1999–2002	120	9	30
Lula 1	2003–2006	189	14	47
Total	**1985–2006**	**1,320**	**100**	**60**

Source: Compiled by the authors from annual reports of the CPT, and Barp and Barp (1998) for the 1985–87 data.

cial relations and understandings that view popular struggles for land rights as an "affront to the established order." The recurrence of human rights violations in the countryside is closely linked to a high rate of impunity surrounding these abuses. Only 8% of murders committed between 1985 and 2006 were prosecuted, and only twenty large landholders who ordered these crimes were convicted.[13] This situation is reinforced by the patrimonial practices found in various echelons of the Brazilian state, the limited presence of public security forces in many parts of the country, the historical affinity between the judiciary and the agrarian elite, and the extreme social inequities found throughout the Brazilian countryside.

4. *Distribution of Residual Land.* A conservative agrarian reform is motivated by a conciliatory instinct that strives to appease rural conflicts while safeguarding the interests of dominant rural sectors. Under these conditions, the govern-

Table 9.3. Agrarian reform in Brazil by region, 1985–2006

	Families in settlements		Area distributed	
Region	Total	%	Total	%
North	313,592	38.0	23,521,185	56.9
Northeast	300,074	36.4	9,097,603	22.0
Midwest	132,363	16.0	6,720,901	16.3
Southeast	43,655	5.3	1,252,487	3.0
South	35,648	4.3	742,984	1.8
Brazil	825,332	100.0	41,335,160	100.0

Source: Compiled by the authors based on DATALUTA (2008a).

Note: DATALUTA offers one of the most comprehensive databases on land issues in Brazil. The Center for the Study of Agrarian Reform (Núcleo de Estudos da Reforma Agrária, NERA), of the State University of São Paulo (UNESP) at the Presidente Prudente campus is responsible for compiling these data based on a careful review of the figures for land reform settlements provided by INCRA and the land institutes in the states of São Paulo and Mato Grosso. NERA's activities are coordinated by Professor Mançano Bernardo Fernandes. The figures on settlements presented in this text excluded fifty-five of the 7,575 settlements established between 1985 and 2006, as explained in the introduction chapter of this book (see note 56). These fifty-five settlements are essentially extractive reserves located in the Amazon region, covering a total area of 18,339,543 hectares, in which 35,957 families were settled, averaging 510 hectares per family. The first Lula administration created forty-seven of these extractive reserves.

It is important to emphasize that the number of settler families used here reflects the number of land parcels available at each settlement, and not the actual number of settled families. This figure, therefore, reflects a maximum estimate of the number of settled families. For a more detailed discussion of Brazilian agrarian reform statistics, see Delgado (chap. 2, this volume), Fernandes (chap. 5, this volume), Carter (chap. 1, this volume), as well as Melo (2006: 220–23).

ment normally reacts to peasant land struggles without a clear agenda for the transformation of land tenure arrangements. As a result, its predominant logic is to create settlements in areas that are more convenient to the state and less annoying for the landed elite. This has led to a residual distribution of land. The standard practice here is to allocate land in relatively remote and deprived areas, typically in agricultural frontier regions, and to scatter these communities over a vast territory.

Brazil's experience illustrates this dynamic clearly. As noted in table 9.3, its land reform settlements have been established mainly in the Amazonian frontier and other poor parts of the country. More than 70% of the land allocated between 1985 and 2006 took place in the Amazon, in the country's northern region and neighboring states of Mato Grosso and Maranhão. The most intense pressure for land reform, however, has taken place in the south and southeastern parts of Brazil. Between 1988 and 2006, these two regions—which are the country's most developed and have its highest land values—registered half of all land occupations but had only 9% of all beneficiary families, in an area that covers only 5% of all the territory distributed by the Brazilian state.[14]

The conservative practice of dispersing agricultural settlements dilutes many of the positive impacts derived from land reform. The geographic isolation of these communities reduces their access to markets, public services, and sources of nonfarm work. This dispersion also decreases possibilities for cooperation among the settlers and weakens their political influence at the local level. All this limits the opportunities to alter the balance of forces in the countryside. The higher concentration of settlements found in places like the Pontal de Paranapanema region in the state of São Paulo, the southeastern portion of the state of Pará, and the western part of Santa Catarina, came about as a result of local struggles and possibilities for land expropriation, and were not the outcome of a territorial policy toward land reform.

5. *Insufficient Support for Settlements.* The vast majority of settlers come from conditions of extreme poverty. Given this situation, Brazil's agrarian legislation and the administrative rules governing INCRA have established a variety of ancillary programs to assist new settlers and ensure access to resources needed to guarantee their subsistence and help generate some farm income. In an optimal situation, the consolidation of a settlement would require at least five years of direct and constant support from the state. However, the gap found between these government norms and their actual implrmentation in most settlement areas has been remarkable, particularly in the two decades that followed President Sarney's 1985 land reform initiative. The state's failure to allocate agricultural credits and resources for housing, education, health, sanitation, electricity, roads, and the purchase of farming equipment forced the MST and other peasant groups to pressure the federal government to abide by the legal norms underpinning these public policies.

A 2002 survey conducted in all of Brazil's agricultural settlements revealed that nearly one-half of the communities created between 1995 and 2001 offered precarious living conditions.[15] One-third of these settlements had no permanent homes, one-half lacked drinking water, and 55% had no electricity.[16] In these settlements, 29% of families with school-age children had no access to primary schools and 77% had no access to secondary education. Furthermore, 38% of the settlements had no regular health services and 62% lacked emergency clinics. Meanwhile, more than one-half of the settlements had no internal roads or access to public transportation.[17] Another study conducted between 2000 and 2001 found that one-third of the settlers had not obtained the farm loans promised by INCRA. Of those who received these funds, 59% indicated they had experienced problems of delay or other hurdles in getting these resources.[18] This precarious situation undermined development prospects for these settlements and fueled internal conflicts during this period, as illustrated in the case studies reviewed by Elena Calvo-Gonzalez and Wendy Wolford in chapters 11 and 12 in this volume.

Table 9.4. Agrarian reform in Brazil, by presidential period, 1979–2006

President	Period	Families in settlements			Area distributed		
		Total	Annual average	%	Total	Annual average	%
Figueiredo	1979–84	53,926	10,785	6.1	4,710,611	942,122	10.2
Sarney	1985–89	92,178	18,436	10.5	5,091,049	1,018,210	11.1
Collor & Franco	1990–94	57,194	14,299	6.5	2,895,903	723,076	6.3
Cardoso 1	1995–98	299,863	74,966	34.1	12,222,613	3,055,653	26.5
Cardoso 2	1999–02	155,491	38,873	17.7	6,768,771	1,692,193	14.7
Lula 1	2003–06	220,606	55,152	25.1	14,356,824	3,589,206	31.2
Total	**1979–2006**	**879,256**	**32,565**	**100.0**	**46,045,771**	**1,705,399**	**100.0**

Source: Compilation prepared by based on DATALUTA (2008a).

The five characteristics of a conservative agrarian reform—land allocations made under social pressure, a sluggish and complicated administrative process, frequent violations of human rights amid widespread impunity, distribution of residual land, and insufficient support for settlements—were discernible during all the national governments constituted between 1985 and 2006. There were, of course, some noticeable differences between these administrations. The creation of land reform settlements gained momentum under the government of Fernando Henrique Cardoso, after the massacres of landless peasants in Corumbiara (1995) and Eldorado dos Carajás (1996) (see table 9.4). The pace slowed down during Cardoso's second administration, yet rebounded under Lula's first term, amid a significant rise in peasant land mobilization.

There was no significant difference in the number of families settled under the Cardoso and Lula governments. During Cardoso's two terms, an average of 56,919 landless families received a farm plot each year, 1,768 families more than the annual average in Lula's first term. Moreover, as table 9.5 shows, the Lula administration increased land distribution in the peripheral regions of the country. Almost one-half of the families settled and nearly three-quarters of the territory distributed under his government were given out in the Brazilian north, where there was less social pressure for land. In contrast, between 2003 and 2006, one-third of the mobilizations in the countryside—land occupations, protest camps, and demonstrations—took place in the south and southeastern part of the country. In fact, these two regions alone accounted for 39% of all the participants in these mobilizations. Yet under Lula's first term, these seven states ended up with less than 3% of the nation's land allocations and only 7% of its beneficiary families.

In other aspects, the Lula government was less conservative than its predecessors. His administration exhibited a more open and fluid relationship

Table 9.5. Social pressure and agrarian reform under Lula, 2003–6, by percentage according to each national region

| | Social pressure | | Agrarian reform | |
Regions	Mobilizations	Peasants mobilized	Families settled	Area
North	12.1	9.9	46.7	72.7
Northeast	38.6	33.2	33.9	18.9
Midwest	15.8	17.8	12.4	5.6
Southeast	16.6	13.2	4.6	2.1
South	17.0	25.9	2.4	0.7

Source: Compilation prepared by the authors with data from the CPT (2004, 2005, 2006, 2007) for social pressure, and DATALUTA (2008a) for agrarian reform settlements. *Social pressure* comprises land occupations, protest camps, and demonstrations carried out by rural workers.

with rural social movements, some of which exercised influence on the political appointments made to the Ministry of Agrarian Development and INCRA. The Lula government also provided greater financial and logistical support to help consolidate Brazil's reform settlements and fostered various educational and rural development initiatives that benefitted the peasantry. The federal government's credit program for small farmers and settlers, the National Program for the Strengthening of Family Agriculture (PRONAF), quadrupled between the 2002–03 and 2006–07 harvests to nearly US$5 billion. The funds for the National Education Program in Agrarian Reform (PRONERA) and its partnerships with public universities and technical schools increased from an annual average of US$3.4 million before 2003 to US$16.3 million over the next four years. The Program for Technical, Social, and Environmental Assistance for Agrarian Reform (ATES), more than tripled its coverage after 2003, serving 555,000 families by 2006. Moreover, the program "Light for All" launched by the Lula government's Ministry of Mines, Energy and Communications had extended rural electrification to 6.1 million people by mid-2007.[19]

These and other public programs were implemented in a context of recurrent lobbying and pressure from rural social movements. A number of these government projects were actually conceived and proposed by the MST and other peasant associations. The Food Purchase Program (PAA), for example, was established in 2003 at the request of a number of these groups. This program, of notable success in recent years, guarantees government purchase of farm goods raised by settlers and other peasant farmers. This foodstuff is then distributed to various state institutions and served in meals offered in public schools, hospitals, prisons and so on. Another illustration of this trend can be gleaned from the Lula government's decision to hire 1,800 new employees for INCRA, which boosted its administrative capacity by 40%. This measure was the result of an agreement made with the MST in the wake of its impressive 2005 march to Brasília, in which 12,000 people walked for sixteen days and 220 kilometers to support agrarian reform.[20]

Despite his longstanding promise to enact a progressive land distribution plan, President Lula retained Brazil's conservative inertia toward agrarian matters, attenuating it only in part. Lula's rural policies were shaped by the government's decision to maintain the Cardoso's economic policies and promote the expansion of agribusiness farming. As such, the Lula government undertook a series of measures that accorded ample political protection and funds to support a model of agricultural production based on large industrial farms, oriented mostly to the production of agro-export commodities. In effect, between 2003 and 2007, state support for the rural elite was seven times greater than that offered to the nation's family farmers, even though the latter represented 87% of Brazil's rural labor force and generated the bulk of the food consumed by Brazilians.[21]

The consolidation of an elite-driven pattern of rural development has reinforced mechanisms of social exclusion and curtailed prospects for the redistribution of land, wealth, and power. In contrast to small-scale family farming, agribusiness production concentrates income, generates little employment, and has a high environmental cost, due to extensive mono-cropping, intensive use of pesticides, and notable contribution to the destruction of forests and other natural resources. In sum, the Lula government's clear preference for an agribusiness model of development thwarted the possibility of carrying out a more progressive agrarian reform.[22]

Land Reform Settlements:
Diversity and Advances amid Precarious Conditions

Land reform settlements are far from homogenous. Rather, they encompass a wide array of territorial units, highly diversified in their economic, social, political, and cultural development. These different dimensions can combine in multiple ways within a given settlement, depending, among other factors, on the number of families involved, their geographical and social background (including previous labor, associational, religious, and political experiences), the micro-region of the country where the community was established, the history of their mobilization to access land, and the organizational resources available during the struggle *on* the land.

Some land reform communities are composed by only five families, while others contain more than 1,500 families, or roughly 7,500 people. Some settlements are located in isolated portions of the Amazonian rainforest, while others are found in the metropolitan area of São Paulo, next to large industrial factories. Some settlements were set up in the semi-arid region of the northeast, where agricultural production hinges on irrigation, the prospect of which has been either remote or unreachable. Other settlements were established on Brazil's most fertile soils, like those found in the western region of the state of Paraná.

The assorted background of landless workers affects the settlements' internal dynamics and organizational capacity. Among the landless one finds the sons and daughters of family farmers, peasants with insufficient land, rural workers, squatters, tenants, rubber tappers, forest gatherers, artisanal gold miners, and people from riverbank communities. Other settlers spent time living in urban shantytowns and returned to the countryside due to the lack of work and concern over rampant crime and drug-related violence. This demographic trend gained visibility in some states during the early 2000s. In Rio Grande do Sul, a significant number of settlers found in the state's southern half—particularly in the municipalities of Canguçu, Bagé, Hulha Negra, and Santana do Livramento—migrated back to the countryside after losing their jobs in the state's industrial centers. In the metropolitan regions of São Paulo and Porto Alegre, some settlements offer a mix of rural and urban features. In these *rururbano* communities some family members will toil on their small farm plot as others commute to the city for work. Here, it is common to find a mixed batch of families, some of peasant origin and others with no previous experience in agriculture.

The social diversity of landless workers adds a layer of complexity to the relations found in an agrarian reform settlement and can hinder efforts to establish a sense of community among settlers. Given the broad scope for cultural and personal misunderstandings, and potential disagreements over the settlement's organization, the rise of internal quarrels in any of these areas is almost inevitable. The likelihood for these conflicts tends to be higher in the earlier stages of community life, in the more isolated and unattended settlements, and in areas where peasants were relocated to a distant region from their place of origin. Such disputes can hinder economic development and undermine the formation of new social and political identities in these communities.

Amid the heterogeneity of these settlements one can find elements of commonality among their peasant dwellers. One of the largest land reform surveys in Brazil found that 94% of the settlers came from rural areas or had once worked in agriculture. According to this report, education levels in these communities are discernibly low; one-third of the settlers had never been to school and 87% had never studied beyond the fourth grade.[23] Though marked by a life of poverty, with few employment opportunities, the settlers were generally hopeful about achieving greater stability and a more dignified future for their families. Many attributed this inspiration to the collective experience of fighting for land.

Table 9.6. Perceptions of living conditions in land reform settlements

Improvements expressed by settlers	%
Quality of life	91
Housing	79
Education	70
Physical security	68
Nutrition	66
Purchasing power	62
Health	53
Access to credit	81
Family future	87
Settlements with children living on their plot	80
Settlements with associations	96

Source: Heredia, Medeiros, Palmeira, Cintrão, and Leite (2004: 337, 347).

Note: The survey data are not based on a national polling sample, but draw on the most comprehensive research done on the subject. Of the 1,568 households interviewed, only 9% claimed their quality of life had "not improved."

For all the hostility against land redistribution, and the inadequate levels of state assistance and precarious situation of most agrarian settlements, the establishment of these communities has brought important advances for rural development in Brazil. Between 1985 and 2006, the creation of these rural settlements has enabled 5.1 million people living in extreme poverty to gain access to a reliable source of employment, income, and nutrition.[24] The substantial improvements in the lives of the settlers are underlined clearly in table 9.6, which presents the findings of one the main surveys of Brazilian land reform communities.[25]

The most discernable impact of Brazil's agrarian reform measures can be observed at the local level, especially in municipalities that hold a higher concentration of settlement projects. As Sonia Bergamasco and Luiz Norder illustrate in chapter 10 in this volume, the rural population has actually increased or remained stable in these localities. Thus, by mitigating the exodus toward urban centers, the creation of these rural communities has helped reduce the growth of shantytowns that form a ring-belt around most Brazilian cities.

In addition, many local economies have benefited significantly from the establishment of land reform settlements in their district. Studies have shown that landless peasants generally experience a notable improvement in their purchasing power after they are settled on the land. This has led to a greater consumption of food, clothing, household appliances, and construction material, along with farming equipment and other agricultural inputs. Through increased consumption, farm production, disbursal of government credit, and the creation of rural cooperatives and small agro-industries, these rural communities have helped boost their local economies by stimulating commerce and construction work. Moreover, the greater availability and diversity of farm products in the area have strengthened local farmers' markets, lowered the cost of food, and improved the quality of nutrition in various municipalities across the country.[26]

Far from simply providing an endpoint to a popular struggle, these rural settlements have often served as a launch-pad for new peasant demands and fostered alternative spaces for public participation.[27] In effect, the struggles for and on the land have contributed to the formation of new generation of popular leaders, ushered-in novel forms of grassroots organization, and improved the capacity of peasants for dialogue and negotiation with state authorities. These experiences have fueled the development of social capital among settlers, nurtured organizing skills and a disposition to participate in associational life, while instilling greater awareness of citizenship rights.[28]

The social dynamic stirred with the creation of agrarian settlements and the inclusion of new local voters, has changed the political landscape of many municipalities. Over the years, numerous settlers have taken part in elections to run the local rural trade unions, serve on the municipal council, and, on rarer occasions, compete for the mayor's office or seats in the State Assembly, and even the National Congress. Other settlers have been actively involved in setting up and running farm cooperatives and supporting the organization of new social movements. All this has strengthened the representation of popular interests and expanded the scope of public discussion, thereby abetted the democratization of local power in various parts of Brazil.

Far from being an expensive policy, land reform has proved to be a cost-effective program for creating new jobs. Indeed, studies show that it has been far less expensive than generating employment in the industrial, commercial, and service sectors of the economy.[29] Agrarian reform also offers a wide range of additional benefits and multiplier effects that go well beyond its economic impact. In short, along with stabilizing and improving the living conditions of 825,000 landless peasant families, the creation of these agrarian settlements has enhanced self-esteem among these rural workers and helped extend basic citizenship rights in the Brazilian countryside.

Building Capabilities amid the Struggle:
MST Innovation and Organizational Strength

The struggle on the land must be understood in light of Brazil's conservative agrarian reform. These conditions shape and explain much of the MST's strengths, weaknesses, and constraints. The movement's internal sophistication and endurance since the 1980s were clearly influenced by this context. The state's slow and restricted approach to the creation of land reform settlements, and meager support to these communities, compelled the MST to launch several initiatives to get the federal government to carry out its promises in favor of agrarian reform. Over time, this situation induced the movement to bolster its operational capacities, both to demand the enactment of the settlers' rights and to develop a range of ancillary activities. All this led to the formation of different task teams within the MST—known in the movement's own parlance, as "sectors and collectives"—along with the creation of various cooperatives, educational centers, media outlets, and artistic groups. This process engendered a complex organizational network, operating at national, state, regional, and local levels.

The MST's current structure reflects two important historical legacies. The first stems from the decision taken in 1986, at the First National Meeting of Settlers, where the movement upheld the principle of maintaining a unified struggle of landless and settler peasants. This strategic definition gave cohesion to both mobilizations *for* land and *on* the land. It also helped promote solidarity between different MST groups and generations.[30]

The second historical legacy was shaped by the social conditions in which the movement was born. The MST originated in southern Brazil, in one of the most developed regions of the country, with a strong state and a resourceful civil society. These conditions influenced the movement's character in many subtle ways, notably by reinforcing its disposition and capacity to organize, train, and instill a sense of discipline among its activists. Such aptitudes were diffused widely through the movement's territorial expansion and strong investment in educating its cadres.

MST activists from the south played a significant role in extending the movement across Brazil and setting up many of its task teams. Since the mid-1990s, however, the presence of movement leaders from other regions has grown considerably, especially with the MST's rapid expansion in the Brazilian northeast. In fact, by 2006, half of all MST settlers were from this part of the country (see table 9.7).

The struggle on the land enabled the MST to complement its public activism for land redistribution with the creation of numerous projects aimed at developing its settlements and sustaining the movement. By combining its grassroots mobilizations, negotiations with public authorities, and formation of a

Table 9.7. Settlements linked to the MST, estimated by region, 2006

Region	Settlements No.	Settlements MST %	Settlements Region %	Families settled No.	Families settled MST %	Families settled Region %	Area distributed (ha) No.	Area distributed (ha) MST %	Area distributed (ha) Region %
North	39	1.9	2.0	8,613	6.4	2.4	481,331	13.1	1.8
Northeast	983	48.9	27.7	66,101	49.2	22.0	1,640,113	44.5	17.9
Midwest	125	6.2	12.0	14,737	11.0	10.5	662,205	18.0	8.9
Southeast	221	11.0	32.9	14,077	10.5	31.1	265,986	7.2	20.8
South	644	32.0	86.9	30,913	23.0	84.4	635,523	17.2	84.3
Brazil	**2,012**	**100.0**	**26.4**	**134,440**	**100.0**	**15.4**	**3,685,158**	**100.0**	**8.0**

Source: Calculated by the authors with data from the MST (2007a) and DATALUTA (2008a).

Note: MST percentages (MST %) are based on the total number of MST settlements. Region and Brazil percentages (Region %) are based on the total number of settlements established in each region and all of Brazil. The estimated number of settlements linked to the movement in 2006 was produced as follows: using MST data for its 2004 settlements, disaggregated by state, we obtained a percentage of MST settlements over the total number of settlements created between 1979 and 2004, based on DATALUTA figures. We then applied this percentage to DATALUTA's total number of settlements, settled families, and area distributed between 1979 and 2006, in each Brazilian region. For a state-by-state estimate of MST settlements see table 9.16.

wide range of ancillary activities, the MST fashioned a multifaceted organizational web. Table 9.8 offers a synthesis of the thirteen sectors and collectives established by various working groups within the MST, between 1988 and 2006. Each initiative has its own story. Yet all emerged through a collective decision-making process and consultation, in the quest to address specific needs and challenges raised during the fight for agrarian reform and the social transformation of Brazil. Born amid the struggle *for* land, the MST gained strength by continuing this struggle *on* the land and expanding the movement's horizons there from.

The MST's task teams operate at multiple levels of the organization. The national coordination for each team is composed of two representatives from each state, a man and a woman, along with activists responsible for handling critical responsibilities in each area. For example, the Communications Task Team also includes the professional journalists that work in the movement's media outlets. The people responsible for the MST's cooperatives and for providing technical assistance to the settlers are also involved in coordinating the Production, Cooperation and Environment Task Team. At the state level, the teams are organized in a similar way, with representatives from various regions in the state. Many of these task team leaders are from MST settlements organized around collective farming practices, as these production methods are more likely to free up people to work as full-time movement activists.

Table 9.8. MST sectors and collectives

Sector/ collective	Year created	Background	Goals and main activities
Political education (*Formação*)	1988	Starts with workshops offered by the CPT. Between 1986 and 1989, MST activists attend courses sponsored by CUT, Brazil's main labor confederation. In 1987, the MST begins training cadres involved in organizing the movement in new states, prompting the sector's creation the following year. In 1990, the MST founds its first National School for Political Education, the Contestado Training Center, in Caçador, Santa Catarina.	Foster knowledge, class consciousness, and critical analysis among MST cadres, its rank-and-file members, and activists from other popular movements. Provides technical trainings on various topics. With the support of several Brazilian universities, in 1999, it began offering a course on "Brazilian society and politics" and "Brazilian thinkers." In 2005, it inaugurated the Florestan Fernandes National School, on a large campus located in Guararema, São Paulo.
Education	1988	Initial stirrings begin in the first schools set up in landless camps and settlements in Rio Grande do Sul. These iniatives gain momentum in 1987 with the organization of the First Meeting of MST educators in São Mateus, Espírito Santo, leading to the creation of a national sector the following year.	Ensure access to education for all MST participants. Promotes policies that guarantee adequate schools for its rural communities. Supports teaching methods inspired by Paulo Freire's pedagogy, geared toward peasant lifestyles, while nurturing principles of cooperation, ecological preservation, and social justice. Oversees the movement's educational activities, from childcare centers, elementary and secondary schools, and adult literacy, to technical vocation schools and university-level programs.
Mass front (*Frente de massa*)	1989	Organizing landless rural workers and getting them involved in the struggle for land reform has been a major task since the movement's onset. In 1985, the MST creates its first mobilizing groups (*grupos motores*) to fine-tune its mobilization tactics in response to the rise of the UDR, a violent landlord group. The sector was consolidated during a phase of internal restructuring within the movement.	Serves as the MST's main entryway. Recruits people to take part of its landless camps. Provides continuous support throughout their land struggle. Coordinates activities carried out by various sectors in each landless camp and manages relevant negotiations with public authorities. Enlists experienced activists to support land struggles in other Brazilian states.

Table 9.8 continued

Sector/ collective	Year created	Background	Goals and main activities
Finance	1989	Early monetary support is provided mostly by Catholic and Lutheran church agencies. In 1989, the MST establishes guidelines to promote greater financial autonomy and encourage its members to sustain their activities by tapping into local resources.	Encourage self-reliance through adequate financial planning, monitoring, and accounting practices. Seeks to decentralize the movement's fundraising activities. Oversees the administration of MST assets.
Projects	1989	Emerges together with the MST's finance unit, but becomes a separate sector with the formation of the movement's finance team.	Obtain funds from national and international donors to support the MST's struggle for land reform, to develop its settlements, raise awareness and educate its members, and promote human rights in the countryside. Strives to diversify the MST's sources of revenue.
Production cooperation and environment	1992	Initial organizing begins in 1986, during the First National Meeting of Settlers, held in Cascavel, Paraná. In the following years, the MST creates its first coops and thereafter begins to establish bodies to coordinate efforts between them, which leads to the development of the Confederation of Agrarian Reform Cooperatives of Brazil (CONCRAB), in 1992, later reorganized as a sector in 2002.	Improve productivity and environmental stewardship in MST settlements, by promoting coops and other forms of mutual aid, agro-industries, alternative trade practices and agro-ecology. Helps coordinate the MST's coops and credit unions. Mobilizes settlers, lobbies and negotiates with the state to ensure proper implementation of farm credit policies, technical assistance, housing and infrastructure development in MST settlements.
International relations (*)	1993	During the early years international contacts are handled by the finance and projects sectors. Between 1988 and 1992, the MST takes an active part in organizing a Latin American network of popular movements, known as the "Continental Campaign for Indigenous, Afro, and Popular Resistance," which prompted the collective's formation.	Maintains relationships with groups of Friends of the MST established in fourteen European and North American countries. Responsible for managing ties with the international affiliates of La Via Campesina, the Latin American Coordinator of Rural Organizations (CLOC), and the World Social Form. Coordinates visits from foreign delegations.

Sector/ collective	Year created	Background	Goals and main activities
Human rights	1995	In the MST's first decade, activists collect data and denounced human rights violations in the countryside in various international forums. Lawyers are asked to handle emergency cases. The massacres of landless peasants in Corumbiara (1995) and Eldorado dos Carajás (1996) give an added momentum to the creation of this sector.	Provides legal advice to the MST and other peasant movements through the National Network of Popular Lawyers (RENAP), which was set up in 1996. In collaboration with RENAP it organizes workshops to prepare its lawyers and educate rural workers on legal issues. Offers courses to instruct MST activists on conflict mediation, and puts out various publications on human rights.
Communication	1997	Originates informally with the creation of the *Jornal Sem Terra*, the MST's monthly newspaper, set up in 1981, in Rio Grande do Sul. The publication becomes the movement's official news outlet in 1984, and is run by a collective. At its Third National Congres, in 1995, the MST agrees to enhance its public outreach and reorganize this sector.	Conveys the movement's goals, ideas, and activities to its members and the general public through various media vehicles. Offer sources of information and opinion that provide alternative viewpoints to those generated by the nation's large media corporations. As such, it strives to enrich and expand the contours of public debate in Brazil.
Health	1998	Stems from the MST's own health care activities carried out at its landless camps and settlements. These are initally supported by the Catholic Church's health agency (the *Pastoral da Saúde*) and various public clinics. At a 2000 workshop in Cajamar, São Paulo, the sector adopts a holistic view of health issues and intensifies its critique of the profit-driven approach to medicine, propelled by the pharmaceutical-hospital industry.	Upholds the principle of treating health care as a basic human right and struggles to ensure adequate and equitable public services in this regard. Promotes a holistic approach to health. Seeks to consolidate Brazil's Unified Health System (SUS), by enhancing popular accountability and thwart efforts aimed at treating health care as a market commodity. Supports preventative health practices and alternative therapeutic approaches. Encourages MST members to cultivate medicinal herbs and promotes public policies that embrace their use.

Table 9.8 continued

Sector/ collective	Year created	Background	Goals and main activities
Culture	2000	Starts as a collective within the education sector, formed during a 1996 music workshop held in Brasília. The collective evolves into a sector with the support of activists involved in the communication and political education sectors.	Promotes artist expressions linked to MST struggles, through music, theater, film and video, graphic arts, literature and poetry. Nurtures a sense of aesthetics that blend MST concerns and folk traditions. Supports various cultural groups and events. Maintains ties with artists and intellectuals who sympathize with the movement.
Gender	2000	The first women's collective is formed in 1985, at the MST's First National Congress, in Curitiba, Paraná. MST women help establish the National Network of Rural Workers (ANMTR) in 1995. The MST's Second National Women's meeting, held in Brasília in 1979, boosts efforts to create this sector. That same year, MST women take part of the ANMTR's campaign to ensure that all rural women workers have proper national identity cards.	Champions gender equality in Brazilian society and within the MST, by challenging patriarchal family norms and traditional values grounded on *machismo*. Encourages women to participate in MST struggles and activities. In the late 1990s, it helps institute childcare centers at all MST meetings and events. In 2003, it obtains support for a rule guaranteeing gender parity in all MST decision-making bodies. Sponsors workshops on gender-related issues in partnership with other sectors.
Youth (*)	2006	Emerges out of discussions at the Youth Assemblies held during the 2005 National March for Agrarian Reform. The collective is set up the following year at a National Seminar for Young Men and Women Engaged in the Struggle, held in Guararema, São Paulo.	Encourages youth in MST landless camps and settlements to organize and take part in the movement's struggle. Supports consciousness-raising activities among young activists. Seeks to strengthen ties with popular urban youth groups, from the *favelas* and metropolitan peripheries.

Source: Representatives of MST task teams and collectives. The authors acknowledge the collaboration of Antônio Pasquetti, Carlos Belé, Gleisa Campigotto, Milton Fornazieri, Edgar Kölling, Evelaine Martines, Dulcinea Pavan, João Paulo Rodrigues, Neuri Rossetto, Gislei Siqueira, Miguel Stédile, Ney Strozake, and Lourdes Vicente, for facilitating information that helped us prepare this table. In addition, we consulted Fernandes (2000).

Starting in the late 1980s, the MST's task teams began to set up and register a number of associations and institutes. Because of their legal status, these associations have been able to sign service contracts with different state agencies and receive funds from national and international donors. Among the organizations set up by MST cadres are a number of production coops and collective farm associations that can be found in settlements across Brazil; the Settlers' Cooperative System (SCA); the National Association for Agricultural Cooperation (ANCA); the Confederation of Agrarian Reform Cooperatives of Brazil (CONCRAB); the Technical School for Coop Administration (TAC); the Technical Institute for Training and Research in Agrarian Reform (ITERRA); the Josué de Castro Educational Institute; several credit unions; the Copertchê Work Cooperative; BioNatur Natural Seeds; the Florestan Fernandes National School; the Latin American School of Agroecology (ELA), and diverse media outlets.

The gradual development of these organizations in the course of the struggle *on* the land strengthened the MST's internal structure and logistical capacity. The assimilation of new interests and activities, along with the movement's territorial expansion, increased the number of cadres engaged in the various MST decision-making bodies. By 2008, there were approximately 2,000 activists dedicated to such endeavors.[31] The struggle *on* the land has also brought about a number of qualitative changes within the movement. Through it, the MST began to discover a series of novel challenges and embrace new causes which expanded the MST's political horizon. All this helped forge a sharper understanding of the broader implications of its struggle to transform Brazil's unjust land tenure. Newfound concerns over gender issues, ecology, human rights, health, cultural diversity, food sovereignty, national development, and international solidarity began to inform and complement the MST's traditional emphasis on class analysis. Amid these eclectic ideas, it fashioned a more holistic view of the process of social change. In this way, the movement's early critique of Brazil's landlords and their vast and mostly unproductive estates evolved to include a trenchant critique of the country's development model. This, in turn, fueled the MST's disposition to contest the global expansion of agribusiness corporations and their support for an agro-system based on large-scale, industrial production of monocrops.

Three MST Sectors:
  Education; Production, Cooperation and Environment; and Communication

This section provides an overview of the development of three MST sectors created between 1988 and 1997. Their brief history illustratrates the movement's ability to forge an increasingly sophisticated popular organization. Each of these task teams is the product of collective decisions made in a context of struggle and adversity, and developed through a process of trial and error, with frequent reevaluations and adjustments. All three sectors also reveal a trend toward the "globalization of the MST," as described by Bernardo Mançano Fernandes (chap. 5, this volume). This impulse gained added traction with the movement's 1996 affiliation to La Via Campesina, an international coalition of peasant associations founded in 1992, with members in Asia, Africa, Europe, and the Americas. Since the late 1990s, La Via Campesina has helped the MST and its Brazilian allies forge a consistent critique of global agribusiness and neoliberal policies toward agriculture adopted by institutions like the World Trade Organization.

Education Sector

The MST's investment in the education of its members and cadre is probably unparalleled in the world history of peasant associations. The chronology presented in table 9.9 draws attention to some of the main developments in this regard.

Table 9.9. The Education Sector: A basic chronology

Year	Event
1982	The first school for the children of landless peasants is set up at the Nova Ronda Alta camp in Rio Grande do Sul.
1987	The first National Meeting of MST Teachers is held in São Mateus, Espírito Santo.
1988	The Education Sector is organized.
1989	The MST helps establish the Development, Education and Research Foundation (FUNDEP) in Três Passos, Rio Grande do Sul, in partnership with rural trade unions linked to CUT-Rural and other popular movements.
1990	The first teaching course for MST educators is instituted in Braga, Rio Grande do Sul.
1990	The MST begins to produce its own teaching materials with the support of intellectuals involved in promoting popular education.
1990	The National Center for Political Education (or *Formação*) is established in Caçador, Santa Catarina.
1991	The MST conducts its first youth and adult literacy workshops for illiterate settlers in Rio Grande do Sul.
1993	The Technical School for Coop Administration (TAC) is created in Braga, Rio Grande do Sul.
1995	The Technical Institute for Training and Research in Agrarian Reform (ITERRA) and the Josué de Castro Educational Institute are founded in Veranópolis, Rio Grande do Sul.
1995	MST teachers take part of the first university training courses, co-sponsored with the Federal University of Espírito Santo. A similar agreement is reached with the Federal University of Paraíba, in 1998, and thereafter with several other Brazilian universities.

Year	Event
1995	The MST receives the Itaú/UNICEF award for "Education and Participation."
1996	The first National Training Workshop for Kindergarten Teachers takes place in Caçador, Santa Catarina, which leads to the formation of numerous childcare centers for children under the age of six.
1996	The MST signs an agreement with the Ministry of Education and the University of Brasília to train 7,000 adult literacy teachers.
1997	The first National Meeting of Agrarian Reform Teachers is held in Brasília. This event prompts the federal government to institute the National Agrarian Reform Education Program (PRONERA), coordinated by the Ministry for Agrarian Reform. The program, however, remains seriously underfunded.
1997	The first Itinerant School is set up in Rio Grande do Sul to care for the children of landless families as they move their protest camps from one locale to another.
1998	The MST convenes a National Conference "For Rural Education" in Luziânia, Goiás, which fuels interest in developing a new national program for rural education.
1998	ITERRA and the Northwest Regional University of the State of Rio Grande do Sul (UNIJUI) sponsor the MST's first university-level Education Program.
1999	The first National Meeting of Landless Children is organized in Porto Alegre.
1999	The first National Meeting of Elementary School Teachers, Fifth to Eighth Grades is held in Esteio, Rio Grande do Sul, in partnership with the state government's Secretary of Education.
2000	Construction of the Florestan Fernandes National School (ENFF) begins in Guararema, São Paulo.
2000	The Cardoso government cuts off funding for PRONERA in reprisal for the MST's ongoing pressure for agrarian reform and critique of its neoliberal policies.
2002	Other peasant movements active in La Via Campesina take part of ITERRA's teacher-training programs and a National Seminar "For Rural Education," held in Brasília.
2003	The new Lula government restores PRONERA and provides a substantial budget increase. The MST signs agreements with several universities to establish special study programs for its activists.
2005	The Florestan Fernandes National School is inaugurated at a large campus in Guararema, São Paulo. La Via Campesina partners from Brazil and abroad attend training courses at the new school.
2006	The first Meeting of MST Teachers for Youth and Adults Literacy from the north and northeast regions of Brazil takes place in Caruaru, Pernambuco.
2006	At the MST's request, the Ministry of Education agrees to fund a degree-granting program in Rural Education and engages seven universities to run this new initiative.
2007	A new Campaign for Youth and Adult Literacy is launched during the MST's Fifth National Congress in Brasília.

Source: Compiled by the authors in consultation with members of the MST's Education and *Formação* (Political Education) Sectors.

Table 9.10. MST achievements in education, 1984–2007

Activities accomplished	Numbers
Elementary schools set up	1,800
Elementary school teachers prepared	8,000
Students in primary and secondary public schools	250,000
Youth and adult literacy students	20,000
Youth and adult literacy teachers	2,000
Child care and kindergarten teachers	500
Teacher-training and education students at ITERRA and partner schools	1,200
Agro-technical students at ITERRA and partner schools	1,300
Health education and nursing students	200
Medical school students in Cuba	120
Partnerships with public and private universities	60
Pedagogical books written and published	63
National and international awards for excellence in education	5

Source: MST Education Sector.

The quantitative results achieved in education, summarized in table 9.10, reveal the size and scope of the pedagogical work carried out by this dynamic and well-established task team within the MST.

These achievements also include important qualitative results. Over the last two decades the MST has invested significant efforts to create its own pedagogical methods, strongly influenced by the ideas of Paulo Freire and other national and international intellectuals concerned with popular education.[32] The teaching method and materials developed by this sector have sought to reinforce core MST values, namely those that underscore the importance of collective struggle, organization, participation, citizenship rights, social justice, solidarity, education, cultural diversity, and ecological integrity. Adding to this, the MST has worked with progressive scholars to develop "a peoples' history of Brazil," through the study and historical re-interpretation of past forms of popular resistance.[33]

MST critics argue that its pedagogy is based on "ideological" and "fundamentalist" ideas. *Veja* magazine, Brazil's leading news weekly, has gone as far as to compare the MST schools to "madrassas," the Muslim boarding schools accused of fostering extreme Islamic views.[34] To be sure, the movement has never hidden its desire to educate its members in ways that would stimulate their engagement in the struggle to promote greater social justice in Brazil. In this regard, its teachings have never exhibited any pretense of neutrality. This stems from the MST's recognition and belief that education is a crucial instrument in the struggle over hegemony, that is, the dominant consensus around the ideas, values, and perceptions of what is considered "realistic," "possible," and "desirable" in a society. In all this, the movement has been quite eclectic in its sources of inspiration and generally open to constructive contributions from people unaffiliated to the group. Without this disposition one could not explain the MST's willingness to have its activists take courses at programs cosponsored by sixty Brazilian universities. If the movement's critics are correct, one would have to conclude that Brazil's most prestigious universities, including the University of São Paulo (USP), the University of Campinas (UNICAMP), the Federal University of Rio de Janeiro (UFRJ), and the State University of São Paulo (UNESP), share the same "ideological" and "fundamentalist" ideas ascribed to the landless movement.

Production, Cooperation, and Environment Sector

This task team is emblematic of the ancillary activities the MST had to organize to develop the productive capacity of its settlements. Its challenges in this area have been formidable. For one, this sector has been compelled to mobilize the settlers through public activism, to demand that the government implement various support programs related to agricultural credits, housing, technical assistance, road construction, the installation of electrical power-grids, and other public services. Adding to this, it has had to counteract the influence of agribusiness firms that have sought to induce many settlers to accept their capital and technology-intensive production model, ill-suited for the long-run sustainability of the family farm economy. Amid these challenges, the sector created its own technical assistance program and tried out various arrangements to promote cooperation among its settlers and settlements (see table 9.11).

Table 9.11. Production, Cooperation, and Environment Sector: A basic chronology

Year	Event
1983	The first collective farm settlements are formed in Ronda Alta, Rio Grande do Sul, sponsored by the state government's Department of Agriculture and the local Catholic Church.
1986	The MST convenes its first National Settlers Meeting in Cascavel, Paraná, which leads to the formation of a National Settlers' Commission (CNA).
1986	At the MST's request, the federal government institutes a Special Credit Program for Agrarian Reform (PROCERA).
1989	The MST has 400 production associations, operating at various organizational and output capacity levels.
1989	New legal opportunities enabled by the 1988 Constitution prompt the MST to dissolve its National Settlers' Commission and evaluate the possibility of creating a network of coops.

Table 9.11 continued

Year	Event
1989	The movement organizes its first Farm Production Coops (CPAs) in Rio Grande do Sul, based on the Cuban collective farm model.
1991	The MST's production sector is set up as the Cooperative System of Settlers (SCA), which stimulates the creation of new CPAs and the organization of coop networks operating at regional, state, and national levels.
1992	The Confederation of Agrarian Reform Cooperatives of Brazil (CONCRAB) is founded in Curitiba, Paraná.
1993	A Technical School for Coop Administration (TAC) is inaugurated in Braga, Rio Grande do Sul. This school eventually becomes part of the Technical Institute for Training and Research in Agrarian Reform (ITERRA).
1994	The production sector evaluates the crisis and break up of various CPAs. The movement decides to invest greater efforts in demanding state support for the development of its land reform settlements.
1996	The Cardoso government institutes the Lumiar Project to provide technical assistance to the settlers.
1996	The MST resolves to develop its own service co-ops and credit unions. The production sector decides to support CREDITAR, a credit union operating in Cantagalo, Paraná, and to establish a new credit union, CRENHOR, in Sarandí, Rio Grande do Sul.
1997	The first organic seeds production coop, BioNatur, is organized in Hulha Negra, Rio Grande do Sul.
1998	CONCRAB embraces an agro-ecological production model and begins to offer workshops promoting this approach to agriculture.
2000	The Cardoso government cancels the Lumiar Project in reprisal for the MST's ongoing pressure for agrarian reform and critique of its neoliberal policies.
2002	CONCRAB is reconstituted as the Production, Cooperation and Environment Sector.
2002	Agreements between the MST, the federal government, and various state governments, restore technical assistance programs for the settlers.
2005	The Latin American School for Agro-Ecology (ELA) is created in Lapa, Paraná, with the support of the state government of Paraná, the Federal University of Paraná, and the government of Venezuela.
2005	The national expansion of the BioNatur Network leads to the creation of the Land and Life National Cooperative (CONATERRA).
2006	The MST collaborates in the establishment of the Paulo Freire Latin American Institute for Agro-Ecology, in Barinas, Venezuela.

Source: Compiled by the authors through consultations with leaders of the Production, Cooperation and Environment Sector; and information found in CONCRAB (1998).

Since the origins of the movement, MST settlers have been encouraged to organize and join farm co-ops and other peasant enterprises. The first experiments in collective farm production were strongly supported by progressive church and state agents, yet exhibited varying levels of success. In the late 1980s, the MST began to promote the formation of a new system of collective work based on Cuba's farm management model, which became known as the Farm Production Cooperatives (CPAs). These collectivized farms were pursued more intensely under President Fernando Collor de Mello's administration (1990–92), at a time when many movement leaders believed the CPAs could serve as "islands of resistance" to the government's repressive measures against their organization. By 1991 the MST had installed two dozen CPAs. Most of these co-ops, though, were short-lived. The following year, the MST created a national Confederation of Agrarian Reform Cooperatives of Brazil (CONCRAB), and in 1993 set up a Technical School for Coop Administration (TAC), which offered the settlers basic management skills for running these new cooperatives.

During Cardoso's first presidential term, and particularly in the aftermath of the landless massacre at Eldorado dos Carajás, the MST gained greater access to public funds for its new cooperatives and agro-industries. These developments boosted the sector's organizational capacity. By 1997, it had founded nine statewide cooperatives. Moreover, between 1997 and 2000, the number of agro-industries in MST settlements—producing milk, beef, yerba mate, *cachaça* (Brazilian rum), *farofa* (manioc flour), fruit jams, bread, and other food products—jumped from twenty-five to eighty processing centers.[35]

In the late 1990s, Brazilian farm cooperatives suffered an economic slump that affected many coops linked to CONCRAB. This situation fueled internal debates as to the merits and viability of developing a cooperative system within a capitalist economy. The impasse generated as a result of this discussion sapped some of the MST's interest in creating new coops. Even under these adverse circumstances, the movement continued to support various forms of cooperation among its settlers. The anti-MST offensive unleashed during Cardoso's second administration, forced CONCRAB's technical staff and other activists to mobilize and lobby intensely to ensure government compliance with agreements made to disburse farm and housing credits, provide technical assistance, and other services.

The results of the 2002 presidential vote ushered in a more auspicious climate for MST dialogue with public officials. The Lula government's preferential option, nonetheless, for an agribusiness rural development model led to various constraints. For instance, funding for family farmers increased during these years, but it did so mostly in ways designed to integrate these peasants into the production and retail-supply chains controlled by agribusiness corporations. This administration also restricted the funds to develop small agro-industries in the settlements. Moreover, it inhibited their formation by maintaining a stringent set of regulations that favored large-scale food processing plants over smaller ones. During this time, then, the MST focused mainly on organizing new service and retail cooperatives. By 2008, the movement had set up a total of 161 co-ops, including four credit unions, and 140 agro-industries.[36]

The downturn in Brazil's agricultural economy, following the adoption of a monetary stabilization plan and various neoliberal measures in the mid-1990s, led the MST to question its own production model and search for alternatives to agro-industrial farming. Gradually, it began to adopt an environmental agenda and sustainable agricultural practices. In 1998, CONCRAB decided to embrace agro-ecological principles and promote these ideas among MST settlers through workshops, technical assistance, and other outreach efforts. The movement's first agro-ecological association, BioNatur, an organic seed co-op, was set up prior to this, in 1997, in Hulha Negra, Rio Grande do Sul. The initiative started with twelve families linked to the Settler's Regional Cooperative (COOPERAL). This co-op, founded in 1991, specialized early on in supplying vegetable seeds to several private firms. Eventually, it decided to build a processing plant and register this activity as a business company. Many settlers and advisers, though, began to question the cooperative's reliance on agro-industrial practices and succeeded in shifting the entire production line to organic seeds by 1997.

BioNatur grew in the late 1990s with the inclusion of new peasant families and the technical assistance and agro-ecology trainings offered by regional MST leaders. Yet in the early 2000s, it experienced a management crisis that led to a decline in production and sales. The MST's response was counterintuitive. Rather than focus solely on resolving the internal crisis, in 2003 it decided to scale up and relaunch the organization as the BioNatur National Seed Network. This decision was inspired by La Via Campesina's global campaign, "Seeds: Heritage of the People for the Good of Humanity," and was developed in clear opposition to the genetically modified seeds (GMOs) propagated by agribusiness corporations like Monsanto and Syngenta. After extensive grassroots consultation, BioNatur members agreed to restructure their organization and revise their agro-ecology trainings. In 2005, BioNatur farmers from the states of Rio Grande do Sul, Santa Catarina, and Paraná agreed to create the Land and Life National Cooperative (CONATERRA), with headquarters in Candiota, Rio Grande do Sul. The following year the coop incorporated a new group of MST settlers from Minas Gerais. By the end of 2007, BioNatur had become the largest producer of organic seeds in Latin America, with 117 crop varieties and an annual yield of twenty tons of seeds, generated by 300 families living in twenty Brazilian municipalities.[37]

Agro-ecology is certainly not a universal practice among MST settlers. In many settlements in southern Brazil it is quite common to see peasants sow their fields with genetically modified soybeans, despite opposition to this from movement leaders. The BioNatur experience, nonetheless, underscores the MST's growing interest in agro-ecology and the broad potential for organic farming in Brazil's land reform settlements.

Communication Sector

The landless movement's first initiative in public communication dates back to 1981, when activists in solidarity with the landless camp at Natalino's Crossing, in Rio Grande do Sul, began to publish the *Jornal Sem Terra* (The Landless Newspaper). This monthly bulletin became the MST's official news outlet in 1984. Its headquarters were transferred subsequently from Porto Alegre to São Paulo, in keeping with the movement's national expansion. During the early years, the *Jornal* continued to print its regular editions despite severe financial constraints. Efforts to improve the movement's public outreach were given a boost at the MST's Third National Congress, in 1995, which adopted the slogan, "Land Reform: A Struggle for All." The Communication Sector originated as a result of this process two years later, during the MST's first National March for Agrarian Reform, which culminated with a massive rally in Brasília on the first anniversary of the Eldorado dos Carajás massacre. Among other goals, this mobilization was designed to strengthen the MST's relations with urban popular movements and trade unions and enhance its image in Brazilian society. Building on this agenda, the MST went on to create several news media and publishing venues over the following decade (see table 9.12).

Various MST news outlets emerged in association with other partners. The monthly radio program *Vozes da Terra* (Voices of the Earth) was started originally with the University of Santos, and continued with the Catholic University of São Paulo. The weekly newspaper, *Brasil de Fato*, and news agencies *Radioagência NP* and the *Chasque* Agency, were established with the support of other popular movements related to La Via Campesina, the *Consulta Popular*, and the Social Ministry of the Catholic Church.

The *Expressão Popular* Publishing House was set up to print books geared toward improving the intellectual capacity of grassroots activists, and provide texts at below-market prices, thanks to the volunteer work of many of its staff members. *Brasil de Fato* and two news agencies offer news accounts and analyses prepared by professional journalists and accomplished writers. Their goal is to present a progressive, popular perspective on peasant and labor issues, and address a wide range of themes dealing with human rights, the environment, national politics and economics, international affairs, and proposals aimed at fostering a *projeto popular* (people's project) to transform Brazilian society.[38]

Table 9.12. Media linked to the MST, 2007

Media associated with MST Media	Year created	Frequency	Distribution
Jornal Sem Terra	1981	monthly	20,000 copies printed
Sem Terra Magazine	1997	bimonthly	7,000 copies printed
MST web page	1997	daily	3,000 hits per day, on average
Community radio stations[a]	1997	daily	30 stations located in different parts of the country
Vozes da Terra radio program	2000	monthly	Distributed to close to 1,500 community stations
Letraviva Newsletter	2000	monthly	Distributed to more than 60,000 email addresses

Media supported by the MST media[b]	Year created	Frequency	Distribution
Expressão Popular press	1999	—	171 books published; 730,000 copies printed
Brasil de Fato	2003	weekly	50,000 copies printed
Radioagência NP news agency	2004	daily	Reports distributed to 100 radio stations
Chasque news agency	2005	daily	Reports distributed to 20 radio stations in the South

Source: The MST Communication Sector and Editora Expressão Popular.

Notes:
a. The MST's first community radio station was set up in 1997. Others soon followed with the promulgation of the 1998 radio broadcasting law, which authorized the creation of these community-owned stations.
b. Entities sponsored and supported by the MST, but run by independent councils.

In the early 2000s, the MST began to organize workshops to train its activists in popular communication and inaugurated its first course on the subject, in 2001, at the Josué de Castro Institute of Education, in Veranópolis, Rio Grande do Sul. These activities, along with the acquisition of new video equipment, increased the sector's capacity to produce documentaries on the movement's struggle. In 2005, the Communication Sector launched a project known as *Cinema na Terra* (Cinema on the Land), to show movies at hundreds of landless camps and settlements across the country. The initiative's democratizing impact is corroborated by the fact that, at the time, 60% of the Brazilian people had never attended a movie theater.[39]

MST Assets and Capabilities

The MST's endurance and growth owe much to its ability to make the best of the opportunities and obstacles on hand. Brazil's new political freedoms and entrenched barriers to agrarian reform have shaped the MST's evolution and capacity to generate various organizational assets. These political capabilities have fueled the movement's territorial expansion and in-house sophistication. In the process, the MST has developed seven sources of power: its mobilization capacity, multifaceted yet flexible organization, strategic creativity, quest for financial independence, resourceful allies, investment in popular education, and mystique and discipline—all of which are briefly reviewed here.

Mobilization Capacity

The movement possesses a large membership and the adroit ability to mobilize masses of people. In 2006, the MST had an estimated membership of 1.1 million people, supported by 20,000 activists engaged in coordinating movement activities on various issues and levels.[40] That same year, the MST led 55% of all land occupations in Brazil and was active in more than half of all popular demonstrations in the countryside.[41] The movement has sponsored some of the largest and most elaborate mass mobilizations in Brazilian history. In April 1997, it gathered 100,000 people at a rally in front of Brazil's National Congress. In May 2000, it mobilized 30,000 peasants in simultaneous occupations of federal buildings in thirteen state capitals. Five years later it led a 125-mile march to Brasília with 12,000 people. No other popular organization in Brazil has exhibited the MST's resilience and capacity for mass mobilization.

Multifaceted, Flexible Organization

The MST is not a bureaucratic organization. Rather, it operates through a complex and scattered network of collective groups. Its multiple instances of coordination—at national, state, regional, and local levels—function in a fairly decentralized but cohesive manner. Though consistent and synchronized in many of its tactics, the MST allows for variation in its regional and local undertakings. Its decision to establish a weblike structure, sustained through group deliberations, was taken during the movement's early days in order to avoid personalized decisions and to cushion the impact of attempts to repress or bribe its leadership. The effort to reach consensus through collective dialogue has its costs, but also facilitates group integration and improves the execution of its decisions. The MST's indifference to bureaucratic formalities accounts partially for its reluctance to set up an official, protocol-laden structure that would oversee the entire movement.[42] Still, over time, it has strengthened its professional support. The MST's main national and state offices employ full-time staff organizers and technical advisers, who earn modest stipends. Most of the movement's activism is carried out by volunteers.

Strategic Creativity

The MST has learned to seek and devise homegrown solutions to a wide range of practical problems. This led the movement to develop an inventive ethos, open to experimentation and renewal. The MST sharply exhibits its ingenuity in the way its local activists plan and carry out its massive and peaceful land occupations, a generally risky endeavor conducted with tactical acumen. Throughout its history the MST has shown a discernable capacity for innovation and adaptation. All this owes much to the movement's practical disposition, its collective decision-making process, and its ability to learn from past mistakes. The MST's resourcefulness can be gleaned from the way it developed its task teams and incorporated new themes into its historic struggle for land reform. Its newfound enthusiasm for agro-ecology, and the decision taken in 2003 to guarantee full gender equality within the organization's leadership structure, is illustrative of this.

Quest for Financial Independence

As a poor people's movement, the MST has faced ongoing challenges in securing material resources needed to sustain its activities. Early concerns about becoming too dependent on a handful of external supporters led the movement to diversify and decentralize much of its fundraising efforts. At the local level, the MST receives regular contributions from its cooperatives and members, and occasional assistance from municipal governments. Aid is also channeled through an assortment of civil society groups, including religious institutions, trade unions, student groups, artists, non-governmental organizations (NGOs), and educational institutions. Federal and state governments have funded various educational and agricultural projects, and they often provide food rations for the movement's landless camps. Between 1995 and 2005, three associations linked to the MST received US$19.2 million from the federal government. This sum, it is worth noting, amounts to only 4% of the federal grants awarded to the main associations representing the nation's agrarian elite.[43] International sources of support for the MST have generally come from church organizations, solidarity groups, foundations, NGOs, and development agencies run by governments in Europe, Canada, Cuba, and Venezuela. In the early 2000s, the European Union contributed US$1.3 million to help build the MST's own university campus.[44] Cuba and Venezuela, in turn, have provided full scholarships for 120 MST medical students.[45]

Resourceful Allies

The movement's birth and ongoing expansion would not have been possible without the contribution of numerous partners in Brazilian civil and political society. Over time, the movement became adept at capitalizing on sympathetic pockets in the state, including those in the federal land reform agency, INCRA. Its strongest supporters in civil society include liberal sectors of the Catholic and mainline Protestant churches, urban and rural trade unions, as well as progressive NGOs, university professors, students, musicians, and actors. The MST has also played an active role in several Brazilian networks such as the National Forum for Agrarian Reform and Justice in the Countryside, the *Consulta Popular*, the Coordination of Social Movements, and the church-sponsored Popular Assembly. In political society, the movement has enjoyed the backing of left-leaning political parties, notably the Workers Party (PT). The MST's international ties strengthened considerably during the 1990s. After receiving Sweden's Alternative Nobel Prize in 1991, it established solidarity groups in fourteen European and North American countries. In 1994, following several years of active engagement with other popular groups in Latin America, the movement helped create the Latin American Coordinator of Rural Organizations (CLOC). Two years later, it joined and became a leading proponent of La Vía Campesina, which, by 2008, had expanded to include 168 peasant associations from sixty-nine countries around the globe. The MST has also maintained close ties to the World Social Forum, since its first gathering in Porto Alegre in 2001.

Investment in Popular Education

The movement has placed a uniquely strong emphasis on educating and raising popular consciousness among its participants. Since its early days, the movement has helped organize hundreds of schools and devoted significant resources to the preparation of its cadres. Between 1988 and 2002, more than 100,000 activists took part in hundreds of workshops organized by the Political Education sector, covering a wide range of topics. In early 2005 the movement inaugurated its first university, the Florestan Fernandes National School (ENFF), named after a renowned Brazilian intellectual, on an attractive campus built by 1,100 volunteers, near the city of São Paulo. The workshops and degree programs offered at the ENFF and other MST institutions for higher education are often administered by professors from leading Brazilian universities. These programs and workshops complement the intense pedagogical experience that takes place during the movement's collective struggles. As many settlers have described it: "the landless camp was where I earned my university degree." MST mobilizations, in particular, have helped its participants overcome previous sentiments of disempowerment and fatalism and foster a strong sense of agency. In this way, the movement has nurtured feelings of dignity, self-confidence, and social responsibility among its members.[46]

Mystique and Discipline

Under the auspices of the church and liberation theology, the movement learned to cultivate a sense of *mística* (mystique) among its participants. It has done so by creating a rich symbolic repertoire—its flag, songs, chants, theater, poetry, and stirring speeches—that is displayed in ritual gatherings, which stimulate feelings of shared sacrifice, camaraderie, and idealism, and offer moments of festive commemoration. All this has helped nourish an intense social energy, forceful convictions, and a strong sense of identity.[47] Among MST activists one often hears expressions of deep emotional attachment, such as: "I love the MST" or "The movement is my family."

Alongside these strong dispositions, the movement normally exhibits a well-composed and orderly lifestyle. By disciplining passions and other raw impulses into more methodical forms of behavior, the MST has helped nurture what Norbert Elias describes as a "civilizing process."[48] Feelings of enhanced self-control and greater self-esteem have inclined MST participants to channel their contentious behavior through constructive means. The movement's sense of mystique and discipline are interwoven in subtle ways. Together, they elicit and channel the emotions that give vitality, courage, and perseverance to the MST's struggles. They are its intangible sources of power.

Constant Challenges

The struggle *on* the land has shaped the MST's growth, endurance, and innovation in crucial ways. Indeed, its unusually long life for a social movement owes much to the assets and capabilities forged during this process. Throughout this time, the MST has faced constant challenges to its survival and integrity as a popular movement. In combing through its history one can find evidence of many valorous deeds and a variety of shoddy actions. Those who wish to find defects in the MST will have no difficulty in doing so. Of course, comparable blemishes and blunders can be found in popular movements all around the globe, even those led by heroic figures like Mahatma Gandhi, Martin Luther King Jr., and Nelson Mandela. History has taught us that all efforts to achieve far-reaching transformations through popular mobilization carry unavoidable elements of risk, turmoil, and disaster. These factors were discernable during the struggle for India's independence, the civil rights movement in the United States, and the fight to end South Africa's apartheid regime.[49] The struggle for social justice and ecological integrity in the Brazilian countryside could not be any different.

There are enormous hazards and challenges to the MST's work in organizing, educating, and mobilizing marginalized sectors of Brazilian society. Error and deficiencies are inevitable in this process. The MST's mobilization strategies, management practices, and relations with allies are not always propitious, transparent, and trouble-free. Adding to this, there is always a risk that the movement might stifle its participatory practices; bureaucratize its organization; routinize its mobilization tactics; mishandle its educational programs; hollow out its sense of *mística*; and exhaust its impetus for social change. Aside from these dangers, its activists are unlikely to shed traditional norms found in Brazilian society, such as machismo, racism, domineering leadership styles, and clientelism, with effortless ease. These problems and shortcomings are well known to those who have followed the MST closely. Yet those who have done so are also aware of the significant efforts made to overcome these dilemmas and mitigate the perils at stake.

Some Brazilian intellectuals would prefer to accentuate the pitfalls inherent to popular movements like the MST. Their efforts to tarnish the movement's public image have received generous attention from the nation's media establishment. These professors have accused the MST of being a "highly centralized," "Leninist organization," controlled by an "elite revolutionary vanguard." Anyone familiar with the MST's inner dealings, however, knows that such depictions are a gross caricature, with no serious empirical support.[50] If the MST was as "highly centralized" as some claim, it would have in all likelihood splintered off a long time ago into numerous factions, in the tradition of many other leftist and sectarian groups. Those unfamiliar with the MST have obvious difficulties in understanding the complexity of its decisionmaking process, weblike articulation, internal fluidity, and capacity for adaptation.

Its hostile opponents and domestic difficulties, however, are not the MST's main problems. Rather, its principal challenge stems from Brazil's position in the global political economy and various structural developments related to this. In the early twenty-first century, Brazil's economy was engrossed in a major agribusiness export boom, to markets mostly in China, Russia, and the European Union. This trend has intensified Brazil's agro-industrial production model and its dependency on a handful of multinational agribusiness conglomerates—such as Monsanto, Syngenta, Bayer, BASF, Cargill, Bunge, and ADM—that dominate global markets for seeds, chemical inputs, and agricultural trading.[51] All Brazilian governments since the military regime have championed this capitalist model of development in the countryside (see Delgado, chap. 2, this volume), which became more globalized with the trade liberalization policies adopted in the 1990s. This configuration cemented a powerful triple alliance between the Brazilian state, the landed elite, and global agribusiness corporations, strongly supported by the financial sector and media establishment.

These structural developments have strengthened the hands of forces inclined to banish agrarian reform from the nation's public agenda. The territorial expansion of agribusiness firms through the acquisition of huge tracts of land to produce soybeans, beef, cellulose, agro-fuels, and other export commodities has set off a new land rush in many parts of the Brazilian countryside and led to a reconcentration of landownership. This situation has created a formidable set of obstacles to the expansion of peasant agriculture in Brazil.

Yet all these developments have also elicited various countertrends and many doubts as to the sustainability of this rural development model. Indeed, it is far from clear as to whether this export boom and land rush will have staying power over the coming years, or whether the triple alliance will remain as stable as it has been since the late 1990s. Agro-export booms, after all, are vulnerable to shifts in global prices, trade regulations, market completion, weather conditions, and new consumer demands.

The twenty-first century promises to be an era of mounting concern for the ecology of the planet. Viewed from this perspective, the agribusiness model of industrial farming runs the serious risk of becoming an archaic practice, due to its high environmental cost and many health hazards. The model's penchant to create vast areas of monoculture that rely on intense pesticide use and high energy consumption; its contamination of water and soil; its rapacious destruction of the Amazonian rain forest and the Cerrado's savannah; and menace to biodiversity; have triggered numerous voices of dissent and acts of defiance.[52]

All this suggests that the prospects for agrarian reform will depend on the future of the world's appetite for agro-industrial commodities, the planet's ecological well-being, and the civic awareness created around it. Over time, the adoption of new consumer habits and state policies designed to preserve Mother Earth through sustainable farming practices could open up new possibilities for the global resurgence of peasant agriculture.

In the meantime, the MST will continue to resist and serve as a symbol and source of inspiration to those who share the hope of making "another world possible." Jonas, the young MST activist, explains why.

> The most impressive thing about the movement is the way it restores people's feeling of dignity. It can take a person who has been excluded from society, without any rights, without a sense of purpose in life, and reintegrate that person into society; give him a new opportunity in life. This is a very powerful thing.
>
> We have to fight for the generations that will come after us, so that they can have better days ahead. That's when I think about my son. We need to fight to try to build a better future for our children. I would like my son to carry on with the struggle for his own children too; and for his children to continue our fight as well. If I stop struggling, I won't give my child the example he needs to continue this fight, either with the MST or another movement striving for the liberation of our society, the liberation of our poor people.
>
> It's really a passion. If I had to explain why I'm in the movement, it'd be hard for me to do it with words. It's something that stirs deep inside. It's a sense of *mística*. I think the *mística* gives the movement a clear sense of purpose. Despite all the problems and challenges ahead, you know that the cause is just. If it's just, it's worthy, and if it's worthy we have to fight for it. That's my philosophy of life.[53]

Table 9.13. Human rights violations in rural Brazil, total and percentage per presidential period, 1988–2006

President	Period	Murders		Assassination attempts		Death threats	
		Total	%	Total	%	Total	%
Sarney	1988–89	167	5	168	5	287	8
Collor	1990–92	179	2	223	3	607	7
Franco	1993–94	99	2	99	2	366	7
Cardoso 1	1995–98	172	3	197	3	424	6
Cardoso 2	1999–2002	120	4	223	7	554	17
Lula 1	2003–2006	189	3	291	5	1,023	19
Total	1988–2006	926	3	1,201	4	3,261	10

President	Period	Torture		Physical attacks		Arrests	
		Total	%	Total	%	Total	%
Sarney	1988–89	72	2	2,032	60	668	20
Collor	1990–92	206	2	6,644	77	757	9
Franco	1993–94	126	2	4,296	77	605	11
Cardoso 1	1995–98	124	2	4,081	59	1,861	27
Cardoso 2	1999–2002	124	4	931	28	1,388	42
Lula 1	2003–2006	137	3	1,796	33	1,979	37
Total	1988–2006	789	2	19,780	60	7,258	22

Source: Prepared by the authors from CPT annual reports.

Notes: Percentage based on the total number of human rights violations in the countryside per presidential period.

There were no data available for the first three years of the Sarney presidency in any category except for murders; see table 9.2.

Table 9.14. Agrarian reform in Brazil, by presidential period and region, 1979–2006

| | | Brazil Families settled | | | Area distributed | | |
President	Period	Total	Annual average	% per period	Total	Annual average	% per period
Figueiredo	1979–1984	53,927	10,785	6.1	4,710,611	942,122	10.2
Sarney	1985–1989	92,178	18,436	10.5	5,091,049	1,018,210	11.1
Collor & Franco	1990–1994	57,194	14,299	6.5	2,895,903	723,976	6.3
Cardoso 1	1995–1998	299,863	74,966	34.1	12,222,613	3,055,653	26.5
Cardoso 2	1999–2002	155,491	38,873	17.7	6,768,771	1,692,193	14.7
Lula 1	2003–2006	220,606	55,152	25.1	14,356,824	3,589,206	31.2
Total	**1979–2006**	**879,259**	**32,565**	**100.0**	**46,045,771**	**1,705,399**	**100.0**

| | | Northeast Families settled | | | Area distributed | | |
President	Period	Total	Annual average	% per period	Total	Annual average	% per Period
Figueiredo	1979–1984	2,330	466	4.3	67,293	13,459	1.4
Sarney	1985–1989	27,728	5,546	30.1	938,074	187,615	18.4
Collor & Franco	1990–1994	14,671	3,668	25.7	422,890	105,723	14.6
Cardoso 1	1995–1998	121,559	30,390	40.5	3,476,733	869,183	28.4
Cardoso 2	1999–2002	59,798	14,950	38.5	1,517,357	379,339	22.4
Lula 1	2003–2006	76,318	19,080	33.9	2,742,549	685,637	18.9
Total	**1979–2006**	**302,404**	**11,200**	**34.4**	**9,164,896**	**399,441**	**19.9**

| | | Southeast Families settled | | | Area distributed | | |
President	Period	Total	Annual average	% per period	Total	Annual average	% per period
Figueiredo	1979–1984	1,661	332	3.1	28,502	5,700	0.6
Sarney	1985–1989	5,459	1,092	5.9	131,412	26,282	2.6
Collor & Franco	1990–1994	2,297	574	4.0	51,247	12,812	1.8
Cardoso 1	1995–1998	16,567	4,142	5.5	453,843	113,461	3.7
Cardoso 2	1999–2002	9,386	2,347	6.0	319,236	79,809	4.7
Lula 1	2003–2006	9,946	2,487	4.6	296,749	74,187	2.1
Total	**1979–2006**	**45,316**	**1,678**	**5.2**	**1,280,989**	**47,444**	**2.8**

Source: Prepared by the authors based on DATALUTA (2008a).

North Families settled			Area distributed		
Total	Annual average	% per period	Total	Annual average	% per period
41,425	8,285	76.8	3,896,793	779,359	82.7
40,412	8,082	43.8	3,274,601	654,940	64.3
33,077	8,269	57.8	2,063,962	515,991	71.3
93,907	23,477	31.3	5,010,284	1,252,596	41.0
44,118	11,030	28.4	2,757,799	689,450	40.7
102,078	25,520	46.7	10,414,339	2,603,585	72.7
355,017	**13,149**	**40.5**	**27,417,978**	**1,015,481**	**59.6**

Midwest Families settled			Area distributed		
Total	Annual average	% per period	Total	Annual average	% per period
7,536	1,507	14.0	706,883	141,377	15.0
12,667	2,533	13.7	623,708	124,742	12.3
5,013	1,253	8.8	313,681	78,420	10.8
54,510	13,628	18.2	2,998,386	749,597	24.5
33,055	8,264	21.3	1,986,373	496,593	29.3
27,118	6,780	12.4	798,753	199,688	5.6
139,899	**5,181**	**16.0**	**7,427,748**	**275,103**	**16.1**

South Families settled			Area distributed		
Total	Annual average	% per period	Total	Annual average	% per period
975	195	1.8	11,140	2,228	0.2
5,912	1,182	6.4	123,154	24,631	2.4
2,136	534	3.7	44,123	11,031	1.5
13,320	3,330	4.4	283,267	70,817	2.3
9,134	2,284	5.9	188,006	47,002	2.8
5,146	1,287	2.4	104,434	26,109	0.7
36,623	**1,356**	**4.2**	**754,124**	**27,124**	**1.6**

Table 9.15. Agrarian reform settlements in Brazil, 1979–2006

Region and state	Settlement Number	%	Families settled Number	%	Area distributed Number	%
North	**1,605**	**21.1**	**355,017**	**40.6**	**27,417,978**	**59.6**
AC	117	1.5	19,755	2.3	1,432,079	3.1
AM	67	0.9	32,144	3.7	1,432,079	15.9
AP	33	0.4	9,930	1.1	1,573,071	3.4
PA	868	11.4	200,300	22.9	11,626,771	25.3
RO	138	1.8	49,043	5.6	2,667,919	5.8
RR	50	0.7	21,062	2.4	1,568,183	3.4
TO	332	4.4	22,813	2.6	1,214,863	2.6
Northeast	**3,548**	**46.6**	**300,174**	**34.3**	**9,137,374**	**19.9**
AL	105	1.4	8,356	1.0	70,713	0.2
BA	592	7.8	45,697	5.2	1,543,959	3.4
CE	377	5.0	22,939	2.6	816,204	1.8
MA	926	12.2	124,862	14.3	4,242,081	9.2
PB	247	3.2	13,423	1.5	246,941	0.5
PE	473	6.2	29,785	3.4	445,968	1.0
PI	405	5.3	37,520	3.1	1,143,703	2.5
RN	272	3.6	19,477	2.2	496,631	1.1
SE	151	2.0	8,115	0.9	131,074	0.3
Midwest	**1,044**	**13.7**	**139,899**	**16.0**	**7,427,784**	**16.2**
DF & GO	350	4.6	20,554	2.3	842,202	1.8
MS	158	2.1	26,990	3.1	616,738	1.3
MT	536	7.0	92,355	10.6	5,968,844	13.0
Southeast	**671**	**8.8**	**45,316**	**5.2**	**1,280,989**	**2.8**
ES	81	1.1	4,072	0.5	40,915	0.1
MG	319	4.2	21,390	2.4	884,292	1.9
RJ	54	0.7	5,229	0.6	64,890	0.1
SP	217	2.9	14,625	1.7	290,892	0.6
South	**741**	**9.7**	**36,623**	**4.2**	**754,124**	**1.6**
PR	300	3.9	19,066	2.2	402,052	0.9
RS	304	4.0	12,001	1.4	259,674	0.6
SC	137	1.8	5,556	0.6	92,398	0.2
Brazil	**7,609**	**100.0**	**874,799**	**100.0**	**45,990,527**	**100.0**

Source: Prepared by the authors based on DATALUTA (2008a).

Note: Further details about the criteria used in preparing these statistics can be found in the note accompanying table 9.3.

Table 9.16. Settlements linked to the MST, estimated by
region and state, 2006

Region and state	Settlements No.	Settlements State %	Settlements MST %	Families settled	Area distributed
North	**39**	**2.0**	**1.9**	**8,613**	**481,331**
AC	—	—	—	—	—
AM	—	—	—	—	—
AP	—	—	—	—	—
PA	16	1.8	0.8	3,682	213,727
RO	15	8.9	0.7	4,367	237,554
RR	—	—	—	—	—
TO	8	2.5	0.4	564	30,050
Northeast	**983**	**27.7**	**48.9**	**66,101**	**1,640,113**
AL	22	21.3	1.1	1,776	15,027
BA	92	15.5	4.6	7,099	239,838
CE	243	64.3	12.1	14,470	525,190
MA	56	6.0	2.8	7,488	525,190
PB	27	11.0	1.4	1,478	27,196
PE	348	73.6	7.3	21,928	328,320
PI	19	4.7	1.0	1,303	54,159
RN	45	16.5	2.2	3,222	82,149
SE	131	86.8	6.5	7,047	113,827
Midwest	**125**	**12.0**	**6.2**	**14,737**	**662,205**
DF & GO	60	17.1	3.0	3,507	143,709
MS	29	18.4	1.4	4,961	113,371
MT	36	6.8	1.8	6,268	405,125
Southeast	**221**	**32.9**	**11.0**	**14,077**	**265,986**
ES	62	76.6	3.1	3,120	31,350
MG	16	5.0	0.8	1,070	44,215
RJ	9	15.9	0.4	834	10,345
SP	134	61.9	6.7	9,054	180,076
South	**644**	**86.9**	**32.0**	**30,913**	**635,523**
PR	223	74.3	11.1	14,174	298,902
RS	295	96.9	14.6	11,635	298,902
SC	126	91.9	6.3	5,103	84,869
Brazil	**2,012**	**26.4**	**100.0**	**134,440**	**3,685,158**

Source: Prepared by the authors based on MST (2007) and DATALUTA (2008a).

Note: State and region percentage (State %) derived from the total number of
settlements created in each state and region between 1979 and 2006. MST percentage
(MST %) based on the total of MST settlements nationwide. For details on how this data
calculated see the note to table 9.7.

Notes

The authors wish to thank all the people who provided the information needed to prepare this chapter, especially Miguel Stédile, Edgar Jorge Kölling, Roseli Salete Caldart, Álvaro Delatorre, and Bernardo Mançano Fernandes. A brief section of this chapter was published ealier in Carter (2011). Translated from the Portuguese by Miguel Carter.

1. Jonas Iora, interview by Miguel Carter, Viamão, Rio Grande do Sul, July 9, 2003.
2. Montero (2005: 71).
3. "Public activism" refers to a type of social conflict that is organized, politicized, visible, autonomous, periodic, and nonviolent in orientation, as explained in Carter (chap. 6, this volume).
4. For an analysis of the segmented and isolated character of conservative agrarian reform policies, see Garcia (1973).
5. Hostility toward the MST and other popular movements engaged in the struggle for land reform have taken various forms, including acts of defamation in the nation's mainstream media; frequent use of punitive investigations led by Parliamentary Commissions of Inquiry in the National Congress and various state legislatures; infiltration and espionage by national security agencies; repression of protest mobilizations; criminalization of landless leaders; and killings of peasant activists and other advocates of agrarian reform.
6. Estimates of land availability for redistribution are from Sampaio et al. (2003: 43 and table 5.1.1.1). The number of families that could potentially benefit from land reform is derived from Del Grossi, Gasques, Silva, and Conceição (2001).
7. The agrarian reform plan prepared by Plinio de Arruda Sampaio and his team of experts would have advanced several elements of a progressive agrarian reform; see Ministério de Desenvolvimento Agrário (MDA) (2003). Sue Branford (chap. 13, this volume) explains in further detail the outcome of this plan, which was partially rejected by the Lula government. On the main elements of a "progressive approach to agrarian reform" in Brazil, see Carvalho (2003).
8. All contributors to this book agree on the crucial role that social pressure has played in prompting the Brazilian state to redistribute land.
9. Heredia, Medeiros, Palmeira, Cintrão, and Leite (2004: 40–43). This data was generated by one of the leading studies on the impact of land reform settlements in Brazil. Commissioned by the Ministry of Agrarian Development and conducted by a team of scholars from Rio de Janeiro, the research conducted surveys among settlers in six areas of the country that held a high concentration of settlements. For an abridged version of this study in English, see Heredia, Medeiros, Palmeira, Cintrão, and Leite (2006).
10. Data for the 1988 to 2006 period are from DATALUTA (2008); and CPT (1992: 12) for the year 1987. Further insights on the human rights situation in the Brazilian countryside can be found in the CPT's annual reports; and Sydow and Mendonça (2007).
11. Information on the number of demonstrations and landless camps organized between 2003 and 2006 is from the CPT's annual reports (2004, 2005, 2006, 2007). The number of people in landless camps is based on an estimate of five members per family. The number of protesters includes an unknown number of people who may have participated in more than one protest act.
12. The average time lapse it has taken to settle a landless family—from the moment they join a landless movement and make their first legal petition for land—is based on consultations with representatives from the National Network of Popular Lawyers (RENAP) and the CPT's National Office, made in 2004.

13. CPT (2007).
14. Statistics on land occupations from 1988 to 2006 are from DATALUTA (2008).
15. Sparovek (2003: 169).
16. Sparovek (2003: 111–14).
17. Settlements in the north and northeast regions were generally more precarious than those in the south and southeast parts of the country; Sparovek (2003: 100–101). The same study found that the projects implemented between 1985 and 1994 were better off than the newer settlements. Still, on some matters the margin of difference appeared to be quite small (2003: 98–99).
18. Heredia, Medeiros, Palmeira, Cintrão, and Leite (2004: 215–22).
19. Data on PRONAF, PRONERA, and ATES are from MDA (2006: 129, 76–77, 71). The figures for the program *Luz para Todos* (Light for All) are from the Ministry of Mines, Energy and Communications (2007).
20. According to the MDA (2006: 69), INCRA's budget more than tripled between 2003 and 2006, from US$0.55 billion to US$1.75 billion.
21. As per the Ministry of Agriculture, Livestock and Provision (Ministério de Agricultura, Pecuária e Abastecimento; MAG) (2008), between the 2003/2004 and 2007/2008 harvest seasons, the federal government provided US$80.8 billion in credit for agribusiness farming and US$11.4 billion for peasant farmers. On the percentage of rural labor engaged in family farms, see Oliveira (2004: 16).
22. For the Minister of Agrarian Development, Guilherme Cassel, the Lula government's main emphasis has been on enhancing the "quality of land reform settlements" rather than fostering their "quantitative" growth; see Parpadellas and Marques (2008). Critical reviews of the Lula government's agrarian policies can be found in Oliveira (2006), Instituto de Estudos Socioeconômicos (INESC) (2006), and MPA, MST, MAB, MNC, CPT, and ABRA (2006). According to Guilherme Delgado, the second Lula administration "abandoned agrarian reform"; see Pereira Filho (2008). On the economic policies of Lula's first term in office, see Filgueiras and Gonçalves (2007).
23. Heredia, Medeiros, Palmeira, Cintrão, and Leite (2004: 287–88).
24. The number of people estimated to have benefited from land distribution between 1985 and 2006 is based on DATALUTA figures for the total sum of settler families, multiplied by 6.2 people per each parcel of land allocated, according to the average family size found in the survey conducted by Heredia, Medeiros, Palmeira, Cintrão, and Leite (2004: 120–24).
25. Heredia, Medeiros, Palmeira, Cintrão, and Leite (2004). Additional studies of land reform settlements, and constructive analyses of their merits and drawbacks, can be found in Medeiros and Leite (1999, 2004); Linhares, Medeiros, Padrão, and Alentejano (2002); Schmidt, Marinho, and Rosa (1998); Sauer (1998); Romeiro, Guanziroli, Palmeira, and Leite (1994); and Medeiros, Barbosa, Franco, Esterci, and Leite (1994).
26. The study undertaken by Heredia, Medeiros, Palmeira, Cintrão, and Leite (2004: 216) found that 93% of the settler families who obtained a government farm credit had never received any public financing before. The same study calculated that, on average, each settled family received a monthly income of US$177, during the 1998/1999 harvest; of which 69% came from its farm production, 14% from other jobs, and 17% from social security payments (2004: 233–41). On the settlement's impact on the diversification of local farm production and stimulus for local commerce, see Bergamasco and Norder (chap. 10, this volume) and Medeiros and Leite (2004).
27. As an illustration, Heredia, Medeiros, Palmeira, Cintrão, and Leite (2006: 287) found

that in 71% of settlements surveyed, settlers had to mobilize and put pressure on local officials to get a public school installed in their community.

28. On the contribution of the struggle on the land for the development of citizenship rights, see Heredia, Medeiros, Palmeira, Cintrão, and Leite (2004: 139–42), Medeiros and Leite (2004: 47–49) and Carter (2011). According to Heredia et al. (2004: 303), 8% of the settlers surveyed had taken part in popular education workshops aimed at raising political awareness, with 77% of the respondents doing so after joining the settlement.

29. A study conducted by INCRA calculated that each family plot cost an average of US$10,940 in 2004. The finding by Heredia, Medeiros, Palmeira, Cintrão, and Leite (2004: 128) that a typical farm parcel employs three people aged fifteen years and older means that the average cost of generating a job through land reform stood at US$3,640. This cost was much less than the value of creating employment in the industrial, commercial, and services sectors of the economy, which were 128%, 190%, and 240% more expensive, respectively, than generating a job on a family farm. This calculus builds on Leite (2006b: 152–54).

30. The decision to maintain an organic unity between the struggles led by landless workers and those led by land reform settlers was made at the first National Meeting of Settlers, which took place in Cascavel, Paraná, and was attended by MST representatives from eleven states. This resolution buried a proposal to create a separate organization to represent the settlers alone; see Stédile and Fernandes (1999: 92) and Branford and Rocha (2002: 132).

31. Data estimated by Horacio Martins de Carvalho on the basis of more than two decades of fieldwork with the MST.

32. On the MST's pedagogical work, see Arenhart (2007); Arroyo, Caldart, and Molina (2005); Menezes (2003); Branford and Rocha (2002: 109–25); Kane (2001: 90–110); and Caldart (2000).

33. This reinterpretation of Brazilian history "from below" has been influenced by Marxist historians such as E. P. Thompson.

34. The *Veja* article is by Weinberg (2004). Critique of the MST's "fundamentalist" views can be found in Navarro (2002a, 2002b) and Martins (2000a: 18–19, 2005).

35. Fernandes (2000: 243–44).

36. MST (2009).

37. An account of BioNatur's history was provided to the authors by leaders of this cooperative, courtesy of Álvaro Delatorre. Data on BioNatur's production are from CPT-Northeast (2008) and MST (2006). On the MST's gradual adoption of agro-ecology, see Correia (2007).

38. For further details on the media outlets linked to the MST, see www.mst.org.br; www.expressaopopular.com.br; www.radioagencianp.com.br; www.agenciachasque.com.br; and www.brasildefato.com.br.

39. Folha Online (2007).

40. The data sources used to calculate the MST's 1.1 million members are explained in Carter's introductory chapter to this volume (see note 17). The figure of 20,000 MST activists was estimated by the authors based on more than two decades of research work on this movement.

41. Authors' calculus based on CPT (2007b: 83–89, 176–99).

42. In the words of Joao Pedro Stédile, one of the movement's best known leaders: "Some people like to formalize everything. We don't. This is why the anarchists seem to like us. If something doesn't work, we undo it and try something else. We don't have a bu-

reaucratic mindset" (Stédile and Fernandes 1999: 94). The indifference to organizational charts and centralized information explains the great difficulties encountered by the authors in collecting data on the thirteen task teams that operate within the MST, presented in table 9.8. Based on our experience, it appeared that the movement was not very concerned about compiling such basic information.

43. Between 1995 and 2005, five associations representing rural elite interests received US$509.6 million from the federal government; a sum twenty-seven times larger than that made available to support MST projects in education, agriculture, and health. Despite these vast disparities, virtually all of the intense congressional and media scrutiny has been on the monies allocated to MST-related associations and not the monies that subsidize the associations controlled by wealthy ranchers and planters. These figures were compiled from data made available in a congressional report organized by the federal deputy João Alfredo Telles Melo (2006: 127, 177). As explained in Melo (2006: 184–88), agrarian elite associations that received funds from the federal government are: the National Agriculture and Livestock Confederation (CNA), the Brazilian Rural Society (SRB), the Organization of Brazilian Cooperatives (OCB), the National Service for Learning about Cooperatives (SESCOOP), which is close to the OCB, and the National Service for Rural Learning (SENAR), which is linked to the CNA and its twenty-seven state affiliates, including the federations of agriculture and livestock of Rio Grande do Sul (FARSUL), São Paulo (FAESP), and Goiás (FAEG).

44. Arruda (2005).

45. MST (2009: 17).

46. Caldart (2000) and Quirk (2008).

47. On the MST's *mística* and symbolic repertoire, see Vieira (2007), Carter (2002), Hoffman (2002), and Bogo (2002).

48. Elias (1982).

49. For telling accounts of the US civil rights, Indian, and South African liberation movements—their triumphs, shortcomings, and intricacies—see Branch (1988, 1998); Collins and Lapierre (1997); Mandela (1995); and Marx (1992).

50. To suspect, as some do, that the frequent media appearances of certain MST leaders are symptomatic of the movement's autocratic demeanor ignores the fact these people have been designated to serve as spokespersons for the organization and handle its public relations. Such misrepresentations hardly correspond to what Zander Navarro, one of the main MST critics, describes as a "Leninist structure" (2002a: 216–17, 2002b); see also Navarro's interviews with Arruda (2003), and Martins (2000a: 145). These views are further examined in Carter's concluding chapter in this volume. The MST's governing structure and internal dynamic have not been as thoroughly analyzed, in an empirical way, as other aspects of the movement have been. For its in-house rules, see MST (2005c). Other internal aspects of the organization are discussed in Harnecker (2003); Branford and Rocha (2002); and Fernandes (2000).

51. On the power of global agro-food corporations, see ActionAid International (2006).

52. Recognized environmentalists in Brazil, such as Lutzenberger (2001), have sharply criticized the industrial model of agriculture; see also Moreira (2000). For an analysis of the future of the Brazilian peasantry, see Carvalho (2005).

53. Jonas Iora, interview by Miguel Carter, Viamão, Rio Grande do Sul, July 9, 2003.

Sonia Maria P. P. Bergamasco and

Luiz Antonio Norder

10 Rural Settlements and the MST in São Paulo
From Social Conflict to the Diversity of Local Impacts

São Paulo is Brazil's most populous and urban state. It is also the nation's industrial and financial heartland and boasts one of the country's most modern and productive agricultural economies. Since the onset of the last century, the state's manufacturing plants have clustered around the city of São Paulo and a few other large towns in the state's interior. Most of São Paulo's smaller municipalities, however, experienced economic and demographic decline during the second half of the last century. In fact, this trend reversed the significant growth that had taken place in these rural towns during the first part of the twentieth century.

The expansion of capitalist agriculture had a major impact on these developments. Agricultural modernization through large-scale cultivation of sugarcane, corn, and oranges, in particular, led to the formation of a new class of temporary rural workers. The expansion of huge, usually inefficient cattle ranches kept many of the state's rural properties operating at lower productivity levels than those required by existing agrarian laws. This was the background during the 1980s when various social and political conflicts over land issues emerged in São Paulo. These disputes helped strengthen the popular organizations that mobilized for agrarian reform. As result of this social pressure, numerous land reform settlements with an assorted set of characteristics were established in São Paulo.

This chapter analyzes these settlements in light of the impact they have had on the quality of life and work in these new rural communities, as well as their demographic, social, and economic effects on their local districts. The first two sections provide a brief historical review of land reform developments in São Paulo. They examine the rise of the Landless Rural Workers Movement (MST) in a context shaped by the mobilization of other landless groups and by a variety of government responses to these land claims. The ensuing two sections draw on field research conducted in four municipalities in São Paulo to probe how land reform settlements have impacted their local setting.[1] This chapter highlights two basic findings: the general improvement of living conditions among the settlers; and the innovative effects these rural communities have had on local politics, civil society, commerce, and rural development, through the gradual consolidation of public policies designed to support of peasant farmers.

History, Social Conflicts, and the MST

The state of São Paulo initiated its first land distribution program in 1960. Known as the *Revisão Agrária*, it emerged in the wake of a budding public debate over agrarian reform, and at the request of urban groups interested in expanding food supplies and neutralizing what they viewed as the "communist incursion" in the Brazilian countryside. The program's goal was to settle up to 1,000 families a year throughout the state. However, the political power of its conservative opponents and the high costs of land compensations—which required a full cash payment in advance, by state law—undermined the initiative's viability. In the end, only two rural settlements were set up, benefiting 175 peasant families, most of whom received a farm parcel on public land.[2]

The military regime that came to power in 1964 opted to colonize the agrarian frontier in the country's midwest and northern region rather than pursue land reform. Its agricultural modernization policies brought extensive changes to the traditional coffee-growing regions in the states of São Paulo, Rio de Janeiro, Minas Gerais, and northern Paraná. The sharecroppers (*colonos*) and other non-wage-earning laborers on the coffee plantations experienced a rapid process of change and proletarianization. Many of these people became migrant or temporary rural workers (*boias frias*). Others migrated to the main urban centers in search of work.

With the country's gradual redemocratization in the late 1970s and early 1980s, various social movements, religious groups, trade unions, and political parties mobilized to put agrarian reform back on the nation's public agenda. During that time, conflicts erupted in the Pontal do Parapanema region, in the westernmost section of the state, over the construction of hydroelectric dams in Porto Primavera, Taquaruçu, and Rosana. Hundreds of small farmers were resettled as a result of the flood waters. Simultaneously, longstanding agrarian disputes gained new relevance during this period, in particular the struggle led by squatters (*posseiros*) at the Primavera estate in Andradina, which the landlord had appropriated through fraud. The estate's expropriation in 1980 and the subsequent two-year struggle to ensure the actual creation of a rural settlement were supported by the Catholic Church's Pastoral Land Commission (CPT) and Community Base Churches (CEBs). This struggle was also backed by the Federation of Agricultural Workers of the State of São Paulo (FETAESP) and some political parties, especially the Workers Party (PT) and the Brazilian Democratic Movement Party (PMDB). These and other mobilizations carried out by different landless groups and their allies helped reignite São Paulo's agrarian debate.

The MST began organizing the landless movement in São Paulo in 1984, at a time when a variety of social and political organizations were engaged in the struggle for land reform in this state. The CPT's regional branch in São Paulo played a crucial role in this process. The MST's First National Congress, held in January 1985, in Curitiba, gave the São Paulo movement an added boost. Later that year, the MST established its first statewide office at the headquarters of Brazil's main labor confederation, the Unified Workers' Central (CUT), located in the city of São Paulo.[3]

The MST's expansion in the state of São Paulo introduced new organizing strategies and mobilization tactics in the effort to spur land redistribution. These innovations underscored the importance of building a mass movement capable of politicizing the land struggle. This orientation had various effects on the MST's approach to mobilizing its rural workers and handling its political alliances. Decisions taken within its landless camps often underscored a sharp division between camp coordinators and the rank-and-file members, its leaders and followers. This dynamic facilitated the rise of internal conflicts and the formation of several dissident organizations. These splits were usually triggered by a variety of motives, ranging from political and ideological differences to administrative and personal disputes. The MST's development in São Paulo was also affected by a climate of tension, conflict, and competition with other organizations active in the struggle for agrarian reform, including the CPT, independent landless groups, and rural trade unions.[4]

MST mobilizations in the late 1980s raised public awareness of popular demands for land reform in the state of São Paulo, and helped improve the overall effectiveness of this struggle. The movement's centralized structure, however, left rural workers with less influence on its decision-making process. As Bernardo Mançano Fernandes describes it, in its early phase, the MST in São Paulo neglected its "political socialization" work within the landless camps. As a result, "the movement's land occupations and mass mobilizations incorporated a growing number of families, but a majority of these were largely alienated and passive participants in the land struggle."[5]

The MST's "rediscovery" of the Pontal do Paranapanema in 1990 turned this region into the epicenter of land disputes in the state of São Paulo. In fact, conditions in this area were ripe for such conflicts. Most of the Pontal's farmland, which covered a territory of over a million hectares, had been illegally usurped toward the end of the nineteenth century and converted into vast cattle ranches during the first half of the twentieth century. MST land struggles and the creation of dozens of settlements over the subsequent years had a significant political impact at the state level and in the area's local districts, and considerable

Map 10.1. São Paulo

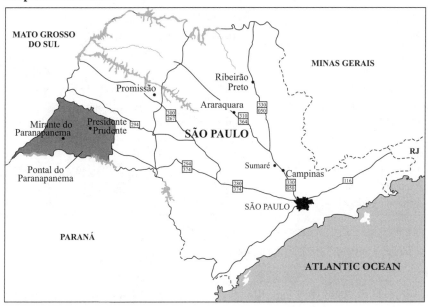

repercussions on the national scene. By 1997, the MST had more than 5,000 families living in landless camps scattered across the Pontal. These mobilizations prompted the state government to recover some of the public lands that had been misappropriated and establish new settlements on these estates, after paying the ranchers cash compensations for all "improvements" made on the land.[6] Another area of conflict in the 1990s revolved around the tree plantations set up by the state-owned rail company, Paulista Railways S.A. (FEPASA). After a series of land occupations, 715 peasant families were settled in 14,000 hectares of land reserved to produce railway sleepers. This trend ended, however, in 1998, when the rail company was privatized.

Land Reform Settlements in São Paulo

The diversity of agrarian settlements in the state of São Paulo is the upshot of a number of factors, three of which will be examined here. These include the distinct life histories of settlers; different organizations sponsoring landless and settler groups; and, assorted policy instruments designed to establish and support these agrarian communities.

The landless camps run by the MST, CPT, and other organizations attracted people from widely disparate life experiences, related to different family and work trajectories, along with varying educational, cultural, and political backgrounds. Some peasant farmers, namely, squatters, tenants, sharecroppers, and small landholders displaced by the construction of hydroelectric dams, fought

Table 10.1. Participation in popular organizations in three São Paulo settlements

Municipality Settlement	Association	Cooperative	Rural trade union	MST	CPT	Other	None
Araraquara							
Montre Alegre I	14	—	42	—	—	—	57
Montre Alegre II	—	18	27	—	—	—	54
Sumaré							
Sumaré I	22	33	77	33	11	22	33
Sumaré II	30	—	40	20	10	30	60
Promissão							
Agrovila Campinas	50	60	10	50	40	10	—
Agrovila Bonifácio	16	8	33	—	—	8	58
Agrovila Penápolis	8	—	8	—	—	16	75

Source: Bergamasco and Aubrée (2002).

Note: Multiple answers provided. All figures are in percentages.

to stay on the land they had tilled for many years. Other settlements were set up by former plantation workers in São Paulo's sugarcane estates. Organized by their trade union, these workers were invited to give up their appalling living conditions in the shantytowns encircling the main cities across the state and struggle for a piece of farmland to improve their life opportunities. Adding to this mix, an influx of migrants from various parts of the country began to engross São Paulo's landless movements after the mid-1980s. Some of these migrants sought to return to the countryside after a disappointing life in the city. Others were keen on staying in a rural setting.

Along with this heterogeneous composition, São Paulo's land struggle involved a variety of popular groups, each bearing their own organizational style and ways of managing their camps and settlements. All told, the MST has organized about half the state's landless camps. Other encampments were set up by the CPT, the CUT-Rural, the Federation of Rural Workers of São Paulo (FERAESP), the Liberation Movement for Landless Peasants (MLST), or local landless groups such as the Landless Farmers Movement (MAST), the Life Land Movement (MTV), and the United Landless Movement (MUST). This multiplicity of landless groups has affected the dynamics of settlement life, where one often finds parallel activities carried out by more than one peasant association, sometimes in a competitive fashion. In a nutshell, São Paulo's settlements reflect the assorted pattern of land conflicts that have taken place in this state, its variegated landless movements, and multiple associations vying to play an active role in these rural communities (see table 10.1).

The data displayed in table 10.1 exemplify the variety of organizations involved in the effort to create and support rural settlements in São Paulo. It also

Table 10.2. Land reform settlements in São Paulo, 1979–99

Public Policy	Period 1973–83	Period 1984–88	Period 1989–94	Period 1995–99	Total families	Number of settlements
Federal	164	1,108	578	1,264	3,114	33
State	—	663	509	3,837	5,009	97
Dam resettlement	523	978	—	—	1,501	11
Total	687	2,749	1,087	5,101	9,624	141

Source: INCRA, "José Gomes da Silva" Land Institute of the State of São Paulo (ITESP), MST.

shows the variations that can be found in a single community. Here, the settlers in Sumaré exhibited a more intense and diversified pattern of participation, as did the families that formed the Campinas Agrovila at the Reunidas settlement in the municipality of Promissão. In effect, all of these families had participated in the same landless camp set up in the metropolitan outskirts of Campinas.

Over 9,600 families received a farm plot in São Paulo between 1980 and 1999, in 141 settlements.[7] Of this total, 5,716 families (almost 60%) were settled in the Pontal do Paranapanema, mostly between 1995 and 1999. These settlements were established under different government land policies. Such measures have included settlements in areas expropriated by the federal government; the resettlement of people displaced by the construction of hydroelectric dams; and settlements in areas that had been usurped by large landholders and subsequently restored to the state government's domain, as detailed in table 10.2.[8]

In the 1980s and 1990s, the federal government set up thirty-three settlements in the state of São Paulo for 3,114 families. The two largest ones were in Promissão and Andradina, with 629 and 343 families, respectively. Thirteen settlements included less than 100 families and eleven had fewer than fifty families. Two state laws approved in 1985 facilitated efforts to recover misappropriated public lands and redistribute São Paulo's state-owned properties, which by 1999 comprised over half of the settlements in this state.[9] Heightened land conflicts in the Pontal do Paranapanema intensified the creation of agrarian settlements on these public territories. From 1995 to 1999, 3,300 families received a land parcel in the Pontal region through these state government programs, 86% of all such beneficiaries.

In sum, the process of land redistribution in São Paulo has involved four basic features. First, practically all of the agrarian settlements established in this state were preceded by social conflicts made visible through various protest mobilizations, notably, land occupations and the organization of landless camps. Government land policies instituted in response to this popular pressure were largely improvised, ad hoc, and erratic. Consequently, most settlements were

Table 10.3. Seven rural settlements surveyed in São Paulo: An overview

Settlement	Municipality	Year set up	Families	Government sponsor
Bela Vista do Chibarro	Araraquara	1989	167	Federal
Santa Clara	Mirante do Paranapanema	1994	46	State
São Bento	Mirante do Paranapanema	1994	185	State
Estrela D'Alva	Mirante do Paranapanema	1995	31	State
Fazenda Reunidas	Promissão	1987	629	Federal
Sumaré I	Sumaré	1984	26	State
Sumaré II	Sumaré	1986	28	State

Source: Medeiros and Leite (2004).

generally of small size, set up in isolation from each other, and scattered widely across the entire state, with the exception of the communities established in the Pontal do Paranapanema region. Finally, these land policies benefited only a small portion of the state's landless workers, and thus had minimal impact on São Paulo's agrarian structure and labor market, as a whole. Still, in a few local districts, the effects of these reform measures were far from negligible, as we will show next.[10]

Land Reform Settlements: Local Dynamics and Impact

This section examines the effects of agrarian settlements on the development of different municipalities of the state of Sao Paulo: Araraquara, Mirante do Paranapanema, Promissão, and Sumaré. It begins with an overview of demographic, social, economic, and landownership trends in these districts. The analysis then draws on field data collected in seven settlements, located in these four municipalities, to assess the life and work histories of those residing in these communities, as well as their sources of income and living conditions. These settlements were instituted in different periods, with dissimilar populations, and in distinct economic regions of the state, as presented in table 10.3.

The contrasting patterns of rural development in these four municipalities can be discerned in table 10.4. In particular, one can observe substantial differences in the proportion of farms that rely on family labor and the percentage of farmland devoted to cattle ranching. As will be shown, in some locales these variations were affected by the settlements that were established in these areas.

Agricultural production in Araraquara has been influenced strongly by two

Table 10.4. Four districts surveyed in São Paulo: Basic rural indicators, 1995–96

	Farmland area (ha)	No. of farms	Pasture area (ha) (%)	People employed	Farm area per person employed (ha)	Family labor (%)	Permanent wage earner (%)
Aranquara	50,000	489	74	3,994	12.5	23	n.d.
Mirante do Praranpanema	97,000	1,471	86	3,721	26.0	78	13
Promissão	63,600	1,127	52	5,123	12.4	77	19
Sumaré	2,276	n.d.	13	1,762	1.3	11	84

Source: IBGE, Censo Agropecuário 1995–96.

mono-crops, oranges and sugarcane. In 1995–96, the municipality's orange crop occupied almost 19,000 hectares of farmland, while sugarcane took up 12,000 hectares, followed by 1,900 hectares of corn. The livestock industry included 13,400 head of cattle and the poultry industry, almost 600,000 chickens. Araraquara's agriculture was significantly modern by the standards of the day. Its land usage and capital-labor ratio were much higher than other districts in São Paulo. One study even ranked the Araraquara region as Brazil's fifteenth-most-modern agricultural setting.

Mirante do Paranapanema, located in São Paulo's western Presidente Prudente region, offered a different economic profile. Its extensive livestock industry included 109,000 heads of cattle, while its main agricultural crops were sugarcane, cotton, corn, and beans. The municipality's levels of agricultural modernization were well below São Paulo's state average, and its population was classified as "rural very poor."[11] Its settlements had been established later than the ones included in this survey. The drop in the district's average farm size between 1985 and 1995, along with the decline in the Gini coefficient used to measure land inequality, was the direct result of land redistribution measures taken in the area.

Promissão's agricultural economy in the mid-1990s was also built on cattle farming. Only one-third of the district's farmland, located in São Paulo's midwest region, was used for temporary crops, mainly sugarcane and corn. The higher levels of family labor and smaller landholdings found in this district underscore the importance of its family farm tradition. Each farm worker in Promissão occupied an area of 12.5 hectares, compared to the average of 27 hectares in the region of Lins and the state average of 19.2 hectares. The Reunidas settlement, established in 1987, has had a discernible effect in absorbing local labor power and altering the municipality's landholding tenure (see table 10.5).

Sumaré, a district in the metropolitan region of Campinas, one of São Paulo's main industrial belts, presented a very different situation. In the mid-1990s

Table 10.5. Land distribution in surveyed districts: Gini index and average farm size, 1975–95

Municipality	1975 Gini	1975 Average farm size	1985 Gini	1985 Average farm size	1995 Gini	1995 Average farm size
Araraquara	0.817	137.4	0.789	181.2	0.796	102.4
Mirante do Paranapanema	0.813	79.7	0.801	111.4	0.755	65.9
Promissão	0.813	130.4	0.769	93.2	0.685	56.4
Sumaré	0.640	37.9	0.687	34.5	0.527	31.6

Source: IBGE. Gini coefficients prepared by Prof. Rodolfo Hoffmann.

Note: Average farm size in hectares.

half of the area's farmland was occupied by sugarcane plantations. Scarcely 270 hectares of land were used for permanent crops and 300 hectares for cattle pasture. Horticulture and the poultry industry were strong components of the district's highly modernized agricultural setting, which exhibited high levels of land use and capital-labor ratio compared to the rest of the state.

All four municipalities experienced perceptible, albeit different, patterns of changes in land tenure and rural demography. Between 1985 and 1995 the average farm size decreased in each district, countering the main trend found in the state of São Paulo. During the same period, the Gini index for land inequality fell in three of these districts, and grew very slightly in Araraquara, one of the modern agricultural hubs in this state. The transformations in Promissão and Mirante do Paranapanema were clearly affected by the land reform settlements set up in these two districts. Promissão exhibited the largest reduction in average farm size and the largest drop in the Gini land coefficient, along with substantial growth of its rural population. Its number of farms nearly doubled from 1985 to 1995, while the landholdings between 10 and 20 hectares—the size of farm plots at the Reunidas settlement—nearly tripled. The demographic data for Mirante do Paranapanema should be appraised in light of the extensive number of families settled in neighboring districts. Still, the figures show a reduction in land concentration.

São Paulo's land reform beneficiaries and the area allocated for this have been quite small, compared to the size of the state's rural population and farmland. However, in many districts the creation of settlements has actually boosted the area's rural population (see table 10.6). In addition, they have had a noticeable impact on the local economy and municipal politics.

Urbanization in Brazil has often led to the rise of huge metropolises, usually linked to state capitals and a few other large cities. This process of urban concentration was accompanied by a remarkable demographic and economic de-

Table 10.6. Urban and rural population in surveyed districts, 1970–2000

Municipality	Population	1970	1980	1991	2000
Araraquara	Urban	84,459	118,781	156,465	173,569
	Rural	15,979	9,341	10,266	8,902
Mirante do Paranapanema	Urban	7,175	8,538	10,545	9,833
	Rural	14,734	6,921	4,634	6,380
Promissão	Urban	15,609	15,877	22,093	25,635
	Rural	4,935	4,345	5,888	5,470
Sumaré	Urban	15,335	95,825	225,528	193,937
	Rural	7,739	6,026	1,342	2,786

Source: IBGE.

Note: The data in this historical series do not include the population that lived in the areas that ended up forming other towns during this period.

cline of many small rural towns. This was due in no small part to the upward redistribution of wealth engendered by a pattern of rural modernization, which enhanced inequities in the access to land, farm credits, agro-technologies, rural infrastructure, and income.[12] The economic deterioration of small rural towns was facilitated, in particular, by this model's propensity to increase local dependency on agro-industrial resources generated in distant parts of the state or country.[13]

The creation of land reform settlements has helped reverse the trend toward urbanization in several districts. In Promissão and Mirante do Paranapanema the rural population dropped between 1970 and 1980, yet increased in the following two decades. By contrast, the urban population rose sharply in Araraquara and Sumaré, which became major economic hubs within their region.

Migration and Labor Trajectories Prior to the Settlement

Many land reform beneficiaries in São Paulo migrated to this state from neighboring Minas Gerais and Paraná, as well as the Brazilian northeast. Those born in São Paulo comprised slightly more than one-half of the families interviewed in the seven settlements surveyed in this state. Land mobilizations in the Pontal do Paranapanema, in fact, attracted migrants from many parts of the country. Most landless migrants initially came to São Paulo looking for other jobs, and only joined the encampments after holding various other—usually precarious—forms of employment. In addition to interstate patterns of migration, a number of landless families had engaged in extensive intrastate migration in search for work.

The vast majority of settlers were employed before receiving a land reform farm plot. One-third of the families interviewed held an urban job prior to their move to the settlement; one-fourth of the families were wage earners in nearby towns. Among the settlers in the Pontal do Paranapanema region, the number of people with a history of urban employment was lower, yet the proportion of temporary rural workers was higher, at roughly 40% to 50% of those surveyed. The preponderance of people with paid jobs who joined the struggle to obtain a settlement plot suggests that their involvement in this mobilization was motivated by more than just a quest for employment.

The living and working conditions of the bulk of the settlers were significantly transformed by their access to land. Prior to joining the landless camp, practically none of those interviewed claimed to have had any real possibility of obtaining land, although 90% of the settlers had worked in agriculture before. Most of them had been sharecroppers and tenants, and a few squatters.

Many of the settlers witnessed firsthand the socioeconomic changes in São Paulo's coffee-growing region, from the 1960s on, with the eradication of coffee trees and their replacement with sugarcane fields, orange plantations, and cattle pastures. These transformations altered the main forms of rural labor at the time—land tenant arrangements, sharecropping, and other forms of non-wage-earning work—and replaced them with temporary and migrant farm workers. All these developments coincided with the expansion of industry and greater demand for urban labor. But the economic crisis of the 1980s, and the industrial decline that continued into the 1990s, generated an auspicious context for the revival of the land struggle.

The vast majority of rural workers who decided to join the land fight did so as part of a family project. Their goal was to gain a farm plot of their own and work as independent farmers. As such, they would no longer have to toil under the dominance of landlords and rural bosses, as farm workers, sharecroppers, or tenants of large estates. For these households, the act of joining a land reform settlement meant they could leave behind a life trajectory beset by continual migration, precarious and underpaid labor, and poor and unreliable housing conditions. Hence, at minimum, for these families the experience of moving into a land settlement helped stabilize livelihood sources and living conditions.

Family Profile and Living Conditions

This section summarizes field data collected in 2002 through surveys conducted with household heads in seven São Paulo settlements. This research gathered information on their age, education, housing arrangements, family situation, access to healthcare facilities, and the quality of their nutrition.[14]

Age The typical head of household in a São Paulo settlement was a man between forty-five and sixty years old. The survey also found that 17% of the settlers were older than sixty. In the Sumaré and São Bento settlements, more than one-third of family heads had surpassed this age. In these communities, it was common to find more than one nuclear family living on the same farm plot, with the new families of the settlers' sons and daughters residing close by.

Education Close to a one-fourth of the lot owners were illiterate. Nine out of ten households surveyed were headed by a person who was either illiterate or had had less than four years of schooling.[15] Fewer than 10% of the family heads had eight or more years of schooling, whereas less than 1% had completed any college coursework. Children attended school for the first four years within the settlement, but were then obliged to travel by bus to the nearest town to complete their primary and secondary education. Even large settlements such as the Reunidas community offered no schools beyond fourth grade. A major point of contention and political negotiation with local authorities often revolved around the settlers' access to municipal school buses.

Housing Home construction in the settlements has helped stimulate local economies and improve ties with the business community. Overall, the settlers' found a significant improvement in their housing conditions.[16] Compared to their previous homes, a greater percentage of people had houses made of brick, rather than the more modest wooden constructions. Despite this, the number of families with dirt floors—an unsanitary condition—rose from 6% to 11%. Nearly 80% of all sewage deposits were made in individual nonaseptic pits, while another 13% of households dumped these in open areas, namely rivers and ditches. Nevertheless, close to 80% of families surveyed claimed that their housing situation had improved since moving to the settlement and 10% said it remained the same, while only 5% saw a decline in their housing quality. Levels of satisfaction over the housing situation were generally higher in the older settlements than in the newer ones. These positive appraisals were linked to the fact that people were living in their own houses, rather than the precarious rentals and temporary shacks of previous years.

Family Nearly half of the settlers surveyed had all of their family members living on the farm plot. The same study found a high number of residents in each household. In Promissão, half of the families included six or more people. All of this suggests that the settlements have provided a place where the settlers' married children can build their own house and continue working on the family farm or in the neighboring area. In looking for outside work, men have usually found temporary odd jobs, while women labored mostly as domestic servants. Thus, these family farms have served as a haven for the settlers' older children by offering housing, food, and a social support network. Many of these young people have found that their added labor on the farm can actually lead to more profitable ventures than earnings made from the unstable jobs found in the vicinity.

Health Some settlements, like in Bela Vista do Chibarro and São Bento, had their own health clinics. Others, like the Estrela D'Alva and the Santa Clara, relied on the clinics set up in neighboring settlements. The Sumaré settlers had to rely on in-town public health services. A similar situation was found at the Reunidas settlement, with the exception of one of its agro-villas, which had a part-time health post. Medical care at most settlements was precarious. The need for better health provision was perceptible in many of these communities, given their large population and the incidence of many chronic diseases.

Food Among those surveyed, 72% said their access to food had improved since moving to the settlement, while only 2.5% indicated it had gotten worse. Close to 20% of households claimed there were no substantial changes in their diet. The peasant tradition of growing food for the family's own consumption has been of great importance to the settlers. This practice has undoubtedly improved the quality of their nutrition and explains much of their satisfaction and sense of progress regarding their access to food.[17]

Family Income and Economic Integration

A survey conducted in 2002 found that the settlers' main economic activity was in agriculture. Less than 2% of family heads worked as wage earners outside of their farm plots. This indicates that the settlements had absorbed rural workers from the labor market. The same survey found that 58% of the settlers had improved their income since receiving a farm plot, compared to 16% who felt it had declined. One-fourth of the respondents noted no variation in their purchasing power. Prior to joining the settlement many family heads held low-paying urban jobs.[18]

On average, the settler's farm income was five times higher than that earned from other sources. A family's average monthly income was US$266, of which $228 was obtained from the farm and $38 from other venues.[19] The family's monthly average farm income exhibited notable variations. In the Estrela D'Alva settlement the average net farm income was $180 per month, while in Sumaré this figure reached $246 per lot. The main sources of external income were social security benefits (at a monthly average of $15 per family) and earned wages (at an average of $14 per month).

Over 35% of households earned more than monthly minimum wages through the sale of their farm products. Yet 30% of families surveyed made less than one-half a month's minimum wage. Their main income originated from social security benefits or wages received while working outside the farm plot. Discernible contrasts were found among the settlements surveyed. Settlements in the Pontal do Paranpanema had lower family incomes due in part to the region's weak labor market for rural workers. As a rule, settler income issues should be appraised in context, and consider all of their forestalled expenditures, compared to urban households with similarly low incomes. These peasant families, after all, do not have to pay rent for their homes or cover transportation costs to get to work, and can grow much of their basic food,

Dynamics in the regional labor market have had a significant bearing on a settlements' possibilities for economic integration. Opportunities for alternative forms of employment and income were much greater in the Sumaré settlements, located near a metropolis with more than two million inhabitants, than those in the more isolated Pontal region, where farm products were a far more important source of family income.

Settlers usually bought and sold their products in local shops, and by doing so helped boost their local economy. This development has been particularly noticeable in smaller towns and appreciated by their business community. In the words of the president of Teodoro Sampaio's Chamber of Commerce:

> We see Pontal do Paranapanema's agrarian reform as the industry that never came to our region. Nowadays we understand that this development was really good for us, and is still good. We hope it will continue. . . . Among the merchants in our town, we estimate that 40% of our new business derives from the land reform settlements.[20]

In the communities surveyed in the Pontal do Paranapanema, about 30% to 50% of household purchases were made in local shops. The settlements in Sumaré and Araraquara were located close to larger cities with a bustling commerce, which diluted much of the settlers' economic influence. By contrast, in the much smaller town of Promissão, a district in which the Reunidas settlement represented 10% of the area's population, the ties between the settlers and the local business community were far more substantial.[21]

Rural Settlements and Regional Development

Land reform settlements can influence their local community, yet are also very susceptible to their surroundings. These conditions can shape the settlers' prospects and capabilities for local engagement in decisive ways. In Sumaré, for example, the settlers were able to draw on their proximity to large urban centers and close ties with various political and civil society organizations—notably the PT, CUT-Rural, MST, non-governmental organizations (NGOs), universities, and schools—to gain public notoriety. This recognition, in turn, helped secure the appointment of settlement reps in the cabinet of a municipal government with close to 200,000, mostly urban, inhabitants. This group of settlers, in fact, has been the subject of significant media attention since 1983, when they helped organize the region's first landless camps. Thanks to these ties with local media services, the Sumaré settlers have played an active role in publicizing demands for agrarian reform in São Paulo, especially in the Campinas region.

The Reunidas settlement in Promissão presents a different dynamic. The settlers in this community were recruited by two different landless groups, one led by the CPT and other by the MST. The latter group originated from the landless camps that were set up in the outskirts of Campinas in 1983. At the Reunidas camp, a running feud between the local leaders of each group fueled an intense rivalry among the two contingents, which eventually led to the camp's division. With the estate's expropriation, INCRA brought in another group of landless workers, organized by the local rural trade union and supported by municipal government authorities. From its onset, then, the Reunidas settlement was plagued by internal rifts, due largely to divergent backgrounds of its participants and sponsoring groups.

The 629 families that comprise the Reunidas settlement had a considerable economic and demographic impact on Promissão, given the district's population size of 30,000 inhabitants. Because of its internal divisions, though, it was unable to elect a settler to the municipal chamber until 2004, when a dissident MST leader garnered enough votes to win a council seat as a PT candidate. Overall, though, the Reunidas community exhibited far less political clout on the local scene than the Sumaré settlers.

The families in Araraquara's Bela Vista settlement did not have the same political influence as the Sumaré settlers or the demographic relevance of the Promissão settlers. Most of the Bela Vista families were recruited by local rural trade unions. Another group had taken part of an MST camp in Campinas, and a third contingent was initially organized by the CPT in Promissão. Given the settlement's location in the heart of São Paulo's sugarcane and ethanol production center, this community of 167 peasant families gained prominence through their symbolic resistance to the dominant rural development model in this region, based on large-scale industrial agriculture. Bela Vista settlers demonstrated it was possible to succeed as farmers by eschewing sugarcane and orange monocultures, in ways that allowed them to diversify their food production and sell their goods in local markets. Adding to this, the settlements strong rural union links helped reaffirm the trade union's commitment to agrarian reform.

The community in Araraquara held a major internal debate over whether or not to cultivate sugarcane. The dispute was sparked by an agreement made by a few settlers to lease their farm plot to local sugar mills. Some Bela Vista families and agricultural advisors argued for the advantages of growing sugarcane, knowing this would make them dependent on the agribusiness conglomerates that dominate the sugar-ethanol complex. Others insisted on the need to forge alternative models of agriculture, by developing technical and social instruments that would allow them to diversify their farming production. Such views underscored the importance of promoting agro-ecological methods and taking advantage of local assets and opportunities, by growing labor intensive crops, particularly vegetables and fruit, among other possibilities.

The settlements in the Pontal do Paranapanema faced a steeper challenge. This stemmed largely from the region's cattle ranch economy, based on large and scarcely productive estates, which displayed the lowest levels of agricultural modernization in the state of São Paulo. The areas extensive environmental and soil degradation made it difficult for the settlers to start raising crops. In addition, the long distances between the farms and the region's main commercial centers created yet another development obstacle. All these elements help explain the precarious conditions and greater levels of poverty found in the Pontal settlements, most of which were linked to the MST. The large influx of settlers in this region, however, has compelled the government to increase public investment in the Pontal region, in an effort to stimulate economic growth and reverse the area's demographic decline.

Final Considerations

This study presented two basic findings. The first underscored the crucial role of the state in shaping the development prospects of land reform settlements. The second highlights the importance of these communities for the diversification of São Paulo's rural population and production matrix.

The local and regional impacts of land reform measures are highly contingent on the effectiveness of a set of ancillary policies designed to provide the settlers with housing, electricity, roads, farm credits, and access to public education, health care and transportation. These social rights are enshrined in the nation's Constitution and its agrarian laws. Aside from improving the quality of life of the settlers, these policies also generate numerous public sector jobs in their communities, for teachers, healthcare workers, agronomists and other professionals.

Farm credit policies have a major impact on development trends in agriculture and on the options available for family farmers. The priorities established by these credit programs and their multiple development effects—over the short, medium and long run—warrant much greater scrutiny that that accorded thus far. Public sector policies in São Paulo have been directed almost exclusively to finance the state's agro-industrial modernization project, centered on the promotion of a handful of export commodities, notably, sugarcane, corn, cotton and orange juice. This model of agriculture favors large-scale farming methods that depend on heavy pesticide uses and degrade the environment. Moreover, compared to alternative forms of agriculture, it relies on higher production costs and generates fewer jobs and revenue per hectare of land. Indeed, the adoption of these farming methods, in a context beset by meager state support for these settlements, have led a number of settlers to bankruptcy.[22]

State shortcomings in the promotion of sustainable rural development policies were compounded by the inefficient administration of programs established to provide settlers with housing, farm credits, technical assistance, and an adequate infrastructure. Adding to their slow and irregular provision of public services, the agencies responsible for managing these programs had a tendency to operate in a very top-down fashion. Their staff workers rarely consulted with the settlers and mostly ignored peasant proposals for alternative production projects. This demeanor undermined the possibilities of exploiting the creative potential found in these farming communities.

For all these drawbacks, however, land reform settlements have had a noticeable impact in the development of their local regions, particularly in the case of smaller rural districts. What is more, a substantial portion of settlers have been able to establish successful family farms that are productive, technically competent, and profitable.

None of these successes would have been possible without the recruitment and mobilization of landless rural workers by various popular organizations, notably, the MST, CPT, and rural trade unions. These groups prodded the federal and state governments to create 217 land reform settlements in São Paulo, between 1980 and 2006. In doing so, they established rural communities that helped transform local land tenure arrangements and the enveloping socioeconomic milieu, as demonstrated by our case studies in the Pontal do Paranapanema and Promissão regions. Elsewhere, they ushered in new local political actors and alternative development ideas, as noted in the review of the Sumaré and Araraquara cases. As such, these settlements have helped diversify São Paulo's agricultural economy and improved the prospects for family farming in this state. They have also generated alternative food crops and fostered innovative trade practices. All this has broadened the range of options available in a part of Brazil dominated by the agribusiness approach to rural development, with its large monoculture plantations, industrial production methods, and powerful conglomerates that control the seed, chemical input, and retail markets for agro-commodities.

In essence, then, the creation of land reform settlements in São Paulo has uplifted thousands of impoverished people, by improving their living conditions and providing a stable source of livelihood. It has also fostered alternative associational and commercial arrangements, innovative farm technologies, and the gradual consolidation of public policies intended to support peasant farmers. All these changes have fueled a new balance of social and political forces in numerous rural districts of São Paulo. But perhaps its main consequences lie in the elements of an alternative development paradigm nurtured by the forces undergirding Brazil's land reform movement. The new ideas, experiences, and projects nurtured by these groups stand in sharp contrast with the prevailing trends in São Paulo and the rest of the country.

The modernization of São Paulo's industry and agriculture during the twentieth century was heavily clustered around a few metropolitan hubs and rural regions. This excluded many parts of the state from the benefits of São Paulo's economic growth, and led to the decline of many small rural towns. While generating substantial wealth, this model of development came at a very high price. It spurred the unwieldy expansion of a few huge metropolises plagued by sharp social disparities, considerable levels of urban violence and insecurity, and precarious access for many of its inhabitants to housing, sanitation, jobs, and other basic human needs. In the countryside, this approach to modernization established a production model detached from its ecosystem and the everyday life of its communities.

Agrarian reform settlements that have succeeded in creating a more autonomous peasant economy, rooted in its ecological milieu, challenge this dominant model of development. The initiatives and aspirations that fuel their alternative paradigm prioritize issues of enduring relevance to Brazil—namely, the need to generate jobs, support economic growth in rural communities, preserve the environment, and strengthen public policies aimed at reducing poverty and social inequality.

Notes

Translated from the Portuguese by Miguel Carter.

1. This section draws on a survey conducted in São Paulo between February and May 1998, as part of a nationwide study of land reform settlements that was coordinated by Medeiros and Leite (2004). The sample in São Paulo included 10% of all households surveyed in each settlement. Our fieldwork was carried out with Leonardo de Barros Pinto and Rosângela A. Pereira de Oliveira.
2. On the timid efforts to redistribute land in São Paulo during the early 1960s, see Tolentino (1990) and Bergamasco et al. (1991).
3. For the MST's history in São Paulo, see Fernandes (1996a, 2000: 66–69, 147–50).
4. Fernandes (1996a:170–71, 1998).
5. Fernandes (1996a: 170–71).
6. The Pontal de Paranapanema region has had a long history of land conflicts. Dozens of lawsuits were filed in the early decades of the twentieth century to challenge the widespread illegal land grabbing that had taken place in this region. Many of these cases dragged on for years. The state government, however, only began a more substantial redistribution of the area's large cattle ranches—set up through fraudulent land titles— after 1990, when 800 MST families occupied the Nova Pontal estate in the district of Teodoro Sampaio. On the land struggle in the Pontal region and the various landless movements that emerged in the region after the mid-1990s, see Fernandes (1996a: 101–13, 158–211; 1998).
7. The total number of settlements in São Paulo includes areas where farmers displaced by the construction of hydroelectric dams, built in the early 1980s, were resettled. Five of these hydroelectric projects were erected in the Pontal do Paranapanema region and two in the Andradina region. In total, they displaced 1,501 families, close to 15% of all those settled in the state by 1999.

8. Government land policies also included efforts to formalize land titles—especially in the Ribeira Valley, a region that includes the state's main natural conservation area—and initiatives to demarcate territories belonging to indigenous groups and the afro-descendants of runaway slaves who set up maroon communities (*quilombolas*).

9. Barbosa and Leite (1990).

10. São Paulo had close to 135,000 farms in the mid-1990s. Between 1970 and 1995, the number of agricultural laborers fell from 1,357,113 to 914,954; of which a substantial number were temporary workers.

11. Kageyama and Leone (1999).

12. Faria (1991).

13. Santos (1988).

14. Bergamasco and Aubrée (2002).

15. These data are similar to the findings of the Brazilian Census of Agrarian Reform Settlements published in Schmidt, Marinho, and Rosa (1998). In some northeastern states, close to one-half of the settlers were illiterate. National statistics also suggest a rough parity between the settler's number of schooling years and that of his or her spouse.

16. As the studies by Lopes (1995) and Leone (1994) demonstrate, a settler's housing situation offers an important parameter by which to gauge his or her social conditions.

17. An analysis of the broader debate over food security and rural development can be found in Norder (1998, 2004). These studies also present relevant nutrition data collected at the Reunidas settlement.

18. Bergamasco and Aubrée (2002).

19. Bergamasco and Aubrée (2002). The monthly average was weighted by the population in each settlement. The exchange rate used was 1.20 Brazilian reais to each US dollar, based on the average rate for 2002.

20. Antonio Celestino dos Santos Neto, president of Teodoro Sampaio's Chamber of Commerce, interview with the authors, Teodoro Sampaio, SP, April 1998.

21. Land reform communities in Promissão gained an added boost of 203 families with the creation of the Dandara settlement, in November 2004.

22. Useful accounts of such failures among settlers can be found in detailed case studies of the Araraquara and Promissão communities, see Barone (2002) and Norder (2004), respectively.

16. Occupation of the Jaguarão estate in Bagé, Rio Grande do Sul, 1997.
Photo courtesy of CPT Archives.

17. The police interrupt a statewide MST assembly at the Annoni settlement, in Rio
Grande do Sul, and treat its participants as criminals, 2008. Photo courtesy of
Leonardo Melgarejo.

18 *(below)*. The mother of Oziel Pereira cries over the death of her son, executed by the police in Eldorado dos Carajás, Pará, 1996. © Sebastião Salgado / Amazonas Images.

19 *(opposite, top)* and **20** *(opposite, bottom)*. Burial and wake for the nineteen landless peasants killed during the police massacre in Eldorado dos Carajás, Pará, 1996.

19 Courtesy of João Ripper.

20 © Sebastião Salgado / Amazonas Images.

21 *(opposite, top)*. Schools at the landless camp of Taquarusu, in the Pontal do Paranapanema, São Paulo, 1996. Photo courtesy of CPT Archives

22 *(left)*. School at the Santa Clara camp in Sergipe, 1996. © Sebastião Salgado / Amazonas Images.

23 *(above)*. The MST's Florestan Fernandes National School in Guarema, São Paulo, 2005. Photo courtesy of MST Archives.

24. More than 1,400 children take part in the MST's Fifth National Congress, 2007. Photo courtesy of João Zinclair.

25. Celebrating the government's recognition of the new Chico Mendes settlement in Pernambuco, 2008. Photo courtesy of Verena Glass.

26. Harvesting crops at the May 23 settlement in São Paulo, 2009.
    Photo courtesy of Douglas Mansur.
27. Hauling hay at the Annoni settlement in Rio Grande do Sul, mid-1990s.
    Photo courtesy of João Ripper.

28. Family at the Conquista da Fronteira settlement, in Santa
    Catarina, 1996. © Sebastião Salgado / Amazonas Images.
29. Lula visits the Annoni landless camp in Rio Grande do Sul, 1986.
    Photo courtesy of MST Archives.

30. João Pedro Stédile at a workshop held at the Florestan Fernandes National School, 2009. Photo courtesy of Max Love da Rocha.

31. Adão Pretto *(center)* and Father Arnildo Fritzen *(right)* at the MST's First National Congress, 1985. Photo courtesy of CPT Archives.

32. Bishop Pedro Casaldáliga (*seated*) in São Felix do Araguaia, Mato Grosso, 1982. Photo courtesy of Prelacy of São Felix Archives.

33. Bishop Tomás Balduíno at the Martyr's Pilgrimage, late 1980s. Photo courtesy of CPT Archives.

11 Community Building in an MST Settlement in Northeast Brazil

Maliene was standing in the middle of an open field trying to fetch her cow. She paused, took a breath, and for the hundredth time, cursed it. The cow somehow seemed to understand her words and ran even farther away. Maliene turned toward me and in a purposely loud voice denounced the lack of interest her neighbors had in helping her. Together we walked slowly toward the cow while she recounted that the few neighbors who still lived at the community's *agrovila* (residential area)—feigning ignorance of her situation—would not come out to help her. But it had not always been so. In a story frequently retold to me, when she arrived at the landless encampment she was determined to get Nestor, her husband, out of there and back to their hometown, where they had a small house and where her family was getting by. According to Maliene, the allure of land was too powerful for her husband, because he was born and brought up in the countryside. In addition, getting to know all the people at the encampment and seeing how people helped each other out building a new kind of community encouraged him to stay and he pressured her to do the same. Today, however, Maliene was not in the mood for telling happy stories.

"*Isso aquí não dá certo não*" (things here aren't working out), Maliene mumbled, as she walked back home in defeat. This statement captured not only her anger at having lost the morning milk, but also her complaints about the lack of support from her neighbors. This same expression was often used by Novo Mirante settlers when referring to their lack of faith in the settlement project. During these times, they would share doubts about their prospects of living off the land.[1] They would also acknowledge growing reservations about the possibility of building a community in which people cared for each other—a community in which people would also have access to health, education, and a much better quality of life than what they had left behind. This was the project that drew Maliene's husband to the Landless Rural Workers Movement (MST). As presented by regional MST leaders in meetings prior to the land occupation, this project would allow their family to live off the land and take part in a community that would ensure their well-being and offer a better quality of life. Like Nestor, other people had similar hopes when they participated in the occupation of an estate belonging to the descendant of a traditional and powerful landlord family in northeast Brazil.

This chapter offers an ethnographic analysis of the different expectations, criticisms, and ambivalences toward the MST's community-building project in a northeast settlement. Among the settlers, recurrent perceptions of "failure" in developing a successful community reflect the importance they attached to the creation of an economically viable and socially cohesive community. This, after all, was a goal that led them to join the MST, to endure sacrifices during the struggle for land, and remain loyal to the movement thereafter. More subtly, perhaps, the perceptions of failure shed light on the different meanings that settlers ascribe to what in essence constitutes a special symbol: their community life.[2]

The initial years of settlement life are usually fraught with feelings of disenchantment. This chapter examines these perceptions and explores a variety of community conflicts dealing with the settlers' choice of residence, participation in collective farm work, extensive use of gossip, and various attributions of blame for the settlement's inadequate infrastructure. It argues that the feelings of failure reveal a lack of common understanding of what it means to live in a community. "Failure," in this sense, reflects an inability to forge a basic consensus on the meanings attached to this symbol. In attributing blame for their situation, the settlers combine ideas held prior to their participation in the new community with notions developed through their involvement in a politicized and politicizing social movement. The analysis offered here will review the ways in which failure is accepted and examine the strategies through which it is actively challenged. In addition, it will cast light onto how the movement's political ideas filter into the settlers' consciousness and affect their views of community life.

Novo Mirante Settlement: A Community in the Making

The Novo Mirante settlement is located in what was once a traditional sugarcane plantation along the northeast coast.[3] The original, unproductive estate was first occupied by the MST in October 1996. After suffering a police eviction in November, the landless contingent reoccupied the area two weeks later. The federal government land reform bureau, INCRA, expropriated the estate in December 1997, close to fourteen months after the area was first occupied. Novo Mirante's 299 hectares of land were divided into thirty family plots of 8 hectares each. The remaining 59 hectares were reserved for common usage. This part of the settlement included an *agrovila* (residential area) and an area for cattle grazing. Turnover in the settlement has been relatively high and by 2002, one-third of the original thirty families had left the community. The Novo Mirante settlers came from a variety of backgrounds. Most, however, had worked in agriculture before and had held odd jobs in urban centers.

Among the settlers, levels of commitment to the community and the MST were quite varied. Some were actively engaged in the settlement activities and were strongly supportive of the MST, while others were more detached. Different views about participation in the community and the MST were at the root of many conflicts among settlers, as well as between the settlers and their regional MST leaders.

For the MST settlers one of the movement's most attractive ideas was the possibility of taking part in a community in which interpersonal solidarity and humane values would prevail. This concept is central to the MST's socialist ideals and is featured prominently in its literature, written for both internal and external audiences. It is assumed here that the MST's role is to instill and nuture these values among all of its members, including leaders, settlers, participants in its encampments, and close supporters.[4] For the MST, then, its land reform settlements are strategic places in which the values of the "new man and woman" are to be encouraged and disseminated in order to foster social change in Brazil. These values, it is believed, can be achieved by closely following MST directives. The emphasis here is on self-discipline and control of other people's behavior, in what Eliane Brenneisen describes, drawing on Michel Foucault, as the "MST's micro-politics of power." The "new man and woman" are expected to evolve through the redeeming power of collective action and collective work. Participation in these new communities would enable MST members to help spread socialist practices as movement activists, by offering concrete examples of its potential application to Brazilian society.[5]

Generally, two types of settlers could be identified here. Some held stronger attachments to the MST. This group included those who had mobilized to occupy the estate or joined the movement shortly after. Their ideas about what sort of community to expect were shaped by their prior participation in MST meetings, media depictions of the movement, conversations with friends engaged in the MST, and, especially, the intense fourteen-month experience of taking part in a landless camp. Other settlers joined the community after the settlement had been officially established, to replace the ten families that eventually left the area. These people were less exposed to MST ideals given that their participation in the movement was limited to occasional meetings and a few demonstrations.

MST settlers, to be sure, are not a tabula rasa on which ideals and visions of society and community are simply imprinted.[6] At Novo Mirante, each settler brought his or her own combination of prior experience and understanding of community. For most settlers this included the experience of living in urban shantytowns. In fact, urban lifestyles shaped many of their ideas and affected their lingering distaste and appreciation for city life. Compared to their overcrowded and violent existence in the shantytowns, the new settlement offered significant improvements. Yet settlers also missed the access to many services and opportunities available in urban areas. Others appreciated the greater anonymity and privacy found in larger cities. For some settlers, everyday life in the community was socially oppressive, given the overabundance of gazing eyes ready to judge their behavior. Their community interactions and relations with regional MST leaders were also affected by prior labor practices under oppressive urban or rural bosses. Adding to this, settlers were also influenced by the idealized images created about land reform settlements elsewhere, particularly those formed by the descendants of European immigrants in southern Brazil.[7]

Thus, an array of experiences and ideas shaped the different expectations Novo Mirante settlers had of their community. Most of the original settlers, though, held equally divergent views on the cause of their disenchantment and perceptions of failure. The explanations and attributions given for this "failure" varied both among the settlers and the context in which they were expressed. In effect, some people would offer explanations in one setting that would be contradicted by those presented in another situation.

Community Spirit and Expectations

Anthropological definitions of *community* usually presuppose a set of common interests that create binding ties among a group of people. Not all the settlers in Novo Mirante could identify the settlement as "their" community, given the novelty of the ties between them and the variety of interests vested in the settlement. Whether settlers chose to identify mostly with their kin, their fellow settlers, or even the wider imagined community of landless people is crucial for understanding their sense of duty and obligation. All this also had a significant impact on their concept of community.

When Maliene voiced her anger toward the neighbors who had not helped her fetch her cow, she was echoing a common complaint among settlers that credited the settlement's failure to the lack of community spirit among its members. Such beliefs could be found among settlers with high and low degrees of commitment to the MST project. It was a discourse particularly favored by those who had endured the encampment experience, since this was commonly felt to involve a period of intense community spirit. This time was often remembered with nostalgia, as a period when everyone was full of hopes and plans and felt a sense of belonging together. Yet Novo Mirante settlers all agreed that the community spirit forged during the struggle for land had vanished.

This feeling of disenchantment is a recurrent phenomenon among new land reform settlers. José de Souza Martins argues that the heightened experience of community during the time of landless encampment is grounded on the euphoria of the festive atmosphere, stemming mostly from its provisional and transcient nature. These, he notes, are not "authentic" communities but residual ones, and as such are especially vulnerable to internal difference. The struggle for land alone, Martins sustains, does not constitute a powerful enough filter or base on which to sustain identity claims.[8]

Some settlers argued that the relatively high turnover rate at the settlement, well over the 20% national average reported in 1992,[9] meant there was little time to get to know all the new families, much less develop the kind of community ties they had forged with other settlers at the landless camp.[10] Many of the original settlers complained that the new settlers were not fully committed to agrarian reform.

The fact that they had not experienced the hardships of the land struggle was frequently held against them as proof that their sole interest was to obtain a land parcel, to the detriment of supporting the MST's broader struggle. This accusation, though, was also directed toward other settlers who had taken part in the camp but became detached from the community. As discussed in the following two sections, this detachment can include both physical and emotional dimensions, exemplified by the decision to leave the agrovila and disengage from the community's work brigade.

Where to Live? The Agrovila versus the Individual Farm

Most Novo Mirante settlers attributed people's change of behavior in their community to the spatial dispersion that took place after the state sanctioned their new settlement. Of the thirty houses built with government funds to accommodate all the settlers in a U-shape agrovila, only half remained occupied two years later. Some settlers built alternative accommodations on their plot of land in order to prevent petty theft and minimize the hour-long trek from the agrovila to their farm plot. These accommodations ranged from temporary shacks where they spent a couple of days a week to fully finished adobe houses where they lived permanently. In addition, three settlers never brought their families to live at the settlement and maintained their main households in the peripheries of neighboring towns. Others detached themselves from the agrovila by purchasing a house and taking up permanent residency in a hamlet closer to their plot of land. All these people, nonetheless, maintained a mostly empty house in the agrovila, which was theirs by right of being a settler. This situation created a sense of a spatial and social vacuum for the families that remained in the residential compound.

Between 2001 and 2002, during my fieldwork in Novo Mirante, three settlers "gave up on agrarian reform," an expression commonly used to describe people who decide to leave the settlement permanently and return to the urban areas where they had lived previously.[11] The departing settlers were allowed to propose a candidate to take their place, subject to the ratification by the settlement's assembly and final approval by INCRA. Two of the new settlers were from a neighboring town and preferred to remain in their existing homes. A third came from a nearby community and had actually taken part in the MST occupation of the Novo Mirante estate. Yet, since more families were encamped than could be accommodated in the new settlement, he was offered land in a more distant location, which he declined. This settler also decided to remain in his current house with a small vegetable garden rather than move to the agrovila. During the same period, three other settlers left the settlement without informing the assembly or INCRA of their intentions to give up the land. Their houses remained vacant and their plots idle, adding to the feeling of emptiness among the agrovila residents.

The settlers living in the agrovila saw this as a sign of weakening commitments toward the community. Although many who lived off the settlement continued to attend weekly work brigades and take part in the settlement's assemblies, their absence from the daily life of the community created an atmosphere in which close personal contact was significantly reduced. This contrasted sharply with the encampment experience. The settlers who had taken up residency on their farm plots argued that their commitment to the MST was not about where they lived but was represented through their daily labor on the land.

Dona Marcela, a single mother with a school-age daughter, was the first woman who chose to leave the agrovila. Her decision to move to her own farm plot was opposed by some of the settlers in the agrovila, who circulated a petition to prevent her move. Because other settlers who had taken up residency in their land plot were single men or male-headed households, Dona Marcela felt betrayed and discriminated against when she heard of the petition. She could hardly believe that her fellow settlers would try to prevent her from leaving the agrovila simply on the grounds that she was a woman, questioning "what was a woman doing down in the *mato* (wild forest) by herself." Her detractors also worried about the lack of school-aged children in the agrovila and noted that this was bringing the community spirit down. Their resistance, though, emboldened Dona Marcela. Using her savings, she bought a small house in a hamlet close to her plot. Unlike her home in the agrovila, the new one had access to electricity. This allowed her to start a micro-business producing and selling soap that helped her augment her farm income. Dona Marcela's entrepreneurial success made her the target of envious gossip at the agrovila, which in turn increased her resentment toward some members of the community.

Another woman settler subsequently followed in Dona Marcela's footsteps and moved to her own farm plot, where she erected an adobe shack. Her children were sent to a nearby elementary school. After a settlement assembly meeting to discuss the lack of children in the agrovila's school, she and another family grudgingly agreed to move back to the agrovila and to send their children to its school. These families conceded to the community's wishes to demonstrate their commitment to the MST.

Communal Land and Collective Work

The Novo Mirante settlers agreed early on to establish a production model based on the allocation of eight hectares to each family, while designating one-fifth of the settlement's area as communal land. To tend to their common property, the settlement assembly instituted a collective work brigade, which mandated a compulsory weekly participation of one-half-day's time. After a while, however, the collective work brigade (*coletivo*) became a polemical issue among settlers, as all agreed it was not functioning at its best. The explanations for this failure, however, were diverse. Some settlers felt it was an MST imposition and actively boycotted it by not showing up or by keeping their productivity at a minimum. Others remained committed to the project and showed up at the weekly work brigades on a regular basis.

Jackson, for example, resented the fact that a lot of the coletivo days were devoted to fixing the fences that prevented cattle from wandering off the settlement because he had no cattle of his own. While he supported the idea of collective work, he disagreed with the way it was organized and saw this as an MST obligation. Jackson defended a more flexible approach, where different task groups would agree on carrying out specific activities. "If so and so have cattle," he explained, "and want to keep the fences in order, because it is their interest to do so, then they should get together and reach their own agreement." This approach, he insisted, would relax the coletivo's rigid format and help avert perceptions of forced participation. Other settlers, however, considered this and other forms of resistance to the coletivo as a sign of detachment from the community, or at worst, a frontal attack on the movement, given the demobilizing effects produced by the absence of dissenting members.

Settlers frequently invoked moral economy ideas and principles grounded on a sense that all community members were responsible for each other's well-being and prosperity. Sometimes, though, this led to transgressive deeds. Once, Maliene, her visiting godson, and I went to collect cashew nuts. We started in the settlement's communal land where there were many cashew trees, only to discover that all the cashews had already been gathered. When the godson proposed that we go back home, Maliene directed us toward the plot of Rosendo, an elderly settler who was not a permanent resident in the settlement. Once there, in a hushed voice she ordered her godson to pull up the barbed wire so we could get onto Rosendo's farm. There we collected as many cashews as could fit into our buckets, while leaving many behind on the ground.

As we walked home Maliene kept complaining about Rosendo's meanness, and how she had even overheard him inviting a man from the neighboring community to go pick up the cashews on his plot. Maliene was outraged that he would invite an outsider when he knew that there were people in the settlement community that needed the cashews as well. Deep inside, though, I sensed she felt guilty at having trespassed on Rosendo's plot. All the way back she joked with her godson about how I had come from afar to teach her how to "steal." The violation of Rosendo's property rights was justified in a similar logic used to legitimize the occupation of an unproductive estate: the owner did not need it to survive. Maliene's justification appealed to a sense of moral duty, while ultimately blaming me, an outsider, for her act of transgression.

Inadequate Infrastructure, MST Leaders, and the Object of Blame

For the thirty landless families who endured the hardship of the fourteen-month occupation of the Novo Mirante estate, the actual expropriation and conversion of the area into a land reform settlement, in late 1997, seemed like a dream come true. Four years later, however, much of what was promised to the settlers by INCRA and regional MST leaders remained either totally or partially undelivered. Along the dirt road that led to the settlement there stood electricity poles without any wiring connection. According to a story frequently told by settlers, this problem was due to corrupt collusion between municipal authorities and regional MST leaders.

At the agrovila's entrance stood an empty health clinic, which was never staffed or stocked with medicines of any kind. The only health service available to the settlement was provided by a municipal government program that hired and trained a settler from a different community to visit Novo Mirante on a regular basis and provide referrals to medical facilities in the nearest town. Therefore, for urgent and everyday medical care the settlers needed to travel to town and seek attention at the chronically underfunded public health clinics. As an alternative, settlers could turn to each other for assistance or seek treatment from local faith-based healers.

The houses promised to the thirty settlers were not in much better shape. Indeed, none of them were properly completed. After the expropriation of the estate the families had to wait for more than a year to obtain the federal government resources needed to construct their houses. Once provided, the funds were insufficient to build the houses according to the standards that had been originally agreed upon. All of the houses were only partially plastered. The concrete floors were never put in, and the septic tanks were never installed as promised. The settlers disagreed on who to blame for all this. Some pointed their fingers at INCRA, while others suggested regional MST leaders had put their hands in the coffers. All agreed that the movement activists had been poor brokers on their behalf.

Additionally, at the center of the agrovila stood an unfinished school building. Some claimed that the building materials had been stolen from the construction site. Others insisted that the money to pay for those materials was never delivered in full. As a result the settlers agreed to borrow one of the unoccupied houses in their residential compound to use as a temporary school building. Among the other unfinished constructions was a fully furbished electric well that had gone to waste for lack of electricity.

The inadequate facilities and services provided to the settlers elicited bitter feelings within the community. On some days, even the most enthusiastic proponents of the MST could be heard murmuring words of disapproval with regard to their regional leaders. This could be noticed particularly on the days these movement activists paid a rushed visit to the settlement, driving at high speeds in a car, which settlers assured me had been paid for with their money, to request greater participation at an MST event or ask for resources to help support other settlements and landless camps.

Dona Marina, a widow with seven children and a fervent supporter of the MST's ideals, exemplifies the views of a loyal movement critic. Dona Marina is known in the community as a regular participant of MST meetings and marches. Often she attends these gatherings with two of her daughters who live in the settlement. She hopes these activities will help broaden their life experience and nurture the passion she has for the movement's struggle for justice.

Dona Marina's experience with community organizing goes back to her participation in the rural trade union, at her hometown. After taking part in the trade union's successful effort to create a land reform settlement and community association similar to the one in Novo Mirante, she came into contact with MST leaders who convinced her to join their national struggle for agrarian reform and social change. According to these activists, the Brazilian state was at the service of national and international elites. Only the organization and mobilization of the dispossessed, they argued, could challenge their domination and help rebalance Brazilian society.[12] Stirred by these shared political ideas and values, Dona Marina agreed to leave her settlement and join the MST. In spite of her commitment to MST ideals, however, she eventually became very critical of the role that regional leaders had played in the development of the Novo Mirante settlement. She could not forgive the long delays in setting up the electrical grid and could empathize with her fellow settlers who felt let down by the MST. Still, Dona Marina continued to believe in the MST's project to reshape Brazilian society in a more just way.

On a trip we took to the MST's state meeting Dona Marina insisted that Novo Mirante's "failure" needed to be measured against the success of other settlements. We sat together while our team assembled the black plastic tarp shack in which we would sleep and put together an improvised kitchen. She kept pointing at a group of busy people behind us who were building barracks out of plastic and wooden poles at a much faster rate than our boys. Their tent-building skills mirrored, according to Dona Marina, the much better organization of their home settlements. As she looked at our semi-erected barrack, Dona Marina shook her head with disappointment at her fellow settlers. For her, the Novo Mirante settlers had not maintained the commitment they had during the encampment years, when the land struggle kept people united and actively engaged. Among her neighbors, a progressive loss of faith in the MST had taken place, as she put it, "because what the leaders had promised never arrived, and you know how some people take things literally. They forget that it's always a struggle, they forget to struggle. That's why."

This line of reasoning was also invoked by MST regional leaders. Attributing the community's failure to the setters' lack of commitment toward the MST both exonerated these leaders and offered a concrete solution: more involvement in settlement activities and MST-sponsored events. Greater participation in MST struggles, after all, would expand the movement's reach and thereby strengthen the position of its leaders.

The mistrust toward these leaders, though, was widely shared in the settlement. Even Dona Marina had openly opposed some of their decisions. During one of the assembly meetings she played an instrumental role in defending the settlement's decision not to lend its tractor to another land reform community. Although the regional leaders claimed it would only be a temporary exchange, Dona Marina argued that these activists could not be entrusted with returning the tractor. "I am telling you," she affirmed, "we know these leaders well. If that tractor leaves we will never set eyes on it again and we will receive nothing in exchange!"

Like other settlers, she felt that MST regional leaders were exploiting their position within the MST for personal benefit and discrediting the entire movement.[13] Although critical of the detachment of some of her community members, she understood their weariness. Even though she blamed these activists for not doing their best to "deliver the goods," Dona Marina was not inclined to treat her relations with MST leaders in a clientelistic fashion.

Other settlers, however, assumed this clientelistic perspective quite openly. One afternoon, I was sitting with Vítor, someone who could be classified as a "weekday settler," because his family had not joined him in the settlement and he traveled on some weekends to visit them. Vítor had asked me to tell him the story of how I had ended up in Brazil, a favorite among settlers. He then told me that he too could have traveled as well. He had a friend who had migrated to the southeast part of the country looking for a job and some adventure. But Vítor could not muster the courage to join him, even though his friend had bought him a bus ticket to São Paulo.

Years later his friend returned to the northeast. Though unsuccessful in the big city, he was determined to go back to the south, this time to try his luck with an agrarian reform community, which, according to hearsay, was due to receive a lot of money from the government. Again, Vítor shied away from joining his friend and never heard back from him. His thoughts lingered on whether the riches to be found in land reform communities in the south were genuine or merely an enticement for a hillbilly like him to join his friend in the adventure. All this left Vítor with the feeling that he had not taken advantage of opportunities in his life. That is why, several years later, when he heard on the radio that landless people had occupied the Novo Mirante estate he packed a few belongings and told his wife that he was going to join them. He arrived at the landless camp and was asked only to produce his national identification card and express his intention of joining the MST struggle.

Throughout the encampment Vítor assumed that the settlement phase would bring ample financial resources. Thus, he endured the hardships and persisted in his determination to gain a plot of land. All this time, though, he missed his wife, who had a job in a factory and did not want to risk her steady income for the uncertainty of the MST, and longed for his daughters. As soon as he managed to get his own farm plot, he resolved to never be away from his family for more than a month. His original plans to supplement his wife's earnings with the income from the land, by drawing on government subsidies and the sale of farm produce, were cut short due to the lack of credit support and other production problems. Vítor became disillusioned. He lost the dreams he had about land reform and how this would help him significantly improve his family's living standards. Nevertheless, given his past experience with long-term unemployment, he held on to the settlement in the hope that things would change in the future.

As with other settlers, he too blamed regional MST leaders for playing a key role in the settlement's "failure." During our conversation Vítor kept referring to how he had been somewhat *iludido* (deceived) into pursuing agrarian reform. I thought he was referring to his old friend's story and made a comment about the "myth" of migration. Vítor stared blankly at me. When I reminded him of the story he had told me, he laughed and said that it was not his friend he was disappointed with, but rather the MST leaders who had reinforced the expectations planted by his friend. After all, he reasoned, "whenever one hears something from one person, one can doubt it, but when you hear it from several people, and you want to believe it, you end up believing it." Vítor attributed the lack of support for the settlement to these activists, claiming that their strategies had been ineffective in obtaining the goods promised by the government. These MST activists, he asserted with anger, "ought to come and live here permanently, to see what it's like to breathe the kerosene we burn to light our houses for lack of electricity." In short, from Vítor's more clientelistic perspective the object of blame centered on the MST brokers who had not delivered on their promises.

Beyond Clientelism? MST and Education in the Settlement

Though tempting, it would be quite simplistic to argue that the settlers were involved in mere clientelist relations with the MST.[14] In fact, clientelist attitudes were entwined with demands for both enhanced autonomy and added MST involvement in their community. This was particularly the case with the local school, seen by many as one of the greatest disappointments in settlement life.

According to MST discourse, an important advantage of life in its settlements rests on the improved access to education. As Carter and Carvalho, chapter 9 in this volume, underscore, education plays a central role in the movement's beliefs and organizational structure. Inspired by Paulo Freire's *Pedadogy of the Oppressed*, the movement argues that the education provided by the Brazilian state is geared toward supporting the interests of the ruling classes. To counter this situation, the MST has created a state-funded educational structure that has enabled the movement to run its own schools, teacher-training programs, and even university courses. The emphasis here is on educating people for life in the countryside and not migration to urban centers.[15] The MST's Education Sector oversees the movement's main activities in this regard, including the set up and staffing of temporary elementary schools in its encampments, as well as its adult literacy classes. Of all of the MST's achievements, those in the field of education appear to be particularly striking. In Novo Mirante, nonetheless, the MST's role in running the local school proved to be one of the most contentious issues in everyday settlement life.

Aside from the lack of a proper building, the agrovila's school suffered from frequent teacher turnovers. In three years alone, the school had seen the rotation of four teachers. Some of these teachers were close to the regional MST leaders. Others were hurriedly appointed by the municipal government, responsible for paying teacher salaries, in order to avoid leaving the pupils without classes. Consequently, not all of the teachers working in the school were committed to the MST's educational principles. Even those inspired by the movement's pedagogy had to deal with the fact that most students were actually not from Novo Mirante, but from a neighboring settlement linked to the local rural workers trade union. The school's only teacher was obliged to adapt her lesson plans to include children of different ages and grades, and from parents who were both members and nonmembers of the MST. The teacher I spoke with claimed she received little support from the MST's regional Education Sector, and therefore followed the same curriculum offered by other public schools. As such, the Novo Mirante settlement school offered no improvement on what the children experienced elsewhere.

Over time, settlers grew more dissatisfied with the teacher's performance, and some began to enroll their children in other schools. The teacher, in turn, resented the lack of parental support. Some parents claimed the teacher and

MST leaders had excluded them from the school's planning process. Both settlers and the teacher were disappointed with the movement's absent role in mediating this conflict and insisted on the need for closer MST supervision of its schools. As with other proposed solutions to local dilemmas, here again, many settlers demanded greater MST involvement in their community development.

Strategies of Resistance and Understanding Failure

Settlers coped with their discontent and made sense of their endurance in the settlement by devoting a great deal of time to discussions about their situation, and particularly the lives of their neighbors. Gossip was widely practiced within the community, and the settlers seemed to spend too much time at it. Anthropologists have seen gossip as a way of maintaining group unity, morality, and history through the constant checking of behaviors against common expectations.[16] Yet different expectations held among the settlers made gossip a highly contentious issue and a particularly annoying problem for some. People gossiped within their families, with friends from neighboring communities, and with visiting relatives. According to most accounts, gossip was notably intense during the settlement's collective workdays, which offered an opportunity to "catch up on the news."

Among those settlers who had taken part in the original occupation, the coletivo was often seen as a remnant of the communal lifestyle that held people together during the encampment period. As an arena shaped by what was believed to be a common set of values and shared understanding of community, it was not surprising to see the coletivo serve as a site for evaluating the behavior of community members. Some settlers, though, refused to take part in the coletivo because they disapproved of the intense gossiping that took place during these activities. In doing so, they not only refused to share the values related to the subjects of gossip, but also turned themselves into objects of rumor. At least one of the settlers I interviewed attributed her decision to leave the settlement to the ruinous effects of gossip. Complaining about the community's unbearable atmosphere of gossip and its judgmental reviews of her life, she returned to her home village to "be finally left alone."

Not all social gatherings, however, gravitated around gossip. Some settlers devoted a great deal of effort at building a healthier sense of community. They invested time and energy into organizing social events to reunite settlers by celebrating people's birthdays, as well as the anniversary dates of the land occupation and the official establishment of their settlement. Some of the participants in these events were also actively involved in efforts that led to the creation of parallel communities, in the form of various evangelical churches.

Evangelicals and Religious Expression

The relationship between Pentecostal churches and social movements is a controversial issue. Evangelicals are often viewed as a demobilizing force. The reality, however, is that some evangelicals (*crentes* as they are commonly known in Brazil) have managed to successfully combine participation in both kinds of grassroots organizations.[17] In Novo Mirante more than one-third of its members were or had been at some point involved with an evangelical church. Some were highly active in both their church and in the MST. Other settlers, though, particularly those not involved in these churches, viewed the strict behavioral codes imposed by some of these churches—such as the prohibitions on drinking, smoking, or dancing, and the tendency to separate themselves from those who are "of the world"—as an indication that these evangelical settlers were more uptight and prone to disengage from activities aimed at binding the community together. Other settlers, however, showed a willingness to accommodate their *crente* neighbors.

For example, Dona Marina, who is a nominal Catholic, was part of the committee responsible for organizing the settlement's anniversary party. Hoping to include all community members, she proposed that one of the evangelicals prepare the liturgy for the event and got other settlers to agree with her. The evangelicals in charge of the celebration used it to promote their faith among the non-crentes. Most of the non-crentes were relaxed about the event's proselytizing slant. As one of them interpreted it, "it was a celebration of God. After all, our God and their God are one and the same." Still, a few of the settlers were troubled by the all the proselytizing, but willing to accept it as a concession to their evangelical neighbors.

Some regional MST leaders, however, did not share the same tolerance. In fact, these activists had opposed the presence of certain evangelical groups in MST camps and were known to have made patronizing remarks about people's religious affiliation.[18] In a conversation with one of these leaders I heard him vent his outrage toward a woman from a neighboring settlement who had given up her gas stove and other personal belongings to her local congregation of the Universal Church of the Kingdom of God (*Igreja Universal do Reino do Deus*). He depicted this woman as an ignorant bigot who was conned into giving away her valuable assets. The irony lost on this leader is that the MST also urges its members to give resources and time to support their organization.

Comparable reactions by MST activists could be seen as an expression of anxiety over their settlers' allegiances. As José David Caume argues, the MST relies on the settlers remaining within the movement in order to expand its organizational reach and power.[19] Thus affiliations to other groups that make claims on the resources and ideological positions of MST settlers could, at times, be seen as a threat to the movement's capacity to maintain hegemonic influence over its settlements.

Conclusion

The importance given by Novo Mirante settlers to building a sense of community reminds us of the need to evaluate the success of land reform settlements in terms that go beyond standard economic and material indicators, and include issues relevant to their social and moral well-being. Throughout this chapter I have tried to convey what settlers felt about their community, by examining their perceptions of community failure and the local strategies designed to counteract this sensation.

By analyzing the explanations for community failure we find that there were primarily three targets of blame at stake: the settlers, the regional MST leaders, and the government. The settlers were portrayed as lazy, uncommitted, or detached physically and ideologically by both other settlers and MST leaders. Regional MST activists, in turn, were often depicted as uncooperative, inept, and untrustworthy. The government, on the other hand, was blamed for the lack of resources to support the settlement and for not mediating some of the conflicts between settlers and MST leaders.

Discussions among settlers as to who should do more to offset these alleged failures were common. Some settlers argued in favor of a greater MST presence in their settlement, noting that without the MST's strong leadership, their adherence to the movement's values would wane, and with it the hope of building a tight-knit community. Yet others insisted that the control exerted by MST leaders needed to be reduced given their poor commitment to the movement's core values. According to these settlers, regional MST leaders were overly concerned with advancing their personal interests and political ambitions. This accusation was often combined with a demand for more government supervision to prevent these activists from abusing their power. Despite all these criticisms, settlers like Dona Marina refused to project their disappointments onto the entire movement, or convey a loss of faith in the MST's goal to change Brazilian society.

Some of the settlers who wanted to reduce the MST's control over the settlement were not eager to hand more power to the settlers themselves. Rather, they preferred to see a stronger government presence. In their view, the government had shirked its duties to provide them with the resources necessary to their success as family farmers. Increased state involvement was needed first and foremost to improve public investment in their community. Though seeking empowerment in many of the radical ways advocated by social movements and alternative development models, the settlers' vision of community building was hardly dismissive of the state. Instead, it perceived the state as a legitimate and necessary force, with important intervening powers to avert local abuses.

Land reform settlements, as seen here, are not closed and established societies, but communities engaged in an ongoing process of creation and evolution. Various values and meanings of what it is to build a community are bound to induce all sorts of problems and conflicts among its members. The strategies developed by Novo Mirante settlers to resist perceptions of failure suggest that there are many possible solutions to the problem. The future success of Novo Mirante, and perhaps many other land reform settlements in Brazil, would seem to hinge significantly on the ability to foster common pursuits among its participants.

Notes

The author would like to thank all the settlers at Novo Mirante for their help, hospitality, and friendship during field research.

1. The settlement's main productive project, pineapple cultivation, was not very successful. Settlers blamed regional MST leaders for imposing a crop and variety that required a lot of technical advice and care; see Calvo-González (2005).

2. According to Anthony P. Cohen, symbols are "those [social categories] whose meanings are the most elusive [such as justice, goodness, patriotism and duty], [whose] range of meanings can be glossed over in a commonly accepted symbol precisely because it allows its adherents to attach their own meanings to it. They share the symbol, but not necessarily the meaning" (1985: 15).

3. The name of the settlement and that of all settlers cited in this text are pseudonyms. I undertook two main periods of ethnographic research; nine months in the 2001–2 and three months in 2003. During both visits to the Novo Mirante I was engaged as a participant observer and carried out semistructured interviews with twenty of the thirty settler families. I also interviewed three settlers who had permanently left the settlement and attended public events organized by the MST in the settlement's region as well as in the state capital.

4. For a useful account of MST membership as constituting an "imagined" community of *sem terras* (landless people), in a way akin to Benedict Anderson's classic term, see Wolford (2003b: 506).

5. Eliane Brenneisen (2002: 23). Elsewhere she argues that the MST articulates a "pedagogy of suffering," which maintains that the creation of a "new man and woman" is forged through the deprivations suffered during the land struggle. Rather than politicizing the landless participants, as the MST would hope, she sees these sufferings as producing a "pedagogy of resignation," with depoliticizing effects on many members; see Brenneisen (2003: 68). For a similar line of interpretation on these issues, see Caume (2002a, 2006).

6. An early MST publication described preexisting cultural dispositions among movement participants as grounded on, "individualism, personalism, spontaneity, anarchism, immobilism, accommodation, sectarianism or radicalism, liquidationism, aventurism, and self-sufficiency"; see Morais (1986: 27, 39, author's translation). These traditional dispositions were seen as a hindrance to the success of the MST model, which encouraged the adherence to socialist values; see Harnecker (2002: 45).

7. To the best of my knowledge, none of the Novo Mirante settlers had direct contact with MST settlements in the south. Their understanding of these places was derived mostly from third-party accounts and media depictions. The descendants of European immigrants who inhabit many of the MST settlements in southern Brazil are a legacy of the nineteenth-century policy aimed at "whitening" the nation; see Santos (2002). The

whitening of the south led that part of the country to be identified as a more educated and "refined" Brazil. According to Christine de Alencar Chaves, this racialized model of a nation, with an allegedly strong work ethos and greater organizational capacity in the south, vis-à-vis the supposedly lazier, racially mixed population in the remainder of the country, can be found in the discourse of some MST leaders from the south (2000: 339).

8. Martins (2003c: 25). José de Souza Martins further notes that the encampment period can also lead to a process of cultural and social loss, whereby the "old values and references lose meaning. . . . And the new values that are announced there still have no meaning, because they are still not concrete" (2003c: 50).

9. See the Food and Agriculture Organization's (FAO) 1992 report, cited in Brenneisen (2002: 277).

10. The new settlers joined the community with a financial disadvantage since by law all of them inherited the debt accrued by their predecessors from the government-subsidized loans, known as the start-up (*fomento*) credits.

11. To be sure, not all people who left the settlement had "given up on agrarian reform." During my research I came to know two former MST settlers from nearby communities who abandoned the MST due to disagreements with regional leaders but subsequently joined other landless movements active in the area.

12. For an example of the MST's view of the state, see Bogo (1999: 26). Wendy Wolford refers to this as an "oppositional class" vision of society, and argues that the MST's "imagined community" is built around it (2003b: 507).

13. These feelings of exploitation and perceptions of MST leaders as being self-interested are fuelled by rumors suggesting that some MST activists enjoy a lavish lifestyle with apartments and cars paid for with the organization's money. The "careerism" of young MST activists within the movement structure and the participation of some of them as political candidates (mainly through the PT), in a nation where politicians are generally viewed as self-interested creatures, contribute further to these feelings; see Navarro, as cited in Branford and Rocha (2002: 121).

14. Elsewhere, I have argued that local MST leaders mimic, at times, the behavior of traditional rural bosses (*patrões*); see Calvo-Gonzalez (2004).

15. For a more in-depth analysis of the MST model of education, see Kolling, Nery, and Castagna (1999) and Caldart (2000). Zander Navarro, however, claims that the MST's critique of the state as "bourgeois" while exhibiting an eagerness to accept state resources represents a "core contradiction" between the movement's ideology and practice (2002a: 30).

16. Gluckman (1963).

17. For relevant discussions about evangelicals and social movements, see Fernandes (1977) and Novaes (1985).

18. Jadson José Cardozo Araújo, researcher from the Federal University of Bahia, personal communication, Salvador, Bahia, October 2001.

19. Caume (2002b: 5).

12 MST Settlements in Pernambuco
Identity and the Politics of Resistance

The Landless Rural Workers Movement (MST) is one of the most well-organized and effective grassroots social movements in Brazilian history. It is the first rural social movement in Brazil able to claim a national membership. Its high level of organizational discipline and ideological coherence has allowed the movement to coordinate land occupations, public demonstrations, marches, and cultural events that cut across geographical regions, social classes, and cultural identities.

The underlying diversity of conditions throughout rural Brazil has required the MST to simplify the demands of its membership, however. The strength of the rural poor lies in their numbers, but only if they are organized and represented as relatively unified. In the MST, as in any social movement, membership is not a discrete variable, where a person is either in or out: rather, membership is arranged along a continuum and at any given time, some members are more accurately represented than others. People join movements for a number of different reasons and the act of joining does not preclude questioning, rejecting, or even deliberately misunderstanding the organization's ideology, tactics, and ultimate goals. Studies of social movements like the MST, however, rarely focus on the ambivalent or half-hearted members; instead model settlements and model members tend to be singled out by activists and scholars alike.

In this chapter, I analyze the MST's attempts to organize rural sugarcane workers in the northeastern state of Pernambuco. I argue that we will have a fuller understanding of mobilization within the MST if we self-consciously ground the movement in people and places, so that distinct localized trajectories are analyzed against the framework of the movement as a whole.

When the MST was first formed in southern Brazil in 1984, movement leaders and supporters recognized the importance of "spread[ing] to all regions of the country, particularly the northeast."[1] Becoming a Brazilian movement rather than a regional one would be a challenge, however, because the peasant culture that shaped the MST in southern Brazil was not evident everywhere in the country. One example was the coastal sugarcane area of Pernambuco in northeastern Brazil, which movement leaders considered particularly important for mobilization because of the region's high level of poverty and long history of collective resistance.[2] MST leaders argued that although organized labor was much more powerful there than the peasantry, a common desire for land united people across different social classes.[3] According to Jaime Amorím, a movement leader from the southern state of Santa Catarina who has led the MST in Pernambuco since he moved there in 1989, the MST was able to build its membership in northeastern Brazil because, "we picked an issue that united everyone—the land. Land is a necessity. Land is the word that unifies. Land became the element of the struggle. You offer the workers the opportunity to have land—but through an occupation that they participate in."[4]

A quarter of a century later, the MST's strategy of expansion appears to have been a success. The coastal sugarcane region of Pernambuco is now considered a stronghold of movement influence and support. The number of settlements per capita and per hectare in the region makes it one of the most active land reform sites in the country. Behind the numbers, however, is a complicated story of local politics and cultural norms regarding the relationship between land and labor.

It was not easy for the MST to build its membership in the sugarcane region. Rural plantation workers did not immediately respond to agrarian reform as an opportunity to maintain their way of life, as the sons and daughters of small farmers in southern Brazil did. It was often difficult to convince plantation workers to forego wage labor for subsistence production on the land, and there was little in the cultural repertoire of plantation labor that legitimated the notion of engaging in direct-action land occupations. As a result of the cultural differences between the MST's original members and plantation workers in the northeast, the movement did not succeed in building its membership there until the mid-1990s when a generalized crisis in the sugarcane industry threw hundreds of thousands of people out of work.[5] This economic crisis met with expanded political resources for agrarian reform because MST leaders mobilized rural workers, and state officials proposed restructuring land tenure relations as a way of addressing the economic crisis.

The fieldwork for this chapter was conducted in the municipality of Água Preta, in the southern sugarcane region of Pernambuco. In 2001, Água Preta was characterized by the largest concentration of land in the sugarcane region, as well as the highest number of land reform settlements in Pernambuco. Between 1992 and 2000, twelve former plantations in the municipality were expropriated and distributed among 926 families.[6] One of the settlements closest to town, which forms the basis of this case study, had been a large-scale sug-

Map 12.1. Pernambuco

arcane plantation before its expropriation in 1996. I call the settlement Flora, although that is not its real name. Forty-six families lived on the settlement. Thirteen families received land after occupying the area with MST in 1996. The remaining thirty-three families were given a farm plot as a result of a law that allows all rural workers or tenants associated with a property first priority in a land expropriation. By 1999, the settlement was publicly affiliated with the MST.[7]

Long after the MST succeeded in articulating the struggle for land in Água Preta, however, the social relationships between people and place that characterized the difficult mobilization period continued to shape dynamics within the movement's membership. Sugarcane as a commodity may have been in crisis, but sugarcane as a culture lived on, nourished by the plants' famously deep roots.[8] Rural workers joined the MST, but many of them continued to privilege wages over farming. They had a social history of household land use on the plantations and they valued their new position as landholders, but property signified stability and status rather than livelihood. These culturally embedded understandings of material space—in this case, land—are what I refer to as "spatial imaginaries."[9] Rural workers who joined the MST brought with them very different spatial imaginaries than their small farmer counterparts in southern Brazil, and these could not be easily erased by membership in the movement. To the contrary, they influenced movement dynamics from the household and settlement to the national levels.

The continued importance of spatial imaginaries influenced by plantation labor became evident when production began to revive again, three years after world prices fell to a ten-year low of six cents a pound, in 1999. By 2003, many of the settlers in Água Preta had begun planting sugarcane again and almost all of them had left the MST. This decision to leave the movement was not a simple economic one, however. The MST lost its position in Água Preta because it assumed that the people who joined the movement necessarily wanted land, and it presumed that meanings associated with land on the plantation could—and should—be easily transformed through participation in movement activities. Ultimately, the MST and the rural workers could not reconcile their perceptions of what it meant to own land.

Sugarcane and the MST in the Zona da Mata Sul

Sugarcane production in northeastern Brazil has been shaped by the vagaries of nature, world market conditions, and political pacts negotiated among regional and national elites.[10] All of these macro-level processes or relationships are refracted through local power relations where a relatively small plantation elite has wielded monopoly control over land and labor for almost 500 years.[11] Sugarcane produced in northeastern Brazil generated considerable fortunes for these plantation elites, but provided little long-term development. The crop's origins in slavery and monoculture left legacies of inequality, poverty, and paternalism that are openly evident today. Most of the sugar was produced for export and finished goods were purchased in Europe rather than manufactured at home. Rather than modernize their methods or diversify production, plantation owners weathered periodic economic downturns, droughts or floods, and occasional episodes of political unrest by manipulating local land-use and labor arrangements. During and after the slave period, they provided more land for their workers to plant subsistence crops when prices were low, and planted cane "right up to the front door" when prices were high.[12] As a result, even though production in the sugarcane region appeared to change very little over the past 500 years, the normative understandings of "appropriate" behavior as well as the relationship between workers and the land have been constantly reworked among the different social classes.[13]

In the late 1800s, as plantation owners made the transition from slave to free labor, rural workers would provide their services for a fixed number of days in return for a place to live and land to plant on.[14] Throughout the depressed years of the early 1900s, this relationship allowed plantations to continue producing and rural workers to maintain subsistence production on small plots of land. As international demand for sugarcane increased in the 1950s, however, plantations rationalized production by expelling their resident workers or taking away their right to land. The right to farm was gradually (and unevenly) replaced by the right to labor. The trend toward what Anthony Pereira calls *full proletarianization* continued throughout the late 1900s as revolution in Cuba and successive oil crises contributed to high sugarcane/ethanol prices.[15]

During the military dictatorship (1964–85), the rural unions built a strong presence in rural Pernambuco. In 1963, rural workers won the right to a formal set of legal protections under the Rural Labor Statute (*Estatuto de Trabalho Rural*). This statue formalized the rural workers' rights to holiday pay, bonuses, medical care, sick leave, and the right to form labor unions. Consequently, rural trade unions became relatively privileged representatives of the rural poor. In fact, the state Federation of Agricultural Workers of Pernambuco (FETAPE), which represented sugarcane workers, was one of the strongest state federations in the country.

The 1963 Rural Labor Statute codified labor relations but failed to protect the rural workers' rights to land. The 1965 Small Farm Law (*Lei do Sitio*), which would have guaranteed all rural workers up to two hectares of land for subsistence production, was never enforced. Coming on the heels of the 1964 Rural Land Statute, the Small Farm Law may even have compelled plantation owners to expel their workers from the plantation because possession threatened to become as important as ownership in making a claim to land. Although the rural poor organized in trade unions and peasant leagues, labor relations were steadily formalized and access to land became increasingly rare.[16]

In 1989, when MST activists undertook their first land occupation in Pernambuco, they expected to be supported by the governor of the state, Miguel Arraes. Arraes had won national and regional fame as an advocate for the rural poor because he implemented the Rural Labor Statue in 1963. In exile during much of the military dictatorship, Arraes returned as governor of Pernambuco in 1988. MST leaders did not realize that in planning their occupation, they were stepping into a long-standing political dispute between peasant activists and rural trade union leaders. Loosely defined, this dispute pits peasant advocates for land reform (supported by the Catholic Church and historic Peasant Leagues) against rural trade union supporters of labor reform (backed by FETAPE). To the MST's surprise, Governor Arraes sent the military police to expel the landless squatters shortly after the occupation, a decision attributed to the state government's desire "to keep the social movements under its control."[17]

In the 1990s the context for MST mobilization shifted. The sugarcane industry in Pernambuco entered into another period of extreme crisis that suggested a possible end of the industry, or at the very least, the need for significant restructuring of both production and land tenure relations.[18] Starting in 1989, newly elected federal and state government officials initiated a series of measures aimed at dismantling the generous system of production subsidies that supported the region's producers. Concomitantly, international demand for Brazilian sugar began to decrease sharply with the rise of new global producers and increasing demand for new artificial sweeteners. By 1995, 44% of the sugarcane refining distilleries in Pernambuco were classified as "paralyzed or functioning with difficulty."[19]

In response to the economic crisis, the federal and Pernambuco governments started to coordinate plans to redistribute land in the sugarcane region. According to these policymakers, agrarian reform represented a rapid means for transforming land tenure relations in support of Pernambuco's working poor, while "rationalizing" the sugarcane industry. As stated in a 1998 government

Table 12.1. Land occupations and agrarian reform settlements in Pernambuco, 1989–97

Year	Land occupations		Settlements	
	No.	No. of families involved	No.	No. of families settled
1989	3	500	—	—
1990	5	300	2	42
1991	3	400	5	205
1992	9	1,250	1	135
1993	12	2,000	4	550
1994	15	2,500	5	720
1995	19	4,500	7	744
1996	35	3,500	17	1,320
1997	51	8,500	16	1,700

Source: MST-PE.

report, "The crisis of the sugarcane industry in the northeastern tropical forest region is a crisis of the [productive] model. The crisis provides a unique opportunity to carry out sweeping structural changes that will eliminate the concentration of landholdings and monocultural production, in order to benefit the economic development of the region with equality and social justice."[20] In the early 1990s MST activists in the region increased the intensity of land occupations and succeeded in expediting the creation of dozens of new land settlements (see table 12.1).

The expropriation of traditional sugarcane plantations transformed Pernambuco's coastal region. Former plantation bosses, administrative and rural workers, cane cutters, and MST squatters alike were given the rights to small plots of land. These new land reform beneficiaries were offered grants for short-term subsistence and materials to build a house. The federal government also promised subsidized loans to plant alternative crops and raise livestock.

Building Membership in the Sugarcane Region

For MST members who had been small family farmers before joining the movement, becoming settlers represented a return to a familiar form of production and social reproduction. In the southern state of Santa Catarina, the sons and daughters of small farmers joined the MST because two decades of militarized agricultural policy had hastened the end of the regional frontier.[21] These landless farmers were not always the poorest in the rural areas; their parents often had access to land. But they joined the MST because there was little other land available that they could afford to purchase or to which they could migrate.

Stories of Amazonian colonization gone awry had filtered through to local communities, and landless farmers were increasingly desperate to find land of their own, where they could begin a family.[22] When MST activists—affiliated with local community leaders—began organizing occupations, these landless farmers joined the movement to maintain their way of life. Pushed by what their "cultural toolkits"[23] led them to see as necessity, and pulled by the strong ties of community and household support, landless farmers in Santa Catarina were some of the first to join the MST in the struggle for land.[24]

For rural workers in Pernambuco, life on the settlements was very different than life on the former plantation. As rural workers, their cultural toolkits had been shaped by occupational hierarchies inscribed onto the physical landscape. Sugarcane production required only a few skilled workers along with a vast number of unskilled cane cutters employed for the harvest season. Occupational hierarchies ran vertically from the plantation owner to skilled laborers, including administrative workers and team leaders, to unskilled cane cutters and handlers. When workers were removed from the plantations and forced to live in the small cities scattered throughout the sugarcane region, in the decades following the 1950s, only a few retained or won the use of small farms in the interior of the plantation. Despite the formulation of the Small Farm Law in 1965, plantation owners continued to award these small plots of land as "gifts" to show preference or appreciation to particular workers. These workers had more security on the plantation and in their jobs than their counterparts in the cities because they could plant subsistence crops, flowers, and fruit trees around their house, and they could fish in the nearby rivers or streams.

The dynamic history of access to land on the plantation gave rise to a social memory of land use, albeit a very different one than that of the small farmers in southern Brazil. Rural workers associated access to land with a time when plantation owners were more honorable and provided well for their workers. Land signified stability, social status, and a certain sense of security that came from subsistence production. Even with this social memory of land, however, the rural workers did not consider land a "right." They were trained by the rural unions to fight for legal rights through juridical means and they were very nervous when MST activists suggested they occupy land that technically belonged to someone else. They wanted land only if, as one settler said, the "government gave it to them without any problems." As one rural worker who received land through his ties to the former plantation explained in 2003, "We all owe what we have today to the movement. I myself, I owe everything to it, I only don't agree with this business of invading land. Who wants to have what is theirs, and then arrive and see it invaded? I have this house here and I leave, and when I get back, it's invaded?"

As the sugarcane crisis deepened, however, rural workers began to join the MST. In Água Preta there were two distinct groups. One included the squatters that took part in the MST-led occupation. The other and larger group was composed of former plantation employees. The squatters joined the movement largely due to the sugarcane crisis and increased difficulties in finding steady work. When MST activists began mobilizing in the region, they jumped at the chance to secure a more stable livelihood. One settler described how she and her husband decided to join the MST: "A man came and asked my husband if he wanted a piece of land, you know? And my husband said that he did, because he lived working for others and paying rent in the city. One day it was here, the next day there, living in the stables because we didn't have a house to live in. It was too much suffering."

The second group of settlers joined the MST after they received land on the settlement. These settlers did not necessarily have to join the MST, but in Água Preta most chose to do so because the movement had become an important political actor in the region. With the crisis of the sugarcane plantations and the breakdown of traditional labor relations, plantation owners left the region and rural workers began to lose both membership and spirit.[25] By the mid-1990s, it was MST activists who were mediating the relationship between settlers and local politicians. In Água Preta, one of the local MST leaders was an agronomist who was asked by the mayor, Eduardo Coutinho (first elected in 1996, re-elected in 2000 and 2004), to serve as technical consultant on the settlements. Coutinho was considered a relatively progressive politician. He was a member of the Brazilian Socialist Party (PSB), the party of Miguel Arraes. Although the MST had close but informal ties at the national level with the left-wing Workers' Party (PT), local political traditions and parties are often privileged on the settlements. This is particularly true in the northeast where patronage politics, referred to *coronelismo* (boss politics), are an enduring legacy of plantation society. As mayor, Coutinho appeared to support agrarian reform in Água Preta, and he maintained a close connection to the settlements through Antonio, the agronomist. Antonio had grown up in Água Preta but moved to Bahia in his early twenties to manage a cattle farm. There he learned about the MST. Upon his return to Água Preta in 1996, he purchased a farm plot on Flora (a practice frowned upon by INCRA, the National Institute for Colonization and Agrarian Reform, though hardly uncommon in the northeast). Antonio joined the MST as a settler, and in consultation with the mayor's office and MST leaders, was appointed to serve as an agronomist for several settlements in the region.

As an agronomist and MST activist, Antonio had considerable influence in the settlements and with the local mayor. On different occasions he negotiated with the mayor for donations of medical supplies; access to bus transportation for MST contingents traveling to the state capital, Recife; and food provisions for an MST encampment on the side of the road near the Água Preta hospital. In 2000, the mayor provided a bus for settlers who wanted to attend the

MST's national Congress in Brasília. As one MST activist said, "At that time, we never needed to go to the INCRA offices in Recife for a mobilization, for transportation, or even for food. The mayor always went to our meetings, and gave speeches, he participated in everything. Whenever settlers affiliated with the MST needed the mayor's office, the doors were open." Former plantation residents who gained a settlement plot often joined the MST to ride on the coattails of its political clout. In an exchange reminiscent of their plantation days, these settlers regularly brought Antonio fresh bundles of manioc and helped maintain his plot of land.

When Flora was first created in 1996, there were considerable tensions between the MST squatters and the previous residents. The latter group did not immediately join the MST. The landless group who occupied the plantation was in fact much poorer than the former plantation employees. The MST squatters were generally of a lower status, working in the sugarcane industry's most insecure positions as undocumented laborers (*clandestinos*) on daily or seasonal contracts. They had few connections in Água Preta and little capital to begin planting on their land. By contrast, many of the previous residents had lived in the municipality all their lives. They knew the settlement well and could begin clearing land for settlement immediately. Despite their differences, the two groups of settlers began to cooperate over political matters soon after the settlement was formed.

Every land reform settlement in the country is required by INCRA to form an association and convene the settlers regularly to conduct settlement business. The associations are led by an elected group of representatives: a president, vice president, treasurer, and three secretaries. In Flora's first internal election the previous residents helped select their former boss's son as president of their new association, who along with his mother had received a parcel of land from INCRA. The move was reminiscent in many ways of events that had taken place during the formation of the first Peasant League in 1955. Many of the former plantation residents, however, felt like they had been tricked, and subsequently formed a coalition with the MST squatters to oust the young plantation boss. After six months, they succeeded in electing a new association president.[26] The need to cooperate over settlement politics encouraged the former residents to align themselves with the MST. As one settler put it, "We saw that it wasn't going to go well because if we all individually asked for little things from INCRA, we would end up with nothing." Some of the former residents were ambivalent about becoming MST members. But they joined the movement nonetheless because it was the one organization that represented the settlement as a whole. As one settler who had been an administrator on the plantation said when asked if he was part of the movement:

SETTLER (S): I am now part of the movement because truly I live in the settlement and in any case I have to be a member because, whether I want to or not, we need to arrange things within the movement.

RESEARCHER (R): And do you pay the movement something?

S: They [the people from the movement] charge a fee, and so I paid some fees and now we are waiting for them to tell us what we need to pay next.

R: How was it decided that you would pay?

S: The president of the association decided. He got together with the agricultural extension agents (who were all MST activists) to make some charges that would be put into practice with the settlers.

R: Have you ever spoken with the militants, the leaders of the MST?

S: Until now I have never been close to the MST leaders because I truly don't know them well, no. I only speak with the agronomists who have to talk with them. But I am not very close to these MST leaders, no. I hardly know them.

R: Do you support the MST?

S: I support the MST.

R: Have you participated in some mobilization, a march, or something like that?

S: Until now not that I know of.

R: Does the movement help you today?

S: No, up to this point, the movement hasn't helped me with anything.

By 1999, when field research for this chapter was conducted, all of Flora's settlers considered themselves to be MST members and were treated as such by MST activists, the local mayor, and INCRA officials. The settlements in Água Preta were well-organized and enthusiastically represented by a handful of veteran MST organizers, including Antonio. The MST's flag waved proudly from the settlement *agrovila* (housing compound) and was clearly visible from the nearby road. These MST members perceived their membership in the movement in ways that differed significantly from their counterparts in southern Brazil: they were not small farmers before winning land and they had little experience with diversified family farming, but the MST considered them as important to their mobilization efforts as the landless peasants.

Once on the settlement, however, the history of plantation life would continue to shape the relationship between the movement and the two groups of settlers. Prior to joining the movement, MST organizers and state agents had been quite conscious of their different origins. But once on the settlements all members began to be treated alike. The underlying tensions, due to the contradiction between old and new spatial imaginaries, would subsequently influence the MST's political trajectory in the sugarcane region.

Three years after the sugarcane industry hit bottom, prices began to revive again. After falling for six straight years, a drop in sugarcane production in India and Cuba led to a price increase in 2000 and 2001. Continued deregulation of the industry also allowed a greater percentage of production to be exported. Moreover, a drought in southern Brazil in 2001 increased demand for sugarcane from the northeast region. The price rise prompted Pernambuco's distilleries in the region to start planting and processing sugarcane again.

By 2003, most of the settlers in Água Preta had covered their land with sugarcane. They had weathered the sugarcane crisis by planting subsistence crops on their land and receiving money from the government, both in the form of investment credit and short-term welfare assistance. Although they had participated actively in discussions about alternative crops to sugarcane, the new higher prices offered the lure of greater profits. By 2003, all of the Flora settlers had abandoned the MST. Three people, including two former MST squatters, had sold their land. Yet all of the others remained in place. There are many reasons why the MST was unable to retain its members during the new sugarcane surge. The two most important factors relate to agricultural production policies and local politics.

When MST leaders first began mobilizing in the sugarcane region, one of their priorities was to convince people that land was (and should be) the key element for both production and social reproduction. The former rural workers (MST squatters and residents alike) were discouraged from planting large-scale commodity crops, especially sugarcane. Indeed, sugarcane was equated with the evils of colonization, exploitation, and poverty. Agronomists affiliated with the MST encouraged the settlers to move into subsistence garden crops, high-value fruits for sale on local markets, and small-scale livestock production.

These production plans were conveyed to the settlers through a credit program called PROCERA (the Special Credit Program for Agrarian Reform), established and funded by the federal government. PROCERA is a special credit program for all agrarian reform settlers in the country. It offers annual production loans (*custeio*), as well as a one-time investment loan.[27] Both loans are administered by the Bank of Brazil. Although the exact funding amount varied, in 1999 settlers were entitled to an annual loan of up to R$2,000 (close to US$1,000 at the time) as well as a one-time investment loan of up to R$7,500 (roughly US$3,750). The settlers were only obliged to repay half of all their subsidized loans.[28]

In accordance with government specifications, these loans for production and investment were not given directly to the settlers. "Projects" (as they were called) for both production and investment were drawn up in conjunction with a trifecta of experts, including state agrarian reform officials, lending agents with the Bank of Brazil, and MST-affiliated agricultural extension agents such as Antonio.

In every region of the country, these projects focused on a few key crops that land reform settlers could produce for the market. Government and bank officials were particularly concerned with the profitability of the projects, so as to ensure proper repayment of the loan. In Pernambuco's sugarcane region, the annual production projects were slated for banana and coconut crops while the investment projects were to be used for raising cattle. For the annual production loan in 1999, the settlers in Água Preta were required to plant at least 200 banana trees, following specific recommendations in terms of fertilizer and pesticide use. For the longer-term investment credit, expected to arrive in 2000, they were required to fence in their land, plant pasture, and purchase between three and six cows. Local MST leaders hoped to secure further funding through the state-run Northeast Bank to establish a fruit-processing plant that would make, among other things, the region's popular banana candies.

Bank of Brazil, INCRA, and MST representatives held different priorities in relation to these projects. The bank sought to ensure repayment. INCRA hoped to foster conditions that would reduce future dependency on the government. The MST tried to obtain as much credit as possible for its settlers to succeed on the land. In all cases, however, production decisions were based on the ability of the settlers to generate income from their family farms. For the settlers, this included a serious flaw: the projects measured income in terms of farm sales rather than in wages, as was the custom when they worked on the plantations. The settlers argued that the detailed calculations of their production costs and benefits had not taken into account their labor cost. Time settlers would spend building fences, planting pasture, tending to the bananas and coconut trees, among other things, was not accounted for by the experts who assumed the settlers were now family farmers, not wage earners. One settlement president described the bank's calculations in the following terms: "Look, the bank has already drawn up the project guidelines, but if you divide things up like this, we are going to work for free. We are going to plant pasture to feed the cows for free. We are going to do a lot of things for free around here."

To ensure compliance with the project, agronomists in Água Preta were required to fill out project evaluations for each individual settler. As Antonio insisted at a settlement meeting, "Now more than ever we need to do our things right. We have an extension agent, we have an agronomist, we have assistance, and so we need to make sure that from now on things happen in a natural yet competent way. We have to produce this banana so that in the year 2000 we can pay the bank back without having to sell our land."

The settlers themselves were not consulted about the formulation of the production projects. Logistical and cultural difficulties encouraged a centralized decision-making process. It was difficult to physically reach all of the settlers and even harder to envision them agreeing on an alternative crop to sugarcane. At the same time, it was widely believed that plantation workers lacked the experience to establish their own production agendas on the model of the small, family farm. Asked if the settlers had been consulted about the investment project, the president of the settlement responded, "No, the boys from the movement said: 'we're going to do a project.' And we said 'ok.' And they said 'we are going to do a project to plant coconut trees and we are going to do a project with cows.' And so other people said, 'I don't want cows, I want sheep.' Every person wanted a different thing, and afterwards they said to us that it was going to be coconuts and cows, and that was it."

In fact, the PROCERA projects were predicated on removing the settlers from the one area in which they could reasonably claim agricultural expertise: sugarcane production. MST leaders insisted that the settlers not plant sugarcane on their land, urging the settlers to plant bananas in places that were once privileged for sugarcane. At settlement meetings, MST leaders described the long, dark history of sugarcane in the region and associated it with legacies of inequality, labor exploitation, and environmental damage. Leaving sugarcane behind, they argued, would be a true sign that they have become both family farmers and MST members. Planting sugarcane, then, came to be seen as a sign of feeble political consciousness and an act of defiance to the movement. As one MST leader said in 2003, "The rebellious settlements, who do not obey and follow our instructions, are the ones that plant sugarcane. They have sugarcane in their heads. They think that sugarcane is the future, that sugarcane makes money, although in reality we know that sugarcane is a monoculture, and doesn't have a future. It's just a waste, just work. There are other crops that we could plant instead."

Agricultural production, then, became a zero-sum issue, with MST leaders insisting that things had to be one way or the other: either sugarcane or subsistence and alternative crops. Consequently, for the settlers, planting sugarcane meant one was rejecting the movement. As a settlement president explained, "We used to plant sugarcane here because that's what did well. But since the movement doesn't want us to plant it, well, it is a huge fight. I have sugarcane here in the front of my house, and it's a huge fight whenever people from the movement come. But I spent two years just losing money, I lost it all. And then I said, 'I'm done.' So we started planting sugarcane."

The movement faced powerful traditions and legacies in its uphill effort to convince the settlers to plant alternative crops. Most of the settlers had grown up in the sugarcane region and spoke admiringly of sugarcane as a "good crop" that was "exported all over the world as sugar." Their resistance to planting banana trees went beyond a mere dependence on sugarcane. Their thoughts about this were also affected by the nature and social meaning of the banana trees themselves. As plantation workers, they were rarely allowed to plant bananas.

If anything, plantation owners would only allow them to grow annual subsistence crops like manioc and corn. The proprietors, after all, feared that perennial crops could be used to prove a squatter had rights to that land.[29] One of the settlers clarified the point by noting that his former plantation boss, "never gave anyone land to plant. He even knocked down all the trees that we planted . . . because he thought the workers would take over his land." Another worker described his situation this way: "We were free to plant food crops. The mill owner just didn't want us to plant bananas. If a person planted bananas, the administrator would pull them up. So we had to plant them in secret."

The lack of experience in planting bananas, and the government's meager support with technical assistance, despite the promise to send plenty of extension agents to all the settlements, led the settlers to plant the banana trees improperly, in overcrowded rows, without space for the roots to spread. Asked if he had received instructions from any extension agents, one of the settlers queried back, "To show me how to plant? No, not yet. They tell us to plant bananas and not sugarcane. But they haven't come here to explain to us how to work on the land. Not yet."

The difficulties in carrying out the new production plans, coupled with the rise in sugarcane prices, prompted most settlers to pull up their banana trees and plant sugarcane instead. Contracts were for delivery to local sugar mills, and many settlers found work on neighboring plantations for R$7 a day (approximately US$2.40 in 2003).[30] The MST's depiction of sugarcane in zero-sum terms prompted the settlers to leave the movement when they began planting sugarcane. They did not necessarily leave the MST because they wanted to, but because they believed that planting cane excluded them de facto from the movement.

New Local Developments: MST Leaders and Municipal Politics

At the same time, the settlers left the MST because there was a shift in political leadership and they no longer felt adequately represented by the movement activists. In 2000, Antonio began spending more time away from the settlements. He worked hard on the mayor's reelection campaign, visiting all of the local settlements and advocating for the mayor under the banner of the MST. When the mayor easily won reelection, Antonio left the movement to begin working as the mayor's right-hand man. This change led to a more general shift in leadership when a new regional leader, Eduardo, was brought in to replace Antonio.

The new regional MST leader was an enthusiastic and idealistic young man. Deeply committed to the movement, Eduardo came to Água Preta with different ideas about how to serve as an MST leader. He looked to national MST leaders to provide guidelines on what to do in the sugarcane region. Movement activists, he claimed, ought to move around regularly or they would become too familiar with local norms and customs to understand the organization's problems in a more objective way.

Eduardo tried to teach the settlers a new "way of doing politics," encouraging them to leave behind the paternalistic, "relational politics" of the old plantation era. In his view, the settlers needed to embrace the more modern notion of universal citizenship rights, including the rights to basic political freedoms and sustainable livelihoods to which all Brazilians were entitled. Previous regional MST activists, he argued, had become mired in plantation politics, leading the settlers to confuse movement leaders with their former patrons.[31] The former leaders, he said, were "always dominating discussions and acting like the old plantation bosses."

The settlers' understanding of their rights, however, was grounded on traditional clientelistic views rather than the universalist notions of human rights and citizenship. Their conceptions of rights called for the presence of a benevolent patron, who would offer protection and assistance in times of need. These dissonant views led the settlers to perceive Eduardo as a politically incompetent leader, while praising Antonio as a powerful leader. Eduardo was especially criticized by settlers for not providing the resources the settlers had come to expect from the movement, a charge affected in large part by the Cardoso government's budget cuts for agrarian reform.

Adding to all this, the new MST leader violated local political norms by supporting an MST candidate for state deputy in the local 2002 elections over the mayor's son who was also a contender. Eduardo and other MST leaders stressed that the settlers had every right to vote their conscience. But in the view of many settlers, the MST's decision to withhold support for the mayor's son reduced the municipal government's assistance to their community. Most Flora residents saw this as a mistake. One of them described the changes that had taken place under the new MST leader as follows.

SETTLER (S): With the former MST leader in the sugarcane region, everything worked differently. At times we needed some medicine and we always went to look for it in other settlements. We always had medicine, we always had a car, everything happened in a different way. Now with this new leader, there's just his car and the other leader's motorcycle. . . .

RESEARCHER (R): And the other leader, does she come here to help?

S: No, she just comes to talk. She's the MST coordinator here. There are some people who need things, they need a food basket, a bit of medicine, and so, whether you think it's good or bad, you have to go and ask the mayor. Because the MST won't take care of these things now! This new leader has done nothing. By the end of the winter there were three people in the settlement going through a terrible crisis.

R: What sort of crisis?

S: They didn't have the means to survive, and so they came looking for me, and I went to the mayor's office and I talked to a young woman there and I got together three food baskets. But the movement . . . well, I talked to the two MST leaders and I told them how it was with these people (who were going through a crisis) but they didn't do anything for them. And that's why we want to organize ourselves, call a meeting and get out of the movement.

R: How strange! When I was here before the movement was so strong.

S: Yes, it was, when you were here before, no one needed food. There was one time when we had more than 200 food baskets! (Arranged for by Antonio.) And so if anyone needed anything, we would take out some food and give it to them. The leader at that time said: if you need anything, just have to ask. . . . In those days there was more incentive to be part of the movement. Now there is no incentive.

The MST's 2001 leadership change, and the negative impact it had on the settler's affiliation to the movement, highlights the personal nature of local politics in this and other parts of Brazil. It also underscores the importance of culture in framing the struggle for social change. Antonio and other local leaders reproduced a style of leadership that made sense to the settlers. They knew how to play the local political game while introducing new forms of collective organization. Dissatisfied with their new leaders and their inability to provide material assistance, the settlers drew on a strategy quite common in situations of conflict with the plantation owner: they simply left. As one of the settlers that had taken part of the land occupation and encampment put it, "I decided to get out of the movement because it wasn't working for me. All this running around and I was getting nothing for myself. . . . I prefer to be working on my farm plot, struggling at my own pace, than to be at all those meetings."

Conclusion

The path that the settlers in Água Preta took from their successful mobilization in September 1999 to their withdrawal from the movement four years later was a gradual one. It was not predetermined by the structural conditions of the settlers' history as plantation workers, nor was it a product of individual interests triumphing over the good of the collective. Instead, it was shaped by conjunctural events and processes perceived through subjective spatial imaginaries produced in the sugarcane plantations.

As plantation workers, the settlers possessed a social memory of the value of land, and most were grateful for the opportunity to own a farm plot. They built houses on their land, planted fruit trees, flowers, and vegetables, and, for a while, were active partners of the MST project. Even as the settlers argued with MST leaders over what crops to plant, they jealously guarded their new identity as settlers because access to land signified a "place in the world." As landowners they had more status in the community and more stability in their own lives. Freed from the *cativeiro* (captivity) of the plantation, they were masters of their own land, and on those nine hectares they did as they pleased. As one settler who had been born on a former plantation in Água Preta said, "In my opinion, things are better now because here on the settlement there isn't anyone who orders you around. We do what we want and whatever you have on your land is yours. Now we plant what we want and no one sticks their nose in." Access to land brought with it some certainty about the future, a certainty that had been denied to plantation workers whose most effective form of resistance was to exit and migrate from one sugar mill to the next. In the words of one worker, "I don't live all that well now, but compared to the life that I used to have, I am better off than when I lived knocking about the world."

The settlers' historical relationship to the land, however, contradicted certain idealized notions of peasant production. Though they planted their fruits and vegetables, they vigorously defended their attachment to sugarcane production. Their right to own land was framed by cultural values developed in the context of their life as plantation workers. For the settlers, land was not just a means of production but a way of improving one's political standing, and consequently, uplifting one's economic position. Implicitly, then, the settlers rejected a key assumption held by MST leaders and government officials, namely, that owning a small plot of land was synonymous with becoming a peasant.

The history of mobilization in the sugarcane town of Água Preta is clearly a specific one, but it should not be read as a regional exception. It is a story of how material histories shape particular renderings of space. These different spatial imaginaries affect who joins the movement and how they participate in it. Amorim may be right in asserting that the search for land unified people around Brazil. But as we have seen here, "the land" means different things to different people and, as a result, membership in the MST also looks different in different places.

The lesson for the study of social mobilization more broadly is that regardless of how coherent and unified a movement appears individual subjectivities rarely conform. Movements gain ideological and discursive coherence by formulating simple and powerful foundational statements, what Jeffrey Rubin calls "strategic essentialisms,"[32] which do important political work. Scholarly and journalistic analyses frequently accept these statements at face value and in doing so tend to treat social movements as unified entities. In the case of the MST, leaders speak for the movement as a whole, while public actions such as demonstrations and land occupations are assumed to signify broadly shared intentions. The important task of social movement analysis is to understand the effect of strategic essentialisms on the ground, in movement experiences, and in people's lives.

Notes

1. Branford and Rocha (2002: 21).
2. Branford and Rocha (2002: 44).
3. There is extensive literature on the distinction between the peasantry and rural workers as political groups in the sugarcane region. For a discussion of mobilization among rural workers, see Pereira (1997) and Andrade (1980). For a presentation of the peasantry's political battles, particularly the formation of the Peasant Leagues, see Forman (1975) and Julião (1972).
4. Unless stated otherwise, all direct quotes are from field research conducted by the author in 1998–99, 2001, and 2003. Pseudonyms are used for the names of settlements and settlers because the interviews dealt with sensitive subjects of movement allegiance and historical memories.
5. Andrade and Andrade (2001).
6. The data are from the mayor's office, 2001.
7. As part of my field research in Brazil, I interviewed all of the families on this settlement, along with close to 200 MST settlers in Santa Catarina and Pernambuco. In addition, I met with many MST leaders, local politicians, and small farmers living near the settlements, as well as agrarian reform agents and agricultural day laborers living in urban peripheries. The interviews in Água Preta varied in style, but most included an extensive tour of the settler's property, lunch, and a two- to three-hour open-ended interview.
8. Muniz (2004).
9. Wolford (2003a).
10. A considerable literature deals with the economic, political, and social conditions on sugarcane plantations in the northeast, given its status as the "cradle of civilization" in Brazil. For a history of colonial sugarcane production, see Schwartz (1985). On the transition from old-fashioned mills to modern sugarcane factories, see the nostalgic sociology of Freyre (1978). For a history of the transition from slavery to free labor, see Eisenberg (1974) and Galloway (1989). For an analysis of the sugarcane region as a product of elite discourse, see Muniz (2004).
11. Schwartz (1985).
12. Andrade (1988), Eisenberg (1974), and Sigaud (1979).
13. Andrade (2001), Freyre (1978), and Sigaud (2004).
14. This relationship between subsistence production and market conditions seems to have characterized both the colonial and postcolonial period. Although there were clearly variations from mill to mill, the relationship between planter and worker (whether slave or free) was probably more "human" when market conditions were less favorable; see Eisenberg (1974). The best discussion of the mutual relationship between subsistence and export production is in Schwartz (1992: 65–103). Also see Barickman (1994) and Eisenberg (1974).
15. Pereira (1997).
16. According to Maybury-Lewis, between 1950 and 1960 the mill owners cut their permanent labor force in half (1994: 65).
17. Fernandes (2000: 110) and Branford and Rocha (2002: 44). Some of the squatters were eventually offered land, but in a region far from the coast, where it was difficult to plant without adequate government support.
18. Lima and Silva (1995).
19. Lins et al. (1996: 2).

20. MEPF (1998: 1).
21. See Cazella (1992) and Paulilo (1996).
22. Wright and Wolford (2003: 45–47).
23. Swidler (1986).
24. Wolford (2003a).
25. Rosa (2003).
26. The settlers joined again soon thereafter to organize a public demonstration to have the former plantation boss removed from his beautiful house (the *Casa Grande*) on the settlement. This mobilization, however, failed because the former boss had close ties to local judges who dismissed the MST's requests to have the house expropriated.
27. PROCERA was created in 1986 but only became effective in 1993. It was merged into the broader funding program for small family farmers in 2001, a decision contested at the time by the MST.
28. The annual loans were to be paid back at the end of each year, at which time the settlers would be eligible for new short-term loans. The investment loan was to be paid back over seven years, with a two-year grace period and low interest rates.
29. The constitutional definition of *direito de posse*, or right of possession, allowed a person who was producing on land the possibility of a legal claim to the land, or *revindicação de posse*. This legal tool derived from the colonial period when the Portuguese monarchy attempted to encourage colonization and proper land use; see Wright (2001) and Andrade (1988). One well-documented effect of the law has been to push landowners to move tenants around frequently in an attempt to ensure they would not be able to claim rights to the land; see Stolcke (1988).
30. Most of the settlers were working in the mill, Barra D'Ouro, which was paying more than the going wage of R$5 (close to US$1.70) per day.
31. Notes from an MST regional meeting, in the municipality of Belem de Maria, Pernambuco, February 17, 2003.
32. Rubin (2004).

PART IV

The MST, Politics, and Society in Brazil

13 Working with Governments
The MST's Experience with the Cardoso and Lula Administrations

Since its emergence in the late 1970s, the Landless Rural Workers Movement (MST) has ridden a roller coaster in its relationship with the authorities, with marked highs and lows. With hindsight, the 1980s can be seen as a period of expansion, not just for the MST, but for many social movements. The MST was often in conflict with the authorities but this did not prevent it from growing rapidly and spreading all over the country.[1] There was a climate of optimism among the militants, particularly when they began to work more closely with the Workers' Party (PT), the left-wing party set up by Luis Inácio Lula da Silva and other dissident trade unionists in the early 1980s. Many MST activists joined the PT and campaigned tirelessly for the party in the 1989 presidential elections when, after a slow start, Lula gained momentum in the last few weeks and seemed to many of his supporters to be heading for victory.

Lula's defeat left the MST reeling. "We were badly hurt," said João Pedro Stédile, the MST's main strategist. "Lula's defeat was a political defeat for mass movements in Brazil, after a ten-year period of growth. It affected us along with the rest. We were in our adolescence. We were still a weak movement and we felt as if we'd been orphaned."[2] Although the new president, Fernando Collor de Mello, had presented himself during the electoral campaign as the defender of the *descamisados* (the shirtless ones), he came from a wealthy family in the northeast state of Alagoas and his commitment was with the land-owning oligarchy. His government refused even to talk to MST leaders and it unleashed a violent campaign against the movement, cutting off funds for agrarian reform and turning a blind eye on the landowners' efforts to evict them from their camps with the use of illegal militias. MST activists confessed later that for a period they were even worried that the movement might not survive.

After millions of Brazilians had taken part in street protests, President Collor was forced to resign in late December 1992, just hours before he would have been impeached for corruption. It was a great relief to the MST, particularly because Vice President Itamar Franco, who replaced him, was more sympathetic toward the movement. But Itamar Franco was only an interlude. A new phase for the MST—and for Brazil as a whole—began in January 1994, when Fernando Henrique Cardoso, a former left-leaning sociologist, took over as president. Unlike Itamar Franco, he was in for the long haul.

In his electoral campaign Cardoso had promised to settle 280,000 landless families on the land but in his first two years in office he did little. He had other priorities. A late—but no less fervent—convert to neoliberalism, he believed that Brazil should dismantle trade barriers and allow the sharp shock of competition to shake up the agricultural sector, even if thousands of farmers were driven out of business by the flood of cheap imported food. Raul Jungmann, who Cardoso was later to appoint as his minister of agrarian reform, recalled a conversation he held with the president in 1995. "We decided that there was little point in trying to intervene in the process of agricultural modernization, which was destroying so many jobs," he said. "In the developed, capitalist world, the towns are full and the countryside is empty. We thought there was simply no point in trying to keep rural families in the countryside. We weren't as arrogant as to think we could reverse a tendency of capitalism."[3]

However, Cardoso—and his minister-in-waiting—were soon to change their minds. The main reason for this shift was growing MST mobilization. Aware that Cardoso considered peasant farming to be a moribund economic activity that would be swept away by agribusiness, the movement decided to fight to prove the president wrong. As thousands of small-scale farmers were losing their livelihoods, the movement found it easy to recruit new members and was able to organize a wave of land occupations and demonstrations. The agronomist Francisco Graziano, at the time a leading Cardoso aide, recalls the atmosphere: "The MST, demanding agrarian reform, had its foot on the accelerator. Thirty years after the defeat of the Peasant Leagues [an influential movement of rural workers in the northeast], sickles and hoes were on the front pages of the newspapers once again."[4]

The situation, which was becoming increasingly tense, erupted on April 17, 1996, when at least nineteen *sem terra* (landless rural workers) were killed in a clash with military policemen in Eldorado dos Carajás in the south of Pará. The state government had sent in the police to break up a group of some 1,500 sem terra families, who were blockading a federal highway after the government had refused to listen to their demand for land. Although accounts differ as to how precisely the bloodshed began, it seems that a military policeman started to shoot, after a deaf-mute MST activist ignored his order to move off the road.

The event—which became known as the Massacre of Eldorado dos Carajás—caused a furor at home and abroad.[5] At first, Cardoso tried to ride out the storm, dismissing the killings as a manifestation of the "archaic" Brazil that he was trying to eradicate but soon the torrent of outrage caused him to reconsider. While trying in the short term to defuse the anger by publicly promising on television to punish the military policemen responsible for the killings, he also realized that he would only prevent such incidents reccurring in the future if he tackled the underlying causes by giving greater priority to agrarian reform. He decided to detach the national land agency, INCRA, from the Ministry of Agriculture, where it had been languishing as a small and largely inoperative unit, and to create a brand new Extraordinary Ministry for Land Policy. Its main responsibility, he said, would be to provide land for the landless. In what at first seemed a bizarre appointment, given Jungmann's known views on the out-dated nature of the peasantry, Cardoso selected him as the new minister.

The paradox was soon explained: Jungmann's primary mission was not to turn the peasantry into an important productive force but to defuse social unrest by settling potentially disruptive landless families onto plots of land in distant regions where their energy would be absorbed in a day-by-day struggle for economic survival. According to Bruno Konder Comparato, Cardoso's advisors worked out that the government could settle 280,000 families on the land in four years and that this would seriously weaken not only the MST but all the other landless movements as well: "The landless movements would lose force, on the one hand, by losing militants, and, on the other, by losing legitimacy among the general public, who would realize that their demands were being met."[6]

Jungmann set about this task with the single-minded determination and energy that were to characterize his years in office. But, far from demobilizing the MST as Jungmann hoped, the land settlement program had the opposite effect: it convinced landless families that they could persuade the government to do what they wanted if they applied pressure. On February 17, 1997, the MST began one of its most ambitious initiatives to date: a National March for Agrarian Reform, Employment and Justice. Leaving from three different corners of Brazil, 1,500 sem terra spent two months marching on foot before reaching Brasília on April 17, the first anniversary of the Eldorado dos Carajás massacre. At first, Jungmann played down the importance of the march, telling Brazil's leading weekly magazine, Veja, "the MST is a numerically small movement. They are bringing 1,500 people to Brasília. Rotary and Lions have far more people."[7] But huge crowds welcomed the march. "It was not just that people flocked in the thousands [actually close to 100,000 at the final demonstration in Brasília] to express support for the movement," said Osvaldo Russo, a former president of INCRA.[8] "It was also the quality of the mobilization. The MST captured the mood of the moment." Expressing themselves in simple direct language, the activists, many of them uneducated, spoke a new language of idealism, optimism, and commitment. Cardoso had no option but to receive the MST leaders in the presidential palace and listen to their demands.

Even though the government publicly welcomed the march, it was privately shocked at the scale of public support. "For the first few years in power, the Cardoso government was not particularly concerned about the growth of the MST," said Osvaldo Russo. "It might even have seen it as an ally in its drive to modernize the old agrarian elite. But the march on Brasília changed all that. The government became scared. For the first time it became worried that the MST might actually overthrow the government. They felt they had to stop it." With hindsight, it is clear that April 1997 was a turning point; one that ushered in another tough period for the movement.

While continuing to instruct INCRA to settle thousands of families on the land in the old way, Jungmann gradually constructed a new strategy. First, he began to develop a new form of agrarian reform, one that was geared to the market. "I am not carrying out the agrarian reform program that the left has dreamed of," he said at the time. "But I am carrying out the only kind that is possible in today's world. To think that a classic program of agrarian reform is possible in today's world is dangerous nonsense."[9] The new scheme, called the *Banco da Terra* (Land Bank), had the support of the World Bank, which was promoting market-oriented land distribution in several other developing nations at this time, including South Africa, Guatemala, and Colombia. The idea was to decentralize the process: groups of landless families would get together in their region, find a landowner who was prepared to sell, and negotiate directly with him. It was only when agreement had been reached in principle that the parties would contact the Bank of Brazil for a loan. The families would be given a three-year grace period but after that would be expected to pay back the loan, plus interest, over seventeen years. They were expected to fill market niches that were of no interest to the big capitalist farmers, usually because they were too labor intensive.[10]

The scheme was controversial. The MST leaders were opposed to it from the beginning, largely because it weakened the movement politically. One of the MST's great strengths has always been its ability to put pressure on the federal government by mobilizing thousands of activists. If the federal government were to be marginalized from the process, then the MST would lose its central target. But the MST was not alone in its criticisms. Other organizations, such as the National Confederation of Agricultural Workers (CONTAG), attacked the scheme for putting land beyond the reach of the vast majority of landless families by insisting that the families pay the market price for their plots. Although they said that the program might be useful for a small group of rural families, particularly small landholders wishing to purchase an additional plot, they, like the MST, were opposed to it becoming the dominant form of access to the land.

In the meantime, the government intensified its political attack on the MST. In early 2000 the movement began a new phase, in which it attempted to broaden its struggle to other sectors of society. After a wave of land occupations in April, about 5,000 sem terra occupied public buildings in fourteen state capitals and another 25,000 took part in demonstrations all over the country. These actions occurred simultaneously on what was, at the time, the most comprehensive and best-coordinated day of action ever organized by the movement. Most of the state governors reacted angrily to the actions, particularly to the occupation of state offices. The toughest response came from Jaime Lerner, the governor of Paraná, who ordered 800 policemen to stop the MST activists who were heading for the state capital, Curitiba, in forty buses. When the unarmed activists got out of the buses, they clashed with the police; about fifty people were injured, and one sem terra, a thirty-eight-year-old man, was killed.

Cardoso reacted furiously to the MST's actions. He said the MST had "overstepped the limits of democracy" and blamed the movement for the death of its activist, saying that this should be "a warning to all those who have opted for provocation and for disrespect for democracy and citizenship."[11] Admitting that he had been taken by surprise by the MST's actions, he held emergency talks with Jungmann and then announced what became known as "the anti-MST package." In a determined attempt to deprive the MST of its main tactic—land occupation—the president announced new regulations by which INCRA would be unable for two years to expropriate an estate invaded by the MST; the limit was to be increased to five years if the estate was invaded for a second time (as frequently happened after evictions). The president also gave the police and security forces a bigger role in dealing with the MST.

In what clearly was a coordinated offensive, the right-wing press and media ran a series of stories alleging corruption or financial irregularities on MST settlements. On the back of these reports, the government felt able to launch an extensive investigation into the movement's finances. For some time Jungmann had been unhappy with the arrangement by which MST settlements benefited from Lumiar, a technical assistance project set up by INCRA. Although INCRA paid the wages of the agronomists, the settlements had won the right to select the agronomists, saying that they could only work with people who broadly supported the movement. Jungmann now accused these agronomists of being involved in financial irregularities and summarily sacked all 1,200 of them, causing severe problems for the settlements. He said that in the future local governments, many of which were known to be hostile to the MST, would select the agronomists.

The restructuring of Lumiar was only the beginning. In what was to prove a much more damaging policy, Jungmann cut off most financial support. Under the terms of the country's agrarian reform legislation prior to the Banco da Terra, the state-owned Bank of Brazil had supplied settlers with subsidized farm credit. The system was far from perfect, for the money was insufficient and often arrived late, but it was absolutely essential for the survival of the settlements. Jungmann decided that the bank would no longer make bulk payments to settlements or cooperatives for them to distribute to their members but would distribute the loans directly to individual farmers. The sudden change caused severe disruptions. Many poorly educated settlers found it extremely difficult to wend their way through the bank bureaucracy. Others for unexplained reasons were declared ineligible.

So the Cardoso years brought mixed results for the MST. During the first administration (1995–98) the government settled 260,000 families on eight million hectares of land. As Jungmann frequently said, it was the biggest program of agrarian reform ever carried out in Brazil. But the program had serious shortcomings: most of the families were settled on marginal land in isolated regions of the country,[12] and, particularly after the march in April 1997, families were provided with vastly inadequate financial and technical support. In his second administration (1999–2002) Cardoso changed track: he tried unsuccessfully to promote market-oriented agrarian reform, and he attempted deliberately to weaken the MST through both an orchestrated press campaign and severe reductions in financial support. Toward the end of Cardoso's second term, the previous Cardoso aide, Francisco Graziano, angrily commented: "Brazil has produced the largest—and the worst—program of agrarian reform in the world."[13]

This all created a very difficult situation for the MST in 2001 and 2002. Many families said that they had not experienced such problems since the Collor government in 1990 and 1991. It was partly for this reason that so many MST families reacted with such delight when Lula won the presidential election in October 2002. Finally Brazil would be governed by a man who knew what it was like to be poor.

The Lula Government and the MST

Since its founding in the early 1980s, the PT repeatedly promised that, once it gained power, it would carry out a far-reaching program of agrarian reform. In its origins the PT was undoubtedly an urban party, set up by industrial workers to offer a radical alternative to the inherently conservative programs being proposed by other political parties that were being formed as the military regime lost momentum and new political space opened up. Yet from the outset the PT strongly identified with the rural poor, particularly Brazil's four million landless families. Indeed, few who have listened to Lula talking about the rural poor can doubt his personal commitment to bettering their lot. Speaking just before the election in 2002 at a rally in Fortaleza, the capital of Ceará, one of the poorest states in the northeast, Lula said with tears in his eyes:

> When I arrived, several men and women came up to me, crying and saying that I am their last hope. I know that I cannot betray the dreams of millions

and millions of Brazilians who are backing me. Any other President of the Republic can be elected and not do anything. The Brazilian people are used to this. But I don't have that right, for there are people in the crowd who have been supporting me for 10, 20, 30 years.[14]

There were few contacts between the MST and the PT during most of the 1980s, as both struggled to establish themselves at a regional level. In some ways, this was not surprising, for the PT was created in São Paulo, while the MST emerged in the southern states of Rio Grande do Sul, Santa Catarina, and Paraná about 1,000 kilometers to the south. At key moments in the MST's struggle for survival, PT politicians expressed solidarity, often at considerable personal risk, but these were largely individual—rather than organizational—gestures.

In the 1990s contacts increased as the PT sought to gain the MST's support in its bid to win municipal, state, and national elections. The meetings were not always amicable. Some PT activists, particularly urban trade unionists, saw the MST as a very junior partner that only represented the peasantry, which they—like Cardoso and most orthodox economists—tended to see as a "moribund force," that is, a social sector that was fast disappearing with the rapid mechanization of agriculture. The MST leaders resented this attitude and, in turn, were critical of the PT's growing involvement in electoral politics at the expense, they thought, of strengthening the grass roots. Even so, behind the squabbling both organizations recognized that they were allies in a common struggle and sought to help each other's development. At the grass roots, where the ideological differences were often blurred, collaboration went much further. Indeed, many activists were simultaneously members of both organizations. In many regions the MST openly campaigned for the PT and, not infrequently, an MST activist stood as the PT candidate in the local election.

Throughout this period the PT insisted that, even though its strategy for achieving power was different from the MST's, it was equally committed to agrarian reform. The PT's best-known politician—Lula—made three unsuccessful bids at securing the presidency before finally achieving victory in October 2002. In each of the electoral programs he presented to the country, agrarian reform figured as a priority objective. The PT's thinking is clearly expressed in a document published in 2001 by Instituto Cidadania, a think tank set up by Lula. Agrarian reform, it stated, would be a key element in what would be the flagship program of the first Lula government—*Fome Zero* (Zero Hunger):

Land concentration in the country has gained today disastrous proportions: data from the 1995/96 Farming Census shows that . . . farms of 1,000 hectares or more represent less than 1% of the farms but cover 45.1% of the total area. This state of affairs has profound historical causes, reflecting the fact that Brazil, despite this immense land concentration, never carried out a program of agrarian reform sufficient . . . to permit a more equitable use of the land.

The expulsion of the rural population, growing proletarianisation and unemployment, along with the existence of immense, unproductive *latifúndios* [large landed estates], meant that social tension in the countryside was constant. . . . The modernization of agriculture, with increasing mechanization . . . meant that large numbers of rural laborers lost that their jobs, which exacerbated even further Brazil's agrarian problem.

The Zero Hunger Project is a vehement advocate of a massive process of land distribution as a structural development policy.[15]

The MST could not have put it better itself. It is scarcely surprising that, although the movement itself did not openly endorse the Lula candidacy, thousands of MST activists, from both the leadership and the grass roots, campaigned for the PT in the 2002 elections. The MST national executive also quietly agreed to reduce the number of land occupations in the election year, so as not to lay the PT open to accusations of being allied with a "violent" movement that was promoting "illegal actions."

In the run up to the election, Lula travelled all over the country, reaching isolated rural areas. Everywhere he went he spoke with passion and conviction, promising land to the landless. On one occasion he said, "With one flourish of my pen I'm going to give you so much land that you won't be able to occupy it all."[16] As several commentators have observed, he offered people the chance to become part of a big project, a shared dream.

When Lula was elected president on October 27, 2002, MST activists shared in the euphoria that swept across the country. Finally, it seemed that Brazil, one of the most socially unjust countries in the world, was going to change forever. "I think Lula's triumph is a key moment in Brazil's history, like the abolition of slavery or the proclamation of the Republic," commented Francisco de Oliveira, a leading Marxist sociologist. "It may be the point in which we move on from a passive history, in which the country is led by the dominant blocs, to an active history in which the dominated classes have a big impact on state policies."[17]

Landless peasants believed that finally their hour had come. Thousands of families spontaneously moved into provisional camps that the MST and other landless organizations had hurriedly erected on roadsides all across the country. These families hoped that they would be some of the first to benefit when the massive program of agrarian reform, so long promised by Lula, was enacted. "Expectations are so great that it is impossible to stop the families," said Paulo de Oliveira Poleze, an advisor to CONTAG in March 2003. Largely because of this wave of mobilization early in the year, 2003 broke all records. According to the Catholic Church's Pastoral Land Commission (CPT) 124,634 families, involving 623,170 people, took part in land occupations or moved into road camps, more than ever before. At the same time, about half a million people took part in demonstrations for agrarian reform across the country.[18]

Although more cautious than the grassroots activists, MST leaders were infected by the general climate of optimism. On July 2, 2003, an MST delegation met Lula in the presidential palace. Before the TV cameras Lula donned on a red MST cap, saying he regarded agrarian reform as a "historic commitment." Clearly buoyed by the upbeat mood of the meeting, the MST coordinator, João Pedro Stédile, commented afterward: "They [the landowners] lost the elections, but they thought it was just a little game, that they could go on doing whatever they like to protect their privileges. And now they're realising that agrarian reform is for real."[19]

However, change did not come as quickly as the thousands of families hoped. For months, the government prevaricated, saying that it had to put its house in order before it could implement reform. Finally, it called in Plínio de Arruda Sampaio, one of the country's foremost agrarian experts and a founding member of the PT. "In July 2003 Lula had been in power for over six months and no progress at all had been made in delivering agrarian reform," he said. "The MST was putting on pressure and Lula was becoming embarrassed by the delay. He called in Miguel Rossetto [the Minister of Agrarian Development] and asked him urgently to draw up a plan. The minister asked me to coordinate the process and I accepted."[20]

Sampaio set to the task with strong willpower. He signed up a team of eight university lecturers, all experts in agrarian matters, and got authorization for fifty INCRA employees to work with him, providing statistical data. He also made contact with the main rural social movements—the MST, CONTAG, the Movement of Small Farmers (MPA), and several others. "So often the movements are presented with completed programs and then asked to comment on them," said Sampaio. "I wanted them involved from the beginning, helping with the formulation of the program."

Sampaio soon ran into problems. "Many of the people working in the MDA [Ministry of Agrarian Development] didn't believe in what I was doing," he said. "The dominant thinking under the Cardoso government had been that agrarian reform was neither necessary nor possible. The people in charge then had argued that the historic moment for agrarian reform had passed and that capitalism had taken hold of the countryside. They said that the peasantry had no future. They believed that those family farmers who could find themselves a role in agribusiness should do so, and that those that couldn't should either migrate to the cities or be cared for by a government welfare program."

New people were in charge of the MDA but the old thinking was still ingrained in many sectors. During the Cardoso years key leaders in the huge rural trade union, CONTAG, had been won over to this way of thinking and no longer really believed that a progressive agrarian reform was possible, though they paid lip service to the idea. Because Lula had frequently expressed his intention to carry out a radical program of agrarian reform, he was not expected to appoint CONTAG sympathizers to key positions within the MDA. But, as he had shown earlier in his career as a leading trade unionist, Lula was a firm supporter of consensual politics. He believed that people with very different views could work together, if they sat around a table and worked things out. In a way, he is similar to former US president L. B. Johnson who, when he decided to retain J. Edgar Hoover as the head of the FBI, said that he would "rather have him inside the tent pissing out, than outside the tent pissing in." So, while appointing an MST sympathizer to head the MDA, he also brought in CONTAG representatives, and nominated Roberto Rodrigues, an ally of the powerful agribusiness lobby, to head the ministry of agriculture. "CONTAG was given three important secretariats within MDA—Technical Assistance, Rural Credit and Territorial Reorganization," said Sampaio. The idea was to bring the main actors together so that they could hammer out a compromise but, in practice, in the agricultural sector as elsewhere, this did not happen and this policy led to delays and setbacks.

As Sampaio sought to formulate his plan, this latent conflict within the ministry erupted. While the radical faction in the ministry enthusiastically collaborated with Sampaio, those aligned with the old guard obstructed his work. Sampaio forced the minister to intervene. "I had made it clear to him from the very beginning that agrarian reform for me meant the expropriation of the *latifúndio*," he said. "So I demanded that he give me the autonomy to draw up a plan that reflected this commitment." Rossetto ceded and gave Sampaio the authority to draw up a plan outside the control of CONTAG.

Sampaio said that, in drawing up the plan, he considered two aspects to be fundamental: the quantitative and the qualitative. "Quantitatively, we had to draw up a program of agrarian reform that would expropriate enough land from the *latifúndio* to make a real rupture with the old system of land tenure. We needed to change the economic, social and political structures. Agrarian reform means strengthening the peasantry. The process must be strong enough to alter the Gini coefficient [the index for measuring land concentration] by ten or twenty percent." Sammpaio's first challenge was "how to get enough people on the land to cause a rupture, not a total rupture but enough to start off a process." He calculated that they would need to settle one million families over four years. This was clearly an ambitious target, given INCRA's depleted resources, but it was feasible; Brazil had enough underused land and families desperate for a plot of land. Moreover, Sampaio did not set out to disrupt Brazil's neoliberal economic system, which is dependent on exports from the large, modern farms in the hands of the agribusiness elite. "The idea was, in the beginning at least, to create two poles—the peasantry and agribusiness. In time, the peasantry would grow stronger and perhaps challenge agribusiness, but this would be another phase."

Qualitatively, Sampaio was brimming with ideas about how to make peasant farming economically viable. "We could guarantee the families a minimum income through bank loans and the anticipatory purchase of their crops. We worked out that we should fix this income at three-and-a-half minimum wages [equivalent to about US$250 a month] per family. It's not much but it's a beginning. The government buys a lot of food, for school meals, for the armed forces, for hospitals, for the *Fome Zero* program [to combat hunger], which is intended to benefit 10 million people. The government could set up a scheme by which it would guarantee to buy basic foodstuffs—rice, beans, corn—from agrarian reform settlements."

In October 2003 Sampaio presented his plan to the minister. It called for the settling of one million families on the land in four years, from 2004 to 2007. To enable the government to obtain this land at reasonable cost, it recommended, first, that the government should take over all *terra grilada* (land usurped illegally by large landowners), and, second, that it should change the criteria by which a latifúndio is deemed unproductive and thus available for forcible purchase. At the moment, the criteria are set at such a low level that much of the land is being used at well below its full potential and is therefore deemed productive. Sampaio argued that the plan would provide 3.5 million jobs, directly and indirectly, and would thus help solve Brazil's serious social crisis.

Sampaio's research showed that it was perfectly possible for Lula to have adopted his plan, despite the PT's lack of a majority in Congress. "We didn't need to change the Constitution or even to get Congressional approval," he said. "The President could have implemented the plan with presidential decrees. The process would have been made easier with changes in one or two laws but this wasn't necessary." What was required, however, was political will. "The government needed to give agrarian reform great priority and to mobilize the population around the program. We needed popular support for a quick, surgical intervention to get rid of the *latifúndio*." According to Sampaio, the cost was high but not exorbitant. "We calculated that it would have cost about US$1 billion over the three years. For a country that spends US$70 billion in servicing its debt every year, this is affordable."

Even before he officially presented his plan, Sampaio became aware of the resistance he faced. "I thought our program was very reasonable but it frightened a lot of people." The minister called him in on several occasions. "We don't have the money, Plínio, to carry out the kind of program you want. We've got to achieve a high primary surplus on our fiscal account in order to satisfy the IMF [International Monetary Fund] and foreign creditors. And it's not just this. INCRA, the ministry, all the agencies concerned with agrarian reform, are run-down and ill-equipped. We haven't the technical expertise to carry out a program like this. You've got to be realistic."[21] Sampaio replied to the minister, "No one says it'll be easy, but you can't carry out agrarian reform like any other program. You've got to mobilize people. That's the only way to do it. We must put the country on a war footing and tackle problems as they arise." But this response, said Sampaio, just alarmed people more, particularly in INCRA. In the end, the minister congratulated Sampaio and his team for their contribution and sent them away.

Even though the PT government was not actually carrying out agrarian reform, the unprecedented level of mobilization of the rural poor was enough to alarm the landowners. Working closely with the judiciary, with which they have historically maintained very close links, the landowners evicted thousands of families from their lands (or lands they claimed to own). According to the CPT, the courts authorized the eviction of 35,297 families, involving 176,485 individuals, in 2003; it was the highest figure the commission had ever recorded and, it believes, the highest number ever in Brazilian history. Because the landowners generally sent in their private militias to carry out the evictions, the level of violence also increased: seventy-three rural workers were assassinated, one of the highest numbers ever recorded by the commission. The number of arrest warrants issued by the courts also increased by 140%.[22]

Perhaps surprisingly, the alleged "modern" farmers, practicing agribusiness, were as violent as the old oligarchs. The CPT's report shows that in 2003, even though in absolute terms the huge backward state of Pará in the Amazon basin had, by far, the largest number of violent incidents and deaths, it was the so-called modern state of Mato Grosso, where most of Brazil's soybeans are cultivated, that had the highest number of incidents, relative to its size: in 2003 an incredible 41% of this state's rural population was involved in some kind of land conflict, while landowners evicted—or attempted to evict—6% of the rural population. Nine people in this state were assassinated by gunmen sent in by landowners.[23]

After Sampaio had submitted his plan, it seemed that the government was intending to postpone indefinitely the whole idea of agrarian reform, perhaps because of the fear of antagonizing large rural landowners, who were still a powerful force in Congress. However, in November 2003, the popular movements took to the streets. The National Forum for Agrarian Reform and Justice in the Countryside, which brings together the country's largest rural movements and progressive non-governmental organizations (NGOs), held a demonstration in Brasília. More than four thousand rural workers marched through the city and were met by President Lula in the main park. Displaying once again his extraordinary capacity to captivate an audience, Lula won the rural workers over with his affirmation that he would, indeed, carry out agrarian reform, but "a cautious and careful agrarian reform." "If not," he warned, "the poorest will lose out." At the end of his improvised speech, Lula was warmly applauded.[24] He had won time—not a blank check—and knew he had to deliver something. Shortly afterward, Lula announced a watered-down version of Sampaio's original plan: among other changes, it cut the number of families to be settled on the land by the end of 2007 from one million to 550,000 (and even this, as we will see, proved wildly optimistic). As he announced it, he warmly thanked Sampaio for his work—praise that the former PT deputy must have received with irony, if not bitterness.[25]

The PT's Agrarian Policies

When I spoke in July 2004 to Agrarian Reform Minister Rossetto, a member of a Trotskyist faction within the PT, he denied strongly that the main reason for modifying Sampaio's original proposal was budget restraints. "President Lula is passionately committed to the cause of the sem-terra," he said. "Somehow he will find the resources that are needed. The program had to be changed, not because it was too costly, but because it was not realistic, given the present correlation of social, economic and political forces." For all the noise the MST made, he suggested, peasant families and the landless were politically weak, compared with the power of agribusiness and even traditional landowners.[26] Faced with what he saw as structural constraints, Rossetto said he had developed a three-pronged strategy for his ministry: to strengthen family agriculture, to improve the efficiency of existing agrarian reform settlements, and to carry out an effective program of agrarian reform.

Rossetto knew that he could not gain the support of the MST for this program, for relations were strained given the minister's refusal to endorse Sampaio's program. The antagonism was further fueled by personal animosity between Rossetto and João Pedro Stédile, the leading MST ideologue. On one occasion, Stédile, who is notoriously ironic and short-tempered, sneered at Rossetto for being a Troskyst, saying, "and Trotksy only went to the countryside to pick flowers."[27] So the minister sought the support of CONTAG, hoping to create a power base that was independent from the MST.[28]

By late 2004, Rossetto's first two objectives were being partly achieved. During the Cardoso administration many more peasant families had been forced off the land through bad debts than the government had managed to settle on the land through its agrarian reform program. In practice, this had made a mockery of the government's whole program for it meant that overall land concentration had continued to intensify. Rossetto has sought to reverse this trend, pointing out that it made no sense to settle families on the land unless the government gave them conditions to survive on their plots. Time and again in his speeches and his articles he stressed the importance of small-scale family agriculture to the national economy. "Family agriculture is responsible for most of the food that arrives each day on the tables of Brazilian families," he wrote in a Brazilian newspaper. "It is responsible for 84% of the cassava, 67% of the beans, 58% of the pork and poultry, 52% of the cow's milk, 49% of the corn and 31% of the rice, produced in Brazil. Seven out of every ten rural workers are engaged in family agriculture. Almost 40% of Brazil's gross agricultural output comes from family agriculture."[29]

Along with his efforts to increase the profile of family agriculture in the media, Rossetto took action to improve conditions for small farmers. He rapidly increased the volume of resources to family farmers through the National Program for the Strengthening of Family Agriculture (PRONAF), which is the main program of subsidized credit for family farmers. The volume increased from US$1 billion in 2001/2002 to US$1.9 billion in 2003/2004 to US$4.8 billion in 2006/2007. Even though at times PRONAF credit is still being disbursed late, which creates real problems for small farmers who depend on the money to purchase seeds, the government believes that the program is allowing hundreds of thousands of poor rural families, who would otherwise have been overwhelmed by debts, to stay on the land.

I was given an indication of the importance of this program when I went to the opening of a large new pig factory in the north of Mato Grosso in July 2004. The governor of the state, Blairo Maggi, reputedly the world's largest soybean farmer, and scores of other big maize and soybean producers, attended the event. During the celebratory lunch the agribusiness farmers time and again complained that subsidized credit, so abundant in previous years, was in short supply because it was being siphoned off to small farmers. Their complaint was scarcely justified, for they are by far the biggest beneficiaries of this credit, but it indicated that there has been a real change in priorities. Not surprisingly, the farmers expressed particular venom for Lula, "this ill-prepared populist president."

Rossetto's second goal—to improve the efficiency of agrarian reform settlements—was linked to the first. Along with PRONAF loans, which were supplied at particularly advantageous rates of interest, the families in the settlements benefited from other assistance, such as grants for housing and infrastructure installation. Although there were complaints that disbursements have been late, there was widespread recognition that the quality of assistance has improved.

It was in the third objective—agrarian reform—where the minister faced most problems. The revised version of Sampaio's plan, announced in November 2003, was called the National Program of Agrarian Reform (PNRA). It established the following goals to be achieved by the end of Lula's mandate in December 2006: 400,000 landless families to be given land in agrarian reform settlements, 500,000 *posseiros* (squatter families) to be given legal rights to their plots, and 130,000 families to be given rural credit to purchase land. The government retained Sampaio's goal of benefiting one million families and could thus claim to be carrying out a progressive plan, but it had introduced a fundamental change. Sampaio had planned to take over from the latifúndios enough land to settle one million families in four years—the minimum required to achieve his "rupture"—whereas the government planned to settle only 550,000 families in this way. The other actions—the regularization of land titles and the facilitation of land purchase—did not challenge the existing system of land tenure. As it turned out, not even the revised goals were achieved but, even if they had been, the impact of the program would have been very different from what Sampaio had hoped for.

The MST at times accused Rossetto of merely carrying on with the market-orientated policies adopted by the Cardoso government, but this was not true. Unlike Raul Jungmann, Cardoso's minister of agrarian development, Rossetto did not endorse the World Bank's pet project—the market-based land distribution program known as the Banco da Terra.[30] In fact, at the beginning of his administration, Rossetto quietly delivered the coup de grâce to the Banco da Terra program, which even the World Bank had recognized was not working, largely because so few landless families had enough resources to pay the full market price for land. In its place Rossetto endorsed a new scheme, simply called *Crédito Fundiário* (Land Credit), which CONTAG had already developed with World Bank support. It differed from the Banco da Terra in that it recognized that the rural poor need to be helped with subsidized credit if they are to purchase land. In practice, this scheme was used mainly by *minifundistas* (owners of tiny plots) who wish to purchase more land to make their holding economically viable.[31]

Rossetto made it clear that forcible purchase remained the main mechanism for distributing land to the landless and wanted to introduce changes in the way the process worked. "Agrarian reform was not successful in the past because isolated settlements were created, without infrastructure and with very low productive capacity. We don't want to repeat these economic, social and environmental disasters."[32] Rossetto said that, instead, he wanted to concentrate agrarian reform in larger areas so that they could provide each other with support and jointly market their produce.[33]

Despite these worthy plans, the government did not provide Rossetto with enough money to achieve even his modest goals. By the end of 2004, leading officials in the ministry were giving public vent to their exasperation. At the National Conference of Land and Water, held in Brasília and attended by 9,000 rural workers, mainly MST activists, INCRA president Rolf Hackbart made a public complaint: "We've spent all our budget for land purchase. We're broke. We need more resources."[34] And he called on the activists to put pressure on the government: "The more the poorer sectors of society are organized, the greater our strength to demand the kind of public policies we want. The federal budget is very limited. We have to fight for resources." He even openly criticized the government's orthodox economic policies, when he said that Brazil needed "a new economic model."[35]

The Lula government claimed that, despite the chronic shortage of funds, it achieved a "record for agrarian reform: 381,000 rural workers without land were settled during Lula's first presidential term (2003–6)."[36] However, news reports and the MST claimed that the figures had been artificially inflated by including families that had been settled under previous governments or that were living in forest reserves. Almost one-half of the families, they said, were not genuine, new beneficiaries.[37] Whatever the truth behind the numbers game, it is clear that the Lula government failed to deliver the kind of agrarian reform defended so passionately by Plínio Sampaio. Its efforts did not lead to a rupture with the old system of land tenure, which remained as concentrated as ever.

The MST in a Predicament

The first Lula government has been, in an odd way, a difficult period for the MST. There is no doubt that at the beginning of his term the leaders of the MST were excited and optimistic. They did not believe that the government would deliver agrarian reform easily but thought that the installation of a leftist government would change the balance of power within the country so that real change would become possible. In an interview with a university magazine in early 2003, Stédile said,

> Certainly, what we've got now is a change in the correlation of forces. In the previous administration the government was an ally of the *latifúndio*, and the forces in favor of agrarian reform—the MST and the other social movements—struggled against the *latifúndio* and against the government. Now, with a government elected on a program of change, the government will also be combating the *latifúndio*. But change in the correlation of forces does not by itself bring about the kind of real agrarian reform that will reduce land concentration. The rhythm and the scale of agrarian reform will be determined by the capacity of the social movements to organize and to mobilize the rural poor who struggle for agrarian reform.[38]

However, as the months passed and no real change occurred, MST activists began to lose heart. For a while Lula managed through his own personal charisma to defuse the discontent. Despite the outraged reaction of landowners, Lula wore the red MST cap on several occasions when speaking to activists and encouraged them to carry on mobilizing. On one occasion, when he was talking to peasant farmers, he stated, "I want to say to the worker comrades who are here that you shouldn't be afraid of making demands. You shouldn't be intimidated. You must go on demanding what you think it is important to demand."[39] Never before had a president spoken like this to the rural poor, and it was music to their ears.

As it became increasingly clear, though, that the PT government was not delivering the kind of agrarian reform that it wanted; the MST faced a difficult choice. In spite of all the setbacks, the PT government had undoubtedly brought some benefits to the MST: it had not repressed the movement and it had improved conditions for peasant farming. Moreover, agribusiness sectors and the conservative media were persistently calling on the government to repress the movement, which Lula just as persistently was refusing to do. It was evident that any other government led by Brazil's major political parties was likely to deal more harshly with the movement. For this reason, and because the grass roots of the movement still felt affection for Lula, the MST decided not to adopt a position of outright opposition to the government.

Instead, the leaders aligned the movement with the left wing of the PT, which was becoming increasingly exasperated with Lula's insistence on adhering strictly to the neoliberal model, and it began to criticize, not Lula himself, but the policies his government was implementing. In December 2003, Stédile declared, "We can no longer accept that the government says there's no money for agrarian reform. We can't accept that Rossetto is left with a bit of the government's odd change, while the banks are receiving US$30 billion just in debt servicing."[40] At the same time the MST went on working closely with the government, particularly the Ministry of Agrarian Reform. "Dialogue is important," declared MST leader Gilmar Mauro. "We respect the government's autonomy and they respect ours. That's how we operate."[41]

In 2004, Stédile began to analyze quite carefully why the PT government was unable to achieve even the modest goals it had set itself for agrarian reform.

> First of all, the government is not administering adequately the instruments of the state so that the bodies, such as INCRA, that are needed for agrarian reform are not working smoothly. Secondly, there is a macroeconomic contradiction which is paralyzing the process of agrarian reform. The government is carrying on with neoliberalism, which leads to fewer jobs, more income concentration, more subordination to the banks, greater priority to exports. Agrarian reform though goes in the opposite direction. It's a policy for distributing income, for encouraging the local production of food, for generating employment.[42]

So why did Lula decide to carry on with neoliberal policies?

> I don't think Lula is a dishonest person, but he made a bet. He calculated that he could make alliance with the right, including financial capital, and still carry out reforms. But these allies are very strong, so he is now ruling with a highly adverse correlation of forces.

So when could the situation change?

> I personally now think that real agrarian reform will only come about in a new historical moment with the renaissance of mass movements in general, with the renaissance of the Brazilian people. It doesn't depend on the

government, which is very divided, and it doesn't depend just on the MST. It is going to depend on broader changes. So our criticism of the government isn't over their diagnosis. It's over the fact that it is doing very little to change the correlation of forces. It seems as if it thinks it is in charge of a small local government. It accepts things as they are and is just concerned in administering well the budget. The government has lost the political initiative. It hides itself behind reality, saying that the conditions aren't right to do anything. But the art of politics, the art of being a leader in a class struggle, is precisely this: to create conditions so that the impossible becomes possible. To administer the status quo, we don't need left-wing parties. The right is far more efficient.[43]

Plínio de Arruda Sampaio had a similar explanation. "When the PT was created in the late 1970s, it decided on two lines of development: within state institutions, with the objective of winning electoral power, and outside state institutions, with the objective of using direct popular pressure to change the nature of the state." In the early days the second line of action was crucial, he said. However, as the years went by, the option for direct action weakened. "To press for changes in the state, it is necessary to have a strong proletariat and/or a strong peasantry. But in the 1980s and 1990s the proletariat was weakened by massive unemployment, caused first by the debt crisis and then by neo-liberal reforms. And the peasant mobilization, organized by the MST, was in its infancy." In contrast, the PT's growth within the state institutions was very rapid. "The conditions were very favorable for this. The PT offered a new, ethical way forward, a real alternative to the old, corrupt parties." The PT realized that it could actually win power through the electoral route. "The PT leaders were aware that the other 'leg' wasn't developing," said Sampaio. But they reassured themselves. "Once we get into power, we'll reform the state. But, in order to be elected, the PT found that it had to compromise and make alliances with the old parties. Now that it actually has power, it finds that it is bound hand-and-foot, unable to revolutionize the state as it had always intended."[44]

In June and July 2005 a massive corruption scandal engulfed the Lula government. Even though not all the allegations made against leading members of the Lula government were fully substantiated at the time, it became clear that the administration had been involved in some extremely murky political deals. Most left-wing activists lost any remaining hope that Lula might deliver a progressive government. Although at first, it seemed that Lula might be forced out of office, he survived and even managed to get reelected for a second term. His reelection was due, above all, to a bedrock of support for Lula among very poor Brazilians, particularly in the northeast of Brazil, who had benefited from the government's social programs and knew little of—and cared less about—scandals in far-off Brasília.

Despite misgivings among many of its members, the MST campaigned for Lula during the second round of the 2006 elections, although it showed little of the enthusiasm it had displayed during the 2002 elections. The admiration, bordering on adulation, that many core MST activists had once felt for Lula was lost forever. The decision to support Lula was based on political pragmatism. The MST sought to avoid a victory for Geraldo Alckmin (the conservative candidate of Cardoso's Party of Brazilian Social Democracy, PSDB), which would have brought the Right back to power and its policies aimed at criminalizing the MST. Moreover, it sought to protect the new benefits received during the Lula administration, particularly in the realm of education, farming credit, and settlement improvement programs. Unlike previous elections, land reform barely registered in Lula's campaign platform for 2006.

Throughout his first term, Lula was forced to make further concessions to the traditional political parties. Part of the new alignment was an even closer relationship with agribusiness. In early 2007, Lula became a highly enthusiastic advocate of ethanol, even praising Brazil's sugar barons as "national heroes." For the MST, who had long argued that, while millions of Brazilians were living in poverty in the country's shanty towns, huge tracts of land should not be used for the cultivation of agro-based fuels, the message could not have been clearer: agrarian reform was off the political agenda. During its history of close to three decades, the MST has almost always relied on its own organizational capacity to make advances. To the bitter disappointment of many MST activists, the Lula government has proved to be no exception.

Notes

1. For a description of the MST's expansion in the 1980s, see Branford and Rocha (2002).
2. Stédile and Fernandes (1999: 68).
3. Raul Jungmann, interview by the author, Brasília, DF, August 10, 2000.
4. Graziano (1996: 12).
5. A more detailed assessment of the Eldorado dos Carajás massacre can be found in Ondetti, Wambergue, and Afonso (chap. 8, this volume); also see Branford and Rocha (2002: 129–47).
6. Comparato (2000: 64).
7. *Veja*, April 23, 1997, news article quoted in Comparato (2000: 61).
8. Osvaldo Russo, interview by the author, Brasília, DF, August 12, 2000.
9. Raul Jungmann, interview by the author, Brasília, DF, August 10, 2000.
10. Branford and Rocha (2002: 191).
11. Folha de São Paulo (2000a), Franca (2000), and Folha de São Paulo (2000b).
12. A report published by the Brazilian Chamber of Deputies found that three-quarters of the eight million hectares allocated for land reform lay in the Amazon Basin; see Câmara de Deputados (1998: 18).
13. Quoted in *Informes Brasil* (2002).
14. Quoted in Branford and Kucinski (2003: 73).

15. Instituto Cidadania (2001: 36).
16. Quoted in Scolese (2004c: A.18).
17. Quoted in Branford and Kucinski (2003: 7).
18. Comissão Pastoral da Terra (CPT) (2004: 7).
19. Quoted in Brazil Network Newsletter, London, August 2003.
20. Plínio de Arruda Sampaio, interview by the author, São Paulo, SP, July 16, 2004. All quotes from Sampaio are taken from this interview.
21. Ibid.
22. CPT (2004: 7).
23. CPT (2004: 7).
24. Scolese, Costa and Figueiredo (2003), Folha de São Paulo (2003).
25. In the wake of the mid-2005 corruption accusations that brought down key Lula advisors and prominent party leaders, Plínio made one last bid to get the party back to what he thought were its origins by standing in the internal elections for the PT presidency. After losing, he resigned from the PT in late 2005 to join a new left-wing party founded by PT dissidents, the Socialism and Freedom Party (PSOL).
26. Miguel Rossetto, interview by the author, Brasília, DF, July 14, 2004. Rossetto's point here is partly shared by Bernardo Mançano Fernandes, who sees the MST as having "a strong political cause," but being quite weak since it "involves only 1 per cent of the Brazilian population." Quoted in Scolese (2004d).
27. Quoted in Glass (2003).
28. Teixeira (2004).
29. Cited in Jornal do Brasil, July 13, 2004.
30. For the story of the defeat of the Banco da Terra, see Branford and Rocha (2002: 185–94).
31. The MST and Via Campesina have been criticized by some agrarian exports, such as Gerson Teixeira (2004), for their uncompromising hostility to this program. These experts say that the movements are failing to recognize that, in some circumstances, rural credit can play a useful role, without implying that market-based land distribution should be the main venue for reform.
32. Miguel Rossetto quoted in Carta Capital, April 20, 2004, p. 25.
33. Rossetto failed to achieve this goal. Because of a shortage of funds, the only region of the country where the government was able to acquire sizeable areas was the Amazon basin, where land was still cheap. But this meant that landless families were settled on distant, inhospitable land, with little of the support they required. In this regard, the Lula government continued the policies of the Cardoso administration, which at the time the PT had criticized so vociferously.
34. Quoted in Suwwan (2004).
35. Quoted in Suwwan (2004).
36. Cited in Valente (2007).
37. Valente (2007) and Osava (2007).
38. Revista PUC-VIVA (2003:28).
39. Quoted in Scolese (2004a).
40. Quoted in Agência Carta Maior, December 21, 2003.
41. Quoted in Scolese (2004a).
42. João Pedro Stédile, interview by the author, e-mail exchange, November 3, 2004.
43. Ibid.
44. Plínio de Arruda Sampaio, interview by the author, São Paulo, SP, July 16, 2004.

14 The MST and the Rule of Law in Brazil

Few subjects so exercise commentators and politicians in Brazil than the real or imagined relationship between the Landless Rural Workers Movement (MST) and the rule of law, or *Estado de Direito*. A typical example of this can be found in the open letter sent by Raul Jungmann, the Minister of Agrarian Reform in President Cardoso's government, to President Luiz Inácio Lula da Silva in July 2003, he writes,

> President, no democrat can sacrifice the Rule of Law in name of the fight against poverty and social exclusion. I am sure you understand this. The MST and the UDR,[1] for different reasons, do not. Agrarian reform has been carried out in two contexts; that of rupture or institutional normality. Rupture is in nobody's interests. Normality implies the strict and rigid adherence to the law—whether we like it or not. Mr President, follow the law and make others follow it.[2]

The implication is clear: first, that the MST's restricted worldview means that questions of poverty and social exclusion are invariably set upon a collision with more broadly based rule of law imperatives; and second, that Brazil's reconnection with "institutional normality" makes it imperative for the president to uphold the rule of law at all times, even if this is to the detriment of allies like the MST.

This is powerful language. It strikes a historical chord with Brazilians who recall the military coup of 1964 and its costly aftermath; and at the same time makes a point of universal significance in terms accessible to all generations. It proposes a highest common denominator by appealing to people's sense of fair play, firmly rejecting the idea that any individual or organization should be considered above the law, and offering a clear way forward: follow the law and make others follow it. What could be simpler than that?

This chapter argues that this is precisely the problem with the way the discussion is framed. The picture presented of both the MST *and* law is deceptively simple, representing little more than a caricature. Of course caricatures have their uses, and public letters must take short cuts in the interest of clarity, but why would someone like Raul Jungmann, one of the sharpest intellects in the Cardoso government, with a deep understanding of the issues involved and the dangers of oversimplification, adopt this type of limiting discourse? Part of the answer is that he remains a politician and the text is a political document and not just a statement of legal orthodoxy. It skillfully takes a sideswipe at the Lula administration by highlighting a vulnerability, namely how a government of the Left can reconcile rule of law imperatives with direct action tactics deployed by its ally in opposition, the MST. By far the most crucial part of the letter, however, consists in the claims it makes about law in general and the MST in particular. In this respect it offers not so much a distorted caricature as a remarkably faithful and succinct portrayal of dominant legal and political discourses. For this reason it cannot be dismissed lightly and was chosen as our point of departure.

This chapter addresses some of the issues raised by orthodox discourses like Jungmann's, but from an entirely different perspective. We begin by acknowledging the uncomfortable nature of the MST's relations with prevailing legal orthodoxy, but then go on to briefly examine their nature, origins, and extent. Typically, critics emphasize the points of friction (of which there are many) and trace (in our view erroneously) their origins exclusively back to the MST and its supposed unilateral failure to "understand" the rule of law. Constructing the problem thus raises the stakes to a supposed clash between the MST and law. In fact, Jungmann's letter suggests that it heralds nothing less than an assault upon democracy itself.[3] This view invites the conclusion that containment, with repressive measures if necessary, is the best course of action. Indeed, Jungmann has gone on to say that it is high time for "law's truncheon to be brought down upon the MST."[4]

The approach of this chapter differs. In acknowledging the tension between the MST and prevailing legal orthodoxy we ask how much this reveals about the movement's approach to legality, and how much it reveals about the legal system itself and the attitudes of those who operate it. The suggestion is that we are dealing with a multilateral equation. Titanic clashes or assaults upon democracy are not the issue. Indeed, aspects of legality may actually be fortified by the MST's actions.

The second part of this chapter emphasizes positive interactions between the MST and the rule of law rather than points of friction. It underscores the importance of unpicking these relations, as well as examining the MST's record, which does not conform to the lawless stereotype. The overall picture that emerges, however uneven and localized, is that of an increasingly rich interplay between legal practitioners and the MST. The latter, it turns out, has quite a sophisticated legal discourse and strategy. Similarly, albeit to a more limited extent given that this is a major part of the challenge, we find that the legal sphere is the subject of internal contestation in addition to external social pressure.

The third and final section draws these threads together in the light of President Luiz Inácio Lula da Silva's administration. His 2002 election and 2006 reelection undoubtedly gave a distinctive new slant to the MST's relationship with the state in general and the rule of law in particular. If the rhetoric was to be believed, land questions had acquired a new urgency. Gone was the repressive tension that had underlain relations between the movement and all the post-dictatorship administrations. Temperamentally, at least, significant sectors of Lula's government, including the president himself, were favorably disposed toward land reform. This raised the tantalizing possibility that, for the first time in decades, a fundamental reorientation of the state—and its corollary, a loosening of the legal regime and decriminalization of landless struggles— might take place. But it also raised the difficult question of how a government of the Left would respond to rule of law imperatives on the one hand, and to a social movement known for tactics of direct action, on the other.

Tensions between the MST and Legal Orthodoxy

Social and Political Origins

There is an element of inevitability governing the MST's difficulties with the established legal order. While this is partly due to the movement's chosen course of action, methods, and self-conception, it also derives from the movement's social origins, that is, to the fact that the MST was a product of, and not just a response to, circumstances. These circumstances, especially the extent of social polarization, are well known. As noted in Carter's introductory chapter and Delgado, chapter 2, this volume, land and income inequality in Brazil are stark. Absolute poverty has been an endemic problem for rural families, of whom more than three million in the mid-2000s lived on a maximum income of roughly US$1 per capita per day. It is a grave mistake to imagine that legal conflicts arising from the release of these structural tensions is the product of "irresponsible leadership." Time and again, whether in South Africa, Poland, or, indeed, Brazil during the 1970s and 1980s, events suggest wider social forces are at work. The MST's supposed failure to "understand" the rule of law simultaneously belittles these tensions and exaggerates leadership volition.

A sense of proportion, then, is needed when considering rural conflicts that occur under the banner of the MST. All too often they are reduced—ad absurdum—to the terrain of "movement or leadership irresponsibility" when in fact something more significant is happening. Consider the marked growth of groups similar to the MST. The numbers speak for themselves.[5] To be sure, the MST is by far the most vocal and powerful of these groups and exercises a de facto leadership role, but that still begs the question why so many others have followed suit and adopted similar tactics of mass occupation? Whatever the answer, a spontaneous mass outbreak of law breaking is not it. Like the MST, these movements should be understood as distinctive responses to and "products" of circumstances rather than straitjacketed with repressive legal discourses and actions.

Another way to understand the origins of conflict between the MST and legal orthodoxy is by posing the following question: what were and are the alternatives to conflict? In fact, the alternatives had been tried and found wanting. The MST was born of a strong sense of past failures, including the assassinations of rural trade union leaders, the glacial pace of land reform, and the excessively debilitating legalistic culture of existing rural organizations.[6] Not even the prospect of more radical rural unions, following the upheavals of the late 1970s, could persuade MST organizers to throw in their lot with these groups. The argument, which finally prevailed, was that while unions could only organize individual workers as members, the MST could derive strength from the organization of families—men, women, and children—in mass occupations without the restriction of municipal limits, to which legislation also subjected unions. Mobilizing beyond traditional borders—geographic and legal—would give the movement its national characteristic as well as the capacity to concentrate large groups of people in small areas without the usual restrictions. In this sense, leadership did indeed play a vital role in shaping the movement and to this extent is responsible for the path undertaken and its consequences.

But what of the substantive critique offered by orthodox rule of law advocates? Is the MST acting beyond the law, thereby "threatening democracy" itself?[7] The illegality argument is usually based on two pillars. The first, although less significant, arises from specific cases of law breaking and their depiction as representative of the movement as a whole. Undoubtedly, this is one of the most difficult questions facing the movement. However, in an organization of the MST's size, operating under extremely stressful conditions, it is not surprising that laws have been broken. That is one reason why, for instance, the movement has long banned alcohol from encampments, since it often gave rise to fights. Over the years, the process of conflict has seen thefts, damage to property, and the killing of landowners, military police, and even fellow members. Opponents have been quick to latch on to these events, seeing in them the possibility of tarnishing the movement's image and embarrassing its leadership. Crucially, though, they do not form part of the MST's modus operandi. If they did then rule of law arguments would hold more weight. Instead, they must be seen for what they are, as episodic exceptions to the rule, no matter how tragic or unwelcome for those directly involved.

The same claim to exceptionality, however, cannot be made for the second target of criticism: land occupations. On the contrary, these form an indispensable part of the MST's whole operation. Without them its survival would either be compromised or the movement would be institutionalized. To this extent, the allegation that the movement is embarked upon a systematic confrontation with the law itself is far more serious. Before addressing this issue, some reference to the operation of Brazil's legal system is required.

Failures of the Legal System

In the absence of clarification the impression created so far has been of a fully functional and largely impartial legal order where due process prevails. Like Gandhi's comment on Western civilization, though, "it would be a very good idea." Arguably the only consistent feature of Brazil's justice system is its inconsistency, namely its capacity to deviate from many of the basic premises advanced by a range of rule of law advocates. The system is notoriously unjust, bureaucratic, cripplingly slow, and saturated with class bias. Because detailed consideration of these points is beyond the scope of this chapter, our remarks' are confined to a few brief illustrations of this last point: class bias.

Even senior figures working within the system have acknowledged major class divisions. In 2000, for instance, Deputy Attorney General for Human Rights Wagner Gonçalves observed that "in Brazil there is a very strong complex of formal and informal mechanisms that protect people with political and economic power." He went on to note that the Brazilian penal system was "profoundly selective": "The chances of a poor person succumbing to the long arm of the law are incomparably greater than those of a rich person."[8]

The differences abound. When a college-educated person goes to prison, assuming that matters get this far, he or she has the right, *enshrined in law* (article 295 of the penal code), to be held in a separate cell away from their less-educated countrymen and women who are held in grossly overcrowded cells. This says a lot for the system. In the case of politicians, the situation remains unequal but is different. For years they attained near untouchable status. In his Oxford Centre speech, Gonçalves, confirmed that "in Brazil, if the author of a crime is a parliamentarian there is a 95% chance that he will not have to respond for the crime he committed."[9] An illustrative case took place in September 2003, when Brazil's attorney general was compelled to halt investigations into the fraudulent emission of hundreds of millions of dollars of land bonds during Senator Jader Barbalho's tenureship of the land reform ministry back in the late 1980s. Despite the colossal magnitude of the crime, the passage of time and destruction of crucial evidence had undermined the prospects of a successful prosecution. At one point in the lengthy proceedings, Barbalho was imprisoned for precisely five hours. The contrast with landless workers is striking. Menial crimes routinely attract custodial sentences. An extreme example occurred in March 1999 when five workers from the state of Pernambuco were imprisoned for a period of six months. Their crime was the theft of eight goats to feed seventy families encamped near the Santa Rita ranch, in São Bento do Una.

Given the class biases of Brazilian justice, it is no wonder that the MST's relationship with the law is difficult. The situation is compounded by Kafkaesque absurdities of which the emphasis upon the vindication of procedure to the exclusion of substantive issues is perhaps the most notable. However, any notion that the MST is uniquely disadvantaged, or a "victim," must be qualified. To a large extent movement members are in exactly the same position as the majority of Brazilians who, according to many studies, have little faith in the system. In a 2003 poll, only 12% of the respondents claimed to have "total confidence" in the judiciary.[10]

Although a blindfolded statue of Themis, the Greek god of justice, sits outside the Supreme Court denoting impartiality, other more negative and powerful representations grip the popular imagination. These include common expressions like: *A lei é para o ingles ver* (The law is for appearances, literally, for the English to see); *Da justiça, o pobre só conhece castigos* (From justice the poor only know punishment), and *Há uma lei para o rico e outra para o pobre* (There's one law for the rich and another for the poor). Arguably the most potent, damning, and illuminating aphorism is attributed to Brazil's greatest twentieth-century statesman and legislator, Getúlio Vargas: *Aos meus amigos tudo, para os inimigos, a lei* (For my friends everything, for my enemies the law). The underlying message of these examples is clear: justice is selective.

Thus there is a universal dimension to tensions between the MST and legal orthodoxy. One feature that clearly distinguishes the movement from the vast majority of other victims, though, is the organized nature of its challenge and the equally systematic nature of the legal response. This gives the conflict an eminently political character.

For many observers politics and law do not mix. The MST is perceived as intruding upon the tranquil and "normal" functioning of the legal system. Such an account is one-sided. Historically speaking it was landowners who dominated legal spaces, through imperial and republican arrangements, and gave the law its highly sectarian character. That Brazil retains an acutely polarized rural social structure illustrates the adaptability and tenacity of landed interests and the degree to which courts and legislatures sustain those interests. Orthodox rhetoric's substitution of ahistorical notions of legal neutrality deliberately overlooks these constitutive social and historical dimensions. Proponents suggest that the line must be drawn somewhere for the common good—"strict and rigid adherence to the law, whether we like it or not"—but rarely acknowledge how it has been redrawn repeatedly to suit landed interests. Although the acknowledgment of law's historical, and especially contemporary, permeability by social forces would move the debate forward, this presents real difficulties for orthodox advocates. Legal change resulting from social pressure is inadmissible because it calls into question law's supposed origins and neutrality and raises the prospect that lines will be redrawn by the most aggressive groups, in this case, the MST and the Rural Democratic Union (UDR). And yet, when one looks at the extent of the threat to legal "neutrality" it becomes clear that any pressure brought to bear upon the system by the MST is nothing compared to that still exercised by landowners—whether by the UDR (a comparatively easy target) or infinitely more powerful mainstream economic and political groupings like the Agricultural and Livestock Confederation of Brazil (CNA), which still exercises a veto over government policy.

Elective affinities felt by many legal practitioners toward landed interests reinforce these imbalances from within. The agrarian ombudsman, a senior judge by profession, acknowledges that 50% of his colleagues believe his more progressive ideas, based on constitutional notions of the social function of property, are "not in accordance with the Civil Code, which says that whoever registers land is its absolute owner, and that consequently it is wrong to speak of a social question.[11] With a starting point like this, the actions of the MST and other rural labor organizations look more like an attempt to rebalance the social and legal order than an effort to subvert it or democracy.

Diverse Legal Currents

In the light of the foregoing discussion we return to the question of whether occupations are lawful. Although we have seen that profound historical and social imbalances structure the legal order, which in turn favors the landed status quo, the legal order is not entirely closed. Indeed, from a strictly legal perspective the status of occupations depends upon the weight attached to various seemingly contradictory legal documents and clauses. Put at its simplest, defenders of the status quo regard the Civil Code as the main bulwark of property rights, while reformers see the 1988 Constitution's concepts of property, especially what is termed its "social function," as the highest expression of property rights and the overriding qualification upon all prior formulations.

Thus to urge the president to "follow the law and make others follow it" begs the question: whose law and on whose terms? Matters are further complicated by the Constitution's failure to offer a sufficiently unambiguous program. Instead, it was marked by immense social and political pressures at the drafting stage. Florestan Fernandes, a deputy on the left of the political spectrum, described the result as a "patchwork quilt," while José Sarney, the former right-wing Brazilian president (1985–90), called it a "Frankenstein's monster."[12] Whatever the metaphor, the stitching is evident. Faced with the impossibility of resolving underlying social tensions, the Constituent Assembly framing the constitution simply farmed out the most contentious issues to other fora for later consideration and, as it would turn out, litigation. Thus although the Constitution asserts the conditions under which the state can and cannot appropriate property for the purposes of agrarian reform, it does so through an elaborate legal, administrative, economic, and social web mediated by judges, politicians, and administrative agencies, such as the National Institute for Colonization and Agrarian Reform (INCRA). Conflict was built in from the start.

A complex battle is now being waged inside the legal establishment for hegemony. However, rather than occurring along a single front, it is expressed in terms of multiple skirmishes and sometimes in quite fluid and episodic formations. Even those taking part are not necessarily fully aware of the ramifications of their own decisions. Indeed, many would reject the notion that they fall into any kind of "camp" at all, since their decisions are taken on a case-by-case basis, often on extremely narrow legal points.[13] Highly restrictive judicial interpretations of property rights form part of a tradition that goes back centuries. Although the alternatives start from a position of institutional and cultural weakness, they are neither weak nor new in doctrinal terms. On the contrary, academic studies examining the social function of property can trace their pedigree back to antiquity and to nineteenth-century Catholic social teaching among others.[14] But just as the Catholic Church developed its immense political and cultural presence in Latin America by ostracizing radical alternatives, so too the legal order developed in close proximity with landed classes, while marginalizing the alternatives.

The failure to establish the supremacy of the 1988 Constitution illustrates the difficulty of reversing such ingrained patterns of behavior. As the following section makes clear, that is precisely why the contribution made by groups like the MST to the debate is potentially so important. In sum, most of the tensions between the MST and the legal order can be traced to the latter's fabric and operating dynamics rather than to the MST's supposedly irresponsible or lawless approach.

In fact there is more to relations between the MST and legality than tension alone. A variety of reciprocal determinations are at work, occasionally with unexpected consequences. Arguably, the MST's very emergence is a prime example of this. Although the movement was the brainchild of the Left and progressive religious organizations, it also emerged as a direct response to the huge legal limitations imposed by the military dictatorship and largely retained by the legal establishment immediately following the transition to democracy. A common perception among MST supporters during the early 1980s was that progressive initiatives were hamstrung by these laws and would remain so unless the connection was broken and entirely new methods and structures developed.

Developing Alternative Conceptions of Legality

This section develops a number of themes. It argues that although the MST's relationship to law was initially marked by mutual ideological hostility, that situation has long since developed into one where, no matter how fraught relations may be, law's potentialities are recognized. The change was neatly symbolized in June 2000 by a front cover of *Caros Amigos* magazine that pictured an MST leader holding up a copy of the Brazilian Constitution under the caption: "The Weapons of the MST."[15] Some detailed examples of these "weapons" are discussed, as well as the shift from what I term a defensive conception of legality to an offensive conception that appreciates law's potentialities. We also examine the increased willingness on the part of legal practitioners (prosecutors, judges, and legal theorists) to recognize the contribution and potentialities of the movement itself. Far from measuring up to Raul Jungmann's description, it turns out that the MST offers a fundamental reference point for interpretations of legality together with the crucially important practical impetus for change so frequently lacking in legal discourses. This last theme is continued into the third and final section, which deals with the Lula administration.

Legal Conservatism and the Imperative for Change

Law's class character, and consequent inability to deliver progressive social change, understandably left deep marks on the MST. In its early days the movement was compelled to develop uncompromising methods, notably the mass occupation of properties, as part of its strategy to propel land reform forward. Contestation and conflict came to be seen as the primary motor of political change. Perhaps because of its success, this perspective left little scope for fuller consideration of the role that law might play. It came to be viewed either with a mixture of hostility and suspicion, or at best as an afterthought. A typical example of the latter occurred in October 1987 with the simultaneous occupation of seven locations across the state of Rio Grande do Sul. Although the occupations themselves were meticulously planned and executed, simultaneously shocking the political establishment and capturing the public imagination, there was little evidence of legal planning. Sympathetic lawyers scurried hundreds of kilometers from one occupation to the next and then back to the courts, improvising the best defense they could to legal counterattacks. With relatively minor variations this pattern of neglect would be repeated throughout Brazil. The MST's daring and imaginative political offensive contrasted starkly with its restrictive conception of legality.

Although it would take several years for the MST to overcome its legal conservatism, the case for doing so was present at the outset. The success of mass occupations and their remarkable capacity to establish a progressive social and political agenda and counter many aspects of landowner power, including violence, created a paradox: simultaneously relegating law to the shade and enhancing its significance. After all, occupations not only created victories and landowner defensiveness, but also engendered a backlash: the reinvigoration of parliamentary and violent extraparliamentary landowner networks and court-based responses. Legal success offered landlords a great prize: the prospect of enlisting the direct support of the state and delegitimizing the movement. For if the courts sided with landowners, imposed an injunction, and the MST resisted, the military police could then be summoned to arrest MST members and halt occupations in their tracks. Clearly, the MST's underdevelopment of legal expertise, at its simplest, the failure to present an adequate defense in court because lawyers were unavailable, was leaving the movement badly exposed. Either it would have to reconsider the question of law or risk fighting with one arm tied behind its back.

There was no Damascene conversion to the virtues of the established legal order. Instead the movement gradually moved from defensive conceptions of law to more offensive—that is, proactive—ones. Undoubtedly, the MST's painstaking construction of legal personnel networks and arguments strengthened its hand. But this still left landlords with massive legal firepower (backed by monetary and other advantages). The playing field is anything but level. Representing landowners is so lucrative that some lawyers leave the ranks of INCRA, the land agency, to join those of landowners, and in many cases, litigating, advising, and researching on behalf of landless workers represents a costly personal undertaking. Were it not for the dedicated body of lawyers and paralegals willing to offer these services on a voluntary basis, the MST's legal presence would be a fraction of its current size.

According to MST leaders, serious discussion of legal issues, like the possibility of forming an in-house legal team instead of relying on the goodwill of the Catholic Church's Pastoral Land Commission (CPT), began in the early 1990s. This was a direct response to the wave of violence unleashed by President Fernando Collor de Mello's administration (1990–92). Until then, the approach had been both deliberately and inadvertently piecemeal. On the one hand, the MST did not wish to go down the route adopted by other organizations that, it believed, had become so enamored with individual lawyers and legal niceties that, in effect, political and movement imperatives had been subordinated to legal ones. On the other hand, though, a relationship of convenience had developed with third parties, like the CPT. "Why change it?" was the attitude.

For radical independent lawyers like Jacques Alfonsin, who provided legal services just as occupations were taking off in Rio Grande do Sul, the movement's arm's length approach in the mid-1980s was inadequate and difficult to deal with on a personal level. "At the beginning I almost felt like an appendage, an excrescence," he said.[16] Like many lawyers he would be called in to assist occupations at the last minute, or in their aftermath. A tension clearly existed between the internal political dynamics of a vibrant social movement still operating under semiclandestine conditions and externally constituted legal demands. The MST felt that lawyers could never "solve" fundamental problems (e.g., accelerate expropriations) on its behalf and that the key to changing social attitudes and pressuring the state into land reform lay with mass mobilizations. If it came down to a choice between who was going to be subordinated, then it would have to be the lawyers, not movement actions.

Whatever the substantive merits of the MST's position, in practical terms, the choice was not as stark as this. Legal action could be expanded and enhanced without compromising the movement's strategic objectives. Indeed, over time even leaders like João Pedro Stédile came to recognize that, "clearing up after the milk was spilt" was not an adequate policy.[17] Gradually, therefore, a more sophisticated, expanded, and assured concept of militant legal action emerged that was in harmony with the MST's imperative of political autonomy. Evidence of this shift comes in the early 1990s with the development of in-house legal services that drew directly upon MST resources and the increased support given by the movement for the National Network of Popular Lawyers (RENAP), officially created in 1996.

The emergence of a more coherent legal strategy, or consciousness, partly arose in response to external shocks such as the repression of the Collor administration and the host of court-based and paramilitary countermeasures undertaken by landowners in the 1990s. Prior to this, legal consciousness was incipient and episodic. Over time, however, the movement's exchanges with the radical legal profession became second nature. Lawyers like Jacques Alfonsin were instrumental in the development of RENAP and legal dialogues in the mid-1990s. Another lawyer, Luis Eduardo Greenhalgh, also provided the movement with assistance during its early struggles, for example at the occupation, in 1985, of the Annoni ranch in Rio Grande do Sul. As a radical lawyer and politician of national standing, Greenhalgh was used to straddling the contradictory worlds of politics and law in a way that better suited the movement. Although this may have helped cement the close relationship he enjoyed, it hardly constituted an autonomous legal consciousness. Dependence on the personal characteristics of an individual lawyer, no matter how brilliant, represented a precarious foundation. As if to underline the point, it was Greenhalgh himself who took the lead in setting up the MST's in-house legal services.

The Worker's Party (PT) provided yet another support network through sympathetic lawyers and leading figures like Plinio de Arruda Sampaio. Like Greenhalgh, Alfonsin, and many others, Sampaio was separate from, but closely linked to, the movement's fortunes from its earliest days. Sampaio's background also straddled the worlds of law and politics. He was a PT heavyweight in the legal sphere (making a notable contribution to those chapters of the 1988 Constitution dealing with the separation of powers and the role of the attorney general's department), and was deeply involved in agrarian questions (hence his citation as a possible Minister of Agrarian Reform under President Lula da Silva, and his appointment as head of the commission that elaborated the National Agrarian Reform Plan [PNRA]). Numerous exchanges with such figures aided the development of a more mature and nuanced legal conception. Vigorous exchanges also took place between the MST and the radical legal education network, the People's Juridical Support (AJUP). It organized seminars for lawyers and militants, produced specialized pamphlets, and actively supported the movement; but Miguel Pressburger, one of AJUP's leading figures and a Marxist lawyer, was openly critical of the MST's lack of legal policies, arguing that these failed to exploit its scope for action. Finally, of course, there was the CPT upon which, as noted earlier, the MST greatly depended and whose influence is still felt today. In short, change was more than just the product of external shocks; it was also part of a wider process of critical reflection going back to the mid-1980s.

The development of in-house legal services during the early 1990s, under the official heading of Human Rights Sector, undoubtedly represented a major step forward. At last the movement could systematize its legal policies; offer a point of contact for the agglutination and coordination of external legal support; comment officially upon individual cases; represent the legal plight of landless workers at a national level; and produce legally oriented publications. It should be stressed, however, that this was not a legal service in the usual mold. The connection between movement and lawyers was intended to be organic. Instead of contracting outside professionals, the movement began training its own cadres, like the head of the Human Rights Sector, Juvelino Strozake, the son of landless workers and an MST activist. His university education was sponsored by the movement, and he was given vital practical training by a skilled lawyer, Luiz Eduardo Greenhalgh, whose political and legal judgments the movement respected. These characteristics would help ensure the legal department meshed fully with the movement's wider objectives.[18]

The MST's tightly controlled model of organic legal growth came at a price. It was slow and therefore bound to be limited in scale, a major problem when dealing with social conflicts scattered across a country of Brazil's dimensions. Some attempts were therefore made to break these limits through agreements, established with both the Cardoso and Lula governments, providing federal funds to retain lawyers to work on certain human rights cases.[19] In no way did the subcontracting of functions at the periphery imply a loss of control at the center. An extended division of labor and professionalization of legal services was perfectly in keeping with the movement's political and legal objectives.

Providing the MST with material leverage—enough lawyers in the right place and at the right time—was obviously a vital task, but so too was broadening its range of legal arguments. Intellectual leverage could not be established in isolation or organically: the movement had to reach out. In this context RENAP would prove highly significant. It offered to the MST both lawyers, which the movement's internal resources could never hope to match, and a vital network of information exchange.

RENAP also had repercussions within the MST.[20] Central to RENAP's agenda is what Jacques Alfonsin described as the "need to bring together and concentrate law professionals, to improve the provision of legal advice, and to debate and clarify legal defence strategies—especially in relation to criminal and civil matters arising from the struggle for agrarian reform."[21] For RENAP members, steeped in radical legal theory and activist struggles, this meant attempting to consolidate an alternative model of legal action by questioning their role as legal professionals; developing jurisprudence that challenged orthodox interpretations; propagating these concepts through pamphlets, meetings, courses, and information technology networks; and seeking a close working relationship with the MST (among others) that stressed not only the latter's autonomy (and in this sense the limited nature of legal action), but RENAP's autonomy as well. The constant dialogue with the MST would give RENAP initiatives their vital grounding, but also would help the MST reorient its legal agenda from a conservative/defensive posture to one grounded in more offensive/radical notions of legality.

From Defensive to Offensive Legality

Although Stédile accepts that substantive changes have taken place, he is keen to stress that these occurred primarily as a function of politics rather than law.[22] Certainly it is true that the movement never lost strategic control over its legal dealings or found itself in awe of law or lawyers. No matter how insightful Greenhalgh's legal advice might be, it was overruled on several occasions.[23] Thus, offensive legality had its limits. It was developed within constraints imposed by the MST and the wider social struggle.

Notwithstanding these limits, legal action did possess its own logic and qualities. Just as Stédile emphasizes that movement activities should "lead society to support us," there can be little doubt that occasionally law constituted a vital bridge in this process. Events in the Pontal do Paranapanema, which first marked the MST in the nation's consciousness, bear this out.[24] As Stédile says:

> It is obvious that the Pontal was very important from an ideological perspective, because in the Pontal there were 700,000 hectares of public land: the status of the property, which belonged to the state, had already been clearly decided in the courts. It had been illegally seized [*grilhada*[25]] by large landowners and figures from São Paulo's aristocracy, indeed the ex-governor, Roberto Costa de Abreu Sodré was a *grilheiro* from the region. The fact of having made occupations and organised the movement here acquired greater symbolic value on account of these aspects.[26]

In other words, the politics of occupation, near the epicenter of landed, industrial, and media power, was complemented by the legal situation. Whatever their de facto power, which was immense, in de jure terms landowners found themselves in a vulnerable position, a fact not lost on the movement and made much of in the course of its public pronouncements. In private negotiations too, with centrist and conservative local town mayors, law exercised a bridge-building capacity. According to José Rainha, the MST's chief spokesperson at the time, "we won over the mayors and isolated the landowners, because there was no way of saying 'no,' because the land was public."[27] Thus, no longer was law simply used to defend the movement from attack; it was also used in a wide variety of contexts to put others on the defensive. Consider, for example, the attitude of landless workers themselves, who are said to be reluctant law breakers.[28] If true, Rainha's affirmation that the Pontal's legal situation made it "a great deal easier" to organize workers is significant. He could claim "we're not the illegal ones; you [the landlords] are because the law says that the land belongs to the state."[29] The MST was using a legal claim as an aid to mobilization.

Although the MST's legal claim was aided by the devolved status of land, activists simultaneously relied on another prop of wider significance: the idea that the state had failed to accord landless workers fundamental collective rights enshrined in the 1988 Constitution. Thus, struggles over devolved land were part of a much broader process of struggle in the social, political, *and* legal fields. Offensive legality's task was to develop the legal imagination and tools capable of undertaking these struggles in all their diversity and universality. Finding a "trump card," like the 1958 decision confirming the devolved status of land in the Pontal, could not be relied on elsewhere. Indeed, court victories alone were not enough, as the fact that it took thirty-five years to *begin* to establish the 1958 court's writ so powerfully illustrates. Instead cards had to be manufactured through painstaking work inside and outside the courts.

Changing Legal Culture

Judicial conservatism resides at the heart of Brazil's legal system, and nowhere is this more evident than in questions pertaining to property. While the movement has always looked beyond the horizons of law, it has come to recognize that these cultures must be contested head on, rather than written off and accepted as forms of oppression. Contestation here neither constitutes an overestimation of movement power nor a sign of its institutionalization. Rather, it is viewed simply as a necessary part of the struggle.

Although the uphill nature of that struggle is clear for all to see, favorable shifts do occur sometimes. In March 1996, for example, one of Brazil's highest courts, the *Superior Tribunal de Justiça*, was asked to decide upon the merits of a petition for habeus corpus (HC.4.399 SP) made by six leading MST members preventively imprisoned following a wave of occupations in the Pontal.[30] In a landmark ruling the court concluded that their actions could not be characterized as a crime under the terms of the penal code because the subjective intentions of the petitioners was furtherance of agrarian reform, rather than theft of property. Their intentions were, in the words of the judges, "substantively distinct" from those alleged by prosecutors. The court also noted the connection between the inaction of the state on land reform, the constitutional imperative for change, and MST activities. The implication was clear. Given the monumental failure on the part of the political class there was a corresponding need to understand the circumstances in which workers felt compelled to occupy land. A comment one often hears from the MST captures this well: "From the point of view of our legislation, if there was political will, there would be no need for land occupations."[31]

The court's decision touches on many of the themes discussed in this chapter. The ruling would become an important piece of ammunition in the MST's arsenal. Through networks like RENAP, as well as the MST's own legal service, the precedent was used in countless other legal actions, albeit with varying degrees of success. The case was also used to cement further the legal aspects of the movement's claim to legitimacy, both before the public and internally, among members. Finally, the case clearly showed that even within Brazil's conservative legal establishment, there were sectors—at the very highest levels—willing to embrace theses advanced by MST lawyers.

The 1996 ruling by the High Court illustrated other issues. Although the judges failed to detail judicial failures, reserving criticism for politicians instead, they did emphasize the importance of a contextual approach and substantively oriented legal reasoning, rather than the purely formal variety characteristic of prevailing legal orthodoxy.[32] This was not a revolution in legal thinking, or the radical kind of reasoning proposed by some legal scholars and judges,[33] but it did represent a symbolic break with tradition and an implied criticism of colleagues. The presence on the panel of Luiz Vicente Cernicchiaro, a leading intellectual in penal affairs who chaired the committee examining reform of the Penal Code, gave the decision added weight. It could not be written off lightly. As such the MST would keep it in the public and judicial eye over the years to come.[34]

For the MST the central issue is not to "sacrifice the rule of law in name of the combat against poverty and social exclusion," but to regain those aspects of law's rule that deal favorably with questions of poverty and social exclusion but which have been buried under the immense weight of other institutional, political, and class imperatives. Regaining law's progressive potential and pushing its boundaries is not just a matter of legal archaeology. New precedents have to be set. One example of this occurred in December 1999, near the town of Matão, in São Paulo state. Six hundred landless families occupied an area devoted to the intensive cultivation of sugarcane, land that was deemed productive. In so doing, the MST appeared to have placed itself on a collision course with the 1988 Constitution, which makes a crucial distinction between so-called productive and unproductive property. According to article 185 the expropriation of productive properties is "not permitted." Closer examination reveals that the movement was not on a collision course with the Constitution, but rather with highly restrictive constitutional interpretations. It was attempting to reestablish the validity, indeed primacy, of other constitutional clauses, notably article 186, which asserts that in order to be accorded legal protection, property must *simultaneously* fulfill its "social function."[35]

A striking feature of the Matão occupation is that from the outset activists were acutely aware of and drew attention to the legal implications of their actions. This was offensive legality at work. As one leader explained, "it is essential that land fulfils its social function, and occupations are one means of carrying out this debate in society."[36] To the surprise of many, the lower court validated the movement's main argument, namely that the property in question was failing to fulfill its social function because of local pollution and the systematic abuse of labor rights. Thus the occupants were allowed to stay. This ruling established an important new precedent. It seemed the MST had an arguable case after all, a remarkable fact given the greater public, political, and judicial hostility toward occupations of productive property.

A shift in legal culture appeared to be taking place. The MST's arguments even received support from local and state prosecutors. A few days before the occupation began, prosecutors and other state officials issued an open letter dealing with the social function of property in much the same terms as those advanced by the MST.[37] Far from coincidental, the letter indicated increased cross-fertilization between the movement and various legal practitioners.[38]

Though unusual, the Matão case highlights a broader trend: the increasing responsiveness of Brazilian legal professionals toward innovative strategies advanced by the MST. Furthermore, the occupation underlines the movement's capacity for creative case construction. Legal issues were woven into the very fabric of this occupation and the MST was more than happy to draw attention to this fact. Throughout, though, the essential driving force remained the unresolved nature of the social and legal contradictions themselves.

The Lula Administration

The election in November 2002 of Luiz Inácio Lula da Silva as president raised tantalizing possibilities as well as thorny questions about the relationship between the MST, the law, and the state. Clearly, the most important issue was the extent to which the presidency would address social contradictions and mark the emergence of a new and radical partnership for agrarian reform, and the beginning of the end of the long cycle of conflict between state and society. Here the role of law was critical since the government could exercise its authority in clearing cultural and legislative obstacles to land reform; could use its constitutional powers in making senior judicial and other appointments, including the attorney general; and could adopt a more benign tone in its public pronouncements, instead of, as Raul Jungmann suggested, "articulate with the security and justice sectors of the states and with the federal police and democratically crack down [*baixar o pau*] in cases of excess by the MST."[39]

The best that can be said of both Lula administrations is that they did not adopt Jungmann's advice. To be sure there were rhetorical ambiguities at the heart of the administration in its legal discourse toward the MST. This oscillated between brinkmanship and conciliation. The former largely came from its so-called hard men, José Genoino and José Dirceu. "Do not doubt the authority of the government," the latter pointedly said at the end of July 2003, following a round of land occupations and tension with the movement. "Acts and actions cannot be allowed to prejudice the democratic rule of law," said Genoino. Almost simultaneously (June 2003) though, other ministers, like Miguel Rossetto (Agrarian Development), were negotiating with judges in the Pontal do Paranapanema in order to accelerate legal procedures and thereby hasten the acquisition of land that might be used to defuse a volatile situation.

The appointment of key legal personnel also appears to send out mixed messages. On the one hand, Claudio Fontelles's appointment as attorney general was a positive development. A progressive with a longstanding interest in land issues and a well-worked-out position, he felt able to criticize the MST when it occupied public buildings and President Cardoso's ranch, in March 2002, contending that such practices, including the occupation of productive property, were illegal and therefore undermined movement legitimacy. But he also confronted basic tenets of legal orthodoxy. In one article he emphasized the futility of bringing repressive penal policies to bear on food thefts in northeast Brazil because their cause essentially lay in the persistence of centuries-old structures of injustice.[40] On August 14, 2003, he took aim at another target, property, which he contended was "not absolute": "you cannot do with an area what you like. Use must be destined toward a social function. The constitution impregnates within the notion of property the notion of solidarity." For properties that were underutilized or held for speculative purposes "social movements can, in a peaceful and orderly fashion, go in and plant and produce."[41]

Although these statements fell well short of claims made by the MST, they represented a clear departure from Fontelles's predecessor, not to mention the repressive approach adopted by Cardoso's minister of justice, Nelson Jobim.[42] For the first time ever, Brazil's most senior prosecutor was publicly endorsing a key argument advanced by the MST: that property was not absolute and could, under certain circumstances, be occupied. Setting the tone in this way would encourage and embolden young prosecutors to question landowner claims instead of taking them at face value. It also strengthened the MST's wider public claims. Fontelles's declarations generated newspaper headlines and predictable criticism from landed interests.[43]

However, when it came to judicial appointments to the Federal Supreme Court (composed of eleven individuals), timidity dominated. A wave of retirements under Lula meant that in contrast to Cardoso, who only appointed three judges during his two terms, the new president was in the privileged position of making five appointments in one term. Instead of leaving an indelible mark, it is arguable that the government's choice quickly came to haunt it when, in August 2003, the Federal Supreme Court rejected the first major expropriation order signed by Lula. The manner of the defeat, on procedural grounds, again seemed to confirm the assertion made to me by one judge that, "With the Brazilian judiciary, if you have an able lawyer you can almost eternalise the discussion!"[44]

Clearly one should not read too much into one decision, but it is symptomatic of a general malaise. Advancing the cause of land reform within the courts has always been a difficult task. It appears likely to remain so for years to come.[45] Perhaps in recognition of past failures, the strength of Lula's popular mandate, and the extent to which the courts were now on trial for any policy failures, the High Court judges involved in the São Gabriel case reiterated their support for agrarian reform. However, their rhetorical support sat uncomfortably alongside their rejection of one of the few practical measures capable of achieving it. MST leaders like Mário Lill asked a pertinent question, "if the judges don't permit agrarian reform within the law, what is left to us?"[46]

As for the law itself, in one of many mixed signals to the MST and right-wing sectors, the government refused to reverse the August 2001 measure designed by the Cardoso administration to choke off occupations at the source.[47] The measure forbade INCRA from auditing any ranch for a period of two years subsequent to any occupation. Lula's retention of the measure was the symbolic equivalent of Tony Blair retaining anti–trade union legislation. Substantively, though, it was more complex. Since its passage, the MST had, quite literally, worked its way around the measure by occupying properties adjacent to intended targets.

In both symbolic and substantive terms, however, the government's failure to update agricultural productivity indices has been far more significant. Dating back to 1975, these indices take no account whatsoever of massive leaps in productivity and Brazil's newfound status as an agricultural superpower: only the most hopelessly unproductive properties can be expropriated, thereby artificially restricting the supply of land available for redistribution. Thus the problems accumulate. Despite promises made by President Lula on the eve of his second electoral victory, he has refused to take on the agricultural lobby by updating the indices. An unholy alliance of propertied classes—from the most advanced to the most antediluvian—has succeeded in preventing the MST and INCRA from getting their foot in the door for fear that their remit may expand uncontrollably. Such fears are, in my view, exaggerated. But they underline just how ideologically driven landed power remains, in all its forms, at the onset of the twenty-first century. While the Lula government has increased public funding for land reform and family farming, ultimately it has done nothing to undermine those power relations.

Conclusion

This chapter could have been renamed "The Devil in the Detail" for the rule of law in Brazil depends greatly on correlations of force at a given moment in time, micropolitical arrangements, and the willingness of operators of the legal system to use their powers in a particular way. A notion like the rule of law fails to capture these dynamics and in Jungmann's hands becomes a highly schematic frame of reference.

In fact, the disjuncture between narrowly conceived rule of law rhetoric on the one hand, and reality on the other, is exemplified by Jungmann's own conduct. Between 1999 and 2000, as minister of Agrarian Development he was faced with a major clash involving landowners from Rio Grande do Sul who did not want their properties audited on the one side, and INCRA, the local judiciary, and MST, who felt that inspectors should be allowed to audit properties freely as the law prescribed. Far from demanding the rule of law, Jungmann simply circumvented it. The head of the land agency, a former prosecutor with a declared desire to make the law "stick," was sacked. Land productivity indices were kept artificially low so that landowners could clear this hurdle and hold onto their land. To be sure, Jungmann had his reasons (as he doubtless has for now urging an authoritarian approach on the part of Lula), but a purist notion of the rule of law is clearly not one of them.[48]

Abstract decontextualized approaches to law and its institutions are unsustainable and unhelpful. Indeed, for all Jungmann's rhetorical inflexibility and emphasis upon "institutional normality," he recognized just how flawed and perverse that normality was. The punitive approach of many legal practitioners toward landless workers, and the glacial speed with which the legal system resolved problems while they accumulated apace, posed a major obstacle to agrarian reform. In order to overcome some of these obstacles Jungmann created the office of the National Agrarian Ombudsman. Its head, a high ranking judge, explained that this was an attempt to "treat agrarian questions in an informal manner, without bureaucracy, without costs to the various parties, and as close to the events as possible."[49] Typically, though, the institution's chances of success depended not on the formal trappings of office, but on the ombudsman's own personal authority and skill. Even so judicial culture remained an obstacle. As the ombudsman freely admitted, his progressive legal theses on land issues were rejected by a substantial portion of the Brazilian judges.[50] Against such profound divisions and institutional contradictions, it seems reasonable to question what Jungmann and others mean by the "strict and rigid adherence to the law."

As for the MST's relationship to law, this must be seen as an integral and legitimate part of legal processes that have long been divided. That an organization of its social expressiveness and stature should at last contribute to reshaping the debate on the nature and function of law, instead of merely accepting the consequences of others' designs, is surely a healthy and long overdue development. Many observers have failed to pick up this point or seem unwilling to do so. They acknowledge the movement's political impact, but seem incapable of recognizing its positive legal ramifications, preferring to remain trapped within an artificially restrictive notion of the rule of law to which not even they can live up to.

To this extent, relations with the Lula administration do mark a significant shift in tone. Despite Genoino's assertion that "Acts and actions cannot be allowed to prejudice the democratic rule of law," it is also clear that this administration is far more at home with the idea of social movement pressure than any of its predecessors. In the same speech, for instance, Genoino referred to the right of social movements to continue to make demands, and the corresponding obligation of the government to manage its alliances in such a way as to bring about reform.

Far from bringing about reform, the government's alliances have only engendered disunity within the PT's own ranks and provoked the emergence of a new more radical Socialism and Freedom Party (PSOL). In the minds of many observers the evident lack of leadership shown by Lula has raised the question of whether the MST might finally turn its back on both the political and legal process in some sort of "radical" break. A look at the recent past shows why not. The fact remains that over the course of the Sarney, Collor, and Cardoso administrations, with all their attendant limitations, the MST strengthened its engagement with the legal field. There is nothing about the Lula administration that would suggest a reversal of this tendency. If anything, the highest echelons of the legal establishment are more receptive now than ever before. To assume that the MST will suddenly become disillusioned with the political process is to make a critical error about the illusions originally held by the organization. Its history suggests that while change from the top is to be welcomed, it must be pushed for from below. It is in this context that legal action has come—and will continue—to play an indispensable part of the struggle.

Notes

An early version of this chapter appeared in the October 2007 edition of *Law, Social Justice and Development*.

1. The Rural Democratic Union (UDR) is the most militant and visceral of the right-wing landowner organizations. It successfully lobbied to defeat land reform legislation in the late 1980s and on subsequent occasions. Throughout its ups and downs it has engaged in violent confrontation with rural groups, including the MST. According to one study,

though, it has also sought to integrate its own version of social movement discourse; see Payne (2000).

2. Jungmann (2003).

3. Jungmann (2003).

4. See "Jungmann diz ser preciso 'baixar o pau da lei' no MST," *Folha de São Paulo*, August 29, 2003.

5. As discussed in Bernardo Mançano Fernandes (chap. 5, this volume), and Marcelo Rosa (chap. 15, this volume), the MST is only one of dozens of organizations active in rural conflicts and land occupations.

6. For a more extended discussion of this issue, particularly as it related to the National Confederation of Workers in Agriculture (CONTAG), see Medeiros (1989: 92). She notes that with the emergence of the military dictatorship in the 1960s, and the generalized climate of fear and demobilization of rural workers that resulted, "the struggle for "rights," within legal parameters, came to constitute the *basic* directive to action of CONTAG" (my emphasis). She concludes that "The point of departure that comes to guide the practise of CONTAG is that rights existed but were not respected. . . . In this way the recourse to legal justice became the framework of action."

7. This is another charge leveled at the MST by Jungmann (2003).

8. Wagner Gonçalves, speech delivered to the conference "The Institutional and Political Challenges of Human Rights Reform in Brazil," organized by the Oxford Centre for Brazilian Studies, St Antony's College, October 13, 2000. His point was underlined in a special edition of the Brazilian weekly *Veja* (August 15, 2007) dealing with "the plague of impunity" from its ruling classes. One article on "Why corrupt officials do not go to prison" examined ten high-profile corruption investigations (between October 2003 and December 2004) of politicians, businessmen, and public officials. Legal loopholes and appeal mechanisms were so successfully exploited by lawyers that the initial figure of 245 arrests was distilled into sixty-four convictions and only two imprisonments. These, it should be emphasized, are instances where the justice system spent considerable sums in the investigative phases.

9. Wagner Gonçalves, speech, October 13, 2000.

10. The same study commissioned by the Brazilian Bar Association revealed that 30.9% of respondents had "no faith whatsoever" in the judiciary and 26.7% only had "partial confidence" in the institution. Among the chief reasons cited for lack of confidence in the justice system as a whole were unequal application of the law; privileging white people and the rich (24.3%); and corruption involving judges, prosecutors, and lawyers (22%); see Jornal do Brasil Online (2003a).

11. Desembargador Gercino da Silva, interview by author, Brasília, DF, October 25, 1999.

12. For a comprehensive guide to the Brazilian Constitution, see Silva (2004).

13. The August 14, 2003, decision of eight Federal Supreme Court judges to annul Lula's presidential decree expropriating 13,200 hectares in Rio Grande do Sul carried tremendous political weight. The expropriation was the largest of its kind ever proposed in Rio Grande do Sul and would have allowed 530 families to be settled. However, the key question before the judges was not so much whether the property was productive or not, but whether the landowner in question had been properly served with notice of an impending audit by INCRA. Lawyers for the landowner argued that the agency had failed in its legal duty while lawyers on behalf of the president argued that notification had taken place but that access to the property had been impeded by landowners. The agency had returned later but neglected to issue a new notification. It was the absence

of the new notification—and the landowner's participation in the audit—that formed the basis of the landowner's case. One of Lula's own appointees sided with the majority, who on administrative grounds rejected the arguments made on behalf of the president of the Republic. Another Lula appointee, however, suggested that the landowner had contributed to the situation through his own reluctance to be notified. For a highly critical analysis of the socio-legal background to the case, see Miguel Stédile (2003). A critical evaluation of the legal background to the case is set out in Görgen (2003). The decision of each judge can be accessed on the Supremo Tribunal Federal's site (http://stf.gov.br/) under *mandado de seguranca* (injunction) no. MS24547.

14. For a thorough discussion of the notion of the social function of property by one of Brazil's leading legal theorists on the subject, see Marés (2003).

15. See *Caros Amigos*, 4 (39) (June 2000): front cover.

16. Jacques Alfonsin, interview by author, Porto Alegre, RS, June 24, 1997.

17. João Pedro Stédile, interview by author, Campinas, SP, March 18, 2000.

18. Indeed, once Strozake was qualified, Greenhalgh would note that in dealing with movement affairs, "these days I am subordinated to him." Luis Eduardo Greenhalgh, interview by author, São Paulo, SP, September 3, 1999.

19. Already under the Cardoso administration some fifteen lawyers were contracted in this way. Under Lula this number was expanded to twenty-five in an agreement made between INCRA on the one hand and on the other the CPT and the National Association for Agricultural Cooperation (ANCA), a non-governmental organization (NGO) linked to the MST. That agreement expired in March 2005, but others have now taken its place. While detractors see this as a waste of money, proponents argue that such work, which encompasses the defense of all militants in rural areas rather than just those of the MST, is essential given the conflictive nature of the rural sphere and the absence of an effective system of public defenders.

20. For an extended discussion of RENAP's early formation and subsequent development, see Gorsdorf (2004).

21. Cited in Gorsdorf (2004: 96).

22. One example is the movement's use of *manutenção de posse,* (maintenance of possession) as a means of *forestalling* counterattacks. When an area is occupied it is common for landowners to seek the *reintegração de posse* (literally meaning the reintegration of possession) via the courts. The maintenance of possession is one means of trying to forestall such a move. The apparent simplicity of possession belies a host of legal complexities with massive social and political ramifications. By way of introduction, consider these comments from Jacques Alfonsin: "In the vast majority of *ações possessorias* [possession actions] what is of importance is not so much the title of land ownership, but the occupation. The proceedings that the owners undertake generally rely on the title. The judge never asks whether that person is actually *occupying* this area. With a mere glance at the land register the judge grants the injunction. We have a longstanding struggle to get judges to see this otherwise. The *reintegração de posse,* the action they most frequently use, presupposes possession. And yet these people often don't have possession. They may be living in the United States, in England, or elsewhere. They undertake legal proceedings and the judge grants it to them. So even from the point of view of positive law the actions of the judge are highly debatable. In an area where the person does not have possession, they undertake proceedings for the reintegration of possession. Why does he go for a reintegration of possession? Because these proceedings involve an injunction." Jacques Alfonsin, interview by author, Porto Alegre, RS, June 24, 1997.

23. Luis Eduardo Greenhalgh, interview by author, São Paulo, SP, September 3, 1999.

24. I devote two chapters of my book on the Pontal do Paranapanema to this topic, see Meszaros (2013). For further background on this region, see Leite (1998) and Fernandes (1996a), as well as the publications by São Paulo's state land agency, Instituto de Terras do Estado de São Paulo (ITESP) (1998a, 1998b) and Fernandes and Ramalho (2001).

25. The origin of the term is said to lie in the practice of taking *grilos* (crickets) and locking them up in a drawer with fictitious deeds. When the crickets died they would secrete liquids that would discolor the paper, prematurely aging it. A slightly different version has it that the crickets eat the paper, thereby aging its edges, and their excrement discolors it. In both instances, though, authentication of the document would be completed by networks of corrupt notaries.

26. João Pedro Stédile, interview by author, Campinas, SP, March 18, 2000.

27. José Rainha, interview by author, Teodoro Sampaio, SP, March 20, 2000.

28. To the best of my knowledge there is no systematic inquiry into the attitudes of landless workers towards the rule of law. The idea that law is a meaningful category of reference in people's lives needs to be treated with caution. Leonilde Sérvolo Medeiros notes that even in situations of extreme violence perpetrated by landowners, rural workers often do not look to law for mediation of conflicts. This may be because of fear of the consequences, unawareness of its provisions, or lack of access. But she also acknowledges that other factors might be in play: "in many situations, at least apparently, domination is exercised without contestation in a complex imbrication between consent . . . and coercion" Medeiros (2002a: 186).

29. José Rainha, interview by author, Teodoro Sampaio, SP, March 20, 2000.

30. I discuss this ruling in Meszaros (2000).

31. See Movimento dos Trabalhadores Rurais Sem Terra (MST) (1998: 3).

32. For a critical analysis of the Brazilian judiciary, see Dallari (1996).

33. At the beginning of the 1990s the Alternative Law movement emerged with considerable force in Rio Grande do Sul. On both theoretical and practical grounds a group of judges questioned claims that Brazilian justice was in any way value neutral and even whether value neutrality was a workable proposition. For practitioners and academics who came to ally themselves to the group a key issue was how to conceptualize the legal order's failure to address issues of substantive inequality while developing practical alternatives to it. For a useful introduction to the subject, see Andrade (1996). For an example of its practical application to the Public Ministry see the work of two public prosecutors, Machado and Goulart (1992).

34. On the back of this decision the MST's in-house legal service produced a pamphlet with the title "Land Occupations are Constitutional, Legitimate and Necessary"; see MST—Setor de Direitos Humanos (1997).

35. It pays to read articles 184, 185, and 186 in their entirety rather than as freestanding objects. Article 184 permits the state to expropriate lands that are not fulfilling their "social function" and to destine these toward agrarian reform. Article 185 deals with the protection of productive land, while article 186 deals with property's social function. The Article 185 reads: "The social function is met when the rural property complies simultaneously with, according to the criteria and standards prescribed by law, the following requirements: I—rational and adequate use; II—adequate use of available natural resources and preservation of the environment; III—compliance with the provisions that regulate labor relations; IV—exploitation that favors the well-being of the owners and laborers" (Vajda, Zimbres, and Souza 1998: 121).

36. Gilmar Mauro, interview by author, Brasília, DF, August 10, 2000.

37. This letter, issued on December 13, 1999, became known as the *Carta de Ribeirão Preto (Letter of Ribeirão Preto)*.

38. The launch of a Manifesto for Agrarian Reform in July 2003 is not specifically directed to the MST but is symptomatic of a broader legal support for agrarian reform. The document, signed by thirty leading practitioners (including judges, prosecutors, lawyers, and law professors) outlined the legal case for agrarian reform as well as expressing the hope that progressive case law would at last inform the views of other practitioners. A copy of this manifesto can be found at Rede Social de Justiça e Direitos Humanos (2003).

39. See Jungamann's quote in Estado de São Paulo (2003a), July 29, 2003.

40. The article, entitled "A fome não faz de famintos criminosos" is cited in Estado de São Paulo (2003b).

41. Estado de São Paulo (2003b).

42. In 1997, Minister Nelson Jobim tried to target more MST activists for prosecution by enlisting the support of the Public Ministry in states where tension was particularly high. In the case of São Paulo his overtures were firmly rejected.

43. See Jornal do Brasil Online (2003b, 2003c) and Estado de São Paulo (2003c).

44. Urbano Ruiz, member of the Association of Judges for Democracy, interview by author, São Paulo, SP, September 2, 1999. For details of this case, see note 13 above.

45. In a 2004 interview, the fourth judge appointed by Lula, Eros Roberto Grau, affirmed his view that the figure of the politically neutral judge was a fiction. When asked to comment on a loaded question, namely whether social movements are in conflict with the spirit of the law, he retreated arguing that it would be "imprudent to pass comment" and "the federal constitution must be respected by all sides"; see Cruz and Freitas (2004).

46. See Estado de São Paulo (2003d).

47. The legal measures introduced under the Cardoso administration to thwart MST land occupations are the Ministry of Agrarian Development (MDA) Portaria (ordinance) no. 62 of March 27, 2001, and *Medida Provisória* (presidential decree) no. 2.183-56, of August 24, 2001, both of which can be found on INCRA's website, available at: http://www.incra.gov.br/estrut/snda/iriv.htm and http://www.incra.gov.br/estrut/pj/medidas/2109.htm, respectively.

48. I briefly discuss the motivations in Meszaros (2000).

49. Author interview with Judge Gersino José da Silva Filho, Agrarian Ombudsman, Brasília, October 25, 1999.

50. See the ombudsman's comments above.

15 Beyond the MST
The Impact on Brazilian Social Movements

The Landless Rural Workers Movement (MST) has had a significant influence on Brazil's contemporary struggle for agrarian reform. Its mobilization strategies have become emblematic symbols of the demand for land redistribution.

Social scientists of various disciplines and leanings assume that the MST's relative success can be understood by analyzing its formation, internal structure, conflicts, and their direct consequences. This approach owes much to the movement's image as a path-breaking social actor. Its landless camps with black tarp–covered shacks, long-distance marches, and occupations of state-owned buildings, after all, represent a novel form of grassroots mobilization in Brazil.[1] Along with the allure sparked by these activities, scholars have also focused on the country's sharply unequal agrarian structure and attributed MST effectiveness to Brazil's historic need for land reform. The movement's success, however, also encompasses issues that go well beyond the nation's agrarian scene.[2]

This chapter highlights a particular contribution: the MST's role in fostering a new pattern of interaction between the Brazilian state and social movements, replicated in a variety of urban and rural settings. The argument unfolds in two parts. First, it shows that MST actions contributed in a decisive way to the creation of a number of grassroots groups driven by a host of demands other than land redistribution. It demonstrates this by providing an overview of four such movements, all of which have had historically close ties with the MST: the Peasant Women's Movement (MMC), the Movement of People Affected by Dams (MAB), the Small Farmers' Movement (MPA), and the Homeless Workers Movement (MTST).[3]

The chapter then examines the MST's impact on Brazil's rural trade union movement and the formation of other landless groups that have drawn inspiration on the MST's mobilization template.[4] This section builds on a case study of Pernambuco. In the mid-2000s, this state had fifteen organizations engaged in land struggles, the largest concentration of such groups in any part of the country.[5] A review of these developments will show how the MST's pattern of mobilization has been adopted by other poor people's movements and became the main formula for advancing popular claims in contemporary Brazilian politics.[6] This new dynamic had an important influence on state interactions and policies dealing with a wide range of historically disadvantaged groups.

A Single Pattern for Many Processes

The landless movement's early mobilizations among the *colonos* (family farmers) of southern Brazil, during the late 1970s and early 1980s, brought together groups of small farmers afflicted by an array of conflicts that permeated Brazilian society. Its first landless camps involved sons and daughters of colonos unable to purchase a farm plot as result of rising rural property prices. They also included families that had lost their farms due to the construction of hydroelectric dams, and people who had returned from failed colonization schemes in the Amazonian region. These landless camps became a symbol of struggle and hope for thousands of peasant families who took shelter under their black-tarp shacks. Moreover, they inspired and engaged the support of various progressive groups—dissenting politicians, religious activists, trade unionists, and intellectuals—who came to see these camps as an exceptional site for political contestation.

The intense exchanges that took place between these emerging landless groups and their political supporters helped establish a new generation of popular leaders among the landless peasants of southern Brazil. The ambiance enveloping these first camps also served as a stimulus for the development of other initiatives at the grass roots. Over time, then, land mobilizations in the southern region inspired the creation of a number of other social movements, which are briefly reviewed here.

From Land to Water: Movement of People Affected by Dams

The Movement of People Affected by Dams (MAB) emerged out of the same political and geographical context that gave rise to the MST. Its early stirrings started in 1980 when a group of university professors, pastoral agents, and peasant families opposed to the federal government's plan to build a series of hydroelectric dams on the Uruguay river, in northern Rio Grande do Sul, formed a commission to gather information on the families to be dislodged by the dam's reservoir. The Regional Commission of People Affected by Dams (CRAB) evolved subsequently into a movement by adopting various protest tactics to demand, at first, a fair compensation for those affected by the dam's construction and, eventually, the cancellation of these large construction projects.[7] The formal shift from a regional committee to a national movement took place in March 1991. By then MAB members had embarked on the development of an organization akin to that of the MST, with active branches in various parts of the country.

CRAB leaders were very familiar with the landless peasant camps that had been set up near the village of Ronda Alta in the early 1980s, scarcely 100 kilometers away from the epicenter of their own struggle. In these camps they met with many peasants that had lost their farms due to the construction of hydroelectric dams in the 1970s. CRAB's initial organization, made up of people displaced by dams and their supporters, was akin to the first commissions established by landless peasants to travel to Porto Alegre and present their demands before state authorities. This similarity contributed to CRAB's early legitimacy.

CRAB and the landless movement in northern Rio Grande do Sul played a pivotal role in the formation of their own national organizations. Their territorial expansion was shaped by their shared ability to organize at the grass roots, connect popular sector groups scattered across Brazil, frame their claims as rights, and pursue their demands vis-à-vis state authorities. Though run independently, MST and MAB have often collaborated on various activities. Many MAB activists have taken part of MST trainings and joined the landless movement in numerous mobilizations. Both groups, in fact, have common protest tactics and symbols. MAB has sponsored the occupations of various dam construction sites in order to enhance its bargaining position. Like the MST, its members also march with red flags and wear red caps with emblems that identify their movement. The MST has continued to offer valuable support for Brazil's anti-dam movement, thanks to its larger organizational structure.

Over the years, MAB spearheaded several campaigns to stop the development of large hydroelectric plants. In cases that appeared to be irreversible, the movement would lead negotiations with dam contractors and investors to protect the rights of the affected families. By 2006, MAB included ten regional organizations that were active in seventeen Brazilian states, including, Ceará, Paraíba, and Sergipe in the northeast; Bahia and the Jequitinhonha Valley in Minas Gerais; Mato Grosso; Goiás; Tocantins and Maranhão; Rondônia; Pará; São Paulo; and Paraná, Santa Catarina, and Rio Grande do Sul in the south.[8]

From Land to Gender: The Peasant Women's Movement

Brazil's movement for land reform generated a momentum and space that facilitated discussions on a variety of other social issues, including women's rights and their political participation. The first women's groups were formed in the MST's landless camps during the early and mid-1980s with the support of pastoral agents. Discussions within this nascent network of women study circles, linked to the MST and rural trade unions, fueled awareness of the need to advance their agenda independently from the church, the trade unions, and the landless movement.[9]

One of the first campaigns organized by these peasant women centered on obtaining state recognition as "rural women workers," a legal category that would confer this segment of the agricultural workforce the same rights to health care and pension benefits granted to urban women and male farm workers. Over time, the peasant women also started to question the patriarchal structure of the rural organizations of which they were a part. As a result, they began to insist on more positions of leadership in the rural workers unions, MST, and other social movements, and call for their effective participation in the committees formed to negotiate policy demands with state authorities.

Though active in the MST's struggle for land redistribution, many of women engaged in this alternative network felt the problem of gender inequality transcended their fight for agrarian reform and needed to be addressed by peasant women in an autonomous way. These discussions stimulated the creation of the Rural Women Workers' Movement (MMTR) in 1989. Similar to the MST and MAB, this new movement emerged largely out of organizing activities that took place in northern Rio Grande do Sul.

The MMTR eventually expanded to various other parts of the country and did so by engaging women's groups linked to the MST and rural trade unions. In all this, the MMTR retained its organizational autonomy and became one of the most active women's groups in Brazil, notably during the 2000s. A National Coordination Committee of Rural Women Workers set up in 1995 helped strengthen the MMTR's network by bringing together peasant women linked to several different rural groups: the MST, MAB, the Pastoral Land Commission (CPT), the Church's Pastoral Service for Rural Youth (PJR), several rural trade unions, a number of local rural movements, and eventually the Small Farmers Movement (MPA).[10]

In 2004, the MMTR joined La Via Campesina's international network of peasant associations. This decision was preceded by an internal debate that led to a rebranding of the organization's name to the MMC. The MMC's first National Congress was held in March 2004 and attended by 1,500 delegates from sixteen states.[11] Like the MST, the MMC members regularly employ different mobilization tactics to advance their claims and pressure the state to enforce their rights. They sponsor workshops and other activities aimed at promoting political activism among peasant women.

In March 2006, women activists linked to the MMC and MST invaded and destroyed part of a tree seedling plantation and laboratory owned by Aracruz Cellulose, a large pulp mill conglomerate. This contentious episode occurred in Barra do Ribeiro, close to the state capital of Rio Grande do Sul, Porto Alegre, which was then hosting the United Nation's Food and Agriculture Organization (FAO) Second International Conference on Agrarian Reform and Rural Development. The protest action taken at the Aracruz facilities sought to draw attention to the indiscriminate expansion of large-scale eucalyptus plantations.

La Via Campesina advocates charged these agribusiness corporations of creating vast "green deserts" that undermined biodiversity, local food production, and the sustainability of family farming. This conspicuous and atypical episode generated national headlines. Thirty-seven activists were subsequently charged with breaking the law.

From Land to Credit: The Small Farmers Movement

With the MST's territorial expansion and consolidation a number of new challenges appeared on the scene. One that gained particular salience in the 1990s concerned the access to farm credit. This issue was raised by new land reform settlers and embraced soon thereafter by other peasant farmers. These demands were fueled in many ways by the MST's relative success in establishing land reform settlements in many parts of the country, in areas once dominated by large cattle ranches and plantations oriented mostly to the production of export commodities.

The first government program established to provide farm credit to the new settlers was the Special Credit Program for Agrarian Reform (PROCERA), which was instituted in 1985 to "increase the agricultural production and productivity of land reform beneficiaries, by promoting their full integration into the market, and thus allowing their 'emancipation,' or rather, independence from the government's guardianship, along with obtaining property titles to their new landholdings."[12] PROCERA, however, only became effective in 1993, as a result of a series of MST mobilizations to demand land expropriations and state support for its settlers.

Other small farmers also began to mobilize for agricultural support policies, particularly in southern Brazil. In 1996, MST activists helped organize many of these peasants into the MPA. This new movement—like the MST, MAB, and MNC—was also started in northern Rio Grande do Sul. In fact, the mobilization that prompted the MPA's formation was a large protest camp of 15,000 peasant families that called on the federal government to provide emergency relief to family farmers that had lost their crops due to a prolonged drought. The camp's long rows of black tarp shacks were mounted on the outskirts of the town of Sarandi, scarcely 20 kilometers from the site of the 1981 encampment at Natalino's crossing that gave birth to the MST.

Through their joint mobilizations in the late 1990s, the MST and MPA helped foster several new government programs geared toward peasant farmers, notably the National Program for the Strengthening of Family Agriculture (PRONAF), among other initiatives administered by the Ministry of Agrarian Development. MST and MPA have continued to collaborate closely through the La Via Campesina network. Their common advocacy efforts and protest actions have facilitated important changes in the state's agricultural policies. Prior to the 1990s, the state's rural priorities were geared almost entirely to support large landholders and commercial farmers. The rise of a new wave of peasant movements, however, created the conditions needed to introduce a series of new public programs aimed at benefiting small landholders. Despite these reforms, the state's historic largesse toward the landed elite has remained basically intact.

From the Countryside to the City: The Homeless Workers Movement

The MST's impact on other grassroots groups has not been confined solely to rural areas. In the 1990s, its organizing and mobilization strategies were also replicated by urban popular movements, which began to alter in a radical way traditional forms of protest in Brazil's major cities. During the 1970s and ealy 1980s the country's larger metropolis experienced a surge of neighborhood associations, formed to get state agencies to provide basic public services such as sanitation, electricity, and street pavement. These urban groups became an important space for political socialization under the military regime, when strikes and other demonstrations were severely repressed, since their demands for local improvement were rarely perceived as a sign of serious political contestation.[13]

These neighborhood associations have remained active in several Brazilian cities. But after the mid-1990s, the most visible urban movements were not the ones engaged in the effort to improve public services in the *favelas* (shantytowns) or middle-class neighborhoods. By then a new wave of mobilization began to coalesce around the demands of the *sem-teto* or homeless movement, composed of poor city dwellers who lacked access to housing and the means to obtain it.[14]

The homeless movement's newfound prominence in urban Brazilian struggles is directly related to the MST's success in the countryside. This stems from more than just their similarity in name. Like their landless counterparts, the main mobilization strategy of the homeless is carried out through the occupation of buildings and undeveloped urban properties.[15] When the homeless movement occupies a vacant parcel of land it also sets up a protest camp like the MST with black-tarp shacks and the group's flag displayed on a tall flagpole. In some cities, notably in the state of São Paulo, the movement has occupied abandoned buildings, both public and privately owned, and demanded state authorities to transform these constructions into residential units.[16]

More than a dozen homeless movements had emerged in Brazil by the late 2000s, most of which have remained active in specific metropolitan areas, in particular Porto Alegre, São Paulo, and Recife. The MST has played an influential role in bolstering many of these groups by offering workshops for its activists. Other supporters include Catholic agencies that work among the urban poor and left-wing political parties.[17] The most important of these associations is the Homeless Workers Movement (MTST), which was founded in 1997, and has operated mainly in the cities of Recife and São Paulo.

In 2003, more than 10,000 MTST members occupied a large area in the metropolitan region of São Paulo donated by the state government to the Volkswagen car company. A village of hundreds of black-tarp shacks was created overnight on the site. The action and close similarity to MST's protest tactics triggered national news headlines. These urban mobilizations have, in effect, helped consolidate a distinct way of asserting popular claims Brazil.[18] These popular sector groups have gained societal recognition by infusing their takeover of public spaces with a *movement approach* grounded on occupations and protest camps organized in both urban and rural settings.

The MST and Rural Trade Unions: The Case of Pernambuco

Since their creation in the early 1960s, the rural workers unions have served as the nation's main political representative for Brazil's agricultural labor force. This section will show the MST's significant impact on these unions through a case study of the country's largest rural trade union association, the Federation of Agricultural Workers of Pernambuco (FETAPE).

Following the 1964 military coup d'état and the suppression of the Peasant Leagues and other independent movements in the countryside, the rural trade unions became the only legal form of political representation available to underprivileged rural people. Their monopoly of representation rested on two pillars: the struggle to enforce existing rural labor laws and the effort to provide their members with access to state-funded medical and retirement programs.[19] Various other demands were raised at trade union congresses conducted in the course of more than four decades, including repeated calls for land reform. Still, the agrarian question was not deemed a central topic of discussion among national union leaders.[20]

Since its founding in 1963, the National Confederation of Agricultural Workers (CONTAG) has been strongly influenced by FETAPE leaders. As such, historically, CONTAG's decisions have been affected by the experience of rural trade unions in Pernambuco, and particularly the sugarcane plantation workers in the state's coastal region, or Zona da Mata. There, FETAPE had shown a combative spirit by organizing, in 1980, the first rural labor strike under the military regime. After the mid-1990s, FETAPE rekindled its organization by sponsoring hundreds of land occupations. These undertakings were instrumental in changing CONTAG's approach to the struggle for agrarian reform and illustrate the MST's impact on other Brazilian popular movements.[21]

The sugarcane industry in Pernambuco entered a period of steady decline following President Collor de Mello's decision to abolish the federal government's marketing board—the Sugar and Alcohol Institute—and terminate a series of subsidies that had kept the industry afloat. Thousands of sugarcane plantation workers were laid off as a result, many of them without the compensations required by existing labor laws. This situation prompted a dramatic decline in union participation. Trade union leaders explained this demobilization in terms that were quite similar to the plantation owners: the economic crisis had reduced the number of jobs available in agriculture and produced a vast reserve of unemployed laborers, hence the drop in union membership.[22]

During this time, labor leaders found it very difficult to deploy traditional strategies for pressing their claims on sugarcane plantation owners—such as strikes, court injunctions, and wage campaigns—because of the bankrupt status of many of these estates. Other landlords could dismiss calls for wage increases by alleging financial constraints as a result of the region's economic downturn. The massive layoffs of sugarcane workers also led to a substantial decline in union dues, which were normally deducted from the plantation payrolls. This sudden drop in funding weakened the union's capacity for mobilization.[23] Even some of the strongest trade unions in the region experienced a rapid deterioration of their once well-built organizations. Among union leaders, all these developments enhanced perceptions of a serious crisis.

In 1992, a senior and respected union president in the Zona da Mata's southern region agreed to support a group of MST organizers. Working in close collaboration with the landless activists, the union leader helped sponsor the occupation of an unproductive sugarcane estate, the first major land takeover in the region.[24] After this, a handful of other trade unions teamed up with the MST to establish an unprecedented wave of land occupations in the Zona da Mata. FETAPE itself, however, was not involved in the initial land mobilizations. In fact, the unions engaged in these struggles did so without any coordination among themselves.

Still, in 1993, FETAPE created a new secretariat to handle agrarian reform issues. At the time, FETAPE leaders had strong misgivings about the MST's mobilization strategy, especially the "illegality" of its land occupations. This tactic, after all, countered the federation's longstanding practice of operating within the state's legal framework, a tradition that facilitated the unions' survival and expansion under the military regime. Adding to this, federation leaders viewed the idea of trespassing on someone's private property to set up a landless camp and call for the area's redistribution as foreign and hazardous.

In other words, FETAPE's ability to associate its demands with a movement that operated outside of the union structure required more than just setting up an internal secretariat to deal with agrarian problems. Land takeovers upset the federation's customary ways, which were forged over three decades of successful engagement.[25] Thus, initially, FETAPE's support for the MST and trade unions involved in land occupations strived to maintain a clear separation between the landless families and plantation workers, and preserve an explicit division of labor between the two groups.[26]

FETAPE and the MST remained close until 1995, when all federal and state government agencies in Pernambuco required that a FETAPE representative accompany any negotiation involving rural workers. This requirement, however, changed in mid-1995, following a clash between landless workers and the police. Thereafter, the MST began to negotiate directly with the federal government's land reform agency, INCRA. The end of FETAPE's mediation efforts on behalf of the MST signaled a definitive split between the two groups. From that point on, the MST and FETAPE began organizing their own land occupations and demonstrations. The MST's newfound recognition among sugarcane workers propelled a surge of land occupations in the Zona da Mata. These developments gave the movement ample exposure in the state and local news media, and wider recognition in various progressive forums. As a result, MST land occupations in Pernambuco jumped from fifteen in 1994 to seventy-three in 1999.[27]

FETAPE's internal elections in 1996 ushered in few changes at the helm of the federation, with the exception of one position: that of the secretary for agrarian reform. By selecting a new young union leader with close connections to the MST, and familiarity with its mobilization tactics, senior FETAPE officials indicated an interest in stepping up the federation's involvement in land struggles. Soon thereafter, FETAPE and the MST embarked on an intense competition over their land occupations. Indeed, nowhere in Brazil was the rivalry between the landless movement and a rural workers federation as intense as it was in Pernambuco.

All the changes brought about by the bankrupt plantations, the rising number of unemployed sugarcane workers, and newfound competition with the MST, prompted Pernambuco's rural trade unions to adopt a new style of making demands. These transformations at the state level were soon reflected in CONTAG's national debates. The 1998 election of yet another FETAPE-trained leader to CONTAG's helm gave added force to these concerns. In fact, during his campaign, this leader promised to increase CONTAG's support for land occupations carried out by rural trade unions in various parts of Brazil.

Thus, one can conclude that transformations that took place in Pernambuco's rural workers federation, as a result of its competition with the MST, had a direct influence on the orientation of Brazil's national rural labor confederation. A number of other federations, such as the FETAEMG in Minas Gerais, FETAG-BA in Bahia, and FETAGRI-PA in Pará, have since adopted the main tactics and symbols of Brazil's struggle for agrarian reform, by engaging in land occupations and setting up landless camps with rows of black-tarp shacks and banners flying on high masts.

None of these trends led Pernambuco's unions to become an MST-like organization. Still, by joining the wave of land occupations, spurred further by the federal government's budding interest in land redistribution, trade union leaders found an effective way to revive the rural workers movement in other parts of the country, including the Amazon region (see Ondetti, Wambergue, and Afonso, chap. 8, this volume.) The trade unions' decision to adopt elements of the MST's mobilization strategy, in a context beset by a diminished number of hired rural laborers, helped increase the unions' public visibility, while opening new venues for dialogue and negotiation with state authorities.

The links between social movements and the state are crucial in understanding how land occupations and other grassroots mobilizations have become a way of asserting citizenship rights in Brazil. The development of rights requires, after all, that they be sanctioned by the state. Land struggles in this country can no longer be confined to matters of territorial redistribution. Groups engaged in land mobilizations have also actively pursued other basic rights, by calling for, among other demands, state policies to contain the violence inflicted by rural landlords and reverse the state's historic neglect toward the rural poor by providing access to decent public health care and schools.

The Movement Approach: The Consolidation of the MST Model

Pernambuco also offers an auspicious terrain in which to examine the impact of MST land struggles and competition with rural workers unions on the rise of new forms of collective action. In early 2004 there were more than seventy organizations in Brazil engaged in MST-like mobilizations for land. Pernambuco alone accounted for fifteen of these associations.[28] Most of these groups were formed by former MST or trade union activists that had left their organizations for a variety of reasons. Some were older people with families to care for, who found it difficult to devote as much time to the movement as the younger MST activists, who were mostly single. Others held jobs that required considerable time investment.[29] Hence, with few opportunities to rise in the MST or union hierarchy, yet fully aware of the potential involved in organizing a landless group, they drew on their personal network of family, friends, and neighbors to create—with INCRA's endorsement—their own landless movements. All of these groups imitated the MST's organizational model. They designed their own flags, wore caps with their movement's logo, set up landless camps with rows of black-tarp shacks on unproductive landholdings, and staged sit-ins in public buildings. In other words, they adopted what I describe as the *movement approach*.

Drawing on their small town base, these groups became a legitimate venue for garnering state attention and fostering local participation. These movements offered an alternative space for community leaders that had been excluded from the rural workers unions; as was the case with the founders of two of these associations, the Brazilian Landless Workers Movement (MTBST) and the Brazilian Rural and Urban Workers Movement (MTRUB). Barred from holding leadership positions in their local trade union, both individuals joined an MST landless camp, where they learned the basic elements of the movement approach, and then decided to form their own movements. A similar split led to the creation of the Struggle in the Countryside Organization (OLC). This group emerged as an offshoot of FETAPE and was led by a former trade union activist who sought to prioritize the fight for land reform over the union's traditional defense of labor rights. Prior to his rise as a union leader, the OLC founder had collaborated informally with the MST. He then went on to promote the MST model within the union movement. After leaving FETAPE, the leader drew on his network of union contacts and supporters to establish a new landless organization.

Most of these landless groups were started in the late 1990s, during a surge of MST and FETAPE land occupations and the formation of various new land reform settlements. Their mobilization and recognition by the state have helped draw public attention to the problems faced by the poorest inhabitants of the Zona da Mata, a region of Brazil where the grip of its powerful landlord class has remained quite strong.

The movement approach deployed here and in other parts of the country can thus be viewed as an instrument through which impoverished people can achieve an element of social recognition. These forms of collective action have enabled many people to be treated as legitimate political subjects by state agents. All this has not only fostered their social inclusion, but provided an auspicious context in which, as Émile Durkheim writes, individual and group differences "are highlighted, made conspicuous and multiplied."[30] The MST's arrival to this region and mobilization for agrarian reform triggered a growing dispute over the access to public funds, which until then were an exclusive resource of the area's large plantation owners.

The Pernambuco case helps challenge the assumption of many scholars and opinion leaders that view the people involved in these landless movements as motivated solely by the desire to obtain land in order to preserve a traditional lifestyle and model of social reproduction. The situations reviewed here refute the reductionist views inherent in such observations, particularly those of José de Souza Martins who regards such people as "community and asset entrepreneurs oriented by traditional and conservative values of land, labor, family, community and religion."[31] To the contrary, the findings presented here suggest that people's involvement in these grassroots movements have catalyzed a process that breaks with traditional patterns of behavior and social hierarchies in the Zona da Mata region. By participating in these movements, rural workers have actually cultivated ideas and dispositions that challenge their previous subordination to local landlords.

Active involvement in these social movements enables participants to take part of a process of social differentiation, through the development of new political spaces and, above all, by gaining exposure to new social values. People do not turn to these movements for lack of options, but decide to join them among other alternatives, such as migrating to the city or pursuing the same activities they had done before. If they opt to go to a landless camp, they can choose between one sponsored by the MST, the rural trade unions, or other landless movements.[32] Contrary to Martins's argument, then, living in the countryside does not foreclose all available options to people involved in land struggles. These new popular organizations have facilitated the life transformation of thousands of people who consider these movements legitimate, and who, by joining their struggles, have helped transform them. Indeed, the MST is no longer what it was when it arrived in Pernambuco, and neither is the region's old structure of social domination. It is therefore senseless to argue as some scholars do that the MST has merely replaced the old patterns of dependency with a new form of subordination.

Conclusions

This chapter has offered an analysis of the MST's significance for Brazilian society and politics based on a review of its direct and indirect influence on other social movements. In doing so, it constructed an argument ground on three main processes.

First, the MST has developed a new pattern of struggle for agrarian reform in contemporary Brazil, grounded on the formation of grassroots movements and the use of direct action tactics, like occupying of rural estates and public buildings. Given its voluntary membership base, the MST does not represent the entirety of land claimants in Brazil, not even those of smaller regions like Pernambuco's Zona da Mata. Through its actions and ability to establish a novel pattern of rural mobilization, however, the MST stimulated the creation of other landless groups and propelled the rural trade unions to join the struggle for land reform.

Second, MST demands, after the early 1990s, began to encompass issues that went beyond the call for land redistribution and called for a variety of public policies in support of peasant farming. These claims produced a similar effect to the MST's struggle for the expropriation of large rural estates, in that they also extrapolated the movement's immediate interest and affected other groups experiencing similar needs. The rise of the Small Farmers Movement emblemizes this dynamic, as does the Peasant Women's Movement. The latter, in fact, drew inspiration from the groups of women formed in the landless camps and rural trade unions, as it mobilized to foster greater gender equity within these popular organizations and other societal spaces. In both cases, the MST facilitated crucial networks and opportunities to enhance the organizing skills of people who helped create these movements, and thus ensure that the demands for adequate farm policies and gender equality would be promoted in a collective and autonomous fashion.

Third, the MST has inspired existing groups to advance their claims in a new way. The Movement of People Affected by Dams, for one, started as a regional commission set up in northern Rio Grande do Sul to gather information and petition state officials. However, as a result of its workshops with the MST and other joint activities, it gradually began to adopt a movement approach. The competition stirred between the MST and rural workers unions in the Zona da Mata had a similar impact, in that it produced a new generation of union leaders that gained stature within their organizations by employing MST tactics. These developments revitalized Pernambuco's rural trade union movement. They helped garner media attention and strengthened FETAPE's capacity to negotiate with the state, on traditional concerns over wages and retirement benefits, as well as several other new demands.

None of these developments would have taken place if the MST had acted simply as a "mediator" between preestablished groups and the state, as Martins and other scholars insist.[33] To the contrary, the MST has played an active role in forging new social perceptions and identities—grounded on categories linked to gender, peasant farming, and landlessness—which, over time, have clustered families and individuals around specific movements. It was in the MST landless camps after all that participants began to cultivate their self-image as "landless people."

These new categories, though, became effective only with the transformation of traditional patterns of state behavior, brought about through a set of popular collective actions. As a result, Brazil has seen the diffusion of what I characterize as the *movement approach*—that is, a form of collective expression grounded on a set of actions and procedures fashioned by the MST that regulate activities carried out by movement activists and, most significantly, by state agents.[34] Indeed, the movement approach has become so compelling that, in practice, only groups that follow and replicate its method are treated as legitimate actors by INCRA's regional authorities.

Over the last quarter of a century, the MST has become one of the most revealing examples of the fact that, in Brazil, there are no benefits to be gained by treating the concepts of state and civil society in a dichotomous manner.[35] By mobilizing ordinary people in tandem with public officials, this social movement has effectively changed the country's history of collective action in a profound way.

Notes

Translated from the Portuguese by Miguel Carter.

1. See Sigaud (2000) and chapter 9 in this volume.
2. This chapter is informed by research activities carried out in Rio Grande do Sul between 1994 and 1999, and 2004–05. On the broader agrarian process involved, see Tavares dos Santos (1985).
3. All of these movements, with exception of the MTST, have joined La Via Campesina, an international network of peasant associations, see Fernandes's chapter 5 in this volume.
4. According to INCRA, in 2003 seventy-two groups were involved in different land struggles across Brazil.
5. Further details on the groups involved in land struggles throughout Brazil can be found in Fernandes (tables 5.4 and 5.5, chap. 5, this volume).
6. Borges (2003).
7. On MAB's historical development, see Vainer (2009), Moraes (1996), and Navarro (1996a). On the CPT's influence in the movement's formation, see Poletto (chap. 4, this volume).
8. Guedes (2006: 19).
9. According to my research findings in Rio Grande do Sul's Ronda Alta region, the first landless camp set up at the Macali farm in 1979 included a group involved with women's issues. For information on the MMC's early history, see Stephen (1996) and Navarro (1996a).
10. See www.mmcbrasil.com.br.
11. These representatives came from the southern states of Rio Grande do Sul, Santa Catarina, and Paraná; the southeastern states of Minas Gerais and Espírito Santo; the midwest state of Mato Groso do Sul; the northeastern states of Alagoas, Bahia, Maranhão, Paraíba, and Sergipe; and the northern states of Acre, Amazonas, Roraima, and Tocantins. The only state delegation that participated in the Congress, yet declined to join the new organization was from Pernambuco, which retained the original name, MMTR.
12. Rezende (1999: 1).
13. Boschi (1987).
14. In Portuguese the term *sem-teto*—literally "roofless"—recalls the term for landless, *sem terra*.
15. The tactic of occupying buildings did not originate in Brazil, yet gained impetus in the country thanks to the MST's success in using similar strategies. On the use of building occupations as a social movement tactic in Europe, see Argiléz and López (2004).
16. Another homeless group, the National Movement to Struggle for Housing (MNLM), has been active mostly in southern Brazil.
17. I witnessed several joint activities between the MST and the homeless movement while conducting fieldwork in Pernambuco in 2002 and 2003.
18. Sigaud (2000).
19. Sigaud (1980).
20. Medeiros (1981).
21. On FETAPE's involvement in land occupations, see Rosa (2004b), which is based on a study sponsored by the Latin American Social Science Council (CLACSO) in 2003–04.
22. See the document "Seminário Regional" (1993: 40).
23. According to several union leaders I interviewed, the number of hired sugarcane workers fell from roughly 240,000, at the time of the 1980 strike, to less than 60,000 laborers in 2000.

24. The MST's first land occupation in Pernambuco took place in 1989, but ended in failure due to the lack of support from the rural trade unions and the state governor, Miguel Arraes. Though left-leaning, he viewed the occupation as an illegitimate act and ordered its eviction. MST subsequently established contact with trade union leaders from the Zona da Mata region in 1992. These meetings led to the joint organization of the first successful land occupation in Pernambuco, which targeted a large and bankrupt sugarcane plantation; see Sigaud (2000).

25. Pernambuco's main newspapers questioned FETAPE's new support for land occupations in various news articles and editorials that treated these activities as acts of political disorder.

26. Anonymous interview with a FETAPE director in Recife, September 2001.

27. Figures based on statistics provided by the MST; for further details, see Wolford (table 12.1, chap. 12, this volume).

28. Data on the groups engaged in land mobilizations in Pernambuco were provided by local INCRA officials in September 2002.

29. Additional information on these landless movements can be found in Rosa (2004a).

30. Durkheim (1995: 360).

31. Martins (2000a: 49). This chapter contests Martins's sociological interpretation of the agrarian reform debate. In it, he treats these elements of reductionism, not only as an empirical finding, but mostly as a political strategy, designed to preserve the truth status of partial theories that pretend to be universal ones. As such, Martins's (2000a) defense of an idealized view of the peasantry vis-à-vis his detractors (in various social movements, political parties, and intellectual circles) mummifies the peasantry in a way that allows him (2000b) to promote his standing as an eminent intellectual and sociologist of the "ordinary man." Here, the simpler the rural man, the truer his own theory.

32. Rosa (2004a, 2006).

33. Martins (1996: 158).

34. On the *movement approach*, see Rosa (2004a).

35. The MST has straddled both state and civil society categories since its origin. In fact, its most visible leader, João Pedro Stédile, helped to organize the first landless camps while employed by the state government of Rio Grande do Sul. More recently, since the early 1990s, the MST has regularly called on the federal government to hire more civil servants to staff INCRA and allocate greater funds for its activities.

Challenging Social Inequality
Contention, Context, and Consequences

The Landless Rural Workers Movement (MST) is undeniably a controversial movement in Brazil. It not only stands at the cutting edge of meaningful transformations in the country, in many regards, it is Brazil's cutting edge. No other Brazilian movement embodies the strength, incisiveness, and aspirations for fundamental social change represented by the MST. The chapters in this book provide a sympathetic yet nuanced assessment of this, grounded on extensive research and field experience.

This conclusion pulls together key findings and ideas in this collection and assesses their main implications for social change in Brazil. There are three sections to this chapter. The first, "Contention," opens with an examination of the principal arguments leveled against the MST's struggle for agrarian reform and delineates the broader contours of the debate at hand. The second section, "Context and Complexity," draws on the findings in this book to suggest ways in which a sharper understanding of the landless movement can be reached. The final section, "Consequences," examines the formidable obstacles to land reform in Brazil; the role of public activism in effecting change; and the radical democratic implications of the MST's fight for social justice.

Contention

This book takes part in a broader public debate over agrarian reform in Brazil. The insights offered here are rarely conveyed by the country's media establishment. Instead, the mainstream press has given ample attention to public intellectuals with very critical views of the MST's social struggle. Four of the best-known critics are: José de Souza Martins, Zander Navarro, Francisco Graziano, and Denis Lerrer Rosenfield.[1] Through their academic writings, newspaper columns, and press interviews, all four scholars have played a key role in legitimizing skeptical views of agrarian reform and reinforcing harsh appraisals of the MST. Their arguments employ three basic lines of attack. The first depicts the MST as an "anachronistic, backward-looking movement" and is inclined to treat agrarian reform as an "outdated" policy. The other contends that land reform has turned out to be a "failure." The third form of assault sustains that the MST's confrontational relations with Brazil's governing institutions represent a "threat" to democracy.

For Martins, one of Brazil's most renowned rural sociologists, the MST is the local equivalent to the English Luddite movement, a short-lived popular uprising in the early nineteenth century famed for wrecking new factory machines. Incited by similar "fundamentalist" beliefs, he insists, the MST "refuses to recognize the institutional legitimacy and actions of the government and the state." In fact, according to Martins, the movement's actions and demands represent a "pre-political and precarious attempt to demolish the political order."[2]

Martins further asserts that the MST and its church ally, the Pastoral Land Commission (CPT), are led by radicalized middle-class intermediaries—professional activists, intellectuals, and clergy members—who filter the authentic voices and usurp the real demands of the rural poor. The ideological and partisan interests of these middle-class activists, he contests, ignore the peasantry's essentially "traditional and conservative values of land, work, family, community and religion." What's more, their "apparent radicalism" does not address the "real roots of the problem," but rather serves to "maintain the social inequities . . . (they) seek to change."[3] In Martins's view, the crux of Brazil's agrarian impasse resides in the land reform activists themselves, who "manipulate" and "use" the rural poor in ways that replicate the old oligarchic patterns of landlord domination.[4] In other words, because of their misbegotten ideas the MST and CPT, not the landlords and their agribusiness allies, have become the main obstacles to progress in the countryside.

Navarro, a fellow sociologist, considers that, "The MST has lost its reason to exist, since the time for land reform has past. In fact, it ceased to be a historic and national necessity a long time ago, under any point of view."[5] Urbanization and the successful development of agribusiness in Brazil have neutralized land reform's raison d'être, as this policy is no longer necessary to stimulate the rural economy. Any mobilization against this historical trend is pointless.[6] Navarro further describes the MST as an "anti-systemic" and "anti-state" organization, driven by a hardened Marxist disposition toward non-institutional venues of action.[7] He argues that the MST stopped being a social movement in the 1990s. Instead, it degenerated into a "semi-clandestine," "orthodox Leninist" organization, run by a small revolutionary cadre. The MST, Navarro stresses, is sustained through "non-democratic" practices, a "militarist ethos," and the "quasi-religious devotion" of its activists. The group's training centers reproduce the "childish Leninism" of its national leaders and instill a "pathetic ideological mystification" of the world.[8]

The MST's authoritarian disposition is such, Navarro adds, that it even "refuses to establish any type of political alliances with other popular organizations in the countryside." Rather, "it seeks to combat them, and if possible, to dominate them."[9] The MST, he claims, controls its land reform settlements through autocratic impositions and manipulations, including the extortion of settlers who depend on the organization for the allocation of public funds.[10]

Graziano, a former federal deputy and head of INCRA during the Cardoso administration, insists that the modernization of large landholdings have extinguished the traditional *latifundia* (vast and mostly unproductive rural estates). Because of this, Brazil has little or no more land to redistribute in its more developed regions.[11] For Graziano, "the main proof" that land reform is an "outdated recipe" can be "found in the resounding failure of the majority of existing rural settlements." Agrarian reform "has done nothing to help reduce poverty in our country." To the contrary, the demand on scarce resources from the public treasury, "subtracts benefits for other social policies, producing waste."[12] If anything, he claims, agrarian reform is responsible for exacerbating poverty in the countryside, notably by producing rural *favelas* (shantytowns).[13]

Agrarian reform erred, according to Graziano, when "it lost its historic economic justification and was directed towards the realm of social policy. By trying to . . . assist the poor and those excluded from society, it left behind its (economic) rationality and drifted towards voluntarism." Destitute people cannot "become competitive farmers."[14] Most people mobilized by the MST, he argues, are undeserving claimants: "From the poorest to the well-off, shopkeepers, butchers, street peddlers, prostitutes, all of them want to put their little finger in this business of getting land for free, pretending to be landless."[15] For Graziano, "The millions of landless people" that land reform proponents put forth "simply don't exist; they are the product of a chimera, an ideological dream."[16] The MST, in his view, is "an authoritarian guerrilla organization" that is "undermining democracy" by abetting acts of "agrarian terrorism" with its land occupations.[17]

Rosenfield treats the MST and CPT as both criminal and revolutionary organizations. He charges them with, "Property invasions, kidnapping, illegal possessions of weapons, disrespect for the law, and the destruction of property (along with) the generalized use of violence." The MST and CPT's real revolutionary intentions can be discerned from the "glamorization of violence" in their songs and poetry, as well as their affection for Che Guevara.[18] Along with Brazil's main labor confederation, the Unified Workers' Central (CUT), these organizations aim to "suppress the market economy, the rule of law, and representative democracy, that is, our liberties."[19]

Rosenfield warns his readers not to be fooled by the MST's demand for land distribution, its calls for introducing a system of national plebiscites, its petition to reduce Brazil's record-high interest rates, and its representation of socialism in moral terms, because behind this façade, the MST is really bent on establishing a totalitarian communist system based on the Soviet and Cuban model.[20] The title of Rosenfield's book describes the MST as a "threat to democracy." His dire conclusions, though, are based principally on the exegesis of six texts: a CPT songbook, two issues of an MST magazine, a history publication on the landless movement, and two minor documents apprehended during a police raid at an MST camp.[21]

These four intellectuals have helped sanction recurrent media depictions of the MST as an "authoritarian, violent, manipulative, revolutionary organization that mobilizes false landless people." As such, they have endorsed a public image that treats the landless movement as a "danger" to the Brazilian state and its democratic regime. The tacit proposition, here, clearly underpins conservative calls to curtail MST demands and restrain their protest activities.

Such critiques of the MST shed greater light on its authors than on the phenomena they are keen to attack.[22] The extreme character of many of their statements, their gross oversimplifications, gratuitous charges, and the dearth of empirical evidence underlying many of their appraisals suggests that these intellectuals are more interested in deploying a "rhetoric of intransigence," in Albert O. Hirschman's fitting term, than facilitating a constructive dialogue.[23] Their restrictive and ahistorical understanding of democracy is certainly worrisome.

None of the texts surveyed here consider Brazil's stark social inequities a central analytical problem. Their main disagreement is with the MST and its struggle for land redistribution, rather than the underlying social dilemma. This outlook reveals much about the authors' political position on the classic Right-Left divide. According to philosopher Norberto Bobbio, "the essence" of this distinction,

> is the different attitude that both parts—the people of the *right* and the people of the left—show systematically towards the idea of equality: the moral conduct and political action of those that claim to be of the *left* gives greater importance to that which makes (humans) equal, or to ways in which factors of inequality can be mitigated or reduced; those that claim to be of the *right* are convinced that inequalities cannot be eliminated, and ultimately have no desire to see their elimination.[24]

Contemporary MST critics generally treat land and income inequality as a peripheral matter, an afterthought, a distant feature in the nation's social landscape. By contrast, progressive scholars and activists tend to consider such disparities a key national dilemma. In their view, Brazil's glaring social inequality warrants extensive research, debate, and energetic public intervention.

These contrasting perspectives, no doubt, shape basic perceptions and appraisals of the MST. For conservatives and neoliberals, the MST is an anachronistic nuisance, a "lunatic" fringe group. Yet for socialists and progressive liberals, the MST is a contemporary movement of vital positive significance.[25] Appraisals of Brazil's public debate over agrarian reform cannot ignore the full implication of Bobbio's distinction: subjective dispositions concerning the problems of inequality are bound to affect the contentious views at stake.

Context and Complexity

This book underscores the importance of understanding the MST's struggle for agrarian reform through an enhanced appreciation for context and complexity. This outlook draws on a methodological effort to: (1) interpret the MST and Brazil's agrarian reform process through a historical lens; (2) invest substantial time and efforts in garnering empirical evidence, notably through extensive fieldwork in the countryside; and (3) sharpen awareness of this phenomenon through a comparative perspective. The following comments address some of the principal issues raised by MST critics. They do so by building on these methodological concerns and gleaning insights presented throughout this book.

History is essential for appraising the MST's broader significance for Brazil. It provides a crucial framework for interpreting its struggle and comprehending the enduring forces, institutions, and practices that have sustained land inequality in the Brazilian countryside. Guilherme Costa Delgado (chap. 2, this volume) and Leonilde Sérvolo de Medeiros (chap. 3, this volume), in particular, touch on key historical legacies: the vast *sesmaria* land grants to privileged colonial Portuguese families; the institution of slavery; and the formation of a society based on sharp class inequities, in a nation ruled by a predominantly authoritarian and patrimonial elite, embedded in a context of international economic dependence. The Land Law of 1850 enshrined Brazil's large landholding oligarchy. Thereafter and throughout the first half of the twentieth century, the landlord class was able to block the extension of basic citizenship rights to peasants, including the right to form associations and, through literacy requirements, the right to vote.

Land reform's forceful entry on the nation's public agenda took place in the mid-1950s, as a result of peasant mobilizations in the northeast. The federal government's first land reform proposal, in 1964, was thwarted by a military coup, which suppressed all reform activists and curtailed the newly formed, independent peasant organizations. Representatives of Brazil's landlord class were active participants in the demise of the nation's democratic regime. In fact, large landholders were prime beneficiaries of the ensuing two decades of authoritarian rule. During this time, vast sums of public monies were injected to modernize parts of the countryside, while preserving the existing land tenure system. In the Amazon, the government subsidized the creation of huge estates. Under the military regime, the state effectively championed the creation of a new rural bourgeoisie, based on an agribusiness model of development, oriented toward international markets.

Brazil's redemocratization in the early 1980s opened the way for a new cycle of peasant mobilizations that placed agrarian reform back on the national agenda. In reaction, the landlords strengthened their own organizations and reinstituted the practice of hiring gunmen to assassinate their opponents. Drawing on their political influence, representatives of the landlord class were able to thwart the implementation of President José Sarney's 1985 agrarian reform program and defeat progressive measures for land distribution in the 1988 Constitution. The 1982 international debt crisis and the neoliberal policies introduced in the 1990s affirmed the large landholders' enduring strength, as agribusiness exports became a leading source of revenue to repay Brazil's foreign and domestic creditors. Even under Brazil's democratic regime, agricultural subsidies, rural development programs, and the state's execution of agrarian laws and taxes, have consistently favored the landlords over the peasantry. Between 1995 and 2005, each of the largest landlords had access to $1,587 in government funds for every dollar made available to a landless family.[26]

A critical examination of these historical barriers to land reform casts the MST in an alternative light. If anything, it helps portray the movement as one engaged in a strenuous, uphill struggle to transform a society based on extreme disparities of wealth and power, long sustained by unfair state policies. Indeed, a close review of Brazilian history allows for an interpretation of the landless movement that turns the conservative imputations of backwardness, failure, and threat on their head. Archaic, here, is Brazil's deeply unequal land structure, not the movement trying to overcome it. Disappointing land reform results shed light on Brazil's landlord-friendly state, rather than the policy's actual merit. Moreover, as the historical record shows, the greatest obstacle and menace to Brazilian democracy has come from the landlord class, not the peasantry. In fact, contemporary efforts to extend modern citizenship rights and enhance the quality of democracy are imperiled by the steadfast defenders of the nation's status quo, not its landless groups. All this casts the MST as a modernizing and democratic force in Brazilian society, unlike the depictions conveyed by its critics.

Attention to historical evidence is also important for understanding specific developments. For instance, during the late 1990s and early 2000s, conservative analysts were quick to explain the MST's antagonism toward the Cardoso government as the result of the movement's adoption of "fundamentalist," "anti-state," and "revolutionary" ideas. A more comprehensive view of this period, however, suggests a different line of interpretation. While it is true that the Cardoso administration distributed more land than all of his predecessors combined, its efforts were basically reactive and defensive in nature. They were not propelled by a programmatic drive to support peasant agriculture and transform the nation's agrarian structure. Instead, as Bernardo Mançano Fernandes, Sue Branford, and other contributors to this book show, these policies were prompted by growing MST mobilizations and intense public protest over two police massacres of landless peasants. Cardoso's land reform program coincided with his decision to transform Brazil's development model and establish a neoliberal state, fully integrated with the global market. After the MST's 1997 national march to Brasília, the Cardoso government began to view the movement's rising popularity, strong ties with the rival PT, and forceful critique of its neoliberal policies with growing apprehension.

Responding to this perception of threat, the second Cardoso administration ushered in a discernable effort to undermine the MST. The government cut back public funding for agrarian reform and farm credits. With World Bank support, it instituted a local, market-based approach to land distribution, which severely undercut the MST's capacity for collective action.[27] Furthermore, the government began to criminalize the movement's protest activities, penalizing all land occupations, while coordinating an offensive with leading news outlets to denigrate the MST's favorable public image, by running stories alleging corruption within the MST.[28] What's more, the Cardoso government fired 1,200 agronomists working with land reform settlements and significantly reduced the staff of the national land reform agency, INCRA. During this time, the number of INCRA employees in the state of Rio Grande do Sul, for example, was cut down by nearly 85%.[29] The federal government's retreat on agrarian reform coincided with the 1999 devaluation of the national currency, which facilitated agribusiness export, enhanced land market values, and reduced opportunities for government land purchases.

In light of these facts, it is hard to view the MST's harsh reaction to the Cardoso government as impelled by purely "dogmatic" ideological beliefs, or any sense of "Luddism," "pseudo-military adventurism," "childish Leninism," and "regressive utopia." A more reasonable explanation would simply treat this as a political conflict of interests and values. Just as the Cardoso administration was at liberty to pursue a policy of state retrenchment and market liberalization, so was the MST entitled to believe that these actions would hinder the implementation of land reform and other public efforts to reduce social inequality.

A concern for historical facts, then, enhances an appreciation for the many complexities at stake. Uniform depictions of the MST should be treated with caution, given the assorted settings, processes, and impacts at stake. Moreover, any serious effort to grasp its actions requires ongoing field experience. Given the movement's dynamic and innovative character, frozen images can become outdated over a brief lapse of time.[30] The following comments provide a framework for analyzing different and intricate aspects of the MST's struggle for agrarian reform. These features include the MST's mobilizations; relations with the state and rule of law; mobilizing resources; motivations; and settlements.

Mobilizations

As the contributors to this book demonstrate, MST mobilizations combine lawful protest and acts of civil disobedience. They generally include masses of people and the participation of entire families. The movement's main pressure tactics, as others and I have shown, involve organizing protest camps, long distance marches, demonstrations, road blockades, hunger strikes, sit-ins in public buildings, and land occupations of mostly idle farms. MST mobilizations regularly take place amid ongoing lobbying activities and negotiations with public authorities. Ondetti, Wambergue, and Afonso underscore the fact that the MST's modern form of contention has actually helped restrain rural violence in the Amazonian frontier. In contrast to traditional squatter land struggles, MST mobilizations are massive in scale, well-organized, family-inclusive, and geared toward making explicit demands on the state. In this way and unlike the squatters, the MST is able to avert direct confrontation with gunmen often hired by landlords. By channeling social conflict through nonviolent means, the MST has actually played a civilizing role in the Brazilian countryside.

On sporadic occasions, mobilizations undertaken by the MST have sparked brawls with the police or resulted in damage to property. Rarer still, some of these clashes and internal power tussles in land reform settlements have ended in tragic deaths. These situations merit a careful analysis. For one, it is important to acknowledge that land struggles in Brazil and elsewhere are hardly a "tea party." Given the stakes and nature of the conflict, a measure of rough play is almost unavoidable. Brazil has over seventy landless organizations and scores of informal groupings engaged in local land struggles. Compared to these other groups, the MST is the most disciplined movement. The sense of self-restraint nurtured among its activists has helped maintain a nonviolent orientation toward land conflicts. Violence, as George Mészáros underscores, is not part of the MST's modus operandi. If anything, MST activists are far more likely to suffer from wanton physical violence than inflict it upon others.

Injuries produced in the context of MST mobilizations are generally accidental, rather than intentional. Careful scrutiny of the facts will find that many of these incidents are actually the result of police provocations or acts of self-defense amid violent attacks by landlord militias. Press coverage of the MST tends to spotlight these physical clashes, while underreporting the many other (less dramatic) efforts made to resolve the underlying impasse in a peaceful manner. In doing so, they distort the overall character of MST mobilizations.

Relations with the State and Rule of Law

All contributors to this book have found the MST to be keenly engaged with the state. Lygia Maria Sigaud's study of landless struggles in Pernambuco, in particular, demystifies the assumptions that the MST is intrinsically hostile toward the state. The bellicose rhetoric between the state and peasant groups, she contends, masks a relationship that also includes elements of close cooperation and mutual dependency. In fact, state actions have rendered the MST's protest camps a legitimate instrument for establishing entitlement claims among the rural poor. Marcelo Rosa extends this point further and argues that the MST is responsible for the emergence of a new pattern of interaction between the Brazilian state and social movements. Nowadays, he observes, public officials are inclined only to recognize grassroots groups that adopt the MST's "movement form."

Others, like myself, highlight the MST's general disposition to negotiate with state authorities, while using pressure tactics to improve its bargaining power. In my chapter on Rio Grande do Sul, I described the movement's involvement in running the state's agrarian reform bureau under a PT governor. Wendy Wolford depicted a pattern of close interactions between MST leaders and local governments in Pernambuco's coastal region. Ondetti, Wambergue, and Afonso claimed that MST mobilizations have enhanced the presence of the federal government in the Amazonian frontier. Branford's review of the MST's historic links with the PT and support for the party's election campaigns denoted a longstanding and practical MST recognition of the importance of democratic institutions.

The idea of a fundamental opposition between the MST and the law, Mészáros asserts, oversimplifies what is an altogether complex and rich relationship. It omits a fact relevant to many social movements around the world and in history, namely, their role as architects of an alternative legal order. The movement's difficulties with Brazil's legal system cannot ignore the country's historic rural inequities and oligarchic domination of legal institutions; the judiciary's own cripplingly bureaucratic, class-biased procedures; and enduring human rights violations and impunity in the countryside. Amid these predictable clashes with the law, the MST has also taken an active part in the nation's debates over the interpretation of existing laws. Through its dedicated and expanding National Network of Popular Lawyers (RENAP), which includes more than 500 attorneys, the movement and its allies are frequently involved in running legal cases and lobbying higher echelons of the judiciary. In one of its major victories, a 1996 decision by one of Brazil's highest courts ruled that land occupations designed to hasten reform were "substantially distinct" from criminal acts against property. According to Mészáros, MST clashes with the law should also be appraised in terms of their long-term contributions toward rebalancing the nation's social and legal order, rather than simply dismissed as acts of subversion. In sum, for all its radical rhetoric and street opposition, a closer examination of the movement's regular activities reveals a myriad of constructive interactions with Brazil's political institutions.[31]

Mobilizing Resources

Over the years the MST has cultivated its own mobilizing resources and has grown to become a highly complex and sophisticated grassroots organization. Bernardo Mançano Fernandes, Horacio Martins de Carvalho, and I describe the MST as a multidimensional, networklike organization, composed of various decentralized yet well-coordinated layers of representation and collective decision making. The MST's national, state, and regional branches are also organized into different task sectors dealing with an array of practical issues—from education; human rights; grassroots organization and training; finances; international relations; production, cooperation, and the environment to gender; health; and culture. In addition, the movement has created legally registered organizations that help channel public and international resources for its educational programs and agricultural development projects.

The MST is a mass movement operating in a continent-size nation with a decentralized state and significant political freedoms. People are at liberty to join and leave the movement. Moreover, its members are regularly exposed to adverse and even hostile information on the MST through the mass media. Under these circumstances, it is hard to imagine a poor people's organization ever succeeding on a national scale with a "militaristic" leadership that "controls," "indoctrinates," and "manipulates" its followers, as some analysts suggest. Rather, the MST's organizational success seems to reflect other attributes, notably, the movement's ability to marshal a consensus through internal debates and collective decision-making bodies; its ample experience in coordinating an array of activities; its capacity to maintain a flexible, versatile, and innovative organization; its substantial investment in consciousness-raising and educational efforts; and the discipline and intense commitment of its activists.[32]

The MST would not exist without the support of a broad constellation of social and political actors. Since its early years, as Ivo Poletto, Fernandes, and I highlighted, the MST has relied on the support of significant sectors of the Catholic Church, a number of Protestant congregations, rural and urban trade unions, student groups, middle-class professionals, NGOs, and progressive politicians from the PT and other political parties. Over the years, the MST has taken part in numerous national and international coalitions and developed an extensive network of overseas supporters. The nature, scope, and intensity of its interactions with other groups have naturally varied over time and from place to place. As Rosa, Ondetti, Wambergue, and Afonso showed in the cases of Pernambuco and Pará, MST relations with other peasant groups can oscillate between close cooperation and bitter competition. To infer, however, from the normal frictions of movement politics that the MST is a closed organization and is hostile toward forming partnerships with other groups ignores the fact that the MST has long played an active role in several national, regional, and local networks and coalitions advocating social change.[33]

Motivations

The chapters in this book suggest that motivations within the MST are varied, wide-ranging, and often quite malleable. These can change during the course of a struggle; are susceptible to their situational dynamic; and are affected by their historical and cultural milieu. Sigaud claimed that people join MST land struggles in hope of finding a quick solution to their impoverished lives. She sees this as a strategic gamble and argues that its participants, under other circumstances, would easily opt for a better alternative. While acknowledging the importance of material calculus, especially in the initial impetus to join the land struggle, Fernandes and I suggested that other impulses—such as feelings of indignation, peasant identity, moral economy views of the land, and political consciousness—can also play an important role in sustaining the land struggle.

In chapter 6, I grouped many of these motivations under Max Weber's concept of ideal interest (or value-rational) behavior. Ideal interests are characterized by a passionate yet strategic approach to the fulfillment of nonnegotiable goals. These motivations are nurtured through MST's mobilizations and regular display of symbols—flags, songs, chants, marches, and ritual gatherings—that stir courage, vitality, and persistence among its participants. Ideal interests, I argued, usually generates intense social energy, which can help neutralize various collective action problems and fuel the movement's endurance.

Elena Calvo-González's ethnographic account of a new settlement community revealed that this phase tends to be a period of frustration and disenchantment within the MST. Amid the nostalgia for the tight-knit community life experienced during the landless encampment and disappointments over the inadequate infrastructure provided to the new settlement, the settlers must cope with power relations within their own community and in their interaction with regional MST leaders. Calvo-González's close view of an MST settlement reminded us that everyday interactions are usually messier than those represented in the broader and more stylized depictions of the movement. Wolford's review of a settlement community in Pernambuco's sugarcane region highlighted the impact of cultural legacies in understanding different conceptions of the land. Unlike family farmers in other parts of Brazil, plantation workers have historically lived off the land as wage earners. Their desire to own land is mainly about having a space where they can be free from outside controls. In this setting, settlers tend to exhibit a strong individualist ethos, which weakens the MST's influence and collective action efforts.

Settlements

As the chapters by Carvalho and Carter, and by Sonia Maria P. P. Bergamasco and Luiz Antonio Norder clearly emphasized, land reform settlements in
Brazil cannot be easily pigeonholed. These communities exhibit great diversity
in their geographical location, size, level of economic development, organizational capacity, political awareness, cultural resources, family composition, and
origin. Significant variations can also be found within settlements and between
their many sponsors. Over a quarter of the nation's settlements are linked to the
MST. Outside observers often ignore or downplay these distinctions and erroneously equate all land reform issues with the MST.

Actual cases of settlement failures need to be evaluated in context, rather
than simply imputed on particular failings. Carvalho and I described how the
Cardoso administration and predecessors largely neglected the land reform
settlements created under their auspices, by failing to provide adequate infrastructure and financial credit. According to a 2002 government survey of all
settlements created between 1995 and 2001, 55% of these communities had no
electricity, 49% had no proper drinking water, 29% lacked elementary schools,
77% were deprived of schooling beyond the primary level, and 62% had no access to emergency health care. Moreover, many of these settlements were created in inaccessible regions, distant from local markets and public services.
Despite these precarious conditions, the same study found that on a national
average only 12% of all settlement farm plots distributed had been abandoned.[34]

Notwithstanding such limitations, leading surveys of land reform communities have actually shown a general improvement in life conditions for most settlers.[35] Bergamasco and Norder's study of settlements in the state of São Paulo,
for example, found that 80% of the settlers claimed to have upgraded their
housing conditions, 72% said they were eating better, and 58% had increased
their income levels. In their study, the average family income was $266 per
month, a relatively modest sum. Yet the fact that settlers don't have to pay rent,
can grow much of their own food, and live in a generally safe environment,
suggests that many are likely to have a better quality of life than that found
in most urban favelas. Land reform settlements, the authors add, also provide
greater family security, while facilitating the revitalization of small rural towns
through the diversification and reactivation of local economies.

Purely economic evaluations of land reform's merits, advanced by Graziano,
Navarro, and other conservative analysts, offer a very limited measurement
criterion. In fact, leading international organizations, like the United Nation's
Development Program and the World Bank, have long adopted a more comprehensive set of development indicators, which go well beyond the conventional calculations of income and economic productivity. The contributors to
this book share this growing consensus within the field of development studies,

and in doing so have anchored their appraisals of land reform settlements on broader notions of well-being, rather than mere monetary results.[36]

The observations raised here concerning MST mobilizations, relations with the state and rule of law, mobilizing resources, motivations, and settlements offer an alternative view of the MST that contrasts in many ways with mass media depictions and academic critiques outlined at the onset of this chapter. These observations do not imply that the movement should be spared criticism. The MST is certainly not a society of angels. Some conservative insights, however exaggerated and distorted, contain kernels of truth. Still, the rhetoric of reaction employed by the MST's intellectual critics hinders more than facilitates the prospects of understanding the movement and its impact on Brazil. An appreciation for context and complexity are needed to go beyond many of their crude caricatures. A historical framework and comparative perspective, along with solid empirical data, ongoing field experience, and proper conceptual tools, can decisively improve the accuracy through which this phenomenon is perceived— and foster a more constructive dialogue among contending views.

The Consequences

The MST's struggle for agrarian reform provides a number of intriguing insights and lessons. Three of these will be highlighted here: the nature of the obstacles to social reform; the need for grassroots public activism to overcome these barriers; and the radical democratic impetus implicit in comparable struggles for social justice. The following comments pursue these three themes in greater detail.

Obstacles to Change

This book sheds light on the many and significant barriers to land reform in Brazil. Their resilience is related to the combination of four basic features: their multidimensional, systemic, historical, and political qualities. The first two traits point to a variegated, complex, and interrelated set of factors that operate in a weblike synergy. The historical and political features address the impact of tradition, previous development trajectories, institutions, and practices that shape the distribution of power in Brazilian society and politics. Each of the features involved in maintaining Brazil's agrarian inequities is examined briefly below.

A comprehensive assessment of Brazil's impediments to land reform requires an awareness of the *multidimensional* issues and levels of analysis at stake. Among the key factors that need to be kept in mind are the influences of: (1) global forces, economic arrangements, and financial institutions; (2) the national development model, including its patterns of production, trade, and distribution; (3) the state, its composition, legal framework, capacity, and disposition; (4) the political regime, its representational formulas, political parties, and electoral practices; (5) the government, its orientation, policies, and will-power; (6) social class structure, mobility, and power correlations; and (7) civil society's configuration, resources, media access, and ideas.

These many obstacles operate in *systemic* mode. They do not function in isolation, but are interconnected in a variety of ways. As such, they generally feed on each other and create a self-sustaining cycle that bolsters impediments and resistance to change. The 1982 debt crisis, for example, and neoliberal development model adopted in the 1990s, amid global financial pressures and the dissemination of fashionable economic ideas, empowered Brazil's large landholders. As Delgado observes, much of the revenue needed to pay Brazil's foreign and domestic creditors has come from agribusiness exports. In the early years of the twenty-first century, the landlords drew on this fact—along with their strong representation in Congress, close ties to the Ministry of Agriculture, and considerable influence on the mass media—to generate a momentum that weakened President Lula's longstanding promise to implement a progressive land reform program. Academic efforts to delegitimize the MST, undertaken by scholars such as Martins, Navarro, Graziano, and Rosenfield, have also contributed to this situation. Their easy traction and diffusion in the nation's conservative press have helped foster a more hostile climate of opinion toward land reform and its proponents. Landlord representatives in civil and political society have deployed these arguments to their advantage.[37] In this way, civil society–based initiatives, organizations, and ideas have served to uphold Brazil's conservative interests, by drawing on numerous strategic and elective affinities.

Brazil's principal obstacles to agrarian reform are also distinctly *historical* in nature. Lest there be any doubt, the nation's exclusionary development process, sharp social inequities, influential landlord class, bourgeoning agribusiness sector, oligarchic politics, weak representation of popular sectors in civil and political society, conservative judiciary, and ineffective state protection of basic human rights, have deep roots in Brazil's past. Together, these elements nurture a powerful inertia in support of the status quo.

Finally, the barriers to reform are notably *political* in character. They are related to broader power struggles in society, shaped by class configurations and political conflicts over access to state resources and protection. Furthermore, they are tied to an array of institutional mechanisms and practices that limit the political representation of popular sector interests. Brazil's patrimonial tradition; disjointed state bureaucracy; overrepresentation of conservative rural interests in Congress due to the malapportionment of legislative seats; inchoate party system; political clientelism and widespread vote buying among the poor; high costs of election campaigns; and elite control of the mass media outlets; have all reinforced the nation's "government by and for the few."[38] Prospects for agrarian reform are predictably diminished when conservative opponents draw on these and other political mechanisms to stifle the impetus for change.

All this suggests that Brazil's barriers to land reform are intimately tied to its authoritarian and patrimonial legacies.[39] In fact, its landlord-friendly, agribusiness model of rural development was designed and bankrolled by the military regime. Since then, the state's conservative inertia has remained largely unabated, despite the regime's political democratization, its laws favoring agrarian reform, and discernible popular demand for land redistribution.

The state's protection of landlord interests is manifest through numerous practices. As noted by Delgado, rural property taxes, for instance, continue to be negligible. State oversight of the land market remains notably weak. Fraudulent land appropriations are prevalent in many parts of the country, especially the Amazon frontier. Potential areas for redistribution, which comprise close to one-third of the nation's territory, have remained mostly unaffected by government reform policies. The state's lax enforcement of agrarian laws has enabled large landholders to accumulate vast areas of unproductive land as reserve value. Furthermore, compensations for land expropriations are commonly inflated well beyond market value, thanks to the government's generous payment criteria and the judiciary's traditional deference toward landlord petitions.

The weight of Brazil's conservative inertia on agrarian matters explains, to a considerable degree, the Lula administration's decision not to revise the more than three-decades-old productivity index used to determine land expropriations, despite having a legal mandate for this. Lula's executive order would have greatly facilitated land expropriations throughout Brazil. Yet the fear of galvanizing media opposition and resistance from the influential *bancada ruralista,* the largest congressional voting bloc linked to landlord and agribusiness interests, led the Lula government to default on a longstanding promise to its landless allies.

For all their powerful weight and objective character, Brazil's obstacles to land reform are also affected by an important subjective valuation. The same hurdles after all can be perceived in different ways. For some, these impediments add to an insurmountable fait accompli. Others, however, see them as a challenge to overcome. Conservatives assume there are no viable or desirable alternatives. They explicate and justify what exists, and often conclude, as Navarro does, that "the time for land reform has passed." By contrast, progressives insist on defying the odds. In this, they share a spirit of resistance akin to that emblemized in the World Social Forum's motto, "Another World Is Possible." These contrasting dispositions are elegantly captured by William Sloan Coffin Jr. "Hope," he writes, "criticizes what is, hopelessness rationalizes it. Hope resists, hopelessness adapts."[40] In today's Brazil, the beacon of hope lies not among reform skeptics, but with those who—despite the odds—continue to struggle for its progressive implementation.

Public Activism

The venue through which the MST challenges Brazil's stark social disparities is as noteworthy as the impetus itself. Latin American history records no other social movement as long lasting, large, and sophisticated as the MST. The movement's surprising success has been intimately entwined with its capacity to engage in a distinct form of social struggle: public activism. As explained in my chapter on Rio Grande do Sul, this approach to social conflict entails an organized, politicized, visible, autonomous, periodic, and nonviolent form of social confrontation. The goal here is to draw public attention, influence state policies, and persuade other societal actors. Public activism deploys modern repertoires of contention to exert pressure on the state while striving to negotiate with its authorities.

The MST's public activism has been instrumental in reinstating land reform on Brazil's national agenda. It has played a decisive role in the creation of over 2,000 agricultural settlements linked to the MST, benefiting by 2006 an estimated 135,000 landless families, through the distribution of 3.7 million hectares of land, an area the size of Switzerland or the state of West Virginia. Moreover, the movement's pressure politics and lobbying have contributed significantly to an unprecedented distribution of public resources to the rural poor, through land purchases, farming and housing credits, infrastructural development, technical assistance, educational programs, and the creation of over 300 rural cooperatives and food processing plants linked to the MST.[41]

Contrary to the opinion of its conservative critics, the movement's embrace of public activism has actually contributed to the advancement of democracy in Brazil by: (1) strengthening civil society through the organization and incorporation of marginalized sectors of the population; (2) fostering a civilizing process in the countryside, by harnessing, articulating, and disciplining social frustrations and deploying these through constructive actions at the grassroots level;[42] (3) highlighting the importance of public activism as a catalyst for social development and providing an impetus for the mobilization of other popular sector groups; (4) facilitating the extension and exercise of basic citizenship rights—civil, political, and social rights—among the poor; (5) underscoring the state's vital responsibility in protecting human rights and fostering equity enhancing reforms; (6) emphasizing the value of education, consciousness raising, self-dignity, and personal responsibility among its participants; and (7) engendering a sense of utopia, hope, and affirmation of ideals imbued in Brazil's long-run, complex, and open-ended democratization process.[43]

Brazil's struggle for agrarian reform suggests that public activism may well be an indispensable instrument for inequality reduction in starkly disparate societies. Such environments, of course, tend to produce daunting obstacles to change. All this implies that an amiable, purely institutionalized, top-down attempt to foster reform is more than likely to end up in empty government promises and innocuous initiatives. Under sharply unequal contexts—as in South Africa's apartheid regime and the United States's racial segregation policies in the South—the barriers to change need to be tackled with concerted, forceful, and disruptive pressure from below. If coupled with a bargaining process at the top, this societal drive can foster an auspicious momentum for state innovation and reform policies. Brazil's struggle for agrarian reform shows that it would be disingenuous, at best, to expect a major impetus for the redistribution of wealth to involve anything less than a tough touch.

Radical Democracy

The MST experience provides a telling lesson for the prospects of inequality reduction in the twenty-first century. During the twentieth century, the three leading formulas for dealing with the problems of wealth disparity were market economics, social revolution, and political democracy. Market economics assumed that consistent economic growth would eventually reduce both poverty and inequality.[44] Social revolutions, relying largely on Marxian inspiration, upheld the need for a violent takeover of the state and drastic impositions of equalizing measures. Political democracies offered a constitutional framework allowing basic civil liberties, political competition, and mass participation in the election of governing representatives. The regime's own incentive structure, it was argued, would lead to the redistribution of wealth over the long run, namely through the development of state welfare policies.

In practice, however, each approach presented serious drawbacks. Market economics generally ignored power asymmetries and their effects on the development process. Economic growth in highly unequal societies is more likely to fuel income disparity than bridge its gap, as Brazil's so-called economic miracle of the 1970s visibly showed.[45] Social revolutions often ushered traumatic episodes of violence and dreadful human rights violations. In their wake, revolutionary elites often instituted draconian policies with devastating social costs, as witnessed during the Soviet Union's industrialization process and China's Great Leap Forward.[46] Political democracy, on the other hand, has not offered clear solutions to the inequality problem either. In the 1990s, most of Latin America experienced economic growth and democratic regimes. Yet income disparity, though remaining stable in Brazil, actually increased in most other Latin American countries.[47] In Latin America, unlike the Western European and North American experience, democracy's positive long-term impact appears to be quite uncertain; and obviously of no consolation to those in dire need.

Brazil's struggle for agrarian reform provides glimpses of an alternative pathway to reducing durable social inequities. The impetus, here, can be construed as one geared toward engendering a form of radical democracy. This approach draws on political democracy's "enabling institutional milieu,"[48] but argues that this framework alone is not enough. Radical democracy stresses the importance of autonomous popular organizations, their mobilization, and their participation in development efforts. Popular engagement can be strengthened through the creation of state partnerships with grassroots groups and their representation in public agencies responsible for executing social policies. A radical democracy incorporates many elements of what Philippe C. Schmitter defined as a societal corporatist model for interest representation based on horizontal state-society linkages.[49] While valuing economic growth, this approach to inequality reduction insists that the poor be included in a productive process that is ecologically sustainable and provides wide access to basic consumer goods and social services.

The radical democratic course, then, combines four basic elements: (1) public activism; (2) institutional mechanisms for developing state-society partnerships and effective societal accountability;[50] (3) a responsive government leadership, sympathetic to grassroots demands; and (4) a functioning state, capable of investing public resources for social welfare and the economic development of the poorest strata in society. The first three features presuppose a political democracy. The latter two explain the MST's support for the political Left and defense of a national development model led by a robust state, rather than powerful economic actors.

The radical democratic approach to inequality reduction is certainly not devoid of problems and practical limitations. Its relevance, however, cannot be easily dismissed. Underlying this formula is a cumulus of experience and ideas that warrant closer attention. The MST's contributions to this debate are apt to stir passionate arguments and fuel creative solutions in the years to come.

The effort to redress Brazil's yawning societal gap calls for innovative ideas, audacious experiments, and an appreciation for the "constructive impatience," in Amartya Sen's fitting term, of groups like the MST.[51] Alternative forms of impatience are apt to be far less edifying. In a mid-2006 letter addressed to "the archaeologist of the future," Luis Fernando Veríssimo, one of Brazil's most beloved humorists, wondered if his country had reached its "last years of patience." In his usual down-to-earth style, Verissimo wrote,

> All of Brazil's manifestations of social unease, up until Lula's election, had been polite petitions to our dominant minority requesting that they hand back the nation to its excluded majority. Throughout this time it was impossible to imagine what would happen if these good manners faded away, when a society in desperation began to demand an end to the criminal incompetence that had for years defrauded people from access to health care, security, education and work, in order to give the banks greater profits, offer assurances to the speculators and a good life to the few. When "give it back!" became a call to war.

Brazil always belonged to a self-perpetuated minority, but never, in the past, has the nation's majority had as clear a notion of their internal banishment, of their exile without leaving their place. Lula's election, among other things, conveyed this newfound recognition. . . . And since Lula frustrated peoples' hope for change by continuing the same economic policies of the previous government, what I could tell the archaeologist of the future is that we may be living Brazil's last years of patience. Although nobody seems to have the least fear that that which is not returned for better will have to be given back for worse.[52]

Notes

The author would like to thank Ralph Della Cava and Kristina Svensson for their valuable comments and suggestions. All translations from the Portuguese and Spanish were prepared by the author.

1. The ideas espoused by all three analysts have received ample attention in Brazil's mainstream media. Martins, a professor emeritus of the Universidade de São Paulo, is Brazil's most prolific rural sociologist. Navarro is a sociology professor at the Universidade Federal do Rio Grande do Sul. Both were once advisors to the MST and the CPT. After the mid-1990s, Martins and Navarro each had a personal falling out with these organizations and served as consultants to the Cardoso government. Graziano was a close advisor to President Cardoso. He writes a regular column for three of the nation's leading newspapers and directs an NGO dedicated to the promotion of agribusiness interests. Rosenfield is a philosophy professor at the Universidade Federal do Rio Grande do Sul. He writes frequently for two of Brazil's leading dailies. The reader should know that Leslie Bethel, director of the University of Oxford's Centre for Brazilian Studies, and I originally asked Martins to write the conclusion for this book; however, he politely declined our request.

2. Martins (2000a: 18–19, 26). Fernando Henrique Cardoso offers a similar appraisal in his presidential memoir. He describes the MST as belonging "to a niche of resistance to modernity that is a conveyer of a regressive utopia." According to Cardoso, the landless movement looks at the world "through the rearview mirror" (2006: 70).

3. Martins (2000a: 49, 60).

4. Martins (2003b: 27, 44); see also Navarro (2002a: 229, 2003). For a more caustic view of the CPT's and MST's "brainwashing" of the rural poor, see Rosenfield (2006: 240, 257, 326, 329, and 373).

5. Interview with Navarro, in Scolese (2003).

6. Interview with Navarro, in Agencia Folha (2003).

7. Navarro (2002a: 208, 211, 2002b: 279).

8. Navarro (2002b: 277, 2002a: 206–7).

9. Navarro (2002b: 279); see also Navarro (2002a: 218).

10. Navarro (2002a: 215–17).

11. Graziano (2004: 133).

12. Graziano (2004: 38–39).

13. Graziano (2004: 108). Drawing on a book published by a journalist linked to the ultraconservative Catholic group Tradition, Family and Property (TFP), Graziano describes

one of the MST's historic communities in Rio Grande do Sul, the Annoni settlement, as "the largest rural *favela* in Latin America." He assures the reader that this claim is true because "nobody has disproved it" (2004: 128–29). When I visited the Annoni settlement, however, in mid-2005, I encountered a quite prosperous farming community, with three cooperatives, five agro-industries, three supermarkets, and a large grain silo. Since 1996, these settlers have repeatedly elected one of their own as a local town mayor.

14. Graziano (2004: 239, 72).
15. Graziano (2004:161).
16. Graziano (2004: 244)
17. Graziano (2004: 304, 72, 2006).
18. Rosenfield (2006: 220–21, 228–38, 253–54).
19. Rosenfield (2006: 247).
20. Rosenfield (2006: 252–53, 303, 309, 301, and 311).
21. The two books in question are Comissão Pastoral da Terra (CPT/RS) and Comunidade Pe. Josino dos Freis Capuchinhos e Franciscanos—Tupanciretã, RS (2003) and Mitsue Morissawa (2001). In addition, Rosenfield analyzes two magazine issues of the MST's *Revista Sem Terra*, published in 2005; and two unpublished documents apprehended during a 2003 police raid at a landless encampment in Rio Grande do Sul, including the personal agenda of a local MST leader. Rosenfield's ideas are not informed by any relevant field experience.
22. Martins's and Navarro's embittered disenchantment with their erstwhile friends in the CPT and MST are no doubt influenced by their personal falling out as mentors of both organizations. Theirs, in many ways, is a professorial-like reprimand of their former pupils. Navarro, for instance, describes the MST's "fundamentalist perspective of political action" as "entirely disassociated with Brazil's agrarian reality" (2002b: 267). Instead, he adds, it "grasps on to its vulgar Marxism," completely ignoring important theoretical advances made by "Western Marxist" scholars (2002b: 279–80). Martins's interpretive essays written in the 2000s carry the same message. The following quote from his book *O Sujeito Oculto* [The Hidden Subject], is revealing of his current views and a good illustration of his writing style. He asserts, "Much is said about agrarian reform. But the substantive aspects of the struggle for land and land reform are lost in intricate ideological babbles, unfounded affirmations and inconsistent proposals. The landless workers move about in a difficult search, they follow guidelines that are alien to them; they fumble without a consistent theoretical reference, oriented by intermediary groups that have serious theoretical failures and inadequate sensitivity towards proper theoretical and interpretive ideas. They get lost in the uncertainties typical of those who harbor a just obsession that does not nourish itself on well-founded reflections and continuous critical examinations of their own actions" (Martins 2003c: 22). As it seems, then, all would be in much better shape if only the land reform activists had "duly listened to their enlightened professors."
23. Hirschman (1991: 7).
24. Bobbio (1995: 15). The Left, Bobbio adds, "draws on the conviction that most of the inequalities it abhors, and would like to make disappear, are social, and thus removable." By contrast, the Right "draws on the opposing conviction, that sees [these inequities] as natural, and as such unchangeable" (1995: 146). For the historic Left, the concentration of private property, according to Bobbio, has been "one of the main, if not the most significant, obstacle to equality" between human beings (1995: 167).

25. The distinction between neoliberal and socialist views of the MST builds on Sampaio's (2010) arguments. For a neoliberal depiction of the MST as a "lunatic" group, see the opinion article by Naím (2004), editor of *Foreign Policy*, a prestigious journal published by the Carnegie Endowment for International Peace.

26. See table 1.6 in my introductory chapter to this book.

27. On the World Bank's land policies in Brazil, see Sauer and Pereira (2006); Pereira (2005, 2010); Martins (2004); and Barros, Sauer, and Schwartzman (2003).

28. For further details on this onslaught against the MST, see Branford (chap. 13, this volume) and Comparato (2000).

29. See my chapter on Rio Grande do Sul in this volume.

30. As Horatio Martins de Carvalho well noted, "The MST is very hard to pin down, it's constantly shifting and evolving. In this sense, the MST is like a gust of wind. Each visit to an MST settlement generates some novelty—new problems to address, new ideas to discuss" (Carter 2004a: 9).

31. For a more comprehensive discussion of the MST's multifarious interactions with the state, see Carter (2011). On the movement's complex relations with the rule of law, also see also Laureano (2007) and Hammond (1999).

32. In fact, for all the imputations of "Leninism" and efforts to disqualify the MST as a social movement, academic detractors like Navarro never define what a "Leninist organization" is and largely ignore the vast scholarly literature on social movements.

33. At the national level, the MST has been active in a number of other progressive Brazilian networks and organizations, such as the National Forum for Agrarian Reform and Justice in the Countryside, the Brazilian Association for Agrarian Reform (ABRA), *Consulta Popular*, the National Network of Popular Independent Lawyers (RENAPE), the Coordination of Social Movements (CMS), and more recently, the church-sponsored Popular Assembly.

34. See Sparovek's interview with Lerrer (2003: 321). Sparovek's (2003) study, sponsored by the FAO and Ministry of Agrarian Development, is the most extensive survey of land reform settlements in Brazil.

35. The main reference in this regard is the excellent study undertaken by Heredia, Medeiros, Palmeira, Cintrão, and Leite (2004).

36. On these development views, see Sen (1999), Chambers (1997), and Narayan (2000). For a thoughtful application of Sen's ideas to Brazil's agrarian reform debate, see Leite, with Ávila (2006a).

37. A clear illustration of this took place in 2005, when an investigative commission of Brazil's National Congress, controlled by representatives of the rural elite, approved a report with scathing attacks on the MST, which was even accused of "terrorism." The conservative politicians responsible for preparing the document made ample use of the ideas expounded by Navarro, Graziano, and other MST detractors; see Lupion (2005). For a critical appraisal of this report, see Sauer, Souza, and Tubino (2006)

38. Montero (2005: 51). Useful references on these obstacles can be found in my introductory chapter to this volume.

39. The notion of "authoritarian legacies" employed here draws on Hite and Cesarini (2004).

40. Coffin (2005: 19).

41. For sources and a brief discussion of these numbers, see my introductory chapter, and Carter and Carvalho (chap. 9, this volume).

42. The concept of a "civilizing process," which arises through the disciplining of passions

and other raw impulses into more methodical forms of behavior, is based on Elias (1982).

43. This approach to democratization draws on Whitehead (2002). These contributions to democracy are discussed further in Carter (2009).

44. For a highly influential statement in this regard, see Kuznets (1954).

45. Between 1966 and 1976 annual GDP growth averaged an impressive 9.2%, yet income inequality rose sharply, by 24% between 1960 and 1977, from 0.50 to 0.62 on the Gini coefficient scale (Fishlow 1972; Paes de Barros, Henriques, and Mendonça 2000).

46. Russia's communist revolution and reign of terror under Joseph Stalin is estimated to have cost at least 12 million lives. The gigantic famine that followed Chairman Mao Zedong's Great Leap Forward caused the death of no less than 20 million Chinese. I am grateful to my colleague Eric Lohr, a Russian history professor at American University, for his insights on the Soviet era, e-mail communication, March 13, 2006. The number of Chinese deaths is from Spence (1990: 583), based on figures that are currently widely regarded as low estimates.

47. Karl (2003: 138)

48. O'Donnell (2004: 11).

49. Schmitter's (1974) seminal article contrasts "societal corporatism" with "state corporatism," which is based on a vertical integration of social groups.

50. On societal forms of accountability, see Smulovitz and Peruzzotti (2000).

51. Sen (1999: 11).

52. Verissimo (2006).

Miguel Carter

Broken Promise
The Land Reform Debacle under the PT Governments

The chapters in this volume have dealt with the past, yet also presage the future. In them, murmurings of a great betrayal have been made. And if not a betrayal, at the very least, a striking failure on the part of the governments led by the Workers Party (PT) to live up to the party's historic promise of agrarian reform.

A study I prepared found many signs that corroborate this interpretation.[1] This chapter is not the place to examine these issues at length. Rather, it will provide a general contour of the evidence on hand, then set the findings in context and briefly evaluate their impact on Brazil's Landless Rural Workers Movement (MST). In closing, I will draw out two paradoxes that emerge from this discussion and weigh on the future of Brazil's democracy, its peasantry, and the ecological fragility of our planet.

The Evidence

A review of the historical facts related to the PT's rural policies under the governments of Luiz Inácio Lula da Silva and Dilma Rousseff go a long way in corroborating the concerns raised throughout this volume. This includes a succinct assessment of land reform activity, the stocks of land available for redistribution and their potential beneficiaries, and the state's manifold relations, under the PT, with the nation's agrarian and corporate elite.

Sharp Decline in Land Redistribution

The evidence on this matter is hard to quibble with. As figure E.1 shows, land reform activity increased under Lula's first term, but experienced a significant drop under his second term. In turn, by 2012, Dilma's administration had benefited fewer families through land distribution than any other Brazil-

Figure E.1. Land reform beneficiary families in Brazil, annual average per presidential period, 1979–2012

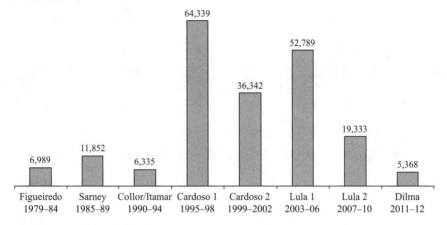

Source: Author's calculations based on DATALUTA (2013) for figures from 1979 to 2011 and INCRA (2013) for 2012 data.

Note: The numbers published in figure E.1 differ slightly from the statistics presented elsewhere in this book (see Carter; Fernandes; and Carter and Carvalho, chapters 1, 5, and 10, respectively), because they are based on the actual number of land beneficiaries rather than the settlement capacity. Moreover, these figures did not compute DATALUTA and INCRA's data for 132 forest settlements established in the Amazon region between 1985 and 2012. Though of great importance to the region, these areas overstretch the definition of an agricultural settlement and are in reality much closer to a nature reserve. Compared to the typical family farm plots found throughout Brazil, the size of land allocations in these areas is huge, with an average 998 hectares of land per family. All of these settlements bear an official INCRA title as either a forest or extractive reserve. These 132 forest settlements amount to only 1.5% of all settlements created in Brazil, but their land mass comprises 37.8 million hectares of land, a territory the size of Italy and Austria combined; 45% of all the land distributed from 1979 to 2012. According to INCRA, these territories have the capacity to settle as many as 37,934 families; 3.7% of all such beneficiaries in Brazil. The Lula government created 83% of these settlements and distributed 89% of these forested domains.

ian government since 1979. The data presented in figure E.2, on the number of estates expropriated by the federal government, confirm the overall trend. They also reveal that the period under President Fernando Henrique Cardoso was more auspicious for farmland redistribution than an entire decade of PT administrations.

Land reform was, in effect, banished from Dilma's 2010 presidential campaign and conspicuously absent in her flagship antipoverty program, *Brasil Sem Miseria*. The plan made no mention of Brazil's problem of peasant landlessness and historic land inequities, even though half of the 16.2 million Brazilians afflicted by extreme poverty were identified as rural inhabitants.[2]

Figure E.2. Rural estates expropriated by Brazil's federal government, 1985–2012

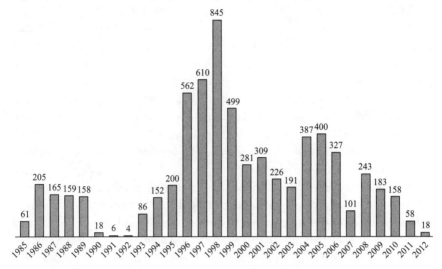

Source: INCRA (2012).

State Reluctance to Distribute Vast Areas of Farmland Available for Reform

One-third of Brazil's national territory is held in estates that have no official land titles or are deemed unproductive according to signed affidavits by their own proprietors. Even if one were to subtract all the forest areas held in private estates, Brazil would still have 182 million hectares of farmland available for reallocation, a territory twice the size of Venezuela. Under the PT, the Brazilian state has made no concerted effort to enforce the constitution's requirement that rural properties perform a "social function." More strikingly, it has not engaged in a serious attempt to recover the 86.4 million hectares of misappropriated land in the hands of the nation's agrarian elite, a domain half the size of Iran.[3]

All the while, Brazil held a large number of impoverished people who could have benefited from land redistribution. According to a 2010 government study, this figure involved close to 4.2 million families, a population roughly the size of Australia's.[4]

Generous State Subsidies and Concessions for Wealthy Planters

The PT's rural development policies have retained a highly lopsided support for the country's agribusiness farmers. Between 2003 and 2012, the PT administrations assigned US$288.1 billion or 88% of all federal agricultural credits, to corporate farms. On average, each corporate estate received US$356,729 to US$9,079 for each family farmer. This amounted to a 133% overpayment for each hectare of corporate farm.[5] The PT administrations also continued to provide financial assistance to the associations run by Brazil's landed elite, including the Brazilian Confederation of Agriculture and Livestock (CNA), the Brazilian Rural Society (SRB), the Organization of Brazilian Cooperatives (OCB), and related institutes. Under Lula, the funds made available to these privileged groups were twenty-one times larger than the monies channeled to MST-related projects in education, cooperatives, human rights, and health care.[6]

Along with these direct subsidies, the PT administrations facilitated various tax breaks, debt renegotiations, and public investments designed to benefit agribusiness farmers. For instance, it retained the 1996 Kandir law that spares all levies on agricultural exports and approved legislation in 2004 that greatly reduced taxes on fertilizer and pesticide imports. In 2006, Lula deferred the public debts of agribusiness co-ops and granted them special exemptions on federal dues.[7] Commercial growers have also benefited considerably from state investments in agricultural research, rural extension services, and large infrastructure projects, such as irrigation systems in the northeast, along with roads, railways, and ports, developed mostly to reduce export costs for agro-commodities.

The list of privileges continues. Brazil's landed elite have made a sizeable profit from the government's compensation for land expropriations. This is the upshot of the exceptionally high interest payments of up to 21% annually, close to 15% in real interest rates. These payment rules have allowed landlords to double the real value of their properties in as few as seven years of court litigation. In 2009, interest charges alone consumed 62% of the state's total expenditures on land expropriations.[8]

Under Lula's second term, the government also issued large land concessions to the nation's agrarian elite. In 2008, it set up a program, *Terra Legal*, to provide property titles in the Amazon region for estates of up to 1,500 hectares of land. This was fifteen times larger than the land titles previously allocated for family farm holdings in this part of Brazil. The program was devised to legalize 67.4 million hectares of land in the Amazon, of which an estimated 40 million hectares—an area almost as big as California—were occupied illegally by *grileiros*, or large land grabbers.[9]

In 2009, on the heels of a Federal Supreme Court ruling that led to the eviction of commercial rice farmers from an indigenous reserve in Roraima, Lula ordered that six million hectares of federal land—a domain twice the size of Belgium—be donated to the state government of Roraima to, essentially, assuage the wealthy planters who had threatened to resist the court order. To enact the legal transfer, the government crafted a special provision that dispensed the land's mandatory use for agrarian reform.[10]

Lax State Enforcement of Laws Affecting Landlord Interests

Implementation of agrarian, property tax, environmental, and labor laws that touch on traditional rural elite privileges remained considerably weak under the PT governments. Examples of this abound. The general reluctance to fully enforce the nation's agrarian reform laws, or recover the public land taken over by the grileiros, were complemented by Lula's decision to backtrack on his promise to revise the greatly outdated productivity index (based on 1975 census data) employed to determine land expropriations, despite a clear legal mandate for this.

What's more, during the Lula administration, Brazil's negligible levies on rural properties declined even further to a trifling 0.06% of the nation's tax base, notably after 2005, when in a bow to landed interests, Lula transferred the authority to collect this tariff to municipal governments.[11] Adding to this, US $4.3 billion in fines issued by Brazil's environmental protection agency, IBAMA, mostly to large rural property owners, were pardoned in 2012 when Dilma ratified a new and highly controversial Forestry Code.[12]

Labor rights also continued to be routinely violated in the countryside. A study conducted by two leading Brazilian universities found that only 1% of the estates surveyed were in compliance with the nation's rural labor laws.[13] More egregious yet, both traditional landlords and agribusiness firms have been known to commit various abusive practices against their workers, including contemporary forms of slave labor. Between 2003 and 2012, the Pastoral Land Commission (CPT) gathered information on 63,417 cases of enslaved workers, involved mostly in rural activities. Of the 2,569 estate owners accused of engaging in such practices, a few were compelled by the courts to pay back wages and labor fines. Yet none were ever sentenced to prison or had their landholdings expropriated, which is surprising considering the flagrant violation of constitutional norms governing rural properties.

High levels of impunity have also persisted with regard to the assassinations of peasant, indigenous, and human rights activists in the countryside, where, according to the CPT, between 1985 and 2012, merely 8% of the 1,239 cases of rural violence that led to the assassination of 1,645 people have been brought to trial. And only twenty-two of the landlords responsible for ordering such executions have been sentenced to prison.[14]

Acquiescence to the Nation's Corporate and the Financial Elite

The PT's alignment with agribusiness interests and their goal of transforming Brazil into a global agricultural and agro-fuel powerhouse, explain Lula's and Dilma's support for the formation of huge Brazilian agro-food conglomerates, like JBS-Friboi in meat, Brasil Foods in poultry, and Ambev in beverages. In similar fashion, PT governments have backed the formation and global expansion of other Brazilian corporate giants—often referred to as "national champions"—such as Vale in mining; Petrobras in oil and gas; Companhia Siderúrgica Nacional in steel; Pão de Açucar in retail; Odebrecht in construction, petrochemicals and agrofuels; and Andrade Gutierrez in telecommunications and

Figure E.3. Interest payments on Brazil's national debt, compared to other federal government expenditures, 2003–12 (in US$ billions)

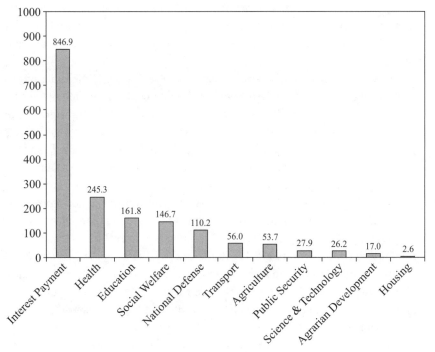

Source: Banco Central (2013); Senado Federal (2013) INESC (2005, 2006, 2007, 2009)

public infrastructure. Much of this has been carried out in collaboration with the state-owned Brazilian Development Bank (BNDES), which has underwritten their market growth, when not dominance, in various countries across Latin America, Africa, and other parts of the world.

The most glaring sign of the PT's overall submission to Brazil's economic elite can be found in the gargantuan transfers of public money to banks and other financial investors. Between 2003 and 2012, the Lula and Dilma administrations paid US$846.9 billion in interest rates to the nation's creditors; a sum that totaled 6.4% of Brazil's GDP during this entire period. As revealed in figure E.3, this amount is basically the equivalent of the federal government's combined expenditures on health, education, social welfare, national defense, transport, agriculture, public security, science and technology, agrarian development, and housing over the same decade.[15]

The vast transfer of wealth to the financial sector was the end result of the Central Bank's soaring interest rates, among the highest in the world. Real interest rates, in fact, averaged 8% from 2003 to 2012, peaking at 14% during Lula's first year in office.[16]

Together, the colossal bonanza bestowed on financial speculators, the state's collaboration in the creation of mega Brazilian corporations, and the significant privileges conferred to the nation's agrarian elite, evoke the twisted image of a starkly unequal country offering "socialism for the rich" . . . under the rule of a left-leaning Workers Party.

Context, Caveats, and Impact

The PT governments' decision to uphold the interests of the nation's rural elite did not take place in a vacuum. Rather, this was strongly shaped by the enveloping political economy, in particular the fierce financial shakedown during Lula's 2002 presidential campaign, along with an agro-mineral export boom fueled by high international commodity prices and the concomitant consolidation of Brazil's agribusiness sector. This development context reinforced the agrarian elite's historic political clout and grip on relevant state institutions, such as the Ministry of Agriculture. It also galvanized these forces to muster their allies in various public institutions—the National Congress, State Assemblies, Judiciary, Public Ministry (attorney general's office), and the Union's Court of Accounts (TCU or federal comptroller's bureau)—along with numerous civil society organizations, and the corporate news media, to launch a veritable assault against land reform proponents, both within the Lula administration and particularly among popular sector groups.

The climate of animosity stirred against the landless struggle, and, above all, the MST, enabled these conservative forces to raise the political cost of pursuing land redistribution. During this time, the agrarian elite and its supporters invested considerable efforts to criminalize the MST—its leaders, protest tactics, and development projects—both to delegitimize its demands and weaken its mobilization capacity.[17]

The PT administrations displeased their conservative detractors on three major points. First, both Lula and Dilma resisted extensive media and agrarian elite pressure to criminalize MST activities. Moreover, throughout this time, a substantial number of PT officials in Congress and in state and municipal governments remained sympathetic to rural popular movements and were inclined to lend a hand in times of need. Finally, the PT boosted state funding for several policies designed to expand welfare assistance, foster economic opportunities, and improve living conditions for family farmers. These included fairly successful initiatives, like the conditional cash transfer program, Bolsa Familia, a boost in agriculture credits for small holders, and the government's Food Acquisition Program (PAA), set up to purchase produce from family farmers. All these policies, along with the government's efforts to extend rural electrification, improve agricultural extension services, fund adult literacy and university courses for land reform settlers, and provide water access to rural communities in the northeast's dry hinterland, have been widely appreciated by the rural poor, yet were often viewed with mistrust by the rural elite.

Many of these pro–family farm programs remain embryonic, tied up in cumbersome regulations, and short-funded. Compared to the sums provided to corporate farmers, the resources for these programs represent trifling amounts. Still, they offer new tangible benefits that have given Brazil's rural masses, in the words of an MST leader, "a first little taste of the nation's pie."[18]

The PT's success in alleviating extreme poverty in Brazil has not revamped the country's grim social reality. In 2012, Brazil still had 42 million people living in poverty, 9.4 million of them in rural areas. The drop in relative income inequality—to a Gini coefficient of 0.522 in 2012, still set Brazil among the fifteen most unequal societies in the world. This decline, however, was offset by an increase in absolute income inequality.[19] In rural areas, income disparities stood at a Gini coefficient of 0.727, higher than that of any other country on the globe.[20] Much of this is closely related to Brazil's stubbornly high land concentration, which persisted at a Gini coefficient of 0.856 in 2006, on par with that of the previous decade. In 2006, only 0.9% of the landowners controlled 43% of the nation's farmland.[21]

The MST was hard hit by the PT's land reform debacle. After all, this was the third major historical defeat of a national agrarian reform movement in Brazil. In previous setbacks—the 1964 military coup against President João Goulart and President José Sarney's decision to abandon the land reform plan adopted in 1985—progressives were clearly overwhelmed by conservative forces. Yet this third historical defeat was far more perplexing and disturbing, given the PT's background and vociferous commitment to land redistribution in the 1980s and 1990s. Many MST activists, particularly those who had volunteered great efforts to campaign for Lula and the PT, felt deeply demoralized. As one movement leader explained,

> Our defeat took a huge toll on the subjective disposition of our militants. Several began to question if it was still possible to carry out an agrarian reform in Brazil, under a capitalist state, or under the existing Brazilian state. . . . Even those who were skeptical about Lula had pinned their hopes on some progress toward land redistribution under a PT government. . . . All this disappointment has affected people's beliefs and hopes in a popular project for Brazil. Our activists, after all, need more than food and water to survive. They also need to share a mystique, to believe, to have dreams and nurture a sense of utopia, in order to fight for social change.[22]

By 2008, the MST had entered a phase of retrenchment and resistance, characterized by a diminished capacity to influence state policies through public activism. A comparison between the first five years of the Lula administration,

2003–07, and the next five years, 2008–12, offers an instructive picture. During the second period, the number of land occupations carried out by all peasant groups in Brazil fell by half (to 1,428 land takeovers) while the number of people involved in these actions declined by 65% (to 140,270 families).[23] In contrast, the number of demonstrations remained roughly the same, which suggests an overall shift in protest tactics, to a greater reliance on marches, sit-ins, and road blockades.

The decline in land occupations, however, varied considerably between regions and states, thus rendering it difficult to establish a distinct national trend. Still, it is generally agreed that the Bolsa Familia program, greater employment prospects, higher minimum wage, and expanded social security coverage, created new opportunities for subsistence among the rural poor. These conditions, in varying ways and degrees, diminished the pool of new recruits available for the MST's landless camps.

More than anything else, though, the drop in the number of landless camps and land occupations was the direct result of the PT governments' decision to curtail its land reform activity, notably after 2007. This situation removed a crucial incentive for poor people to join the struggle for land reform. It compelled landless families to endure several more years of mobilization than originally anticipated, while diminishing the confidence that they would gain a farm plot at the end of this grueling effort. In states like Pernambuco, by late 2012, roughly half of the MST's 15,000 landless families had been encamped for ten years or more. In early 2013, the state's longest surviving contingent of landless peasants reached eighteen years of existence.[24]

The MST's retrenchment was also affected by significant cutbacks in its access to public resources for various grassroots development projects, especially after 2009. This situation forced the movement to downsize its professional staff by more than half and curb its living stipends for many full-time activists.[25]

Lula's determination to embrace Cardoso's economic orthodoxy and side with the agribusiness sector put the MST on a tight-rope. For movement leaders, the cost of breaking up with Lula was simply too high. Lula, after all, was a popular president among much of the MST's rank-and-file. Unlike his conservative adversaries, Lula did not treat the movement as a "national threat." To the contrary, his administration offered several programs that were quite advantageous for peasant farmers. Consequently, the MST brass took the pragmatic decision to align with the PT's left and attack the government's neoliberal measures while sparing Lula himself. In 2006 and 2010, the MST campaigned to defeat the PT's more conservative opponents of the Party of Brazilian Social Democracy, PSDB, out of fear for the return of the criminalization policies of the Cardoso era. "If it's bad with the PT," the reasoning went, "it would be worse without it."

For all these setbacks, the MST has remained active and defiant. Various gestures—notably, its continued mobilization, organizational investments and adaptations, innovative framings, and quest to expand and strengthen its alliances—indicate it is gearing up for the long haul and unlikely to fade away from the national scene any time soon. Crucial in all this will be its ability to mobilize resources and adjust its tactics in a context of diminished opportunities for growth and land redistribution.

A sign of its enduring mobilization capacity can be gleaned from the fact that, even in a period of retreat, between 2008 and 2012, the MST took part in 2,712 protest actions across Brazil, 56% of all such events. During this time it also mobilized three-fourths of all the people involved in land occupations throughout Brazil, that is, close to 100,000 families.[26]

Since the mid-2000s, some of the movement's most radical actions were spearheaded by MST women, who have assumed a much greater role within the organization. In particular, women played a key part in deepening the movement's critique of the agribusiness complex. As an outgrowth of this process, they joined with other Via Campesina women in organizing a number of direct and symbolic clashes with a handful of global corporations, especially in the pulp-mill sector.[27]

In a more discrete manner, the MST continued to invest significant resources in developing training centers for its cadres and was running more than forty of these movement schools in 2013. In collaboration with the federal government, it also provided MST members with access to adult literacy courses and special study programs that were set up in sixty-five Brazilian universities and technical schools.[28]

The movement's budding interest in agro-ecology gained solid footing during the 2000s and led to various undertakings with its Via Campesina allies, including scores of workshops, along with the creation of four institutes for agro-ecological learning and research, in the states of Paraná (2005) and Pará (2009) and in Venezuela (2006) and Paraguay (2008). This trend also comprised efforts to lobby the government for a national program to promote organic farming, which was launched by President Dilma in 2013.

In September 2010 the MST teamed up with seventy-three civil society organizations—including peasant movements, trade unions, universities, and medical research centers, church agencies, NGOs, and consumer groups—to establish a National Campaign Against Pesticides and For Life. The venture helped raise public awareness of the health risks associated with the sharp rise in farm pesticide use in Brazil and drew attention to the grossly inadequate control over the use of these chemicals. In 2009, Brazil became the world's leading consumer of these products, exposing each of its inhabitants to an average 4.5 liters of agro-toxic compounds.[29] The antipesticide movement has given the MST a platform on which to forge new partnerships in support of agro-ecology and family farming among urban groups, notably health care professionals, medical scientists, consumer groups, and food industry unions. This campaign has also offered the MST a novel frame on which to legitimize its calls for an alternative rural development modethat addresses the growing concerns over the public health consequences and costs of industrial farming.

The MST's quest to strengthen alliances with popular organizations operating in the Brazilian countryside reached a new climax in August 2012, when it joined twenty-six other associations to celebrate a Unified Meeting of Workers and Peoples of the Countryside, Waters and Forests. The landmark event, held in Brasília with over 7,000 activists representing all of the main popular civil society groups in rural Brazil, commemorated the fifty-first anniversary of a similar gathering in Belo Horizonte, in 1961. A public statement issued at the meeting laid out a trenchant critique of corporate agriculture and the Brazilian state's support for a rural development model based on social exclusion and "an ultra-predatory exploitation of nature."[30] Its call for a radical transformation of the nation's countryside illustrates the main demands on which these organizations have converged. They include support for agrarian reform, agro-ecology, and family farming; food, energy, and territorial sovereignty; gender equality; peasant and indigenous-friendly education policies; and the democratization of Brazil's mass media.

Paradoxes

In assessing the broader implications of the PT government's decision to sideline land reform, two critical paradoxes can be discerned. One probes the PT's dramatic turnabout on this issue, its new alliance with the agrarian elite, and the deeper consequences of this for the future of Brazil's democracy. The other explores the prospects of the nation's peasantry in light of the planet's mounting environmental crisis. Both arguments, etched out here in preliminary form, seek to encourage a much-needed public conversation on these matters.

As is well known, the PT has experienced a substantial transformation since its founding in the early 1980s. Over the course of more than three decades, it transitioned "from a labor-based movement to an institutionalized and electoral-professional"[31] catchall party, nominally on the left of Brazil's increasingly narrow political spectrum. Well into the early 2000s, the party retained discernable elements of its founding spirit, an affinity with popular movements and an anti-oligarchic ethos. After reaching the helm of the Brazilian government in 2003, its tactical détente with the agribusiness sector evolved into a newfound appreciation of its contribution to Brazil's export economy and innovative agro-fuel technology. This new sentiment was facilitated, in part, by the assumption—advanced by some scholars and repeated ad nauseam in the mainstream press—that corporate farming represented a sharp modern break from the country's traditional latifundios and plantation economy, given its capital and technology-intensive production, and modern management practices.

For this assumption to work, however, it was necessary to obscure or ignore the fact that in many crucial aspects the new agrarian elites were not so different from the old. As with the previous rural oligarchy, the new one has revealed an inclination to hoard vast tracts of land (much of it for speculative purposes), produce mostly export commodities, exploit its workers (particularly in the sugarcane industry), rely on the state for support and protection, hinder efforts to advance human rights and democracy among the rural poor, and generate wealth for a few. In today's agriculture, this oligarchic thrust is compounded by strong linkages between these corporate farms and a handful of global firms—Monsanto, Syngenta, Cargill, Bunge, ADM, Dupont, Bayer, and BASF—that dominate most of the world's modern rural economy. In effect, the PT's newfound amity with the agribusiness sector mirrors its acquiescence, and even embrace, of other oligopolies in Brazil, related to finance, oil, mining, construction, and mass communication, among other industries.

This is a worrisome development. Mega business enterprises create enormous power asymmetries that undermine, in various ways, basic democratic freedoms and notions of political equality. This model of capitalism, grounded on unbridled corporate power and influence, is detrimental for democratic accountability, as eminent scholars such as Robert Dahl, Sheldon Wolin, Joseph Stiglitz, Robert Reich, and others, remind us well.[32] Extraordinarily huge firms—some, in fact, deemed "too big to fail" or even "prosecute"—are a force for de-democratization wherever they control the commanding heights of the economy.

It is an ironic turn of history that the PT, Brazil's once-eminent anti-oligarchic party, when in power, became an enthusiastic promoter of this type of capitalism, both at home and abroad. For in doing so, the PT has reinforced the corrosive and oligarchic sway this model of capitalism has had—and will continue to have—on Brazilian politics.

All this gains added poignancy if one considers what the PT has forgone. Compared to the agrarian elite, its erstwhile allies among the peasantry and rural workers have played a far more constructive role in advancing Brazil's long-term and open-ended democratization process. As Charles Tilly elucidates, this has been accomplished both through "explicit programs" and as "by-products of their action."[33]

The MST and its allies have favored democratization by challenging the country's entrenched inequities and fighting to extend basic citizenship rights—civil, political, and social rights—among the rural poor. In the process, they have enhanced political awareness and capabilities among this population. As a counterhegemonic force, these peasant groups have helped enrich the country's public debate, by keeping a substantial spectrum of dissent alive.[33] More subtle and significantly, perhaps, their approach to economic development—based on family farms, cooperatives, vibrant local markets, and civil society associations—is far more conducive to meaningful democratic politics than corporate agriculture.

If the first paradox underscores a serious loss for Brazil's agrarian reform movement, the second draws attention to a new window of opportunity for such reforms, albeit one set in a context of dire menace. Since the late 2000s, several UN agencies and the World Bank have issued reports dealing with climate change and agriculture that have essentially made the same calls advanced by the MST and La Via Campesina in support of a paradigmatic shift from large-scale industrial farming to agro-ecology, family farms, and greater food sovereignty.[35]

The global food system, according to these studies, is responsible for the emission of approximately half of the greenhouse gases that are warming our planet and fueling climate change. Brazil, after China, is the world's second-largest contributor to such gases originating from agriculture. The bulk of these emissions stem from agribusiness farming—namely, through deforestation and the conversion of new farmland, nitrogen use in synthetic fertilizers, methane gases from livestock, food waste, and fossil fuels burned while transporting farm products, within country and overseas.[36] The environmental costs of corporate agriculture are compounded by the health costs associated with the increasing use of pesticides and antibiotics in industrial farming, related, in many cases, to new pests, plagues, and outbreaks in cancer and neurological diseases.

The rationale for shifting to agro-ecology and smaller-scale holdings is reinforced by solid environmental and economic sustainability arguments, as corroborated by Brazil's agricultural census data. Compared to corporate agriculture, family farms are 74% less likely to use pesticides.[37] They are also twice as efficient in their land use and produce most of the food consumed in this country. Furthermore, family farms create 9.1 times more employment than agribusiness holdings and offer a much higher return on public investments. For every US$100,000 in government farm credits, family farmers generate 266% more wealth and provide 21.1 more jobs.[38]

Herein lays the crux of this paradox. In an era of rising concern for the ecological fragility of our planet, many of the world's leading scientists and global policy makers have come to recognize the kernels of ecological wisdom found among the alleged "backward people" and "historical residues" of modernity—the peasants, indigenous communities, forest gatherers, artisanal fisher-folk, and nomadic pastoralists.

In this quest for an epochal transformation, it is not just the values of agro-ecology that are stake. Hidden in all this is an implicit recognition that the meek of the earth might have much to teach us about the ethos of frugality, humility, generosity, and respect for the ecological integrity of life.

Notes

The author would like thank Ralph Della Cava and Patrick Quirk for their helpful comments on the text, and Anderson Antonio da Silva for his valuable assistance in processing relevant data. A word of gratitude is also due to Bernardo Mançano Fernandes, Ariovaldo Umbelino de Oliveira, Múria Carrijo Viana, and Cinair Correia da Silva for making available some of the information used to prepare this chapter.

1. Carter (2014).
2. *Brasil Sem Miseria*'s plan to eradicate extreme poverty in the countryside includes welfare payments, job trainings, technical assistance, microcredit, and state food purchases from family farmers, but no land redistribution. The Centro Brasileiro de Análise e Planejamento, CEBRAP'S (2012: 23) study on Brazil's social inequality sums up the skepticism toward this program found among academics and grassroots activists: "The fight against inequality here appears to be largely rhetorical." The program seeks "to improve living conditions" among the extremely poor "while at the same time creating positive statistics and electoral dividends. . . . [We see] the technocratic elite staking its bet on a quick-fix agenda, which instead of fighting inequalities contributes to their solidification." Also see Arruda's (2012) interview with João Pedro Stédile. On Lula's and Dilma's rural policies, see Oliveira (2010), Sauer (2014) and Teixeira (2013b).
3. According to Oliveira (2013), INCRA's 2010 land registry included 218,957 large and medium-size rural property with "unproductive" estates, based on information provided by the owners in signed affidavits. Together, these idle farms encompassed a land mass of 190 million hectares, an area three times the territory of France.
4. Instituto de Pesquisa Econômica Aplicada, IPEA (2010: 244).
5. Author's calculations are based on Ministério da Agricultura, Pecuária e Abastecimento (2013) and Instituto Brasileiro de Geografia e Estatística (2009a). More broadly, on the political economy of Brazilian agribusiness, see Delgado (2012).
6. This estimate draws on Melo (2006: 127, 177).
7. Sauer (2010).
8. Brazil's inflation rate between 2003 and 2012 averaged 5.9% annually, according to Instituto de Pesquisa Econômica Aplicada, IPEA (2013), far below the interest payments made for land expropriations. In all such expropriations, landowners received cash payment upfront for all improvements made on the estate, along with agrarian bonds covering 80% of the land value; see Zanatta (2010) and Teixeira (2012).
9. The *Terra Legal* program rescinded legal norms that required its applicants to live and work on their farms, as peasant households normally do. Moreover, no provisions were made to prevent a *grileiro*, or large land grabber, from parceling his land among family members or close associates; see Texeira (2013), Oliveira (2010), Comissão Pastoral da Terra-Santarém (2010), Biernaski (2009). As Ariovaldo Umbelino de Oliveira (2010: 59), a noted Brazilian scholar on agrarian issues, caustically underscored, "President Lula's [*Terra Legal*] decree earned him a distinct place in the history of Brazil's *grilagem* [public land theft], as the third national ruler, after Emperor Dom Pedro II and the dictator Getúlio Vargas, to have enacted a law in support of the country's *grileiros*."
10. Oliveira (2010: 40–41).
11. Teixeira (2013a).
12. The new Forestry Code, according to The Nature Conservancy, is expected to reduce the nation's conservation area by as much as 40%; see Reuters (2013). The legislation was strongly supported by the agribusiness lobby and the *bancada ruralista*, the powerful rural elite caucus in Congress, and opposed by a wide spectrum of civil society

organizations and national celebrities, including a host of environmental, peasant, religious, and youth organizations, and prominent scientists and artists. On the value of IBAMA's fines for environmental destruction, see Vaz and Magalhães (2012).

13. The survey on rural labor conditions was carried out by the Federal University of Minas Gerais and the Fundação Getúlio Vargas, see Instituto de Pesquisa Econômica Aplicada IPEA (2010: 245).

14. For the number of enslaved workers, see Comissão Pastoral da Terra CPT (2013, 2012, 2005, and 2004). On human rights violations in rural areas, see Centro de Documentação Dom Tomás Balduíno (2013) and Comissão Pastoral da Terra (2013).

15. Interests payments are for both foreign and domestic debt, the latter representing 97.8% of Brazil's sovereign debt; see Banco Central (2013a). Annual average interest rates are based on data from Banco Central (2013b). Federal government expenditures for 2003–6 and 2008–9 are from Instituto de Estudos Socioeconômicos (2005, 2006, 2007, 2009, 2010), while 2007 and 2010–12 expenditures are from Senado Federal (2013).

16. The data for real interest rates draws on Banco Central (2013) and Instituto de Pesquisa Econômica Aplicada, IPEA (2013).

17. For a more detailed assessment of the conservative onslaught, see Carter (2014).

18. Neuri Rossetto, personal communication, São Paulo, December 15, 2009.

19. Instituto de Pesquisa Econômica Aplicada, IPEA (2013). On the rise of absolute income inequality in Brazil, amid a decline of relative inequality, see Kakwani (2013). Between 2003 and 2013, the number of Brazilian billionaires swelled by nearly six-fold, from eight to forty-six; see Geromel (2013). In 2013, it was reported that the assets owned by 124 Brazilians alone equaled 12.3% of the nation's GDP; see Exame (2013).

20. Instituto de Pesquisa Econômica Aplicada, IPEA (2010: 214).

21. Sauer and Leite (2012: 506). According to INCRA's land registry, large rural estates increased their control of the nation's farmland by 104 million hectares, or 48%, between 2003 and 2010, mostly in the Amazon region; see Teixeira (2011: 5).

22. Maria Gorete de Sousa, author's interview by telephone, São Luiz, Maranhão, September 24, 2013.

23. Author's calculations are based on DATALUTA (2013); Centro Dom Tomas Balduíno, CPT (2013).

24. Jaime Amorim, author's interview by telephone, Caruaru, Pernambuco, November 30, 2012.

25. Gustavo Augusto Gomes de Moura, author's interview by telephone, Brasília, September 23, 2013.

26. Author's calculus based on DATALUTA (2013); Centro Dom Tomas Balduíno, CPT (2013).

27. On the more assertive role of MST women, see Peschanski (2013).

28. By 2013, the National Education Program in Agrarian Reform (PRONERA) had benefited close to half million land reform settlers. On the MST's leadership training schools, see Plummer (2008).

29. ABRASCO (2012: 13–17). On the National Campaign Against Pesticides and For Life, see http://www.contraosagrotoxicos.org/.

30. See Encontro Unitário dos Trabalhadores, Trabalhadoras e Povos do Campo, das Águas e das Florestas (2012). Among the twenty-seven national associations that sponsored this event were CONTAG, CUT, all the Via Campesina movements, FETRAF, the Articulation of Indigenous Peoples of Brazil (APIB), church networks like the CPT and CIMI, and various NGOs, including Greenpeace and Oxfam Brasil.

31. Hunter (2011: 307). On the PT's transformation, also see Hunter (2010), Singer (2012), and Kingstone and Ponce (2010).
32. Dahl (2006, 1998), Wolin (2008), Stiglitz (2013), and Reich (2007, 2012).
33. Tilly (2004: 142–143).
34. On the MST's contribution to democracy in Brazil, see Carter (2009, 2011).
35. United Nations Conference on Trade and Development, UNCTAD (2013), De Schutter (2010), and International Assessment of Agricultural Knowledge, Science and Technology for Development (2009).
36. United Nations Conference on Trade and Development (2013: 2–21).
37. Instituto Brasileiro de Geografia e Estatística, IBGE (2009b: 217); pesticide use compares farms with plantation areas under and above 100 hectares.
38. Author's calculations are based on Instituto Brasileiro de Geografia e Estatística, IBGE (2009a) and Ministério da Agricultura, Pecuária e Abastecimento (2013).

Abramovay, Ricardo. 1992. *Paradigmas do capitalismo agrário em questão*. São Paulo: Hucitec/Anpocs.

ActionAid International. 2006. *Power Hungry: Six Reasons to Regulate Global Food Corporations*. Johannesburg: ActionAid International.

Adriance, Madeleine Cousineau. 1995. *Promised Land: Base Christian Communities and the Struggle for the Amazon*. Albany: State University of New York Press.

Agencia Folha. 2003. "Sociólogo vê ação leviana do governo." *Folha de São Paulo*, September 22. Available at http://www1.folha.uol.com.br/folha/brasil/ult96u53655.shtml. Accessed on September 25, 2003.

Akram-Lodhi, A. Haroon, Saturnino M. Borras Jr., and Cristóbal Kay. 2007. *Land, Poverty and Livelihoods in an Era of Globalization: Perspectives from Developing and Transition Countries*. London: Routledge.

Aldighieri, Mário. 1993. *Josimo: A terra, a vida*. São Paulo: Loyola.

Alier, Verena Martinez, and Michael Hall. n.d. "From Sharecropping to the Colonato." Mimeo.

AllRefer.com. 2006a. "Country Studies—Iraq." Available at http://reference.allrefer.com/country-guide-study/iraq/iraq55.html. Accessed on April 10, 2006.

AllRefer.com. 2006b. "Country Studies—Syria." Available at http://reference.allrefer.com/country-guide-study/syria/syria64.html. Accessed on April 10, 2006.

Américas Watch. 1991. *Violência rural no Brasil*. São Paulo: Human Rights Watch/Núcleo de Estudos da Violência, USP/Comissão Teotônio Vilela.

Aminzade, Ronald R., and Doug McAdam. 2001. "Emotions and Contentious Politics." In *Silence and Voice in the Study of Contentious Politics*, edited by Ronald R. Aminzade, Jack A. Goldstone, Doug McAdam, Elizabeth Perry, William H. Sewell Jr., Sidney Tarrow, and Charles Tilly, 14–50. Cambridge: Cambridge University Press.

Andrade, Lédio Rosa de. 1996. *Introdução ao direito alternativo brasileiro*. Porto Alegre: Livraria do Advogado Editora.

Andrade, Manuel Correia de. 1980. *The Land and People of Northeast Brazil*. Albuquerque: University of New Mexico Press.

Andrade, Manuel Correia de. 1988. *Área do sistema canavieiro*. Recife: Superintendencia do Desenvolvimento do Nordeste.

Andrade, Manuel Correia de. 2001. *Historia das usinas de açúcar de Pernambuco*. Recife: Editora da Universitária da UFPE.

Andrade, Manuel Correia de, and Sonia Correia de Andrade. 2001. *As usinas de Pernambuco e a crise atual*. Recife: UNTEPPE.

Andrade, Sonia Correia de. 2001. *A Cana de açúcar na região da mata Pernambucana*. Recife: CNPQ/FJN/UFPE.

Antunes, Ricardo. 1988. *A Rebeldia do trabalho: O confronto operário no ABC Paulista, as greves de 1978/80*. São Paulo: Editora Ensaio/UNICAMP.

Arendt, Hannah. 1987. *A condição humana*. 3rd ed. Rio de Janeiro: Forense Universitária.

Arenhart, Deise. 2007. *Infância, educação e MST: Quando as crianças ocupam a cena*. Chapecó: ARGOS Editora Universitaria.

Argiléz, Ramon Adell, and Miguel Martínez López. 2004. *Dónde están las llaves? El movimiento okupa, práticas sociales y contextos sociales*. Madrid: Catarata.

Arroyo, Miguel Gonzalez, Roseli Salete Caldart, and Mônica Castagna Molina, eds. 2005. *Por uma educação do campo*. Petrópolis: Vozes.

Arruda, Roldão. 2003. "'Ofensiva do MST será estorvo político para Lula': Para o sociólogo Zander Navarro, Movimento pode atrapalhar programa de reforma agrária." *Estado de São Paulo*, May 5.

Arruda, Roldão. 2012. "'Governo Dilma foi tomado por tecnocracia de segundo escalão,' diz Stédile." *Blog do Estado de São Paulo*, April 16. http://blogs.estadao .com.br/roldao-arruda/governo-dilma-foi-tomado-por-tecnocracia-de-segundo-escalao-diz-stedile/. Accessed on April 30, 2012.

Arruda, Roldão. 2005. "MST inaugura escola de US$1,3 mi." *O Estado de São Paulo*, January 16.

Aryal, Gokarna Raj, and Ghan Shyam Awasthi. 2006. "Agrarian Reform and Access to Land Resource in Nepal: Present Status and Future Perspectives/ Action." Centro de Estudios Rurales y de Agricultura Internacional. Available at http://www.cerai.es/fmra/archivo/nepal.pdf. Accessed on May 4, 2006.

Asselin, Victor. 1982. *Grilagem: Corrupção e violência em terras do Carajás*. Petrópolis: Vozes.

Associação Brasileira de Saúde Coletiva, ABRASCO (2012). *Dossiê ABRASCO, Parte 1: Agrotóxicos, segurança alimentar e saúde*. Rio de Janeiro: ABRASCO.

Avelino Filho, George. 1994. "Clientelismo e política no Brasil: Revisitando velhos problemas." *Novos Estudos, CEBRAP*, 38 (March): 225–40.

Bacha, Edmar Lisboa. 1976. *Os mitos de uma década*. Rio de Janeiro: Paz e Terra.

Banco Central. 2005. *Relatorio resumido da execução orçamentaria do governo federal, janeiro a abril de 2005*. Available at http://www.stn.fazenda.gov.br. Accessed on May 17, 2007.

Banco Central. 2013a. "Boletim do BC: Relatorio Annual." Available at http://www .bcb.gov.br/?boletimano. Accessed on September 12, 2013.

Banco Central. 2013b. "Histórico das taxas dos juros." Available at http://www.bcb .gov.br/?copomjuros. Accessed on September 12, 2013.

Barbosa, Maria Valéria, and Sérgio Pereira Leite. 1990. *Reforma agrária em terras públicas: Contradições de um governo democrático*. Jaboticabal: Universidade Estadual Paulista; Faculdade de Ciências Agrárias.

Barelli, Walter, and Ruth Vilela. 2000. "Trabalho escravo no Brasil." *Estudos Avançados* 38 (January–April): 7–29.

Barickman, Bert J. 1994. "'A Bit of Land, Which They Call Roça': Slave Provision Grounds in the Bahian Reconcavo, 1780–1860." *Hispanic American Historical Review* 74 (4): 649–87.

Barone, Luiz Antonio. 2002. "Conflito e cooperação: O jogo das racionalidades sociais e o campo político num assentamento de reforma agrária." Ph.D. diss., Universidade Estadual Paulista em Araraquara.

Barp, Wilson José, and Ana Rosa Baganha Barp. 1998. "Tendência da violência no espaço agrário: Uma análise estatística." In *Conflitos no campo, Brasil 97*, 14–17. Goiânia: CPT.

Barros, Flavia, Sergio Sauer, and Stephan Schwartzman, eds. 2003. *Os impactos negativos da política de reforma agrária de mercado do Banco Mundial.* Brasília: Rede Brasil sobre Organizações Financeiras Multilaterais, MST, Via Campesina, FIAN, CPT, Environmental Defense.

Barros, Marcelo, and José L. Caravias. 1988. *Teologia da terra.* Petrópolis: Vozes.

Barros, Marcelo, and Artur Peregrino. 1996. *A festa dos pequenos: Romarias da terra no Brasil.* São Paulo: Paulus.

Barros, Ricardo Paes de, Mirela de Carvalho, Samuel Franco, and Rosane Mendonça. 2006. "A Queda recente da desigualdade de renda no Brasil." In *Desigualdade de renda no Brasil: Uma análise da queda recente*, edited by Ricardo Paes de Barros, Miguel Nathan Foguel, and Gabriel Ulyssea, 107–27. Brasília: IPEA.

Barros, Ricardo Paes de, Ricardo Henriques, and Rosane Mendonça. 2000. "A estabilidade inaceitável: Desigualdade e pobreza no Brasil." In *Desigualdade e pobreza no Brasil*, edited by Ricardo Henriques, 21–47. Rio de Janeiro: IPEA.

Basset, Thomas J., and Donald E. Crummey, eds. 1993. *Land in African Agrarian Systems.* Madison: University of Wisconsin Press.

Baumeister, Eduardo. 1992. "Algunas lecciones de los procesos de reform agraria." In *Honduras: El ajuste estructral y la reforma agraria*, edited by Hugo Noé Pino and Andrew Thorpe, 1–23. Tegucigalpa: Editorial Guaymuras.

Benson, Todd. 2005. "Brazil's 'Temple of Luxury' Becomes a Symbol of Excess." *New York Times*, July 16. Available at http://www.nytimes.com/2005/07/15/business/worldbusiness/15iht-daslu.html?pagewanted=all&_r=0. Accessed on September 3, 2006.

Beozzo, Pe. José Oscar. 1994. *A Igreja do Brasil: de João XXIII a João Paulo II, de Medellin a Santo Domingo.* Petrópolis: Vozes.

Beraba, Marcelo. 2005. "Crítica diaria." *Folha de São Paulo*, July 14.

Bergamasco, Sonia Maria Pereira, and Mario Aubrée, eds. 2002. *A dinâmica dos assentamentos de trabalhadores rurais e seus efeitos sobre o espaço social e físico.* Relatório da Pesquisa: Campinas, Faculdade de Engenharia Agrícola/ Universidade Estadual de Campinas; Paris, Centre de Recherches sur le Brésil Contemporain/Ecole des Hautes Etudes em Sciences Sociales.

Bergamasco, Sonia Maria Pereira, Vera Lúcia Botta Ferrante, and Terezinha D'Aquino. 1991. "Assentamentos rurais em São Paulo: A roda viva de seu passado/presente." In *Ciências Sociais Hoje*, 253–80. São Paulo: Vértice/ANPOCS.

Bergamo, Mônica. 2005a. "ACM chora e defende empresária." *Folha de São Paulo*, July 14, p. B8.

Bergamo, Mônica. 2005b. "Com Alckmin, passeando na Daslu." *Folha de São Paulo*, June 6, p. E2.

Berger, Christa. 1998. *Campos em confronto: A terra e o texto.* Porto Alegre: Editora da Universidade/UFRGS.

Bermeo, Nancy G. 1986. *The Revolution within the Revolution: Worker's Control in Rural Portugal.* Princeton, N.J.: Princeton University Press.

Berry, Albert. 1998. *Poverty, Economic Reform and Income Distribution in Latin America.* Boulder, Colo.: Lynne Rienner.

Bezerra, Gregório. 1979. *Memórias. Segunda parte: 1946–1964.* Rio de Janeiro: Civilização Brasileira.

Biernaski, Dom Ladislau. 2009. "Oficializada a grilagem da Amazônia." *Conflitos no Campo, Brasil 2009,* 168–69. São Paulo: Expressão Popular.

Bingswanger-Mkhize, Hans P., Camille Bourguignon, and Rogier van den Brink, eds. 2009. *Agricultural Land Redistribution: Toward Greater Consensus.* Washington, D.C.: World Bank.

Birdsall, Nancy, Carol Graham, and Richard H. Sabot, eds. 1998. *Beyond Tradeoffs: Market Reforms and Equitable Growth in Latin America.* Washington, D.C.: Inter-American Development Bank.

Birdsall, Nancy, and Juan Luis Londoño. 1997. "Asset Inequality Matters: An Assessment of the World Bank's Approach to Poverty Reduction." *American Economic Review* 87 (2) (May): 32–37.

Birdsall, Nancy, and Richard Sabot. 1994. "Inequality as a Constraint on Growth in Latin America." *Development Policy, Inter-American Development Bank* 3 (3) (September): 1–5.

Bispos do Centro-Oeste. 1973. "Marginalização de um povo: O grito das Igrejas." *SEDOC* 6 (1973–74): 903–1021. Petrópolis: Vozes.

Bispos e Superiores Religiosos do Nordeste. 1973. "Eu ouvi os clamores do meu povo." *SEDOC* 6 (1973–74): 607–29. Petrópolis: Vozes.

Bobbio, Norberto. 1995. *Derecha e izquierda: Razones y significados de uma distinción política.* Madrid: Taurus.

Bobo, Kimberly A., Jackie Kendall, and Steve Max, eds. 1996. *Organizing for Social Change: A Manual for Activists in the 1990s.* Santa Ana, Calif.: Seven Locks Press.

Bogo, Ademar. 1999. *Lições da luta pela terra.* Salvador: Memorial da Letras.

Bogo, Ademar. 2002. *O vigor da mística.* Caderno de Cultura No. 2. São Paulo: ANCA.

Borges, Antonadia. 2003. *Tempo de Brasília: Etnografando lugares-evento da política.* Rio de Janeiro: Relume-Dumará.

Borras, Saturino M., Jr. 2006. "The Underlying Assumptions, Theory, and Practice of Neoliberal Land Policies." In *Promised Land: Competing Visions of Agrarian Reform,* edited by Peter Rosset, Raj Ptel, and Michael Courville, 99–128. Oakland, Calif.: Food First Books.

Borras, Saturnino M., Marc Edelman, and Cristóbal Kay, eds. 2008. *Transnational Agrarian Movements Confronting Globalization.* Oxford: Wiley-Blackwell.

Boschi, Renato. 1987. *A arte da associação.* Rio de Janeiro: Vértice.

Branch, Taylor. 1988. *Parting the Waters: America in the King Years, 1954–63.* New York: Simon and Schuster.

Branch, Taylor. 1998. *Pillar of Fire: America in the King Years, 1963–1965.* New York: Touchstone.

Branford, Sue. 2005. "Brazil's Landless Squeeze Government." *BBC News,* May 28.

Branford, Sue, and Oriel Glock. 1985. *The Last Frontier: Fighting over Land in the Amazon*. London: Zed Books.

Branford, Sue, and Bernardo Kucinski. 2003. *Politics Transformed: Lula and the Workers' Party in Brazil*. London: Latin America Bureau.

Branford, Sue, and Jan Rocha. 2002. *Cutting the Wire: The Story of the Landless Movement in Brazil*. London: Latin American Bureau.

Brenneisen, Eliane. 2002. *Relações de poder, dominação e resistência: O MST e os assentamentos rurais*. Cascavel: Edunioeste.

Brenneisen, Eliane. 2003. "Assentamento Sepé Tiaraju: Persistencias do passado, fragmentos do presente." In *Travessias: Estudo de caso sobre a vivência da reforma agrária nos assentamentos*, edited by José de Souza Martins, 53–107. Porto Alegre: Editora da UFRGS.

Breton, Binka Le. 1997. *A Land to Die For*. Atlanta: Clarity Press.

Breton, Binka Le. 2002. *Vidas roubadas: A escravidão moderna na amazônia brasileira*. São Paulo: Loyola.

Brockett, Charles. 1998. *Land Power and Poverty: Agrarian Transformation and Political Conflict in Central America*. Boulder, Colo.: Westview Press.

Brum, Argemiro Jacob. 1988. *Modernização da agricultura, Trigo e soja*. Petrópolis: Vozes.

Bruno, Regina. 1997. *Senhores da terra, senhores da guerra. A nova face política das elites agroindustriais no Brasil*. Rio de Janeiro: Edur/Forense Universitária.

Buainain, Antônio Márcio, ed. 2008. *Luta pela terra, reforma agrária e gestão de conflitos no Brasil*. Campinas: Editora da UNICAMP.

Buarque, Cristovam. 1994. *O que é a apartação? O apartheid social brasileiro*. São Paulo: Editora Brasiliense.

Buarque, Sergio C. 1997. "Proposta de reestruturação do setor sucro-alcooleiro e negociação de divida por terra para assentamentos de reforma agrária." Paper prepared for the workshop on the Reestruturação do Setor Sucro-Alcooleiro e Reforma Agrária na Zona da Mata de Pernambuco, Recife.

Caldart, Roseli Saldete. 2000. *Pedagogía do Movimento Sem terra: Escola é mais do que escola*. 2nd ed. Petrópolis: Vozes.

Calvo-González, Elena. 2004. "Power, Mediation and the Construction of Community: A Case Study of a Landless Movement Settlement in Brazil and an Indigenous Agrarian Community in Mexico." Ph.D. diss., University of Manchester.

Calvo-González, Elena. 2005. "Ruralidad re-emergente: Estrategias de vida, producción y agrotecnología en un asentamiento de reforma agraria en el Nordeste brasileño." In *Gente de campo: Patrimonios y dinámicas rurales en México*, edited by Esteban Barragán López. Zamora: El Colegio de Michoacán.

Câmara de Deputados. 1998. *Relatório da Comissão Externa destinada a averiguar a acquisação de madeiras, serrarias e extensas porções de terras por grupos asiáticos*. Brasília: Câmara de Deputados.

Camargo, Aspásia A. 1973. "Brésil, Nordest: Mouvements paysans et crise populiste." Ph.D. diss., École pratique des hautes études, Centre d'etudes des mouvements sociaux.

Camargo, Aspásia A. 1981. "A questão agrária: Crise de poder e reformas de base (1930–1964)." In *História geral da civilização brasileira: O Brasil republicano*, edited by Boris Fausto, vol. 3, 121–224. São Paulo: Difel.

Campos, André, Alexandre Barbosa, Marcio Pochmann, Ricardo Amorin, and Ronnie Silva, eds. 2005. *Os ricos no Brasil: Atlas da exclusão social.* Vol. 3. São Paulo: Editora Cortez.

Canuto, Antônio. 2002. "Acentos no trajeto dos 25 anos da CPT." In *Nas pegadas do povo da terra: 25 anos da Comissão Pastoral da Terra*, edited by Ivo Poletto and Antônio Canuto, 83–164. São Paulo: Loyola.

Cardoso, Fernando Henrique. 1977. *O capitalismo e escravidão no Brasil meridional: O negro na sociedade escravocrata do Rio Grande do Sul.* 3rd ed. Rio de Janeiro: Paz e Terra.

Cardoso, Fernando Henrique. 1991. Preface to *A tragédia da terra: O fracasso da reforma agrária no Brasil*, by Francisco de Graziano Neto, 9–12. São Paulo: IGLU/FUNEP/UNESP.

Cardoso, Fernando Henrique. 2006. *A arte da política: A história que vivi.* Rio de Janeiro: Civilização Brasileira.

Carta Maior. 2006. *El foro mundial sobre la reforma agraria.* Available at http://www.fma.org/memoria_CartaMaior.pdf, accessed August 24, 2008.

Carter, Miguel. 2002. "Ideal Interest Mobilization: Explaining the Formation of Brazil's Landless Social Movement." Ph.D. diss., Columbia University.

Carter, Miguel. 2003. "The Origins of Brazil's Landless Rural Workers' Movement (MST): The Natalino Episode in Rio Grande do Sul (1981–84). A Case of Ideal Interest Mobilization." Working Paper CBS-43-03, Centre for Brazilian Studies, University of Oxford.

Carter, Miguel. 2004a. "The Landless Rural Workers' Movement (MST) and Agrarian Reform in Brazil: Conference Report, October 17, 2003." Centre for Brazilian Studies, University of Oxford.

Carter, Miguel. 2004b. "Shaping Civil Society: Political Opportunities, Mobilizing Resources and Patterns of Contention." Unpublished manuscript.

Carter, Miguel. 2007. "Land Mobilizations in Rio Grande do Sul, 1978–2006." Unpublished database, American University.

Carter, Miguel. 2009. "The Landless Rural Workers Movement and the Struggle for Social Justice in Brazil." In *Rural Social Movements in Latin America: Organizing for Sustainable Livelihoods*, edited by Carmen Diana Deere and Fredrick S. Royce, 87–115. Gainesville: University Press of Florida.

Carter, Miguel. 2011. "The Landless Rural Workers Movement and Democracy in Brazil." Special issue, *Latin American Research Review* 45.

Carter, Miguel. Forthcoming. *Stroessner vive: Legados autoritarios y democracia en el Paraguay, 1989–2008.* Asunción: DEMOS/Servilibro.

Carter, Miguel. 2014. "Agrarian Dominance, Acquiescence and Resistance in Brazil, 2003–2014." Unpublished manuscript.

Carvalho, Abdias Vilar de. 1985. "A Igreja e a questão agrária." In *Igreja e questão agrária*, edited by Vanilda Paiva, 68–109. São Paulo: Loyola.

Carvalho, Horácio Martins de. 2002. "A emancipação do movimento no movimento de emancipação social continuada (resposta a Zander Navarro)." In

Produzir para viver: Os caminhos da produção não capitalista, edited by Boaventura de Sousa Santos, 233–60. São Paulo: Civilização Brasileira.

Carvalho, Horácio Martins de. 2003. "Governo Lula e a contra reforma agrária no Brasil." *Revista ADUSP—Associação dos Docentes da USP* 29 (May): 13–19.

Carvalho, Horacio Martins de, ed. 2005. *O campesinato no século XXI: Possibilidades e condicionantes do desenvolvimento do campesinato no Brasil*. Petrópolis: Vozes.

Carvalho, José Murilo de. 2006. *Cidadania no Brasil: O longo caminho*. 8th ed. Rio de Janeiro: Civilização Brasileira.

Casaldáliga, Dom Pedro. 1971. *Uma Igreja da Amazônia em conflito com o latifúndio e a marginalização social*. Petrópolis: Vozes.

Castro, Edna M. R. de, and Jean Hébette, eds. 1990. *Na trilha dos grandes projetos: Modernização e conflito na Amazônia*. Cadernos NAEA 10. Belém: Universidade Federal do Pará, Núcleo de Altos Estudos Amazônicos.

Castro, Josué de. 1966. *Death in the Northeast*. New York: Random House.

Caume, David José. 2002a. "Assentamento 16 de Março: Discursos e práticas instituíntes de um espaço gerenciado pelo poder." Paper presented at the XL Congresso Brasileiro de Economia e Sociologia Rural/SOBER, Passo Fundo, RS, July.

Caume, David José. 2002b. "Práticas de poder e resistência social em assentamentos de reforma agrária." Paper presented at the XI Congresso Latino Americano de Sociologia Rural/ALASRU, Porto Alegre, RS.

Caume, David José. 2006. *O MST e os assentamentos de reforma agrária: A construção de espaços sociais modelares*. Passo Fundo/Goiânia: Universidade de Passo Fundo/Universidade Federal de Goiás.

Cazella, Antony Ademir. 1992. "Assentamentos rurais e cooperação agrícola: Políticas conflitantes." Master's thesis, Curso de Pós-Graduação em Desenvolvimento, Agricultura e Sociedade, Universidade Federal Rural de Rio de Janeiro.

Cehelsky, Marta. 1979. *Land Reform in Brazil: The Management of Social Change*. Boulder, Colo.: Westview.

Central Intelligence Agency (CIA). 2008. *The World Factbook*. Available at https://www.cia.gov/library/publications/the-world-factbook/. Accessed on March 25, 2008.

Centro Brasileiro de Análise e Planejamento, CEBRAP. 2012. *The Real Brazil: The Inequality Behind the Statistics*. London: Christian Aid.

Centro de Documentação Dom Tomás Balduíno, CPT. 2013. "Assassinatos e Julgamentos 1985/2012," "Ocupações/Retomadas 2012" and "Manifestações de Luta, Brasil 2000–2012." Digital database.

Chalmers, Douglas A., Carlos M. Vilas, Katherine Hite, Scott B. Martin, Kerianne Piester, and Monique Segarra, eds. 1997. *The New Politics of Inequality in Latin America: Rethinking Participation and Representation*. New York: Oxford University Press.

Chambers, Robert. 1997. *Whose Reality Counts? Putting the Last First*. London: ITDG.

Chaves, Christine de Alencar. 2000. *A marcha nacional dos sem terra: Um estudo sobre a fabricação do social*. Rio de Janeiro: Relume Dumara.

Coffin, William Sloan, Jr. 2005. *Credo*. Louisville, Ky.: Westminster John Knox Press.

Cohen, Anthony P. 1985. *The Symbolic Construction of Community*. New York: Tavistock.

Cohen, Jean. 1985. "Strategy or Identity: New Theoretical Paradigms and Contemporary Social Movements." *Social Research* 52 (4): 663–716.

Colburn, Forrest D., ed. 1989. *Everyday Forms of Peasant Resistance*. Armonk: M. E. Sharpe.

Colette, Christine. 2006. "The Jarrow Crusade." Available at http://www.bbc.co .uk/history/society_culture/protest_reform/jarrow_01.shtml. Accessed on January 20, 2006.

Collins, Larry, and Dominique Lapierre. 1997. *Freedom at Midnight: The Epic Drama of India's Struggle for Independence*. New Delhi: Vikas.

Comisión Económica Para América Latina (CEPAL). 2004. *Anuario estadístico de América Latina y el Caribe, 2004*. Available at http://www.eclac.cl/. Accessed on May 19, 2006.

Comissão Pastoral da Terra (CPT). 1976. "CNBB apoia CIMI e CPT." *Boletim da CPT,* 3 (7) (November–December): 9.

Comissão Pastoral da Terra (CPT). 1977. "CNBB apoia CIMI e CPT." *Boletim da CPT,* 3 (10) (May–June). The entire issue is related to the topic mentioned in the related endnote.

Comissão Pastoral da Terra (CPT). 1986 and 1987. *Conflitos de terra no Brasil*. Goiânia: CPT.

Comissão Pastoral da Terra (CPT). 1988 to 2013. *Conflitos no campo: Brasil*. Goiânia: CPT.

Comissão Pastoral da Terra (CPT). 1997. *A luta pela terra: Comissão Pastoral da Terra 20 anos depois*. São Paulo: Paulus.

Comissão Pastoral da Terra (CPT). 1999b. *Trabalho escravo no Brasil contemporâneo*. Edited collection. São Paulo: Edições Loyola.

Comissão Pastoral da Terra (CPT). 2007. "Assassinatos e julgamentos 1985–2006." Setor de Documentação. Digital database.

Comissão Pastoral da Terra-Nordeste (CPT-NE). 2008. "IV Encontro da BioNatur debate desafios da agroecologia." Available at http://www.cptpe.org.br/ modules.php?name=New&file=article&sid=1300. Accessed on August 8, 2008.

Comissão Pastoral da Terra-Rio Grande do Sul (CPT-RS) and Comunidade Pe. Josino dos Freis Capuchinhos e Franciscanos—Tupanciretã, RS. 2003. *Cantos: Cantando com a Mãe Terra*. Porto Alegre: CPT-RS.

Comissão Pastoral da Terra, CPT-Santarém (2010). "Carta Aberta da CPT sobre o Programa Terra Legal." *Manuscript*, June13. Available at http://terra aguadireitos.blogspot.com/2010/07/carta-aberta-da-cpt-sobre-o-programa .html. Accessed on September 3, 2013.

Comparato, Bruno Konder. 2000. *A ação política do MST*. São Paulo: Editora Expressão Popular.

Confederação das Cooperativas de Reforma Agrária do Brasil (CONCRAB). 1998. *Sistema de cooperativista dos assentados*. Cadernos de Cooperação Agrícola No. 5. 2nd ed. São Paulo: CONCRAB.

Confederação Rural Brasileira (CRB). 1955. *Revista Gleba* (December).

Conferência Nacional de Bispos do Brasil (CNBB). 1980. *Igreja e problemas da terra*. São Paulo: Paulinas.

Cornia, Giovanni Andrea, ed. 2004. *Inequality, Growth, and Poverty in an Era of Liberalization and Globalization*. Oxford: Oxford University Press.

Corporación Latinobarómetro. 2004. *Informe—Resumen Latinobarómetro 2004: Una Década de Mediciones*. Santiago, Chile. Available at http://www.latino barometro.org. Accessed on May 30, 2007.

Corporación Latinobarómetro. 2006. *Informe Latinobarómetro 2006*. Santiago, Chile. Available at http://www.latinobarometro.org. Accessed on May 30, 2007.

Corporación Latinobarómetro. 2007. *Latinobarómetro Report 2007*. Santiago, Chile. Available at http://www.latinobarometro.org. Accessed on May 3, 2008.

Correia, Ciro. 2007. "MST en marcha hacia la agroecologia: Una aproximación a la construcción histórica de la agroecologia en el MST." Master's thesis, Universidad Internacional de Andalucía, Universidad de Córdoba.

Costa, Francisco de Assis. 1998. "Grande empresa e agricultura na Amazônia: Dois momentos, dois fracassos." *Novos cadernos do NAEA* 12 (94): 1–43.

Costa, Luciana Miranda. 1999. *Discurso e conflito: Dez anos de disputa pela terra em Eldorado do Carajás*. Belém: UFPA/NAEA.

Costa, Luiz Flávio Carvalho, and Raimundo Santos, eds. 1998. *Política e reforma agrária*. Rio de Janeiro: MAUD.

Cuban Economic Research Project. 1965. *Cuba: Agriculture and Planning, 1963–1964*. Coral Gables, Fla.: University of Miami.

Cunha, Paulo Ribeiro da. 2007. *Aconteceu longe demais: A luta pela terra dos posseiros em Formoso e Trombas e a revolução brasileira (1950–1964)*. São Paulo: Editora da Unesp.

Central Única dos Trabalhadores (CUT) and Confederação Nacional dos Trabalhadores na Agricultura (CONTAG). 1999. *Desenvolvimento e sindicalismo rural*. São Paulo: Projeto CUT/CONTAG.

Dacanal, José Hildebrando, and Sergius Gonzaga, eds. 1979. *RS: Economía e política*. Porto Alegre: Mercado Aberto.

Dahl, Robert. 1971. *Polyarchy: Participation and Opposition*. New Haven, Conn.: Yale University Press.

Dahl, Robert A. 1998. *On Democracy*. New Haven: Yale University Press.

Dahl, Robert A. 2006. *On Political Equality*. New Haven: Yale University Press.

Dallagnol, Wilson. 2001. *As romarías da terra no Rio Grande do Sul*. Porto Alegre: CPT.

Dallari, Dalmo de Abreu. 1996. *O poder dos juizes*. São Paulo: Saraiva.

Da Ros, César Augusto. 2006. "As políticas agrárias durante o governo Olívio Dutra e os embates sociais em torno da questão agrária gaúcha." Ph.D. diss., Universidade Federal Rural de Rio de Janeiro.

DATALUTA, Banco de Dados da Luta pela Terra. 2008. Núcleo de Estudos da Reforma Agrária (NERA), Universidade do Estado de São Paulo (UNESP), Presidente Prudente. Available at http://www.fct.unesp.br/nera.

DATALUTA. 2013. "Assentamentos de Reforma Agrária—RA (Atualizado em 31/12/2011)." Digital database. Núcleo de Estudos de Reforma Agrária (NERA), Universidade Estadual de São Paulo (UNESP), Presidente Prudente.

Deere, Carmen Diana, and Frederick S. Royce, eds. 2009. *Rural Social Movements in Latin America: Organizing for Sustainable Livelihoods.* Gainesville: University Press of Florida.

Deere, Carmen Diana, and Leonilde Servolo de Medeiros. 2007. "Agrarian Reform and Poverty Reduction: Lessons from Brazil." In *Land, Poverty and Livelihoods in an Era of Globalization,* edited by A. Haroon Akram-Lodhi, Saturnino M. Borras Jr., and Cristóbal Kay, 80–118. London: Routledge.

De Janvry, Alain. 1981. *The Agrarian Question and Reformism in Latin America.* Baltimore: Johns Hopkins University Press.

De Janvry, Alain, Gustavo Gordillo, Jean-Philippe Platteau, and Elisabeth Saudolet, eds. 2001. *Access to Land, Rural Poverty, and Public Action.* Oxford: Oxford University Press.

Delfim Neto, Antônio. 1963. "Problemas econômicos da agricultura brasileira." Boletim no. 46, Cadeira 25. São Paulo: Faculdade de Ciências Econômicas e Administrativas da USP.

Delfim Neto, Antônio. 1965. "O café do Brasil." No. 3. São Paulo: Estudo ANPES.

Delfim Neto, Antônio, Affonso Celso Pastore, and Eduardo Pereira de Carvalho. 1969. *Agricultura e desenvolvimento no Brasil.* São Paulo: Estudo ANPES.

Delgado, Guilherme C. 1985. *Capital financeiro e agricultura no Brasil.* São Paulo: Ícone-UNICAMP.

Delgado, Guilherme C. 2003. "O setor de subsistência na economia e na sociedade brasileira: gênese histórica, reprodução e configuração contemporânea." Revista de conjuntura 4 (16). Brasília: Conselho Regional de Economia do Distrito Federal.

Delgado, Guilherme. 2012. *Do 'capital financeiro na agricultura' à economia do agronegócio: mudanças cíclicas em meio século (1965–2012).* Porto Alegre: Editora da Universidade/UFRGS.

Delgado, Guilherme C., and José Flores Filho. 1998. "Determinantes da queda recente do preço da terra no Brasil." *Economia—ensaios* 12–13 (2–1). Uberlândia.

Del Grossi, Mauro Eduardo, José Garcia Gasques, José Graziano da Silva, and Júnia Cristina P. R. da Conceição. 2001. "Estimativas das famílias potenciais beneficiárias de programas de assentamentos rurais no Brasil." *Transformações da agricultura e políticas públicas,* edited by José Garcia Gasques and Júnia Cristina P. R. da Conceição, 457–78. Brasília: IPEA.

Della Cava, Ralph. 1989. "The 'People's Church,' the Vatican and the Abertura." In *Democratizing Brazil,* edited by Alfred Stepan, 143–67. New York: Oxford University Press.

Departamento Intersindical de Estatística e Estudos Socioeconômicos (DIEESE). 2006. *Estatísticas do meio rural.* Brasília: Ministério do Desenvolvimento Agrário.

Desai, A. R. 1986. *Agrarian Struggles in India after Independence.* New Delhi: Oxford University Press.

De Schutter, Olivier. 2010. *Report submitted by the Special Rapporteur on the Right to Food,* 16th Session of the Human Rights Council, United Nations General Assembly. December 20.

Desmarais, Annette Aurélie. 2007. *La Vía Campesina: Globalization and the Power of Peasants.* Ann Arbor, Mich.: Pluto.

Desmarais, Annette Aurélie. 2009. "La Vía Campesina: Globalizing Peasants." In *Rural Social Movements in Latin America: Organizing for Sustainable Livelihoods*, edited by Carmen Diana Deere and Fredrick S. Royce, 33–54. Gainesville: University Press of Florida.

Diskin, Martin. 1989. "El Salvador: Reform Prevents Change." In *Searching for Agrarian Reform in Latin America*, edited by William C. Thiesenhusen, 429–50. Boston: Unwin Hyman.

Dorner, Peter. 1992. *Latin American Land Reforms in Theory and in Practice: A Retrospective Analysis*. Madison: University of Wisconsin Press.

Dos Santos, Andrea Paula, Suzana Lopes Salgado Ribeiro, and José Carlos Sebe Bom Meihy. 1998. *Vozes da marcha pela terra*. São Paulo: Edições Loyola.

Downie, Andrew. 2005. "A Stone's Throw from Poverty, Brazil's Daslu Glimmers." *Christian Science Monitor*, July 12. Available at http://www.csmonitor.com/2005/0712/p04s01-woam.html. Accessed on September 4, 2006.

Dreifuss, Armand René. 1981. *1964: A conquista do estado: Ação política, poder e golpe de classe*. Petrópolis: Vozes.

Durkheim, Émile. 1995. *Da divisão do trabalho social*. São Paulo: Martins Fontes.

Eckert, Córdula. 1984. "Movimento dos Agricultores Sem Terra no Rio Grande do Sul: 1960–1964." Master's thesis, Universidade Federal Rural de Rio de Janeiro.

Eckstein, Shlomo, Gordon Donald, Douglas Horton, and Thomas Carroll. 1978. *Land Reform in Latin America: Bolivia, Chile, Mexico, Peru, and Venezuela*. World Bank Staff Working Paper 275. Washington, D.C.: World Bank.

Edwards, Bob, Michael W. Foley, and Mario Diani, eds. 2001. *Beyond Tocqueville: Civil Society and the Social Capital Debate in Comparative Perspective*. Hanover, N.H.: University Press of New England.

Eisenberg, Peter. 1974. *The Sugar Industry in Pernambuco: Modernization without Change, 1840–1910*. Berkeley: University of California Press.

Eisenberg, Peter L. 1977. *Modernização sem mudança: A indústria açucareira em Pernambuco: 1840/1910*. Rio de Janeiro/Campinas: Paz e Terra/Unicamp.

El-Ghonemy, M. Riad. 2001. "The Political Economy of Market-Based Land Reform." In *Land Reform and Peasant Livelihoods: The Social Dynamics of Rural Poverty and Agrarian Reform in Developing Countries*, edited by Krishna B. Ghimire, 105–33. London: Cromwell Press.

Elias, Norbert. 1982. *Power and Civility*. New York: Pantheon.

Elias, Norbert. 1991. *Qu'est-ce que la sociologie?* Marseille: Editions de L'aube.

Elias, Norbert. 1997. *Os alemães: A luta pelo poder e a evolução do habitus nos séculos XIX e XX*. Rio de Janeiro: Jorge Zahar Editores.

Emmi, Marília Ferreira. 1985. *A oligarquia do Tocantins e o domímio dos castanhais*. Belém: NAEA/UFPA.

Encontro Unitário dos Trabalhadores, Trabalhadoras e Povos do Campo, das Águas e das Florestas. 2012. "Declaração do Encontro Unitário dos Trabalhadores, Trabalhadoras e Povos do Campo, das Águas e das Florestas: Por terra, território e dignidade!" Available at http://encontrounitario.wordpress.com/2012/08/22/declaracao-do-encontro-nacional-unitario-dos-trabalhadores-e-trabalhadoras-e-povos-do-campo-das-aguas-e-das-florestas/. Accessed on March 30, 2013.

Enríquez, Laura J. 1991. *Harvesting Change: Labor and Agarian Reform in Nicaragua, 1979–1990*. Chapel Hill: University of North Carolina Press.

Esterci, Neide. 1987. *Conflito no Araguaia: Peões e posseiros contra a grande empresa*. Petrópolis: Vozes.

Esterci, Neide. 1994. *Escravos da desigualdade: Estudo sobre o uso repressivo da força de trabalho hoje*. Rio de Janeiro: CEDI/Koinonia.

Exame. 2013. "Apenas 124 pessoas concentram mais de 12% do PIB do Brasil." *Exame*, September 9. Available at http://exame.abril.com.br/economia/noticias/124-pessoas-mais-ricas-do-brasil-correspondem-a-12–3-do-pib?page=2. Accessed on September 17, 2013.

Fajolles, David. 2000. "Mamucaba: L'Attente." Rio de Janeiro: Museu Nacional. Relatório de Pesquisa.

Faoro, Raymundo. 1957. *Os donos do poder: Formação do patronato político brasileiro*. Vols. 1 and 2. Rio de Janeiro: Editora Globo.

Faria, Vilmar Evangelista. 1991. "Cinqüenta anos de urbanização no Brasil: Tendências e perspectivas." *Novos Estudos, CEBRAP*, 29, 98–119.

Federal Reserve Bank of St. Louis. 2006. *Brazil/US Foreign Exchange Rate*. Available at http://research.stlouisfed.org/fred2/categories/15. Accessed on March 27, 2006.

Fernandes, Bernardo Mançano. 1996a. *MST: Formação e territorialização*. São Paulo: Editora Hucitec.

Fernandes, Bernardo Mançano. 1996b. "Reforma agrária e modernização do campo." *Terra Livre* 11–12: 153–75. São Paulo: Associação dos Geógrafos Brasileiros.

Fernandes, Bernardo Mançano. 1997. "A judiciarização da luta pela reforma agrária." *GEOUSP-Revista de pós-graduação em geografia*. São Paulo: Departamento de Geografia da FFLCH-USP, 35–39.

Fernandes, Bernardo Mançano. 1998. "A luta pela terra no Pontal do Paranapanema." Paper presented at the Encontro regional do projeto de intercâmbio em pesquisa social em agricultura, Araraquara, São Paulo.

Fernandes, Bernardo Mançano. 1999. *MST, Movimento Dos Trabalhadores Rurais Sem Terra: Formação e territorialização*. São Paulo: Editora Hucitec.

Fernandes, Bernardo Mançano. 2000. *A formação do MST no Brasi*. Petrópolis: Vozes.

Fernandes, Bernardo Mançano. 2001. *Questão agrária: Pesquisa e MST*. São Paulo: Cortez.

Fernandes, Bernardo Mançano. 2005. "Movimentos socioterritoriais e movimentos socioespaciais." *Observatorio social de America Latina* 16: 273–84.

Fernandes, Bernardo Mançano. 2008. "Questão agrária: Conflitualidade e desenvolvimento territorial." In *Luta pela terra, reforma agrária e gestão de conflitos no Brasil*, edited by Antônio Márcio Buainain, 173–224. Campinas: Editora da Unicamp.

Fernandes, Bernardo Mançano, Anderson Antonio Silva Girardi, and Eduardo Paulon. 2004. "Questões da Via Campesina." Anais do VI Congresso Nacional de Geógrafos. Goiânia: Associação dos Geógrafos Brasileiros.

Fernandes, Bernardo Mançano, and Jean Yves Martin. 2004. "Movimento socio-territorial e 'globalização': Algumas reflexões a partir do caso do MST." *Lutas sociais*, Programas de Estudos Pós-graduados em Ciências Sociais, Pontifícia Universidade Católica de São Paulo, 12: 161–72.

Fernandes, Bernardo Mançano, and Cristiane Barbosa Ramalho. 2001. "Luta pela terra e desenvolvimento rural no Pontal do Paranapanema." *Estudos Avançados* 15 (43) (September–December): 239–54.

Fernandes, Bernardo Mançano, Arlete Meneguette, Diana da Cruz Fagundes, and Gleison Leal. 2003. "Insertion socio-politique et criminalisation de la lutte pour la terre: Occupations de terre et assentamentos ruraux dans le Pontal do Paranapanema, São Paulo." *Cahiers du Bresil Contemporain* 51/52: 71–94.

Fernandes, Rubem César. 1977. *O Debate entre sociólogos a propósito de pentecostais*. Cadernos do ISER 6. Rio de Janeiro: ISER.

Ferranti, David de, Guillermo E. Perry, Francisco Ferreira, and Michael Walton. 2004. *Inequality in Latin America: Breaking with History?* Washington, D.C.: World Bank.

Figueira, Ricardo Rezende. 2000. "Porque trabalho escravo?" *Estudos Avançados* 14 (38) (January/April): 31–50.

Figueira, Ricardo Rezende. 2004. *Pisando fora da própria sombra: A escravidão por dívida no Brasil contemporâneo*. Rio de Janeiro: Civilização Brasileira.

Filgueiras, Luiz, and Reinaldo Gonçalves. 2007. *A economia política do governo Lula*. Rio de Janeiro: Contraponto.

Fishlow, Albert. 1972. "Brazilian Size Distribution of Income." *American Economic Review* 62 (2) (May): 391–402.

Flake, Oliver. 2006. *Focus on Brazil: Agricultural Production and Trade*. U.S. Department of Agriculture (February). Available at http://oalp.okstate.edu/files/Brazil_2006/Oliver_Flake2.pdf. Accessed on May 24, 2006.

Folha de São Paulo. 2000a. "MST invade prédios em 12 capitais." *Folha de São Paulo*, May 3, p. 1.

Folha de São Paulo. 2000b. "Morte deve servir de alerta, diz porta-voz." *Folha de São Paulo*, May 4, p. 6.

Folha de São Paulo. 2003. "Lula vai até o MST, pede calma e defende Palocci." *Folha de São Paulo*, November 22, p. A1.

Folha Online. 2007. "Maioria dos brasileiros nunca foi a cinema ou museu, diz estudo." *Folha de São Paulo*, April 30. Available at http://www1.folha.uol.com .br/folha/ilustrada/ult90u70716.shtml. Accessed on June 19, 2008.

Food and Agriculture Organization (FAO) and Instituto Nacional de Colonização e Reforma Agrária (INCRA). 2000. *Novo retrato da agricultura familiar: O Brasil redescoberto*. Brasília: FAO/INCRA.

Forman, Shepard. 1975. *The Brazilian Peasantry*. New York: Columbia University Press.

Foweraker, Joe. 1982. *A luta pela terra: A economia política da fronteira pioneira no Brasil de 1930 aos dias atuais*. Rio de Janeiro: Zahar Editores.

Foweraker, Joe, and Todd Landman. 1997. *Citizenship Rights and Social Movements: A Comparative and Statistical Analysis*. Oxford: Oxford University Press.

Fox, Jonathan, ed. 1990. *The Challenge of Rural Democratisation: Perspectives from Latin America and the Philippines*. London: Frank Cass.

Franca, William. 2000. "FHC descarta negociar sob pressão com os sem-terra." *Folha de São Paulo*, May 3, p. 5.

Freyre, Gilberto. 1978. *The Masters and the Slaves*. New York: Knopf.

Fundação Getúlio Vargas. 2004. *Conjuntura econômica* 58 (11) (August).

Gacitúa-Marió, Estanislao, and Michael Woolcock, eds. 2005a. *Exclusão social e mobilidade no Brasil*. Brasília: IPEA/Banco Mundial.

Gacitúa-Marió, Estanislao, and Michael Woolcock, with Marisa von Bulow. 2005b. "Uma avaliação da exclusão social e da mobilidade no Brasil." *Exclusão social e mobilidade no Brasil*, edited by Estanislao Gacitúa-Marió and Michael Woolcock, 1–18. Brasília: IPEA/Banco Mundial.

Galbraith, John Kenneth. 1977. *The Age of Uncertainty: A History of Economic Ideas and Their Consequences*. Boston: Houghton Mifflin.

Galloway, Jack H. 1989. *The Sugar Cane Industry: An Historical Geography from Its Origins to 1914*. Cambridge: Cambridge University Press.

Gamson, William. 1992. "The Social Psychology of Collective Action." In *Frontiers in Social Movement Theory*, edited by Aldon D. Morris and Carol McClurg Mueller, 53–76. New Haven, Conn.: Yale University Press.

Ganuza, Enrique, Ricardo Paes de Barros, Lance Taylor, and Rob Vos, eds. 2001. *Liberalización, desigualdad y pobreza: América Latina y el Caribe en los 90*. Buenos Aires: Universidad de Buenos Aires and Programa de Naciones Unidas para el Desarrollo.

Garcia, Afrânio, Jr. 1983. *Terra de trabalho*. Rio de Janeiro: Paz e Terra.

Garcia, Afrânio, Jr. 1990. *O Sul: Caminho do roçado*. São Paulo: Marco Zero.

Garcia, Antonio. 1973. *Sociologia de la reforma agraria em América Latina*. Buenos Aires: Amorrotu Editores.

Gasques, José Garcia, and Júnia Cristina P. R. da Conceição. 1998. "A demanda por terra para a reforma agrária no Brasil." Anais do 36° Congresso de Economia e Sociologia do Rural (SOBER). Foz do Iguaçu.

Gasques, José Garcia, and Júnia Cristina P. R. da Conceição, eds. 2001. *Transformações da agricultura e políticas públicas*. Rio de Janeiro: IPEA.

Gasques, José Garcia, and Carlos Monteiro Villa Verde. 2003. "Gastos públicos na agricultura: Evolução e mudanças." *Texto para discussão* 48 (April).

Gehlen, Ivaldo. 1983. "Uma estratégia camponesa de conquista da terra e o estado: O caso da Fazenda Sarandi." Master's thesis, Universidade Federal do Rio Grande do Sul.

Gehlen, Ivaldo. 1991. "Terres de lutte e luttes pour la terre: Étude sur le mouvement social pour la terre et la reforme agraire au Sud du Bresil." Ph.D. diss., Universite de Paris X–Nanterre.

Geromel, Ricardo. 2013. "All You Ever Needed to Know about Brazilian Billionaires (and More)." *Forbes*, April 4. Available at http://www.forbes.com/sites/ricardo geromel/2013/04/18/all-you-ever-needed-to-know-about-brazilian-billionaires-and-more/. Accessed on May 15, 2013.

Ghimire, Krishna B., ed. 2001. *Land Reform and Peasant Livelihoods: The Social Dynamics of Rural Poverty and Agrarian Reform in Developing Countries*. London: Cromwell.

Glass, Verena. 2003. "Sem Terra e intelectuais criticam a política agrária." *Agência Carta Maior*, October 29.

Gluckman, Max. 1963. "Gossip and Scandal." *Current Anthropology* 4 (3): 307–16.

Góes, Cesar Hamilton Brito. 1997. "A Comissão Pastoral da Terra: História e ambivalencia da ação da Igreja no Rio Grande do Sul." Master's thesis, Universidade Federal do Rio Grande do Sul.

Goeth, Pe. Ernesto. 1994. "Lições pastorais do Sul 3 na década de 70." *Pastoral da Igreja no Brasil nos anos 70: Caminhos, experiências e dimensões*, edited by Instituto Nacional de Pastoral, 83–101. Petrópolis: Vozes.

Goodman, David. 1989. "Rural Economy and Society." In *Social Change in Brazil 1945–1985: The Incomplete Transition*, edited by Edmar L. Bacha and Herbert S. Klein, 49–98. Albuquerque: University of New Mexico Press.

Goodwin, Jeff, and James M. Jasper, eds. 2004. *Rethinking Social Movements: Structure, Meaning and Emotion*. Lanham, Md.: Rowman and Littlefield.

Goodwin, Jeff, James M. Jasper, and Francesca Poletta, eds. 2001. *Passionate Politics: Emotions and Social Movements*. Chicago: University of Chicago Press.

Görgen, Frei Sérgio Antônio. 1989. *O massacre da Fazenda Santa Elmira*. 2nd ed. Petrópolis: Vozes.

Görgen, Frei Sérgio Antônio, ed. 1991. *Uma foice longe da terra: Repressão aos sem-terra em Porto Alegre*. Petrópolis: Vozes.

Görgen, Frei Sérgio Antônio. 1997. "Religiosidade e fé na luta pela terra." In *A reforma agrária e a luta do MST*, edited by João Pedro Stédile, 279–92. Petrópolis: Vozes.

Görgen, Frei Sérgio Antônio. 2004. *Marcha ao coração do latifúndio*. Petrópolis: Vozes.

Görgen, Frei Sergio Antonio, and João Pedro Stédile, eds. 1991. *Assentamentos: A resposta econômica da reforma agrária*. Petrópolis: Vozes.

Görgen, Sérgio. 1998. *A resistência dos pequenos gigantes: A luta e a organização dos pequenos agricultores*. Petrópolis: Vozes.

Gorsdorf, Leandro Franklin. 2004. "Advocacia popular na construção de um novo senso comum jurídico." Ph.D. diss., Universidade Federal do Paraná, Curitiba.

Graziano, Francisco. 1996. *Qual reforma agrária? Terra, pobreza e cidadania*. São Paulo: Geração Editorial.

Graziano, Xico. 2004. *O carma da terra*. São Paulo: A Girafa.

Graziano, Xico. 2006. "Terrorismo agrário." *Estado de São Paulo*, May 23.

Grindle, Merilee S. 1986. *State and Countryside: Development Policy and Agrarian Politics in Latin America*. Baltimore: Johns Hopkins University Press.

Grynszpan, Mário. 1987. "Mobilização camponesa e competição política no estado do Rio de Janeiro (1950–1964)." Master's thesis, PPGAS, Universidade Federal Rural de Rio de Janeiro.

Guanziroli, Carlos Enrique, and Isabella Fernandes. 1987. *Reforma agrária em terras da Igreja: São Miguel, relato de uma experiência*. Petrópolis: Vozes.

Guedes, André D. 2006. "Projeto identitário, discurso e pedagogia na constituição de um sujeito coletivo: O caso dos atingidos por barragens." Master's thesis, Rio de Janeiro, IPPUR/UFRJ.

Guimarães, Alberto Passos. 1982. *A crise agrária*. Rio de Janeiro: Paz e Terra.

Guimarães, Alberto Passos. 1989. *Quatro séculos de latifúndio*. 6th ed. Rio de Janeiro: Editora Paz e Terra.

Hammond, John L. 1999. "Law and Disorder: The Brazilian Landless Farmworkers' Movement." *Bulletin of Latin American Research* 18 (4): 469–89.

Hammond, John L. 2004. "The MST and the Media: Competing Images of the Brazilian Landless Farmworkers' Movement." *Latin American Politics and Society* 46 (4): 61–90.

Handelman, Howard. 1981. *The Politics of Agrarian Change in Asia and Latin America.* Bloomington: Indiana University Press.

Handy, Jim. 1994. *Revolution in the Countryside: Rural Conflict and Agrarian Reform in Guatemala, 1944–1954.* Chapel Hill: University of North Carolina Press.

Harnecker, Marta. 2003. *Landless People: Building a Social Movement.* São Paulo: Editora Expressão Popular.

Harnecker, Marta. 2002. *Sin tierra: Construyendo un movimiento social.* Madrid: Siglo Veintiuno Editores de España.

Healy, Kevin. 2001. *Llamas, Weavings, and Organic Chocolate: Multicultural Grassroots Development in the Andes and Amazon of Bolivia.* Notre Dame, Ind.: University of Notre Dame Press.

Hecht, Susanna B., and Alexander Cockburn. 1989. *The Fate of the Forest: Developers, Destroyers, and Defenders of the Amazon.* New York: Verso.

Henriques, Ricardo, ed. 2000. *Desigualdade e pobreza no Brasil.* Rio de Janeiro: IPEA.

Heredia, Beatriz. 1979. *A morada da vida.* Rio de Janeiro: Paz e Terra.

Heredia, Beatriz, Leonilde Sérvolo de Medeiros, Moacir Palmeira, Rosângela Cintrão, and Sergio Leite. 2004. *Impactos dos assentamentos: Um estudo sobre o meio rural brasileiro.* Brasília: Núcleo de Estudos Agrários e Desenvolvimento Rural.

Heredia, Beatriz, Leonilde Medeiros, Moacir Palmeira, Rosângela Cintrão, and Sérgio Pereira Leite. 2006. "Regional Impacts of Land Reform in Brazil." In *Promised Land: Competing Visions of Agrarian Reform,* edited by Peter Rosset, Paj Patel, and Michael Courville, 277–300. Oakland, Calif.: First Food Books.

Hirschman, Albert O. 1982. *Shifting Involvements: Private Interest and Public Action.* Princeton, N.J.: Princeton University Press.

Hirschman, Albert O. 1991. *The Rhetoric of Reaction: Perversity, Futility and Jeopardy.* Cambridge, Mass.: Harvard University Press.

Hite, Katherine, and Paola Cesarini. 2004. *Authoritarian Legacies and Democracy in Latin America and Southern Europe.* Notre Dame, Ind.: Notre Dame University Press.

Hoffman, Leandro Sidinei Nunes. 2002. "Da cruz à bandeira: A construção do imaginário do Movimento Sem Terra/RS, 1985–1991." Ph.D. diss., Universidade Federal do Rio Grande do Sul.

Hoffmann, Rodolfo. 1998. "A Estrutura fundiária no Brasil de acordo com o cadastro do INCRA: 1967 a 1998." Unpublished manuscript, UNICAMP/INCRA.

Hoffmann, Rodolfo. 2001. "A distribuição da posse da terra no Brasil de acordo com as PNADs de 1992 a 1999." In *Transformações da agricultura e políticas públicas,* edited by José Garcia Gasques and Júnia Cristina P. R. da Conceição, 441–55. Brasília: IPEA.

Hoffmann, Rodolfo. 2004. "Distribuição da renda e da posse da terra no Brasil." Unpublished manuscript, Instituto de Economia, UNICAMP.

Hoffmann, Rodolfo, and José Graziano da Silva. 1999. "O Censo Agropecuário de 1995–96 e a distribuição da posse da terra no Brasil." Paper presented at the XXXVII Congresso Brasileiro de Economia e Sociologia Rural/SOBER, Foz do Iguaçu.

Hooglund, Eric J. 1982. *Land Revolution in Iran, 1960–1980*. Austin: University of Texas Press.

Houtzager, Peter P. 1997. "Caught between State and Church: Popular Movements in the Brazilian Countryside, 1964–1989." Ph.D. diss., University of California, Berkeley.

Houtzager, Peter P. 2001. "Collective Action and Political Authority: Rural Workers, Church, and State in Brazil." *Theory and Society* 30 (1): 1–45.

Huber, Evelyne, and Frank Safford, eds. 1995. *Agrarian Political Structure and Political Power: Landlord and Peasant in the Making of Latin America*. Pittsburgh: University of Pittsburgh Press.

Hunter, Wendy. 2010. *The Transformation of the Workers' Party in Brazil, 1989–2009*. New York: Cambridge University Press.

Hunter, Wendy. 2011. "Brazil: The PT in Power." *The Resurgence of the Latin American Left*, edited by Steven Levitsky and Kenneth M. Roberts, 306–24. Baltimore: Johns Hopkins University Press.

Huntington, Samuel P. 1968. *Political Order in Changing Societies*. New Haven, Conn.: Yale University Press.

Inayatullah, ed. 1980. *Land Reform: Some Experiences in Asia*. Vol. 4. Kuala Lumpur: Asian and Pacific Development Administration Centre.

Indiaagronet Agriculture Resource Center. 2006. "Ceiling Limits on Land Holdings." Available at http://www.indiaagronet.com/indiaagronet/AGRI_LAW/CONTENTS/Ceiling.htm. Accessed on March 1, 2006.

Informes Brasil. 2002. 67 (February).

Instituto Brasileiro de Geografía e Estatística (IBGE). 1996. *Censo Agropecuário 1996.* Vol. 1. Rio de Janeiro: IBGE.

Instituto Brasileiro de Geografía e Estatística (IBGE). 2001. *Censo Demográfico 2000: Características da população e dos domicílios—Resultados do universo.* Rio de Janeiro: IBGE.

Instituto Brasileiro de Geografía e Estatística (IBGE). 2005a. *Censos Demográficos.* Available at http://www.ibge.gov.br/. Accessed on October 15, 2008.

Instituto Brasileiro de Geografía e Estatística (IBGE). 2005b. *Estudos e pesquisas: Economia.* Available at http://www.ibge.gov.br/home/estatistica/economia/pibmunicipios/2005/tab01.pdf. Accessed on April 10, 2008.

Instituto Brasileiro de Geografía e Estatística (IBGE). 2007a. *Censo Agropecuário de 1995–1996.* Available at http://www.ibge.gov.br/. Accessed on August 26, 2007.

Instituto Brasileiro de Geografía e Estatística (IBGE). 2007b. "Censo Agropecuario 2006: Resultados preliminares do censo confirmam expansão da fronteira agrícola na região Norte." Comunicação Social (December). Available at http://www1.ibge.gov.br/home/presidencia/noticias/noticia_impressao.php?id_noticia=1064. Accessed on April 15, 2008.

Instituto Brasileiro de Geografía e Estatística (IBGE). 2007c. *Estudos e pesquisas: Indicadores Sociais 2007.* Available at http://www.ibge.gov.br/home/estatistica/populacao/condicaodevida/indicadoresminimos/sinteseindicsociais2007/indic_sociais2007.pdf. Accessed on April 8, 2008.

Instituto Brasileiro de Geografia e Estatística (IBGE). 2009a. *Censo agropecuário 2006: Agricultura familiar, primeiros resultados—Brasil, grandes regiões e unidades da federação.* Rio de Janeiro: IBGE.

Instituto Brasileiro de Geografia e Estatística (IBGE). 2009b. *Censo Agropecuário 2006: Brasil, Grandes Regiões e Unidades da Federação.* Rio de Janeiro: IBGE.

Instituto Cidadania. 2001. *Projeto fome zero: Uma proposta de política de segurança alimentar para o Brasil.* Porto Alegre: Instituto Cidadania.

Instituto de Estudos Socioeconômicos (INESC). 2006. "Reforma agrária no governo Lula: Residual e periférica." *Nota Técnica* 105 (March).

Instituto de Estudos Socioeconômicos (INESC). 2010. "Orcamento e Direitos na Execucao da LOA 2009." *Nota Técnica,* no. 164 (April).

Instituto de Estudos Socioeconômicos (INESC). 2009. "Execução Orcamentaria do Governo Federal, 2008." *Nota Técnica,* no. 149 (April).

Instituto de Estudos Socioeconômicos (INESC). 2005/2007. "Orçamento," 4: 7 (July 2005): 5: 9 (March 2006), 6: 10 (April 2007).

Instituto Nacional de Colonização e Reforma Agrária (INCRA). 2003c. "Projetos de reforma agrária conforme fases de implementação: Período de criação do projeto, 01/01/1900 até 24/07/2003." Unpublished database.

Instituto Nacional de Colonização e Reforma Agrária (INCRA). 2010. *Reforma Agrária: Pesquisa sobre a qualidade de vida renda e produção nos assentamentos de reforma agraria.* Brasília: INCRA.

Instituto Nacional de Colonização e Reforma Agrária (INCRA). 2012. "Evolução da desapropriação de terras no Brasil: Decretos emitidos pelo Governo Federal, 1985–2012." Unpublished document, December 14.

Instituto Nacional de Colonização e Reforma Agrária-Rio Grande do Sul (INCRA-RS). 2003a. "Banco de relatórios de projetos de assentamento." Unpublished document, INCRA-RS.

Instituto Nacional de Colonização e Reforma Agrária-Rio Grande do Sul (INCRA-RS). 2003b. "Invasões de terra no Rio Grande do Sul: Periodo maio de 1978 e 10 de março de 2003." Unpublished document, INCRA-RS.

Instituto Nacional de Colonização e Reforma Agrária-Rio Grande do Sul (INCRA-RS). 2005. "Projetos de assentamentos no Estado do Rio Grande do Sul." Unpublished document, INCRA-RS.

Instituto Nacional de Colonização e Reforma Agrária-Rio Grande do Sul (INCRA-RS). 2008. "Projetos de assentamentos no Estado do Rio Grande do Sul." Unpublished document, INCRA-RS.

Instituto de Pesquisa Econômica Aplicada (IPEA). 2001. *Políticas sociais: Acompanhamento e análise.* No. 3 (Agosto). Brasília: IPEA.

Instituto de Pesquisa Econômica Aplicada (IPEA). 2003. *Políticas sociais: Acompanhamento e análise.* No. 6 (Fevereiro). Brasília: IPEA.

Instituto de Pesquisa Econômica Aplicada (IPEA). 2005. *Radar Social.* Brasília: IPEA.

Instituto de Pesquisa Econômica Aplicada (IPEA). 2009. *IPEA Data*. Available at http:www.ipeadata.gov.br. Accessed on October 20, 2009.

Instituto de Pesquisa Econômica Aplicada (IPEA). 2010. *Perspectivas da política social no Brasil*. Brasília: IPEA.

Instituto de Pesquisa Econômica Aplicada (IPEA). 2011/2013. *IPEA Data*. Available at www.ipeadata.gov.br. Accessed on various dates.

Instituto de Terras do Estado de São Paulo (ITESP). 1998a. *Mediação no campo: Estratégias e ação em situações de conflito fundiário*. Cadernos ITESP 6. São Paulo: ITESP.

Instituto de Terras do Estado de São Paulo (ITESP). 1998b. *Terra e cidadãos: Aspectos da ação de regularização fundiária no Estado de São Paulo*. Cadernos ITESP 4. São Paulo: ITESP.

International Assessment of Agricultural Knowledge, Science and Technology for Development (IAASTD). 2009. *Agriculture at a Crossroads: Synthesis Report*. Washington, D.C.: Island Press.

International Labor Organization (ILO). 2008. *Laborista: Database of Labour Statistics*. Available at http://laborsta.ilo.org/. Accessed on September 21, 2008.

International Monetary Fund (IMF). 2008. *Data and Statistics*. Available at http://www.imf.org/external/pubs/ft/weo/2008/01/weodata/weorept.aspx?sy=2000&ey=2007&scsm=1&ssd=1&sort=country&ds=.&br=1&c=223&s=PPPEX&grp=0&a=&pr.x=41&pr.y=11#download. Accessed on April 14, 2008.

Intervozes Coletivo Brasil de Comunicação Social. 2005. *Direito à comunicação no Brasil: Base constitucional e legal, implementação, o papel dos diferentes atores e tendências atuais e futuras*. Projeto de governança global e Campanha CRIS (Communication Rights in the Information Society). São Paulo: Intervozes Coletivo Brasil de Comunicação Social.

Johnston, Bruce F., and John W. Mellor. 1961. "The Role of Agriculture in Economic Development." *American Economic Review* 51 (4) (September): 566–93.

Julião, Francisco. 1972. *Cambão—The Yoke: The Hidden Face of Brazil*. Translated from Portuguese by John Butt. Harmondsworth: Penguin.

Jungmann, Raul. 2003. "Carta Aberta ao Presidente Lula." *Folha de São Paulo*, July 15.

Justino, Patricia, Julie Litchfield, and Laurence Whitehead. 2003. "The Impact of Inequality in Latin America." PRUS Working Paper 21. Poverty Research Unit at Sussex, University of Sussex.

Kageyama, Ângela, and Eugênia Troncoso Leone. 1999. "Uma tipologia dos municípios paulistas com base em indicadores sociodemográficos." Working paper 66. Instituto de Economia, Universidade Estadual de Londrina.

Kaimowitz, David. 1989. "The Role of Decentralization in the Recent Nicaraguan Agrarian Reform." In *Searching for Agrarian Reform in Latin America*, edited by William C. Thiesenhusen, 384–407. Boston: Unwin Hyman.

Kakwani, Nanak. 2013. "Inclusive Development: Defining, Measuring and Analyzing for BRICS Countries." Presentation at IPEA, September 5. Available at http://www.ipea.gov.br/portal/images/stories/PDFs/temasrelevantes/nanak%20presentation%20at%20ipea%202%202.pdf. Accessed on September 29, 2013.

Kane, Liam. 2001. *Popular Education and Social Change in Latin America*. London: Latin America Bureau.

Karl, Terry Lynn. 2003. "The Vicious Cycle of Inequality in Latin America." In *What Justice? Whose Justice? Fighting for Fairness in Latin America*, edited by Susan Eva Eckstein and Timothy P. Wickham-Crowley, 133–57. Berkeley: University of California Press.

Kawagoe, Toshihiko. 1999. "Agricultural Land Reform in Postwar Japan: Experience and Issues." Policy Research Working Paper WPS2111. Washington, D.C.: World Bank.

Kay, Cristobal. 1998. "Latin America's Agrarian Reform: Lights and Shadows." *Land Reform, Land Settlements and Cooperatives* 2: 9–31.

King, Russell. 1973. *Land Reform: The Italian Experience*. London: Butterworth.

King, Russell. 1977. *Land Reform: A World Survey*. Boulder, Colo.: Westview.

Kingstone, Peter R., and Aldo Ponce. 2010. "From Cardoso to Lula: The Triumph of Pragmatism in Brazil." *Leftists Governments in Latin America: Successes and Shortcomings*, edited by Kurt Weyland, Raúl L. Madrid, and Wendy Hunter, 98–123. New York: Cambridge University Press.

Kleinmann, Luiza H. Schmitz. 1986. *RS: Terra e poder. História da questão agrária*. Porto Alegre: Mercado Aberto.

Kolling, Edgar, Israel Nery, and Mônica Castagna. 1999. *Por uma educação básica do campo*. Brasília: Fundação Universidade de Brasília.

Kotscho, Ricardo. 1982. *O massacre dos posseiros: Conflitos de terras no Araguaia-Tocantins*. São Paulo: Brasiliense.

Kuhnen, Frithjof. 1971. "Land Tenure and Agrarian Reform in Asia: A Re-appraisal of Priorities in Agrarian Re-organization for Rural Development." Paper for the Asian Regional Seminar on the Contribution of Rural Institutions to Rural Development, Particularly Employment, New Delhi. Available at http://www.professor-frithjof-kuhnen.de/publications/land-tenure-asia/0.htm. Accessed on January 30, 2006.

Kurtz, Marcus. 2000. "Understanding Peasant Revolution: From Concept to Theory and Case." *Theory and Society* 29 (1): 93–124.

Kuznets, Simon S. 1954. "Economic Growth and Income Inequality." *American Economic Review* 45 (March): 1–28.

Lamounier, Bolívar. 1989. "Brazil: Inequality against Democracy." In *Democracy in Developing Countries: Latin America*, vol. 4, edited by Larry Diamond, Juan J. Linz, and Seymour Martin Lipset, 111–57. Boulder, Colo.: Lynne Rienner.

Lapp, Nancy D. 2004. *Landing Votes: Political Representation and Land Reform in Latin America*. New York: Palgrave Macmillan.

Lara, Francisco, Jr., and Horacio R. Morales, Jr. 1990. "The Peasant Movement and the Challenge of Rural Democratisation in the Philippines." In *The Challenge of Rural Democratisation: Perspectives from Latin American and the Philippines*, edited by Jonathan Fox, 143–62. London: Frank Cass.

Lastarria-Cornheil, Susana. 1989. "Agrarian Reform of the 1960s and 1970s in Peru." In *Searching for Agrarian Reform in Latin America*, edited by William C. Thiesenhusen, 127–55. Boston: Unwin Hyman.

Laureano, Delze dos Santos. 2007. *O MST e a constituição: Um sujeito histórico na luta pela reforma agrária no Brasil*. São Paulo: Expressão Popular.

Leal, Victor Nunes. 1993. *Coronelismo, enxada e voto*. 6th ed. São Paulo: Editora Alfa-Omega.

Leite, José Ferrari. 1998. *A ocupação do Pontal do Paranapanema*. São Paulo: Editora Hucitec.

Leite, Sérgio, with the collaboration of Rodrigo Àvila. 2006a. "Réforme agraire, justice sociale et dévelopment durable." Thematic document No. 4. Conferénce Internationale sur la Réforme Agraire et le Devéloppement Rurale (CIRADR).

Leite, Sérgio. 2006b. "Seis comentários sobre seis equívocos a respeito da reforma agrária no Brasil." *Revista NERA* 8 (9) (July–December): 144–58.

Lenharo, Alcir. 1986a. *Colonização e trabalho no Brasil: Amazônia, Nordeste e Centro-Oeste. Os anos 30*. 2nd ed. Campinas: Editora da Unicamp.

Lenharo, Alcir. 1986b. *Sacralização da política*. 2nd ed. Campinas/São Paulo: Editora da Unicamp/Papirus.

Lenz, Matias Martino, ed. 1980. *A Igreja e a propriedade da terra*. São Paulo: Edições Loyola.

Leone, Eugênia Troncoso. 1994. "Pobreza e trabalho no Brasil: Análise das condições de vida e ocupação das famílias agrícolas nos anos 80." Ph.D. diss., Universidade Estadual de Campinas.

Leroy, Jean-Pierre. 1991. *Uma chama na Amazônia*. Rio de Janeiro: Vozes.

Lerrer, Débora. 2003. *Reforma Agrária: Os caminhos do impasse*. São Paulo: Editora Garçoni.

Lerrer, Débora. 2005. *De como a mídia fabrica e impõe uma imagem: "A degola" do PM pelos sem-terra em Porto Alegre*. Rio de Janeiro: Editora Revan.

Lerrer, Débora Franco. 2008. "Trajetória de militantes sulistas: Nacionalização e modernidade do MST." Ph.D. diss., Universidade Federal Rural do Rio de Janeiro.

Library of Congress. 2003. "Country Studies, Egypt." Available at http://country studies.us/egypt/85.htm. Accessed on June 1, 2006.

Lima, João Policarpo R., and Gerson Victor Silva. 1995. "A economia canavieira de Pernambuco e a reestruturação necessária." *Revista de economia Nordeste de Fortaleza* 26 (2): 181–203.

Lima, Solange, and Bernardo Mançano Fernandes. 2001. *Trabalhadores urbanos nos assentamentos rurais: A construção de novos sujeitos sociais*. Presidente Prudente, CNPq—PIBIC Report, 1999–2001.

Linhares, Elizabeth, Leonilde Medeiros, Luciano Padrão, and Paulo Alentejano. 2002. *Conhecendo assentamentos rurais no Rio de Janeiro*. Rio de Janeiro: CPDA/UFRRJ.

Lins, Carlos Jose Caldas, et al. 1996. *Programa de ação para o desenvolvimento da Zona da Mata do Nordeste*. Recife: SUDENE.

Lipton, Michael. 2009. *Land Reform in Developing Countries*. Abingdon, UK: Routledge.

Loera, Nashieli Cecilia. 2006. *A espiral das ocupações*. São Paulo: Polis; Campinas: Unicamp/IFCH/CERES.

Lopes, Juarez Brandão. 1995. "Política social: Subsídios estatísticos sobre a pobreza e acesso a programas sociais no Brasil." *Estudos Avançados* 9 (24) (August): 141–56.

Loureiro, Walderez Nunes. 1982. "O aspecto educativo da prática política: A luta do arrendo em Orizona, Goiás." Master's thesis, Fundação Getúlio Vargas de Rio de Janeiro.

Lupion, Abelardo. 2005. "Comissão Parlamentar Mixto de Inquérito da Terra, Voto em separado (substitutivo aprovado)." Brasília: Congresso Nacional.

Lustig, Nora, ed. 1995. *Coping with Austerity: Poverty and Inequality in Latin America*. Washington, D.C.: Brookings Institution.

Lutzenberger, José A. 2001. "O absurdo da agricultura." *Estudos Avançados: Dossiê Desenvolvimento Rural* 15 (43) (September–December): 61–74.

Macedo, Marcelo Ernandez. 2003. "'Zé pureza': Etnografia de um acampamento no Norte Fluminense." Ph.D. diss., Universidade do Estado do Rio de Janeiro.

MacEwan, Arthur. 1981. *Revolution and Economic Development in Cuba*. New York: St. Martin's.

Machado, Antônio Alberto, and Marcelo Pedroso Goulart. 1992. *Ministério Público e direito alternativo: O MP e a defesa do regime democrático e da ordem jurídica*. São Paulo: Editora Acadêmica.

Mainwaring, Scott. 1986. *The Catholic Church and Politics in Brazil, 1916–1985*. Stanford, Calif.: Stanford University Press.

Mainwaring, Scott P. 1999. *Rethinking Party Systems in the Third Wave of Democratization: The Case of Brazil*. Stanford, Calif.: Stanford University Press.

Mainwaring, Scott, Daniel Brinks, and Anibal Peréz-Liñán. 2007. "Classifying Political Regimes in Latin America, 1945–2004." In *Regimes and Democracy in Latin America: Theories and Methods*, edited by Gerardo L. Munck, 123–60. Oxford: Oxford University Press.

Mandela, Nelson. 1995. *Long Walk to Freedom: The Autobiography of Nelson Mandela*. New York: Little, Brown.

Marcon, Telmo. 1997. *Acampamento Natalino: História da luta pela reforma agrária*. Passo Fundo: Editora da Universidade de Passo Fundo.

Marés, Carlos Frederico. 2003. *A função social da terra*. Porto Alegre: Editora Sergio Antonio Fabris.

Marshall, T. H. 1992. "Citizenship and Social Class." In *Citizenship and Social Class*, edited by Tom Bottomore, 1–51. London: Pluto.

Martins, José de Souza. 1979. *O cativeiro da terra*. São Paulo: Ciências Humanas.

Martins, José de Souza. 1981. *Os camponses e política no Brasil*. Petrópolis: Vozes.

Martins, José de Souza. 1984. *A militarização da questão agrária no Brasil*. Petrópolis: Vozes.

Martins, José de Souza. 1989. *Caminhada no chão da noite*. São Paulo: Hucitec.

Martins, José de Souza. 1991. *Expropriação e violência: A questão política no campo*. 3rd ed. rev. São Paulo: Hucitec.

Martins, José de Souza. 1996. *O poder do atraso: Ensaios de sociologia da história lenta*. São Paulo: Hucitec.

Martins, José de Souza. 1997. "A questão agrária brasileira e o papel do MST." In *A reforma agraria e a luta do MST*, edited by João Pedro Stédile, 11–76. Petrópolis: Vozes.

Martins, José de Souza. 2000a. *Reforma agrária: O impossível diálogo*. São Paulo: Editora da Universidad de São Paulo.

Martins, José de Souza. 2000b. *A sociabilidade do homem simples*. São Paulo: Editora Hucitec.

Martins, José de Souza. 2003a. *Exclusão social e a nova desigualdade.* 2nd ed. São Paulo: Paulus.

Martins, José de Souza. 2003b. "O sujeito da reforma agrária (estudo comparativo de cinco assentamentos)." In *Travessias: Estudo de caso sobre a vivência da reforma agrária nos assentamentos,* edited by José de Souza Martins, 11–52. Porto Alegre: Editora da UFRGS.

Martins, José de Souza. 2003c. *O sujeito oculto: Ordem e transgressão na reforma agrária.* Porto Alegre: Editora da Universidade/UFRGS.

Martins, José de Souza. 2005. "Uma escola com o nome de Florestan." *O Estado de São Paulo* (February 6), p. A11.

Martins, José de Souza. 2007. "O MST e seus moinhos de vento." *O Estado de São Paulo* (April 22).

Martins, Mônica Dias, ed. 2004. *O Banco Mundial e a terra: Ofensiva e resistência na América Latina, Ásia e África.* São Paulo: Biotempo.

Marx, Anthony W. 1992. *Lessons of Struggle: South African Internal Opposition, 1960–1990.* Cape Town: Oxford University Press.

Maybury-Lewis, Bjorn. 1994. *The Politics of the Possible: The Brazilian Rural Workers' Trade Union Movement, 1964–1985.* Philadelphia: Temple University Press.

McAdam, Doug. 1982. *The Political Process and the Development of Black Insurgency.* Chicago: University of Chicago Press.

McAdam, Doug, John D. McCarthy, and Mayer N. Zald. 1996. *Comparative Perspectives on Social Movements: Political Opportunities, Mobilizing Structures, and Cultural Framings.* Cambridge: Cambridge University Press.

McAdam, Doug, Sidney Tarrow, and Charles Tilly. 2001. *Dynamics of Contention.* Cambridge: Cambridge University Press.

McCarthy, John D., and Mayer N. Zald. 1977. "Resource Mobilization and Social Movements: A Partial Theory." *American Journal of Sociology* 82 (6): 1212–41.

McClintock, Cynthia. 1981. *Peasant Cooperatives and Political Change in Peru.* Princeton, N.J.: Princeton University Press.

Medeiros, Leonilde. 1981. "CONTAG: Um balanço." *Reforma agrária* 11 (6) (November–December): 9–25.

Medeiros, Leonilde Servolo de. 1983. "A questão da reforma agrária no Brasil." Master's thesis, FFCL, Universidade de São Paulo.

Medeiros, Leonilde Servolo de. 1989. *História dos movimentos sociais no campo.* Rio de Janeiro: FASE.

Medeiros, Leonilde Servolo de. 1995. "Lavradores, trabalhadores agrícolas, camponeses: Os comunistas e a constituição de classes no campo." Ph.D. diss., IFCH, UNICAMP.

Medeiros, Leonilde Servolo de. 2002a. "Dimensões políticas da violência no campo." In *O direito achado na rua: Introdução crítica ao direito agrário,* vol. 3, edited by Mônica Castagna Molina, José Geraldo de Sousa Jr., and Fernando da Costa Tourinhi Neto. Brasília /São Paulo: Editora UnB/Imprensa Oficial do Estado de São Paulo.

Medeiros, Leonilde Servolo de. 2002b. *Movimentos sociais, disputas políticas e reforma agrária de mercado no Brasil.* Rio de Janeiro: Editora da Universidade Rural e UNRISD.

Medeiros, Leonilde, Maria Valéria Barbosa, Mariana Pantoja Franco, Neide Esterci, and Sérgio Leite, eds. 1994. *Assentamentos rurais: Uma visão multidisciplinar.* São Paulo: Editora da UNESP.

Medeiros, Leonilde Servolo de, and Sergio Leite, eds. 1999. *A formação dos assentamentos rurais no Brasil: Processos sociais e políticas públicas.* Porto Alegre: Editora da Universidade UFRGS.

Medeiros, Leonilde Servolo de, and Sergio Leite, eds. 2004. *Assentamentos rurais: Mudança social e dinâmica regional.* Rio de Janeiro: MAUAD Editora.

Mello, Mário Lacerda de. 1975. *O açúcar e o homem.* Recife: MEC/Instituto Joaquim Nabuco.

Melo, João Alfredo Telles, ed. 2006. *Reforma agrária quando? CPI mostra as causas da luta pela terra no Brasil.* Brasília: Senado Federal.

Méndez, Juan E., Guillermo O'Donnell, and Paulo Sergio Pinheiro, eds. 1999. *The (Un) Rule of Law and the Underprivileged in Latin America.* Notre Dame, Ind.: University of Notre Dame Press.

Mendonça, Sonia Regina de. 2006. *A Questão agrária no Brasil: A classe dominante agrária: Natureza e comportamento, 1964–1990,* edited by João Pedro Stédile. São Paulo: Editora Expressão Popular.

Menezes Neto, Antonio Julio de. 2003. *Além da terra: Cooperativismo e trabalho na educação do MST.* Rio de Janeiro: Quartet Editora.

Menjivar, Rafael. 1969. *Reforma agraria: Guatemala, Bolivia, y Cuba.* San Salvador: Editorial Universitaria de El Salvador.

Mészáros, George. 2000. "Taking the Land into Their Hands: The Landless Workers' Movement and the Brazilian State." *Journal of Law and Society* 27 (4) (December): 517–41.

Mészáros, George. 2013. *Social Movements, Law and the Politics of Land Reform: Lessons from Brazil.* Abingdon, UK: Routledge-Cavendish.

Ministério de Agricultura, Pecuária e Abastecimento (MAPA). 2008. "Estatísticas: Crédito rural no Brasil." Available at http://www.agricultura.gov.br/. Accessed on July 28, 2008.

Ministério da Agricultura, Pecuária e Abastecimento (MAPA). 2013. "Crédito rural: aplicação de recursos nas safras 2003/4 a 2011/12." Digital report. Available at http://www.agricultura.gov.br/vegetal/estatisticas. Accessed on April 30, 2013.

Ministério do Desenvolvimento Agrário (MDA). 2000. "Novo retrato da agricultura familiar." Brasília: Projeto Cooperação FAO/INCRA.

Ministério do Desenvolvimento Agrário (MDA). 2003. *II PNRA—Plano Nacional de Reforma Agrária: Paz, produção e qualidade de vida no meio rural.* Brasília: MDA.

Ministério do Desenvolvimento Agrário (MDA). 2004. *Relatório da Ouvidoria Agrária 05/2004.* Brasília: MDA.

Ministério do Desenvolvimento Agrário (MDA). 2006. *Desenvolvimento agrário como estratégia: Balanço MDA, 2003/2006.* Porto Alegre: NEAD.

Ministério Extraordinário da Política Fundiária (MEPF). 1998. *Programa Integrado de Reforma na Zona da Mata Nordestina.* Recife: MEPF.

Ministério das Minas, Energias e Comunicações. 2007. "Informativo Luz para Todos." No. 1. Brasília (July). Available at http://200.198.213.102/luzparatodos/downloads/Informativo%2001–23.07.07.pdf. Accessed on July 23, 2008.

Ministério do Planejamento e Coordenação Econômica (EPEA). 1965. "Programa de Ação Econômica do Governo." No. 66 (Síntese). 2nd ed. Doc. no. 1.

Montero, Alfred P. 2005. *Brazilian Politics*. Cambridge: Polity.

Montgomery, John D. 1984. *International Dimensions of Land Reform*. Boulder, Colo.: Westview Press.

Moore, Barrington. 1966. *Social Origins of Dictatorship and Democracy: Landlord and Peasant in the Making of the Modern World*. Boston: Beacon.

Moraes, Maria Estela. 1996. "No rastro da águas: Organização, liderança e representatividade dos atingidos por barragens." In *Política, protesto e cidadania no campo: As lutas sociais dos colonos e dos trabalhadores rurais no Rio Grande do Sul*, edited by Zander Navarro, 137–70. Porto Alegre: Editora da Universidade.

Morais, Clodomir Santos de. 1986. *Elementos sobre a teoria da organização no campo*. São Paulo: MST.

Moreira, Roberto José. 2000. "Críticas ambientalistas à revolução verde." *Estudos sociedade e agricultura* 15 (October): 39–52.

Morissawa, Mitsue. 2001. *A história da luta pela terra e o MST*. São Paulo: Expressão Popular.

Morley, Samuel A. 2000. *La distribuición del ingreso en América Latina y el Caribe*. Santiago: Fondo de Cultura Económica/CEPAL.

Morris, Aldon D., and Carol McClurg Mueller, eds. 1992. *Frontiers in Social Movement Theory*. New Haven, Conn.: Yale University Press.

Movimento dos Pequenos Agricultores (MPA), Movimento dos Trabalhadores Rurais Sem Terra (MST), Movimento dos Atingidos por Barragens (MAB), Movimento das Mulheres Camponesas (MNC), Comissão Pastoral da Terra (CPT), Associação Brasileira de Reforma Agrária (ABRA). 2006. "Balanço das medidas do governo Lula (2002–2006) em relação a agricultura camponesa e reforma agrária no Brasil." Public statement, March 26.

Movimento dos Trabalhadores Rurais Sem Terra (MST). 1993. *A cooperação agrícola nos assentamentos*. Cadernos de formação no. 20. São Paulo: Secretaria Nacional do MST.

Movimento dos Trabalhadores Rurais Sem Terra (MST). Setor de Direitos Humanos. 1997. *As ocupaçcõoes de terras são constitucionais, legítimas e necessárias*. São Paulo: MST.

Movimento dos Trabalhadores Rurais Sem Terra (MST). 1998. *A lei e as ocupaçcões de terras*. São Paulo: MST.

Movimento dos Trabalhadores Rurais Sem Terra (MST). 2005a. *Ergue a tua voz: Marcha nacional pela reforma agrária 2005*. Video documentary.

Movimento dos Trabalhadores Rurais Sem Terra (MST). 2005b. "MST entrega pauta da marcha ao ministro Rosetto." *Informativos: Últimas do MST* (May 3). Available at http://www.mst.org.br/informativos/minforma/ultimas721.htm. Accessed on September 29, 2005.

Movimento dos Trabalhadores Rurais Sem Terra (MST). 2005c. *O MST: A luta pela reforma agrária e por mudanças sociais no brasil—Documentos básicos*. São Paulo: Secretaria Nacional do MST.

Movimento dos Trabalhadores Rurais Sem Terra (MST). 2006. "BioNatur leva sementes agroecológicas para todo o país." Available at http://www.mst.org.br/mst/pagina.php?cd=727. Acessed on August 9, 2008.

Movimento dos Trabalhadores Rurais Sem Terra (MST). 2007a. "Assentamentos do MST em 2004." Available at http://www.mst.org.br/mst/pagina.php?cd=1010. Accessed on March 15, 2007.

Movimento dos Trabalhadores Rurais Sem Terra (MST). 2007b. "MST quer novo modelo para reforma agrária." *MST Informa* 5 (139) (August 2).

Movimento dos Trabalhadores Rurais Sem Terra (MST). 2009. *Revista Sem Terra* 11 (January–February): 48.

Movimento dos Trabalhadores Rurais Sem Terra-Rio Grande do Sul (MST-RS). 2003. "Acões do MST-RS, 1979–1996." Available at http://empresa.portoweb .com.br/mstrs/acoes. Accessed on October 7, 2003.

Moyo, Sam, and Paris Yeros, eds. 2005. *Reclaiming the Land: The Resurgence of Rural Movements in Africa, Asia, and Latin America.* London: Zed Books.

Muller, Edward N., and Mitchell A. Seligson. 1987. "Inequality and Insurgency." *American Political Science Review* 81 (2) (June): 425–52.

Muniz, Durval de Albuquerque. 2004. "Weaving Tradition: The Invention of the Brazilian Northeast." *Latin American Perspectives* 31 (2) (March): 42–61.

Naím, Moisés. 2004. "From Normalcy to Lunacy." *Foreign Policy* 141 (March–April): 103–4.

Narayan, Deepa, with Raj Patel, Kai Schafft, Anne Rademacher, and Sarah Koch-Schulte. 2000. *Voices of the Poor: Can Anyone Hear Us?* Washington, D.C.: World Bank.

Navarro, Zander. 1996a. "Democracia, cidadania e representação: Os movimentos sociais rurais no Estado do Rio Grande do Sul, Brasil, 1978–1990." In *Política, protesto e cidadania no campo: As lutas sociais dos colonos e dos trabalhadores rurais no Rio Grande do Sul*, edited by Zander Navarro, 62–105. Porto Alegre: Editora da Universidade.

Navarro, Zander, ed. 1996b. *Política, protesto e cidadanía no campo: As lutas sociais dos colonos e trabalhadores rurais do Rio Grande do Sul.* Porto Alegre: Editora da Universidade Federal do Rio Grande do Sul.

Navarro, Zander. 2002a. "'Mobilização sem emancipação': As lutas sociais dos sem terra no Brasil." In *Produzir para viver: Os caminhos da produção não capitalista*, edited by Boaventura de Sousa Santos, 189–232. Rio de Janeiro: Civilização Brasileira.

Navarro, Zander. 2002b. "O MST e a canonização da ação coletiva (reposta a Horacio Martins Carvalho)." *Produzir para viver: Os caminhos da produção não capitalista*, edited by Boaventura de Sousa Santos, 261–82. São Paulo: Civili-zação Brasileira.

Navarro, Zander. 2003. "Sociólogo vê ação leviana do governo." *Folha de São Paulo*, September 22.

Navarro, Zander. 2007. "Comédia agrária." *Folha de São Paulo*, April 22.

Navarro, Zander. 2009. "MST tenta se manter vivo no sistema politico." *Gazeta Mercantil*, February 12.

Neiva, Artur Hehl. 1942. "A imigração e a colonização no governo Vargas." *Cultura política*, Rio de Janeiro 2 (21) (November).

Nepomuceno, Eric. 2007. *O massacre*. São Paulo: Editora Planeta do Brasil.

Neves, Delma Pessanha. 1997. *Assentamento rural: Reforma agrária em migalhas.* Niterói: EDUFF.

Noé Pino, Hugo, and Andrew Thorpe, eds. 1992. *Honduras: El ajuste estructral y la reforma agraria*. Tegucigalpa: Editorial Guaymuras.

Norder, Luiz Antonio Cabello. 1998. "A construção da segurança alimentar em assentamentos rurais: Questões, contextos e métodos." *Caderno de Debates* 5. Revista do Núcleo de Estudos e Pesquisas em Alimentação, UNICAMP.

Norder, Luiz Antonio Cabello. 2004. "Políticas de assentamento e localidade: Os desafios da reconstituição do trabalho rural no Brasil." Ph.D. diss., Universidade de Wageningen.

Novaes, Regina Célia R. 1997. *De corpo e alma: Catolicismo, classes sociais e conflitos no campo*. Rio de Janeiro: Graphia.

Novaes, Regina Reyes. 1985. *Os escolhidos de Deus: Pentecostais, trabalhadores e cidadania*. Cadernos do ISER 19. Rio de Janeiro: ISER.

Oberschall, Anthony. 1973. *Social Conflict and Social Movements*. Englewood Cliffs, N.J.: Prentice Hall.

O'Donnell, Guillermo. 1998. "Poverty and Inequality in Latin America: Some Political Reflections." In *Poverty and Inequality in Latin America: Issues and New Challenges*, edited by Víctor E. Tokman and Guillermo O'Donnell, 49–71. Notre Dame, Ind.: Notre Dame University Press.

O'Donnell, Guillermo. 1999. "Polyarchies and the (Un)Rule of Law in Latin America: A Partial Conclusion." In *The (Un)Rule of Law and the Underprivileged in Latin America*, edited by Juan E. Mendez, Guillermo O'Donnell, and Paulo Sergio Pinheiro, 303–37. Notre Dame, Ind.: Notre Dame University Press.

O'Donnell, Guillermo. 2004. "Human Development, Human Rights, and Democracy." In *The Quality of Democracy: Theory and Applications*, edited by Guillermo O'Donnell, Jorge Vargas Cullell, and Osvaldo M. Iazzetta, 9–92. Notre Dame, Ind.: University of Notre Dame Press.

O'Donnell, Guillermo, Jorge Vargas Cullell, and Osvaldo M. Iazzetta, eds. 2004. *The Quality of Democracy: Theory and Applications*. Notre Dame, Ind.: University of Notre Dame Press.

Offe, Claus. 1984. *Problemas estruturais do estado capitalista*. Rio de Janeiro: Tempo Brasileiro.

Oliveira, Ariovaldo Umbelino de. 1991. *A agricultura camponesa no Brasil*. São Paulo: Contexto.

Oliveira, Ariovaldo Umbelino de. 1999. *A geografia das lutas no campo*. São Paulo: Contexto.

Oliveira, Ariovaldo Umbelino de. 2004. "As transformações no campo e o agronegócio no Brasil." In *O agronegócio X agricultura familiar e a reforma agrária*, edited by Secretaria da CONCRAB, 7–81. Brasília: CONCRAB.

Oliveira, Ariovaldo Umbelino de. 2006. "A 'não reforma agrária' do MDA/INCRA no governo Lula." Paper presented at parallel meeting organized by La Via Campesina during the FAO's Conferência Internacional sobre Reforma Agrária e Desenvolvimento Rural, Porto Alegre, March 7–10.

Oliveira, Ariovaldo Umbelino de. 2010. "A questão da aquisição de terras por estrangeiros no Brasil: Um retorno aos dossiers." *Agrária*, no. 12, 3–113. Available at http://www.revistas.usp.br/agraria/article/view/702. Accessed on July 15, 2013.

Oliveira, Ariovaldo Umbelino de. 2013. *Atlas da terra Brasil: Relatório técnico CNPq.* Unpublished text.

Olson, Mancur, Jr. 1965. *The Logic of Collective Action.* Cambridge, Mass.: Harvard University Press.

Ondetti, Gabriel. 2008. *Land, Protest, and Politics: The Landless Movement and the Struggle for Agrarian Reform in Brazil.* University Park: Pennsylvania State University Press.

Osava, Mario. 2007. "Brazil: No Consensus on Success of Land Reform." Inter Press Service, March 22. Available at http://www.ipsnews.net/news.asp?idnews= 3705. Accessed on June 19, 2007.

Otero, Gerardo. 1989. "Agrarian Reform in Mexico: Capitalism and the State." In *Searching for Agrarian Reform in Latin America,* edited by William C. Thiesenhusen, 276–304. Boston: Unwin Hyman.

Ozorio de Almeida, Anna Luiza. 1992. *The Colonization of the Amazon.* Austin: University of Texas Press.

Paige, Jeffrey M. 1975. *Agrarian Revolution: Social Movements and Export Agriculture in the Undeveloped World.* New York: Free Press.

Paiva, Vanilda, ed. 1985. *Igreja e questão agrária.* São Paulo: Loyola.

Palmeira, Moacir. 1971. "Feira e mudança econômica." Simpósio de Pesquisas: Museu Nacional/Centro Latino-Americano de Pesquisas em Ciências Sociais. Unpublished document.

Palmeira, Moacir. 1977. "Casa e Trabalho: Notas sobre as relações sociais na *plantation* tradicional." *Contraponto* 2 (2) (November): 103–14.

Palmeira, Moacir. 1985. "A diversidade da luta no campo: Luta camponesa e diferenciação do campesinato." In *Igreja e questão agrária,* edited by Vanilda Paiva, 43–51. São Paulo: Loyola.

Palmeira, Moacir, and Sérgio P. Leite. 1998. "Debates Econômicos, Processos Sociais e Lutas Políticas." In *Política e reforma agrária,* edited by Raimundo Santos and Luiz Flávio de Carvalho Costa, 92–165. Rio de Janeiro: Mauad.

Parpadellas, Sérgio, and Hugo Marques. 2008. "Guilherme Cassel: 'Stédile agride o bom senso.'" *IstoÉ* 20 (January): 7–10.

Partido dos Trabalhadores (PT). 1998. *Resoluções de encontros e congressos 1979–1998.* São Paulo: PT.

Partido dos Trabalhadores (PT). 2002. *Vida digna no campo: Desenvolvimento rural, política agrícola, Agrária e de segurança alimentar.* São Paulo: PT.

Paulilo, Maria. 1996. *Terra a vista . . . e ão Longe.* Florianopolis: Editora da Universidade Federal de Santa Catarina.

Pausewang, Siegfried. 1983. *Peasants, Land and Society: A Social History of Land Reform in Ethiopia.* Munich: Weltforum-Verlag.

Payne, Leigh A. 2000. *The Armed Right Wing, Uncivil Movements: The Armed Right Wing and Democracy in Latin America.* Baltimore: Johns Hopkins University Press.

Pereira, Anthony W. 1997. *The End of the Peasantry: The Rural Labor Movement in Northeast Brazil, 1961–1988.* Pittsburgh: University of Pittsburgh Press.

Pereira, Anthony W. 2000. "An Ugly Democracy? State Violence and the Rule of Law in Postauthoritarian Brasil." In *Democratic Brazil: Actors, Institutions and*

Processes, edited by Peter R. Kingstone and Timothy J. Power, 217–35. Pittsburgh: University of Pittsburgh Press.

Pereira, João Marcio Mendes. 2005. "A política agrária contemporânea do Banco Mundial: Matrizes políticas, base intelectual, linhas de ação e atualizações estratégicas." Unpublished manuscript.

Pereira, João Marcio Mendes. 2010. *A política de reforma agrária de mercado do Banco Mundial: Fundamentos, objetivos, contradições e perspectivas.* São Paulo: Hucitec.

Pereira Filho, Jorge. 2008. "Lula abandonou a reforma agrária." *Brasil de Fato* (April 23). Available at http://www.brasildefato.com.br/v01/agencia/entre vistas/lula-abandonou-a-reforma-agraria-diz-pesquisador/?searchterm=lula %20abandonou%20a%20reforma%20agraria%20pereira%20filho. Accessed on April 25, 2008.

Peschanski, João Alexandre. 2013. "Gender, Internal Politics and Tactical Innovation in the Brazilian Landless Workers' Movement." Paper presented at the Latin American Studies Association Meeting in Washington, D.C., May 30.

Pessoa, Jadir de Morais. 1999. *Revanche camponesa.* Goiânia: UFG.

Petit, Pere. 2003. *Chão de promessas: Elites políticas e transformações econômicas no Estado do Pará pós-1964.* Belém: Paka-Tatu.

Pierruci, Antônio Flávio Oliveira, Beatriz Muniz de Souza, and Cândido Procópio Ferreira de Camargo. 1986. "Igreja católica: 1945–1970." In *O Brasil republicano: Economia e cultura (1930–64)*, vol. 4, edited by Boris Fausto, 343–80. São Paulo: Difel.

Pinheiro, Paulo Sergio. 1997. "Popular Responses to State-Sponsored Violence in Brazil." In *The New Politics of Inequality in Latin America: Rethinking Participation and Representation*, edited by Douglas A. Chalmers, Carlos M. Vilas, Katherine Hite, Scott B. Martin, Kerianne Piester, and Monique Segarra, 261–80. New York: Oxford University Press.

Pinho, Pericles Madureira. 1939. *O Problema da sindicalização rural.* Rio de Janeiro: n.p.

Plummer, Dawn M. 2008. "Leadership Development and Formação in Brazil's Landless Workers Movement (MST)." M.A. thesis, The City University of New York.

Poletto, Ivo. 1985. "A CPT, a Igreja e os camponeses." In *CPT: Conquistar a terra, reconstruir a vida*, 29–66. Petrópolis: Vozes.

Poletto, Ivo. 2002a. "Testemunhas do processo germinal: CPT, fruto e vivência do pentecostes dos anos 70." In *Nas pegadas do povo da terra*, edited by Ivo Poletto and Antonio Canuto, 25–40. São Paulo: Loyola.

Poletto, Ivo, ed. 2002b. *Uma vida a serviço da humanidade: Diálogos com Dom Tomás Balduíno.* São Paulo: Rede e Loyola.

Poletto, Ivo. 2003. "A CNBB e a luta pela terra no Brasil." In *Presença pública da Igreja no Brasil: Jubileu de ouro da CNBB*, edited by Instituto Nacional de Pastoral, 333–52. São Paulo: Paulinas.

Poletto, Ivo, and Antônio Canuto, eds. 2002. *Nas pegadas do povo da terra.* São Paulo: Loyola.

Pontifícia Universidade Católica de Minas Gerais, Instituto de Desenvolvimento

Humano and Programa das Nações Unidas para o Desenvolvimento. 2004. *Educação: Objetivo 2, atingir o ensino básico universal*. Belo Horizonte: PUC Minas/ IDHS. Available at http://www.virtual.pucminas.br/idhs/o2_pnud/ODM_WEB/ livro_2_dividido/livro2a_capitulos1e2.pdf. Accessed on April 8, 2008.

Prado, Caio, Jr. 1966. *A revolução brasileira*. São Paulo: Brasiliense.

Prado, Caio, Jr. 1994. *A formação do Brasil contemporâneo*. 23rd ed. São Paulo: Editora Brasiliense.

Prakesh, Gyan. 1994. "Subaltern Studies as Postcolonial Criticism." AHR Forum piece. *American Historical Review* 99 (5): 1475–90.

Presidência da República. 1962. "Plano Trienal de Desenvolvimento Econômico e Social, 1963–65." Brasília: Presidência da República.

Projeto de Reflorestamento Econômico Consorciado e Adensado (RECA). 2003. *Nosso jeito de caminhar: A história do projeto Reca contada por seus associados, parceiros e amigos*. Brasília: Ministério do Meio Ambiente.

Prosterman, Roy L., and Jeffrey M. Riedinger. 1987. *Land Reform and Democratic Development*. Baltimore: Johns Hopkins University Press.

Przeworski, Adam, Michael E. Alvarez, José Antonio Cheibub, and Fernando Limongi. 2001. "What Makes Democracies Endure?" In *The Global Divergence of Democracies*, edited by Larry Diamond and Marc F. Plattner, 167–84. Baltimore: Johns Hopkins University Press.

Putnam, Robert D. 1993. *Making Democracy Work: Civic Traditions in Modern Italy*. Princeton, N.J.: Princeton University Press.

Quirk, Patrick. 2008. *Emotions and the Struggle of Brazil's Landless Social Movement (MST)*. Saarbrucken: VDM.

Quizón, Antonio B., and Teresa L. Debuque. 1999, October 6–7. "An Overview of Agrarian Reforms in Asia." Report for WCARRD 20/20 Conference. Philippines: ANGOC. Available at http://64.233.161.104/search?q=cache:AXK37fAnnocJ: www.asiacaucus.net.ph/development/arrd/ar_2000_1209_01.htm+agrarian+ reform+land+ceiling&hl=en. Accessed on February 10, 2006.

Rangel, Ignácio. 1961. *Questão agrária brasileira*. Rio de Janeiro: Presidência da República/Conselho de Desenvolvimento Econômico.

Reich, Robert. B. 2007. *Supercapitalism: The Transformation of Business, Democracy and Everyday Life*. New York: Vintage Books.

Reich, Robert. 2012. *Beyond Outrage: What Has Gone Wrong With Our Economy and Our Democracy, and How to Fix It*, expanded edition. New York: Random House.

Reinhardt, Nola. 1989. "Contrast and Congruence in the Agrarian Reforms of El Salvador and Nicaragua." In *Searching for Agrarian Reform in Latin America*, edited by William C. Thiesenhusen, 451–82. Boston: Unwin Hyman.

Reuters. 2013. "Novo Código Florestal fez país perder até 40% de áreas protegidas, diz ONG." *Globo*, May 27. Available at http://g1.globo.com/natureza/noticia/ 2013/05/novo-codigo-florestal-fez-pais-perder-ate-40-de-areas-protegidas-diz-ong.html. Accessed on August 10, 2013.

Rezende, Gervásio Castro. 1981. "Crédito rural subsidiado e preços da terra no Brasil." Working paper no. 42. Rio de Janeiro: IPEA-INPES.

Rezende, Gervásio. 1999. *Programa de Crédito Especial para Reforma Agrária*

(*PROCERA*): *Institucionalidade, subsídio e eficácia*. Working paper no. 648. Rio de Janeiro: IPEA.

Ricci, Rudá. 1999. *Terra de ninguém: Representação sindical rural no Brasil*. Campinas: Editora da UNICAMP.

Riedinger, Jeffrey M. 1995. *Agrarian Reform in the Philippines: Democratic Transitions and Redistributive Reform*. Stanford, Calif.: Stanford University Press.

Romeiro, Adhemar, Carlos Guanziroli, Moacir Palmeira, and Sérgio Leite, eds. 1994. *Reforma agrária: Produção, emprego e renda—O relatório da FAO em debate*. Petrópolis/Rio de Janeiro: Vozes/IBASE/FAO.

Rosa, Marcelo. 2000. "O sem terra partido ao meio: Um estudo das relações entre assentados e municípios receptores na região da Grande Porto Alegre, RS." Master's thesis, CPDA, Universidade Federal Rural de Rio de Janeiro.

Rosa, Marcelo. 2001. "Espetáculo e cotidiano: Pequenas vozes na luta do MST." *Cultura Vozes* 95 (3): 83–93.

Rosa, Marcelo Carvalho. 2004a. "O engenho dos movimentos: Reforma agrária e significação social na Zona Canavieira de Pernambuco." Ph.D. diss., Sociology, Instituto Universitário de Pesquisas do Rio de Janeiro, IUPERJ.

Rosa, Marcelo. 2004b. "Sobre os sentidos das novas formas de protesto social no Brasil: Os impactos das ações do MST sobre o sindicalismo rural." In *La cultura en las crisis latinoamericanas*, edited by Alejandro Grimson, 43–62. Buenos Aires: Clacso.

Rosa, Marcelo. 2006. "Uma região em movimento: As lutas por terra e a transformação das estruturas de poder e significação social na Mata Pernambucana." *Revista Brasileira de Estudos Urbanos e Regionais (ANPUR)* 8: 41–58.

Rosa, Marcelo C. 2003. "Sindicalismo rural e movimentos sociais: Notas sobre o caso Pernambucano." Paper presented at the twenty-seventh ANPOCS Meeting in Caxambu (MG), October 21–25. Available at http://sindicalismo.pessoal .bridge.com.br/Marcelointero3.rtf. Accessed on May 1, 2006.

Rosenfield, Denis Lerrer. 2006. *A democracia ameaçada: O MST, o teológico-político e a liberdade*. Rio de Janeiro: Topbooks Editora.

Rosset, Peter, Raj Patel, and Michael Courville, eds. 2006. *Promised Land: Competing Visions of Agrarian Reform*. Oakland, Calif.: Food First Books.

Rubin, Jeffrey. 2004. "Meanings and Mobilizations: A Cultural Politics Approach to Social Movements and States." *Latin American Research Review* 39 (3): 106–42.

Rueschemeyer, Dietrich. 2005. "Addressing Inequality." In *Assessing the Quality of Democracy*, edited by Larry Diamond and Leonardo Morlino, 47–61. Baltimore: Johns Hopkins University Press.

Rueschemeyer, Dietrich, Evelyne Huber Stephens, and John D. Stephens. 1992. *Capitalist Development and Democracy*. Chicago: University of Chicago Press.

Sader, Eder. 1988. *Quando novos personagens entraram em cena*. Rio de Janeiro: Paz e Terra.

Sampaio, Plínio de Arruda. 2010. "O impacto do MST no Brasil de hoje." *Combatendo a desigualdade social: O MST e a reforma agrária no Brasil*, edited by Miguel Carter, 397–408. São Paulo: Editora da UNESP.

Sampaio, Plínio de Arruda, et al. 2003. "Proposta do Plano Nacional da Reforma Agrária." Unpublished manuscript. Brasília.

Sampaio, Plínio de Arruda, et al. 2005. "Proposta de Plano Nacional de Reforma Agrária." *Revista da Associação Brasileira de Reforma Agrária* 32 (1) (August–December): 108–86.

Santos, Milton. 1988. *Metamorfoses do espaço habitado*. São Paulo: Paz e Terra.

Santos, Sales Augusto dos. 2002. "Historical Roots of the 'Whitening' of Brazil." *Latin American Perspectives* 29 (1) (January): 61–82.

Santos, Wanderley Guilherme dos. 1979. *Cidadania e justiça: A política social na ordem brasileira*. Rio de Janeiro: Campus.

Sartori, Giovanni. 1987. *The Theory of Democracy Revisited*. Chatham, N.J.: Chatham House.

Sauer, Sergio. 1998. *Reforma agrária e geração de emprego e renda no meio rural*. São Paulo: ABET.

Sauer, Sérgio. 2010. "Lobby Ruralista: Dinheiro público para o agronegócio." *Le Monde Diplomatique Brasil*, 1 April. Available at http://www.diplomatique.org .br/artigo.php?id=654. Accessed on December 10, 2011.

Sauer, Sérgio. 2010. *Terra e modernidade: A reinvenção do campo brasileiro*. São Paulo: Expressão Popular.

Sauer, Sérgio. 2014. "O Governo Lula no campo: compromissos e embates nas políticas agrárias e agrícolas." *Trajetória e dilemas da reforma agrária no Brasil*, edited by Lauro Mattei. (Forthcoming).

Sauer, Sérgio and Sérgio Pereira Leite. 2012. "Expansão agricola, preços e apropriação de terra por estrangeiros no Brasil." *RESR, Piraicicaba-SP* 50, 3 (July–September): 503–24.

Sauer, Sérgio, and João Marcio Mendes Pereira, eds. 2006. *Capturando a terra: Banco Mundial, políticas fundiárias neoliberais e reforma agrária de mercado*. São Paulo: Expressão Popular.

Sauer, Sérgio, and Marcos Rogério de Souza. 2007. "Movimentos sociais na luta pela terra: Conflitos no campo e disputas políticas." Unpublished manuscript.

Sauer, Sérgio, Marcos Rogério de Souza, and Nilton Tubino. 2006. "O parlamento e a criminalização dos movimentos de luta pela terra: Um balanço da CPMI da Terra." Unpublished manuscript.

Scalabrin, Leandro Gaspar. 2008. "'Estado de Exeção' no Rio Grande do Sul e a criminalização do MST." Unpublished manuscript.

Scheper-Hughes, Nancy. 1992. *Death without Weeping: The Violence of Everyday Life in Brazil*. Berkeley: University of California Press.

Schmidt, Benício, Danilo Nolasco Marinho, and Sueli Couto Rosa, eds. 1998. *Os Assentamentos de reforma agrária no Brasil*. Brasília: Editora da Universidade de Brasília.

Schmink, Marianne, and Charles H. Wood, eds. 1984. *Frontier Expansion in Amazonia*. Gainesville: University Press of Florida.

Schmink, Marianne, and Charles H. Wood. 1992. *Contested Frontiers in Amazonia*. New York: Columbia University Press.

Schmitter, Philippe C. 1971. *Interest Conflict and Political Change in Brazil*. Stanford, Calif.: Stanford University Press.

Schmitter, Philippe C. 1974. "Still the Century of Corporatism?" *Review of Politics* 36 (1) (January): 86–131.

Schneider, Sérgio. 2003. *A Pluriatividade na agricultura familiar.* Porto Alegre: Editora da Universidade Federal Rural do Rio Grande do Sul.

Schwartz, Stuart B. 1985. *Sugar Plantations in the Formation of Brazilian Society: Bahia, 1550–1835.* New York: Cambridge University Press.

Schwartz, Stuart B. 1992. *Slaves, Peasants, and Rebels: Reconsidering Brazilian Slavery.* Urbana: University of Illinois Press.

Schwartzman, Simon. 2004. *As causas da pobreza.* Rio de Janeiro: Editora da FGV.

Scolese, Eduardo. 2003. "Revogar MP é 'tiro no pé,' diz especialista." *Folha de São Paulo,* March 23.

Scolese, Eduardo. 2004a. "Cobrado, Lula diz que MST deve reivindicar." *Folha de São Paulo,* June 29, p. A6.

Scolese, Eduardo. 2004b. "'É hora de os ministros desligarem telefones e trabalharem.' Diz Stédile." *Folha de São Paulo,* April 8, p. A4.

Scolese, Eduardo. 2004c. "Na gestão Lula, renasce associação que pressiona por reforma agrária." *Folha de São Paulo,* March 7, p. A18.

Scolese, Eduardo. 2004d. "'O MST está numa sinuca de bico." *Folha de São Paulo,* January 19, p. A6.

Scolese, Eduardo. 2005. *A Reforma Agrária.* Folha Explica. São Paulo: PubliFolha.

Scolese, Eduardo, Patrícia Costa, and Talita Figueiredo. 2003. "Lula pede ao 'amigo' MST que o julgue só no fim do governo." *Folha de São Paulo,* November 22, p. A4.

Scott, James C. 1985. *Weapons of the Weak: Everyday Forms of Peasant Resistance.* New Haven, Conn.: Yale University Press.

Scott, James C. 1990. *Domination and the Arts of Resistance: Hidden Transcripts.* New Haven, Conn.: Yale University Press.

Selligson, Mitchell A., and John T. Passé-Smith, eds. 2003. *Development and Under-Development: The Political Economy of Global Inequality.* Boulder, Colo.: Lynne Rienner.

Seminário Regional. 1993. "Crise e reestruturação no complexo sucro-alcooleiro do Nordeste." Recife: Unpublished manuscript.

Sen, Amartya. 1992. *Inequality Reexamined.* Cambridge, Mass.: Harvard University Press.

Sen, Amartya. 1997. *On Economic Inequality.* Oxford: Oxford University Press.

Sen, Amartya. 1999. *Development as Freedom.* Oxford: Oxford University Press.

Senado Federal. 2013. "Siga Brasil: Portal do Orcamento." Available at http://www12.senado.gov.br/orcamento/loa. Accessed on September 15, 2013.

Singer, André. 2012. *Os sentidos do Lulismo: Reforma gradual e pacto conservador.* São Paulo: Companhia das Letras.

Serbin, Kenneth P. 2000. *Secret Dialogues: Church-State Relations, Torture, and Social Justice in Authoritarian Brazil.* Pittsburgh: University of Pittsburgh Press.

Shanin, Teodor, ed. 1987. *Peasant and Peasant Societies.* 2nd ed. Oxford: Blackwell.

Sigaud, Dom Geraldo de Proença, Dom Antonio de Castro Mayer, Plinio Corrêa de Oliveira, and Luiz Mendonça de Freitas. 1960. *Reforma agrária: Questão de consciência.* São Paulo: TFP.

Sigaud, Lygia. 1979. *Os clandestinos e os direitos.* São Paulo: Duas Cidades.

Sigaud, Lygia. 1980. *Greve nos engenhos.* Rio de Janeiro: Paz e Terra.

Sigaud, Lygia. 1999. "Les paysans et le droit: Le mode juridique de règlement des conflits." *Informations Sur Les Sciences Sociales* 38 (1): 113–47.

Sigaud, Lygia. 2000. "A forma acampamento: Notas a partir da versão Pernambucana." *Novos Estudos CEBRAP* 58: 73–92.

Sigaud, Lygia. 2004. "Armadilhas da honra e do perdão: Usos sociais do direito na Mata Pernambucana." *Mana* 10 (1): 131–63.

Sigaud, Lygia. 2005. "As condições de possibilidade das ocupações de terra." *Tempo Social: Revista de Sociologia da USP* 17 (1) (June): 255–80.

Sigaud, Lygia M. 1986. "A luta de classe em dois atos: Notas sobre um ciclo de greves camponesas." *Dados* 29 (3): 319–34.

Sigaud, Lygia, David Fajolles, Jérôme Gautile, Hernán Gómez, and Sergio Chamorro Smircic. 2006. "Os Acampamentos da reforma agrária: História de uma surpresa." In *Ocupações de terra e transformações sociais*, edited by Benoit de L' Estoile and Lygia Sigaud, 29–63. Rio de Janeiro: FGV Editora.

Silva, Anderson Antonio, and Bernardo Mançano Fernandes. 2006. "Ocupações de terras, 2000–2005: Movimentos socioterritoriais e espacialização da luta pela terra." In *Conflitos no Campo, Brasil 2005*, 96–108. Goiânia: CPT.

Silva, Gerson F. da. 1985. "Animação Cristã no meio rural." In *Igreja e questão agrária*, edited by Vanilda Paiva, 149–52. São Paulo: Loyola.

Silva, José Alfonso da. 2004. *O curso de direito constitucional positivo.* São Paulo: Malheiros.

Silva, José Gomes da. 1987. *Caindo por terra: Crises da reforma agrária na Nova República.* São Paulo: Editora Busca Vida.

Silva, José Gomes da. 1989. *Buraco negro: A reforma agrarian na Constituínte.* São Paulo: Paz e Terra.

Silva, Lígia Osorio. 1996. *Terras devolutas e latifúndio: Efeitos da Lei de 1850.* Campinas: Editora da UNICAMP.

Sindicato das Indústrias do Açúcar de Pernambuco (1999). *Boletins de Safra (1989–1999).* Recife: Sindicato das Indústrias do Açúcar de Pernambuco.

Singh, Karori. 1989. *Land Reforms in South Asia: A Study of Sri Lanka.* New Delhi: South Asian Publishers.

Slater, David, ed. 1985. *New Social Movements and the State in Latin America.* Amsterdam: CEDLA.

Smircic, Sergio Chamorro. 2000. "Com a cara e a coragem: Uma etnografia de uma ocupação de terras." Master's thesis, Museu Nacional/Universidade Federal de Rio de Janeiro.

Smith, Peter H. 2005. *Democracy in Latin America: Political Change in Comparative Perspective.* New York: Oxford University Press.

Snow, David A., and Robert D. Benford. 1992. "Master Frames and Cycles of Protest." In *Frontiers in Social Movement Theory*, edited by Aldon D. Morris and Carol McClurg Mueller, 133–55. New Haven, Conn.: Yale University Press.

Snyder, Richard, and David J. Samuels. 2004. "Legislative Malapportionment in Latin America: Historical and Comparative Perspectives." In *Federalism and Democracy in Latin America*, edited by Edward L. Gibson, 131–72. Baltimore: Johns Hopkins University Press.

Sobhan, Rehman. 1993. *Agrarian Reform and Social Transformation: Preconditions for Development.* London: Zed.

Sociedade Nacional da Agricultura (SNA). 1943. "O problema da sindicalização rural." *A Lavoura*, April–June.

Sparovek, Gerd. 2003. *A qualidade dos assentamentos da reforma agrária brasileira*. São Paulo: USP/MDA/INCRA/FAO.

Spence, Jonathan D. 1990. *The Search for Modern China*. New York: Norton.

Stanfield, David J. 1989. "Agrarian Reform in the Dominican Republic." In *Searching for Agrarian Reform in Latin America*, edited by William C. Thiesenhusen, 305–37. Boston: Unwin Hyman.

Stédile, João Pedro, ed. 1997. *A reforma agrária e a luta do MST*. Petrópolis: Vozes.

Stédile, João Pedro. 1999. *A questão agrária no Brasil*. 7th ed. São Paulo: Editora Atual.

Stédile, João Pedro. 2002. *História e natureza das Ligas Camponesas*. São Paulo: Expressão Popular.

Stédile, João Pedro, ed. 2005a. *A questão agrária no Brasil: O debate na esquerda, 1960–1980*. São Paulo: Editora Expressão Popular.

Stédile, João Pedro, ed. 2005b. *A questão agrária no Brasil: O debate tradicional, 1500–1960*. São Paulo: Editora Expressão Popular.

Stédile, João Pedro, ed. 2005c. *A questão agrária no Brasil: Programas de reforma agrária, 1946–2003*. São Paulo: Editora Expressão Popular.

Stédile, João Pedro, ed. 2006. *A questão agrária no Brasil: História e natureza das Ligas Camponesas, 1954–1964*. São Paulo: Editora Expressão Popular.

Stédile, João Pedro, and Bernardo Mançano Fernandes. 1999. *Brava gente: A trajetória do MST e a luta pela terra no Brasil*. São Paulo: Fundação Perseu Abramo.

Stédile, João Pedro, and Frei Sergio Görgen. 1993. *A luta pela terra no Brasil*. São Paulo: Editora Página Aberta.

Stein, Leila. 1991. "Sindicalismo e corporativismo na agricultura brasileira (1930–1945)." Master's thesis, Pontifícia Universidade Católica de São Paulo.

Stepan, Alfred. 2001. *Arguing Comparative Politics*. Oxford: Oxford University Press.

Stephen, Lynn. 1996. "Relações de gênero: Um estudo comparativo sobre organizações de mulheres rurais no Brasil e no México." In *Política, protesto e cidadania no campo: As lutas sociais dos colonos e dos trabalhadores rurais no Rio Grande do Sul*, edited by Zander Navarro, 29–61. Porto Alegre: Editora da Universidade.

Stiglitz, Joseph E. 2013. *The Price of Inequality: How Today's Divided Society Endangers Our Future*. New York: W.W. Norton.

Stolcke, Verena. 1988. *Coffee Planters, Workers, and Wives: Class Conflict and Gender Relations on São Paulo Plantations, 1850–1980*. Houndmills, UK: Macmillan.

Strasma, John. 1989. "Unfinished Business: Consolidating Land Reform in El Salvador." In *Searching for Agrarian Reform in Latin America*, edited by William C. Thiesenhusen, 408–28. Boston: Unwin Hyman.

Stringer, Randy. 1989. "Honduras: Toward Conflict and Agrarian Reform." In *Searching for Agrarian Reform in Latin America*, edited by William C. Thiesenhusen, 358–83. Boston: Unwin Hyman.

Sutton, Alison. 1994. *Trabalho escravo: Um elo na cadeia da modernização no Brasil de hoje*. São Paulo: Edições Loyola.

Suwwan, Leila. 2004. "Presidente do INCRA relaciona agronegocioa à chacina do MST." *Folha de São Paulo*, November 24, p. A4.

Swidler, Ann. 1986. "Culture in Action: Symbols and Strategies." *American Sociological Review* 51 (2) (April): 273–86.

Swinnen, Johan F. M., ed. 1997. *Political Economy of Agrarian Reform in Central and Eastern Europe*. Aldershot: Ashgate.

Sydow, Evanize, and Maria Luisa Mendonça, eds. 2007. *Human Rights in Brazil 2007: A Report by the Network for Social Justice and Human Rights*. São Paulo: Network for Social Justice and Human Rights.

Tarrow, Sidney. 1998. *Power in Movement: Social Movements and Contentious Politics*. 2nd ed. Cambridge: Cambridge University Press.

Tavares dos Santos, José Vicente. 1991. "Crítica da sociologia rural e a construção de uma outra sociologia dos processos sociais agrários." *Ciências Sociais Hoje*, 13–51.

Tavares dos Santos, José Vicente. 1993. *Matuchos: Exclusão e luta, do Sul para a Amazônia*. Petrópolis: Vozes.

Tavares dos Santos, José Vicente, ed. 1985. *As Revoluções Camponesas na America Latina*. São Paulo: Icone.

Teixeira, Gérson. 2003. "A iniciativa da PEC, Proposta de emenda Constitucional." Comissão Pastoral da Terra. Available at http://www.cptnac.com.br/?system= news&action=read&id=1116&eid=56. Accessed on June 5, 2006.

Teixeira, Gerson. 2004. "Por uma releitura da conjuntura agrária Nacional." Unpublished manuscript.

Teixeira, Gerson. 2011. "Agravamento do quadro de concentração da terra no Brasil?" *Boletim DATALUTA—Artigo do mês*. NERA—Núcleo de Estudos, Pesquisas e Projetos de Reforma Agrária (July).

Teixeira, Gerson. 2012. "Crise do Incra reflete a 'periferização política da reforma agrária.'" *Instituto Humanitas Unisinos, IHU On-Line*, August 3. Available at http://www.ihu.unisinos.br/entrevistas/512057-crise-do-incra-reflete-a-periferizacao-politica-da-reforma-agraria-entrevista-especial-com-gerson-teixeira. Accessed on August 20, 2012.

Teixeira, Gerson. 2013a. "O agronegócio e o abismo agrário-ambiental. Entrevista especial com Gerson Teixeira." *Instituto Humanitas Unisinos, IHU On-Line*, January 7. Available at http://www.ihu.unisinos.br/entrevistas/516794-ha-muito-tempo-o-incra-sofre-processo-de-esvaziamento-entrevista-especial-com-gerson-teixeira. Accessed on February 10, 2013.

Teixeira, Gerson. 2013b. "Os rumos atuais da reforma agrária." *Boletim DATALUTA—Artigo do mês*. Presidente Prudente: NERA—Núcleo de Estudos, Pesquisas e Projetos de Reforma Agrária (January).

Telles, Vera. 1994. "Sociedade civil e construção de espaços públicos." In *Anos 90, política e sociedade no Brasil*, edited by Evelina Dagnino, 91–102. São Paulo: Brasiliense.

Thakur, D. 1989. *Politics of Land Reforms in India*. New Delhi: Commonwealth.

Thiesenhusen, William C. 1989a. "Introduction: Searching for Agrarian Reform in Latin America." In *Searching for Agrarian Reform in Latin America*, edited by William C. Thiesenhusen, 1–41. Boston: Unwin Hyman.

Thiesenhusen, William C., ed. 1989b. *Searching for Agrarian Reform in Latin America*. Boston: Unwin Hyman.

Thiesenhusen, William C. 1995. *Broken Promises: Agrarian Reform and the Latin American Campesino*. Boulder, Colo.: Westview Press.

Tilly, Charles. 1978. *From Mobilization to Revolution*. New York: McGraw-Hill.

Tilly, Charles. 1979. "Repertoires of Contention in America and Britain." In *The Dynamics of Social Movements*, edited by Mayer N. Zald and John D. McCarthy, 126–55. Cambridge, Mass.: Winthrop.

Tilly, Charles. 1983. "Speaking Your Mind without Elections, Surveys, or Social Movements." *Public Opinion Quarterly* 47 (4) (Winter): 461–78.

Tilly, Charles. 1986. *The Contentious French*. Cambridge, Mass.: Harvard University Press.

Tilly, Charles. 1998. *Durable Inequality*. Berkeley: University of California Press.

Tilly, Charles. 2002. *Stories, Identities, Political Change*. New York: Rowman and Littlefield.

Tilly, Charles. 2004a. *Contention and Democracy in Europe, 1650–2000*. Cambridge: Cambridge University Press.

Tilly, Charles. 2004b. *Social Movements, 1768–2004*. Boulder, Colo.: Paradigm.

Tilly, Charles. 2005. "Poverty and the Politics of Exclusion." Unpublished manuscript.

Tilly, Charles. 2006. *Regimes and Repertoires*. Chicago: University of Chicago Press.

Tokman, Víctor E., and Guillermo O'Donnell, eds. 1998. *Poverty and Inequality in Latin America: Issues and New Challenges*. Notre Dame, Ind.: Notre Dame University Press.

Tolentino, Célia Aparecida Ferreira. 1990. "A revisão agrária Paulista: A proposta de modernização do campo do governo Carvalho Pinto." Master's thesis, Universidade Federal Rural do Rio de Janeiro.

Touraine, Alain. 1989. *Palavra e sangue: Política e sociedade na América Latina*. Campinas: Trajetória Cultural/Editora da Unicamp.

Tseng, Hsin-yu. 2004. "Land Ownership Transfer and Productivity: Evidence from Taiwan." Unpublished manuscript. Available at http://www.arts.cornell.edu/econ/75devconf/papers/Tseng.pdf. Accessed on March 30, 2006.

Tulchin, Joseph S., ed. 2002. *Democratic Governance and Social Inequality*. Boulder, Colo.: Lynne Rienner.

United Nations Conference on Trade and Development (UNCTAD). 2013. *Trade and Environment Review 2013: Wake Up Before It Is Too Late—Make Agriculture Truly Sustainable Now for Food Security in a Changing Climate*. Geneva: UNCTAD.

United Nations Development Programme (UNDP). 2005. *Human Development Report 2005. International Cooperation at a Crossroads: Aid, Trade and Security in an Unequal World*. New York: UNDP.

United Nations Development Programme (UNDP). 2007. *Human Development Report 2007/2008. Fighting Climate Change: Human Solidarity in a Divided World*. New York: UNDP.

Vainer, Carlos. 2009. "Water for Life, Not for Death: The Anti-dam Movement in Brazil." In *Rural Social Movements in Latin America: Organizing for Sustainable*

Livelihoods, edited by Carmen Diana Deere and Frederick S. Royce, 163–88. Gainesville: University Press of Florida.

Vajda, Istvan, Patrícia de Queiroz Carvalho Zimbres, and Vanira Tavares de Souza, trans. 1998. *Federative Constitution of Brazil, 1988.* Brasília: Senado Federal.

Valente, Rubens. 2007. "Lula engorda reforma agrária com assentamento estadual." *Folha de São Paulo*, February 19, p. A4.

Vaz, Lúcio, and João Carlos Magalhães. 2012. "Código Florestal deve anistiar 75% das multas millionárias." *Folha de São Paulo*, March 5, p. A4.

Veiga, José Eli da. 1990. *A reforma que virou suco: Uma introdução ao dilema agrário do Brasil.* Petrópolis: Vozes.

Veiga, José Eli. 2001. *O Brasil precisa de uma estratégia de desenvolvimento.* Serie Textos para Discussão 1. Brasília: CNDRS/MDA/NEAD.

Veríssimo, Luis Fernando. 2006. "Ao arqueólogo do futuro: Os últimos anos da paciencia." *Carta Maior.* Available at http://agenciacartamaior.uol.com.br/templates/materiaMostrar.cfm?materia_id=11845. Accessed on August 2, 2006.

Via Campesina. 1996. *Memoria de la Segunda Conferência Internacional de la Via Campesina.* Tlaxcala.

Vieira, Else R. P., ed. 2007. *Landless Voices in Song and Poetry: The Movimento dos Sem Terra of Brazil.* Translated by Bernard McGuirk. Nottingham: Critical, Cultural and Communications Press.

Vieira, Oscar Vilhena. 2007. "Inequality and Subversion of the Rule of Law in Brazil." Working Paper CBS-60-05. Oxford: Centre for Brazilian Studies, University of Oxford.

Vigna, Edélcio. 2001. "Bancada ruralista: Um grupo de interesse." *Argumento*, INESC 8 (December): 1–52.

Vigna, Edélcio. 2003. "Mediação de Sementes." *Reforma agrária: Os caminhos do impasse*, interview by Débora Lerrer, 115–25. São Paulo: Editora Garçoni.

Wambergue, Emmanuel. 1999. "Le arbre politique." Master's thesis, Centre National D'Études Agronomiques des Régions Chaudes, Montpellier, France.

Wanderley, Maria de Nazareth B. 2000. "A emergência de uma nova ruralidade nas sociedades modernas avançadas: O 'Rural' como espaço singular e ator coletivo." *Estudos sociedade e agricultura* 15 (October): 87–145.

Weber, Max. 1978. *Economy and Society*, edited by Guenther Roth and Claus Wittich. Berkeley: University of California.

Weinberg, Mônica. 2004. "Madraçais do MST." *Veja* (September 8). Available at http://veja.abril.combr/080904/p_046.html. Accessed on September 10, 2004.

Welch, Cliff. 1999. *The Seed Was Planted: The São Paulo Roots of Brazil's Rural Labor Movement, 1924–1964.* University Park: Pennsylvania State University Press.

Welch, Cliff. 2006. "Movement Histories: A Preliminary Historiography of Brazil's Landless Laborers' Movement (MST)." *Latin American Research Review* 41 (1): 198–210.

Weyland, Kurt. 1996. *Democracy without Equity: Failures of Reform in Brazil.* Pittsburgh: University of Pittsburgh Press.

Whitehead, Laurence. 2002. *Democratization: Theory and Experience.* Oxford: Oxford University Press.

Whitehead, Laurence, and George Gray-Molina. 2003. "Political Capabilities over the Long Run." *Changing Paths: International Development and the New Politics of Inclusion*, edited by P. Peter Houtzager and Mick Moore, 32–57. Ann Arbor: University of Michigan Press.

Wikipedia. 2006. "Salt Satyagraha." Available at http://en.wikipedia.org/wiki/Salt_Satyagraha. Accessed on January 20, 2006.

Wilkie, Mary. 1964. "A Report on Rural Syndicates in Pernambuco." Rio de Janeiro: Centro Latino-Americano de Pesquisas Em Ciências Sociais. Unpublished manuscript.

Wilkinson, Richard, and Kate Pickett. 2009. *The Spirit Level: Why Greater Equality Makes Societies Stronger*. New York: Bloomsbury.

Williams, Donald C. 1992. "Measuring the Impact of Land Reform Policy in Nigeria." *Journal of Modern African Studies* 30 (4): 587–609.

Wolf, Eric. 1973. *Peasant Wars of the Twentieth Century*. New York: Harper and Row.

Wolford, Wendy. 2003a. "Families, Fields, and Fighting for Land: The Spatial Dynamics of Contention in Rural Brazil." *Mobilization* 8 (2): 201–15.

Wolford, Wendy. 2003b. "Producing Community: The MST and Land Reform Settlements in Brazil." *Journal of Agrarian Change* 3 (4) (October): 500–520.

Wolford, Wendy. 2010. *This Land Is Ours Now*. Durham, N.C.: Duke University Press.

Wolin, Sheldon S. 2008. *Democracy Incorporated: Managed Democracy and the Specter of Inverted Totalitarianism*. Princeton: Princeton University Press.

Wood, Charles H., and José Alberto Magno de Carvalho. 1988. *The Demography of Inequality in Brazil*. Cambridge: Cambridge University Press.

Wood, Elisabeth Jean. 2003. *Insurgent Collective Action and Civil War in El Salvador*. Cambridge: Cambridge University Press.

World Bank. 2004. *Inequality and Economic Development in Brazil: A World Bank Country Study*. Washington, D.C.: World Bank.

World Bank. 2005. *World Development Report 2006: Equity and Development*. Washington, D.C.: World Bank.

Wright, Angus. 2001. "The Origins of the Brazilian Movement of Landless Rural Workers." Paper prepared for presentation at the meeting of the Latin American Studies Association, Washington, D.C. (September 6–8).

Wright, Angus, and Wendy Wolford. 2003. *To Inherit the Earth: The Landless Movement and the Struggle for a New Brazil*. Oakland, Calif.: Food First Books.

Yue, Kang. 2004, "Land Ceilings: A Mixed History." *Understanding World Bank Land Policies in Brazil*, organized by Miguel Carter. Unpublished report, School of International Service, American University.

Zaheer, M. 1980. "Policies and Implementation of Land Reforms in Uttar Pradesh, India." In *Land Reform: Some Asian Experiences*, vol. 4, edited by Inayatullah, 183–219. Kuala Lumpur: Asian and Pacific Development Administration Center.

Zald, Mayer N. 1996. "Culture, Ideology and Strategic Framing." In *Comparative Perspectives on Social Movements: Political Opportunities, Mobilizing Structures, and Cultural Framings*, edited by Doug McAdam, John D. McCarthy, and Mayer N. Zald, 261–74. Cambridge: Cambridge University Press.

Zamosc, Leon. 1987. *La cuestión agraria y el movimiento campesino en Colombia.* Ginebra and Bogotá: UNRISD and CINEP.

Zamosc, León, Estela Martínez, and Manuel Chiriboga, eds. 1997. *Estructuras agrarias y movimientos campesinos en América Latina, 1950–1990.* Madrid: Ministério de Agricultura, Pesca y Alimentación.

Zanatta, Mauro. 2010. "Juro leva 62% dos gastos de desapropriação" and "Desapropriação de terras custa R$1 bi por ano só em juros." *Valor Econômico,* May 25.

CONTRIBUTORS

José Batista Gonçalves Afonso is a lawyer and coordinator for the Pastoral Land Commission (CPT) in Marabá, Pará, where he has collaborated with rural social movements for eighteen years. He is the author of several articles on agrarian conflicts and human rights violations in the Amazon region.

Sonia Maria P. P. Bergamasco is an agronomist and professor at the School of Agricultural Engineering at the Universidade Estadual de Campinas (UNICAMP). Over the last forty-five years she has led various research projects in the Brazilian countryside, dealing with family farmers, rural community groups, land reform, and agricultural policies. Among her numerous publications are *Assentamentos rurais no século XXI: Temas recorrentes*, with Julieta de Oliveira and Vanilde de Souza-Esquerdo; *A alternativa dos trabalhadores rurais: Organização social, trabalho e política*, and *O que são assentamentos rurais?*, both with Luiz Norder.

Sue Branford is a journalist who has covered Brazil for the BBC World Service, the *Financial Times*, the *Economist*, the *Guardian*, and other news outlets for thirty-five years. She has also conducted extensive research on the country's agrarian conflicts. Her books include *Cutting the Wire: The Story of Brazil's Landless Movement*, with Jan Rocha; *Politics Transformed: Lula and the Workers' Party in Brazil*; and *Brazil Carnival of the Oppressed: Lula and the Brazilian Workers' Party*, both with Bernardo Kucinski; and *The Last Frontier: Fighting over Land in the Amazon*, with Oriel Glock.

Elena Calvo-González, an anthropologist and lecturer at the Federal University of Bahia, carried out her doctoral fieldwork in land reform settlements in the Brazilian northeast, between 1999 and 2003. She has published several papers based on her ethnographic research.

Miguel Carter is a political scientist and director of DEMOS – Centro para la Democracia, la Creatividad y la Inclusión Social, in Asunción, Paraguay. Prior to this he was a lecturer at American University, in Washington, DC, and served as a research fellow at the University of Oxford's Centre for Brazilian Studies. Carter has carried out research work on land reform and social movements in the Brazilian countryside for over two decades. He is the author of various texts on the MST, including *For Land, Love, and Justice: The Origins of Brazil's Landless Social Movement* (forthcoming, Duke University Press); and two books on Paraguay, *El papel de la Iglesia en la caída de Stroessner*; and *Stroessner Vive: Legados autoritários y democracia en el Paraguay, 1989–2008* (forthcoming, DEMOS/Servilibro).

Horacio Martins de Carvalho, an agronomist and advisor to rural popular movements, has been engaged in agrarian research and peasant advocacy work for five decades. Among his many publications on the MST, land reform, and Brazilian agriculture are two edited volumes, *O campesinato no século XXI: Possibilidades e condicionantes do desenvolvimento do campesinato no Brasil*, and *Sementes, patrimônio do povo a serviço da humanidade*. Carvalho also organized the publication of a nine-volume collection on the social history of the Brazilian peasantry.

Guilherme Costa Delgado, an economist who served at Brazil's Institute for Applied Economic Research from 1976 to 2007, has conducted research on rural economic and social development for four decades. He is a member of the Board of Directors of the Brazilian Association for Agrarian Reform (ABRA) and the author of *Do 'capital financeiro na agricultura' à economia do agronegócio: Mudanças cíclicas em meio século, 1965–2012*; *Capital financeiro e agricultura no Brasil, 1965—1985*; and *Universalização de direitos sociais no Brasil: A previdência rural nos anos 90*, co-edited with José Cardoso Jr., among numerous other publications.

Bernardo Mançano Fernandes is a geographer and professor at the Universidade Estadual Paulista, where he heads the UNESCO Chair for Education in the Countryside and Territorial Development. He has studied the MST and rural development in Brazil for over three decades, during which time he founded and directed UNESP's Núcleo de Estudos, Pesquisas e Projetos de Reforma Agrária, and coordinated the working group on rural development for the Latin American Council of Social Sciences (CLASCSO). His numerous publications include *A formação do MST no Brasil*; *Brava Gente: A trajetória do MST e a luta pela terra no Brasil*, with João Pedro Stédile; *Land Governance in Brazil: A Geo-Historical Review of Land Governance in Brazil*, with Clifford Welch and Elienai Gonçalves; and *Campesinato e agronegócio na América Latina: A questão agrária atual*.

Leonilde Sérvolo de Medeiros is a sociologist and professor in the Graduate Program for Social Sciences in Development, Agriculture and Society at the Federal Rural University of Rio de Janeiro. She has conducted research on agrarian policies and social movements in Brazil for thirty-five years. Her books include *Reforma agrária no Brasil: História e atualidade da luta pela terra*; *Movimentos sociais,disputas poíticas e reforma agrária de mercado no Brasil*; *História dos movimentos sociais no campo*; and *Impactos dos assentamentos: Um estudo sobre o meio rural brasileiro*, with Sergio Leite, Beatriz Heredia, Moacir Palmeira, and Rosângela Cintrão.

George Mészáros is a sociologist and associate professor at the School of Law, University of Warwick, England. His research interests in Brazil go back twenty-five years. Mészáros is the author of *Social Movements, Law and the Politics of Land Reform: Lessons from Brazil* and several scholarly articles on the MST.

Luiz Antonio Norder, a sociologist and professor in the Graduate Program for Agro-ecology and Rural Development at the Federal University of São Carlos, has carried out research in Brazilian land reform settlements for nearly two decades. His publications on this subject include *Memória da luta pela reforma agrária no Brasil: Catálogo da documentação da ABRA no período 1967–2007*, with Diego Campos Arruda; *A alternativa dos trabalhadores rurais: Organização social, trabalho e política*; and *O que são assentamentos rurais?*, both with Sonia Bergamasco.

Gabriel Ondetti is a political scientist and associate professor at Missouri State University. He has studied Brazil's agrarian social movements for fifteen years and is the author of *Land, Protest, and Politics: The Landless Movement and the Struggle for Agrarian Reform in Brazil*, as well as several academic articles on related issues.

Ivo Poletto is a philosopher, theologian, and advisor to various social movements and church organizations, among them the Fórum Mudanças Climáticas e Justiça Social, the National Conference of Bishops of Brazil, Caritas Brasileira, and the Semanas Sociais Brasileiras. Poletto was the Pastoral Land Commission's first national secretary and has been actively involved in the land reform movement for forty-five years. In 2003–4 he served as a special advisor to the Lula government's Zero Hunger Program. Poletto's many publications include *Brasil, Oportunidades perdidas: Meus dois anos no Governo Lula*; *Nas pegadas do povo da terra:25 anos da Comissão Pastoral da Terra*, with Antônio Canuto; *Mestre solidário da vida: Celebrando os 90 anos de Dom Tomás Balduino*; and *Água de chuva: O segredo da convivência com o Semi-Árido Brasileiro*.

Marcelo Carvalho Rosa is a sociologist and professor at the University of Brasília who has conducted research on landless social movements in Brazil and Africa for more than two decades. He is the author of *O engenho dos movimentos: Reforma agrária e significação social na zona canavieira de Pernambuco*; *Ocupações e acampamentos: Estudo comparado sobre a sociogênese das mobilizações por reforma agrária no Brasil*, with Lygia Sigaud and Marcelo Macedo; and *Estado y movimientos sociales: Estudios etnográficos en Argentina y Brasil*, co-edited with Mabel Grinberg and Maria Inés Fernández Alvares.

Lygia Maria Sigaud, an anthropologist and professor at the Museu Nacional, Federal University of Rio de Janeiro, passed away in April 2009, after dedicating four decades of her life to the study of rural struggles and social transformation in Brazil. Her best-known books include *Os clandestinos e os direitos: Estudo sobre os trabalhadores da cana*; *Greves nos engenhos*; *Ocupações de terra e transformações sociais*, edited with Benoît de L'Estoile; and *Empires, Nations, and Natives: Anthropology and State-Making*, edited with Benoît de L'Estoile and Federico Neiburg (Duke University Press).

Emmanuel Wambergue is a tropical agronomist and president of the Cooperativa de Prestação de Serviços in Marabá, Pará. For thirty-eight years, following his relocation from France, he has played an active role in supporting peasant organizations, human rights, and land reform in the Eastern Amazon. During this time he served as regional coordinator for the Pastoral Land Commission and executive director of the Fundação Agrária do Tocantins Araguaia. Wambergue has published several articles on the Amazonian peasantry.

Wendy Wolford is a geographer and associate professor of Development Sociology at Cornell University. Her research work on land tenure and agrarian reform settlements in Brazil covers nearly two decades. Wolford is the author of two books on the MST, *To Inherit the Earth: The Landless Movement and the Struggle for a New Brazil*, with Angus Wright, and *This Land Is Ours Now: Social Mobilization and Sugarcane in the Brazilian Northeast* (Duke University Press), as well as several academic articles on related subjects.

communist insurgency in, 157; extractive reserves in, 37n56, 80, 235, 414; land concentration in, 427n21; land distribution in, 9, 36n56, 37n56, 66n25, 143, 235, 349n12, 350; land fiscal module in, 26; land fraud in, 59, 103, 405, 416; land struggles in, 78, 104, 118, 202; land titling program (Terra Legal) in, 416; as a largely urban frontier, 212; military regime's colonization program in, 8, 117, 149, 179n23, 205, 316, 376; military regime's development policies for, 99, 204–7; mining projects in, 105; MST's first mobilizations in, 122, 125; rainforest destroyed in, 30, 80, 101, 109, 205, 264; rainforest restored in, 109; rural violence in, 132, 135, 197, 342, 398

Amorim, Jaime, 326

Andradina (São Paulo), 275, 279, 291n7

Annoni estate, 154, 158–60, 162, 172, 179n29–30, 361, 410n13, 410

Apartheid; Brazil's social, 12, 35n40; South Africa's, 262, 353, 407

Aracruz, 169, 378

Araraquara (São Paulo), 280–83, 287–88, 290

Arbenz, Jacobo, 17

Argentina, 20

Arraes, Miguel, 314, 317, 389n24

Asia, 53, 138, 250

ATES (Program for Technical, Social and Environmental Assistance for Agrarian Reform), 238

Bacha, Edmar, 12

Bahia (state), 3, 69, 103–4, 383; MST's first mobilizations in, 120

Baixada Fluminense, 71, 73

Balbina dam (Amazonas), 104

Balduíno, Tomás, 32n2, 96, 122, 157, 179n19. See also Photo illustration

Bancada ruralista (Ruralist caucus), 27, 85, 120, 142, 165, 342, 405; estates with slave labor and, 38n76, 108; MST accused of "terrorism" by, 34, 411n37; new Forestry Code championed by,

426n12; political overrepresentation of landlords and, 25, 404; size of, 26, 64. See also Agrarian elites; Legislature

Bangladesh, 14–15, 18

Bank of Brazil, 65n9, 187, 193, 201n30, 320–21, 334–35

Banks. See BNDES; Financial Sector

Barbalho, Jader, 217, 355

Belém (Pará), 206, 210, 215–17

Belém-Brasília Highway, 205

Belgium, 416

Belo Horizonte (Minas Gerais), 74, 86, 423

BioNatur, 249, 254, 256–57

Blair, Tony, 368

BNDES (Brazilian Development Bank), 418

Boff, Leonardo, 32n2

Bolivia, 4, 14, 16, 18, 32n7

Bornhausen, Jorge, 6

Bové, José, 169

Braga (Rio Grande do Sul), 250, 254

Brasília, 85, 90, 107, 198, 345, 348, 423. See also Marches to Brasília

Brasília, MST in, 125, 160, 248, 251, 318, 342

Britto, Antônio, 168–70

Brizola, Leonel, 88n21, 155

Buarque, Cristovam, 35n40

Building occupations, 122, 152, 163, 172, 175, 177; homeless movement carries out, 380; MST's first, 160–61

Bulgaria, 22

Caçador (Santa Catarina), 229, 245, 250–51

Campinas (São Paulo), 279, 281, 287–88

Campos, Roberto, 45

Canada, 13, 24, 260

Canudos, 69, 111n4

Carajás (Pará), 105, 206, 210–11, 213, 332

Cardoso, Fernando Henrique, 332; MST depicted as a "niche of resistance to modernity" by, 409n2; MST leaders meet president, 333; MST occupies family ranch of, 367

Contentious politics. *See* Mobilization tactics; Popular movements; Public activism; Social movements

Contestado, 69, 111n4, 245

Cooperatives, 71, 82, 106, 242, 278, 336, 424; MST history and, 123, 159, 166, 210, 246, 249, 253–56; MST investment in, 9, 125, 137, 151, 243–44, 406, 410n13; MST sustained by its, 260. *See also* CONCRAB; OCB

Coordenação dos Movimentos Sociais (Coordination of Social Movements), 261, 411n33

Corumbiara (Rondônia), 60, 124, 211, 237, 247

Costa Rica, 16–17

Courts, 108, 174, 359, 366, 368–69, 416–17; agrarian elites favored by, 231, 234, 356–358, 360–61, 368–69, 372n22, 399; agrarian elites get overvalued land payments set by, 60–61, 405, 416; agrarian elites limit expropriations through, 120, 233; agrarian elites' sway over, 165; Alternative Law movement questions neutrality of, 373n33; conservatism of Brazilian, 364, 404; land fraud and, 363–64; landless massacre leads to creation of new, 215; land occupations legitimized by, xxix, 364–65, 399; land protest criminalized by, xxviii, 146n12, 169, 172, 342, 419; Lula government and, 366–68; meagre public confidence in, 356, 371n10; MST land occupations and, 164; rural workers and Labor, 82, 194, 201n29. *See also* Land evictions; Land expropriations; Rule of law; Supreme Court

CPT (Pastoral Land Commission), 79, 142, 182, 360, 409n1; agro-ecology fostered by, 107–10, 112n28; in Amazon region, 100, 102; "Brazil's leading human rights organization in the countryside," 22; church support for land reform shored up by, 100, 111; CNBB and, xxv, 96–97, 100; creation of, 91–92, 94–102, 112n16, 178n16; critique of, 392–94, 409n4, 410n22; democratization and, 109–10; ecumenism and, 100; family farmers and, 106; Grito da Terra and, 83; human rights violations documented by, 22, 84, 97, 104, 107–10; Land and Water Conference and, 90; landless camps run by, 276–78, 288, 290; La Via Campesina and, 139; MST activities supported by, 245; MST discrepancies with, 106, 161, 210; MST established with crucial help from, 81, 102, 105–6, 118–19, 155–58, 179n19, 209, 275–76; MST mobilizations backed by, 32, 160, 164, 179n29, 360; MST territorial expansion supported by, 120, 122, 125; peasant women and, 378; people displaced by dams and, 104–5; progressive rural network and, 50, 98, 111n15, 224, 427n30; squatter land struggles and, xxvi, 102–4, 207, 212; violent attacks against pastoral agents linked to, 103, 163. *See also* Land laws; Land Pilgrimage; Liberation theology; Violence

CRB (Brazilian Rural Confederation), 75, 86

Criminalization of popular protest, xxviii, 19, 25, 140, 146, 172, 270n5; Cardoso and, 124–25, 225n38, 397, 421; Collor and, 159; Lula and Dilma resist calls for, 172, 419

Crusius, Yeda, 172

Cuba, 14–16, 18, 22, 254–55, 313, 320, 394; MST sends medical students to, 252, 260

Curionópolis (Pará), 213

Curitiba (Pará), 106, 209, 248, 254, 276, 335

CUT (Unified Workers' Central), 107, 118, 141, 208, 393; MST and, 115, 122, 209, 245, 276, 427n30. *See also* Labor unions

CUT-Rural, 250, 278, 287

CVRD (Vale do Rio Doce Company), 120, 211, 417

Elections (*continued*)
    land reform absent in campaign for
        Dilma and, 414; oligarchic politics
        and, 27, 174, 230, 404, 409; peasant
        involvement in local, 84, 242, 288,
        318, 324; MST supports PT candidate
        for, 159, 165, 331, 336–38, 349, 399;
        PT strategy to attain power and, 337,
        348, 423; public activism and, 152.
        See also Lula
Elias, Norbert, 193, 198, 262, 412n42
El Salvador, 14–17
ENFF (Florestan Fernandes National
    School), 135–36, 146n13, 245, 249,
    251, 261. *See also* Photo illustration
England, 4, 13, 372
Environmental preservation, xxvii, 83,
    262, 291, 423, 425; alternative energy
    matrix and, 105; associations for,
    427n12; CPT and, 108–10; industrial
    agriculture and, 30, 101, 169, 239,
    264, 289, 322, 423, 425; land reform's
    future and, 28, 264, 425; laws and,
    416–17; MST embraces ecological
    principles and, 245–46, 249, 252–54,
    256; peasant farming and, 30, 291,
    425; social function of rural property
    and, 57–58, 89n36, 366, 373n35. *See
    also* Agribusiness; Agro-ecology;
    Amazon; Development model;
    Pesticides
Espírito Santo (state), 100, 120, 245, 250
Ethiopia, 14
Europe, 138, 219, 250, 260, 263, 313;
    Eastern, 14, 18; migrants to southern
    Brazil from, 154, 296, 308n7; MST
    solidarity groups in, 246, 261;
    Western, 48, 219, 407
European Union, 260, 263
Evangelical churches, 305–6; CPT and,
    100
Evictions. *See* Land evictions

FAO (Food and Agriculture Organization
    of the United Nations), 9, 148, 378
FARSUL (Agricultural Federation of the
    State of Rio Grande do Sul), 75, 165,
    168, 172, 273n43

Favelas (shantytowns), 4, 11, 197, 296,
    380, 402; land reform reduces rural
    exodus and growth of, 241; land
    settlements described as rural,
    29–30, 393, 410n13; MST builds ties
    with youth in, 248; MST recruits in,
    131, 151, 165, 181n52, 240, 278; rural
    trade unions organize in, 278
Federal government, xxvi, 208, 300,
    336, 379, 418, 422; budget priorities
    of, 26, 418; fragmentation and
    bureaucratic politics in, 27, 404;
    greater rural presence of, 79, 108,
    203, 210, 217, 219, 399; landed
    interests protected by administrative
    design of, 102, 233; lax enforcement
    of rural land taxes by, 59; legal
    proprietorship of settlements and, 59;
    MST development projects supported
    by, 251, 253–54, 260; MST relations
    with, 117, 161, 168, 236, 243, 334,
    389n35. *See also* Agrarian elites;
    Agro-export commodities; Landless
    camps; Military regime
Federalism, 27
FERAESP (Federation of Rural Workers
    and Wage Earners of São Paulo), 84,
    89n41, 278
Fernandes, Florestan, 357. *See also* ENFF
FETAESP (Federation of Agricultural
    Workers of the State of São Paulo),
    275
FETAG (Federation of Agricultural
    Workers of Bahia), 383
FETAGRI (Federation of Workers in
    Agriculture of Pará), 203, 208,
    215–16, 218, 221, 223–24, 225n39, 383
FETAPE (Federation of Agricultural
    Workers of Pernambuco), 81, 184,
    188, 314, 381–83, 385, 387; news
    media criticizes, 389n25
FETRAF (Family Farm Workers Federa-
    tion), 83, 86, 107, 142, 427n30
FIESP (Federation of Industries of São
    Paulo), 6
Figueiredo, João Batista de Oliveira:
    land distribution under, 237, 266,
    414

Financial sector, 2, 5, 25, 108, 191; agrarian elites allied with, 53, 64, 263; farmland purchased as investment by, 61, 84; "to give the banks greater profits," 2, 347, 408; interest paid on public debt and, 418; shakedown during Lula election campaign and, 419; state-run Northeast Bank and, 321. *See also* Agrarian elites; Bank of Brazil; BNDES

Fontelles, Claudio, 367

Food Purchase Program, 238, 419

Forestry Code, 417, 426n12

Formoso (Goiás), 73, 94

Fortaleza (Ceará), 336

Foucault, Michel, 295

France, 24, 426n3

Franco, Itamar, 123, 164, 332

Freire, Paulo, 94, 245, 252, 254, 304

Fritzen, Arnildo, 149–50, 155–56, 158, 160–61, 178n17, 178n19, 179n30. *See also* Photo illustration

FTAA (Free Trade Area of the Americas), 169

Furtado, Celso, 45, 65n4

General Motors, 169

Germany, 13, 231

GMOs (genetically-modified organisms [seeds]), 2, 107, 109, 169, 256–57

Goiânia, 1, 3, 32n2, 86, 100, 119, 122

Goiás (state), 3, 71–72, 85, 103, 120, 251, 273n43; MST's first mobilizations in, 122

Görgen, Sérgio, 158, 161, 163, 166

Graziano, Francisco (Xico), 332, 336; as an MST critic, 34n25, 391, 393–94, 402, 404, 409n1, 409n13, 411n37

Grito da Terra, 83, 86

Guariba (São Paulo), 82, 86

Guatemala, 14, 16–18, 334

Guimarães, Alberto Passos, 45

Hackbart, Rolf, 345

Health, 78, 84; federal expenditures on, 418; industrial agriculture and, 30, 264, 422–23, 425; landless camps and, 131, 156, 160, 184, 229; land

settlements and, 236, 241, 286, 300, 402; MST and, 32, 135, 166, 247, 249, 252; peasant women and, 378

Hired gunmen, 73, 103, 122, 185, 208, 217, 342; impunity of landlords and, 22, 132; land mobilizations and, 396; MST averts direct confrontation with, 398; private security contractors and, 85. *See also* Agrarian elites; Paramilitary groups

Hirschman, Albert O., 181n59, 394

Homeless movement. *See* MTST

Honduras, 16–18

Hoover, J. Edgar, 340

Hulha Negra (Rio Grande do Sul), 240, 254, 256

Human rights; MST calls for protection of basic, 2, 167–68, 246–47, 249, 406; MST's task team on, 125, 135, 247, 249, 361–63, 400

Human rights organizations; MST origins and, 154, 156; MST supported by, 3, 122, 125, 210. *See also* CPT; RENAP

Human rights violations, 69, 93, 104, 265, 270n5, 399; in the Amazon region, 96, 99, 103, 108, 222; conservative agrarian reform and, 19, 232–34; MST protest against, 2, 168, 247; of peasants and rural activists, 123, 132, 159, 163, 361, 417; popular movements raise cost of, 179n21, 212, 220–21; in the Soviet Union and China, 407. *See also* CPT; Violence

Human rights violations under military rule; attacks on pastoral agents and, 99; Church opposition to, 92, 94–95, 103; popular groups suffer bulk of, 8, 25, 47, 78, 94, 96–97, 182

Hunger strikes, 132, 152, 160, 168, 175–77, 233, 398

Hydroelectric dams, 63, 277; conflicts over the construction of large, 79–81, 104–5, 275, 376–77; MST origins and, 105, 118, 160; resettlements of people displaced by, 279, 291. *See also* Balbina; Itaipu; Itaparica; MAB; Sobradinho; Tucuruí

Land ceiling laws, 14–15, 20

Land Credit program (Crédito Fundiário), 140, 142, 345

Land evictions, 192, 196, 219, 342, 389n24; courts and, 183, 185, 195, 218, 294, 335, 342; dam constructions and, 104; landlord militias carry out, 331, 342; MST origins and, 105, 118, 122, 131, 149, 154; MST resists, 138, 158, 162–64, 168, 179n32; Pará state government delays execution of, 226n50; Peasant Leagues and, 72, 74; rural migration and, 77. See also Indigenous people; Squatter land struggles

Land expropriations, 19, 60, 231, 315, 340, 386, 415; administrative procedure for, 66n22, 88n29, 186, 192, 201n31, 233, 312; Cardoso restricts, 60, 124, 165, 335; compensation for, 60–61, 66, 76, 120, 355, 405, 416, 426n8; constitutional law and, 56, 60, 365–66, 373n35; drop in land value facilitates, 52; judiciary annuls, 143, 172, 233, 368, 371n13; landless massacre and surge in, 60, 215; MST targets influential landlords for, 209, 218; popular mobilizations trigger, 122, 183, 194–98, 208–13, 236, 275, 288, 300; slave labor and, 38n76, 108; statistical data on, 414–15. See also Constituent Assembly of 1988; Productivity Index; Social function of rural property

Land fraud (*grilagem*), 74, 205, 276–77, 291n6, 341, 363–64, 405; etymology of Brazilian term for, 112n21, 147n15, 373n25; lax enforcement of agrarian laws enables, 53–54, 59; Lula government legalizes, 416, 426n9; national territory usurped through, 58, 415; squatter struggles and, 73–74, 103, 118, 126, 202, 206, 275. *See also* Amazon region; Pontal do Paranapanema

Land inequality, 110, 142, 205, 281, 340, 346, 397; agrarian reform reduces local, 282, 290; agribusiness

development model exacerbates, xxv, 44, 51, 56, 263–64; Brazil's persistently high, 24, 116, 144–45, 263, 280, 343, 346; conservative agrarian reform and, 19, 231, 235; global comparison of, 20; as a historic and symbolic Brazilian legacy, 7, 24, 31, 395; peripheral treatment of, 29, 46–47, 71, 394; perverse effects of, 45, 62, 72, 74, 83, 104; popular struggles to overcome, 220, 249; PT tones down earlier critique of, 141; social disparity and, xxiii, 21–22; statistical data on, 7, 20, 23, 29, 57, 66n19, 282, 337, 420

Land Law of 1850, 45, 395

Land laws; agrarian elites benefit from implementation of, 60, 396; Agrarian Law of 1993, 57–58, 182, 196; ancillary programs for settlers and, 236, 289; authoritarian legacies and, 231; CPT promotes study of, 105, 156; fiscal land module and, 26; lax enforcement of, 54, 56–59, 63, 405, 416. *See also* Constituent Assembly of 1988; Land expropriations; Land fraud; Land occupations; Land Statute of 1964; Rural property taxes; Social function of rural property

Landless camps, 115, 150, 163–65, 168, 213, 279, 375; Cardoso and, 123–24; in the early 1960s, 74; identities created at, 197, 387; internal organization of, 119, 131, 136, 155–56, 158; land inequities and conflicts exposed through, 220, 279; Lula and, 217; MST bans alcohol at, 2, 354; MST formation and, 105, 122, 150, 154, 287–88, 376, 389n35; as MST's main recruitment venue, 132, 136; MST origins at Natalino's Crossing and, 119, 155–57, 179n19, 257, 379; MST recruitment slump and, 421; nostalgia for, 296, 302, 305, 401; participants at, 277; pedagogical experience of, 117, 132, 261, 276, 295, 309n8; reasons for joining and leaving, 189–93, 197, 283, 303;

Marxism, 10, 14, 45, 338, 362, 407; MST and, 272n33, 392, 410n22

MASTER (Landless Farmers Movement), 74, 86, 88n21, 119

MASTRO (Movement of Landless Workers of the West), 81

Mato Grosso, 71, 100, 106, 135, 222, 235, 344; MST's first mobilizations in, 125; rural violence in, 66n23, 85, 342

Mato Grosso do Sul (state), 106, 118

Mauro, Gilmar, 347

MEB (Grassroots Education Movement), 94

Medianeira (Paraná), 119

Médici, Emílio Garrastazu, 205

Mendes, Luciano, 3

Mexico, 14, 16–18, 20, 22, 50–51

Military coup of 1964, 43, 64, 116, 118, 150, 351, 420; agrarian elites take part of, 76, 395; land reform debate suppressed with, 8, 46–47, 63, 77, 93–94, 182, 381, 395; religious support for, 92–93

Military regime, 7, 46, 313, 380, 382; agribusiness formation under, 64, 103, 263, 396; autocratic legacies and, 231, 358, 405; Catholic Church and, 92–96, 98–100, 104, 155–57, 207; communist guerrilla defeated by, 204; election rules introduced by, 27; landlord class allied with, xxiv, 8, 78, 84, 116, 395; land policies of, 8, 45, 76, 116–17, 204–5, 275; MST origins and, 118–19, 154–57; opposition to, 80, 96, 99–100, 117–19, 154, 157, 207; rural development policies of, 43, 47, 51, 77, 84, 112n24, 204–6; rural trade unions and, 8, 77–78, 313, 371n6, 381; state repression and control of peasantry during, 8, 25, 77–78, 117, 119, 182. See also Agrarian elites; Agricultural modernization; Amazon region; Human rights violations

Minas Gerais, 75, 82, 104, 256, 275, 283, 383; MST's first mobilizations in, 120

Mining, 59, 101, 112n24, 204–5, 417, 419, 424; Carajás complex and, 105, 206, 210–11; MST and, 211, 222, 240; Serra

Pelada and gold, 157, 206

Mirante do Paranapanema (São Paulo), 280–83

Mística (movement mystique), 6, 136, 138, 155, 174, 262–64, 420; religious origins of MST's, 155, 157, 162, 262. See also Ideal interests; Movement symbols; Music and singing

MMC (Peasant Women's Movement), 107, 139, 180n49, 375, 377–78, 386, 388n11

Mobilization tactics, 73, 196, 378–80; MST, 122, 150, 158, 219–21, 245, 263, 276; popular groups influenced by MST, 220–21, 380, 382–84; as a repertoire of contention, 152, 203, 217, 219. See also Demonstrations; Hunger Strikes; Labor Strikes; Landless camps; Land occupations; Marches; Rural trade unions

Monoculture, 102, 169, 264, 290, 313, 322; eucalyptus plantations and, 120; Green deserts and, 169, 378–79. See also Industrial agriculture; Pesticides

Monsanto, 53, 169, 256, 263, 424

Moral economy of the land, 131, 401

Moses, 149

Movement symbols, 1–3, 7, 136, 184, 199, 319; CPT's use of, 109; land claims conveyed through, 186, 195, 199; Lula puts on MST cap and displays, 3, 339, 346; MST adopts its principal, 122, 161–62; MST as a symbol and source of inspiration, 7, 264, 375–76; MST stirred by its, 136–38, 156, 175, 262, 401; MST task team promotes, 138; popular groups emulate MST's, 184, 377, 380, 383–84. See also Music and singing

MPA (Small Farmers Movement), 83, 86, 107, 339, 378–79, 386; MST's close ties with, 139, 180n49, 375, 379

MTST (Homeless Workers Movement), 375, 380–81, 388n3

Music and signing, 2, 4, 109, 156, 158, 248, 393–94; MST identity affirmed through, 122, 137–38, 262; MST mística and ideals nurtured through, 162, 175, 262, 401

National Agrarian Ombudsman, 357,
369
National Agrarian Reform Plan (PNRA);
of 1985, 43, 50, 164; of 2003, 142, 344,
361
National Congress. *See* Legislature
National debt, 50–53, 55, 61, 348;
agro-exports spurred to pay, xxiv, 28,
43, 50–55, 64, 91, 396, 404; interest
payment on, 2, 341, 347, 418
National Forum for Agrarian Reform
and Justice in the Countryside, 50,
90, 98, 232, 261, 342, 411n33
Navarro, Zander, 309, 405; as an MST
critic, 147n22, 273n50, 391–94, 402,
404, 409n1, 410n22, 411n32
Neoliberalism, 52, 91, 101, 140, 199, 256,
332, 340; agribusiness expansion and,
53–55, 62–64, 140, 263, 396, 404;
Cardoso and, 52–55, 332, 397; Collor
de Mello and, 159, 381; constrained
adjustment to global economy and,
xxiv, 44, 50–51, 53–55, 57, 63; land
reform undercut by, xxiv–xxv, 8, 43;
Lula and, xxviii, 147n27, 347, 421;
MST critique of, 9, 139, 169, 250–51,
254, 397; MST viewed through prism
of, 411n25. *See also* Democracy
Nepal, 15
New Republic, 50, 80
News media, 170, 174, 295, 344, 363,
367; agrarian elites and, 25, 59,
66n22, 140–41, 168, 185–86, 263,
404; agribusiness and, 30, 62, 141,
143, 423; Brazil's corporate oligopoly
in, 10, 168, 247, 404, 424; calls to
democratize Brazil's corporate, 167,
423; early pro-land reform press
and, 72, 74, 86; Eldorado dos Carajás
massacre and, 214; landless-state
cooperation obscured in, 198, 398;
Lula administration fears wrath of,
142, 172, 405; MST criminalized by,
335–36, 347, 397, 419; MST critics
get ample coverage in, 27, 34n25,
151, 263, 391–92, 394, 409n1; MST
march to Brasília and, 3, 6–7; MST
mobilizations ignored by, 163;

MST origins and, 154–57; MST outlets
and, 9, 150–51, 166, 180n46, 243–44,
247, 257–58; MST's ability to garner
public attention and, 116, 164, 203,
212, 216, 222–23, 287; MST treated
with hostility by, 10, 32n6, 34n28,
142, 180n46, 252, 400, 419; social
movements and, 152, 220–21, 383,
387; state subsidies for landed elite
groups and, 273n43. *See also* FETAPE;
Land occupations; Radio
NGOs (non-governmental organizations), 83, 112n28; anti-pesticide
campaign and, 422; land reform
advocacy and, 50, 139, 342, 427n30;
MST-linked, 135, 249, 372n19; MST
supported by, 121, 146n8, 166,
260–61, 287, 400; pro-agribusiness,
34n25, 409n1. *See also* National
Forum for Agrarian Reform and
Justice in the Countryside
Nicaragua, 14–18
Nigeria, 20
North Korea, 14

OCB (Organization of Brazilian Cooperatives), 273n43, 416
Oligarchical politics, 7, 91, 101, 110, 213,
331; agribusiness reinforces, 49–50,
102, 424; Brazilian democracy and,
xxiv, 25–27, 98, 110, 230, 399, 404,
424; historical legacy of, 24, 231, 395;
local power and, 101; MST and, 392;
PT's founding opposition to, 423–24;
state presence and, 210. *See also*
Agrarian elites; Development model;
Elections; Popular movements
Oliveira, Ariovaldo Umbelino de, 426n9
Oliveira, Francisco de, 338

Pakistan, 14–15, 20–21
Palmeira das Missões (Rio Grande do
Sul), 160, 163
Panama, 16
Pará (state), xxvi, 71, 85, 202–26, 236,
342, 422; extractive reserves in,
36n56; MST arrival to, 125, 209–11;
slave labor in, 108

Porto Alegre (Rio Grande do Sul), 9, 165, 170, 240, 251, 257, 377; homeless movement in, 380; MST marches to, 32, 160, 163; MST mobilizations in, 160–61, 163, 180n41; MST origins and, 149, 151, 154, 157; World Social Forum and, 169, 261

Portugal, 14, 22

Prado Júnior, Caio, 45–46

Presidente Prudente (São Paulo), 115, 281

Pressburger, Miguel, 362

Pretto, Adão, 179n27. *See also* Photo illustration

PROCERA (Special Credit Program for Agrarian Reform), 253, 320, 322, 328n27, 379

Productivity Index: Land, 165, 187, 274; agrarian elites oppose revisions to, 30, 59, 66n22; criteria used for, 66n20; Lula refuses to update, 368, 405, 417. *See also* Land expropriations

Progressive agrarian reform, 56, 98, 148n31, 232; definition of, 19; unraveling of Lula's promise to carry out a, xxviii, 239, 339, 404

Promissão (São Paulo), 279–83, 285, 287–88, 290, 292n21

PRONAF (National Program for the Strengthening of Family Agriculture), 83, 238, 344, 379

PRONERA (National Education Program in Agrarian Reform), 238, 251, 427n28

Property rights, 61, 76, 101, 108, 160, 300, 357; absolutist view of, xxviii, 29, 97, 358. *See also* Land expropriations; Social function of rural property

Protestant churches: CPT and, 100, 104; land reform defended by, 91, 110–11; MST backed by, 122, 156, 246, 261, 400. *See also* CONIC; Ecumenism; Evangelical churches

PSB (Brazilian Socialist Party), 317

PSDB (Party of Brazilian Social Democracy), 172, 213, 349

PSOL (Party for Socialism and Liberty), 148n31, 350n25, 370

PT (Workers' Party), 104, 172, 287, 338–39, 341–43, 348, 361; Agrarian Secretariat within, 148n31; electoral route to power and, 337, 348, 423; historic commitment to agrarian reform of, 336–37; left-wing dissent within, 148n31, 347, 350n25, 370, 421; MST campaigns for, 159, 165, 217, 317, 331, 337–38, 399, 421; MST discrepancy with, 337; MST fields candidates linked to, 179n27, 288, 309n13, 337; MST formation and, 118, 122, 276, 337; MST's close ties with, 3, 32n2, 261, 276, 337, 361, 397, 400, 419; MST's fading passion for, 420–21. *See also* Elections; Popular movements

PT (Workers' Party) government; agribusiness and, 415–17, 419, 423–24; concessions to traditional parties under, 348–49; corporate elite and, 417–19; family farmers and, 419; MST collaborates with, 165–66, 399; MST's criminalization opposed by, 172; oligarchical politics and, 424; turnabout on agrarian policies during, 91, 140–42, 147n27, 217, 343–49, 414–17, 420–21, 423–24. *See also* Lula government

PTB (Brazilian Labor Party), 146n5

Public activism, 158, 160, 167, 230, 243, 253, 420; as a catalyst for social development, 28, 406; conditions for, 152, 154–55; as a counterpoint to elite power, 156–57, 168; definition of, xxvi, 151–53; democracy and, 152, 173–74, 406, 408; as an instrument for inequality reduction, 406; modes of, 153–54, 173–74; movement mystique and, 174. *See also* INCRA; Mobilization tactics; Social movements

Public Ministry, 172, 181n55, 374n42, 419

Public opinion, 104, 142, 203, 221, 224, 334; Brazil's unequal democracy and, 11–13; judiciary and, 12, 356; land mobilizations and, 165; MST strategy to influence, 155, 174, 212

Russia, 13, 20, 51, 53, 263, 412n46. *See also* Soviet Union
Russo, Osvaldo, 333–34

Salles, Walter, 2
Salvador (Bahia), 99
Sampaio, Plínio de Arruda, 142, 147n31, 148n31, 270n7, 339–46, 348, 361, 411n25
Santa Catarina (state), 69, 236, 256, 311, 315–16; MST origins in, 118–19
São Felix do Araguaia (Mato Grosso), 99
São Gabriel (Rio Grande do Sul), 143, 172, 368
São Mateus (Espírito Santo), 245, 250
São Paulo (metropolitan area), 4–6, 34n25, 69, 96, 139, 240, 274; homeless movement in, 380–81; labor mobilizations in, 80, 157; MST offices in, 151, 257, 276
São Paulo (state), 4–5, 48, 72, 247–48, 274–92, 337, 365, 402; landed elite in, 75, 85, 211, 363; MST origins in, 118, 120, 275–76
Sarandi (Rio Grande do Sul), 150, 160, 379
Sarney, José, 159, 164, 232–33, 357, 420
Sarney, José: government: land distribution during, 120, 237, 266, 414; National Agrarian Reform Plan of, 50, 85, 120, 137, 159, 208, 396
Scandinavia, 13
Scherer, Vicente, 179n19
Schmitter, Philippe C., 408, 412n49
Second Vatican Council, xxv, 94–95, 100, 155. *See also* Catholic Church
Sergipe (state), 120
Serra, José, 5
Serra Pelada (Pará), 157, 206, 210, 213
Sesmarias, 7, 395
Sierra Leone, 7
Simon, Pedro, 170
Sirinhaém (Pernambuco), 187, 190
Slave labor, 149, 338; contemporary forms of, 84, 107–8, 110, 224, 417; historic legacy of, 7, 24, 29, 69, 313, 395;

non-expropriation of estates with, 29, 38n76, 108. *See also* Bancada Ruralista; Human rights violations
SNA (National Agricultural Society), 70–71, 75, 85, 87n6
Soares, Jair, 170
Sobradinho dam (Bahia), 104
Social exclusion; Church critique of, 45, 96, 99; land reform movement and, 62–63; MST organizes marginalized people to overcome, 28, 167, 262, 264, 406; peasantry confronts, 83, 98; rule of law and, 351, 365. *See also* Agribusiness development model; Apartheid; Development model
Social function of rural properties, xxviii, 43, 58–60, 357, 366–67; Catholic social teaching and, 45, 97, 358; Constitution of 1988 and, 57, 65n18, 81, 89n36, 201n31, 373n35; Land Statute and, 45, 81; negligible enforcement of, 56, 58, 415; productivity criteria and, 66n20. *See also* Constitution of 1988; Environmental preservation
Social inequality; approaches to reduction of, 407–8; democratic development undermined by, 10–13, 25; developing countries compared and, 20–21; Dilma's policies to reduce, 426n2; income disparity in Brazil and, 7, 32n12, 420; Left-Right divide and, 394; MST critique of neoliberalism and, 169, 397
Socialism, 14, 95, 395, 411n25; MST embraces, 161, 295, 308n6, 394
Socialism for the rich, 25, 419
Social movement[s], 74, 199, 203, 242, 392; as architects of an alternative legal order, xxviii, 399; citizenship rights and, 384; land reform placed on nation's agenda by, 118, 275; Lula government improves dialogue with, 237–38, 339, 370; MST as a, 8, 10, 33n19, 150, 262, 310, 406, 411n32; MST innovation and, 386–87, 399; MST inspires other, 9, 221–23, 376;

Social movement[s] (*continued*)
MST's genesis amid a network of, 50, 92, 331; rule of law and, 353, 360, 367, 374n45; state tension and cooperation with, 196–98; theoretical insights on, 151–52, 178n11, 181n55, 219–20, 310, 326. *See also* Civil rights movement; Coordenação dos Movimentos Sociais; INCRA; Land occupations; Mística; Mobilization tactics; Movement symbols; Popular movements; Public activism; Rural social movements

Sodré, Roberto Costa de Abreu, 363

South Africa, 18, 20–21, 262, 334, 353, 407

South Korea, 11, 14–15, 20

Souza, Amaral de, 150, 170

Soviet Union, 14, 18, 21, 394, 407

Soybeans, 54, 101, 342, 344; for export, 22, 263; GMOs, 169, 257

Spain, 13, 34n24

Squatter (*posseiro*) land struggles, 8–9, 73, 79–80, 197, 206–9, 221–22; CPT's "baptism by fire" and, 103; evictions and, 77, 149, 206; MST contrasted with, 105, 126, 203, 209–12, 218, 220, 222, 398; MST influence on, 221, 223; under-counting of, 144, 233. *See also* Land fraud

Squatters (*posseiros*), 59, 102, 240, 277, 284, 323, 344; Church defense of, 79, 99–100, 102–4, 110, 202, 204, 206–7, 212; as a legal category, 74, 194; legitimize land rights through labor, 73, 103, 108; MST origins and, 81, 105, 118, 131, 149, 275; rural trade unions and, xxvi, 8, 78, 118, 202, 208. *See also* Indigenous people

SRB (Brazilian Rural Society), 75, 85, 273n43, 416

Sri Lanka, 14–15

Stalin, Joseph, 412n46

State. *See* Federal government

State governments, 73, 84, 314, 381, 383, 389n35, 416; land distributed by, 122, 150, 154, 166, 253, 277, 279, 291n6; MST makes demands on, 150, 154, 157–58, 169, 213, 314, 389n24; MST partners with, 3, 165–66, 251, 254, 399; policing by, 168, 226n50, 314, 332, 335

Stédile, João Pedro, 159, 272n42, 331, 339, 343, 361, 363; on enforcing agrarian laws, 81; on the Lula government, 346–48; MST origins and, 150, 389n35. *See also* Photo illustration

Stiglitz, Joseph, 424

Stroessner, Alfredo, 17

Strozake, Juvelino, 362

Student organizations; Church-related, 93; MST backed by, 3, 125, 260–61, 400; MST origins and, 122, 156

Sugar, 77, 294, 322–23; agricultural marketing board and, 48, 65n9, 187, 381; for export, 22, 289, 313

Sugarcane cultivation; history of, 200n4, 313; in land reform settlements, xxviii, 312, 320–23, 326

Sugarcane landlords, 186, 189, 313, 316, 382; Lula praises, 349; MST disputes public funds available to, 385; persistent political clout of, 200n4, 385; plantation workers and, 314, 316; use and threat of violence by, 82, 185, 190, 192. *See also* Agrarian elites; Bancada Ruralista; Citizenship rights; Democracy; Military regime; Rural trade unions

Sugarcane plantations; labor demands and, 72–73, 314; labor exploitation in, 70, 73, 77, 313, 424; labor strikes and, 81–82, 86, 88n17, 381–82, 388n23; land struggles target, 183, 185–90, 193–94, 198, 201n32, 278, 382–83

Sugar industry; crisis of, 84, 187, 311, 314, 320, 381–82, 388n23; land occupations amid crisis of, 189, 191, 193–94, 315–18, 383

Sumaré (São Paulo), 279–81, 283–84, 286–88, 290

Suplicy, Eduardo, 3

Supreme Court, 368, 374n45, 416; Lula's first expropriation annulled by, 143, 172, 368, 371n13

Sweden, 23, 261